THE History OF Sacerdotal Celibacy IN THE Christian Church

HENRY C. LEA

THE History OF
Sacerdotal
Celibacy IN
THE Christian
Church

RUSSELL & RUSSELL · NEW YORK

1957

LIBRARY OF CONGRESS CATALOG CARD NUMBER 57-8673

MANUFACTURED IN THE U S. A.

PREFACE

THE following work was written several years since, simply as an historical study, and with little expectation of its publication. Recent movements in several portions of the great Christian Church seem to indicate, however, that a record of ascetic celibacy, as developed in the past, may not be without interest to those who are watching the tendencies of the present.

So far as I am aware, no work of the kind exists in English literature, and those which have appeared in the Continental languages are almost exclusively of a controversial character. It has been my aim to avoid polemics, and I have therefore sought merely to state facts as I have found them, without regard to their bearing on either side of the questions involved.

The scope of the work is designedly confined to the enforced celibacy of the sacerdotal class. The vast history of monachism has therefore only been touched upon incidentally when it served to throw light upon the rise and progress of religious asceticism. The various celibate communities which have arisen in this country, such as the Dunkers and Shakers, are likewise excluded from the plan of the volume. These limitations occasion me less regret since the appearance of M. de Montalembert's " Monks of the West " and Mr. W. Hepworth Dixon's " New America," in which the student will probably find all that he may require on these subjects.

Besides the controversial importance of the questions connected with Christian asceticism, it has seemed to me that a brief history like the present might perhaps possess interest for the general reader, not only on account of the influence which ecclesiastical celibacy has exerted, directly and indirectly, on the progress of civilisation, but also from the occasional glimpse into the interior life of past ages afforded in reviewing the effect upon society of the policy of the Church as respects the relations of the sexes. The more ambitious historian, in detailing the intrigues of the court

v

and the vicissitudes of the field, must of necessity neglect the minuter incidents which illustrate the habits, the morals, and the modes of thought of bygone generations. From such materials a monograph like this is constructed, and it may not be unworthy the attention of those who deem that the life of nations does not consist exclusively of political revolutions and military achievements.

CONTENTS

XIII. MILAN

XIV. HILDEBRAND

XXVII. CALVINISM

SACERDOTAL CELIBACY

THE Latin Church is the great fact which dominates the history of modern civilisation. All other agencies which moulded the destinies of mediæval Europe were comparatively isolated or sporadic in their manifestations. Thus in one place we may trace the beneficent influence of commerce at work, in another the turbulent energy of the rising Third Estate; the mortal contests of the feudal powers with each other and with progress are waged in detached and convulsive struggles; chivalry casts only occasional and evanescent flashes of light amid the darkness of military barbarism; literature seeks to gain support from any power which will condescend to lend transitory aid to the plaything of the moment. Nowhere do we see combined effort, nowhere can we detect a pervading impulse, irrespective of locality or of circumstance, save in the imposing machinery of the Church establishment. This meets us at every point, and in every age, and in every sphere of action. In the dim solitude of the cloister, the monk is training the minds which are to mould the destinies of the period, while his roof is the refuge of the desolate and the home of the stranger. In the tribunal, the priest is wrestling with the baron, and is extending his more humane and equitable code over a jurisdiction subjected to the caprices of feudal or customary law, as applied by a class of ignorant and arbitrary tyrants. In the royal palace, the hand of the ecclesiastic, visible or invisible, is guiding the helm of state, regulating the policy of nations, and converting the brute force of chivalry into the supple instrument of his will. In Central Europe, lordly prelates, with the temporal power and possessions of the highest princes, joined to the exclusive pretensions of the Church, make war and peace, and are sovereign in all but name, owing no allegiance save to emperors whom they elect and popes whose cause they share. Far above all, the successor of St. Peter from his pontifical throne claims the whole of Europe as his empire, and dictates terms to kings. At the other extremity of society, the humble minister of the altar, with his delegated power over heaven and hell, wields in cottage as in castle an authority hardly less potent, and enforces on the populations the behests of his superiors. Even art offers a willing submission to the universal mistress, and seeks the embodiment of its noblest aspirations in the lofty poise of the cathedral spire, the rainbow glories of the painted window, and the stately rhythm of the solemn chant.

This vast fabric of ecclesiastical supremacy presents one of the most curious problems which the world's history affords. Through its perfected organisation the Church wielded its wide and absolute authority, deriving its force from moral power alone, marshalling no legions of its own in battle array, but permeating everything with its influence, walking unarmed through deadly strife, rising with renewed strength from every prostration, triumphing alike over the savage nature of the barbarian and the enervated apathy of the Roman tributary, blending discordant races and jarring nations into one great brotherhood of subjection —such was the papal hierarchy, a marvel and a mystery. Well is it personified in Gregory VII, a fugitive from Rome, without a rood of ground to call him master, a rival pope lording it in the Vatican, a triumphant emperor vowed to internecine strife, yet issuing his commands as sternly and as proudly to prince and potentate as though he were the unquestioned suzerain of Europe, and listened to as humbly by three-fourths of Christendom. The man wasted away in the struggle; his death was but the accident of time : the Church lived on, and marched to inevitable victory.

The investigations of the curious can hardly be deemed misapplied in analysing the elements of this impalpable but irresistible power, and in examining the causes which have enabled it to preserve such unity of action amid such diversity of environment, presenting everywhere by turns a solid and united front to the opposing influences of barbarism and civilisation. In detaching one of these elements from the group, and tracing out its successive vicissitudes, I may therefore be pardoned for thinking the subject of sufficient interest to warrant a minuteness of detail that would otherwise perhaps appear disproportionate. It was by no means the least of the factors in the conquering career of the Church that it required of all to whom it granted the supernatural powers conferred in holy orders that they should surrender themselves to it unreservedly and irrevocably, that they should sunder all human ties, should have no aspirations beyond its service, no family affections to distract their loyalty, no family duties on which to waste its substance, and no ambitions save for the rewards which it alone could bestow.

CHAPTER I

ASCETICISM

THE most striking contrast between the Mosaic Dispensation and the Law of Christ is the materialism of the one, and the pure spirituality of the other. The Hebrew prophet threatens worldly punishments, and promises fleshly rewards : the Son of Man teaches us to contemn the treasures of this life, and directs all our fears and aspirations towards eternity. The exaggeration of these teachings by the zeal of fervent disciples led to the ascetic efforts to subjugate nature, which present so curious a feature in religious history, and of which those concerning the relation of the sexes form the subject of our consideration.

This special phase of asceticism was altogether foreign to the traditions of Israel, averse as they were from all restrictions upon the full physical development of man. Enjoying, apparently, no conception of a future existence, the earlier Hebrews had no incentive to sacrifice the pleasures of the world for those of a heaven of which they knew nothing; nor was the gross polytheism, which the monotheistic prophets combated, of a nature to lead to ascetic practices. The worship of Ashera—probably identical with the Babylonian Beltis or Mylitta—undoubtedly consecrated the sacrifice of chastity as a religious rite, and those who revered the goddess of fertility as one of the supreme deities were not likely to impose any restrictions on the exercise of her powers. We see, indeed, in the story of Judah and Tamar, and in the lamentation of the daughter of Jephthah, that virginity was regarded almost as a disgrace, and that child-bearing was considered the noblest function of woman; while the institution of levirate marriage shows an importance attributed to descendants in the male line as marked as among the Hindu Arya. The hereditary character of the priesthood, moreover, both as vested in the original Levites and the later Tsadukim and Baithusin, indicates conclu-

sively that even among the orthodox no special sanctity
attached to continence, and that the temporary abstinence
from women required of those who handled the hallowed
articles of the altar (1 Sam. xxi. 4–5) was simply a distinction drawn between the sacerdotal class and the laity; for
in the elaborate instructions as to uncleanness there is no
allusion made to sexual indulgence, though the priest who
had partaken of wine was forbidden to enter the Tabernacle,
and defilement arising from contact with the dead was a
disability (Lev. x., xxi., xxii.), while the highest blessing
that could be promised as a reward for obedience to God
was that " there shall not be male or female barren among
you " (Deut. vii. 14). In fact, the only manifestation of
asceticism as a religious ordinance, prior to the Second
Temple, is seen in the vow of the Nazirites, which consisted merely in allowing the hair to remain unshorn, in the
abstinence from wine, and in avoiding the pollution arising
from contact with the dead. Slender as were these restrictions, the ordinary term of a Nazirate was only thirty days,
though it might be assumed for life, as in the cases of
Samson and Samuel; and the vows for long terms were
deemed sufficiently pleasing to God to serve as means of
propitiation, as in the case of Hannah, who thus secured her
offspring Samuel, and in that of Helena, Queen of Adiabene,
who vowed a Nazirate of seven years if her son Izaces should
return in safety from a campaign. The few references to
the custom in Scripture, however, show that it was little
used, and that it exercised no visible influence over social
life during the earlier periods.

When the conquests of Cyrus released the Hebrews from
captivity, the close relations established with the Persians
wrought no change in this aspect of the Jewish faith.
Mazdeism, in fact, was a religion so wholesome and practical
in its character that asceticism could find little place among
its prescribed observances, and the strict maintenance of its
priesthood in certain families, who transmitted their sacred
lore from father to son, shows that no restrictions were
placed upon the ministers of Hormadz, or athravas, though
in the later period of the Achæmenian Empire, after the
purity of ancient Mazdeism had become corrupted, the
priestesses of the Sun were required to observe chastity,
without necessarily being virgins. With the conquests of
Alexander, however, Judaism was exposed to new influences,

and was brought into relation at once with Grecian thought and with the subtle mysticism of India, with which intercourse became frequent under the Greek Empire. Beyond the Indus the Sankhya philosophy was already venerable, which taught the nothingness of life, and that the supreme good consisted in the absolute victory over all human wants and desires. Already Buddha had reduced this philosophy into a system of religion, the professors of which were bound to chastity—a rule impossible of observance by the world at large, but which became obligatory upon its innumerable priests and monks, when it spread and established itself as a Church, thus furnishing the prototype which was subsequently imitated by Roman Christianity. Already Brahmanism had invented the classes of Vanaprasthas, Sannyasis, and others—ascetics whose practices of self-mortification anticipated and excelled all that is related of Christian Antonys and Simeons—although the ancestor worship which required every man to provide descendants who should keep alive the Sraddha in honour of the Pitris of his forefathers postponed the entrance into the life of the anchorite until after he should have fulfilled his parental duties : and we know from the references in the Greek writers to the Hindu gymnosophists how great an impression these customs had made upon those to whom they were a novelty. Already the Yoga system had been framed, whereby absorption into the Godhead was to be obtained by religious mendicancy, penances, mortifications, and the severest severance of self from all external surroundings. All this had been founded on the primæval doctrine of the Vedas with respect to the virtue of *Tapas*, or austere religious abstraction, to which the most extravagant powers were attributed, conferring upon its votaries the authority of gods. With all the absurdities of these beliefs and practices, they yet sprang from a profound conviction of the superiority of the spiritual side of man's nature, and if their theory of the nothingness of mortal existence was exaggerated, yet they tended to elevate the soul, at the expense, it must be confessed, of a regard to the duties which man owes to society.

The influences arising from this system of religious philosophy, so novel to the Semitic races, were tardy in making themselves felt upon the Hebrews, but they became gradually apparent. The doctrine of a future life with rewards and punishments, doubtless derived from Chaldean and Mazdean sources during the Captivity and under the Persian Empire, slowly made its way, and though opposed by the aristocratic conservative party in power—the Tsadukim or Sadducees (descendants of Zadoc, or just men) —it became one of the distinctive dogmas of the Beth Sopherim or House of Scribes, composed of religious teachers, trained in all the learning of the day, sprung from the people, and eager to maintain their nationality against the temporising policy of their rulers. At the breaking out of the Maccabean revolt against Antiochus Epiphanes we find the nation divided into two factions—the Sadducees, disposed rather to submit to the Hellenising tyranny of Antioch, and the Chassidim (the Assideans of the Vulgate), democratic reformers, ready for innovation, and prepared to die in defence of their faith. In the triumph of the Hasmonean revolution they obtained control of the State, and in the development of the Oral Law by the Scribes, supplementing the Torah or Written Law, they engrafted permanently their doctrines upon the ancestral belief. With the tenet of spiritual immortality there followed, as a necessary consequence, the subordination of the present existence to life hereafter, which is the direct incentive to asceticism. The religious exaltation of the stormy period which intervened between the liberation from Antioch and the subjugation to Rome afforded a favourable soil for the growth of this tendency, and rendered the minds of the devout accessible to the influences both of Eastern and of Western speculation. How powerful eventually became the latter upon the Alexandrian Jews may be estimated from the mysticism of Philo.

With their triumph over Antioch, the name of the Chassidim disappears as that of an organised party, and in its place we find those of two factions or sects—the Perushim (Pharisees) or Separatists, who maintained an active warfare, temporal and theological, with the Sadducees, and the Essenes, mystics, who bound themselves by vows, generally including the Nazirate, and withdrew from active life for the benefit of spiritual growth and meditation.

The Essenes cultivated the soil and sometimes even lived in cities, but oftener dwelt as anchorites, using no artificial textures as clothing, and no food save what was spontaneously produced. They mostly practised daily ablu-

tions and admitted neophytes to their society by the rite
of baptism after a novitiate of a year, followed by two
years of probation. Among those who did not live as
hermits, property was held in common, and marriage was
abstained from, and it is to this latter practice doubtless
that reference was made by Christ in the text, " There be
eunuchs which have made themselves eunuchs for the
kingdom of heaven's sake." The Essenes enjoyed high
consideration among the people; their teachings were
listened to with respect, and they were regarded as especially
favoured with the gifts of divination and prophecy. There
can be no doubt that John the Baptist was an Essene;
James of Jerusalem, brother of Jesus, was a Nazirite and
probably an Essene, and Christ himself may reasonably be
regarded as trained in the principles of the sect. His tendencies all lay in that direction, and it is observable that,
while he is unsparing in his denunciations of the Scribes
and Pharisees and Sadducees, he never utters a word of
condemnation of the Essenes.

It is thus easy to understand the refined spirituality of
Christ's teachings, and the urgency with which he called
the attention of man from the gross temptations of earth
to the higher things which should fit him for the inheritance
of eternal life. Yet his profound wisdom led him to forbear
from enjoining even the asceticism of the Essenes. He
allowed a moderate enjoyment of the gifts of the Creator;
and when he sternly rebuked the Scribes and Pharisees for
imposing, in their development of the Oral Law, burdens
upon men not easily to be borne by the weakness of human
nature, he was far indeed from seeking to render obligatory,
or even to recommend, practices which only the fervour of
fanaticism could render endurable. No teacher before
him had ventured to form so lofty a conception of the
marriage-tie. It was an institution of God himself whereby
man and wife became one flesh. " What therefore God
hath joined together let not man put asunder "; and though
he refrained from condemning abstention from wedlock, he
regarded it as possible only to those whose exceptional
exaltation of temperament might enable them to overcome
the instincts and passions of humanity.

When the broad proselytising views and untiring energy
of Paul, the apostle of the Gentiles, were brought to bear
upon the little circle of mourning disciples, it was inevitable

that a rupture should take place. No one in the slightest degree familiar with the spirit of Judaism at that day can have difficulty in understanding how those who still regarded themselves as Jews, who looked upon their martyr, not as the Son of God, but, in the words of Peter, as " Jesus of Nazareth, a man approved of God among you, by miracles and wonders and signs which God did by him in the midst of you," and who held, as is urged in the Epistle of James, firmly to their· Master's injunction to preserve every jot and tittle of the Law, should regard with growing distrust and distaste the activity of the Pharisee Paul, who, like other Pharisees, was ready to encompass land and sea to gain one proselyte, and, more than this, was prepared to throw down the exclusive barriers of the Law, in order to invite all mankind to share in the glad tidings of Salvation. The division came in time, and as the Gentile Church spread and flourished, it stigmatised as heretics those who adhered to the simple monotheistic reformed Judaism which Christ had taught. These became known as the Ebionim, or Poor Men, Essenes, and others, who followed Christ as a prophet inspired by God, who accepted all of the apostles save Paul, whom they regarded as a transgressor of the Law, holding their property in common, honouring virginity rather than marriage, but uttering no precept upon the subject, and observing the Written Law with rigid accuracy. They maintained a quiet existence for four centuries, making no progress, but exciting no antagonism save on the part of vituperative heresiologists, whose denunciations, however, contain no rational grounds for regarding them otherwise than as the successors of the original followers of Christ.

Meanwhile, Pauline Christianity, launched on the tumultuous existence of the Gentile world, had adapted itself to the passions and ambitions of men, had availed itself both of their strength and of their weakness, and had become a very different creed from that which had been taught around the Sea of Galilee, and had seen its teacher expiate on Calvary his revolt against the Oral Law. In its gradual transformation through the ages, from Essenic and Ebionic simplicity to the magnificent sacerdotalism of the Innocents and Gregories, it has felt itself bound to find or make, in its earliest records, some precedent for

every innovation, and accordingly its ardent polemics in
modern times have endeavoured to prove that the celibacy
of its ministers was, if not absolutely ordained, at least
practised from the earliest period.   Much unnecessary
logic and argument have been spent upon this subject
since the demand which arose for clerical marriage at the
Reformation forced the champions of the Church to find
scriptural authority for the canon which enjoins celibacy.
The fact is that prior to the sixteenth century the Fathers
of the Church had no scruple in admitting that in primitive
times the canon had no existence and the custom was not
observed.   The reader may therefore well be spared a
disquisition upon a matter which may be held to be self-
evident, and be contented with a brief reference to some
of the authorities of the Church who, prior to the Reformation, admitted that in primitive times marriage was freely
permitted to the ministers of Christ.

No doctor of the Church did more than St. Jerome to
impose the rule of celibacy on its members, yet even he
admits that at the beginning there was no absolute injunction to that effect; and he endeavours to apologise for the
admission by arguing that infants must be nourished with
milk and not with solid food.   In the middle of the eleventh
century, during the controversy between Rome and Constantinople, Rome had no scruple in admitting that the
celebrated text of St. Paul (1 Cor. ix. 5) meant that the
apostles were married, though subsequent commentators
have exhausted so much ingenuity in explaining it away.
A century later Gratian, the most learned canonist of his
time, in the "Decretum," undertaken at the request of
the papal court, which has ever since maintained its
position as the foundation of the canon law, felt no hesitation in admitting that, before the adoption of the canon,
marriage was everywhere undisturbed among those in
orders, as it continued to be in the Greek Church.   St.
Thomas Aquinas admits that Christ could not properly
require men to leave their wives, and that he did not
enforce it on St. Peter.   There were in the twelfth and
thirteenth centuries few more learned men than Giraldus
Cambrensis, whose orthodoxy was unquestioned, and
who, as Archdeacon of St. David's, vigorously sought to
enforce the rule of continence upon his recalcitrant clergy.
Yet in a strenuous exhortation to them to mend the error

of their ways in this respect, he admits that clerical celibacy has no spiritual or apostolic warrant. That this was universally admitted at the time is manifested by Alfonso the Wise, of Castile, about the middle of the thirteenth century, asserting the fact in the most positive manner, while forbidding marriage to the priests of his dominions, in the code known as Las Siete Partidas.

Gerson, indeed, who, like most of the ecclesiastics of his time, attributes to the Council of Nicæa the introduction of celibacy, seems inclined to justify the change assumed to have been then made, by alluding to the forged donation of Constantine. That the temporalities of the Church could only be entrusted to men cut off from family ties was an axiom in his day, and though he does not himself draw the conclusion, he clearly regarded the supposed accession to the landed estates of the Church as a satisfactory explanation of the prohibition of marriage to its ministers in the fourth century. Shortly afterwards, Pius II, one of the most learned of the popes, had no scruple in admitting that the Primitive Church was administered by a married clergy. Just before the Reformation, Geoffroi Boussard, dean of the faculty of theology of Paris, published, in 1505, a dissertation on priestly continence, in which he positively assumes, as the basis of his argument, that the use of marriage was universally permitted to those in holy orders, from the time of Christ to that of Siricius and Innocent I; and this may be assumed to be the opinion of the University of Paris, for Boussard formally submitted his tract to that body, and its approbation is to be found in the fact that he was subsequently elevated to its chancellorship, and was sent as its delegate to the Council of Pisa. The future antagonist of Luther, the learned Dr. John Eck, in 1512, had no hesitation in instancing celibacy as an example of the laws which the Church had altered to suit the changes of the times.

Even after the Reformation, unexceptionable orthodox authority is found to the same effect. In 1564, Pius IV admitted it in an epistle to the German princes, and explained it by the necessity of the times. Zaccaria, probably the most learned of Catholic polemics on the subject, endeavours to reconcile his belief in the Apostolic origin of clerical celibacy, with the indubitable practice of the primitive Church, by suggesting that while the Apostles commanded the observance of the rule by the clergy in general, yet in special cases they discreetly dispensed with it to avoid greater scandals; and that with the gradual increase of these dispensations the clergy came at length to assume the indulgence as a matter of course without asking for special licences. More logical is the argument brought forward by a priest named Taillard, resisting in 1842 some efforts made to introduce priestly marriage in Prussian Poland. He coolly reasons that if celibacy was not enforced in the primitive Church, it ought to have been—" if the celibacy of the priesthood be not from the beginning of Christianity, it ought to have been there, for, as our holy religion comes from God, it should contain in itself all the means possible to elevate the nations to the highest point of liberty and happiness."

CHAPTER II

ALTHOUGH no thought existed in the mind of Paul, and of his co-labourers in founding the Church of the Gentiles, of prohibiting to his disciples the institution of marriage, there was a distinct flavour of asceticism in some of his teachings, which might readily serve as a warrant to those whose zeal was greater than their discretion, to mortify the flesh in this as in other ways. The Apostle, while admitting that the Lord had forbidden the separation of husband and wife, said of the unmarried and widowers : " It is good for them if they abide even as I. But if they cannot contain let them marry, for it is better to marry than to burn."

And though in one passage he seems to indicate a belief that woman could only be saved by maternity from the punishment incurred by the disobedience of Eve, in another he formally declares that " he that giveth her in marriage doeth well; but he that giveth her not in marriage doeth better," thus showing a marked preference for the celibate state, in which the devout could give themselves up wholly to the service of the Lord.

The Apostle's discussion of these subjects shows that already there had commenced a strong ascetic movement, raising questions which he found hard to answer, without on the one hand repressing the ardour of serviceable disciples, and on the other, imposing burdens on neophytes too grievous to be borne. He foresaw that the former would soon run beyond the bounds of reason, and he condemned in advance the heresies which should forbid marriage; but that the tendency of the faithful lay in that direction was inevitable. In those times, no one would join the infant Church who did not regard the things of earth as vile in comparison with the priceless treasures of heaven, and the more fervent the conviction, the more it

13

was apt to find expression in mortifying the flesh and purchasing salvation by the sacrifice of passions and affections. Such especially would be the tendency of the stronger natures which lead their fellows; and the admiration of the multitude for their superior virtue and fortitude would soon invest them with a reputation for holiness which would render them doubly influential.

There was much, indeed, in the teaching of the Church, and in its relations with the Gentiles, to promote and strengthen this tendency. The world into which Christianity was born was hopelessly corrupt. Licentiousness, probably, has never been more defiant than amid the splendours of the early Empire. The gossip of Suetonius and the denunciations of Juvenal depict a society in which purity was scarce understood, and in which unchastity was no sin and hardly even a reproach. To reclaim such a population needed a new system of morality, and it is observable that in the New Testament particular stress is laid upon the avoidance of fornication, especially after the faith had begun to spread beyond the boundaries of Judea. The early Christians thus were a thoroughly puritan sect, teaching by example as well as by precept, and their lives were a perpetual protest against the licence which reigned around them. It therefore was natural that converts, after their eyes were opened to the hideous nature of the prevailing vices, should feel a tendency to plunge into the other extreme, and should come to regard even the lawful indulgence of human instincts as a weakness to be repressed. Civilisation, indeed, owes too much to the reform which Christianity rendered possible in the relations of the sexes, for us to condemn too severely even the extravagances into which it was sometimes betrayed.

That it was becoming not uncommon for Christians to follow a celibate life is shown by various passages in the early Fathers. St. Ignatius alludes to abstinence from marriage in honour of God as a matter not uncommon, but which was wholly voluntary and to be practised in humility and secrecy, for the virtue of continence would be much more than counterbalanced by the sin of pride. The Apologists, Justin Martyr about the year 150, Athenagoras about 180, and Minucius Felix about 200, all refer to the chastity and sobriety which characterised the sect, the celibacy practised by some members, and the single marriage of others, of which the sole object was the securing of offspring and not the gratification of the passions. Athenagoras, indeed, condemns the exaggerations of asceticism in terms which show that already they had made their appearance among the more ardent disciples, but that they were strongly disapproved by the wiser portion of the Church. Origen seems to regard celibacy as rather springing from a desire to serve God without the interruptions arising from the cares of marriage than from asceticism, and does not hesitate to condemn those who abandoned their wives even from the highest motives. The impulse towards asceticism, however, was too strong to be resisted. Zealots were not wanting who boldly declared that to follow the precepts of the Creator was incompatible with salvation, as though a beneficent God should create a species which could only preserve its temporal existence by forfeiting its promised eternity. Ambitious men were to be found who sought notoriety or power by the reputation to be gained from self-denying austerities, which brought to them followers and believers venerating them as prophets. Philosophers were there also, who, wearied with the endless speculations of Pythagorean and Platonic mysticism, sought relief in the practical morality of the Gospel, and perverted the simplicity of its teachings by interweaving with it the subtle philosophy of the schools, producing an apparent intoxication which plunged them either into the grossest sensuality or the most rigorous asceticism. Such were Julius Cassianus, Saturnilus, Marcion, the founder of the Marcionites, Tatianus, the heresiarch of the Encratitians, and the unknown authors of a crowd of sects which, under the names of Abstinentes, Apotactici, Excalceati, etc., practised various forms of self-mortification, and denounced marriage as a deadly sin. Such, on the other hand, were Valentinus and Prodicus, who originated the mystic libertinism of the Gnostics; Marcus, whose followers, the Marcosians, were accused of advocating the most disgusting practices; Carpocrates, who held that the soul was obliged to have experience of all manner of evil before it could be elevated to God; Basilides, whose sectaries honoured the passions as emanating from the Creator, and taught that their impulses were to be followed. Even the Ebionites did not escape the taint, if Epiphanius is to be believed; and there was also a sect advocating promiscuous intercourse, to whom the name of Nicolites was given in memory of the story of Nicholas, the deacon of the primitive Church, who offered to his fellow-disciples the wife whom he was accused of loving with too exclusive a devotion—a sect which merited the reproof of St. John, and which has a special interest for us, because in the eleventh century all who opposed clerical celibacy were branded with its name, thus affording to the sacerdotal party the inestimable advantage of stigmatising their antagonists with an opprobrious epithet of the most damaging character, and of invoking the authority of the Apocalypse for their destruction.

The Church was too pure to be led astray by the libertinism of the latter class of heresiarchs. The time had not yet come for the former, and men who, in the thirteenth century, might perhaps have founded powerful orders, and have been reverenced by the Christian world as almost equal to Christ himself, were, through their anachronism, stigmatised as heretics, and expelled from the communion of the faithful. Still, their religious fervour and rigorous virtue had a gradually increasing influence in stimulating the development of the ascetic principle, if not in the acknowledged dogmas, at all events, in the practice of the Church, as may be seen when, towards the close of the second century, Dionysius of Corinth finds himself obliged to reprove Pinytus, Bishop of Gnosus, for endeavouring to render celibacy compulsory among his flock, to the manifest danger of those whose virtue was less austere. In all this, unquestionably, the ascetic ideas of the East had much to do, and these were chiefly represented by Buddhism, which, since the reign of Asoka, in the third century B.C., had been the dominant religion of India. A curious allusion in St. Jerome to Buddha's having been born of a virgin, shows a familiarity with details of Buddhist belief which presupposes a general knowledge of that faith; and though the divinised Maya, wife of Suddhodana, is not absolutely described as a virgin in Eastern tradition, yet she and her husband had taken a vow of continence before Buddha, from the Tushita heaven, to fulfil his predestined salvation of mankind and establishment of the kingdom of righteousness, had selected her as the vehicle of his incarnation. Much in the legend of his birth, of the miracles which attended it, of his encounter with the

Tempter, and other details of his life, is curiously suggestive of the source whence sprang the corresponding legend of the life of Christ, more particularly as related in the pseudo-gospels. Not only this, but many of the observances of Latin Christianity would seem explicable by derivation from Buddhism, such as monasticism, the tonsure, the use of beads, confession, penance, and absolution, the sign of the cross, relic-worship, and miracles wrought by relics, the purchase of salvation by gifts to the Church, pilgrimages to sacred places, etc., etc. Even the nimbus which in sacred art surrounds the head of holy personages is to be found in the sculptures of the Buddhist Topes, and the Sangreal, or Holy Cup of the Last Supper, which was the object of lifelong quest by the Christian knight, is like the Patra or begging-dish of Buddha, which was the subject of many curious legends. It is no wonder that when the good Jesuit missionaries of the sixteenth century found among the heathen of Asia so much of what they were familiar with at home, they could not decide whether it was the remains of a pre-existing Catholicism, or whether Satan, to damn irrevocably the souls of men, had parodied and travestied the sacred mysteries and ceremonies, and introduced them in those distant regions. We may there-fore, perhaps, ascribe to Buddhist beliefs at least a portion of the influence which led the Church into the extravagances of asceticism.

The first official manifestation of this growing tendency, applied to the relations of the sexes, is to be seen in the legislation with regard to second marriages. In the pas-sages alluded to above from Athenagoras and Minucius Felix, the fact is referred to that second marriages were already regarded as little better than adulterous, while Justin Martyr denounces them as sinful, in spite of the permission so freely granted by St. Paul for such unions. Though this opinion was branded by the Church as heretical when it was elevated into an article of belief by the Mon-tanists and Cathari, or Puritans, and though even the eminence and piety of Tertullian could not save him from excommunication when he embraced the doctrine, yet the orthodox came very near accepting it, for the Council of Neocæsarea, in 314, forbade priests from honouring with their presence the festivities customary on such occasions, as those who married a second time were subject to penance,

and that of Laodicea, in 352, deemed it a matter of indulgence to admit to communion those who contracted such
unions, after they had redeemed their fault by fasting and
prayer for a certain time—a principle repeated by innumerable councils during the succeeding centuries. So far did
this prejudice extend that as late as 484 we find the Pope,
St. Gelasius, obliged to remind the faithful that such
marriages are not to be refused to laymen. It is by no
means impossible that this opposition to repeated wedlock
may have arisen, or perhaps have been intensified, by a
similar feeling which existed among the Pagans, at least
with regard to the second marriages of women. Moreover,
in Rome the Flamen Dialis was restricted to a single marriage with a virgin, and such was the strictness with which
this was observed that, as the assistance of the Flaminica,
his wife, was necessary to the performance of some religious
rites, he was obliged to resign when left a widower.

Although the Church forbore to prohibit absolutely the
repetition of matrimony among the laity, it yet, at an early
though uncertain period, imitated the rule enforced on the
Flamen Dialis, and rendered it obligatory on the priesthood, thus for the first time drawing a distinct line of
separation between the great body of the faithful and those
who officiated as ministers of Christ. It thus became
firmly and irrevocably established that no " digamus " or
husband of a second wife was admissible to holy orders.
As early as the time of Tertullian we find the rule formally
expressed by him, and he even assures us that the whole
structure of the Church was based upon the single marriages of its ministers. Indeed, the holy rites came to be
regarded as so entirely incompatible with repetition of
wedlock that the Council of Elvira, in 305, while admitting
that in cases of extreme necessity a layman might administer
baptism, is careful to specify that he must not be a
" digamus."

Yet this restriction on the priesthood was not easily
enforced, and already we begin to hear the complaints,
which have followed uninterruptedly for more than fifteen
hundred years, of the evasion or disregard of the regulations
whereby the Church has sought to repress the irrepressible
instincts of humanity. In the early part of the third
century Hippolytus, Bishop of Portus, in his enumeration
of the evil ways of Pope Calixtus, taxes the pontiff with

admitting to the priesthood men who had been married twice, and even thrice, and with permitting priests to marry while in orders. Even the great apostle of celibacy, St. Jerome, expresses surprise that Oceanus should object to Carterius, a Spanish bishop, on the ground that he had had a wife before baptism, and a second one after admission to the Church. The world, he adds, is full of such prelates, not only in the lower orders but in the episcopate, the digamous members of which exceed in number the three hundred prelates lately assembled at the Council of Rimini. Yet this was the formal rule of the Church as enunciated in the Apostolic Constitutions and Canons—bodies of ecclesiastical law not included, indeed, in the canon of Scripture, but yet so venerable that their origin was already lost sight of, and they were everywhere received as authoritative expositions of primitive discipline.

The introduction of this entering-wedge is easily explicable. St. Paul had specified the monogamic condition— "unius uxoris vir"—as a prerequisite to the diaconate, priesthood, and episcopate, and the temper of the times was such as to lead irresistibly to this being taken in its literal sense, rather than to adopt the more rational view that it was intended to exclude those among the Gentiles who indulged in the prevalent vice of concubinage, or who among the Jews had fallen into the sin of polygamy—or those among either race who had taken advantage, either before or after conversion, of the disgraceful laxity prevalent with regard to divorces, for, as we learn from Origen, the rule was by no means obeyed which forbade a divorced person to marry during the lifetime of the other spouse.

When once this principle was fairly established, and when at the same time the efforts of the Montanists to render it binding on the whole body of Christian believers had failed, a distinction was enforced between the clergy and the laity, as regards the marriage-tie, which gave to the former an affectation of sanctity, and which was readily capable of indefinite expansion. It is therefore easy to comprehend the revival, which shortly followed, of the old Levitical rule requiring the priesthood to marry none but virgins—a rule which was early adopted, though it took long to establish it in practice, for as late as 414 we find Innocent I complaining that men who had taken widows to wife were even elevated to the episcopate, and Leo I

devoted several of his epistles to its enforcement. A
corollary to this speedily followed, which required a priest
whose wife was guilty of adultery to put her away, since
further commerce with her rendered him unfit for the
functions of his office; and this again, as subsequent
authorities were careful to point out, afforded a powerful
reason for requiring absolute celibacy on the part of the
clergy, for, in view of the fragility of the sex, no man could
feel assured that he was not subject to this disability, nor
could the faithful be certain that his ministrations were
not tainted with irregularity.   We thus reach the state of
ecclesiastical discipline at the close of the third century, as
authoritatively set forth in the Apostolic Constitutions and
Canons—bishops and priests allowed to retain the wives
whom they may have had before ordination, but not to
marry in orders; the lower grades, deacons, subdeacons,
etc., allowed to marry after entering the Church; but all
were to be husbands of but one wife, who must be neither
a widow, a divorced woman, nor a concubine.

Meanwhile, public opinion had moved faster than the
canons. Ascetic sects multiplied and increased, and the
highest authorities in the Church could not always resist
the contagion. A fresh incitement, indeed, had been
found in the neo-platonic philosophy which arose in the
beginning of the third century. Ammonius Saccas, its
founder, was a Christian, though not altogether orthodox,
and his two most noted disciples, Origen and Plotinus,
fairly illustrate the influence which his doctrines had upon
both the Christian and the Pagan world. As to the latter,
neo-platonism borrowed from Christian and Indian as well
as Greek philosophy, evolving out of them all a system of
elevated mysticism in which the senses and the appetites
were to be controlled as severely almost as in the Sankhya
and Buddhist schools. Commerce between the sexes was
denounced as a pollution degrading to the soul, and the best
offering which a worshipper could bring to the Deity was a
soul absolutely free from all trace of passion. Although
neo-platonism engaged in a hopeless struggle to stay the
advancing tide of Christianity, and thus became its most
active opponent, yet the lofty asceticism which it inculcated
could not be without influence upon its antagonists, were it
only through inflaming the emulation of those who were
already predisposed to regard the mortification of the

flesh as a means of raising the soul to communion with God.

How these motives worked upon an ardent and uncompromising temperament is seen in the self-sacrifice of Origen, showing how absorbing was the struggle, and how intense was the conviction that nature must be conquered at all hazards and by any practicable means, although he himself afterwards condemned this practical rendering of the text (Matt. xix. 12) on which it was founded. Origen was by no means the first who had sought in this way to gain the kingdom of heaven, for he alludes to it as a matter by no means unexampled, and before him Justin Martyr had chronicled with approbation a similar case. In fact, there is said to have been an obscene sect which, under the name of Valesians, followed the practice and procured proselytes by inflicting forcible mutilation upon all who were unhappy enough to fall into their hands; and though their date and locality are unknown to those who allude to them, it would be rash, in view of similar eccentricities existing in more modern times, to pronounce them wholly apocryphal. The repeated prohibitions of the practice, in the canons of the succeeding century, show how difficult it was to eradicate the belief that such self-immolation was an acceptable offering to a beneficent Creator. Sextus Philosophus, an ascetic author of the third century, whose writings long passed current under the name of Pope Sixtus II, did not hesitate openly to advocate it, and though his arguments were regarded as heretical by the Church, they were at least as logical as the practical application given to the texts commonly cited in defence of the prohibition of marriage.

Not all, however, who sought the praise or the merits of austerity were prepared to pay such a price for victory in the struggle with themselves. Enthusiastic spirits, exalted with the prospect of earthly peace and heavenly rewards promised to those who should preserve the purity of virginity and live abstracted from the cares and pleasures of family life, frequently took the vow of continence which had already become customary. This vow as yet was purely voluntary. It bound those who assumed it only during their own pleasure, nor were they, during its continuance, in any way segregated from the world. So untrammelled, indeed, were their actions that Cyprian is

forced to rebuke the holy virgins for frequenting the public
baths in which both sexes indiscriminately exposed themselves, and he does not hesitate to attribute to this cause
much of the ruin and dishonour of its votaries which
afflicted the Church.   Yet this was by no means the severest
trial to which many of them subjected their constancy.
Perhaps it was to court spiritual martyrdom, and to show
to their admirers a virtue robust enough to endure the most
fiery trials, perhaps it was that they found too late that they
had over-estimated their strength, and that existence was a
burden without the society of some beloved object—but,
whatever may have been the motive, it became a frequent
custom to associate themselves with congenial souls of the
other sex, and form Platonic unions in which they aspired
to maintain the purity which they had vowed to God.   At
the best, the sensible members of the Church were scandalised by these performances, which afforded so much
scope for the mockery of the heathen ; but scandal frequently
was justified, for Nature often asserted her outraged rights,
to the shame and confusion of the hapless votaries of an
artificial and superhuman perfection.   Tertullian does not
hesitate to assert that the desire of enjoying the reputation
of virginity led to much secret immorality, the effects of
which were concealed by resort to infanticide.   Cyprian
chronicles, not with surprise but sorrow, the numerous
instances which he had known of ruin resulting to those
who had so fatally miscalculated their power of resistance :
with honest indignation he denounces the ecclesiastics who
abandoned themselves to practices which, if not absolutely
criminal, were brutally degrading : and with a degree of
common sense hardly to be looked for in so warm an admirer
of the perfection of virginity, he advises that those whose
weakness rendered doubtful the strict observance of their
vows, should return to the world and satisfy their longings
in legitimate marriage. The heresiarch Paul of Samosata
affords, perhaps, the most conspicuous example of the
extent to which these and similar practices were sometimes
carried, and, in condemning him, the good fathers of the
Council of Antioch lamented the general prevalence of the
evils thence arising.   Cyprian's prudent consideration for
the weakness of human nature was as yet shared by the
ecclesiastical authorities.   In the order of widows professed, which was recognised by the early Church, the

Apostolic Constitutions enjoin that none should be admitted below the age of sixty, in order to avoid the danger of their infringing their vows by a second marriage, but the writer is careful to add that such a marriage is not to be condemned for itself, but only on account of the falsehood which it occasioned. These widows and virgins were supported out of the tithes of the Church, and were, therefore, necessarily subjected to its control, so that it is evident that there was nothing irrevocable in the vows wherewith they were bound. The change is marked by the end of the century, when widows who thus forsook their order were unrelentingly· and irrevocably condemned, deprived of communion, and expelled from social intercourse.

While the Christian world was thus agitated with the speculative doctrines and practical observances of so many enthusiasts, heretical and orthodox, who seemed to regard the relations between the sexes as the crucial test and most trustworthy exponent of religious ardour, a new dogma arose in the East and advanced with a rapidity which shows how much progress the ascetic spirit had already made, and how ripe were the unsettled minds of zealots to welcome whatever system of belief promised to trample most ruthlessly upon nature, and to render the path of salvation inaccessible to all save those capable of the sternest self-mortification. Towards the end of the third century, the Persian Manes made his advent in the Empire, proclaiming himself as the Paraclete and as a new and higher Apostle. Though his career as an envoy of Christ was stoutly resisted by the orthodox, and though, after a chequered life, he was flayed alive, and his followers in Persia were slaughtered by Varahran I, his Western disciples were more fortunate, and the hateful name of Manichæan acquired a sinister notoriety which maintained its significance for a thousand years. His system was a compound of several faiths, and though it failed in its comprehensive design to bring all mankind together in one form of belief, it yet had features which won for it the enthusiastic adhesion of men of diverse races. The way was already prepared for its reception among both Gentiles and Christians by the prevalence on the one hand of the Mithraic worship, and on the other of Gnosticism. The Dualistic theory was attractive to those who were disheartened in the vain attempt to reconcile the existence of evil with an omnipotent and all-merciful Creator; the

Platonic identity of the soul with the Godhead was a recommendation to the schoolmen; the Brahmanical and Buddhist views as to abstinence from meat and marriage won adherents among the remains of the ascetic sects, and were acceptable even to those among the orthodox who were yielding to the increasing influence of asceticism. The fierce temporal persecution of the still Pagan emperors, and the unavailing anathemas of the Church, as yet confined to mere spiritual censures, seemed only to give fresh impetus to the proselytizing energy of the Elect, and to scatter the seed more widely among the faithful. After this period we hear but little of the earlier ascetic heresies; the system of Manes, as moulded by his followers, was so much more complete, that it swallowed up its prototypes and rivals, and concentrated upon itself the vindictiveness of a combined Church and State. So thorough was this identification that in 381 an edict of Theodosius the Great directed against the Manichæans assumes that the sects of Encratitæ, Apotactitæ, Hydroparastitæ, and Saccofori were merely nominal disguises adopted to elude detection.

That Manichæism, in fact, exercised a substantial influence over orthodoxy is shown in other directions besides that of asceticism. The Eucharist was thus diverted from its original form of a substantial meal—one of the means by which the charity of the Church was administered to the poor—into the symbolical wafer and wine which assimilated it so closely to the Izeshne sacrifice, the most frequent Mazdean rite, and one which, like the Mass, was customarily performed for the benefit of departed souls. Manes, in combining Mazdeism with Christianity, had adopted the Eucharist in the Mazdean form, and had confined the use of the cup to the priesthood; and this lay communion in one element became so well recognised as a test of Manichæism that Leo the Great ordered the excommunication of all who received the sacrament after that fashion. It may therefore be remarked as a curious coincidence that when Manichæism was revived by the Albigenses, in the eleventh and twelfth centuries, the Church, which until then had preserved its ancient custom, adopted the lay communion in one element and adhered to it so rigidly that, as we shall see hereafter, not even the dread of the Hussite schism nor the earnest requests of those who remained faithful during the perils of the Reformation, could induce it to grant the cup to the laity. Lay communion in one element drew a line of distinction between the priest and his flock which the former would not willingly abandon.

Although, in the region of asceticism, the Church might not be willing to adopt the Manichæan doctrine that man's body is the work of the Evil Principle, and that the Soul as partaking of the substance of God was engaged in an eternal war with it, and should thus abuse and mortify it, yet the general tendencies of the religious enthusiasm of the time made the practical result common to all, and there can scarce be doubt that the spreading belief in Manes exercised a powerful influence in accelerating the progress of orthodox asceticism. The fact that as yet the Church was persecuted and had no power of imposing its yoke on others bound it to the necessity of maintaining its character for superior sanctity and virtue; and ardent believers could not afford to let themselves be outdone by heretics in the austerities which were popularly received as the conclusive evidence of religious sincerity. We may therefore easily imagine a rivalry in asceticism which, however unconscious, may yet have powerfully stimulated the stern and unbending souls of such men as St. Antony, Malchus, and Hilarion, even as Tertullian, after combating the errors of Montanus, adopted and exaggerated his ascetic heresies. It would be easy to show from the hagiologies how soon the Church virtually assented to the Manichæan notion that the body was to be mortified and macerated as the only mode of triumphing in the perennial struggle with the Evil Principle, but this would be foreign to our subject. It is sufficient for us here to indicate how narrowly in process of time she escaped from adopting practically, if not theoretically, the Manichæan condemnation of marriage. This is clearly demonstrated by the writings of the orthodox Fathers, who in their extravagant praise of virginity could not escape from decrying wedlock. It was stigmatised as the means of transmitting and perpetuating original sin, an act which necessarily entailed sin on its participants, and one which at best could only look for mercy and pardon and be allowed only on sufferance. It is therefore not surprising if those who were not prepared to join in the progress of asceticism should habitually stigmatise the mortifications of their more enthusiastic brethren as Manichæism in spirit if not in name.

Jovinian, it would seem, did not neglect this ready means of attack; nor was he alone, for Jerome complains that the worldly and dissolute sheltered themselves behind the same excuse, and derided as Manichæans all who were pallid and faint from maceration and fasting. The comparison, indeed, became a not untruthful one, when the Christian and the heretic both adopted the plan of restricting their sacred class from the pleasures of the world—when the Manichæan Elect, who remained unmarried and fasted upon vegetable food, were equivalent to the priesthood, while the Auditors, to whom a larger liberty was allowed, represented the ortho- dox laity. It is by no means improbable that the tenets of the Manichæans have been exaggerated by their opponents in controversy, and that in process of time, when the Church became avowedly ascetic, there was practically little differ- ence on this point between Manichæism and Orthodoxy. St. Augustin, indeed, represents the Manichæan Faustus as arguing that both in doctrine and practice his sect only fol- lowed the example of the Church. He ridiculed the idea that it could prohibit marriage, and asserts positively that it only encouraged those who manifested a desire to per- severe in continence. If this is to be received as an authen- tic exposition of Manichæan principles, it will be seen that the Church was not long in outstripping the heretics.

In fact, even as early as the time of Cyprian, that saint, in allusion to the parable of the sower, had rated the com- parative merits of martyrdom to virginity as one hundred to sixty; while, after martyrdom had gone out of fashion, St. Patrick, in the fifth century, undertook a more elaborate classification in which bishops and doctors of the Church, monks and virgins, were rated at one hundred, ecclesiastics in general and widows professed at sixty, while the faithful laity stand only at thirty. It was therefore a heresy for Jovinian to claim equal merit for maidens, wives, and widows; and though St. Jerome, in controverting this, com- menced by carefully denying any intentional disrespect towards marriage, still his controversial ardour carried him so far in that direction, that he aroused considerable feeling among reasonable men and was obliged formally and repeatedly to excuse himself. His contempt for marriage, indeed, was so extreme that in spite of the recognised primacy of St. Peter, he considered that apostle as decidedly inferior to St. John, because the one had a wife and the other was a virgin—apparently not observing that, as he denied the marriage of all the apostles save Peter, he was thus relegating the head of the Church to the last place among the holy twelve. St. Augustin recognised the difficulty of reconciling the current views of his time with the necessities of humanity when he wrote a treatise for the purpose of proving the difference between the good of marriage and the evil of carnal desire, which, while it perpetuated the species, likewise perpetuated original sin; and he gave a signal example of the manner in which enthusiastic asceticism sought to improve upon the work of the Creator when he uttered the pious wish that all mankind should abstain from marriage, so that the human race might the sooner come to an end. St. Martin of Tours was somewhat less extravagant when he was willing to admit that marriage was pardonable, while licentiousness was punishable and virginity glorious; and he was far behind the enthusiasts of his time, for, while he deplores the miserable folly of those who consider marriage to be equal to virginity, he is likewise obliged to reprove the error of those who were willing only to compare it to lechery—the former belief being evidently much more erroneous than the latter in the Saint's estimation. So a treatise on chastity, which passes under the name of Sixtus III, barely admits that married people can earn eternal life; and it apparently is only the dread of being classed with Manichæans that leads the author to shrink from the conclusions of his own reasoning, and to state that he does not absolutely condemn wedlock or prohibit it to those who cannot restrain their passions. Not a little Manichæan in its tendency is a declaration of Gregory the Great to Augustine the Apostle of England that connubial pleasures cannot possibly be free from sin; and quite as decided is another assertion of the same Pope that the strictness of monastic life is the only possible mode of salvation for the greater portion of mankind. It was the natural practical deduction from this which is drawn by the Penitential of Theodore, when it commands those who contract a first marriage to abstain from entering a church for thirty days, after which they are to perform penance for forty more; while a digamus is subjected to penance for a year, and a trigamus, or one oftener married, for seven years. When marriage was thus regarded as a sin, we can scarcely be surprised at the practical Manichæism of

Epiphanius, who declares that the Church is based upon virginity as on its corner-stone.

This ascetic development, however, was not destined to triumph without occasional efforts at repression. At the close of the third century, the highest authorities of the Church still condemned the ruthless asceticism, which was subsequently glorified as the loftiest achievement of Christian virtue. Thus in the Apostolic Constitutions, the influence of Manichæism and its kindred sects is as yet only manifested by the opposition aroused to their doctrines; and the necessity of that opposition is indicated by the careful and repeated declaration of the purity and sanctity of the marriage-tie, both as regards the priesthood and the laity. Not less instructive is the bare toleration almost grudgingly extended to vows of celibacy, and the cautious restriction which declares that such vows are not to be held as justifying a disparagement of matrimony. No stronger contrast can be looked for than that produced by little more than a century between the rational piety of these provisions and the extravagant rhapsodies of Jerome, Augustin, and Martin. The calm good sense of Lactantius also takes occasion to reprove the extravagance which regarded all indulgence of the natural affections as a sin requiring repentance and pardon. He assumes, indeed, that perpetual continence, as being opposed to the law of nature, is not recommended, but only permitted by the Creator, thus reversing the maxims of the zealots. Equally suggestive are the Apostolic Canons. The sixth of these pronounces deposition on the bishop or priest who separates himself from his wife under pretext of religion; while the fiftieth threatens equally rigorous punishment on the clerk or layman who shall abstain from marriage, from wine, or from meat, not for the purpose of devoting himself to piety, but on account of holding them in abomination—such belief being a slander on the goodness of God, and a calumny on the perfection of his works. Even a hundred years later there is still an occasional protest to be heard, showing how the more moderate section of the Church felt the danger to which she was exposed by intemperate ascetic zeal, and how narrow was the path which she had to trace between orthodoxy and heresy. The Fourth Council of Carthage, in 398, prescribing the examination to which all bishops-elect were to be subjected, specifies for inquiry among other points of faith questions as to whether the candidate disapproves of marriage, or condemns second marriages, or prohibits the use of meat. It shows how readily Manichæism or Catharism might lurk in the asceticism of the most devout.

The tide, however, was fairly on the flood, and the resistance of the more reasonable among ecclesiastics was unavailing. It is true that the influences which were now so powerful could evidently not be applied to the whole body of believers, as they would only result in gradual extinction or in lawless licentiousness; but as the ecclesiastical body was perpetuated by a kind of spiritual generation, it could, without hazarding a decrease of numbers, be subjected to regulations which should render obligatory the asceticism which as yet had been optional. The only wonder, in fact, is that this had not been earlier attempted. Such a rule, by widening the distinction between laymen and ecclesiastics, would be grateful to the growing sacerdotalism which ere long was to take complete possession of the Church. Such a rule, moreover, was not only indicated by the examples of Buddhism and Manichæism, but had abundant precedent among the Pagans of the Empire. More than one passage in classical writers shows that abstinence from women was regarded as an essential prerequisite to certain religious observances, and the existence of this feeling among the primitive Christians, based upon the injunction of Ahimelech, is indicated by St. Paul—and this custom, as sacerdotalism developed, and formalism rendered the life of the minister of the altar a ceaseless round of daily service, would practically separate husband and wife. Moreover, much of the Pagan worship subjected its officials to general restrictions of greater or less severity. Diodorus Siculus states that the Egyptian priests were permitted to have but one wife, although unlimited polygamy was allowed to the people; while Chæremon the Stoic, according to St. Jerome, and Plutarch indicate that they were obliged to observe entire continence. The castration of the Galli, the priests of Rhea at Hierapolis, though explained by the myth of Attys, was evidently only a survival of the fierce asceticism which counterbalanced the licentiousness of the older Phœnician worship. The rites of the Gaditanian Hercules were conducted by ministers obliged to observe chastity, and the foot of woman was not permitted to pollute the sacred precincts of the temple; while the priestesses of Gea Eurysternus at Ægæ were required to preserve the strictest celibacy. The hierophants of Demeter in Athens were obliged to maintain unsullied continence. The priestesses of the Delphic Apollo, the Achaian Hera, the Scythian Artemis, and the Thespian Heracles were virgins. In Africa, those of Ceres were separated from their husbands with a rigour of asceticism which forbade even a kiss to their orphaned children; while in Rome the name of Vestal has passed into a proverb, although it is true that while they were only six or seven in number, the distinguished honours and privileges accorded to them were insufficient to induce parents to devote their children to the holy service, and there was difficulty in keeping the ranks filled.

The earliest recorded attempt by the Church to imitate these restrictions was made in 305 by the Spanish Council of Elvira, which declared, in the most positive manner, that all concerned in the ministry of the altar should maintain entire abstinence from their wives under pain of forfeiting their positions. It further endeavoured to put an end to the scandals of the Agapetæ, or female companions of the clergy, which the rigour of this canon was so well fitted to increase, by decreeing that no ecclesiastic should permit any woman to dwell with him, except a sister or a daughter, and even these only when bound by a vow of virginity. This was simply the legislation of a local synod, and its canons were not entitled to respect or obedience beyond the limits of the churches directly represented. Its action may not improbably be attributed to the commanding influence of one of its leading members, Osius, Bishop of Cordova, and that action had no result in inducing the Church at large to adopt the new rule, for some ten years later were held the more important Councils of Ancyra and Neocæsarea, and the absence of any allusion to it in their proceedings seems to fix for us the discipline of the period in this respect, at least in the East. By the canons of Ancyra we learn that marriage in orders was still permitted, as far as the diaconate, provided the postulant at the time of ordination declared his desire to enjoy the privilege and asserted his inability to remain single. This is even less stringent than the rule quoted above from the Apostolic Constitutions, and proves incontestably that there was no thought of imposing any restriction upon the intercourse between the married clergy and their wives. By the Council of Neo-cæsarea it was provided that a priest marrying in orders should be deposed, but a heavier punishment was reserved for what was then, in reverse of the standard of later times, regarded as the greater sin of licentiousness. That no interference was intended by this with the relations existing between those who had married in the lower grades and their wives, is shown by another canon which deprives of his functions any priest who submitted to the commission of adultery by his wife without separating from her—being a practical extension of the Levitical rule, now by common consent adopted as a portion of ecclesiastical discipline. Yet, even in the East, there was a growing tendency to more rigid asceticism than this, for, about the same period, we find Eusebius stating that it is becoming in those who are engaged in the ministry of God to abstain from their wives, though his argument in justification of this is based upon the multiplicity of occupation, which in civilised society rendered it desirable for those enlisted in the service of the Church to be relieved from family cares and anxieties.

CHAPTER III

THE COUNCIL OF NICÆA

THUS far the Church had grown and strengthened without
any recognised head or acknowledged legislative power.
Each patriarch or metropolitan, surrounded by his provincial synod, established regulations for his own region,
with no standard but the canon of Scripture, being responsible only to the opinion of his compeers, who might refuse
to receive his clergy to communion.   Under this democratic
autonomy the Church had outlived persecution, had repudiated and cast out innumerable successive heresies, and,
thanks to external pressure, had managed to preserve its
unity.   The time, however, had now come for a different
order of things.   Constantine, following the dictates of
his unerring political sagacity, allied himself with the
Christians and professed conversion;   and Christianity,
powerful even when merely existing on sufferance, became
the religion of the state.   As such, the maintenance of its
unity seemed to be a political necessity, to accomplish which
required some central power entitled to general respect and
implicit obedience.   The subtle disputations concerning the
fast-spreading Arian heresy were not likely to be stilled by
the mere *ipse dixit* of any of the Apostolic Sees, nor by the
secular wisdom of crown lawyers and philosophic courtiers.
A legislative tribunal, which should be at once a court of
last appeal and a senate empowered to enact laws of binding
force, as the final decisions of the Church Universal, was
not an unpromising suggestion.   Such an assemblage had
hitherto been impossible, for the distances to be traversed
and the expenses of the journey would have precluded an
attendance sufficiently numerous to earn the title of
Œcumenical;   but an imperial rescript which put the
governmental machinery of posts at the service of the
prelates could smooth all difficulties, and enable every
diocese to send its representative.   In the year 325, there-

fore, the FIRST GENERAL COUNCIL assembled at Nicæa. With the fruitlessness of its endeavours to extinguish the Arian controversy we have nothing to do, but in its legislative capacity its labours had an influence upon our subject which merits a closer examination than would appear necessary from the seemingly unimportant nature of the proceedings themselves.

With the full belief that the canons of a general council were the result of the direct operation of the Holy Ghost, they were of course entitled to unquestioning reverence, and those of Nicæa have always been regarded as of special and peculiar authority, cutting off all debate on any question to which they might be applicable. The third of the series has been the main reliance of sacerdotal controversialists, and has been constantly appealed to as the unanswerable justification for enforcing the rule of discipline which enjoined celibacy on all admitted to holy orders. Its simple phraseology would hardly seem to warrant such conclusion. "The Great Synod has strictly forbidden to bishop, priest, and deacon, and to every ecclesiastic, to have a 'subintroductam mulierem,' unless perhaps a mother, a sister, an aunt, or such person only as may be above suspicion."

This is the only allusion to the subject in the Nicene canons. As it does not include wives among those exempted from the prohibition of residence, we can hardly be surprised that those who believe celibacy to be of apostolic origin should assume that it was intended to pronounce an absolute separation between husband and wife. As the Council of Elvira, however, contains the only enunciation of such a rule, previous to that of Nicæa, and as those of Ancyra and Neocæsarea and the Apostolic Constitutions and Canons, directly or indirectly, allow the conjugal relations of ecclesiastics to remain undisturbed, we are certainly justified in assuming the impossibility that an innovation of so much importance would be introduced in the discipline of the universal Church without being specifically designated and commanded in terms which would admit of no misunderstanding. That the meaning of the canon is really and simply that alone which appears on the surface—to put an end to the disorders and scandals arising from the improper female companions of unmarried priests—is, moreover, I think, susceptible of easy demonstration.

The term "subintroducta mulier"—γυνη συνεισακτος—is

almost invariably used in an unfavourable sense, and is
equivalent to the " fœmina extranea," and nearly to the
" focaria " and " concubina " of later times, as well as to
the " agapeta " and " dilecta " of earlier date.   We have
already seen how Cyprian, seventy-five years before, denounced the agapetæ who even then were so common, and
whose companionship proved so disastrous to all parties,
but the custom continued, and its evil consequences became
more and more openly and shamelessly displayed.   In 314
the Council of Ancyra denounced it in terms implying its
public recognition.   At the close of the same century,
Jerome still finds in it ample material for his fiery indignation ; and his denunciations manifest that it was still a
corroding cancer in the purity of the Church, prevailing
to an extent that rendered its suppression a matter of the
utmost importance.   The testimony of Epiphanius is almost
equally strong, and shows that it was a source of general
popular reproach.   Such a reform was therefore well
worthy the attention of the Nicene fathers, and that this
was the special object of the canon is indicated by Jerome
himself, who appeals to it as the authority under which an
ecclesiastic refusing to separate himself from his agapeta
could be punished ; it was to be read to the offender, and if
he neglected obedience to its commands, he was to be
anathematised.

That it had no bearing upon the wives of priests can,
moreover, be proved by several reasons.   The restriction
on matrimony has never at any time extended below the
subdiaconate, the inferior grades of the secular clergy
having always been free to live with their wives, even in
the periods of the most rigid asceticism.   The canon, however, makes no distinction.   Its commands are applicable
" alicui omnino qui in clero est."   To suppose, therefore,
that it was intended to include wives in its restriction is
to prove too much—the *reductio ad absurdum* is complete.
Equally convincing is the fact that when, towards the close
of the century, the rule of celibacy and separation was
introduced, and Siricius and Innocent I ransacked the
Gospels for texts of more than doubtful application with
which to support the innovation, they made no reference
whatever to the Nicene canon.   Had it been understood at
that period as bearing on the subject, it would have been
all-sufficient in itself.   The reverence felt for the Council of

Nicæa was too great, and the absolute obedience claimed for its commands was too willingly rendered, for such an omission to be possible. That Siricius and Innocent should not have adduced it is therefore proof incontrovertible that it was as yet construed as directed solely against the improper companions of the clergy. If further evidence to the same effect be required, it may be found in a law of Honorius, promulgated in 420, in which, while forbidding the clergy to keep " mulieres extraneæ " under the name of " sorores," and permitting only mothers, daughters, and sisters, he adds that the desire for chastity does not prohibit the residence of wives whose merits have assisted in rendering their husbands worthy of the priesthood. The object of the law is evidently to give practical force and effect to the Nicene canon, and the imperial power under Honorius had sunk to too low an ebb for us to imagine the possibility of his venturing to tamper with and overrule the decrees of the most venerable council. Even in the sixth century the Nicene canon was not yet considered to have the meaning subsequently attributed to it, for otherwise there would have been no necessity for inserting a provision prohibiting the marriage of priests in the account forged at that time of a Roman council said to have been held by Silvester I.

If the proof thus adduced be as convincing as it appears to me, the story of Paphnutius is not so important as to deserve the amount of controversy that has been expended upon it, and a brief reference is all that seems necessary. Socrates and Sozomen relate that while the canons of the council were under consideration, some of the Fathers desired to introduce one interdicting all intercourse between those in orders and their wives. Whereupon Paphnutius, an Egyptian bishop, protested against the heavy burden to be thus imposed upon the clergy, quoting the well-known declaration of St. Paul to the Hebrews respecting the purity of the marriage-bed. The influence of St. Paphnutius was great, for he was a confessor of peculiar sanctity ; the loss of his right eye bore testimony to the severity of the persecutions which he had endured, and his immaculate chastity, preserved from boyhood in a monastery, rendered his motives and his impartiality on the subject unimpeachable. The bishops, who had been on the point of accepting the proposed canon, were convinced, and the project was abandoned.

If this account be true, it of course follows that the third canon has no bearing on the wives of ecclesiastics, and that the enforcement of celibacy dates from a later period than that of the council. Accordingly, when the Nicene canon was found necessary to give authority to the rule, it became requisite to discredit the story of Paphnutius. The first attempt to do this which has come under my observation occurred during the fierce contentions aroused by the efforts of Gregory VII to restore the almost-forgotten law of celibacy. Bernald of Constance has left a record of a discussion held by him in 1076 with Alboin, a zealous defender of sacerdotal marriage, in which the authenticity of the story is hotly contested. Bernald's logic may be condensed into the declaration that he considered it much more credible that Sozomen was in error than that so holy a man as St. Paphnutius could have been guilty of such blasphemy. No reason whatever was vouchsafed when Gregory VII caused the story to be condemned in the Synod of Rome of 1079. In spite of this, Pius IV, in 1564, admitted its authenticity in his epistle to the German princes who had requested of him the concession of sacerdotal marriage. Later writers, from Bellarmine down, have, however, entered into elaborate arguments to prove its impossibility. They rest their case principally on the assertion of the existence of celibacy as a rule anterior to the council, and on its enforcement afterwards; on the fact that Socrates and Sozomen flourished a little more than a century after the council, and that they are therefore untrustworthy; and that the name of St. Paphnutius does not appear in the acts of the council. To the first of these objections the preceding pages afford, I think, a sufficient answer; to the second it can only be replied that we must be content with the best testimony attainable, and that there is none better than that of the two historians, whose general truthfulness and candour are acknowledged; and to the third it may be remarked that of the 318 bishops present, but 222 affixed their signatures to the acts, while Rufinus and Theodoret both expressly assert that Paphnutius was present. That the statement was not discredited until controversialists found it desirable to do so, is shown by its retention in the full account of the proceedings of the council by Gelasius of Cyzicus, in the fifth century, and also by its repetition in the " Historia Tripartita," a condensation of the narratives of Socrates, Sozomen, and Theodoret, compiled in the sixth century by Cassiodorus, whose irreproachable orthodoxy would hardly have permitted him to give it currency if it had then been considered as blasphemous as the writers of the eleventh century would have us believe. In fact, the learned and orthodox Christian Wolff, in his great work on the Councils, rejects as trifling the assertion that the story of Paphnutius is fictitious. His theory of the whole matter is that the Western Church endeavoured to subject the Eastern to its views on the celibacy required of the priesthood; that the effort failed, in consequence of the opposition of Paphnutius, and that the canon adopted had reference merely to the scandals of the Agapetæ.

Various indications have been collected by controversialists to show that for some time after the Council of Nicæa no interference was attempted with married priests. Of these, one or two will suffice.

St. Athanasius, whose orthodoxy it would not be prudent for anyone to question, and whose appearance during his diaconate at the Council of Nicæa first attracted general attention to his commanding abilities, has left us convincing testimony as to the perfect freedom allowed during his time to all classes of ecclesiastics. An Egyptian monk named Dracontius had been elected to an episcopate, and hesitated to accept the dignity lest its duties should prove incompatible with the fulfilment of his vows. To remove these scruples, Athanasius addressed to him an epistle containing various arguments, among which was the declaration that in his new sphere of action he would find no difficulty in carrying out whatever rules he might prescribe for himself. "Many bishops," said the Saint, "have not contracted matrimony, while, on the other hand, monks have become fathers. Again, we see bishops who have children, and monks who take no thought of having posterity." The tenor of the whole passage is such as to show that no laws had yet been enacted to control individual action in such matters, and while rigid asceticism was largely practised, it was to be admired as the result of private conviction, and not as mere enforced submission to an established rule.

Testimony equally unequivocal is afforded by the case of St. Gregory Theologos, Bishop of Nazianzum. He relates that his father, who was likewise a St. Gregory, Bishop of Nazianzum, was converted about the period of

the Nicene Council, and was shortly afterwards admitted
to the priesthood and created bishop. His mother, St.
Nonna, prayed earnestly for male issue, saw her future son
St. Gregory in a prophetic vision, and devoted him, before
his birth, to the service of God. That this occurred after
his father's admission to orders is shown by the address
which he represents the latter as making to him, " I have
passed more years in offering the sacrifice than measure
your whole life," while the birth of a younger son, Cæsarius,
shows that conjugal relations continued undisturbed.
St. Gregory evidently felt that neither shame nor irregularity attached to his birth during the sacred ministry of his
father.

CHAPTER IV

LEGISLATION

THUS far the progress of asceticism had been the result of moral influence alone. Those who saw in the various forms of abstinence and mortification the only path to salvation, and those who may have felt that worldly advantages of power or reputation would compensate them for the self-inflicted restrictions which they underwent, already formed a numerous body in the Church, but as yet had not acquired the numerical ascendancy requisite to enable them to impose upon their brethren the rules which they had adopted for their own guidance. The period was one of transition, and for sixty years after the Council of Nicæa there was doubtless a struggle for supremacy, not perhaps the less severe because at this late date we can but dimly trace its outlines amid the records of the fierce Arian controversy which constitutes the ecclesiastical history of the time, and which absorbed the attention of writers almost to the exclusion of everything else.

The first triumph of the ascetic party was in establishing recognised restrictions on those who had voluntarily assumed vows of celibacy. With them, at least, the case was clear. Aspiring to no rank in the Church, they simply dedicated themselves to God, and pledged themselves to lives of abstinence. Their backsliding caused scandal to the Church, which, if it were held responsible in the eyes of men for their conduct, must necessarily assume the power to control their mode of life, while the fact of simply holding them to the performance of vows solemnly undertaken could not reasonably be regarded as an arbitrary stretch of authority. These voluntary vows, which speedily led to the establishment of the vast fabric of monachism, will form the subject of a subsequent chapter, and need not be further alluded to here.

Another move in the direction of asceticism was the

39

prohibition by the Council of Laodicea in 352 of women serving as priests or presiding over the churches. Although in later Judaism the Temple service was confined to men, the examples of Deborah and Huldah show that in earlier times women were considered as capable of inspiration and were sometimes revered as prophets; the Gentiles, among whom the infant Churches were founded, had priestesses almost everywhere actively employed in the duties of worship and sacrifice; and it would have been strange if women, to whom the propagation of the Gospel was so greatly owing, had not been sometimes admitted to the function of conducting the simple services of the primitive Church. We learn from St. Paul that Phœbe was a deacon (διάκονος) of the Church at Cenchrea; the Apostolic Constitutions contain a regular formula for their ordination; and the canon of Laodicea shows that until the middle of the fourth century they still occasionally occupied recognised positions in the active ministry of the Church. They could not have been numerous, or the references to them in the history of the period would have been more frequent, and the enforcement of their disability for divine service would have required constant repetition in the canons of the general and local synods; but unquestionably the growth of the veneration of the Virgin and of female saints would have sufficed to prevent the inconsistency of regarding women as absolutely unfitted for any function in public worship, had it not been for the rising influence of asceticism, which demanded the separation of the sexes, and insisted upon an artificial purity in all concerned in the ministry of the altar. Even in the tenth century, so good a celibatarian as Atto of Vercelli was perfectly willing to assert that in the early Church, when the labourers were few, women were admitted to share in the ceremonies of divine worship; and, as late as the fourteenth, Bishop Alvaro Pelagio complains that women take orders, though they cannot legally do so, fulminate excommunications, and hear confessions.

Still, as yet, the secular clergy were at liberty to follow the dictates of their own consciences, and if an attempt was made to erect the necessity of ascetic abstinence into an article of either faith or discipline, the Church was prompt to stamp it with the seal of unequivocal reprobation. Eustathius, Bishop of Sebastia, in Cappadocia, himself the son of the Bishop of Cappadocian Cæsarea, Eulalius, carried his zeal for purity to so great an excess that his exaggerated notions of the inferiority of the married state trenched closely upon Manichæism, although his heretical rejection of canonical fasting showed that on other points he was bitterly opposed to the tenets of that obnoxious sect. His horror of matrimony went so far as to lead him to the dogma that married people were incapable of salvation; he forbade the offering of prayer in houses occupied by them; and he declared that the blessings and sacraments of priests living with their wives were to be rejected, and their persons treated with contempt.

There were not wanting those to whom even these extreme opinions were acceptable, and Eustathius speedily accumulated around him a host of devotees whose proselytizing zeal threatened a stubborn heresy. The excesses attributed to their inability to endure the practical operation of their leader's doctrines may be true, or may be merely the accusations which are customarily disseminated when it becomes necessary to invest schismatics with odium. Be this as it may, the orthodox clergy felt the importance of promptly repressing opinions which, although at variance with the creed of the Church, were yet dangerously akin to the extreme views of those who were regarded as pre-eminently holy. Eulalius, the father of the heresiarch, himself presided at a local synod held at Cæsarea, and condemned his son. This did not suffice to repress the heresy, and about the year 362 a provincial council was assembled at Gangra, where fifteen bishops, among whom was Eulalius, pronounced their verdict on Eustathius and his misguided followers, and drew up a series of canons defining the orthodox belief on the questions involved. That they were received by the Church as authoritative is evident from their being included in the collections of Dionysius and Isidor. These canons anathematise all who refuse the sacraments of a married priest, and who hold that he cannot officiate on account of his marriage; also those who, priding themselves on their professed virginity, arrogantly despise their married brethren, and who hold that the duties of wedlock are incompatible with salvation. The whole affords a singularly distinct record of the doctrines accepted at this period, showing that there was no authority admitted for imposing restrictions of any kind on the married clergy. It probably was an effort on the part of

the conservatives of the Church to restrain their more progressive brethren, and they no doubt gladly availed themselves of the wild theories of Eustathius to stigmatise the
extravagances which were daily becoming more influential.
At the same time, they were careful to shield themselves
behind a qualified concession to the ascetic spirit of the
period, for in an epilogue they apologetically declare their
humble admiration of virginity, and their belief that pious
continence is most acceptable to God.

In little more than twenty years after this emphatic
denunciation of all interference with married priests, we
find the first absolute command addressed to the higher
orders of the clergy to preserve inviolate celibacy. So
abrupt a contrast provokes an inquiry into its possible
causes, as no records have reached us exhibiting any special
reasons for the change.

While the admirers of ascetic virginity became louder and
more enthusiastic in their praises of that blessed condition,
it is fair to presume that they were daily more sensible of a
lower standard of morality in the ministers of the altar,
and that their susceptibilities were more deeply shocked by
the introduction and growth of abuses. While the Church
was kept purified by the fires of persecution, it offered few
attractions for the worldly and ambitious. Its ministry
was too dangerous to be sought except by the pure and
zealous Christian, and there was little danger that pastors
would err except from over-tenderness of conscience or
unthinking ardour. When, however, its temporal position
was incalculably improved by its domination throughout
the empire, it became the avenue through which ambition
might attain its ends, while its wealth held out prospects
of idle self-indulgence to the slothful and the sensual. A
new class of men, dangerous alike from their talents or their
vices, would thus naturally find their way into the fold, and
corruption, masked under the semblance of austerest virtue,
or displayed with careless cynicism, would not be long in
penetrating into the Holy of Holies. Immorality must
have been flagrant when, in 370, the temporal power felt
the necessity of interfering by a law of the Emperor Valen-
tinian, which denounced severe punishment on ecclesiastics
who visited the houses of widows and virgins. When an
increasing laxity of morals thus threatened to overcome the

purity of the Church, it is not surprising that the advocates
of asceticism should have triumphed over the more moderate
and conservative party, and that they should improve their
victory by seeking a remedy for existing evils in such laws as
should render the strictest continence imperative on all
who entered into holy orders. They might reasonably
argue that, if nothing else were gained, the change would
at least render the life of the priest less attractive to the
vicious and the sensual, and that the rigid enforcement of
the new rules would elevate the character of the Church by
preventing such wolves from seeking a place among the
sheep. If by such legislation they only added fresh fuel
to the flame; if they heightened immorality by hypocrisy,
and drove into vagabond licentiousness those who would
perhaps have been content with lawful marriage, they only
committed an error which has ever been too common with
earnest men of one idea to warrant special surprise.

Another object may not improbably have entered into
the motives of those who introduced the rule. The Church
was daily receiving vast accessions of property from the
pious zeal of its wealthy members, the death-bed repentance
of despairing sinners, and the munificence of emperors and
prefects, while the effort to procure the inalienability of its
possessions dates from an early period. Its acquisitions,
both real and personal, were of course exposed to much
greater risk of dilapidation when the ecclesiastics in charge
of its widely scattered riches had families for whose provision
a natural parental anxiety might be expected to override
the sense of duty in discharging the trust confided to them.
The simplest mode of averting the danger might therefore
seem to be to relieve the churchman of the cares of paternity,
and, by cutting asunder all the ties of family and kindred, to
bind him completely and for ever to the Church and to that
alone. This motive, as we shall see, was openly acknowledged as a powerful one in later times, and it no doubt
served as an argument of weight in the minds of those who
urged and secured the adoption of the canon.

It appears to me not unreasonable to suppose that all
these various motives lent additional force to the zeal for
the purity of the Church, and to the undoubting belief in
the necessity of perpetual celibacy, which impelled the
popes, about the year 385, to issue the first definite command imposing it as an absolute rule of discipline on the

ministers of the altar. The question evidently was one
which largely occupied the minds of men, and the conclusion was reached progressively. A Roman synod, to which
the date of 384 is conjecturally assigned, answered a series
of interrogatories propounded by the bishops of Gaul,
among which was one relating to the chastity of the priesthood. To this the response was rather argumentatory and
advisory in its character than imperative; the continence
of the higher grades of ecclesiastics was insisted on, but no
definite punishment was ordered for its violation—and no
maxim in legislation is better understood than that a law
without a penalty expressed is practically a dead letter.
Allusion was made to previous efforts to enforce the observance in various Churches; surprise was expressed that light
should be sought for on such a question—for the Gallic
prelates had evidently been in doubt respecting it—and
numerous reasons were alleged in a manner to show that
the subject was as yet open to argument, and could not be
assumed as proved or be decided by authority alone. These
reasons may be briefly summed up as consisting of references to the well-known texts referred to in a previous
chapter, together with a vague assertion of the opinion of
the Fathers to the same effect. Allusion was made to the
inconsistency of exhortations to virginity proceeding from
those who themselves were involved in family cares and
duties, a reasonable view when we consider how much of
ecclesiastical machinery by this time turned on monachism;
and the necessity was urged of bishops, priests, and deacons
preserving the purity requisite to fit them for the daily
sacrifice of the altar and the ministration of the sacraments.
This latter point was based upon the assumption of a similar
abstinence being imposed by the old law on the Levites
during their term of service in the Temple, and the example
of the pagan priesthood was indignantly adduced to shame
those who could entertain a sacrilegious doubt upon a
matter so self-evident. The conclusion arrived at was
definite, but, as I have already remarked, no means were
suggested or commanded for its enforcement.

Not many months later Pope Damasus died, but the
cause was safe in the hands of his successor. Scarcely had
Siricius ascended the pontifical throne, when, in 385, he
addressed an epistle to Himerius, Archbishop of Tarragona,
expressing his grief and indignation that the Spanish clergy

should pay so little regard to the sanctity of their calling as to maintain relations with their wives. It is evident from the tenor of the decretal that Himerius had been unable to enforce the new discipline, and had appealed to Rome for assistance in breaking down the stubborn resistance which he had encountered, for allusion is made to some of the refractory who had justified themselves by the freedom of marriage allowed to the Levites under the old law, while others had expressed their regret and had declared their sin to be the result of ignorance. Siricius adopted a much firmer tone than his predecessor. He indulged in less elaboration of argument; a few texts, more or less apposite; an expression of wonder that the rule should be called in question; a distinct assertion of its application to the three grades of bishops, priests, and deacons; a sentence of expulsion on all who dared to offer resistance, and a promise of pardon for those who had offended through ignorance, allowing them to retain their positions as long as they observed complete separation from their wives, though even then they were pronounced incapable of all promotion— such was the first definitive canon, prescribing and enforcing sacerdotal celibacy, exhibited by the records of the Church.

The confident manner in which the law is thus laid down as incontrovertible and absolute might almost make us doubt whether it were not older than the preceding pages have shown it to be, if Siricius had not confessed the weakness of the cause by adopting a very different tone within a year. In 386 he addressed the Church of Africa, sending it certain canons adopted by a Roman synod. Of these the first eight relate to observances about which there was at that time no question, and they are expressed in the curtest and most decisive phraseology. The ninth canon is conceived in a spirit totally different. It persuades, exhorts, and entreats that the three orders shall preserve their purity; it argues as to the propriety and necessity of the matter, which it supports by various texts, but it does not assume that the observance thus enjoined is even a custom, much less a law, of the Church; it urges that the scandal of marriage be removed from the clergy, but it threatens no penalty for refusal. Siricius was too imperious and too earnest in all that he undertook for us to imagine that he would have adopted pleading and entreaty if he had felt that he possessed the right to command; nor would he have condescended to beg for the removal of an opprobrium if he were speaking with all the authority of unquestioned tradition to enforce a canon which had become an unalterable part of ecclesiastical discipline.

It is observable that in these decretals no authority is quoted later than the Apostolic texts, which, as we have seen, have but little bearing on the subject. No canons of councils, no epistles of earlier popes, no injunctions of the Fathers are brought forward to strengthen the position assumed, whence the presumption is irresistible that none such existed, and we may rest satisfied that no evidence has been lost that would prove the pre-existence of the rule.

CHAPTER V

ENFORCEMENT OF CELIBACY

CELIBACY was but one of the many shapes in which the rapidly progressing sacerdotalism of Rome was overlaying religion with a multitude of formal observances. That which in earlier times had been the spontaneous expression of fervid zeal, or the joyful self-sacrifice of ardent asceticism, was thus changed into a law, bearing upon all alike, and taking no count of the individual idiosyncrasies which might render the burden too heavy for the shoulders of the less fiery though not less conscientious Christian. That it should meet with resistance was to be expected when we consider that the local independence of primitive times had not as yet been crushed under the rapidly growing preponderance of the Roman see. In fact, energetic protests were not wanting, as well as the more perplexing stubbornness of passive resistance.

St. Ambrose admits that although the necessity of celibacy was generally acknowledged, still, in many of the remoter districts, there were to be found those who neglected it, and who justified themselves by ancient custom, relying on precautions to purify themselves for their sacred ministry. In this he gives countenance to the tradition of the Leonistæ, simple Christians whose refusal to adapt themselves to the sacerdotalism which was daily becoming more rigorous and indispensable caused their expulsion from Rome, and who, taking refuge in the recesses of the Cottian Alps, endeavoured to preserve the unadulterated faith of earlier times in the seclusion and privation of exile.

All who revolted against the increasing oppression of the hierarchy were not, however, content to bury themselves in solitude and silence, and heresiarchs sprang up who waged a bold but unequal contest. Bonosus, Jovinian, and Vigilantius are the names which have reached us as the most conspicuous leaders in the unsuccessful attempt to

47

turn back the advancing spirit of the age, and of these Jovinian is the foremost figure. Bonosus, who was Bishop of Sardica, acquired a peculiarly sinister notoriety, for, in his opposition to the ascetic spirit, he adopted a heresy of Tertullian and Photinus, and assailed one of the chief arguments of the admirers of celibacy by denying the perpetual virginity of the Virgin; whence his followers acquired the euphonious title of Bonosiacs. For this he was naturally denounced by Pope Siricius, and his followers were duly condemned by the Council of Capua in 389, while the tireless pen of St. Jerome was called into requisition to refute errors so unpardonable. Notwithstanding this, they continued to flourish, for an epistle of Innocent I to Laurence, Bishop of Segna, proves that the error was openly taught on the eastern shores of the Adriatic in the early part of the fifth century; in 443 the Council of Arles shows their existence in France by promising reconciliation to those who should manifest proper repentance, and that of Orleans as late as 538 still contains an allusion to them; even as late as the middle of the seventh century St. Ildefonso of Toledo wrote a treatise on the subject in which he overwhelmed Jovinian and Helvidius with opprobrious epithets. About the same period the Bonosiacs are the only heretics referred to by name in a canon of the Penitential of St. Columban, as though they were the most prominent misbelievers of the time. The belief even extended to Arabia, where a sect professing it is stigmatised by Epiphanius as Antidicomarianitarians, whose conversion that worthy bishop endeavoured to secure by a long epistle, in which his laboured explanations of the stubborn text of Matthew are accompanied with hearty objurgations of the blasphemous dogma, and an illustrative comparison of the Virgin to a lioness bearing but one whelp.

While Jovinian shared in this particular the error of Bonosus and Helvidius, he did not attach undue importance to it. More practically inclined, his heresy consisted principally in denying the efficacy of celibacy, and this he maintained in Rome itself, with more zeal than discretion. Siricius caused his condemnation and that of his associates in a synod held about the year 390, and succeeded in driving him to Milan, where he had many proselytes. There was no peace for him there. A synod held under the auspices of St. Ambrose bears testimony to the wickedness of his doctrines and to the popular clamour raised against him, and the wanderer again set forth on his weary pilgrimage. Deprived of refuge in the cities, he disseminated his tenets throughout the country, where ardent followers, in spite of contumely and persecution, gathered around him and conducted their worship in the fields and hamlets. The laws promulgated about this time against heresy were severe and searching, and bore directly upon all who deviated from the orthodox formulas of the Catholic Church, yet Jovinian braved them all. The outraged Church called upon its most unscrupulous polemic, St. Jerome, who indulged in the customary abuse which represented the schismatics as indulging in the grossest promiscuous licentiousness and Jovinian as teaching them that all things were permitted to those baptized in Christ, in contradiction to St. Augustin, who admits the sobriety and virtue of Jovinian, in spite of his denying the efficacy of celibacy. All this was insufficient to put down the stubborn schismatics, who maintained their faith until the Church, wearied out with their obstinacy and unable to convert or to silence them, appealed to the secular power for more efficient assistance. Perhaps Jovinian's long career of successful resistance may have emboldened him; perhaps his sect was growing numerous enough to promise protection; at all events, despite the imperial rescripts which shielded with peculiar care the Apostolic city from the presence of heretics, Jovinian in 412 openly held assemblages of his followers in Rome, to the scandal of the faithful, and made at least sufficient impression to lead a number of professed virgins to abandon their vows and marry. The complaints of the orthodox were heard by the miserable shadow who then occupied the throne of Augustus, and Honorius applied himself to the task of persecution with relentless zeal. Jovinian was scourged with a leaded thong and exiled to the rock of Boa, on the coast of Dalmatia, while his followers were hunted down, deported, and scattered among the savage islands of the Adriatic.

Nor was this the only struggle. A wild shepherd lad named Vigilantius, born among the Pyrenean valleys, was fortunate enough to be the slave of St. Sulpicius Severus, whose wealth, culture, talents, and piety rendered him prominent throughout Southern Gaul. The earnest character of the slave attracted the attention of the master; education developed his powers; he was manumitted, and the people of his native Calagurris chose him for their priest. Sent by Sulpicius as bearer of letters to his friends St. Paulinus at Nola and St. Jerome in his Bethlehem retreat, Vigilantius had the opportunity of comparing the simple Christianity of his native mountains with the splendid pageantry of Rome, the elegant retirement of Nola, and the heated controversialism which agitated the asceticism of Bethlehem. Notwithstanding the cordiality of their first acquaintance, his residence with Jerome was short. Both were too earnestly dogmatic in their natures for harmony to exist between the primitive Cantabrian shepherd and the fierce apostle of Buddhist and Mazdean Christianity, who devoted his life to reconciling the doctrines of the Latin Church with the practices of Manichæism. Brief friendship ended in a quarrel, and Vigilantius extended his experiences by a survey of Egypt, where the vast hordes of Nitrian anchorites were involved in civil strife over the question of Origenism. Returning through Italy, he tarried in Milan and among the Alps, where he found the solution of his doubts and the realisation of his ideas in the teaching of Jovinian. He had left Gaul a disciple; he returned to it a missionary, prepared to do battle with sacerdotalism in all its forms. Not only did he deny the necessity of celibacy, but he pronounced it to be the fertile source of impurity, and in his zeal for reform he swept away fasting and maceration, he ridiculed the veneration of relics, and pronounced the miracles wrought at their altars to be the work of demons; he objected to the candles and incense around the shrines, to prayers for the dead, and to the oblations of the faithful.

No doubt the decretals of Siricius had rendered compulsory the celibacy of the priesthood throughout Gaul and Spain. The machinery of the hierarchy may readily have stifled open opposition, however frequent may have been the secret infractions of the rule. This may perhaps have contributed to the success of Vigilantius. Even his former master, St. Sulpicius Severus, and St. Exuperius, Bishop of Toulouse, were inclined to favour his reforms. That they spread with dangerous rapidity throughout Gaul from south to north is shown by the fact that in 404 Victricius, Bishop of Rouen, and in 405 St. Exuperius of Toulouse applied to Innocent I for advice as to the manner in which they should deal with the new heresy. It also counted numerous adherents throughout Spain, among whom even some bishops were enumerated. The alarm was promptly sounded, and the machinery of the Church was brought to bear upon the hardy heretic. The vast reputation and authority of Jerome lent force to the coarse invective with which he endeavoured to overwhelm his whilom acquaintance, and though the nickname of Dormitantius which he bestowed on Vigilantius was a sarcasm neither very severe nor very refined, the disgusting exaggeration of his adversary's tenets, in which he as usual indulged, had doubtless its destined effect. Pope Innocent was not backward in asserting the authority of Rome and the inviolable nature of the canon. In his epistle to Victricius, he repeated the decretal of Siricius, but in a somewhat more positive form; while in the following year (405) he confirmed the vacillating faith of Exuperius by declaring that any violation of the strictest celibacy on the part of priest or deacon subjects the offender to the deprivation of his position. As in the previous effort of Siricius, however, ignorance is admitted as an excuse, entitling him who can plead it to retain his grade without hope of preferment—and the test of this ignorance is held to be the canon of 385. This latter point is noteworthy, for it is a tacit confession of the novelty of the rule, although Innocent laboured at great length to prove both its antiquity and necessity from the well-known texts of St. Paul and the Levitical observances. Yet no intermediate authority was quoted, and punishment was only to be inflicted on those who could be proved to have seen the decretal of Siricius.

The further career of Vigilantius and his sectaries is lost in the darkness and confusion attendant upon the ravages of the Alans and Vandals who overran Gaul during the following year. We only know that Sulpicius and Exuperius, frightened by the violence of Jerome and the authority of Innocent, abandoned their protégé, and we can presume that, during the period of wild disorder which followed the irruption of the Barbarians, what little protection Rome could afford was too consoling to the afflicted Churches for them to risk its withdrawal by resisting on any point the daily increasing pretensions of the Apostolic See to absolute command.

The victory was won, for with the death of Vigilantius

and Jovinian ended the last organised and acknowledged attempt to stay the progress of celibacy in the Latin Church, until centuries later, when the regulation was already too ancient and too well supported by tradition and precedent to be successfully called in question.

In Africa we find no trace of open resistance to the introduction of the rule, though time was evidently required to procure its enforcement. We have seen that Siricius, in 386, addressed an appeal to the African bishops. To this they responded by holding a council in which they agreed " conscriptione quadam " that chastity should be preserved by the three higher orders. This apparently was not conclusive, for in 390 another council was held in which Aurelius, Bishop of Carthage, again introduced the subject. He recapitulated their recent action, urged that the teaching of the Apostles and ancient usage required the observance of the rule, and obtained the assent of his brother prelates to the separation from their wives of those who were concerned in administering the sacraments. The form of these proceedings shows that it was an innovation, requiring deliberation and the assent of the ecclesiastics present, not a simple affirmation of a traditional and unalterable point of discipline, and, moreover, no penalty is mentioned for disobedience. Little respect, probably, was paid to the new rule. The third and fourth Councils of Carthage, held in 397 and 398, passed numerous canons relating to discipline, prescribing minutely the qualifications and duties of the clergy, and of the votaries of the monastic profession. The absence from among these canons of any allusion to enforced celibacy would therefore appear to prove that it was still left to the conscience of the individual. If this be so, the triumph of the sacerdotal party was not long delayed, as might be expected from the rising influence and authority of St. Augustin, whose early Manichæism led him, after his conversion, to be one of the most enthusiastic admirers and promoters of austere asceticism. We may not unreasonably assume that it was through his prompting that his friend St. Aurelius, at the fifth Council of Carthage in 401, proposed a canon, which was adopted, ordering the separation of the married clergy of the higher grades from their wives, under pain of deprivation of office. As before, the form of the canon shows it to be an innovation.

That the rule was positively adopted and frequently submitted to is shown by St. Augustin, who, in his treatise against second marriages, states that, in arguing with those desirous of entering upon those unhallowed unions, he was accustomed to strengthen his logic by citing the continence of the clergy, who, however unwillingly they had in most cases been forced to undertake the burden, still, by the aid of God, were enabled to endure it to the end. Yet it is evident that its enforcement was attended with many difficulties and much opposition, for, twenty years later, at another Council of Carthage, we find Faustinus, the papal legate, proposing that the three higher orders shall be separated from their wives, to which the fathers of the council somewhat evasively replied that those who were concerned in the ministry of the altar should be chaste in all things. No attempt, however, was apparently made to strengthen the resolution by affixing a penalty for its infringement. It was a simple declaration of opinion, and nothing more.

Symptoms of similar difficulty in the rigid enforcement of the canon are observable elsewhere. The proceedings of the first Council of Toledo, held in the year 400, show not only that it was a recent innovation which continued to be disregarded, but also that it had given rise to a crowd of novel questions which required imperatively to be settled, as to the status of the several grades of clerks who were guilty of various forms of disobedience—the prototype and exemplar of innumerable similar attempts at legislation which continued for more than a thousand years to occupy a good part of the attention of almost every council and synod. The prelates of Cis-Alpine Gaul, assembled in the Council of Turin in 401, could only be brought to pronounce incapable of promotion those who contravened the injunction which separated them from their wives. The practical working of this was to permit those to retain their wives who were satisfied with the grade to which they had attained. Thus the priest who saw little prospect of elevation to the episcopate might readily console himself with the society of his wife, while the powerful influence of the wives would be brought to bear against the promptings of ambition on the part of their husbands. The punishment thus was heaviest on the lower grades and lightest on the higher clergy, whose position should have rendered the sin more heinous—in fact, the bishop, to whom further promotion was impossible, escaped entirely from the penalty.

Even as late as 441 the first Council of Orange shows how utterly the rule had been neglected by ordering that for the future no married man should be ordained deacon without making promise of separation from his wife, for contravention of which he was to suffer degradation; while those who had previously been admitted to orders were only subjected to the canon of the Council of Turin, incurring merely loss of promotion. This evidently indicates that the regulation was a novelty, for it admits the injustice of subjecting to the rigour of the canon those who had taken orders without being aware of the obligations incurred; and it is a fair conclusion to suppose that this was a compromise by which the existing clergy gave their assent to the rule for the benefit of their successors, provided that they themselves escaped its full severity. In fact, it seemed to be impossible to make the Church of Gaul accept the rule of discipline. About 459, we find Leo I, in answer to some interrogatories of Rusticus, Bishop of Narbonne, laboriously explaining that deacons and subdeacons, as well as bishops and priests, must treat their wives as sisters. Rusticus had evidently asked the question, and Leo expresses no surprise at his ignorance.

The Irish Church, founded about the middle of the fifth century, although it was to a great extent based on monachism, apparently did not at first order the separation of the sexes. A century later an effort seems to have been made in this direction; but the canons of a synod held in the early part of the eighth century show that priests at that time were not prevented from having wives.

Even where the authority of the decretals of Siricius and Innocent was received with respectful silence, it was not always easy to enforce their provisions. An epistle of Innocent to the bishops of Calabria shows that, within territory depending strictly upon Rome itself, a passive resistance was maintained, requiring constant supervision and interference to render the rule imperative. Some priests, whose growing families rendered their disregard of discipline as unquestionable as it was defiant, remained unpunished. Either the bishops refused to execute the laws, or their sympathies were known to be with the offenders, for the pious layman whose sensibilities were wounded by the scandal felt himself obliged to appeal to the Pope. Innocent accordingly ordered the accused to be tried and to be expelled, while he expressed no little surprise at the negligence of the prelates who were so remiss. It is more difficult to understand the edict of 420, issued by Honorius, to which allusion has already been made (p. 35). This law expressly declares that the desire for purity does not require the separation of wives whose marriage took place before the ordination of their husbands.

These disconnected attempts at resistance were unsuccessful. Sacerdotalism triumphed, and the rule which forbade marriage to those in orders, and separated husband and wife when the former was promoted to the ministry of the altar, became irrevocably incorporated in the canon law. Throughout the struggle the papacy had a most efficient ally in the people. The holiness and the necessity of absolute purity was so favourite a theme with the leading minds of the Church, and formed so prominent a portion of their daily homilies and exhortations, that the popular mind could not but be deeply impressed with its importance, and therefore naturally exacted of the pastor the sacrifice which cost so little to the flock. An instance or two occurring about this period will show how vigilant was the watch kept upon the virtue of ecclesiastics, and how summary was the process by which indignation was visited upon even the most exalted, when suspected of a lapse from the rigid virtue required of them. Thirty years after the ordination of St. Brice, who succeeded St. Martin in the diocese of Tours, rumour credited him with the paternity of a child unseasonably born of a nun. In their wrath the citizens by common consent determined to stone him. The saint calmly ordered the infant, then in its thirtieth day, to be brought to him, and adjured it in the name of Christ to declare if it were his, to which the little one firmly replied, " Thou art not my father ! " The people, attributing the miracle to magic, persisted in their resolution, when St. Brice wrapped a quantity of burning coals in his robe, and pressing the mass to his bosom carried it to the tomb of St. Martin, where he deposited his burden, and displayed his robe uninjured. Even this was insufficient to satisfy the outraged feelings of the populace, and St. Brice deemed himself fortunate in making his escape uninjured, when a

successor was elected to the bishopric.   Somewhat similar
was the case of St. Simplicius, Bishop of Autun.   Even as
a layman, his holy zeal had led him to treat as a sister his
beautiful wife, who was inspired with equal piety.   On his
elevation to the episcopate, still confident of their mutual
self-control, she refused to be separated from him.   The
people, scandalised at the impropriety, and entertaining a
settled incredulity as to the superhuman virtue requisite
to such restraint, mobbed the bishop's dwelling, and
expressed their sentiments in a manner more energetic than
respectful.   The saintly virgin called for a portable furnace
full of fire, emptied its contents into her robe, and held it
uninjured for an hour, when she transferred the ordeal to
her husband, saying that the trial was as nothing to the
flames through which they had already passed unscathed.
The result with him was the same, and the people retired,
ashamed of their unworthy suspicions.   Gregory of Tours,
who relates these legends, was sufficiently near in point of
time for them to have an historical value, even when
divested of their miraculous ornaments.   They bring before
us the popular tendencies and modes of thought, and show
us how powerful an instrument the passions of the people
became, when skilfully aroused and directed by those in
authority.

The Western Church was thus at length irrevocably
committed to the strict maintenance of ecclesiastical celibacy, and the labours of the three great Latin Fathers,
Jerome, Ambrose, and Augustin, were crowned with success.
It is perhaps worth while to cast a glance at such evidences
as remain to us of the state of morals about this period and
during the fifth century, and to judge whether the new
rule of discipline had resulted in purifying the Church of
the corruptions which had so excited the indignation of the
anchorite of Bethlehem, and had nerved him in his fierce
contests with those who opposed the enforced asceticism
of the ministers of Christ.

How the morals of the Church fared during the struggle
is well exhibited in the writings of St. Jerome himself, as
quoted above, describing the unlawful unions of the agapetæ
with ecclesiastics and the horrors induced by the desire to
escape the consequences of incautious frailty.   Conclusions
not less convincing may be drawn from his assertion that

holy orders were sometimes assumed on account of the superior opportunities which clericature gave of improper intercourse with women; and from his description of the ecclesiastics, who passed their lives in female companionship, surrounded by young female slaves, and leading an existence which differed from matrimony only in the absence of the marriage ceremony.

But a short time after the recognition of the rule appeared the law of Honorius, promulgated in 420, to which reference has already been made. It is possible that the permission of residence there granted to the wives of priests may have been intended to act as a partial cure for evils caused by the enforcement of celibacy; and this is rendered the more probable, since other portions of the edict show that intercourse with improper females had increased to such a degree that the censures of the Church could no longer restrain it, and that an appeal to secular interference was necessary, by which such practices should be made a crime to be punished by the civil tribunals. That even this failed lamentably in purifying the Church may be gathered from the proceedings of the provincial councils of the period.

Thus, in 453, the Council of Anjou repeats the prohibition of improper female intimacy, giving as a reason the ruin constantly wrought by it. For those who thereafter persisted in their guilt, however, the only penalty threatened was incapacity for promotion on the part of the lower grades, and suspension of functions for the higher—whence we may conclude that practically an option was afforded to those who preferred sin to ambition. The second Council of Arles, in 443, likewise gives an insight into the subterfuges adopted to evade the rule and to escape detection. About this period a newly-appointed bishop, Talasius of Angers, applied to Lupus of Troyes and Euphronius of Autun for advice concerning various knotty points, among which were the rules respecting the celibacy of the different grades. In their reply the prelates advised their brother that it would be well if the increase of priests' families could be prevented, but that such a consummation was almost impossible if married men were admitted to orders, and that if he wanted to escape ceaseless wrangling and the scandal of seeing children born to his priests, he had better ordain those only who were single. The subject was one of endless effort. In fact, of the numerous councils whose canons have reached us, held in Gaul and Spain during the centuries which intervened until the invasion of the Saracens and the decrepitude of the Merovingian dynasty caused their discontinuance, there is scarcely one which did not feel the necessity of legislating on this delicate matter. It would be tedious and unprofitable to detail specifically the innumerable exhortations, threats, and ingenious devices resorted to in the desperate hope of enforcing obedience to the rules and of purifying the morals of the clergy. Suffice it to say that the constantly varying punishments enacted, the minute supervision ordered over every action of the priesthood, the constant attendance of witnesses whose inseparable companionship should testify to the virtue of each ecclesiastic, and the perpetual iteration of the rule in every conceivable shape, prove at once the hopelessness of the attempt and the incurable nature of the disorders of which the Church was at once the cause and the victim. In short, this perpetual legislation frequently betrays the fact that it was not only practically impossible to maintain separation between the clergy and their wives, but that at times marriage was not uncommon even within the prohibited orders.

Perhaps this may not move our surprise when we glance at the condition of morality existing throughout the Empire in the second quarter of the fifth century, as sketched by a zealous churchman of the period. Salvianus, Bishop of Marseilles, was a native of Trèves. Three times he witnessed the sack of that unfortunate city by the successive barbarian hordes which swept over Western Europe, and he lifts up his voice, like Jeremiah, to bewail the sins of his people, and the unutterable misfortunes which were the punishment but not the cure of those sins. Nothing can be conceived more utterly licentious and depraved than the whole framework of society as described by him, though we may charitably hope that holy indignation or pious sensibility led him to exaggerate the outlines and to darken the shades of the picture. The criminal and frivolous pleasures of a decrepit civilisation left no thought for the absorbing duties of the day or the fearful trials of the morrow. Unbridled lust and unblushing indecency admitted no sanctity in the marriage-tie. The rich and powerful established harems, in the recesses of which their wives lingered, forgotten, neglected, and despised. The banquet, the theatre, and the circus exhausted what little strength and energy were left by domestic excesses. The poor aped the vices of the rich, and hideous depravity reigned supreme and invited the vengeance of Heaven. Such rare souls as could remain pure amid the prevailing contamination would naturally take refuge in the contrast of severe asceticism, and resolutely seek absolute seclusion from a world whose every touch was pollution. The secular clergy, however, drawn from the ranks of a society so utterly corrupt, and enjoying the wealth and station which rendered their position an object for the ambition of the worldly, could not avoid sharing to a great extent the guilt of their flocks, whose sins were more easily imitated than eradicated. Nor does Salvianus confine his denunciations to Gaul and Spain. Africa and Italy are represented as even worse, the prevalence of unnatural crimes lending a deeper disgust to the rivalry in iniquity. Rome was the sewer of the nations, the centre of abomination of the world, where vice openly assumed its most repulsive form, and wickedness reigned unchecked and supreme.

It is true that the descriptions of Salvianus are intended to include the whole body of the people, and that his special references to the Church are but few. Those occasional references, however, are not of a nature to exempt it from sharing in the full force of his indignation. When he pronounces the Africans to be utterly licentious, he excepts those who have been regenerated in religion—but these he declares to be so few in number that it is difficult to believe them Africans. What hope, he asks, can there be for the people when even in the Church itself the most diligent search can scarce discover one chaste amid so many thousands? And when imperial Carthage was tottering to its fall under the assaults of the besieging Vandals, he describes its clergy as wantoning in the circus and the theatre—those without falling under the sword of the barbarian, those within abandoning themselves to sensuality. This, be it remembered, is that African Church which had just been so carefully nurtured in the purest asceticism for thirty years, under the unremitting care of Augustin, who died while his episcopal city of Hippo was encircled by the leaguer of the Vandals.

Nor were these disorders attributable to the irruption of the Barbarians, for Salvianus sorrowfully contrasts their purity of morals with the reckless dissoluteness of the Romans. The respect for female virtue, inherent in the Teutonic tribes, has no warmer admirer than he, and he recounts with wonder how the temptations of luxury and vice, spread before them in the wealthy cities which they sacked, excited only their disgust, and how, so far from yielding to the allurements that surrounded them, they sternly set to work to reform the depravity of their new subjects, and enacted laws to repress at least the open manifestations which shocked their untutored virtue.

When corruption so ineradicable pervaded every class, we can scarce wonder that in the story of the trial of Sixtus III, in 440, for the seduction of a nun, when his accusers were unable to substantiate the charge, he is said to have addressed the synod assembled in judgment by repeating to them the story of the woman taken in adultery, and the decision of Christ. Whether it were intended to be regarded as a confession, or as a sarcasm on the prelates around him, whom he thus challenged to cast the first stone, the tale, whether true or false, is symptomatic of the time that gave it birth.

As regards the East, if the accusations brought against Ibas, Metropolitan of Edessa, at the Synod of Berytus in 448, are worthy of credit, the Oriental Church was not behind the West in the effrontery of sin.

CHAPTER VI

THE EASTERN CHURCH

DURING the period which we have been considering, there had gradually arisen a divergence between the Christians of the East and of the West. The Arianism of Constantius opposed to the orthodoxy of Constans lent increased development to the separation which the division of the Empire had commenced. The rapid growth of the New Rome founded on the shores of the Bosporus gave to the East a political metropolis which rendered it independent of the power of Rome, and the patriarchate there erected absorbed to itself the supremacy of the old Apostolic Sees, which had previously divided the ecclesiastical strength of the East. In the West, the Bishop of Rome was unquestionably the highest dignitary, and when the separation relieved him of the rivalry of prelates equal in rank, he was enabled to acquire an authority over the churches of the Occident undreamed of in previous ages. As yet, however, there was little pretension of extending that power over the East, and though the ceaseless quarrels which raged in Antioch, Constantinople, and Alexandria enabled him frequently to intervene as arbiter, still he had not yet assumed the tone of a judge without appeal or of an autocratic lawgiver.

Though five hundred years were still to pass.before the Greek schism formally separated Constantinople from the communion of Rome, yet already, by the close of the fourth century, the characteristics which ultimately led to that schism were beginning to develop themselves with some distinctness. The sacerdotal spirit of the West showed itself in the formalism which loaded religion with rules of observance and discipline enforced with Roman severity. The inquiring and metaphysical tendencies of the East discovered unnumbered doubtful points of belief, which were argued with exhaustive subtlety and supported by relentless persecution. However important it might be

for any polemic to obtain for his favourite dogma the assent
of the Roman bishop, whose decisions on such points thus
constantly acquired increased authority, yet when the Pope
undertook to issue laws and promulgate rules of discipline,
whatever force they had was restricted to the limits of the
Latin tongue. Accordingly, we find that the decretals of
Siricius and Innocent I produced no effect throughout the
East. Asceticism continued to flourish there as in its
birthplace, but it was voluntary, and there is no trace of
any official attempt to render it universally imperative.
The canon of Nicæa was of course law, and the purity of the
Church required its strict observance, to avoid scandals and
immorality; but beyond this and the ancient rules exclud-
ing digami and prohibiting marriage in orders, no general
laws were insisted on, and each province or patriarchate was
allowed to govern itself in this respect. How little the
Eastern prelates thought of introducing compulsory celibacy
is shown by the fact that at the second General Council, held
at Constantinople in 381, only four or five years before the
decretals of Siricius, there is no trace of any legislation on
the subject; and this acquires increased significance when
we observe that although this council has always been
regarded as Œcumenical, and has enjoyed full authority
throughout the Church universal, yet of one hundred
and fifty bishops who signed the acts, but one—a Spanish
prelate—was from the West.

This avoidance of action was not merely an omission of sur-
plusage. Had the disposition existed to erect the custom of
celibacy into a law, there was ample cause for legislation on
the subject. Epiphanius, who died in the year 403 at a very
advanced age, probably compiled his " Panarium " not long
after this period; he belonged to the extreme school of
ascetics, and lost no opportunity of asserting the most
rigid rule with regard to virginity and continence, which
he considered to be the base and corner-stone of the Church.
While assuming celibacy to be the rule for all concerned in
the functions of the priesthood, he admits that in many
places it was not observed, on account of the degradation of
morals or of the impossibility of obtaining enough ministers
irreprehensible in character to satisfy the needs of the
faithful.

That Epiphanius endeavoured to erect into a universal
canon rules only adopted in certain Churches is rendered

probable by an allusion to St. Jerome, who, in his controversy with Vigilantius, urged in support of celibacy the custom of the Churches of the East (or Antioch), of Alexandria, and of Rome. He thus omits the great exarchates of Ephesus, Pontus, and Thrace, as not lending strength to his argument. Of these the first is perhaps explicable by the latitudinarianism of its metropolitan, Anthony, Bishop of Ephesus. At the Council of Constantinople, held in 400, this prelate was accused of many crimes, among which were simony, the conversion to the use of his family of ecclesiastical property and even of the sacred vessels, and, further, that after having vowed separation from his wife, he had had children by her. Even Egypt, the nursery of monachism, affords a somewhat suspicious example in the person of Synesius, Bishop of Ptolemais. This philosophic disciple of Hypatia, when pressed to accept the bishopric, declined it on various grounds, among which was his unwillingness to be separated from his wife, or to live with her secretly like an adulterer, the separation being particularly objectionable to him, as interfering with his desire for numerous offspring. Synesius, however, was apparently able to reconcile the incompatibilities, for after accepting the episcopal office, we find, when the Libyans invaded the Pentapolis and he stood boldly forth to protect his flock, that two days before an expected encounter he confided to his brother's care his children, to whom he asked the transfer of that tender fraternal affection which he himself had always enjoyed.

It is easy to imagine what efforts were doubtless made to extend the rule, and to render it as imperative throughout the East as it was becoming in the West, when we read the extravagant laudations of virginity uttered about this time by St. John Chrysostom, who lent the sanction of his great name and authority to the assertion that it is as superior to marriage as heaven is to earth, or as angels are to men. Strenuous as these efforts may have been, however, they have left no permanent record, and their effect was short-lived. Within thirty years of the time when Jerome quoted the example of the Eastern Churches as an argument against Vigilantius, Socrates chronicles as a novelty the introduction into Thessalia of compulsory separation between married priests and their wives, which he says was commanded by Heliodorus, Bishop of Trica, apparently to compensate for the amatory character of the " Æthiopica," written in his youth. The same rule, Socrates informs us, was observed in Greece, Macedonia, and Thessalonica, but he asserts that throughout the rest of the East such separation was purely voluntary, and even that many bishops had no scruple in maintaining ordinary intercourse with their wives—a statement easy to be believed in view of the complaints of St. Isidor of P.elusium, about the same time, that the rules of the Church enjoining chastity received little respect among the priesthood.

The influence of Jerome, Chrysostom, and other eminent Churchmen, the example of the West, and the efforts of the Origenians in favour of philosophic asceticism, doubtless had a powerful effect during the first years of the fifth century in extending the custom, but they failed in the endeavour to render it universal and obligatory, and the testimony of Socrates shows how soon even those provinces which adopted it in Jerome's time returned to the previous practice of leaving the matter to the election of the individual. The East thus preserved the traditions of earlier times, as recorded in the Apostolic Constitutions and Canons, prohibiting marriage in orders and the ordination of digami, but imposing no compulsory separation on those who had been married previous to ordination.

Even these rules required to be occasionally enunciated in order to maintain their observance. In 530 a constitution of Justinian calls attention to the regulation prohibiting the marriage of deacons and subdeacons, and, in view of the little respect paid to it, the Emperor proceeds to declare the children of such unions spurious (not even *nothi* or *naturales*), and incompetent to inherit anything; the wife is likewise incapacitated from inheritance, and the whole estate of the father is escheated to the Church—the severity of which may perhaps be a fair measure of the extent of the evil which it was intended to repress. Five years later Justinian recurs to the subject, and lays down the received regulations in all their details. Any one who keeps a concubine, or who has married a divorced woman or a second wife, is to be held ineligible to the diaconate or priesthood. Any member of those orders or of the subdiaconate who takes a wife or a concubine, whether publicly or secretly, is thereupon to be degraded and to lose all clerical privileges; and though the strongest preference is expressed for those who, though married, preserve strict continence, the very phrase employed indicates that this was altogether a matter of choice, and that previous conjugal relations were not subject to any legislative interference.   These same regulations were repeated some ten years later in a law, promulgated about 545, which was preserved throughout the whole period of Greek jurisprudence, being inserted by Leo the Philosopher in his Basilicon, quoted by Photius in the Nomocanon, and referred to as still in force by Balsamon in the thirteenth century.   At the same time, Justinian tacitly admits the failure of previous efforts when he adds a provision by which an unmarried postulant for the diaconate is obliged to pledge himself not to marry, and any bishop permitting such marriage is threatened with degradation.

Bishops, however, were subjected to the full severity of the Latin discipline.   As early as 528, Justinian ordered that no one should be eligible to the episcopate who was burdened with either children or grandchildren, giving as a reason the engrossing duties of the office, which required that the whole mind and soul should be devoted to them, and still more significantly hinting the indecency of converting to the use of the prelate's family the wealth bestowed by the faithful on the Church for pious uses and for charity.   It is probable that this was not strictly observed, for in 535, when repeating the injunction, and adding a restriction on conjugal intercourse, he intimates that no inquiry shall be made into infractions previously occurring, but that it shall be rigidly enforced for the future.   The decision was final as regards the absence of a wife, for it was again alluded to in 548, and that law is carried through the Nomocanon and Basilicon.   The absence of children as a prerequisite to the episcopate, however, was not insisted upon so pertinaciously, for Leo the Philosopher, after the compilation of the Basilicon, issued a constitution allowing the ordination of bishops who had legitimate offspring, arguing that brothers and other relatives were equally prone to withdraw them from the duties of their position.

It is not worth while to enter into the interminable controversy respecting the council held at Constantinople in 680, the canons of which were promulgated in 692, and which is known to polemics as the *Quinisext in Trullo*. The Greeks maintain that it was Œcumenical, and its legislation binding upon Christendom; the Latins, that it was provincial and schismatic : but whether Pope Agatho acceded to its canons or not; whether a century later Adrian I admitted them; or whether their authentication by the second Council of Nicæa gave them authority over the whole Church or not, are questions of little practical importance for our purpose, for they never were really incorporated into the law of the West, and they are only to be regarded as forming a portion of the received ecclesiastical jurisprudence of the East. In one sense, however, their bearing upon the Latin Church is interesting, for, in spite of them, Rome maintained communion with Constantinople for more than a century and a half, and the schism which then took place arose from altogether different causes. In the West, therefore, celibacy was only a point of discipline, of no doctrinal importance, and not a matter of heresy, as we shall see it afterwards become under the stimulus afforded by Protestant controversy.

The canons of the Quinisext are very full upon all the questions relating to celibacy, and show that great relaxation had occurred in enforcing the regulations embodied in the laws of Justinian. Digami must have become numerous in the Church, for the prohibition of their ordination is renewed, and all who had not released themselves from such forbidden unions by June 15th of the preceding year are condemned to suffer deposition. So marriage in orders had evidently become frequent, for all guilty of it are enjoined to leave their wives, when, after a short suspension, they are to be restored to their position, though ineligible for promotion. A much severer punishment is, however, provided for those who should subsequently be guilty of the same indiscretion, for all such infractions of the rule are visited with absolute deposition—thus proving that it had fallen into desuetude, since those who sinned after its restoration were regarded as much more culpable than those who had merely transgressed an obsolete law. Even bishops had neglected the restrictions imposed upon them by Justinian, for the council refers to prelates in Africa, Libya, and elsewhere, who lived openly with their wives; and although this is prohibited for the future under penalty of deposition, and although all wives of those promoted to the episcopate are directed to be placed in nunneries at a distance from their husbands, yet the remarkable admission is made that this is done for the sake of the people, who regarded such things as a scandal, and not for the purpose of changing that which had been ordained by the Apostles.

With regard to the future discipline of the great body of the clergy, the council, after significantly acknowledging that the Roman Church required a promise of abstinence from married candidates for the diaconate and priesthood, proceeds to state that it desires to adhere to the Apostolic canon by keeping inviolate the conjugal relations of those in holy orders, and by permitting them to associate with their wives, only stipulating for continence during the time devoted to the ministry of the sacraments. To put an end to all opposition to this privilege, deposition is threatened against those who shall presume to interfere between the clergy and their wives, and likewise against all who, under pretence of religion, shall put their wives away. At the same time, in order to promote the extension of the Church in the foreign provinces, this latter penalty is remitted, as a concession to the prejudices of the " Barbarians." How thoroughly in some regions sacerdotal marriage had come to be the rule we learn from a reference to Armenia, where the Levitical custom of the Hebrews was imitated, in the creation of a sacerdotal caste, transmitted from father to son, and confined to the priestly houses. This limitation is condemned by the council, which orders that all who are worthy of ordination shall be regarded as eligible.

The Eastern Church thus formally and in the most solemn manner recorded its separate and independent discipline on this point, and refused to be bound by the sacerdotalism of Rome. It thus maintained the customs transmitted from the early period, when asceticism had commenced to show itself, but it shrank from carrying out the principles involved to their ultimate result, as was sternly attempted by the inexorable logic of Rome. The system thus laid down was permanent, for throughout the East the Quinisext was received unquestioningly as a general council, and its decrees were authoritative and unalterable. It is true that in the confusion of the two following centuries a laxity of practice gradually crept in, by which those who desired to marry were admitted to holy orders while single, and were granted two years after ordination during which they were at liberty to take wives, but this was acknowledged to be an abuse, and about the

year 900 it was formally prohibited by a constitution of
Leo the Philosopher. Thus restored, the Greek Church
has preserved its early traditions unaltered to the present
day. Marriage in orders is not permitted, nor are digami
admissible, but the lower grades of the clergy are free to
marry, nor are they separated from their wives when promoted to the sacred functions of the diaconate or priesthood. The bishops are selected from the regular clergy or
monks, and, being bound by the vow of chastity, are of
course unmarried and unable to marry. Thus the legislation of Justinian is practically transmitted to the nineteenth century. Even this restriction on the freedom of
marriage renders it difficult to preserve the purity of the
priesthood, and the Greek Church, like the Latin, is forced
occasionally to renew the Nicene prohibition against the
residence of suspected women.

The strongly marked hereditary tendency, which is so
distinguishing a characteristic of mediæval European
institutions, has led, in Russia at least, since the time of
Peter the Great, to the customary transmission of the priesthood, and even of individual churches, from father to son,
thus creating a sacerdotal caste. To such an extent has
this been carried that marriage is obligatory on the parish
priest, and custom requires that the wife shall be the
daughter of a priest. Some of the results of this are to be
seen in a law of 1867, forbidding for the future the aspirant
to a cure from marrying the daughter of his predecessor or
undertaking to support the family of the late incumbent as
a condition precedent to obtaining the preferment. It
shows how entirely the duties of the clergy had been lost in
the sense of property and hereditary right attaching to
benefices, leading inevitably to the neglect or perfunctory
performance of ecclesiastical duties. We shall see hereafter
how narrowly the Latin Church escaped a similar transformation, and how prolonged was the struggle to avoid it.

One branch of the Eastern Church, however, relaxed the
rules of the Quinisext. In 431, Nestorius, Patriarch of
Constantinople, was excommunicated for his heretical
subtleties as to the nature of the Godhead in Christ. Driven
out from the empire by the orthodox authorities, his followers spread throughout Mesopotamia and Persia, where,
by the end of the century, their efforts had gradually con-

verted nearly the whole population. About the year 480, Barsuma, Metropolitan of Nisibis, added to his Nestorian heresy the guilt of marrying a nun, when, to justify himself, he assembled a synod in which the privilege of marriage was granted not only to priests, but even to monks. In 485, Babueus, Patriarch of Seleucia, held a council which excommunicated Barsuma and condemned his licentious doctrines; but, about ten years later, a subsequent patriarch, Babeus, in the Council of Seleucia, obtained the enactment of canons conferring the privilege of marriage on all ranks of the clergy, from monk to patriarch. Some forty years later a debate recorded between the Patriarch Mar Aba and King Chosroes shows that repeated marriages were common among all orders, but Mar Aba subsequently issued a canon depriving patriarchs and bishops of the right, and subjecting them to the rules of the Latin and Greek Churches.

The career of the Nestorians shows that matrimony is not incompatible with mission-work, for they were the most successful missionaries on record. They penetrated throughout India, Tartary, and China. In the latter empire they lasted until the thirteenth century; while in India they not improbably exercised an influence in modifying the doctrines of ancient Brahmanism, and the Portuguese discoverers in the fifteenth century found them flourishing in Malabar. So numerous were they that during the existence of the Latin kingdom of Jerusalem they are described, in conjunction with the monophysite sect of the Jacobites, as exceeding in numbers the inhabitants of the rest of Christendom.

Another segment of the Eastern Church may properly receive attention here. The Abyssinians and Coptic Christians of Egypt can scarcely in truth be considered a part of the Greek Church, as they are monophysite in belief, and have in many particulars adopted Jewish customs, such as circumcision, etc. Their observances as regards marriage, however, tally closely with the canons of the Quinisext, except that bishops are permitted to retain their wives. In the sixteenth century, Bishop Zaga Zabo, who was sent as envoy to Portugal by David, King of Abyssinia, left behind him a confession of faith for the edification of the curious. In this document he describes the discipline of his Church as strict in forbidding the clericature to illegitimates;

marriage is not dissolved by ordination, but second marriage, or marriage in orders, is prohibited, except under dispensation from the Patriarch, a favour occasionally granted to magnates for public reasons. Without such dispensation, the offender is expelled from the priesthood, while a bishop or other ecclesiastic convicted of having an illegitimate child is forthwith deprived of all his benefices and possessions. Monasteries, moreover, were numerous, and monachal chastity was strictly enforced. These rules, I presume, are still in force. A recent traveller in those regions states that " if a priest be married previous to his ordination, he is allowed to remain so; but no one can marry after having entered the priesthood "—while a mass of superstitious and ascetic observances has overlaid religion, until little trace is left of original Christianity.

CHAPTER VII

MONACHISM

THE Monastic Orders occupy too prominent a place in ecclesiastical history, and were too powerful an instrument both for good and evil, to be passed over without some cursory allusion, although the secular clergy are more particularly the subject of the present sketch, and the rise and progress of monachism is a topic too extensive in its details to be thoroughly considered in the space which can be allotted to it.

In this, as in some other forms of asceticism, we may look to Buddhism for the model on which the Church fashioned her institutions. Ages before the time of Sakyamuni, or the Buddha, the life of the anchorite had become a favourite mode of securing the *moksha*, or supreme good of absorption in Brahma. Buddhism, in throwing open the way of salvation to all mankind, popularised this, and thus multiplied enormously the crowd of mendicants, who lived upon the charity of the faithful, and who abandoned all the cares and duties of life in the hope of advancing a step in the scale of being, and of ultimately obtaining the highest bliss of admission to Nirvana. In the hopeless confusion of Hindu chronology, it is impossible to define dates with exactness, but we know that at a very early period these bhikshus and bhikshunis, or mendicants of either sex, were organised in monasteries (viharas or sangharamas) erected by the piety of the faithful, and were subjected to definite rules, prominent among which were those of poverty and chastity, which subsequently became the foundation of all the Western orders. Probably the oldest existing scripture of Buddhism is the Pratimoksha, or collection of rules for observance by the bhikshus, which tradition, not without probability, ascribes to Sakyamuni himself. In this, infraction of chastity falls under the first of the four Parajika rules; it is classed, with murder, among the most

serious offences, entailing excommunication and expulsion
without forgiveness.   The solicitation of a woman comes
within the scope of the thirteen Sanghadisesa rules, entailing
penance and probation, after which the offender may be
absolved by an assembly of not less than twenty bhikshus.
Other punishments are allotted for every suspicious act, and
the utmost care is shown in the regulations laid down for
the minutest details of social intercourse between the sexes.

Under these rules, Buddhist monachism developed to an
extent which more than rivals that of its possible Western
derivative.   The remains of the magnificent Viharas still to
be seen in India testify at once to the enormous multitudes
which found shelter in them and to the munificent piety of
the monarchs and wealthy men who, as in Europe, sought
to purchase the favour of Heaven by founding and enlarging
these retreats for the devotee.   In China, Buddhism was
not introduced until the first century A.D., and yet, by the
middle of the seventh century, in spite of repeated and
severe persecutions, the number of monasteries already
amounted to 3716, while two hundred years later the persecuting Emperor Wu-Tsung ordered the destruction of no
less than 4600; and at the present day it is estimated that
there are 80,000 Buddhist monks in the environs of Pekin
alone.   When, in the seventh century, Hiouen-Thsang
visited India, he describes the Sangharama of Nalanda as
containing ten thousand monks and novices; and the later
pilgrim, Fah-Hian, found fifty or sixty thousand in the
island of Ceylon.   In the fourteenth century, the city of
Ilchi, in Chinese Tartary, possessed fourteen monasteries,
averaging three thousand devotees in each; while in Tibet
at the present time there are in the vicinity of Lhassa twelve
great monasteries, containing a population of 18,500 lamas.
In Ladak, the proportion of lamas to the laity is as one to
thirteen; in Spiti, one to seven; and in Burmah, one to
thirty.   Great as were the proportions to which European
monachism grew, it never attained dimensions such as these.

Whether the West may have borrowed from the East in
this matter of monachism, or was independently inspired
by similar impulses, is a question which we are not called
upon to answer.   As an historical fact, the first rudimentary
development of a tendency in such direction is to be found
in the vows, which, as stated in a previous section, had
already, at an early period in the history of the Church,

become common among female devotees. In fact, an order of widows, employed in charitable works and supported from the offerings of the faithful, was apparently one of the primitive institutions of the Apostles. To prevent any conflict between the claims of the world and those of the Church, St. Paul directs that they shall be childless and not less than sixty years of age, so that on the one hand there might be no neglect of the first duty which he recognised as owing to the family, nor, on the other hand, that the devotee should be tempted by the flesh to quit the service which she had undertaken.

This admirable plan may be considered the germ of the countless associations by which the Church has in all ages earned the gratitude of mankind by giving to Christianity its truest practical exposition. It combined a refuge for the desolate with a most efficient organisation for spreading the faith and administering charity; and there was no thought of marring its utility by rendering it simply an instrument for exaggerating and propagating asceticism. St. Paul, indeed, expressly commands the younger ones to marry and bring up children; and he could little have anticipated the time when this order of widows, so venerable in its origin and labours, would, by the caprice of ascetic progress, come to be regarded as degraded in comparison with the virgin spouses of Christ, who selfishly endeavoured to purchase their own salvation by shunning all the duties imposed on them by the Creator. Nor could he have imagined that, after eighteen centuries, enthusiastic theologians would seriously argue that Christ and his apostles had founded regular religious orders, bound by the three customary vows of chastity, poverty, and obedience.

In the early Church, as has been already shown, all vows of continence and dedication to the service of God were a matter of simple volition, not only as to their inception, but also as to their duration. The male or female devotee was at liberty to return to the world and to marry at any time; although during the purer periods of persecution such conduct was doubtless visited with disapprobation and was attended with loss of reputation. As, moreover, there was no actual segregation from the world and no sundering of family ties, there was no necessity for special rules of discipline. When, under the Decian persecution, Paul the

Thebæan, and shortly afterwards St. Antony, retired to the desert in order to satisfy a craving for ascetic mortification which could only be satiated by solitude, and thus unconsciously founded the vast society of Egyptian cenobites, they gave rise to what at length became a new necessity. The associations which gradually formed themselves required some government, and the institution of monachism became too important a portion of the Church, both in numbers and influence, to remain long without rules of discipline to regulate its piety and to direct its powers. As yet, however, a portion of the Church, adhering to ancient tradition, looked reprovingly on these exaggerated vagaries. Lactantius, for instance, in a passage written subsequent to the conversion of Constantine, earnestly denounces the life of a hermit as that of a beast rather than of a man, and urges that the bonds of human society ought not to be broken, since man cannot exist without his fellows.

It was in vain to attempt to stem the tide which had now fairly set in, nor is it difficult to understand the impulsion which drove so many to abandon the world. No small portion of pastoral duty consisted in exhortations to virginity, the praises of which were reiterated with ever-increasing vehemence, and the rewards of which, in this world and the next, were magnified with constantly augmenting promises. Indeed, a perusal of the writings of that age seems to render it difficult to conceive how any truly devout soul could remain involved in worldly duties and pleasures, when the abandonment of all the ties and responsibilities imposed on man by Providence was represented as rendering the path to heaven so much shorter and more certain, and when every pulpit resounded with perpetual amplifications of the one theme. Equally efficacious with the timid and slothful was the prospect of a quiet retreat from the confusion and strife which the accelerating decline of the empire rendered every day wilder and more hopeless; while the crushing burdens of the State drove many, in spite of all the efforts of the civil power, to seek their escape in the exemptions accorded to those connected with the Church. When to these classes are added the penitents—prototypes of St. Mary of Egypt, who retired to the desert as the only refuge from her profligate life, and for seventeen years waged an endless struggle with the burning passions which she could control but could not conquer—it is not

difficult to understand how vast were the multitudes unconsciously engaged in laying the foundations of that monastic
structure which was eventually to overshadow all Christendom. Indeed, even the Church itself at times became
alarmed at the increasing tendency, as when the Council of
Saragossa, in 381, found it necessary to denounce the
practice of ecclesiastics abandoning their functions and
embracing the monastic life, which it assumes was done
from unworthy motives.

Soon after his conversion, Constantine had encouraged
the prevailing tendency by not only repealing the disabilities imposed by the old Roman law on those who
remained unmarried, but by extending the power of making
wills to minors who professed the intention of celibacy.
His piety and that of subsequent emperors speedily
attributed to all connected with the Church certain exemptions from the intolerable municipal burdens which were
eating out the heart of the empire. An enormous premium
was thus offered to swell the ecclesiastical ranks, while, as
the number of the officiating clergy was necessarily limited,
the influx would naturally flow into the mass of monks
and nuns, on whose increase there was no restriction, and
whose condition was open to all, with but slender examination into the fitness of the applicant. The rapidly increasing
wealth of the Church and the large sums devoted to the
maintenance of all orders of the clergy offered additional
temptations to those who might regard the life of the
ascetic as the means of securing an assured existence of
idleness, free from all care of the morrow. If, therefore,
during a period when ridicule and persecution were the
portion of those who vowed perpetual continence, it had
been found impossible to avoid the most deplorable scandals,
it can readily be conceived that allurements such as these
would crowd the monastic profession with proselytes of a
most questionable character, drawn from a society so fright-
fully dissolute as that of the fourth century. The fierce
declamations of St. Jerome afford a terrible picture of the
disorders prevalent among those vowed to celibacy, and of
the hideous crimes resorted to in order to conceal or remove
the consequences of guilt, showing that the asceticism
enforced by Siricius had not wrought any improvement.
The necessity of subjecting those bound by vows to
established rules must therefore have soon become generally

recognised; and although, as we have already seen, they were free at any time to abandon the profession which they had assumed, still, while they remained as members, the welfare of the Church would render it imperative to establish rules of wholesome discipline. The first authoritative attempt to check disorders of the kind is to be found in the first Council of Carthage, which in 348 insisted that all who, shunning marriage, elected the better lot of chastity, should live separate and solitary, and that none should have access to them under penalty of excommunication; and in 381 the Council of Saragossa sought to remedy the evil at its root by forbidding virgins to take the veil unless they could furnish proof that they were at least forty years of age.

Although the Church, in becoming an affair of state, had to a great extent sacrificed its independence, still it enjoyed the countervailing advantage of being able to call upon the temporal power for assistance when its own authority was defied, nor was it long in requiring this aid in the enforcement of its regulations. Accordingly, in 364, we find a law of Jovian forbidding, under pain of actual or civil death, any attempt to marry a sacred virgin, the extreme severity of which is the best indication of the condition of morals that could justify a resort to penalties so exaggerated. How great was the necessity for reform, and how little was actually accomplished by these attempts, may be estimated from an effort of the Council of Valence, in 374, to prevent those who married from being pardoned after too short a penance, and from the description which ten years later Pope Siricius gives of the unbridled and shameless licence indulged in by both sexes in violation of their monastic vows.

Thus definite rules for the governance of these constantly increasing crowds of all stations, conditions, and characters, who were obviously so ill-fitted for the obligations which they had assumed, became necessary, but it was long before they assumed an irrevocable and binding force. The treatise which is known as the Rule of St. Orsiesius is only a long and somewhat mystic exhortation to asceticism. That which St. Pachomius is said to have received from an angel is manifestly posterior to the date of that saint, and probably belongs to the commencement of the fifth century. Minute as are its instructions, and rigid as are its injunctions respecting every action of the cenobite, yet it fully displays the voluntary nature of the profession and the lightness of the bonds which tied the monk to his order. A stranger applying for admission to a monastery was exposed only to a probation of a few days, to test his sincerity and to prove that he was not a slave; no vows were imposed, only his simple promise to obey the rules being required. If he grew tired of ascetic life, he departed, but he could not be taken back without penitence and the consent of the archimandrite. Even female travellers applying for hospitality were not refused admittance, and an inclosure was set apart for them, where they were entertained with special honour and attention; a place was likewise provided for them in which to be present at vespers.

A similar system of discipline is manifested in the detailed statement of the regulations of the Egyptian monasteries left us by John Cassianus, Abbot of St. Victor of Marseilles, who died in 448. No vows or religious ceremonies were required of the postulant for admission. He was proved by ten days' waiting at the gate and a year's probation inside, yet the slender tie between him and the community is shown by the preservation of his worldly garments, to be returned to him in case of his expulsion for disobedience or discontent, and also by the refusal to receive from him the gift of his private fortune—although no one within the sacred walls was permitted to call the simplest article his own— lest he should leave the convent and then claim to revoke his donation, as not infrequently happened in institutions which neglected this salutary rule. So, in a series of directions for cenobitic life, appended to a curious Arabic version of the Nicene canons, the punishment provided for persistent disobedience and turbulence is expulsion of the offender from the monastery.

As a temporary refuge from the trials of life, where the soul could be strengthened by seclusion, meditation, peaceful labour, and rigid discipline, thousands must have found the institution of monachism most beneficial who had not resolution enough to give themselves up to a life of ascetic devotion and privation. These facilities for entrance and departure, however, only rendered more probable the admission of the turbulent and the worldly; and the want of stringent and effective regulations must have rendered itself every day more apparent, as the holy multitudes waxed larger and more difficult to manage, and as the

empire became covered with wandering monks, described
by St. Augustin as beggars, swindlers, and peddlers of false
relics, who resorted to the most shameless mendacity to
procure the means of sustaining their idle and vagabond
life.

It was this, no doubt, which led to the adoption and
enforcement of the third of the monastic vows—that of
obedience—as being the only mode by which, during the
period when residence was voluntary, the crowds of devotees
could be kept in a condition of subjection. To what a length
this was carried, and how completely the system of religious
asceticism succeeded in its object of destroying all human
feeling, is well exemplified by the shining example of the
holy Mucius, who presented himself for admission to a
monastery, accompanied by his child, a boy eight years of
age. His persistent humility gained for him a relaxation of
the rules, and father and son were admitted together. To
test his worthiness, however, they were separated, and all
intercourse forbidden. His patience encouraged a further
trial. The helpless child was neglected and abused systematically, but all the perverse ingenuity which rendered him
a mass of filth and visited him with perpetual chastisement
failed to excite a sign of interest in the father. Finally, the
abbot feigned to lose all patience with the little sufferer's
moans, and ordered Mucius to cast him in the river. The
obedient monk carried him to the bank and threw him in
with such promptitude that the admiring spectators were
barely able to rescue him. All that is wanting to complete
the hideous picture is the declaration of the abbot that in
Mucius the sacrifice of Abraham was completed. This
epitomises the whole system—the transfer to man of the
obedience due to God—and shows how little, by this time,
was left of the hopeful reliance on a beneficent God which
distinguished the primitive Church, and which led Athenagoras, in the second century, to argue from the premises
" God certainly impels no one to those things which are
unnatural."

The weaker sex, whether from the greater value attached
to the purity of woman or from her presumed frailty, as well
as from some difference in the nature of the engagement
entered into, was the first to become the subject of distinct
legislation, and the frequency of the efforts required shows
the difficulty of enforcing the rule of celibacy and chastity.

Allusion has already been made to a law of Jovian which, as early as 364, denounced the attempt to marry a nun as a capital crime. Subsequent canons of the Church show that this was wholly ineffectual. The Council of Valence, in 374, endeavoured to check such marriages. The Synod of Rome, in 384, alludes with horror to these unions, which it stigmatises as adultery, and drawing a distinction between virgins professed and those who had taken the veil, it prescribes an indefinite penance before they can be received back into the Church, but at the same time it does not venture to order their separation from their husbands. A year later, the bolder Siricius commands both monks and nuns guilty of unchastity to be imprisoned, but he makes no allusion to marriage. Notwithstanding the fervour of St. Augustin's admiration for virginity and the earnestness with which he waged war in favour of celibacy, he pronounces that the marriage of nuns is binding, ridicules those who consider it as invalid, and deprecates the evil results of separating man and wife under such circumstances, but yet his asceticism, satisfied with this concession to common sense, pronounces such unions to be worse than adulterous. From this it is evident that these infractions of discipline were far from uncommon, and that the stricter churchmen already treated such marriages as null and void, which resulted in the husbands considering themselves at liberty to marry again. Such view of monastic vows was not sustained by the authorities of the Church, for about the same period Innocent I, like St. Augustin, while condemning such marriages as worse than adulterous, admitted their validity by refusing communion to the offenders until one of the partners in guilt should be dead; and, like the Synod of 384, he considered the transgression as somewhat less culpable in the professed virgin than in her who had consummated her marriage with Christ by absolutely taking the veil. It was probably this assumed marriage with Christ—a theory which St. Cyprian shows to be as old as the third century, and which is very strongly stated by Innocent—which rendered the Church so much more sensitive as to the frailty of the female devotees than to that of the men. As yet, however, the stability of such marriages was generally accepted throughout the Church, for, a few years before the epistle of Innocent, we find it enunciated by the first Council of Toledo, which decided that the nun who married was not admissible to penitence during the life of her husband, unless she separated herself from him.

It is evident from all this that an effort had been made to have such marriages condemned as invalid, and that it had failed. We see, however, that the lines had gradually been drawn more tightly around the monastic order, that the vows could no longer be shaken off with ease, and that there was a growing tendency to render the monastic character ineffaceable when once assumed. Towards the middle of the fifth century, however, a reaction took place, possibly because the extreme views may have been found impracticable. Thus Leo I treats recalcitrant cenobites with singular tenderness. He declares that monks cannot without sin abandon their profession, and therefore that he who returns to the world and marries must redeem himself by penitence, for however honourable be the marriage-tie and the active duties of life, still it is a transgression to desert the better path. So professed virgins who throw off the habit and marry violate their duty, and those who in addition to this have been regularly consecrated commit a great crime—and yet no further punishment is indicated for them; and the little respect still paid to the indelible character claimed for monachism is shown by the manner in which the civil power was ready to interfere for the purpose of putting an end to some of the many abuses arising from monastic institutions. In 458 Majorian promulgated a law in which he inveighs with natural indignation against the parents who, to get rid of their offspring, compel their unhappy daughters to enter convents at a tender age, and he orders that, until the ardour of the passions shall be tempered by advancing years, no vows shall be administered. The minimum age for taking the veil is fixed at forty years, and stringent measures are provided for insuring its observance. If infringed by order of the parents, or by an orphan girl of her own free will, one-third of all the possessions of the offender is confiscated to the State, and the ecclesiastics officiating at the ceremony are visited with the heavy punishment of proscription. A woman forced into a nunnery, if her parents die before she reaches the age of forty, is declared to be free to leave it and to marry, nor can she be disinherited thereafter. Fruitless as this well-intentioned effort proved, it is highly suggestive as to the wrongs which were perpetrated under the name of religion, the stern efforts felt to be requisite for their prevention, and the power exercised to annul the vows.

In the East, the tendency was to give a more rigid and unalterable character to the vows, nor is it difficult to understand the cause. Both Church and State began to feel the necessity of reducing to subjection under some competent authority the vast hordes of idle and ignorant men who had embraced monastic life. In the West, monachism was as yet in its infancy, and was to be stimulated rather than to be dreaded, but it was far otherwise in the East, where the influence of the ascetic ideas of India was probably much more direct and immediate. The examples of Antony and Pachomius had brought them innumerable followers. The solitudes of the deserts had become peopled with vast communities, and as the contagion spread, monasteries arose everywhere and were rapidly filled and enlarged. The blindly bigoted and the turbulently ambitious found a place among those whose only aim was retirement and peace; while the authority wielded by the superior of each establishment, through the blind obedience claimed under monastic vows, gave him a degree of power which rendered him not only important but dangerous. The monks thus became in time a body of no little weight which it behoved the Church to thoroughly control, as it might become efficient for good or evil. By encouraging and directing it, she gained an instrument of incalculable force, morally and physically, to consolidate her authority and extend her influence. How that influence was used, and how the monks became at times a terror even to the State, is written broadly on the history of the age. Even early in the fifth century the hordes of savage Nitrian cenobites were the janizaries of the fiery Cyril, with which he lorded it over the city of Alexandria, and almost openly bade defiance to the imperial authority. The tumult in which Orestes nearly lost his life, the banishment of the Jews, and the shocking catastrophe of Hypatia show how dangerous an element to society they were even then, when under the guidance of an able and unscrupulous leader. So the prominent part taken by the monks in the deplorable Nestorian and Eutychian controversies, the example of the Abbot Barsumas at the Robber Synod in Ephesus, the exploits of Theodosius of Jerusalem and Peter of Antioch, who drove out their bishops and usurped the episcopal chairs, the career of Eutyches himself, the blood-thirsty rabble of monks who controlled the Synod of Ephesus and endeavoured to overawe that of Chalcedon, and, in the succeeding century, the insurrections against the Emperor Anastasius which were largely attributed to their efforts—all these were warnings not lightly to be neglected. The monks, in fact, were fast becoming not only disagreeable but even dangerous to the civil power; their organisation and obedience to their leaders gave them strength to threaten seriously the influence even of the hierarchy, and the effort to keep them strictly under subjection and within their convent walls became necessary to the peace of both Church and State.

At the Council of Chalcedon, in 451, the hierarchy had their revenge for the insults which they had suffered two years before in the Robber Synod. A large portion of the monks, infected with Eutychianism, came into direct antagonism with the bishops, whom they defied. With the aid of the civil power, the bishops triumphed, and endeavoured to put an end for the future to monastic insubordination, by placing the monasteries under the direct control and supervision of the secular prelates. A series of canons was adopted which declared that monks and nuns were not at liberty to marry; but while excommunication was the punishment provided for the offence, power was given to the bishops to extend mercy to the offenders. At the suggestion of the Emperor Marcian, the council deplored the turbulence of the monks who, leaving their monasteries, stirred up confusion everywhere, and it commanded them to devote themselves solely to prayer and fasting in the spot which they had chosen as a retreat from the world. It forbade them to abandon the holy life to which they had devoted themselves, and pronounced the dread sentence of the anathema on the renegades who refused to return and undergo due penance. No monastery was to be founded without the licence of the bishop of the locality, and he alone could give permission to a monk to leave it for any purpose.

This legislation was well adapted to the end in view, but the evil was too deep-seated and too powerful to be thus easily eradicated. Finding the Church unable to enforce a remedy, the civil power was compelled to intervene. As early as 390 Theodosius the Great had ordered the monks to confine themselves strictly to deserts and solitudes. Two years later he repealed this law and allowed them to enter the cities. This laxity was abused, and in 466 the Emperors Leo and Anthemius issued an edict forbidding for the future all monks to go beyond the walls of their monasteries on any pretext, except the apocrisiarii, or legal officers, on legitimate business alone, and these were strictly enjoined not to engage in religious disputes, not to stir up the people, and not to preside over assemblages of any nature.

History shows us how little obedience this also received, nor is it probable that much more attention was paid to the imperial rescript when, in 532, Justinian confirmed the legislation of his predecessors, and added provisions forbidding those who had once taken the vows from returning to the world under penalty of being handed over to the *curia* of their municipality, with confiscation of their property, and personal punishment if penniless. Had the effort then been successful, he would not have been under the necessity of renewing it in 535 by a law making over to the monastery, by way of satisfaction to God, the property of any monk presuming to abandon a life of religion and returning to the cares of the world. The prevalent laxity of morals is further shown by another provision according to which the monk who received orders was not allowed to marry, even if he entered grades in which marriage was permitted to the secular clergy, the penalty for taking a wife or a concubine being degradation and dismissal, with incapacity for serving the State. Ten years later, further legislation was found necessary, and at length the final expedient was hit upon, by which the apostate monk was handed over to the bishop to be placed in a monastery, from which if he escaped he was delivered to the secular tribunal as incorrigible. The trouble was apparently incurable. Three hundred and fifty years later, Leo the Philosopher deplores it, and orders all recalcitrant monks to be returned to their convents as often as they may escape. As for the morals of monastic life, it may be sufficient to refer to the regulation of St. Theodore Studita, in the ninth century, prohibiting the entrance of even female animals.

Thus gradually the irrevocable nature of monastic vows became established in the East, more from reasons of State than from ecclesiastical considerations. In the West, matters were longer in reaching a settlement, and the causes operating were somewhat different. Monachism there had not become a terror to the civil power, and its management was left to the Church ; yet, if its influence was insufficient to excite tumults and seditions, it was none the less disorganised, and its disorders were a disgrace to those on whom rested the responsibility.

The Latin Church was not by any means insensible to this disgrace, nor did it underrate the importance of rendering the vows indissoluble, of binding its servants absolutely and for ever to its service, and of maintaining its character and influence by endeavouring to enforce a discipline that should insure purity. During the period sketched above, and for the two following centuries, there is scarcely a council which did not enact canons showing at once the persistent effort to produce these results and the almost insurmountable difficulty of accomplishing them. It would lead us too far to enter upon the minutiæ of these perpetually reiterated exhortations and threats, or of the various expedients which were successively tried. Suffice it to say that the end in view was never lost sight of, while the perseverance of the wrongdoer seems to have rivalled that of the disciplinarian. The anvil bade fair to wear out the hammer, while the confusion and lawlessness of those dismal ages gave constantly increasing facilities to those who desired to escape from the strictness of the ascetic life to which they had devoted themselves. Thus arose a crowd of vagabond monks, *gyrovagi, acephali, circilliones, sarabaitæ,* who, without acknowledging obedience to any superior or having any definite place of abode, wandered over the face of the country, claiming the respect and immunities due to a sacred calling, for the purpose of indulging in an idle and dissolute life—vagrants of the worst description, according to the unanimous testimony of the ecclesiastical authorities of the period.

Thus, up to the middle of the fifth century, no regular system of discipline had been introduced in the monastic establishments of the Latin Church. About that period Cassianus, the first abbot of St. Victor of Marseilles, wrote out, for the benefit of the ruder monasticism of the West, the details of discipline in which he had perfected himself among the renowned communities of the East. He deplores

the absence of any fixed rule in the Latin convents, where
every abbot governed on the plan which suited his fancy;
where more difficulty was found in preserving order among
two or three monks than the Abbot of Tabenna in the
Thebaïd experienced with the flock of five thousand committed to his single charge; and where each individual
retained his own private hoards, which were carefully
locked up and sealed to keep them from the unscrupulous
covetousness of his brethren. How ·little all these efforts
accomplished is clearly manifested when, in 494, we find
Gelasius I lamenting the incestuous marriages which were
not uncommon among the virgins dedicated to God, and
venturing only to denounce excommunication on the
offenders, unless they should avert it by undergoing public
penance. As for widows who married after professing
chastity, he could indicate no earthly chastisement, but only
held out to them the prospect of eternal reward or punishment, and left it for them to decide whether they would
seek or abandon the better part. Still, the irrevocable
nature of the vow of celibacy was so little understood or
respected that in 502 Cæsarius, who had just been translated
from the abbacy of a monastery to the bishopric of Arles,
wrote to Pope Symmachus asking him to issue a precept
forbidding marriage to nuns, to which the pontiff promptly
acceded.

A new apostle was clearly needed to aid the organising
spirit of Rome in her efforts to regulate the increasing
number of devotees, who threatened to become the worst
scandal of the Church, and who could be rendered so
efficient an instrument for its aggrandisement. He was
found in the person of St. Benedict of Nursia, who, about
the year 494, at the early age of sixteen, tore himself from
the pleasures of the world, and buried his youth in the
solitudes of the Latian Apennines. A nature that could
wrench itself away from the allurements of a splendid
career dawning amid the blandishments of Rome was not
likely to shrink from the austerities which awe and attract
the credulous and the devout. Tempted by the Evil Spirit
in the guise of a beautiful maiden, and finding his resolution
on the point of yielding, with a supreme effort Benedict cast
off his simple garment and threw himself into a thicket of
brambles and nettles, through which he rolled until his
naked body was lacerated from head to foot. The experi-

ment, though rude, was eminently successful; the flesh was effectually conquered, and Benedict was never again tormented by rebellious desires. A light so shining was not created for obscurity. Zealous disciples assembled around him, attracted from distant regions by his sanctity, and after various vicissitudes he founded the monastery of Monte Cassino, on which for a thousand years was lavished all that veneration and munificence could accumulate to render illustrious the birthplace and capital of the great Benedictine Order.

The rule promulgated by Benedict, which virtually became the established law of Latin Monachism, shows the more practical character of the Western mind. Though pervaded by the austerest asceticism, yet labour, charity, and good works occupy a much more prominent place in its injunctions than in the system of the East. Salvation was not to be sought simply by abstinence and mortification, and the innate selfishness of the monastic principle was relaxed in favour of a broader and more human view of the duties of man to his Creator and to his fellows. This gave to the institution a firmer hold on the affections of mankind and a more enduring vitality, which preserved its fortunes through the centuries, in spite of innumerable aberrations and frightful abuses.

Still there were as yet no irrevocable vows of poverty, chastity, and obedience exacted of the novice. After a year of probation he promised, before God and the Saints, to keep the rule under pain of damnation, and he was then admitted with imposing religious ceremonies. His worldly garments were, however, preserved, to be returned to him in case of expulsion, to which he was liable if incorrigibly disobedient. If he left the monastery, or if he was ejected, he could return twice, but after the third admission, if he again abandoned the order, he was no longer eligible. Voluntary submission was thus the corner-stone of discipline, and there was nothing indelible in the engagement which bound the monk to his brethren.

Contemporary with St. Benedict was St. Cæsarius of Arles, whose Rule has been transmitted to us by his nephew, St. Tetradius. It is very short, but is more rigid than that of Benedict, inasmuch as it requires from the applicant the condition of remaining for life in the convent, nor will it permit his assumption of the habit until he shall have

executed a deed bestowing all his property either on his
relatives or on the establishment of his choice, thus insuring
the rule of poverty, and depriving him of all inducement to
retire.   The Rule of St. Aurelian of Arles, which dates from
about 550, likewise insists on similar conditions.

The Rule of St. Benedict, however, overcame all rivalry,
and was at length universally adopted; Charlemagne,
indeed, inquired in 811 whether there could be any monks
except those who professed obedience to it.   Under it were
founded the innumerable monasteries which sprang up in
every part of Europe, and were everywhere the pioneers of
civilisation; which exercised a more potent influence in
extending Christianity over the heathen than all other
agencies combined; which carried the useful arts into barbarous regions, and preserved to modern times whatever of
classic culture has remained to us.   If they were equally
efficient in extending the authority of the Roman curia, and
in breaking down the independence of local and national
Churches, it is not to be assumed that even that result was
an unalloyed misfortune, when the centrifugal tendencies of
the Middle Ages were to be neutralised.   Until the thirteenth
century the Benedictines were practically without rivals,
and their numbers and holiness may be estimated by the
fact that in the fifteenth century one of their historians computed that the order had furnished fifty-five thousand five
hundred and five blessed members to the calendar of saints.

Yet it could not but be a scandal to all devout minds that
a man who had once devoted himself to religious observances
should return to the world.   Not only did it tend to break
down the important distinction now rapidly developing
between the clergy and the laity, but the possibility of
such escape interfered with the control of the Church over
those who formed so large a class of its members, and
diminished their utility in aiding the progress of its aggrandisement.   We cannot be surprised, therefore, that within
half a century after the death of St. Benedict, among the
reforms energetically inaugurated by St. Gregory the Great,
in the first year of his pontificate, was that of commanding
the forcible return of all who abandoned their profession—
the terms of the decretal showing that no concealment had
been thought necessary by the renegades in leading a secular
life and in publicly marrying.   Equally determined were
his efforts to reform the abuses which had so relaxed the

discipline of some monasteries that women were allowed
perfect freedom of access, and the monks contracted such
intimacy with them that they openly acted as godfathers to
their children ; and when, in 601, he learned that the monks
of St. Vitus, on Mount Etna, considered themselves at liberty
to marry, apparently without leaving their convent, he
checked the abuse by the most prompt and decided
commands to the ecclesiastical authorities of Sicily.

By the efforts of Gregory, the monk was thus, in theory at
least, separated irrevocably from the world, and committed
to an existence which depended solely upon the Church.
Cut off from family and friends, the door closed behind him
for ever, his only aspirations, beyond his own personal wants
and hopes, could but be for his abbey, his order, or the
Church, with which he was thus indissolubly connected.
There was one exception, however, to this general rule. No
married man was allowed to become a monk unless his wife
assented and likewise became a nun. The marriage-tie was
too sacred to be broken, unless both parties agreed simultaneously to embrace the better life. Thus, on the complaint
of a wife, Gregory orders her husband to be forcibly removed
from the monastery which he had entered and to be restored
to her. We shall see hereafter how entirely the Church in
time outgrew these scruples, and how insignificant the
sacrament of marriage became in comparison with that of
ordination or the vow of religion.

The theory of perpetual segregation from the world was
thus established, and it accomplished at last the objects for
which it was designed, but it was too much in opposition to
the invincible tendencies of human nature to be universally
enforced without a struggle, which lasted for nearly a
thousand years. To follow out in detail the vicissitudes of
this struggle would require too much space. Its nature will
be indicated by occasional references in the following pages ;
meanwhile it will be sufficient to observe how little was
accomplished even in his own age by the energy and
authority of Gregory. It was only a few years after his
death that the Council of Paris, in 615, made it evident that
residence in monasteries was not considered necessary for
women who took the vows, and that the civil power had to
be invoked to prevent their marriage. Indeed, it was not
uncommon for men to turn their houses, nominally at least,
into convents, living there surrounded by their wives and

families, and deriving no little worldly profit from the
assumption of superior piety, to the scandal of the truly
religious. St. Isidor of Seville, about the same period,
copies the words of St. Augustin in describing the wandering
monastic impostors who lived upon the credulous charity
of the faithful; and he also enlarges upon the disgraceful
licence of the *acephali*, or clerks bound by no rule, whose
vagabond life and countless numbers were an infamy to the
western kingdoms which they infested. The quotation of
this passage by Louis-le-Débonnaire, in his attempt to
reform the Church, shows that these degraded vagrants
continued to flourish unchecked in the ninth century; and,
indeed, Smaragdus, in his Commentary on the Rule of St.
Benedict, assures us that the evil had rather increased than
diminished.

Monachism was but one application of the doctrine of
justification by works, which, by the enthusiasm and superstition of ages, was gradually built into a vast system of
sacerdotalism. Through it were eventually opened to the
mediæval Church sources of illimitable power and wealth,
under the sole control of the central head, to which were
committed the power of the keys and the dispensation of
the exhaustless treasure of the merits of the Redeemer and
of the saints. To discuss these collateral themes, however,
would carry us too far from our subject, and I must dismiss
them with the remark that at the period now under consideration there could have been no anticipation of these
ulterior advantages to be gained by assuming to regulate
the mode in which individual piety might seek to propitiate
an offended God. Sufficient motives for the assumption
existed in the evils and aspirations of the moment, without
anticipating others which only received their fullest
development under the skilful dialectic of the Schoolmen.

CHAPTER VIII

THE BARBARIANS

WHILE the Latin Church had thus been engaged in its hopeless combat with the incurable vices of a worn-out civilisation, it had found itself confronted by a new and essentially different task. The Barbarians who wrenched province after province from the feeble grasp of the Cæsars had to be conquered, or religion and culture would be involved in the wreck which blotted out the political system of the Empire. The destinies of the future hung trembling in the balance, and it might not be an uninteresting speculation to consider what had been the present condition of the world if Western Europe had shared the fate of the East, and had fallen under the domination of a race bigoted in its own belief and incapable of learning from its subjects. Fortunately for mankind, the invaders of the West were not semi-civilised and self-satisfied; their belief was not a burning zeal for a faith sufficiently elevated to meet many of the wants of the soul; they were simple barbarians, who, while they might despise the cowardly voluptuaries on whom they trampled, could not fail to recognise the superiority of a civilisation awful even in its ruins. Fortunately, too, the Latin Church was a more compact and independently organised body than its Eastern rival, inspired by a warmer faith and a more resolute ambition. It faced the difficulties of its new position with consummate tact and tireless energy; and whether its adversaries were Pagans like the Franks, or Arians like the Goths and Burgundians, by alternate pious zeal and artful energy it triumphed where success seemed hopeless, and where bare toleration would have appeared a sufficient victory.

While the celibacy, which bound every ecclesiastic to the Church and dissevered all other ties, may doubtless be credited with a considerable share in this result, it could only lead, in the confusion of the time, to additional corruption of morals, already sufficiently corrupt. The chaste purity of the Barbarians at their advent aroused the wondering admiration of Salvianus, as that of their fathers four centuries earlier had won the encomium of Tacitus; but the virtue which sufficed for the simplicity of the German forests was not long proof against the allurements accumulated by the cynicism of Roman luxury. At first the wild converts, content with the battle-axe and javelin, might leave the holy functions of religion to their new subjects, their strength scarcely feeling the restraint of a faith which to them was little more than an idle ceremony; but as they gradually settled down in their conquests, and recognised that the high places of the Church conferred riches, honour, and power, they coveted the prizes which were too valuable to be monopolised by an inferior race. Gradually the hierarchy thus became filled with a class of warrior bishops, who, however efficient in maintaining and extending ecclesiastical prerogatives, were not likely to shed lustre on their order by the rigidity of their virtue, or to remove, by a strict enforcement of discipline, the scandals inseparable from endless civil commotions.

Reference has been made above (p. 58) to the perpetual iteration of the canon of celibacy, and of the ingenious devices to prevent its violation, by the numerous councils held during this period, showing at once the disorders which prevailed among the clergy and the fruitlessness of the effort to repress them. The history of the time is full of examples illustrating the various phases of this struggle.

The episcopal chair, which at an earlier period had been filled by the votes of the people, and which subsequently came under the control of the papacy, was at this time a gift in the hands of the untamed Merovingians, who carelessly bestowed it on him who could most lavishly fill the royal coffers, or who had earned it by courtly subservience or warlike prowess. The supple Roman or the turbulent Frank, who perchance could not recite a line of the Mass, thus leaped at once from the laity through all the grades; and as he was most probably married, there can be no room for surprise if the rule of continence, thus suddenly assumed from the most worldly motives, should often prove unendurable. Even in the early days of the Frankish conquest we see a cultured noble, like Genebaldus, married to the niece of St. Remy, when placed in the see of Laon ostensibly putting his wife away and visiting her only under pretext of religious instruction, until the successive births of a son and a daughter—whom he named Latro and Vulpecula in token of his sin—and we may not unreasonably doubt the chronicler's veracity when he informs us that the remorse of Genebaldus led him to submit to seven years' imprisonment as an expiatory penance. Equally instructive is the story of Felix of Nantes, whose wife, banished from his bed on his elevation to the episcopate, rebelled against the separation, and, finding him obdurate to her allurements, was filled with jealousy, believing that only another attachment could account for his coldness. Hoping to detect and expose his infidelity, she stole into the chamber where he was sleeping and saw on his breast a lamb, shining with heavenly light, indicative of the peaceful repose which had replaced all earthly passions in his heart. A virtue which was regarded as worthy of so miraculous a manifestation must have been rare indeed among the illiterate and untutored nominees of a licentious court, and that it was so in fact is indicated by the frequent injunctions of the councils that bishops must regard their wives as sisters; while a canon promulgated by the Council of Macon, in 581, ordering that no woman should enter the chamber of a bishop without two priests, or at least two deacons, in her company, shows how little hesitation there was in publishing to the world the suspicions that were generally entertained. How the rule was sometimes obeyed by the wild prelates of the age, while trampling upon other equally well-known canons, is exemplified by the story of Macliaus of Brittany. Chanao, Count of Brittany, had made away with three of his brothers; the fourth, Macliaus, after an unsuccessful conspiracy, sought safety in flight, entered the Church, and was created Bishop of Vannes. On the death of Chanao, he promptly seized the vacant throne, left the Church, threw off his episcopal robes, and took back to himself the wife whom he had quitted on obtaining the see of Vannes— for all of which he was duly excommunicated by his brother prelates.

When such was the condition of morals and discipline in the high places of the Church, it is not to be wondered at if the second Council of Tours, in 567, could declare that the people suspect, not indeed all, but many of the arch-priests, vicars, deacons, and subdeacons, of maintaining improper relations with their wives, and should command that no one in orders should visit his own house except in company with a subordinate clerk, without whom, moreover, he was never to sleep; the clerk refusing the performance of the duty to be whipped, and the priest neglecting the precaution to be deprived of communion for thirty days. Any one in orders found with his wife was to be excommunicated for a year, deposed, and relegated among the laity; while the arch-priest who neglected the enforcement of these rules was to be imprisoned on bread and water for a month. An equally suggestive illustration of the condition of society is afforded by another canon, directed against the frequent marriages of nuns, who excused themselves on the ground that they had taken the veil to avoid the risk of forcible abduction. Allusion is made to the laws of Childebert and Clotair, maintained in vigour by Charibert, punishing such attempts severely, and girls who anticipate them are directed to seek temporary asylum in the Church until their kindred can protect them under the royal authority, or find husbands for them.

Morals were even worse among the Arian Visigoths of Spain than among the orthodox believers of France. It is true that priestly marriage formed no part of the Arian doctrines, but as the heresy originated prior to the Council of Nicæa, and professed no obedience to that or any other council or decretal, its practice in this respect was left to such influence as individual asceticism might exercise. Having no acknowledged head to promulgate general canons or to insist upon their observance, no rule of the kind, even if theoretically admitted, could be effectually enforced. How little, indeed, the rule was obeyed is shown by the proceedings of the third Council of Toledo, held in 589 to confirm the reunion of the Spanish kingdom with the orthodox Church. It complains that even the converted bishops, priests, and deacons are found to be publicly living with their wives, which it forbids for the future under threat of degrading all recalcitrants to the rank of lector. The conversion of the kingdom to Catholicism did not improve matters. The clergy continued not only to associate with their wives, but also to marry openly, for the secular power was soon afterwards forced to interfere, and King Recared I issued a law directing that any priest, deacon, or subdeacon connecting himself with a woman by marriage or otherwise, should be separated from his guilty consort by either the bishop or judge, and be punished according to the canons of the Church, while the unfortunate woman was subjected to a hundred lashes and denied all access to her husband. To ensure the enforcement of the edict, the heavy mulct of two pounds of gold was levied on any bishop neglecting his duty in the premises. Recared also interposed to put a stop to the frequent marriages of nuns, whose separation from their husbands and condign punishment were decreed, with the enormous fine of five pounds of gold exacted of the careless ecclesiastic who might neglect to carry the law into effect—a fair measure of the difficulties experienced in enforcing the rule of celibacy. This legislation had little effect, for half a century later the eighth Council of Toledo, in 653, shows us that all ranks of the clergy, from bishops to subdeacons, had still no scruple in publicly maintaining relations with wives and concubines. Such was the state of discipline in Spain when the Saracen conquest, in 711, overwhelmed the Visigothic monarchy.

Italy was almost equally far removed from the ideal purity of Jerome and Augustin. In the early part of the sixth century was fabricated an account of a supposititious council, said to have been held in Rome by Silvester I, and the neglect of celibacy is evident when it was felt to be necessary to insert in this forgery a canon forbidding marriage to priests, under penalty of deprivation of functions for ten years. Even in this it is observable that there was no thought of annulling the marriage, as subsequently became established in orthodox doctrines. Nothing can be more suggestive of the demoralisation of the Italian Church than the permission granted about the year 580 by Pelagius II, for the elevation to the diaconate of a clerk at Florence, who while a widower had had children by a concubine. What renders the circumstance peculiarly significant is the fact that the Pope pleads the degeneracy of the age as his apology for this laxity.

Such was the condition of the Christian world when Gregory the Great, in 590, ascended the pontifical throne.

He was too devout a Churchman, and too sagacious a statesman, not to appreciate thoroughly the importance of the
canon in all its various aspects—not only as necessary to
ecclesiastical purity according to the ideas of the age, but
also as a prime element in the influence of the Church over
the minds of the people, as well as an essential aid in
extending ecclesiastical power, and in retaining undiminished the enormous possessions acquired by the Church
through the munificence of the pious. The prevailing
laxity, indeed, was already threatening serious dilapidation
of the ecclesiastical estates and foundations. How clearly
this was understood is shown by Pelagius I in 557, when he
refused for a year to permit the consecration of a bishop
elected by the Syracusans. On their persisting in their
choice he wrote to the Patrician Cethegus, giving as the
reason for his opposition the prelate's wife and children, by
whom, if they survive, the substance of the Church is wont
to be jeopardised; and his consent was finally given only
on the condition that the bishop-elect should provide competent security against any conversion of the estate of the
diocese for the benefit of his family, a detailed statement
of the property being made out in advance to guard against
attempted infractions of the agreement. That this was not
a merely local abuse is evident from a law of the Visigoths,
which provides that on the accession of any bishop, priest,
or deacon, an accurate inventory of all Church possessions
under his control shall be made by five freemen, and that
after his death an inquest shall be held for the purpose of
making good any deficiencies out of the estate of the
decedent, and forcing the restoration of anything that
might have been alienated.

There evidently was ample motive for a thorough
reformation, and Gregory accordingly addressed himself
energetically to the work of enforcing the canons. In his
decretals there are numerous references to the subject,
showing that he lost no opportunity of reviving the
neglected rules of discipline regarding the ordination of
digami, the residence of women, and abstinence from all
intercourse with the sex. In his zeal he even went so far
as to decree that any one guilty of even a single lapse from
virtue should be for ever debarred from the ministry of the
altar—a law nullified by its own severity, which rendered
its observance impossible. In 587, his predecessor Pelagius

had ordered that in Sicily the Roman rule should be followed of separating subdeacons from their wives, but it appeared cruel to Gregory that this should be enforced on those who had had no warning of such rigour when accepting the sub-diaconate, and one of the earliest acts of his pontificate was to allow them to resume relations with their wives; but he ordered that they should abstain from all service of the altar, and that in future no one should be admitted to that grade who would not formally take a vow of continence. There is not much trace in contemporary history of any improvement resulting from these efforts, and towards the very close of his pontificate, in 602, we find him entreating Queen Brunhilda to exercise her power in restraining the still unbridled licence of the Frankish clergy—a task which he assures her is essential if she desires to transmit her possessions in peace to her posterity. He also endeavoured to reform the perennial abuse of the residence of women, a reform which the Church had been vainly attempting ever since the canon of Nicæa. That Gregory's zeal, however, exercised some influence is manifested by the fact that tradition in the Middle Ages occasionally associated his name with the introduction of celibacy in the Church. The impression which he produced is shown by the wild legend which relates that, soon after issuing and strictly enforcing a decretal on the subject, he happened to have his fish-ponds drawn off, when the heads of no less than six thousand infants were found in them—the offspring of ecclesiastics, destroyed to avoid detection—which filled him with so much horror that he abandoned the vain attempt. Yet in Italy the residence of wives was still permitted to those in orders, under the restriction that they should be treated as sisters; and Gregory relates as worthy of all imitation the case of a holy priest of Nursia who, following the example of the saints in depriving himself of even lawful indulgences, had persistently relegated his wife to a distance. When at length he lay on his death-bed, to all appearance inanimate, the wife came to bid him a last farewell, and placed a mirror to his lips to see whether life was yet extinct. Her kindly ministrations roused the dominant asceticism in his expiring soul, and he gathered strength enough to exclaim, " Woman, depart ! Take away the straw, for there is yet fire here "—which supreme effort of self-immolation procured him on the instant a beatific vision of St. Peter and St. Paul, during which he lapsed ecstatically into eternity.

In considering so thoroughly artificial a system of morality, it is perhaps scarcely worth while to inquire into the value of a virtue which could only be preserved by shunning temptation with so scrupulous a care.

CHAPTER IX

THE CARLOVINGIANS

EVEN the energy and authority of Gregory the Great were powerless to restore order in the chaos of an utterly demoralised society. In Spain, the languishing empire of the Visigoths was fast sinking under the imbecility which invited the easy conquest of the Saracens. In France, Brunhilda and Fredegonda were inflaming the fierce contentions which eventually destroyed the Merovingian dynasty, and which abandoned the kingdom at once to the vices of civilisation and the savage atrocities of barbarism. In Italy, the Lombards, more detested than any of their predecessors, by their ceaseless ravages made the Ostrogothic rule regretted, and gleaned with their swords such scanty remnants of plunder as had escaped the hordes which had successively swept from the gloomy forests of the North across the rich valleys and fertile plains of the mistress of the world. Anarchy and confusion everywhere scarce offered a field for the exercise of the humbler virtues, nor could the Church expect to escape the corruption which infected every class from which she could draw her recruits. Still, among the crowd of turbulent and worldly ecclesiastics, whose only aim was the gratification of the senses or the success of criminal ambition, some holy men were to be found who sought the mountain and forest as a refuge from the ceaseless and all-pervading disorder around them. St. Gall and St. Columba, Willibrod and Boniface, were types of these. Devoted to the severest asceticism, burying themselves in the wilderness and subsisting on such simple fare as the labour of their hands could wring from a savage land, the selfishness of the anchorite did not extinguish in them the larger aims of the Christian, and by their civilising labours among the heathen they proved themselves worthy disciples of the Apostles.

Thicker grew the darkness as Tarik drove the Gothic

fugitives before him on the plains of Xeres, and as the
house of Pepin d'Heristel gradually supplanted the long-
haired descendants of Clovis. The Austrasian Mayors of
the Palace had scanty reverence for mitre and crozier, and
it is a proof how little hold the clergy had gained upon the
respect and affection of the people, when the usurpers in
that long revolution did not find it necessary to conciliate
their support. In fact, the policy of these shrewd and able
men was rather to oppress the Church and to parcel out its
wealth and dignities among their warriors, who made no
pretence of piety nor deigned to undertake the mockery of
religious duties. Rome could interpose no resistance to
these abuses, for, involved alternately in strife with the
Lombards and the Iconoclastic Emperors, the Popes
implored the aid of the oppressor himself, and were in no
position to protest against the aggressions which he might
commit at home.

In Italy, the condition of discipline may be inferred from
the fact that, in 721, Gregory II considered it necessary to
call a synod for the special purpose of condemning incestuous unions and the marriages of nuns, which he declared
were openly practised, and the canons then promulgated
received so little attention that they had to be repeated by
another synod in 732. In fact, the vow of chastity was
frequently taken by widows that they might escape a second
marriage and thus be able to live in shameless licence without being subject to the watchful control of a husband;
and an edict of Arechis, Duke of Beneventum, about the
year 774 orders that all such godless women shall be seized
and shut up in convents. That the secular clergy should
consider ordination no bar to matrimony need therefore
excite little surprise. There is extant a charter of Tale-
sperianus, Bishop of Lucca, in 725, by which he confirms a
little monastery and hospital to Romuald the priest and
his wife—" presbytera sua." The document recites that
this couple had come on a pilgrimage from beyond the Po;
that they had settled on the lands of the Convent of St.
Peter and St. Martin in the diocese of Lucca, where they
had bought land and built the institution which the good
bishop thus confirms to them with certain privileges. He
evidently felt that there was nothing irregular in their
maintaining the connection, and he lays upon them no
conditions of separation.

In France, it may be readily believed that discipline was even more neglected. For eighty years scarce a council was held; no attempts were made to renew or enforce the rules of discipline, and the observances of religion were at length well-nigh forgotten. In 726, Boniface even felt scruples as to associating in ordinary intercourse with men so licentious and depraved as the Frankish bishops and priests, and he applied to Gregory II for the solution of his doubts. Gregory, in reply, ordered him to employ argument in endeavouring to convince them of their errors, and by no means to withdraw himself from their society, a politic toleration of vice contrasting strangely with his fierce defiance of the iconoclastic heresy of Leo the Isaurian, when he risked the papacy itself in his eagerness to preserve his beloved images.

When, however, the new dynasty began to assume a permanent position, it sought to strengthen itself by the influence of the Church. Like the modern Charlemagne, it saw in a restoration of religion a means of assuring its stability by linking its fortunes with those of the hierarchy. A Radical in opposition becomes of necessity a Conservative in power; and the arts which had served to supplant the hereditary occupants of the throne were no longer advisable after success had indicated a new line of policy. As Clovis embraced Christianity in order to consolidate his conquests into an empire, so Carloman and Pepin-le-Bref sought the sanction of religion to consecrate their power to their descendants, and the Carlovingian system thenceforth became that of law and order, organising a firm and settled government out of the anarchical chaos of social elements.

It was the pious Carloman who first saw clearly how necessary was the aid of the Church in any attempt to introduce civilisation and subordination among his turbulent subjects. Immediately on his accession, he called upon St. Boniface to assist him in the work, and the Apostle of Germany undertook the arduous task. How arduous it was may be conceived from his description of the utterly demoralised condition of the clergy, when he appealed to Pope Zachary for advice and authority to assist in eradicating the frightful promiscuous licentiousness which was displayed with careless cynicism throughout all grades of the ecclesiastical body. The details are unfit for translation, but the statement can readily be believed when we see what manner of men filled the controlling positions in the hierarchy.

Charles Martel had driven out St. Rigobert, Archbishop of Rheims, and had bestowed that primatial see on one of his warriors named Milo, who soon succeeded in likewise obtaining possession of the equally important archiepiscopate of Trèves. Milo was himself an indication of the prevailing laxity of discipline, for he was the son of Basinus, his predecessor in the see of Trèves. He is described as being a clerk in tonsure, but in every other respect an irreligious laic, yet Boniface, with all the aid of his royal patrons, was unable to oust him from his inappropriate dignities, and in 752, ten years after the commencement of his reforms, we find Pope Zachary, in response to an appeal for advice, counselling him to leave Milo and other similar wolves in sheep's clothing to the divine vengeance. Boniface, apparently, found it requisite to follow this advice, and the divine vengeance did not come until Milo had enjoyed his incongruous dignities for forty years, when at length he was removed by an appropriate death, received from a wild boar in hunting. He was only a type of many others who openly defied all attempts to remove them. One, who is described as " pugnator et fornicator," gave up, it is true, the spiritualities of his see, but held to the temporalities with a grip that nothing could loosen ; another utterly disregarded the excommunications launched at his head, and Zachary and Boniface at last were fain to abandon him to his evil courses. Somewhat more success, indeed, he had with Gervilius, son and successor to Geroldus, Bishop of Mainz. The latter, accompanying Carloman in an expedition against the Saxons, was killed in battle. Bishop Gervilius, in another foray, recognised his father's slayer, invited him to a friendly interview, and treacherously stabbed him, exclaiming, in the rude poetry of the chronicler, " Accipe jam ferrum quo patrem vindico carum." This act of filial piety was not looked upon as unclerical, until Boniface took it up ; Gervilius was finally forced to abandon the see of Mainz, and it was given to Boniface himself. When such were the prelates, it is not to be supposed that rules of abstinence and asceticism received much attention from their subordinates. Boniface admits, in an epistle to King Ecgberht, that, in consequence of the universal licentiousness, he was compelled to restore the guilty to their functions after penitence, as the canonical punishment of dismissal would leave none to perform the sacred offices. What the Church, however, could not prevent on earth, it at least had the satisfaction of seeing punished in the future life. It was principally for the support given to Milo of Rheims among his many similar misdeeds, that Charles Martel was condemned to eternal torture, which was, as a wholesome example, made manifest to the most incredulous. St. Eucherius, in a vision, saw him plunged into the depths of hell, and on consulting St. Boniface and Fulrad, Abbot of St. Denis, it was resolved to open Charles's tomb. The only tenant of the sepulchre was found to be a serpent, and the walls were blackened as though by fire, thus proving the truth of the revelation, and holding out an awful warning to future wrongdoers.

How much of the licence complained of was indiscriminate concubinage, and how much was merely intercourse with legitimate wives, we have no means of ascertaining. The latter Boniface succeeded in suppressing, for the Church could control her sacraments. The former was beyond his power.

Armed with full authority from Pope Zachary, Carloman and Boniface commenced the labour of reducing to order this chaos of passion and licence. Under their auspices a synod was held, April 23rd, 742, in which all unchaste priests and deacons were declared incapable of holding benefices, were degraded, and forced to do penance. Bishops were required to have a witness to testify to the purity of their lives and doctrines, before they could perform their episcopal functions. For all future lapses from virtue, priests were to be severely whipped and imprisoned for two years on bread and water, with prolongation of the punishment at the discretion of their bishops. Other ecclesiastics, monks, and nuns were to be whipped thrice and similarly imprisoned for one year, besides the stigma of having the head shaved. All monasteries, moreover, were to adopt and follow rigidly the Rule of St. Benedict.

The stringency of these measures shows not only the extent of the evil requiring such means of cure, but the fixed determination of the authorities to effect their purpose. The clergy, however, did not submit without resistance. It is probable that they stirred up the people, and that signs of general disapprobation were manifested at a rigour so

extreme in punishing faults which for more than two
generations had passed wholly unnoticed, for during the
same year Zachary addressed an epistle to the Franks with
the object of enlisting them in the cause. The ill-success
of their arms against the Pagans he attributes to the vices
of their clergy, and he promises them that if they show
themselves obedient to Boniface, and if they can enjoy the
prayers of pure and holy priests, they shall in future have
an easy triumph over their heathen foes. Yet many adulterous priests and bishops, noted for the infamy of their
lives, pretended that they had received from Rome itself
dispensations to continue in their ministry—an allegation
which Zachary of course repelled with indignation.

Carloman, however, pursued his self-imposed task without
flinching. On March 1st, 743, he held another synod at
Leptines, where the clergy promised to observe the ancient
canons, and to restore the discipline of the Church. The
statutes enacted the previous year were again declared to
be in full vigour for future offences, while for previous ones
penitence and degradation were once more decreed.

These regulations affected only Austrasia, the German
portion of the Frankish empire, ruled by Carloman. His
brother, Pepin-le-Bref, who governed Neustria, or France,
was less pious, and had apparently not as yet recognised the
policy of reforming out of their possessions the warrior
vassals whom his father had gratified with ecclesiastical
benefices. At length, however, he was induced to lend his
aid, and in 744 he assembled a synod at Soissons for the
purpose. So completely had the discipline of the Church
been neglected and forgotten, that Pepin was obliged to
appeal to Pope Zachary for an authoritative declaration as
to the grades in which marriage was prohibited. Yet his
measures were but lukewarm, for he contented himself with
simply forbidding unchastity in priests, the marriage of nuns,
and the residence of stranger women with clerks, no special
punishment being threatened, beyond a general allusion to
existing laws.

Thus assailed by both the supreme ecclesiastical and
temporal authorities, the clergy still were stubborn. Some
defended themselves as being legitimately entitled to have
a concubine—or rather, we may presume, a wife. Among
these we find a certain Bishop Clement described as a pestilent heresiarch, with followers, who maintained that his

two children, born during his prelacy, did not unfit him for his episcopal functions; and a synod held in Rome, October 31st, 745, was required for his condemnation, the local authorities apparently proving powerless. Even this was not sufficient, for in January 747 we find Zachary directing Boniface to bring him before a local council, and if he still proved contumacious, to refer the matter again to Rome. Others, again, unwilling to forgo their secular mode of existence, or to abandon the livelihood afforded by the Church, were numerous and hardy enough to ask Pepin and Carloman to set apart for them churches and monasteries in which they could live as they were accustomed to do. So nearly did they succeed in this attempt, that Boniface found it necessary to appeal to Zachary to prevent so flagrant an infraction of the canons, and Zachary wrote to the princes with instructions as to the mode of answering the petition. Others, still more audacious, assailed Boniface in every way, endeavoured to weary him out, and even, rightly regarding him as the cause of their persecution and tribulations, made attempts upon his life.

That he should have escaped, indeed, is surprising, when the character of the age is considered, and the nature of the evils inflicted on those who must have regarded the reform as a wanton outrage on their rights. As late as 748, Boniface describes the false bishops and priests, sacrilegious and wandering hypocrites and adulterers, as much more numerous than those who as yet had been forced to compliance with the rules. Driven from the churches, but supported by the sympathising people, they performed their ministry in the fields and the cabins of the peasants, who concealed them from the ecclesiastical authorities. This is not a description of mere sensual worldlings, and it is probable that by this time persecution had ranged the evil-disposed on the winning side. Those who thus exercised their ministry in secret and in wretchedness, retaining the veneration of the people, were therefore men who believed themselves honourably and legitimately married, and who were incapable of sacrificing wife and children for worldly advantage or in blind obedience to a rule which to them was novel, unnatural, and indefensible.

Boniface escaped from the vengeful efforts of those who suffered from his zeal, to fall, in 755, under the sword of the equally ungrateful Frisians. It is probable that up to the

time of his death he was occupied with the reformation of
the clergy in conjunction with his missionary labours, for in
752 we find him still engaged in the hopeless endeavour to
eject the unclerical prelates, who even yet held over from
the iron age of Charles Martel. His disappearance from
the scene, however, made but little change in the movement
which had owed so much to his zeal.

In 747 Carloman's pious aspirations had led him from a
throne to a cloister, and the monastery of Monte Cassino
welcomed its most illustrious inmate. Pepin received the
whole vast kingdom, and his ambitious designs drew him
daily closer to the Church, the importance of whose support
he commenced to appreciate. His policy, in consolidating
the power of his house and in founding a new dynasty, led
him necessarily to reorganise the anarchical elements of
society. As an acknowledged monarch, a regularly constituted hierarchy and recognised subordination to the laws,
both civil and ecclesiastical, were requisite to the success
of his government and to the establishment of his race.
Accordingly, we find him carrying out systematically
the work commenced by Carloman and Boniface, of
which at first his support had been rather negative than
positive.

Six weeks after the martyrdom of Boniface, Pepin held a
synod in his royal palace of Verneuil, in which this tendency
is very apparent. Full power was given to the bishops in
their respective dioceses to enforce the canons of the Church
on the clergy, the monks, and the laity. The monasteries
were especially entrusted to the episcopal care, and means
were provided for reducing the refractory to submission.
The Rule of Benedict was proclaimed as in force in all conventual establishments, and cloistered residence was strictly
enjoined. All ecclesiastics were ordered to pay implicit
obedience to their bishops, and this was secured by the
power of excommunication, which was no longer, as in earlier
stages, the simple suspension from religious privileges, but
was a ban which deprived the offender of all association
with his fellows, and exposed him, if contumacious, to exile
by the secular power. By the appointment of metropolitans,
a tribunal of higher resort was instituted, while two synods,
to be held each year, gave the opportunity both of legislation and of final judgment. Submission to their decisions

was ensured by threatening stripes to all who should appeal from them to the royal court.

Such are the main features, as far as they relate to our subject, of this Capitulary, which so strikingly reveals the organising system of the Carlovingian polity. Carried out by the rare intelligence and vigour of Charlemagne, it gave a precocious development of civilisation to Europe, transitory because in advance of the age, and because it was based on the intellectual force of the ruler, and not on the virtue and cultivation of a people as yet too barbarous to appreciate it.

The organisation of the Church, moreover, received at the same time an efficient impulse by the institution of the order of canons, founded virtually in 762, the year in which St. Chrodegang, Bishop of Metz, promulgated the Rule for their government. This Rule of course entirely forbids all intercourse with women, and endeavours to suppress it by punishing transgressors with stripes, incarceration, and deposition. The lofty rank of St. Chrodegang, who was a cousin of Pepin-le-Bref, and the eminent piety which merited canonisation, gave him wide influence, which doubtless assisted in extending the new institution, but it also had recommendations of its own which were sufficient to ensure success. By converting the cathedral clergy into monks, bound by implicit obedience towards their superiors, it brought no little increase of power to the bishops, and enabled them to exert new authority and influence. It is no wonder, therefore, that the order spread rapidly, and was adopted in most of the dioceses.

For a century we hear nothing more of sacerdotal marriage —and yet it may be doubted whether clerical morality had really been improved by the well-meant reforms of Boniface. These were followed up by Charlemagne with all his resistless energy, and the importance which he attached to the subject is shown by an epistle of Adrian I denying certain assertions made to the Frankish sovereign, inculpating the purity of the Roman clergy. Adrian, in defending his flock, assumes that the object of the slanders can only have been to produce a quarrel between himself and Charlemagne, who must evidently have made strong representations on the subject to the Pontiff. Under such pressure perhaps there was something less of shameless licentiousness; the episcopal chairs were no longer defiled by the cynical lubricity of unworthy prelates; but in the mass of the clergy the passions, deprived of all legitimate gratification, could not be restrained in a race so little accustomed to self-control, and unchastity remained a corroding ulcer which Charlemagne and Louis-le-Débonnaire vainly endeavoured to eradicate. The former, indeed, we find asking in 811 whether the only difference between clerk and layman is that the former does not bear arms and is not publicly married; while Ghaerbald, Bishop of Liège, a few years before had ordered that all priests maintaining intercourse with their wives should be deprived of their benefices and be subjected to penitence until death.

It would be an unprofitable task to recapitulate the constantly repeated legislation prohibiting the residence of women with the clergy and repressing the disorders and irregularities of the monastic establishments. It would be but a reiteration of the story already related of previous centuries, and its only importance would be in showing by the frequency of the edicts how utterly ineffectual they were. When Louis-le-Débonnaire, in 826, decreed that the seduction of a nun was to be punished by the death of both the partners in guilt; that the property of both was to be confiscated to the Church; and that the count in whose district the crime occurred, if he neglected its prosecution, was to be degraded, deprived of his office, undergo public penance, and pay his full wer-gild to the fisc; the frightful severity of the enactment is the measure of the impossibility of effecting its purpose, and of the inefficiency of the reformation which had been so elaborately prepared and so energetically promulgated by Louis in 817.

But perhaps the most convincing evidence of the debased morality of the clergy, and of the low standard which even the most zealous prelates were forced to adopt, is to be found in a curious fabrication by the authors of the False Decretals. The collection of decretals which they put forth in the names of the early popes embodied their conception of a perfect Church establishment, as adapted to the necessities and aspirations of the ninth century. While straining every point to throw off all subjection to the temporal power, and to obtain for the hierarchy full and absolute control over all ecclesiastical matters and persons, they seem to have felt it necessary to relax in an important point the rigour of the canons respecting sacerdotal purity.

Gregory the Great had proclaimed in the clearest and most definite manner the rule that a single lapse from virtue condemned the sinner to irrevocable degradation, and rendered him for ever unfit for the ministry of the altar. Yet "Isidor Mercator" added to a genuine epistle of Gregory a long passage elaborately arguing the necessity of forgiveness for those who expiate by repentance the sin of impurity, "of which, among many, so few are guiltless." The direct testimony is notable, but not less so is the indirect evidence of the prevalent laxity which could induce such a bid for popularity on the part of high Churchmen like those concerned in the Isidorian forgeries.

Evidence also is not wanting that the denial of the appropriate and healthful human affections led to the results which might be expected, of fearful and unnatural crimes. That the inmates of monasteries, debarred from female society, occasionally abandoned themselves to the worst excesses, or, breaking through all restraint, indulged in less reprehensible but more open scandals, is proclaimed by Charlemagne, who threatened to vindicate the outrage upon religion with the severest punishment. Nor were the female convents more successfully regulated, for the Council of Aix-la-Chapelle, in 836, states that in many places they were rather brothels than houses of God; and it shows how close a supervision over the spouses of Christ was thought requisite when it proceeds to direct that nunneries shall be so built as to have no dark corners in which scandals may be perpetrated out of view. The effect of these efforts may be estimated from a remark in a collection of laws which bears the name of Erchenbald, Chancellor of Charlemagne, but which is rather attributable to the close of the ninth century, that the licentiousness of nuns commonly resulted in a worse crime, infanticide; and, as this is extracted textually from an epistle of St. Boniface to Ethelbald, King of Mercia, it is presumable that the evil became notorious simultaneously with the reform under the early Carlovingians, and continued unabated throughout their dynasty. One device to subjugate nature, adopted in the monasteries, was to let blood at stated intervals, in the hope of reducing the system and thus mitigating the effects of prolonged continence—a device prohibited by Louis-le-Débonnaire, but long subsequently maintained as part of monastic discipline. As regards the secular clergy, even darker horrors are asserted by Theodulf, Bishop of Orleans, and other prelates, who forbade to their clergy the residence of mother, aunt, and sister, in consequence of the crimes so frequently perpetrated with them at the instigation of the devil; and the truth of this hideous fact is unfortunately confirmed by the declarations of councils held at various periods.

If, under the external polish of Carlovingian civilisation, such utter demoralisation existed, while the laws were enforced by the stern vigour of Charlemagne, or the sensitive piety of Louis-le-Débonnaire, it is easy to understand what was the condition of society when the sons of the latter involved the whole empire in a ceaseless tumult of civil war. Not only was the watchful care of the first two emperors withdrawn, but the state was turned against itself, and rapine and desolation became almost universal. The royal power was parcelled out, by the rising feudal system, among a crowd of nobles whose energies were solely directed to consolidating their position, and was chiefly employed, as far as it affected the Church, in granting abbeys and other ecclesiastical dignities to worthless laymen, whose support could only be secured by bribes which the royal fisc could no longer supply. Pagan Danes and infidel Saracens were ravaging the fairest provinces of the empire, and their blows fell with peculiar weight on the representatives of a hated religion. For seventy years previous to the Treaty of Clair-sur-Epte no mass resounded in the walls of the cathedral church of Coutances, so fierce and unremitting had been the incursions of the Northmen. It is therefore no wonder that, as early as 845, the bishops assembled at the Council of Vernon confess that their ecclesiastical authority is no longer sufficient to prevent the marriage of monks and nuns, and to suppress the crowds who escaped from their convents and wandered over the country in licentiousness and vagabondage. To restrain these disorders they are obliged to invoke the royal power to cast into prison these reprobates and force them to undergo canonical penance.

During this period of anarchy and lawlessness, the Church was skilfully emancipating itself from subjection to the temporal power, and was laying the foundation of that supremacy which was eventually to dominate Christendom. While its aspirations and ambitions were thus worldly, and its ranks were recruited from a generation trained under such influences, it is easy to believe that the disorders which Charlemagne himself could not repress grew more and more flagrant. Even the greatly augmented power of the papacy added to the increasing licence, although Nicholas I in 861 had ordered the deposition and degradation of all priests convicted of immorality, for the appellate jurisdiction claimed by Rome gave practical immunity to those against whom the enforcement of the canons was attempted. About the year 876, Charles-le-Chauve, in a spirited argument against the pretensions of the popes, calls attention specially to the exemption thus afforded to unchaste priests, who, after due conviction by their bishops, obtained letters from Rome overruling the judgments; the distance and dangers of the journey precluding the local authorities from supporting their verdicts by sending commissioners and witnesses to carry on a second trial beyond the Alps.

This shows that the effort to enforce purity was not as yet abandoned, however slender may have been the success in eradicating an evil so general and so deeply rooted. The nominal punishment for unchastity—loss of benefice and deposition—was severe enough to induce the guilty to hide their excesses with care, when they chanced to have a bishop who was zealous in the performance of his duties. Efforts at concealment, moreover, were favoured by the forms of judicial procedure, which were such as to throw every difficulty in the way of procuring a conviction, and to afford, in most cases, practical immunity for sin, unless committed in the most open and shameless manner. Hincmar, Archbishop of Rheims, the leading ecclesiastic of his day, whose reputation for learning and piety would have rendered him one of the lights of the Church, had not his consistent opposition to the innovations of the papacy caused his sanctity to be questioned in Rome, has left us elaborate directions as to the forms of prosecution in such matters. Notwithstanding his earnest exhortations and arguments in favour of the most ascetic purity, he discourages investigation by means of neighbours and parishioners, or irreverent inquiries on the subject. Only such testimony was admissible as the laws allowed, and the laws were very strict as to the position and character of witnesses. In addition to the accusers themselves, seven witnesses were necessary. Of these, one was required to substantiate the oaths of the rest by undergoing the ordeal,

thus exposing himself and all his fellows to the heavy
penalties visited on perjury, upon the chance of the red-hot
iron or cold-water trial, administered, perhaps, by those
interested in shielding the guilty. If, as we can readily
believe was generally the case, these formidable difficulties
could not be overcome, and the necessary number of witnesses were not ready to sacrifice themselves, then the
accused could purge himself of the sins imputed to him by
his own oath, supported by one, three, or six compurgators
of his own order; and Hincmar himself bears testimony to
the associations which were formed among the clergy to
swear each other through all troubles. Even simpler,
indeed, was the process prescribed not long before by Pope
Nicholas I, who ordered that, when legal evidence was not
procurable, the accused priest could clear himself on his own
unsupported oath.

Under these regulations, Hincmar orders an annual
investigation to be made throughout his province, but the
results would appear to have been as unsatisfactory as
might have been expected. In 874, at the Synod of Rheims,
he complains that his orders have been neglected and
despised, and he warns his clergy that proof of actual
criminality will not be required, but that undue familiarity
with women, if persisted in, will be sufficient for condemnation when properly proved.

In the presence of facilities for escape such as were
afforded by the practice of ecclesiastical law as constructed
by the decretalists, and as expounded by Hincmar himself,
the threats in which he indulged could carry but little terror.
We need not wonder, therefore, if we meet with but slender
indications of priestly marriage during all this disorder, for
there was evidently little danger of punishment for the
unchaste priest who exercised ordinary discretion in his
amours, while the penalties impending over those who
should openly brave the canonical rules were heavy, and
could hardly be avoided by any one who should dare to
unite himself publicly to a woman in marriage. Every
consideration of worldly prudence and passion therefore
induced the priest to pursue a course of illicit licentiousness
—and yet, as the century wore on, traces of entire neglect
or utter contempt of the canons began to manifest themselves. How little the rule really was respected by the
ecclesiastical authorities when anything was to be gained by

its suppression is shown in the decision made by Nicholas I, the highest of high Churchmen, when encouraging the Bulgarians to abandon the Greek Church, although the separation between Rome and Constantinople was not, as yet, formal and complete. To their inquiry whether married priests should be ejected, he replied that though such ministers were objectionable, yet the mercy of God was to be imitated, who causes His sun to shine on good and evil alike, and as Christ did not dismiss Judas, so they were not to be dismissed. Besides, laymen were not to judge priests for any crime, nor to make any investigation into their lives, such inquiries being reserved for bishops. As no bishops had yet been appointed by Rome, the answer was a skilfully tacit permission of priestly marriage, while avoiding an open avowal.

It need awaken no surprise if those who united recklessness and power should openly trample on the canons thus feebly supported. A somewhat prominent personage of the period was Hubert, brother of Teutberga, Queen of Lotharingia, and his turbulent conduct was a favourite theme for animadversion by the quiet monastic chroniclers. That he was an abbot is perhaps no proof of his clerical profession, but when we find his wife and children alluded to as a proof of his abandoned character, it shows that he was bound by vows or ordained within the prohibited grades, and that he publicly violated the rules and defied their enforcement.

The earliest absolute evidence that has reached us, however, of the marriage of a member of the great body of the plebeian clergy, subsequent to the reforms of Boniface, occurs about the year 893. Angelric, priest of Vasnau, appealed to the Synod of Chalons, stating that he had been publicly joined in wedlock to a woman named Grimma. Such an attempt by a priest, the consent of the woman and her relatives, and the performance of the ceremony by another priest, all show the prevailing laxity and ignorance, yet still there were found some faithful and pious souls to object to the transaction, and Angelric was not allowed to enjoy undisturbed the fruits of his sin. Yet even the synod was perplexed, and unable to decide what ought to be done. It therefore only temporarily suspended Angelric from communion, while Mancio, his bishop, applied for advice to Foulques of Rheims, metropolitan of the province, and the ignorance and good faith of all parties are manifested by the fact that Angelric himself was sent to Foulques as the bearer of the letter of inquiry.

With the ninth century the power, the cultivation, and the civilisation of the Carlovingians may be considered virtually to disappear, though for nearly a hundred years longer a spectral crown encircled the brows of the ill-starred descendants of Pepin. Centralisation, rendered impossible in temporal affairs by feudalism, was transferred to the Church, which thenceforth, more than ever independent of secular control, became wholly responsible for its own shortcomings; and the records of the period make only too plainly manifest how utterly the power, so strenuously contended for, failed to accomplish good amid the ignorance and the barbarism of the age.

CHAPTER X

THE TENTH CENTURY

THE tenth century, well characterised by Cave as the " Sæculum Obscurum," is perhaps the most repulsive in Christian annals. The last vestiges of Roman culture have disappeared, while the dawn of modern civilisation is as yet far off. Society, in a state of transition, is painfully and vainly seeking some form of security and stability. The marauding wars of petty neighbouring chiefs become the normal condition, only interrupted when two or three unite to carry destruction to some more powerful rival. Though the settlement of Normandy relieved Continental Europe to a great extent from the terror of the Dane, yet the still more dreaded Hun took his place and ravaged the nations from the Danube to the Atlantic, while England bore the undivided fury of the Vikings, and the Saracen left little to glean upon the shores of the Mediterranean.

When brutal ignorance and savage ferocity were the distinguishing characteristics of the age, the Church could scarce expect to escape from the general debasement. It is rather a matter of grateful surprise that religion itself was not overwhelmed in the general chaos which engulfed almost all previously existing institutions. When the crown of St. Peter became the sport of barbarous nobles, or of a still more barbarous populace, we may grieve, but we cannot affect astonishment, at the unconcealed dissoluteness of Sergius III, whose bastard, twenty years later, was placed in the pontifical chair by the influence of that embodiment of all possible vices, his mother Marozia. The last extreme of depravity would seem attained by John XII, but as his deposition in 963 by Otho the Great loosened the tongues of his accusers, it is possible that he was no worse than some of his predecessors. No extreme of wickedness was beyond his capacity; the sacred palace of the Lateran was turned into a brothel; incest gave a flavour to crime when simple profligacy palled upon his exhausted senses, and the honest citizens of Rome complained that the female pilgrims who formerly crowded the holy fanes were deterred from coming through fear of his promiscuous and unbridled lust.

With such corruption at the head of the Church, it is grotesque to see the popes inculcating lessons of purity, and urging the maintenance of canons which they set the example of disregarding so utterly. The clergy were now beginning to arrogate to themselves the privilege of matrimony; and marriage, so powerful a corrective of indiscriminate vice, was regarded with peculiar detestation by the ecclesiastical authorities, and awoke a far more energetic opposition than the more dangerous and corrupting forms of illicit indulgence. The pastor who intrigued in secret with his penitents and parishioners was scattering the seeds of death in place of the bread of life, and was abusing his holy trust to destroy the souls confided to his charge, but this worked no damage to the temporal interests of the Church at large. The priest who, in honest ignorance of the canons, took to himself a wife, and endeavoured faithfully to perform the duties of his humble sphere, could scarcely avoid seeking the comfort and worldly welfare of his offspring, and this exposed the common property of all to dilapidation and embezzlement. Disinterested virtue would perhaps not be long in making a selection between the comparative evils, but disinterested virtue was not a distinguishing characteristic of the age.

Yet a motive of even greater importance than this rendered matrimony more objectionable than concubinage or licentiousness. By the overruling tendency of the age, all possessions previously held by laymen on precarious tenure were rapidly becoming hereditary. As the royal power slipped from hands unable to retain it, offices, dignities, and lands became the property of the holders, and were transmitted from father to son. Had marriage been openly permitted to ecclesiastics, their functions and benefices would undoubtedly have followed the example. An hereditary caste would have been established, who would have held their churches and lands of right; independent of the central authority, all unity would have been destroyed, and the collective power of the Church would have disappeared. Having nothing to gain from obedience, submission to control would have become the exception, and, laymen in all but name, the ecclesiastics would have had no incentive to perform their functions, except what little influence, under such circumstances, might have been retained over the people by maintaining the sacred character thus rendered a mockery.

In an age when everything was unsettled, yet with tendencies so strongly marked, it thus became a matter of vital importance to the Church to prevent anything like hereditary occupation of benefices or private appropriation of property, and against these abuses its strongest efforts were directed. The struggle lasted for centuries, and it may perhaps be fortunate for our civilisation that sacerdotalism triumphed, even at the expense of what at the moment was of greater importance. I cannot here pause to trace the progress of the contest in its long and various vicissitudes. It will be found constantly reappearing in the course of the following pages, and for the present it will suffice to group together a few evidences to show how rapidly the hereditary tendency developed itself in the period under consideration.

The narrowness of the escape from ecclesiastical feudalisation is well illustrated by an incident at the Council of Tours, in 925, where two priests, *father and son*, Ranald and Raymond, appeared as complainants, claiming certain tithes detained from them by another priest. They gained the suit, and the tithes were confirmed to them and their successors for ever. Even more suggestive is the complaint, some thirty years later, of Ratherius, Bishop of Verona, who objects strenuously to the ordination of the children sprung from these illegal marriages, as each successive father made his son a priest, thus perpetuating the scandal indefinitely throughout the Church; and as he sorrowfully admits that his clergy could not be restrained from marriage, he begs them at least to bring their children up as laymen. This, however, by his own showing, would not remove the material evil, for in another treatise he states that his priests and deacons divided the Church property between them, that they might have lands and vineyards wherewith to provide marriage portions for their sons and daughters. This system of appropriation also forms the subject of lamentation for Atto, Bishop of

Vercelli, whose clergy insisted on publicly keeping concubines—as he stigmatises those who evidently were wives—to whom they left by will everything that they could gather from the possessions of the Church, from the alms of the pious, or from any other source, to the ruin of ecclesiastical property and to the deprivation of the poor. How well founded were these complaints is evident from a document of the eleventh century concerning the churches of St. Stephen and St. Donatus in Aretino. The priests in charge appropriated to themselves all the possessions of the churches, including the revenues of the altars, the oblations, and the confessional. These they portioned out among each other and handed down from father to son as regularly as any other property, selling and exchanging their shares as the interest of the moment might suggest, and the successive transmission of each fragment of property is detailed with all the precision of a brief of title. The natural result was that for generations the religious services of Aretino were utterly disregarded. Sometimes the priestly owners would hire some one to ring the bells, light the candles, and minister at the altar, but in the multitude of ownerships the stipends were irregularly paid, and the officiator refused continually to serve, candles were not furnished, bell-ropes were not renewed, and even the leathers which attached the clappers to the bells were neglected. The church of St. Stephen was the cathedral of Aretino, yet the bishops were powerless to correct these abuses. The marriages of their priests they do not seem to have even attempted to repress, and were quite satisfied if they could occasionally get a portion of the revenues devoted to the offices of religion. The same condition of affairs existed among the Anglo-Saxons. " It is all the worse when they have it all, for they do not dispose of it as they ought, but decorate their wives with what they should the altars, and turn everything to their own worldly pomp. . . . Let those who before this had the evil custom of decorating their women as they should the altars, refrain from this evil custom, and decorate their churches, as they best can; then would they command for themselves both divine counsel and worldly worship. A priest's wife is nothing but a snare of the devil, and he who is ensnared thereby on to his end, he will be seized fast by the devil."

It will be observed that, as the century advanced, sacerdotal marriage became more and more common. Indeed, in 966, Ratherius not only intimates that his clergy were all married, but declares that if the canon prohibiting repeated marriages were put in force, only boys would be left in the Church, while even they would be ejected under the rule which rendered ineligible the offspring of illicit unions; and, in spite of his earnest asceticism, he only ventures to prohibit his clergy from conjugal intercourse during the periods likewise forbidden to laymen, such as Advent, Christmas, Lent, etc. It was not that the ancient canons were forgotten, nor that strenuous efforts were not made to enforce them, but that the temper of the times created a spirit of personal independence so complete that the power of the ecclesiastical authorities seemed utterly inadequate to control the growing licence. About the year 938, Gerard, Archbishop of Lorsch and Papal Legate for Southern Germany, laid before Leo VII a series of questions relating to various points in which the ancient canons were set at naught throughout the region under his supervision. Leo answered by a decretal addressed to all the princes and potentates of Europe, in which he laments over Gerard's statement of the public marriages of priests, and replies to his inquiry as to the capacity of their children for ecclesiastical promotion. The first he pronounces forbidden by the canons, and those guilty of it he orders to be deprived of their benefices. As for the offspring of such marriages, however, he says that they are not involved in the sins of their parents.

The unusual liberality of this latter declaration, however, was not a precedent. The Church always endeavoured to prevent the ordination of the children of ecclesiastics, and Leo, in permitting it, was only yielding to a pressure which he could not withstand. It was a most dangerous concession, for it led directly to the establishment of the hereditary principle. An effort was soon after made, by an appeal to the temporal power, to recover the ground lost, and about the year 940 Otho the Great was induced to issue an edict prohibiting the sons of deacons, priests, and bishops from occupying the positions of notary, judge, or count—the bare necessity of which shows how numerous and powerful the class had already become.

Although, as early as 925, the Council of Spalatro seemed to find nothing to condemn in a single marriage, but threatened excommunication against those who so far forgot themselves as to contract a second, and though by the middle of the century the practice had become generally established, yet some rigid prelates continued to keep alive the memory of the ancient canons by fruitless protests and ineffectual efforts at reform. In 948 the Synod of Engelheim, under the presidency of Marino, Bishop of Ostia and Papal Vicar, condemned such marriages as incestuous and unlawful. In 952, at the Council of Augsburg, the assembled German and Italian prelates made a further and more desperate effort. Deposition was pronounced against the subdeacon, deacon, priest, or bishop who should take to himself a wife; separation of those already married was ordered, and even the lower grades of the clergy, who had not previously been subjected to any such rule, were commanded to observe the strictest continence. An attempt was also made to prevent concubinage by visiting suspected women with stripes and shaving; but there evidently was some difficulty anticipated in enforcing this, for the royal power is invoked to prevent secular interference with the sentence.

This stringent legislation of course proved utterly nugatory, but, futile as it was, it yet awakened considerable opposition. St. Ulric, in whose episcopal town of Augsburg the council was held, addressed a long epistle to the pope remonstrating against his efforts to enforce the rule of celibacy, and arguing the question, temperately but forcibly, on the grounds both of scriptural authority and of expediency. He pointed out how much more obnoxious to divine wrath were the promiscuous and nameless crimes indulged in by those who were foremost in advocating the reform than the chaste and single marriages of the clergy; and the violent distortion of the sacred texts, by those who sought authority to justify the canon, he not unhappily characterised as straining the breast of Scripture until it yielded blood in place of milk.

Despite the inefficiency of these attempts, the clergy were not always allowed to enjoy their unlawful domestic ties in peace, and, where the votaries of asceticism were bold and determined, the contest was sometimes severe. The nature of the struggle is well illustrated by the troubles which arose between Ratherius of Verona and the ecclesiastics of his diocese. In April, 967, John XIII held a council at Ravenna which commanded those who were in holy orders to give up at once either their wives or their ministry, and Otho the Great was induced to issue a precept confirming this peremptory decree. Ratherius had long been vainly wishing for some authority on the subject more potent than the ancient and now obsolete canons, and on his return from Ravenna he summoned a synod for the purpose of promulgating the new regulations. His clergy got wind of his intention; very few of them obeyed the summons, and most of those who came boldly declared that they would neither be separated from their wives nor abandon their functions—in fact, they did not scruple to maintain that marriage was not only permissible, but even necessary to protect the Church from the most hideous vices. The utmost concession he could obtain, indeed, came from a few who endeavoured to excuse themselves on the ground of poverty, which did not enable them to live without the assistance of their wives, and who professed to be willing to separate from them if they could be assured of a regular stipend. Ratherius had passed through too many vicissitudes in his long and agitated career to shrink from the collision, now that he was backed by both the papal and imperial authority. He promptly threw the recalcitrant pastors into prison, declaring that they should lie there until they paid a heavy fine for the benefit of the Cathedral of the Virgin, and he further commanded the presence of those who had failed to appear. The clergy of the diocese, finding that the resistance of inertia was unavailing, took more decided steps, and appealed for protection to the temporal power, in the person of Nanno, Count of Verona. He promptly espoused their cause, and his *missus* Gilbert forbade their obedience to the summons of their bishop for a year. Ratherius remonstrated vehemently against the assumption of Nanno that the priests were his vassals, subject to his jurisdiction, and entitled to protection, and he lost no time in invoking the power of Otho, in a letter to Ambrose, the Imperial Chancellor. The clergy were too powerful; the imperial court decided against the bishop, and before the end of the year Ratherius was forced to retire from the unequal contest and to take refuge in the peaceful abbey of Lobbes, whence he had been withdrawn a quarter of a century before to fill the see of Verona. Three times had he thus been driven from that city, and an intermediate episcopate of Liège, with which one of his periods of exile was gratified, had been terminated in the same abrupt manner by the unruly clergy, unable to endure the severity of his virtue. How great was the revolution, to the unavailing repression of which he sacrificed his life, is shown by his declaration, two years before, that ecclesiastics differed from laymen only in shaving and the tonsure, in some slight fashioning of their garments, and in the careless performance of the Church ritual. The progress of sacerdotal marriage during the preceding quarter of a century is shown by a similar comparison drawn by Ratherius some thirty years before, in which matrimony is included among the few points of difference, along with shaving and the tonsure.

That the Veronese clergy were not alone in obtaining from the secular potentates protection against these efforts on the part of reforming bishops, is evident from the lamentations of Atto of Vercelli. That estimable prelate deplores the blindness of those who, when paternally warned to mend their evil ways, refuse submission, and seek protection from the nobles. If we may believe him, however, they gained but little from this course, for their criminal lives placed them at the mercy of the secular officials, whose threats to seize their wives and children could only be averted by continual presents. Thus they not only plundered the property of their churches, but forfeited the respect and esteem of their flocks; all reverence for them was thereby destroyed, and, living in perpetual dread of the punishment due to their excesses, in place of commanding obedience, they were exposed to constant oppression and petty tyranny.

When prelates so sincere and so earnest as Ratherius and Atto were able to accomplish so little, it is easy to understand what must have been the condition of the dioceses entrusted to the great mass of bishops, who were rather feudal nobles than Christian prelates. St. Wolfgang of Ratisbon might issue thousands of exhortations to his clergy, inculcating chastity as the one indispensable virtue, and might laboriously reform his monasteries, in

which monks and nuns led a life almost openly secular;
but he was well-nigh powerless for good compared with
the potentiality of evil conveyed by the example of such
a bishop as Segenfrid of Le Mans, who, during an episcopate
which lasted for thirty-three years, took to himself a wife
named Hildeberga, and who stripped the Church for the
benefit of his son Alberic, the sole survivor of a numerous
progeny by her whom he caused to be reverenced as his
Episcopissa : or of Archembald, Archbishop of Sens, who,
taking a fancy to the Abbey of St. Peter, drove out
the monks and established a harem of concubines in the
refectory, and installed his hounds and hawks in the
cloister. Guarino of Modena might hope to stem the tide
of licence by refusing preferment to all who would not
agree to hold their benefices on a sort of feudal tenure of
chastity; but he had much less influence on his age than
such a man as Alberic of Marsico, whose story is related
as a warning by Peter Damiani. He was married (for, in
the language of Damiani, "obscæna meretricula" may
safely be translated a wife), and had a son to whom he
transferred his bishopric, as though it had been an hereditary fief. Growing tired of private life, however, he
aspired to the abbacy of Monte Cassino. That humble
foundation of St. Benedict had become a formidable
military power, of which its neighbours the Capuans stood
in constant dread. Alberic leagued with them, and a plot
was laid by which the reigning abbot's eyes were to be
plucked out and Alberic placed in possession, for which
service he agreed to pay a heavy sum, one-half in advance,
and the rest when the abbot's eyes should be delivered to
him. The deed was accomplished, but while the envoys
were bearing to Alberic the bloody tokens of success, they
were met by tidings of his death, and on comparing notes
they found that he had expired at the very moment of
the perpetration of the atrocious crime.

So St. Abbo of Fleury might exhaust his eloquence in
inculcating the beauty and holiness of immaculate purity,
and might pile authority on authority to demonstrate the
punishments which, in this world and the next, attended
on those who disobeyed the rule; yet when he endeavoured,
in the monastery of La Réole, a dependency of his own
great abbey of Fleury, to put his precepts into practice,
the recalcitrant monks flew to arms and murdered him in

the most brutal manner, not even sparing the faithful Adalard, who was reverently supporting the head of his beloved and dying master. Damiani might well exclaim, when bewailing the unfortunate fate of abbots, on whom was thrown the responsibility of the morals of their communities—

> Phinees si imitatur,
> Fugit vel expellitur;
> Si Eli, tunc irridetur
> Atque parvipenditur;
> Odiosus est, si fervens,
> Et vilis, si tepidus.

How little disposed were the ecclesiastical authorities in general to sustain the efforts of puritans like St. Abbo was clearly shown in the Council of St. Denis, convened in 995 for the purpose of restoring the neglected discipline of the Church, when, passing over the object of its assembling, the reverend fathers devoted their whole attention to the more practically interesting question of tithes.

All prelates, however, were not either feudal chiefs or ascetic puritans. Some, who were pious and virtuous, had so far become infected with the prevailing laxity that they regarded the stricter canons as obsolete, and offered no opposition to the domestic aspirations of their clergy. Thus Constantine, abbot of the great house of St. Symphorian of Metz, in his Life of Adalbero II, who was Bishop of Metz from 984 to 1005, actually praises him for his liberality in not refusing ordination to the sons of priests, and attributes discreditable motives to those bishops who insisted on the observance of the canons prohibiting all such promotions. As Constantine was a monk and a disciple of Adalbero, the tone which he adopts shows that the higher prelates and the regular clergy were beginning to recognise sacerdotal marriage as a necessity of the age. This view is strengthened by the fact that no effort to reform an abuse so universal was made at the great Synod of Dortmund, held in 1005 for the special purpose of restoring the discipline of the Church.

How completely, indeed, marriage came to be regarded as a matter of course is manifest when, in 1019, an assembly of German bishops, with the Emperor St. Henry at their head, gravely deliberated over the knotty question whether, when a noble permitted his serf to enter into holy orders,

and the serf, presuming upon his new-born dignities and
the wealth of his benefices, married a free woman and
endeavoured to withhold his children from the servitude
which he still owed to his master, such infraction of his
master's rights could be permitted out of respect to his
sacerdotal character. Long and vehement was the argument among the learned prelates, until finally St. Henry
decided the point authoritatively by pronouncing in favour
of the servitude of the children.

But perhaps the most instructive illustration of the
character and temper of the age may be found in the
three prelates who for more than a century filled the rich
and powerful archiepiscopal see of Rouen. Hugh, whose
episcopate lasted from 942 to 989, was nominated at a
period when William Longsword, Duke of Normandy, was
contemplating retirement from the world to shroud his
almost regal dignity under the cowl of a monk; yet what
little is known of his archbishop is that, though he was a
monk in habit, he was an habitual violator of the laws of
God—in short, we may presume, a man well suited to the
wild, half-pagan times which witnessed the assassination
of Duke William and the minority of Richard the Fear-
less. On his death, in 989, Duke Richard, whose piety
was incontestably proved by the liberality of his monastic
foundations and by his zeal for the purity of his monkish
protégés, filled the vacant see with his son Robert, who
held the position until 1037. Robert was publicly and
openly married, and by his wife Herleva he had three
sons, Richard, Rodolf, and William, to whom he distributed
his vast possessions. Ordericus, the conscientious cenobite of the twelfth century, looks, in truth, somewhat
askance at this disregard of the rules accepted in his own
time, yet no blame seems to have attached to Robert in
the estimation of his contemporaries. The family chronicler
characterises him as " Robert bons clers, honestes hom,"
and assures us that he was highly esteemed as a wise and
learned prelate

> Li secunz fu genz e aperz
> Et si fu apelez Roberz.
> Clere en firent, mult aprist bien,
> Si fi sage sor tote rien;
> De Roem out l'arcevesquié
> Honoré fu mult e preisié.

His successor, Mauger, son of Duke Richard II, and archbishop from 1037 to 1054, was worthy of his predecessors. Abandoned to worldly and carnal pleasures, his *legitimate* son Michael was a distinguished knight, and half a century later stood high in the favour of Henry I of England, in whose court he was personally known to the historian. The times were changing, however, and Mauger felt the full effects of reformatory zeal, for he was deposed in 1054; the see was bestòwed on St. Maurilio, a Norman, who as Abbot of Santa Maria in Florence had been driven out and nearly poisoned to death by his monks on account of the severity of his rule, and the Norman clergy, as we shall see hereafter, experienced their share of suffering in the mutation of discipline.

Notwithstanding this all-pervading laxity, the canons of the Church remained unaltered, and their full force was theoretically admitted. Hopeless efforts, moreover, were occasionally made to re-establish them, as in the Council of Anse in 990, which reminded the clergy that intercourse with wives after ordination was punishable with forfeiture of benefice and deprivation of priestly functions; and in that of Poitiers about the year 1000, which prohibited concubines under pain of degradation. In a similar spirit, a Penitential of the period recapitulates the severe punishments of a former age, involving degradation and fearfully long terms of penance. All this, however, was practically a dead letter. The person who best represents the active intelligence of the age was Gerbert of Aurillac, the most enlightened man of his time, who, after occupying the archiepiscopal sees of Rheims and Ravenna, finally became pope under the name of Silvester II. The lightness with which he treats the subject of celibacy is therefore fairly a measure of the views entertained by the ruling spirits of the Church, beyond the narrow bounds of cloistered asceticism. Gerbert, describing in a sermon the requisites of the episcopal and sacerdotal offices, barely refers to the " unius uxoris vir," which he seems to regard in an allegorical rather than in a literal sense; he scarcely alludes to chastity, while he dilates with much energy on simony, which he truly characterises as the almost universal vice of his contemporaries. So when, in 997, he convened the Council of Ravenna to regulate the discipline of his

Church, he paid no attention whatever to incontinence, while strenuously endeavouring to root out simony.   At an earlier period, while Abbot of Bobbio, in an epistle to his patron, the Emperor Otho II, refuting various calumnies of his enemies, he alludes to a report of his having a wife and children in terms which show how little importance he attached to the accusation.

Such, at the opening of the eleventh century, was the condition of the Church as regards ascetic celibacy. Though the ancient canons were still theoretically in force, they were practically obsolete everywhere. Legitimate marriage or promiscuous profligacy was almost universal, in some places unconcealed, in others covered with a thin veil of hypocrisy, according as the temper of the ruling prelate might be indulgent or severe.   So far, therefore, Latin Christianity had gained but little in its struggle of six centuries with human nature.   Whether the next eight hundred years will show a more favourable result remains for us to develop.

Before proceeding, however, to discuss the events of the· succeeding century, it will be well to give a rapid glance at a portion of Christendom, the isolation of which has thus far precluded it from receiving attention.

CHAPTER XI

WHATEVER of virtue or purity may have distinguished the Church of Britain under Roman domination was speedily extinguished in the confusion of the Saxon occupation. Gildas, who flourished in the first half of the sixth century, describes the clergy of his time as utterly corrupt. He apparently would have been satisfied if the bishops had followed the apostolic precept and contented themselves with being husbands of one wife; and he complains that instead of bringing up their children in chastity, the latter were corrupted by the evil example of their parents. Under Saxon rule, Christianity was probably well-nigh trampled out, except in the remoter mountain districts, to be subsequently restored in its sacerdotal form under the direct auspices of Rome.

Meanwhile, the British Isles were the theatre of another and independent religious movement. Palladius, who assumed the title of Patricius, was sent to Ireland as bishop, in 432, by Cœlestin I. It is not our province to determine whether he is the traditional St. Patrick who Christianised Ireland, or whether a supposititious saint was invented in the seventh century, bearing the same name, as a factor in the struggle between the Romanising party and the supporters of the native Church. It suffices for us to have seen (p. 54) that celibacy was not one of the rules enforced in the infant Irish Church; but this was of comparatively little moment, for that Church was almost exclusively monastic in its character, and preserved the strictest views as to the observance of the vows by those who had once taken them. That the principles thus established were long preserved is evident from an ancient Penitential, presumably Hibernian, which breathes the most vigorous asceticism. A single passing emotion of lust for a woman, not expressed, is visited with seven days' penance, on a measured amount of bread and water. Innocent familiarity with a woman requires forty days' penance, but if a kiss passes between them it is lengthened to a year. Fornication forfeits the tonsure, but if it is not known it can be redeemed with three years of penance, after which the functions are restored. If a child is born, the penalty is nine years of penance, of which seven must be passed in exile, with subsequent resumption of functions —being the same as for homicide. As no punishment is provided for clerical marriage, it was evidently not regarded as supposable.

The missionary career by which the Irish Church repaid the debt that it owed to Christianity is well known, and the form of faith which it spread was almost exclusively monastic. Luanus, one of the monks of Benchor, is said to have founded no less than a hundred monasteries; and when Columba established the Christian religion in Scotland, he carried with him this tendency to asceticism and inculcated it among his Pictish neophytes. His rule enjoins the most absolute purity of mind as well as body; and that his teachings were long obeyed is evident when we find that, a hundred and fifty years later, his disciples are praised for the chastity and zeal of their self-denying lives by the Venerable Bede, who was fully alive to the importance of the rule, and who would have wasted no such admiration on them had they lived in open disregard of it. Equally convincing is the fact that Scotland and the Islands were claimed to be under the supremacy of the see of York, and that during the long controversy requisite to break down their schismatic notions respecting the date of Easter and the shape of the tonsure, not a word was said that can lead to the supposition that they held any unorthodox views on the far more important subject of sacerdotal purity.

When, a hundred and fifty years after the Anglo-Saxon invasion, Gregory the Great undertook the conversion of the islanders, the missionaries whom he despatched under Augustine of course carried with them the views and ideas which then held undisputed sway in Rome. Apparently, however, asceticism found little favour at first with the new converts, rendering it difficult for Augustine to obtain sufficient co-labourers among his disciples, for he applied to Gregory to learn whether he might allow those who could not restrain their passions to marry and yet remain in the ministry.   To this Gregory replied evasively, stating, what Augustine already knew, that the lower grades might marry, but making no reference whatever to the higher orders.   He apparently did not wish to assume the responsibility of relaxing the rule, while willing perhaps to connive at its suspension in order to encourage the infant Anglican Church.   If so, the indulgence was but temporary.

The attempt has been made to prove that marriage was permitted in the early Saxon Church, and support for this supposition has been sought from a clause in the Dooms of King Ina, of which the date is about the year 700, fixing the wer-gild of the son of a bishop.   But the rubric of the law shows that it refers rather to a godson; and even if it were not so, we have already seen how often in France, at the same period, the episcopal office was bestowed on eminent or influential laymen, who were obliged on its acceptance to part with their wives.

These speculations are manifestly groundless.   The Penitential which goes by the name of the celebrated Theodore, who was Archbishop of Canterbury from 668 to 690, forbids the marriage of the clergy under pain of deposition, and all intercourse with such wives was punished by life-long penance as laymen;   not only were digami ineligible to ordination, but also even those who had kept concubines;   the bishop, priest, or deacon who was guilty of fornication was degraded, and all who had been baptized by him were required to be re-baptized—an expression of reprobation which it would be hard to parallel elsewhere in the history of the Church.   The Christianity introduced into Britain was purely Roman, and, although these rules were impossible of rigid enforcement, it is not likely that they were wholly inoperative, in a Church sufficiently enlightened to produce the learning and piety of men like Bede and St. Aldhelm;   where the admiration of virginity was as great as that which finds utterance in the writings of these fathers, and the principles of asceticism were so influential as to lead a powerful monarch like Ina to retire with his queen, Ethelberga, from the throne which he had gloriously filled, to the holy restrictions of a monastic life.

Ecgberht, who was Archbishop of York from 732 to

766, is almost equally decisive in his condemnation of priestly irregularities, though he returned to the received doctrine of the Church that baptism could not be repeated. It is also probable that even the Britons, who derived their Christianity from the older and purer sources of the primitive Church, preserved the rule with equal reverence. At the request of a national council, St. Aldhelm addressed an epistle to the Welsh king, Geruntius, to induce him to reform his Church so as to bring it within the pale of Catholic unity. To accomplish this, he argues at length upon the points of difference, discussing the various errors of faith and discipline, such as the shape of the tonsure, the date of Easter, etc., but he is silent with regard to marriage or concubinage. Had the Welsh Church been schismatic in this respect, so ardent a celibatarian as Aldhelm would certainly not have omitted all reference to a subject of so much interest to him. The inference is therefore justifiable that no difference of this nature existed.

We may fairly conclude that the discipline of the Church in these matters was reasonably well maintained by the Saxon clergy, with the exception of the monasteries, the morals of which institutions appear to have been deplorably and incurably loose. About the middle of the seventh century, John IV reproves the laxity of the Saxon monasticism, under which the holy virgins did not hesitate to marry. In 734 we find Bede, in an epistle to Ecgberht of York, advising him to create suffragan bishoprics and to endow them from the monastic foundations, of which there were a countless number totally neglectful of all monastic discipline, whose reformation could apparently be accomplished in no other way. St. Boniface, whose zeal on the subject has already been sufficiently made manifest, about the year 746 paused in his reformation of the French priesthood to urge upon Cuthbert, Archbishop of Canterbury, the necessity of repressing the vices of the Saxon ecclesiastics. He dwells at considerable length upon their various crimes and misdemeanours—drunkenness, unclerical garments, neglect of their sacred functions, etc.—but he does not accuse them of unchastity, which he could not well have avoided doing had there been colourable grounds for such a charge. In fact, the only allusion connected with the question in his epistle is a request that some restrictions should be laid upon the permissions granted to women and nuns for pilgrimage to Rome, on account of the attendant dangers to their virtue; in illustration of which he states the lamentable fact that scarcely a city in Lombardy, France, or the Rhinelands but had Saxon courtesans derived from this source, to the shame and scandal of the whole Church.

Pope Zachary seconded these representations, and in 747 Cuthbert, yielding to the impulsion, held the celebrated Council of Clovesho, which adopted thirty canons on discipline, to remedy the disorders enumerated by Boniface. Among these, the only ones directed against unchastity relate solely to the nunneries, which were represented as being in a condition of gross immorality. The council does not spare the vices of the secular clergy, and its silence with respect to their purity fairly permits the inference that there was not much to correct with regard to it, for had licentiousness been so prevalent that Cuthbert had feared to denounce it, or had sacerdotal marriage been passed over as lawful, the zeal of St. Boniface would have led to an explosion, and Zachary would not have sanctioned the proceedings by his approval.

The same argument is applicable to the Council of Chelsea, held in 787 by the legates of Adrian I, under the presidency of Gregory, Bishop of Ostia. The vices and shortcomings of the Anglican Church were there sharply reproved, but no allusion was made to any unchastity prevailing among the priesthood, with the exception, as before, of nuns, on whom we may infer that previous reformatory efforts had been wasted; and in an epistle from Alcuin to Ethelred, King of Northumbria, near the close of the century there is the same reference to nuns, without special condemnation of the other classes of the clergy. That this reticence did not arise from any licence granted for marriage is conclusively shown by the interpolation of the word *laicus* in the text I Cor. vii. 2, which is quoted among the canons adopted. To the same effect are the canons of the Council of Chelsea, in 816, in which the only allusion to such matters is a provision to prevent the election of unfit persons to abbacies, and to punish monks and nuns who secularise themselves.

On the other hand, it is true that about this time St. Swithun, after obtaining orders, was openly married; but his biographer states that he had a special dispensation from Leo III, and that he consented to it because, on the death of his parents, he was the sole representative of his family. As Swithun was tutor to Ethelwulf, son of King Ecgberht, the papal condescension is by no means impossible.

Such was the condition of the Anglo-Saxon Church at this period. During the century which follows, the materials for tracing the vicissitudes of the question before us are of the scantiest description. The occasional councils which were held have left but meagre records of their deliberations, with few or no references to the subject of celibacy. It is probable, however, that a rapid deterioration in the strictness of discipline occurred, for even the power of the great Bretwalda Ecgberht was unequal to the task of repressing effectually the first invasions of the Northmen, and under his feebler successors they grew more and more destructive, until they culminated in the anarchy which gave occasion to the romantic adventures of Alfred.

It is to this period of darkness that we must attribute the introduction of sacerdotal marriage, which became so firmly established, and was finally so much a matter of course, that it attracted no special attention until the efforts made for its abrogation late in the succeeding century. When Alfred undertook to restore order in his recovered kingdom, the body of the laws which he compiled contains no allusion to celibacy, except as regards the chastity of nuns. The same may be said of the Constitutions of Odo, Archbishop of Canterbury, to which the date of 943 is attributed, although they contain instructions as to the conduct of bishops, priests, and clerks—whence we may infer that the marriage even of consecrated virgins was not uncommon, and that it was the only infraction of the rule which aroused the opposition of the hierarchy. Simple immorality called forth an occasional enactment, as in the laws of Edward and Guthrun about the year 906, and in those of Edmund I in 944, yet even to this but little attention seems to have been attracted, until St. Dunstan undertook a reformation which was sorely needed.

St. Dunstan himself, although regularly bred to the Church, with the most brilliant prospects both from his distinguished abilities and his powerful kindred, betrothed himself in marriage after receiving the minor orders. His uncle, St. Elphege, Bishop of Winchester—apparently a Churchman of the stricter school—vehemently opposed the union, but Dunstan was immovable in his determination. Elphege, finding his worldly wisdom set at nought, appealed to the assistance of Heaven. His prayer was answered, and Dunstan was attacked with a mysterious and loathsome malady, under which his iron resolution gave way. He sought Elphege, took the monastic vow (the only inseparable bar to matrimony), and was ordained a priest. This stern experience might have taught him charity for the weakness of natures less unbending than his own, but his temperament was not one to pause half-way. If, too, religious conviction urged him to the task of restoring the forgotten discipline of the Church, worldly ambition might reasonably claim its share in his motives. He could not but feel that his authority would be vastly enhanced by rendering the great ecclesiastical body dependent entirely upon him as the representative of Rome, and by sundering the ties which divided the allegiance due wholly to the Church.

The opportunity to effect a reformation presented itself when the young king, Edgar the Pacific, in 963 violated all the dictates of honour and religion in his adventure with the nun at Wilton. Her resistance attested her innocence, and the birth of a daughter did not prevent her subsequent canonisation as St. Wilfreda; but Edgar's crime and remorse were only the more heightened. When the terror-stricken king sought pardon and absolution, Dunstan was prepared with his conditions. Seven years of penitence, during which he was to abstain from wearing the crown, was the personal infliction imposed on him, but the most important portion of the sentence was that by which the vices of the king were to be redeemed by the enforced virtues of his subjects. He promised the founding of monasteries and the reformation of the clergy; and his implicit obedience to the demands of his ghostly judge is shown, perhaps, less in the fact that his coronation did not take place until 973, than in the active measures immediately set on foot with respect to the morals of the ecclesiastics.

That their morals, indeed, needed reformation is the

unanimous testimony of all the chroniclers of the period. Among all the monasteries of England, formerly so noted for their zeal and prosperity, only those of Glastonbury and Abingdon were inhabited by monks. The rest had fallen into ruin, or were occupied by the secular clergy, with their wives, or worse, and were notorious as places of the most scandalous dissipation and disorder. So low was the standard of morality that priests did not even scruple to put away the wives of whom they grew tired, and to form new connections, of open and public adultery; and so common had this become that a code of ecclesiastical law, probably drawn up about this time, reproves this systematic bigamy, and appears to tacitly authorise marriage as legitimate and honourable. One author declares that none but paupers could be found willing to bind themselves by monastic vows; and another asserts, with every show of reason, that the clergy were not only not superior to the laity in any respect, but were even far worse in the scandals of their daily life.

When King Edgar made his peace with the Church by consenting to the vicarious penitence of the priesthood, three rigid and austere monks were the ardent ministers of the royal determination. Of St. Dunstan, the primate of England, I have already spoken. St. Ethelwold, his pupil, Abbot of Abingdon, was elevated to the see of Winchester, and commenced the movement by expelling the occupants of the monastery there. A few who consented to take monastic vows were allowed to remain, and the remainder were replaced by monks; but even St. Ethelwold's rigour had to bend to the depravity of the age, and he was forced to relax the rigidity of discipline in non-essentials in order to obtain recruits of a better class. The difficulties he encountered are indicated by the legend which relates that he was poisoned in his wine and carried from table to his couch in excruciating torment, where he lay hopeless till, reproaching himself with want of faith, he repeated the text—" Et si mortiferum quid biberint, non eis nocebitur," and was cured on the instant. That his canons were quite capable of such an attempt may be assumed from the description given of them in the bull procured by Dunstan from John XIII, authorising their ejection by the king. The pope does not hesitate to stigmatise them as vessels of the devil, hateful to all good

Christians on account of their inveterate and ineradicable wickedness.

The third member of the reforming triumvirate was St. Oswald, Bishop of Worcester, who undertook a similar transformation of the clergy occupying the monastery of St. Mary in his cathedral city. Many promises they made to conform to his wishes, and many times they eluded the performance, till, losing patience with the prolonged procrastination, he one day entered the chapel with a quantity of monkish habits as they were vigorously chanting " Servite Domino in timore," when he made practical application of the text by forcing them to put on the garments and take the vows on the spot, under the alternative of instant expulsion.

These proceedings received the unqualified approbation of Edgar, who in 964, by his " Charter of Oswalde's Law," confirmed the ejection of the recusants who refused to part with their wives, and transferred all their rights and possessions to the newcomers. In the same document he boasted that he had instituted forty-seven abbeys of monks and nuns, and that he hoped to increase the number to fifty. The same year a similar summary process was carried out in the convents of Chertsey and Winchester; and in 966 Edgar was able to boast of the numerous religious houses throughout England which he had purified by replacing lascivious clerks with pious monks.

These efforts, however, tended only to restore these monastic foundations to their original position, and left the secular clergy untouched, except in so far as a few of them were deprived of the comfortable quarters which they had usurped in the abbeys. This immunity it was no part of Dunstan's plan to permit, and accordingly Edgar issued a series of laws restoring the obsolete ecclesiastical discipline throughout his kingdom. By this code a lapse from virtue on the part of a priest or monk was visited with the same penalty as homicide, with a fast of ten years; for a deacon the period of penitence was seven years; for the lower grades, six years. The monk, priest, or deacon who maintained relations with his wife was subjected to the same punishment; but there is no mention of degradation or deprivation of benefice.

The struggle was long, and at one time the three reformers seem to have grown wearied with the stubborn resistance which they met, while the zeal of King Edgar grew more fiery as, with the true spirit of the huntsman, he followed up the prey, his ardour increasing as the chase grew more difficult. In 969 he eloquently addressed Dunstan, Ethelwold, and Oswald, blaming their luke-warmness in the good cause, and promising them every support and assistance in removing this opprobrium from the Church. Stimulated by these reproaches, Dunstan summoned a council which adopted a canon depriving unchaste priests of their benefices. Still the conflict con-tinued, and a charter dated 974, the last year of Edgar's reign, shows that he persevered to the end with unabated zeal.

The contumacious clerks may have been silenced; they were not subdued, and they but waited their opportunity. It came in 975, with the early death of Edgar and with the dissensions caused by his widow, Elfritha, who en-deavoured to deprive of the succession his eldest son, the youthful Edward, fruit of a former marriage. During the confusion, the ejected priests banded together and bribed Elfhere, the powerful Ealdorman of Mercia, together with some other magnates, to espouse their cause. In many abbeys the regulars were expelled and the priests with their wives were reinstated. In East Anglia, however, the nobles took sides with the monks, and, rising in arms, valiantly defended the monasteries. At length, on the accession of Edward, a council was assembled to make final disposition of the question. The married priests were present, and promised amendment; their noble protectors pleaded earnestly for them; the boy-king was moved, and was about to pronounce in their favour, when a miracle preserved the purity of the Church. The council was sitting in the refectory of the monastery of Hyde, the headquarters of the ascetic party; Edward and Dunstan were enthroned separately from the rest, with their backs to a wall on which, between them, hung a small crucifix. At the critical moment, just as the king was yielding, the crucifix spoke, in a low tone inaudible to all save Edward and the primate, " Let not this thing be done "—the mandate was imperative, and the married clergy lost their cause.

Still the stubborn priests and their patrons held out, and another miracle was necessary—this time a more impressive one. A second council was called to discuss the matter, and was held at Calne in 978. During the heat of the argument the floor gave way, carrying with it the whole assembly, except St. Dunstan, who remained triumphantly and miraculously perched upon a joist, while his adversaries lay groaning below, in every variety of mutilation. His triumph, however, was but short. The same year the pious child Edward perished through the intrigues of Elfritha, whose son, Ethelred the Unready, succeeded to the throne. The mixed political and religious character of these events is shown by the canonisation of Edward, who, though yet a child, was regarded as a martyr by the ascetics, whose cause he had espoused.

As Elfritha had evidently sought the alliance of the secular clergy to strengthen her party, her success proved disastrous to the cause of reform. The respite of peace, too, which had blessed the island during the vigorous reigns of Athelstan the Magnificent and Edgar the Pacific, gave place to the ravages invited by the feeble and vacillating policy of Ethelred the Unready; the incursions of the pagan Danes became more and more frequent and terrible; and what little respect had been inculcated for the strictness of discipline was speedily forgotten in the anarchy which ensued.

The efforts of the reformers appear to have extended even to the British churches of Wales, which had followed Saxon example in abandoning celibacy. The Brut y Tywysogion relates that about the year 861 the priests were forbidden to marry without dispensation from the pope; but they did not submit, and the disturbances thus provoked rendered necessary the abandonment of the effort, so that sacerdotal marriage remained unchecked. We shall see hereafter that in the Principality the custom remained in full vigour until the thirteenth century was well advanced.

How thoroughly the work of Dunstan and Edgar was undone in England is sufficiently indicated by the efforts made not long after, with the consent of Ethelred, to introduce some feeble restraints upon the prevailing immorality. About the year 1006 we find the chief monastery of England, Christ Church at Canterbury, in full possession of the secular clergy, whose irregularities were so flagrant that even Ethelred was forced to expel them, and to fill their places with monks. What was the condition of discipline among the secular priests may be guessed from the reformatory efforts of St. Ælfric, who was Archbishop of Canterbury from 995 to 1006. In his series of canons the first eight are devoted to inculcating the necessity of continence; after quoting the Nicene canon, he feels it to be so much at variance with the habits and customs of the age, that he actually deprecates the surprise of his clergy at hearing a rule so novel and so oppugnant to the received practice, " as though there was no danger in priests living as married men "; he anticipates the arguments which they will bring against him, and refutes them with more gravity than success. There is also extant, under the name of St. Ælfric, a pastoral epistle, which is regarded as supposititious by some critics; but its passages on this subject are too similar in spirit to the canons of Ælfric to be reasonably rejected. They show how hopeless was the effort to maintain the purity desired by the ecclesiastical authorities, and that entreaties and exhortations were uttered merely from a sense of duty, and with hardly an expectation of commanding attention. " This, to you, priests, will seem grievous, because ye have your misdeeds in custom, so that it seems to yourselves that ye have no sin in so living in female intercourse as laymen; and say that Peter the Apostle had a wife and children. . . . Beloved, we cannot now forcibly compel you to chastity, but we admonish you, nevertheless, that ye observe chastity, so as Christ's ministers ought, in good reputation, to the pleasure of God."

That these well-meant homilies effected little in reforming the hearts of so obdurate a generation becomes manifest by the proceedings of the Council of Enham, held by King Ethelred in 1009. The priests are there entreated, by the obedience which they owe to God, to observe the chastity which they know to be due. Yet so great was the laxity prevailing that some are stated to have two or more wives, and many to be in the habit of changing their spouses at pleasure, in violation of all Christian law. The council was apparently, however, powerless to repress these scandals by an adequate punishment, and contented itself with promising to those who lived chastely the privileges and legal status of nobles, while the vicious were vaguely threatened with the loss of the grace of God and man.

The injunctions of the council as regards the regular clergy, though not particularly specific in their nature, show that even the monks had not responded to the benefits conferred upon them by Edgar the Pacific, nor fulfilled the expectations of the pious Dunstan. An expression employed, indeed, leads the learned Spelman to suggest that there possibly were two orders of monks, the one married and the other unmarried; but this is probably without foundation.

Such was the condition of the Church when the increasing assaults of the Northman finally culminated in overthrowing the house of Cerdic, and placing the hated Dane upon the throne of England. Cnut's long and prosperous reign, and his earnest veneration for the Church, as shown by his pilgrimage to Rome, may perhaps have succeeded in removing some of the grosser immoralities of the clergy, but that marriage was still openly and unrestrainedly practised by those in orders is evident. The ecclesiastical laws of Cnut exhort priests to chastity in precisely the same words, and with the same promises, as the canons of the Council of Enham, but do not allude to the habit of keeping a plurality of wives; while, in the same chapter, a warning to the whole people against unlawful concubinage would seem to indicate that the clergy and laity were bound by rules identical in strictness.

That the rule of celibacy was recognised as binding only on the regulars, or monks, and that the secular priesthood were at full liberty to marry, is evident from the system of purgation enjoined on them by the same code. The priest who was also a monk (sacerdos regulariter vivens—sacerd þe regollice libbe) could clear himself from an accusation in a simple suit by merely saying mass, and receiving communion, while the secular priest (plebeius sacerdos—mæssepreost þe regol-lif næbbe) is only equal to the deacon-monk (diaconus regularis—diacon þe regollice libbe), requiring two of his peers as compurgators.[1] The

[1] Cnutes Domas c. v. (Thorpe I. 362). To appreciate the full weight of the privileges thus distributed, we should bear in mind how completely, in those times, the various classes of society were distinguished by the facilities afforded them of acquittal in cases of accusation, and by the graduated scale of fines established for injuries inflicted on them. These were most substantial advantages when the wergild, or blood-money, was the only safeguard guaranteed

significance of the distinction thus drawn is rendered clear
by the version of the passage in a curious Latin text of the
code published by Kolderup-Rosenvinge. The chapter is
divided into two, the first one with the rubric " De Sacer-
dotibus," and commencing " Si contigerit presbyterum
regulariter et caste viventem," etc., while the second is
headed " De vulgare sacerdote *non casto*," the meaning
of which is defined in the expression " Si vulgaris presbyter
qui non regulariter vivit." It is thus evident that purity
was expected from those only who had entered into the
obligations of monastic life, and also that the reforms
of Dunstan had caused the ministers of the altar to be
frequently selected from among the monks.

To this period are also, in all probability, to be attributed the " Institutes of Polity, civil and ecclesiastical,"
to which reference has been made in the preceding section
as blaming priests for decorating their wives with the
ornaments belonging to their churches. Unable to denounce efficient penalties for the prevention of such evil
practices, the author is obliged to content himself with
invoking future punishment from heaven, in vague and
meaningless threats—" A priest's wife is nothing but a
snare of the devil, and he who is ensnared thereby on to
his end, he will be seized fast by the devil."

From all this it is evident that the memory of the ancient
canons was not forgotten, and that their observance was
still urged by some ardent Churchmen, but that the customs
of the period had rendered them virtually obsolete, and
that no sufficient means existed of enforcing obedience.
If open scandals and shameless bigamy and concubinage
could be restrained, the ecclesiastical authorities were
evidently content. Celibacy could not be enjoined as a
law, but was rendered attractive by surrounding it with
privileges and immunities denied to him who yielded to
the temptations of the flesh, and who thus in some degree
assimilated his sacred character to that of the laity.

by law for life and limb, and were most important privileges of the
atistocracy. This constitutes the thane-right alluded to in the
Council of Enham, and retained by the laws of Cnut, as attaching to
priests who preserve their chastity. Thus " sacramentum presbyteri
regulariter viventis tantumdem valeat sicut liberalis hominis " (Cnuti
Leg. Sæcul. c. 128—ed. Kolderup-Rosenvinge)—the expression
" liberalis homo " being, in this version, used for the " taynus " or
thane of the other texts.

The Saxon Church thus was practically regardless of
the rule of celibacy when Edward the Confessor ascended
the throne. The ascetic piety of that prince and his
Norman education alike led him to abhor the sensual
indulgences in which he found his subjects plunged, and
he attached himself almost exclusively to the horde of
Norman monks who flocked to his court from across the
Channel. Their influence was all-powerful, and though
reasons of the highest state necessity forced him to ally
himself in marriage with Edith, daughter of the puissant
Duke Godwin, whom Edward hated with all the energy of
his feeble nature, it was not difficult for his artful ghostly
counsellors to persuade him that a vow of virginity, taken
and kept amid the seductions of a throne, would insure
his glory in this world and his salvation in the next. A
minstrel historian describes at length the engagement of
perpetual chastity entered into between Edward and Edith
at their marriage, and though he mentions the popular
derision to which this exposed the royal monk at the
hands of a gross and brutal generation, he is firmly persuaded that the crown of martyrdom was worthily won
and worn—

> Par veincre charnel desir,
> Bein deit estre clamez martir.
> Ne sai cunter en nul estoire
> Rei ki feist si grant victoire,
> Sa char, diable e mund venqui,
> Ki sont troi fort enimi.

How little the royal pair expected this example to be
followed, and how relaxed were all the rules of monastic
discipline, is shown by an anecdote of the period. The
austere Gervinus, Abbot of St. Riquier in Ponthieu, was
always welcomed by them when he visited England, and
on one occasion Queen Edith offered to kiss him. The
abbot's rigidity overcame his courtliness, and he refused
the royal salutation, to the great indignation of the queen,
who ordered certain gifts which she had set apart for him
to be withdrawn. Edward, however, approved of the
action of the monk, and after Edith had been made to
understand his motives she not only joined in applauding
him but demanded that a similar rule should be made
imperative on all the monks of England.
It cannot be doubted that Edward made efforts to

effect a reform among his sensual and self-indulgent subjects, but his want of success is developed in the description
of the Saxon clergy at the time of the Conquest. The
Norman chroniclers speak of them as abandoned to sloth,
ignorance, and the lusts of the flesh; even monastic institutions were matters rather of tradition than of actual
existence, and the monks themselves were hardly distinguishable by their mode of life from the laity. There
doubtless may be some contemptuous exaggeration in this,
and yet one author of the period, who is wholly Saxon in
his feelings, does not hesitate to attribute the ruin of the
Saxon monarchy and the devastation of the kingdom to
the just wrath of God, provoked by the vices of the clergy.

The rule of the Normans removed England from her
isolation. Brought into the commonwealth of Christendom and under the active supremacy of the Holy See,
her history henceforth becomes more closely connected
with the general ecclesiastical movement which received its
irresistible impulsion about this period. That movement
it is now our business to examine.

CHAPTER XII

PETER DAMIANI

In a previous section I have shown the laxity prevailing throughout Continental Europe at the commencement of the eleventh century. It is not to be supposed, however, that even where this was tacitly permitted it was openly and unreservedly authorised. The perversity of a sinful generation might render impossible the enforcement of the ancient canons; they might even be forgotten by the worldly and unthinking; but they were still the law of the Church, and their authority was still admitted by some ardent devotees who longed to restore the purity of earlier ages. Burckhardt, who was Bishop of Worms from the year 1000 to 1025, in his voluminous collection of canons, gives a fair selection from the councils and decretals prohibiting all female intercourse to the clergy. Benedict VIII and the Emperor St. Henry II—whose admiration of virginity was evinced by the personal sacrifice, to which reference has just been made—in 1022 endeavoured in the most solemn manner to reform the universal laxity. At the Synod of Pavia a series of canons was adopted pronouncing sentence of deposition upon all priests, deacons, and subdeacons having wives or concubines, and upon all bishops keeping women near them, while special stress was laid upon the continued servitude of the children of all such ecclesiastics as were serfs of the Church. These canons, signed by the pope and attendant bishops, were laid before the emperor, who indorsed them with his sanction, declared them to be municipal as well as ecclesiastical law, promised that their observance should be enforced by the civil magistrates, and thanked Benedict and his prelates for their vigilance in seeking a remedy for the incontinence of the clergy, the evils whereof swept like a storm over the face of Christendom.

In France, the long reign of Robert the Pious seems

to have been marked with almost entire indifference to the subject, but the accession of his son Henry I was attended with a strenuous effort to effect a reform. The Council of Bourges, held in November 1031, but four months after the death of Robert, may perhaps have been assembled at the request of the dying monarch, desirous of redeeming his own sins with the vicarious penance of his subjects. It addressed itself vigorously to eradicating the evil by a comprehensive series of measures, admirably adapted to the end in view. Priests, deacons, and sub-deacons were forbidden to have wives or concubines, and all such consorts were ordered to be dismissed at once and for ever. Those who refused obedience were to be degraded to the rank of lectors or chanters, and in future no ecclesiastic was to be permitted to take either wife or concubine. A vow of chastity was commanded as a necessary pre-requisite to assuming the subdiaconate, and no bishop was to ordain a candidate without exacting from him a promise to take neither wife nor concubine. Children of the clergy in orders, born during the ministry of their parents, were pronounced incapable of entering the Church, in justification of which was cited the provision of the municipal law which incapacitated illegitimates from receiving inheritance or bearing witness in court; but those who were born after their fathers had been reduced to the condition of laymen were not to be considered as the children of ecclesiastics. As this is apparently the earliest instance of a vow of chastity being imposed in conferring orders, it is as well to remark that this precaution has never been adopted by the Church, but such a duty is considered as implied, and became what was known in the schools as a *votum adnexum*.

Nothing could be more reasonable than these provisions of the council, considered from the high-church standpoint, and nothing better adapted to effect the object in view. All that was wanting was the enforcement of the legislation—and laws, when opposed to the spirit of the age, are not apt to be enforced. How much was really gained by the united efforts of the pope, the emperor, and the Gallican hierarchy can readily be gathered from a few out of innumerable incidents afforded by the history of the period.

The able and energetic, though unscrupulous, Benedict

VIII was no more, and the great House of Tusculum, which ruled the Eternal City, had filled the chair of St. Peter with a worthless scion of their stock, as though to declare their contempt for the lofty pretensions of the Apostolic Episcopate. A fit descendant of the infamous Marozia and Alberic, Benedict IX, a child ten years old at the time of his elevation in 1032, grew up in unrestrained licence, and shocked even the dull sensibilities of a gross and barbarous age by the scandals of his daily life. The popular appreciation of his character is shown by the legend of his appearing after death to a holy man, in the figure of a bear, with the ears and tail of an ass, and declaring that, as he had lived in bestiality, so he was destined to wear the form of a beast and to suffer fiery torments until the Day of Judgment, after which he was to be plunged, body and soul, into the fathomless pit of hell. When the Vicegerent of God, the head of the Christian Church, was thus utterly depraved, the prospect of reforming the corruption of the clergy was not promising, and the good work was not likely to be prosecuted with vigour.

Nor were the members of the hierarchy unworthy of their superior. We hear of Rainbaldo, Bishop of Fiesole, who, not contented with numerous concubines, had publicly married a wife, and whose children were established as a widespread and powerful family—and, what is perhaps more remarkable, this dissolute prelate was gifted with the power of working miracles. The bishops, indeed, at this period were still rather warrior nobles than Christian ministers. Bisantio, the good Bishop of Bari, is praised quite as much for his terrible prowess in battle as for his pious benevolence and munificence; and on his death, in 1035, his flock chose a military official as his successor.

Descending in the scale, we may instance the priest Marino, who, though he lived openly with his wife, was a noted miracle-worker. Among quaint wonders wrought by him it is recorded that water rendered holy by his blessing, when sprinkled over the cornfields, had the power of driving away all caterpillars and other noxious insects. His son, Eleuchadio, was a most venerable man, who subsequently, as abbot of the monastery of the Virgin at Fiano, won the esteem and respect of even the stern Damiani himself. In fact, the pious Desiderius, Abbot of Monte Cassino, better known as pope under the name of

Victor III, declares that throughout Italy, under the pontificate of Benedict, all orders, from bishops down, without
shame or concealment, were publicly married and lived
with their wives as laymen, leaving their children fully
provided for in their wills; and what rendered the disgrace
more poignant was the fact that the scandal was greatest
in Rome itself, whence the light of religion and discipline
had formerly illuminated the Christian world. Another
contemporary writer asserts that this laxity prevailed
throughout the whole of Latin Christendom, sacerdotal
marriage being everywhere so common that it was no
longer punished as unlawful, and scarcely even reprehended.

In becoming thus universal and tacitly permitted it
was not incompatible with the most fervent piety; and
though it may be an evidence of hierarchical disorganisa-
tion, it can no longer be considered as indicating of itself
a lowered standard of morals in the ministers of the Church.
This is forcibly illustrated in the case of St. Procopius,
selected by Duke Ulrich of Bohemia as the first abbot of
the monastery of Zagow. He was regularly bred to the
Church under the care of Bishop Quirillus, and was noted
for the rectitude of his deportment in the priesthood; yet
we learn that he was married during this period, when we
are told that, being disgusted with the hollow vanities
of the world, he abandoned wife and friends for the solitude
of a hermit's cave. Here an accidental meeting with
Duke Ulrich, while hunting, led to the foundation of
Zagow and to the installation of Procopius as its head.

Silently the Church seemed to acquiesce in the violation
of her canons, until at length she appeared content if her
ministers would satisfy themselves with reputable marriage
and avoid the grosser scandals. When Ulrich, Abbot of
Tegernsee, about 1041, deplored the evil influence of a
priest who had two wives living, he seems to have felt
that lawful marriage might be tolerated, but that polygamy
was of evil example in a Christian pastor. So when Albert
the Magnificent, Archbishop of Hamburg, was accustomed
to exhort his clergy to continence and to shun the pesti-
ferous society of women, his worldly wisdom prompted
him to add that, if they were unequal to the effort, they
should at least keep unsullied the bonds of marriage and
should live " si non caste, tamen caute."

If irregularities such as these existed, they are not justly imputable to the Church itself. It can scarcely be a matter of wonder if the clergy, in assimilating themselves to the laity as regards the liberty of wedlock, should also have adopted the licence which in that lawless age rendered the marriage-tie a slender protection for the weakness of woman. Though it was indissoluble according to the teachings of religion, yet the Church, which at that time was the only protector of the feeble against the strong, had not acquired the commanding authority which subsequently enabled it to enforce its decrees everywhere and on all occasions. If, under a vigorous pope, the sentence of excommunication had been able to frighten a superstitious monarch like Robert the Pious, yet the pontiffs of the House of Tusculum were not men to trouble themselves, or to be successful had they made the attempt, to rectify the wrongs perpetrated in every obscure baronial castle or petty hamlet in Europe. The isolation and independence of the feudal system made every freeman, so to speak, the arbiter of his own actions. The wife whose charms ceased to gratify the senses of her husband, or whose temper threatened to disturb his equanimity, stood little chance of retaining her position, if an opportunity offered of replacing her to advantage, unless she was fortunate in having kindred able to resent the wrong which the Church and the law were powerless to prevent or to punish. If, then, the clergy occasionally indulged in similar practices, the evil is not attributable to the licence of marriage which they had usurped. That licence had, at all events, borne some fruits of good, for during its existence we hear somewhat less of the system of concubinage so prevalent before and after this period, and there is no authentic indication of the nameless horrors so suggestively intimated by the restrictions on the residence of relatives enjoined in the frequent canons promulgated at the close of the ninth century.

It is not to be supposed, however, that the race of ascetics was extinct. Amid the licence which prevailed in every class, there were still some men who, disgusted with the turbulent and dissolute world, despairing of salvation among the temptations and trials of active life or the sloth and luxury of the monastic establishments, sought the path to heaven in solitude and maceration. Such men could not but look with detestation on the worldly priests who divided their thoughts between their sacred calling and the cares of an increasing household, and who profaned the unutterable mysteries of the altar with hearts and hands not kept pure from the lusts of the flesh.

Prominent among these holy anchorites was S. Giovanni Gaulberto, who fled from the snares of the world to the forests of Camaldoli, where his austerities, his holiness, and his miracles soon attracted crowds of disciples, who formed a numerous community of humble imitators of his virtues.   Restoring in its strictness the neglected Rule of Benedict, his example and his teaching wrought conviction, and the order of monks which he founded and carried with him to the peaceful shades of Vallombrosa became renowned for its sanctity and purity.   Thus withdrawn by the will of Heaven from the selfish egotism of a hermit's existence, he laboured earnestly to reform the laxity of priestly life in general, and his success was most encouraging.   Moved by his admonitions, self-indulgent clerks abandoned wives and mistresses, devoted themselves to the performance of their sacred functions, or sought in monastic seclusion to make atonement for their past excesses.

Though it may well be supposed that Gaulberto was not unassisted in his efforts, yet all such individual exertions, dependent upon persuasion alone, could be but limited in their influence and temporary in their results.   Reform, to be universal and permanent, required to be authoritative in its character, and to proceed from above downward.   The papacy itself must cease to be a scandal to Christendom, and must be prepared to wield the awful force of its authority, seconded by the moral weight of its example, before disorders so firmly rooted could be attacked with any hope of success.   In 1044, Benedict IX was driven out of Rome by a faction of rebels or patriots, who elected Silvester III as pontiff in his place.   A sudden revolution sent Silvester into exile, and brought Benedict back, who, to complete the confusion, sold the papal dignity to a new aspirant, known as Gregory VI.   The transaction was not one which could decently be recognised by the Church, and Benedict was held incapable of thus transferring the allegiance of Christendom, or of depriving himself of his position.   There were thus three popes, whose conflicting claims to reverence threw all Europe into the doubt and danger of schism, nor could the knotty question be solved by the power of distracted Italy. A more potent judge was required, and the decision was referred, as a matter of course, to the sagacious and energetic Emperor, Henry the Black, whose success in repressing the turbulence of the empire, and whose sincere reverence for the Church, gave reasonable promise of a happy solution of the tangled problem. His proceeding was summary. The three competitors were unceremoniously dismissed, and Henry filled the vacancy thus created by the appointment of Suidger, Bishop of Bamberg, who assumed the name of Clement II.

Henry III was moved by a profound conviction that a thorough and searching reform was vitally necessary to the Church. The conscientious severity of his character led him to have little toleration for the abuses and disorders which were everywhere so painfully apparent. How far his views were in advance of those generally entertained, even by ecclesiastical dignitaries, was clearly manifested as early as 1042, when Gebhardt, Bishop of Ratisbon, urged the claims of his favourite arch-priest Cuno for the vacant see of Eichstedt. Henry refused on the ground that Cuno was the son of a priest, and therefore by the established canons ineligible to the position. The reason, though unanswerable, was so novel that Gebhardt refused to accept it as the true one, and Henry, to pacify him, promised to nominate any other one of the Ratisbon clergy whom Gebhardt might select. The choice fell upon a young and unknown man, also named Gebhardt, whose abilities, brought into notice thus accidentally, rendered him afterwards more conspicuous as Pope Victor II.

Henry did not neglect the opportunity now afforded him of carrying into effect his reformatory views, and in his selection of a pontiff he was apparently influenced by the conviction that the Italian clergy were too hopelessly corrupt for him to expect from them assistance in his plans. Clement exchanged with him promises of mutual support in the arduous undertaking. We have nothing to do with the most crying evil; the one first vigorously attacked, and the one which was productive of the greatest real detriment to the Church—simony. That was everywhere open and avowed. From the blessing of the priest

to the nomination for a primacy, every ecclesiastical act
was the subject of bargain and sale, reduced in many
places to a regular scale of prices. To remove this scandal,
Clement set vigorously to work, and soon found a united
opposition which promised little for the success of the
undertaking. He was doubtless sincere, but he was clearly
alone in his struggle with the fierce Italian prelates, who
were resolved not to abandon the emoluments and indulgences to which they had grown accustomed, and the result
of his efforts did not fulfil the expectations of the more
sanguine aspirants for the purification of the Church.
Even his patron the emperor appears to have doubted his
earnestness in the cause, for we find Henry not only addressing him a letter urging him to fresh exertion, but entrusting
it to Peter Damiani, with a command to present it in
person, and to use all his powers of exhortation to stimulate the flagging zeal of the pope. Damiani refused to
leave his hermitage even at the imperial mandate, but he
enclosed the missive in one of his own, deploring the
unhealed wounds of the Church, recapitulating the shortcomings of Clement, and goading him to fresh efforts, in
a style which savoured little of the reverence due to the
vicegerent of God. The pontifical crown was evidently
not a wreath of roses. Clement sank under its weight, and
died 9th October, 1047, in less than ten months after he
had accepted the perilous dignity.

St. Peter Damiani, who thus introduces himself to our
notice, was one of the remarkable men of the epoch. Born
about the year 988 at Ravenna, of a noble but decayed
family, and the last of a numerous progeny, he owed his
life to a woman of the very class to the extirpation of
which he devoted all the energies of his prime. His
mother, worn out in the struggle with poverty, regarded
his birth with aversion, refused to suckle the infant saint,
and neglected him until his forlorn and emaciated condition
awoke the compassion of a female retainer, the wife of a
priest, who remonstrated with the unfeeling parent until
she succeeded in arousing the sense of duty, and restored
to existence the little sufferer, who was destined to bring
unnumbered woes to all who were of her condition. His
early years are said to have been passed as a swineherd, till
the opportunity for instruction offered itself, which he

eagerly embraced. Retiring at length from the world, he joined the disciples of St. Romuald, who practised the strictest monastic life, either as monks or hermits, at Avellana, near Gubbio. Immuring himself there in the desert, his austerities soon gained for him the reputation of pre-eminent sanctity, and led to his election as prior of the brotherhood. Gifted by nature with an intellect of unusual strength, informed with all the learning of the day, his stern asceticism, his dauntless spirit, and the uncompromising force of his zeal brought him into notice, and marked him as a fitting instrument in the cause of reform. Occasionally, at the call of his superiors, he left his beloved retreat to do battle with the hosts of evil, returning with renewed zest to the charms of solitude, until, in 1057, Stephen IX forced him to accept the cardinal-ate and bishopric of Ostia—the highest dignity in the Roman court. The duties of his episcopate, however, conflicted with his monastic fervour, and after a few years he rendered up the pastoral ring and staff and returned to Avellana, where he died in 1072, full of years and honours. His position and authority can best be estimated from the terms employed by Alexander II, who, when sending him on an important mission to France, described him as next in influence to himself in the Roman Church, and the chief support of the Holy See.

With a nature ardent and combative, worked up to the highest pitch of ascetic intolerance by the introspective musings of his cell, it may readily be conceived that the corruptions of the Church filled him with warm indignation and fierce desire to restore it to its pristine purity. To this holy cause he devoted the last half of his life, and was always ready, with tongue and pen, at the sacrifice of his dearly prized solitude, to further the great movement on which he felt that the future of Christianity depended. The brief hopes excited by the promises of Clement and Henry were speedily quenched by the untimely death of the German pontiff, and the most sanguine might well despair at seeing the odious Benedict IX reinstated as pope. But the emperor was in earnest, and listened willingly to the cry of those who besought him not to leave his work unfinished. Nine brief months saw Benedict again a wanderer, and another German prelate installed in his place. Poppo of Brixen, however, enjoyed his new

dignity, as Damasus II, but twenty-one days, when he
fell a martyr to the cause, perishing miserably, either
through the insalubrious heats of a Roman summer or
the hidden vindictiveness of Italian party rage. It required some courage to accept the honourable but fatal
post, and six months elapsed ere a worthy candidate could
be found. Henry's choice fell this time upon Bruno of
Toul, a prelate to whom admiring biographers ascribe
every virtue and every qualification. As Leo IX he
ascended the pontifical throne in February 1049, and he
soon gave ample evidence of the sincerity with which he
intended to carry out the views of the puritans whom
he represented.

It was significant that he took with him to Rome the
monk Hildebrand, lately released from the service of his
master Gregory VI, who had died in his German exile,
restored by a miracle at his death to the honours of which
he had been adjudged unworthy while living. Still more
significant was the fact that Leo entered Rome, not as
pope, but as a barefooted pilgrim, and that he required
the empty formality of an election within the city, as
though the nomination of the emperor had given him no
claim to his high office. Whether this was the result of
a voice from heaven, as related by the papal historians,
or whether it was done at the suggestion of the high churchman Hildebrand, it showed that the new pontiff magnified
his office, and felt that the line of distinction between
the clerk and the layman was to be sharply drawn and
vigorously defended.

Damiani lost no time in stimulating the stranger to the
duties expected of him by the party of reform. From
the retreat of Avellana he addressed to Leo an essay,
which is the saddest of all the sad monuments bequeathed
to us by that age of desolation. With cynical boldness he
develops the frightful excesses epidemically prevalent
among the cloistered crowds of men, attributable to the
unnatural restraints imposed upon the passions of those
unfitted by nature or by training to control themselves;
and his laborious efforts to demonstrate the propriety of
punishing the guilty by degradation shows how hideous
was the laxity of morals which was disposed to regard such
crimes with indulgence. Like the nameless horrors of
the Penitentials, it is the most convincing commentary on

the system which sought to enforce an impossible exaltation of purity on the ministers of a religion whose outward
formalism had absorbed its internal life.

Leo IX was not long in manifesting his intentions, and
his first point of attack was chosen with some skill, the
ecclesiastical rank of the victim and his want of power
rendering him at once a striking example and an easy
sacrifice. Dabralis, Archbishop of Salona (or Spalatro) in
Dalmatia, was married and lived openly with his wife.
Leo sent a legate to investigate and punish. Called before
a synod, Dabralis could not or deigned not to deny his
guilt, but boldly justified it, as the woman was his lawful
wife, and he instanced the customs of the Greek Church
in his defence. This only aggravated his guilt, and he
was promptly degraded for ever.

Leaving, for a time, the Italian Church for subsequent
efforts at reformation, Leo undertook a progress throughout Northern Europe, for the purpose of restoring the
neglected discipline of those regions. Before the year of
his installation had expired, in November 1049, we find
him presiding with the emperor at a council in Mainz,
where the simony and marriage of the clergy were condemned under severe penalties. That the influence thus
brought to bear had some effect, at least in externals, is
shown by the courtly Albert of Hamburg, who, on returning from the council to his see, revived a forgotten regulation
of his predecessors, in virtue of which the women of ecclesiastics were ordered to live outside of the towns, in order
to avoid public scandal. A few weeks before, in France,
Leo had presided over a national council at Rheims, where
his vigorous action against simony caused numerous vacancies in the hierarchy. The records and canons of this
council contain no allusions to the subject of marriage or
concubinage, but it is altogether improbable that they
escaped attention, for they were indulged in without concealment by all classes of ecclesiastics, and some subsequent
writers assert that they were rigorously prohibited by the
council, but that the injunctions promulgated were unavailing.

Returning to the South, the Easter of 1051 beheld a
council assembled at Rome for the purpose of restoring
discipline. Apparently, the Italian prelates were disposed
to exercise considerable caution in furthering the wishes of
their chief, for they abstained from visiting their indigna-

tion on the guilty priests, and directed their penalties against the unfortunate females. In the city itself these were declared to be enslaved, and were bestowed on the cathedral church of the Lateran, while all bishops throughout Christendom were desired to apply the rule to their own dioceses, and to seize the offending women for the benefit of their churches. The atrocity of this legislation against the wives of priests is all the more noteworthy when contrasted with the tenderness shown to worse crimes committed by men whose high position only rendered their guilt the more heinous. At this council, Gregory, Bishop of Vercelli, was convicted of what, by the rules of the Church, was considered as incest—an amour with a widow betrothed to his uncle. For this aggravated offence he was merely excommunicated, and when, soon after, he presented himself in Rome, he was restored to communion on his simple promise to perform adequate penance.

The reformatory zeal of Leo and of the monastic followers of Damiani was thus evidently not seconded by the Italian Church. A still more striking proof of this was afforded by the attempt to hold a council at Mantua early in 1053. The prelates who dreaded the result conspired to break it up. A riot was provoked between their retainers and the papal domestics; the latter, taken unawares and speedily overpowered, fled to the council-chamber for safety, and Leo, rushing to the door to protect them, was in imminent danger from the arrows and stones which hurtled thickly around him. The reckless plot succeeded, and the council dispersed in undignified haste. Whether Leo was disgusted with his want of success and convinced of the impracticability of the undertaking, or whether his attention was thenceforward absorbed by his unlucky military operations against the rapidly augmenting Norman power in Southern Italy, it is not easy now to ascertain : suffice it to say that no further indications remain of any endeavour to carry out the reforms so eagerly commenced in the first ardour of his pontificate. The consistent Damiani opposed the warlike aspirations of the pontiff, but Leo persisted in leading his armies himself. A lost battle threw Leo into the power of the hated Normans, when, after nine months, he returned to Rome to die, in April 1054, and to be reverenced as a saint after death by those who had withstood him during life in every possible manner.

It is not easy to repress a smile on seeing Leo, who had been so utterly unable to enforce the canons of the Latin Church at home, seriously undertaking to procure their adoption in Constantinople. From his prison, in January 1054, he sent Cardinal Humbert of Silva Candida on a mission to convert the Greek Church. There is extant a controversy between the legate and Nicetas Pectoratus, a learned Greek abbot, on the various points in dispute. I cannot profess to decide which of the antagonists had the advantage on the recondite questions of the use of unleavened bread, the Sabbath fasts, the calculation of Easter, etc., but the contrast between the urbanity of the Greek and the coarse vituperation of the Latin is strikingly suggestive as a tacit confession of defeat on the part of the latter. In view of the frightful immorality of the Italian clergy, there is something peculiarly ludicrous in the mingled anger, contempt, and abhorrence with which Humbert alludes to the marriage of the Greek clergy, which, as he declares, renders their Church the synagogue of Satan and the brothel of Balaam and Jezebel, with other equally courteous and convincing arguments. Humbert attributes priestly marriage altogether to the heresy of the Nicolites, and lays down the law on the subject as inexorably as though it were at the time observed in his own Church.

After an interval of about a year, the line of German pontiffs was continued in the person of Gebhardt, Bishop of Eichstedt (Victor II), whose appointment by the emperor was owing in no small degree to the influence of Hildebrand —an influence which was daily making itself more felt. Installed in the pontifical seat by Godfrey, Duke of Tuscany, his efforts to continue the reformation commenced by his predecessors aroused a stubborn resistance. There may be no foundation for the legend of his being saved by a miracle from a sacramental cup poisoned by a vengeful subdeacon, nor for the rumours that his early death was hastened by the recalcitrant clergy who sought to escape the severity of his discipline. There is some probability in the stories, however, for, during his short pontificate, interrupted by a lengthened stay in Germany and the perpetual vicissitudes of the Neapolitan troubles, he yet found time to hold a synod at Florence, where he degraded numerous prelates for simony and licentiousness; but, whether true or false, the existence of the reports attests at once the sincerity of his zeal and the difficulties of the task.

His death in July 1057 was followed after but a few days' interval by the election of Frederic, Duke of Lorraine —the empire having passed in 1056 from the able hands of Henry III to the feeble regency of his empress, Agnes, as guardian of the unfortunate infant Henry IV—thus releasing the Roman clergy from the degrading dictation of a Teutonic potentate. That Frederic should have abandoned the temptations and ambitions of his lofty station to embrace the austerities of monastic life in the abbey of Monte Cassino, is a sufficient voucher that he would not draw back from the work thus far hopelessly undertaken by his predecessors. Notwithstanding the severity of the canons promulgated during the previous decade, and the incessant attempts to enforce them, Rome was still full of married priests, and the battle had to be recommenced, as though nothing had yet been done. Immediately on his installation, as Stephen IX, he addressed himself unshrinkingly to the task. For four months, during the most unhealthy season, he remained in Rome, calling synod after synod, and labouring with both clergy and people to put an end to such unholy unions, and he summarily expelled from the Church all who had been guilty of incontinence since the prohibitions issued in the time of Leo. One case is related of a contumacious priest whose sudden death gave him the opportunity of striking terror into the hearts of the reckless, for the mutilated funeral rites which deprived the hardened sinner of the consolation of a Christian burial would, it was hoped, prove an effectual warning to his fellows. Feeling the necessity of support in these thankless labours, he forced Damiani to leave the retirement of the cloistered shades of Avellana, and to bear, as Bishop of Ostia, his share of the burden in the contest which he had done so much to provoke—but it was all in vain.

In little more than half a year Stephen found refuge from strife and turmoil in the tomb. The election of his successor, Gerard, Bishop of Florence, was the formal proclamation that the Church was no longer subjected to the control of the secular authority. January 18th, 1058, saw the power of the emperor defied, and the gauntlet thrown for the quarrel which for three centuries was to plunge Central and Southern Europe in turmoil and bloodshed. Henry III had laboured conscientiously to rescue the papacy from the disgrace into which it had fallen. By removing it from the petty sphere of the counts of Tusculum and the barons of the Campagna, and by providing for it a series of high-minded and energetic pontiffs, he had restored its forfeited position, and indeed had conferred upon it an amount of influence which it had never before possessed. His thorough disinterestedness and his labours for its improvement had disarmed all resistance to the exercise of his power, but when that power passed into the hands of an infant but five years old, it was natural that the Church should seek to emancipate itself from subjection; and if almost the first use made of its new-found prerogatives was to crush the hand that had enabled it to obtain them, we must not tax with ingratitude those who were undoubtedly penetrated with the conviction that they were only vindicating the imprescriptible rights of the Church, and that to them was confided the future of religion and civilisation.

In the revolution which thus may date its successful commencement at this period the two foremost figures are Damiani and Hildebrand. Damiani the monk, with no further object than the abolition of simony and the enforcement of the austerities which he deemed indispensable to the salvation of the individual and to the purity of the Church, looked not beyond the narrow circle of his daily life, and sought merely to level mankind by the measure of his own stature. Hildebrand, the far-seeing statesman, could make use of Damiani and his tribe, perhaps equally fervent in his belief that the asceticism of his fellow-labourer was an acceptable offering to God, but yet with ulterior views of transcendently greater importance. In his grand scheme of a theocratic empire, it became an absolute prerequisite that the Church should hold undivided sway over its members; that no human affection should render their allegiance doubtful, but that their every thought and action should be devoted to the common aggrandisement; that they should be separated from the people by an impassable barrier, and should wield an influence which could only be obtained by those who were recognised as superior to the weaknesses of common humanity; that the immense landed possessions of the Church should remain untouched and constantly increasing as the common property of all, and not be subjected to the incessant dilapidations inseparable from uxorious or paternal affections at a time when the restraints of law and of public opinion could not be brought to bear with effect. In short, if the Church was to assume and maintain the position to which it was entitled by the traditions of the canon law and of the False Decretals, it must be a compact and mutually supporting body, earning by its self-inflicted austerities the reverence to which it laid claim, and not be diverted from its splendid goal by worldly allurements or carnal indulgences and preoccupations. Such was the vision to the realisation of which Hildebrand devoted his commanding talents and matchless force of will. The temporal success was at length all that he could have anticipated. If the spiritual results were craft, subtlety, arrogance, cruelty, and sensuality, hidden or cynical, it merely proves that his confidence in the strength of human nature to endure the intoxicating effects of irresponsible power was misplaced. Meanwhile he laboured with Damiani at the preliminary measures of his enterprise, and together they bent their energies to procure the enforcement of the neglected rules of discipline.

The new pope, Nicholas II by name, entered unreservedly into their views. Apparently taught by experience the fruitlessness of additional legislation when the existing canons were amply sufficient, but their execution impossible through the negligence or collusion of the ecclesiastical authorities, he assembled, in 1059, a council of a hundred and thirteen bishops, in which he adopted the novel and hazardous expedient of appealing to the laity, and of rendering them at once the judges and executioners of their pastors. A canon was promulgated forbidding all Christians to be present at the mass of any priest known to keep a concubine or female in his house. This probably remained, like its predecessors, a dead letter for the present, but we shall see what confusion it excited when it was revived and put effectually in force by Gregory VII some fifteen years later. Meanwhile I may observe that it trenched very nearly on the Donatist heresy that the sacrament was polluted in polluted hands, and it required the most careful word-splitting to prevent the faithful from drawing a conclusion so natural.

In addition to this, the council ordered, under pain of excommunication, that no priest who openly took a concubine (or rather a wife), or who did not forthwith separate himself from such a connection already existing, should dare to perform any sacred function, or enjoy any portion of ecclesiastical revenue. Hildebrand, who was all-powerful at the papal court—his enemies accused him of keeping Nicholas like an ass in the stable, feeding him to do his work—has the credit of procuring this legislation. Nicholas, whether acting under the impulsion of Hildebrand and Damiani, or from his own convictions, followed up the reform with vigour. During the same year he visited Southern Italy, and by his decided proceedings at the Council of Melfi endeavoured to put an end to the sacerdotal marriages which were openly practised everywhere throughout that region, and the Bishop of Trani was deposed as an example and warning to others. Damiani was also entrusted with a mission to Milan for the same purpose, of which more anon.

Nor did Nicholas confine his efforts to Italy. His legates in other countries endeavoured to enforce the canons, and apparently had little difficulty in obtaining the adoption of stringent regulations—the more easily acceded to that they were utterly disregarded. Thus his legate Stephen, early in 1060, held councils at Vienne and Tours, where the prohibitions of the Synod of Rome were agreed to, and those who did not at once abandon either their women or their benefices were declared to be degraded for ever, without hope of restitution.

In practice, however, all these measures of reform were scarcely felt except by the lower grades of the ecclesiastical body. The prelates, whose lives were equally flagitious, and far more damaging to the reputation and purity of the Church, were enabled virtually to escape. The storm passed beneath them, and with few exceptions persecuted only those who were powerless to oppose anything but passive resistance. The uncompromising zeal of Damiani was not likely to let a temporising lenity so misplaced and so fatal to the success of the cause remain unrebuked; and he calls to it the attention of Nicholas, stigmatising the

toleration of episcopal sins as an absurdity no longer to
be endured. The occasion of this exhortation was a
commission entrusted by the pope to Damiani, to hold a
friendly conference with the prelates, and to induce them
to reform their evil ways without forcing the authorities to
the scandal of public proceedings. The fear of such results
and the fiery eloquence of Damiani were alike unheeded.
The bishops confessed themselves unequal to the task of
preserving their chastity, and indifferent to the remote
contingency of punishment which had so often been
ineffectually threatened that its capacity for exciting
apprehension had become exhausted. With all the coarseness of monastic asceticism, Damiani describes the extent
of the evil, and its public and unblushing exhibition : the
families which grew and increased around the prelates, the
relationships which were ostentatiously acknowledged, and
the scandals perpetrated in the Church of God. In the
boldest strain he then incites the pope to action, blames
his misplaced clemency, and urges the degradation of all
offenders, irrespective of rank, pointing out the impossibility
of reforming the priesthood if the bishops are allowed full
and undisturbed licence.

This shows that even if the machinery of ecclesiastical
authority was at work to correct the errors of the plebeian
clergy, it was only local and sporadic in its efforts. In
some favoured dioceses, perhaps, blessed with a Puritan
bishop, the decrees of the innumerable councils may have
been put in force, but in the great body of the Church the
evil remained unaltered. During this very year, 1060,
Nicholas again found it necessary to promulgate a decretal
ordering priests to quit their wives or resign their position,
and this in terms which prove how utterly futile had been
all previous fulminations. He also manifested some consideration for temporal necessities by allowing the discarded
wives to live with their husbands under proper supervision.

How complete was the disregard of these commands is
well illustrated by an epistle which about this time Damiani
addressed to the chaplains of Godfrey the Bearded, Duke
of Tuscany. From this we learn that these prominent
ecclesiastics openly defended sacerdotal marriage, pronounced it canonical, and were ready to sustain their
position in controversy. As Duke Godfrey, with the pious
Beatrice his wife, was the leading potentate in Italy, and

as his territories were in close proximity to Rome itself, it is evident that the reform so laboriously prosecuted for the previous ten or fifteen years had thus far accomplished little.

Parties were now beginning to define themselves. The reformers, irritated by their want of success, were for more stringent measures, and when the canonical punishments of degradation and excommunication were derided and defied, they were ready, as we shall see hereafter at Milan, to have recourse to the secular arm, and to invoke the aid of sword and lance. The clergy, finding that passive resistance did not wear out the zeal of their persecutors, that the storm promised to be endless, and warned by the fate of the Milanese, were prepared to adopt an aggressive policy, and to seek their safety in revolutionising the central authority. Perhaps the bishops, whose silence had been secured by the toleration so distasteful to Damiani, began to feel the pressure which he was bringing to bear upon them, and to look forward with apprehension to the unknown evils of the future. If so, they were ready to make common cause with their flocks, and throw into the scale the immense influence due to their sacred character and temporal power. Thus only the occasion was wanting for an open rupture, and that occasion was furnished by the death of Nicholas in July 1061.

The factions of the day had alienated a powerful portion of the Roman barons from the papal party as represented by Hildebrand. They at once united with the Lombard clergy in sending a deputation to the young Henry IV, who was still under the tutelage of his mother Agnes, offering him a golden crown and the title of Patrician. The empire was not indisposed to vindicate its old prerogatives, recently annulled by the initial act of Nicholas limiting the right of papal election to the Roman clergy. The overtures were therefore welcomed, and while Anselmo, Bishop of Lucca, was chosen in Rome, October 1st, 1061, assuming the name of Alexander II, on the 28th of the same month a rival election took place in Germany, by which Cadalus, Bishop of Parma, was invested with the perilous dignity of Anti-pope, and divided the allegiance of Christendom under the title of Honorius II. At least two Italian bishops lent their suffrages to these proceedings—those of Vercelli and

Piacenza—as representatives of the Lombard interest; and, if the testimony of Damiani is to be believed, they were men whose dissolute lives fitly represented the licence which the reformers asserted to be the principal object of the schismatics.

The married or concubinary clergy were now no longer merely isolated criminals, to be punished more or less severely for infractions of discipline. They were a united body, who boldly proclaimed the correctness of their course, and defended themselves by argument as well as by political intrigues and military operations. They thus became offenders of a far deeper dye, for the principles of the Church led irrevocably to the conclusion, paradoxical as it may seem, that he who was guilty of immorality, knowing it to be wrong, was far less criminal than he who married, believing it to be right. What before had been a transgression, to be redeemed by penance and repentance, became heresy—an awful word in those fierce times. The odious name of Nicolites was speedily fastened on the schismatics, and the Apocalyptic denunciations of St. John were universally held applicable to them. According to Damiani, they supported Cadalus in the expectation that his success would lead to a modification in the discipline of the Church, by which the licence to marry would be accorded to all ecclesiastics.

That support was efficient, and it was shortly needed. A revolution suddenly occurred in the politics of Germany. Some dissatisfied nobles and prelates conspired to obtain power by overthrowing the regency of the dowager Empress Agnes. A stroke of daring treachery put them in possession of the person of the boy-king, and the arch-conspirator, Hanno of Cologne, earned his canonisation by reversing at once the policy of the previous administration. In a solemn council held at Osber in 1062, the pretensions of Cadalus were repudiated, and Alexander II was recognised as pope. Still Cadalus did not despair, but with the aid of the Lombard clergy he raised forces and marched on Rome, relying on his adherents within the walls. They admitted him into the Leonine city, where he threw himself into the impregnable castle of Sant' Angelo. Immediately besieged by the Romans, he resolutely held out for two years, in spite of incredible privations, but at length he sought safety in flight with but a single follower. Meanwhile his party, as a political body, had become broken up, and though Henry, Archbishop of Ravenna, still adhered to him, he was powerless to maintain his claims. Finally, in 1067, Alexander held a council at Mantua, cleared his election of imputed irregularity, and was universally recognised.

During this period the " Nicolitan " clergy by no means abandoned their tenets. In 1063, as soon as he could feel reasonably assured of his eventual success, Alexander assembled more than a hundred bishops in council at Rome, where he emphatically repeated the canon promulgated in 1059 by Nicholas II, which was not only a proclamation of his fidelity to the cause of reform, but an admission that the legislation of his predecessor had thus far proved fruitless. Damiani, also, laboured unceasingly with argument and exhortation, but the vehemence of his declamation only shows how widely extended and how powerful the heresy still was. We shall see hereafter that on a mission to Milan, to reduce the married clergy to obedience, he barely escaped with his life; and on another to Lodi, with the same object, the schismatics, after exhausting argument, in support of priestly marriage, threatened him with arms in their hands, and again his saintly dignity came near being enhanced by the honours of martyrdom. Even the restriction upon second marriages was occasionally lost sight of, and such most irregular unions were celebrated with all the ceremony and rejoicings that were customary among laymen in their public nuptials. Yet, notwithstanding the pious fervour which habitually stigmatised the wives as harlots and the husbands as unbridled adulterers, Damiani himself allows us to see that the marriage relation was preserved with thorough fidelity on the part of the women, and was compatible with learning, decency, and strict attention to religious duty by the men. Urging the wives to quit their husbands, he finds it necessary to combat their scruples at breaking what was to them a solemn engagement, fortified with all legal provisions and religious rites, but which he pronounces a frivolous and meaningless ceremony. So, in deploring the habitual practice of marriage among the Piedmontese clergy, he regards it as the only blot upon men who otherwise appeared to him as a chorus of angels, and as shining lights in the Church.

Such considerations as these, however, had no influence in diminishing Damiani's zeal. To Cunibert, Bishop of Turin, whose spiritual flock he thus so much admired, he addressed, about 1065, an epistle reproaching him with his criminal laxity in permitting such transgressions in his diocese, and urging him strenuously to undertake the reform which was so necessary to the purity of the Church. Cunibert apparently did not respond to the exhortation, for Damiani proceeded to appeal to the temporal sovereign of Savoy and Piedmont, Adelaide, widow of Humbert-aux-Blanches-Mains, who was then regent. In an elaborate epistle he urges her to attack the wives, while her bishops shall coerce the husbands; but if the latter neglect that duty, he invites her to interpose with the secular power, and thus avert from her house and her country the divine wrath which must else overtake them. That so strict a Churchman as Damiani should not only tolerate but advise the exercise of temporal authority over ecclesiastics, and this, too, in a matter purely ecclesiastical, shows how completely the one idea had become dominant in his mind, since he was willing to sacrifice to it the privileges and immunities for which the Church had been struggling, by fair means and foul, for six centuries. It would appear, moreover, that this was not the first time that potentates had been allowed, or had assumed, to exercise power in the matter, for Damiani cautions the Countess Adelaide not to follow the example of some evil-minded magnates and make the pretence of reformation an excuse for spoiling the Church.

The zeal of the indefatigable Damiani continued to be as unconquerable as the stubbornness of his adversaries, and some two years later we find him again at work. The date of 1067 is generally attributed to a letter which he addressed to Peter, Cardinal Archpriest of the Lateran, stimulating him to renewed exertions in extirpating this foul disgrace to the Church, and arguing at great length in reply to the reasons and excuses with which the clerical Benedicks continued to defend their vile heresy.

In all this controversy, it is instructive to observe how Damiani shows himself to be the pure model of monkish asceticism, untainted by any practical wisdom and unwarped by any earthly considerations. When Hildebrand struggled for sacerdotal celibacy, the shrewdness of the serpent guided the innocence of the dove, and he fought for what he knew would prove a weapon of tremendous power in securing for the Church the theocracy which was his pure ideal of human institutions. Not a thought of the worldly advantages consequent upon the reform appears to have crossed the mind of Damiani. To him it was simply a matter of conscience that the ministers of Christ should be adorned with the austere purity through which alone lay the path to salvation. Accordingly, the arguments which he employs in his endless disputations carefully avoid the practical reasons which were the principal motive for enforcing celibacy. His main reliance is on the assumption that, as Christ was born of a virgin, so He should be served and the Eucharist be handled only by virgins; and his subsidiary logic consists of mystical interpretations of passages in the Jewish history of the Old Testament. Phineas, of course, affords a favourite and oft-repeated argument and illustration. Allusions to Ahimelech can also be understood, but the reasoning based upon the tower of Sichem, the linen girdle of Jeremiah, and the catastrophe of Cain and Abel is convincing only as to the unworldliness of the recluse of Avellana.

Notwithstanding all his learning and eloquence, the authority of his name, the lustre of his example, and the tireless efforts of his fiery energy, the cause to which he had devoted himself did not advance. The later years of Alexander's pontificate afford unmistakable indications that the puritan party were becoming discouraged; that they were disposed to abate some of their demands, and were ready to make concessions to the refractory spirit which refused obedience both in principle and in practice. Thus, in 1068, a decretal addressed to the authorities of Dalmatia merely threatens suspension until satisfaction is made by those who marry in orders or who refuse to abandon their wives. A somewhat different position was taken with the Venetians. An epistle to the Patriarch of Grado orders the deprivation of those who live in open and undisguised concubinage, but significantly confines its penalties to notorious infractions of the rule, and leaves to God the investigation of such as may be prudently concealed. This manifests a willingness to temporise with offenders whose respect for papal authority would induce them to abstain from defiant disobedience—a pusillanimous tempting of hypocrisy to which the bolder Hildebrand could never have given his consent.   A principle of great importance, moreover, was abandoned when, in 1070, Alexander assented to the consecration of the bishop-elect of Le Mans, who was the son of a priest; and when he stated that this was not a precedent for the future, but merely a concession to the evil of the times, his laxity was the more impressive, since he thus admitted his violation of the canons.   He subsequently even enlarged this special permission into a general rule, with merely the saving clause that the proposed incumbent should be more worthy than his competitors. Alexander, moreover, maintained in force the ancient rule that no married man could assume monastic vows unless his wife gave her free consent, and entered a convent at the same time.   We shall see that in little more than half a century the progress of sacerdotalism rendered the sacrament of marriage powerless in comparison with the vows of religion.

Alexander clearly had not in him the stuff of which persecutors and reformers are made, as, indeed, his merciful liberality in extending over the Jews throughout Europe the protection of the Holy See would sufficiently demonstrate.   At length he, too, was released from earthly cares, and on the day after his decease, on April 22nd, 1073, his place was filled by the man who of all others was the most perfect impersonation of the aggressive churchmanship of the age.

Before proceeding, however, to sketch the stormy pontificate of Hildebrand in its relation to our subject, I must pause to relate the episode of the Milanese clergy. The struggle in that city to enforce the ascetic principles of the reformers gives so perfect an inside view of the reformation itself, and its various stages have been handed down to us with so much minuteness by contemporary writers, that it deserves to be treated by itself as a separate whole.

CHAPTER XIII

MILAN

In the primitive ages of the Church, Milan was at the head of the Northern Vicariate of Italy, as Rome was of the Southern. When the predominance of the latter city became established, the glory of St. Ambrose shed a lustre over his capital which the true Milanese fondly regarded as rivalling that of St. Peter, and the superiority of Rome was grudgingly admitted. In the eleventh century, Milan is found occupying the chief place among the Lombard cities, virtually governed by its archbishop, whose temporal as well as spiritual power rendered his position one of great influence and importance. Yet even at that early period the republican spirit was already developed, and the city was divided into factions, as the nobles and citizens struggled for alternate supremacy.

Milan was, moreover, the headquarters of the hidden Manichæism which, after surviving centuries of persecution in the East, was now secretly invading Europe through Bulgaria, and had already attracted the vigilant attention of the Church in localities widely separated. Its earliest open manifestation was in Toulouse, in 1018; at Orleans, in 1023, King Robert the Pious caused numerous sectaries to expiate their heresy at the stake, where their unshrinking zeal excited general wonder. At Cambrai and Liège similar measures of repression became necessary in 1025; the Emperor Henry III endeavoured at Goslar, in 1052, to put an end to them with the gallows; and traces of them are to be found at Agen about the year 1100; at Soissons in 1114; at Toulouse in 1118; at Cologne in 1146; at Périgord in 1147; in England in 1166, until we can trace their connection with the Albigenses, whose misfortunes fill so black a page in the history of the thirteenth century. Calling themselves Cathari, and stigmatised by true believers under various opprobrious names, of which the commonest was Paterins, their doctrines were those of the ancient Manichæans, their most characteristic tenets being belief in the dualistic principle, and the abhorrence of animal food and of marriage. The prevalence of these dogmas among the Milanese populace furnishes a probable explanation of much that took place during the contest between Rome and the married priests.

Eriberto di Arzago, who filled the archiepiscopal chair of Milan from 1019 to 1045, was one of the most powerful princes of Italy, and though unsuccessful in the revolt which he organised in 1034 against the Emperor Conrad the Salic, his influence was scarcely diminished after his return from the expulsion which punished his rebellion. At the time of his death, Milan was passing through one of its accustomed civil dissensions. The Motta, or body of burgesses, had quarrelled with the nobles and archbishop, and, under the leadership of an apostate noble named Lanzo, had expelled them from the city—an ejection which was followed by an unsuccessful siege of three years. At length, in 1044, Lanzo obtained promise of armed assistance from Henry III, which reduced the nobles to subjection, and they returned in peace. Eriberto died the following year, and the election of his successor caused great excitement. Erlembaldo, the popular chief (*dominus populi*), called the citizens together to nominate candidates, and induced them to select four. One of these was Landolfo Cotta, a notary of the sacred palace, who was brother to Erlembaldo; another was Anselmo di Badagio, Cardinal of the Milanese Church, subsequently Bishop of Lucca, and finally, as we have seen, pope, under the name of Alexander II; the third was Arialdo, of the family of the capitanei of Carinate; and the fourth was Otho, another Milanese cardinal. These four were sent to the emperor, for him to make his selection; but the faction of the nobles despatched a rival in the person of Guido di Valate, who already held the appointment of secretary from the emperor, and who had recommended himself by zealous services, which now claimed their reward. Henry gave the coveted dignity to Guido, to the great surprise and indignation of the popular nominees. Their expostulations were unavailing, and both parties returned—Guido to assume an office harassed by the opposition of the people on whom he had been forced, and the disappointed candidates to brood over the wrongs which had deprived them of the splendid prize. We shall see how thoroughly three of those candidates avenged themselves.

It is observable from this transaction that Milan was completely independent of Rome. The sovereignty of the distant emperor, absorbed in the dissensions of Germany, could press but lightly on the powerful and turbulent city. Rome was not even thought of in creating the archbishop, whose spiritual and temporal power was granted by the imperial investiture. But when, soon after, the German popes had rescued the papacy from the contempt into which it had fallen, its domination over Milan became a necessary step in its progress to universal supremacy, and lent additional vigour to the desires of the reformers to restore the forgotten discipline of the Church in a city so influential.

Marriage at this time was a universal privilege of the Milanese clergy. If we may believe the testimony of one who was almost a contemporary, the candidate for holy orders was strictly examined as to his learning and morals. These being satisfactory, he was, if unmarried, asked if he had strength to remain so, and if he replied in the negative, he could forthwith betroth himself and marry with the ordinary legal and religious ceremonies. Second marriages were not allowed, and the Levitical law as to the virginity of the bride was strictly observed. Those who remained single were objects of suspicion, while those who performed their sacred functions duly, and brought up their families in the fear of God, were respected and obeyed by their flocks as pastors should be, and were eligible to the episcopate. Concubinage was regarded as a heinous offence, and those guilty of it were debarred from all promotion—in this reversing the estimate placed upon the respective infractions of discipline by the Roman Church.

The see of Lucca consoled Anselmo di Badagio for the failure of his aspirations towards the archiepiscopate, and the other disappointed candidates for a while cherished their mortification in silence. Landolfo and Arialdo were inclined to asceticism, and a visit which Anselmo paid to Milan stimulated them to undertake a reform which could not but prove a source of endless trouble to their successful competitor Guido. Leaders of the people, and masters of

the art of inflaming popular passion, they caused assemblies
to be held in which they inveighed in the strongest terms
against the irregularities of the clergy, whose sacraments
they stigmatised as the foulest corruption, whose churches
they denounced as dens of prostitution, and whose property
they assumed to be legitimate prey for the spoiler. Guido
in vain endeavoured to repress the agitation thus produced,
argued in favour of the married clergy, and was sustained
by the party of nobles. In a city like Milan, it was not
difficult to excite a tumult. Besides the influence of the
perennial factions, ever eager to tear each other's throats,
the populace were ready to yield to the eloquence of the
bold reformers. The Manichæan heresy had taken deep
root among the masses, who, afraid to declare their
damnable doctrines openly, rejoiced in any way to undermine the authority of the priesthood, and whose views
were in accordance with those now broached on the
subject of marriage. While these motives would urge
forward the serious portion of the citizens, the unthinking
rabble would naturally be prompt to embrace any cause
which promised a prospect of disturbance and plunder.
Party lines were quickly drawn, and if the reformers were
able to revive a forgotten scandal by stigmatising their
opponents as Nicolites, the party of the clergy and the
nobles had their revenge. The meetings of Landolfo and
Arialdo were held in a spot called Pataria, whence they
soon became known as Paterins—a term which for centuries
continued to be of fearful import, as synonymous with
Manichæans.

Matters could not long remain in this condition. During
an altercation in the church of San Celso, a hot-headed
priest assaulted Arialdo, whom Landolfo extricated from
the crowd at considerable personal risk. Thereupon the
reformers called the people together in the theatre; inflam-
matory addresses speedily wrought up the popular passions
to ungovernable fury; the priests were turned out of their
churches, their houses sacked, their persons maltreated,
and they were finally obliged to purchase a suspension of
oppression by subscribing a paper binding themselves to
chastity. The nobles, far from being able to protect the
clergy, finding themselves also in danger, sought safety in
flight; while the rabble, having exhausted the support
derivable from intramural plunder, spread over the country

and repeated in the villages the devastations of priestly property which they had committed in Milan.

The suffering clergy applied for relief to the bishops of the province, and finding none, at length appealed to Rome itself. Stephen IX, who then filled the papal chair, authorised the archbishop to hold a synod for the purpose of restoring peace. It met, in the early part of 1058, at Fontaneto, near Novaro. The prelates were unanimous in sustaining their clergy, and the reformers Landolfo and Arialdo were excommunicated without a dissentient voice. They disregarded the interdict, however, redoubled their efforts with the people, whom they bound by a solemn oath to adhere to the sacred cause, and even forced the priests to join in the compact. Arialdo then proceeded to Rome, where he developed in full the objects of the movement, and pointed out that it would not only result in restoring purity and discipline, but might also be used to break down the dangerous independence of the Ambrosian Church and reduce it to the subjection which it owed and refused to the apostolic see. The arguments were convincing, the excommunication was removed, and Arialdo returned to his work with zeal more fiery than ever.

Meanwhile the nobles had taken heart and offered armed resistance to the Patarian faction, resulting in incessant fights and increasing bloodshed. Nicholas II, who by this time had succeeded Stephen IX, sent Hildebrand and Anselmo di Badagio on a mission to Milan, with instructions to allay the passions which led to such deplorable results, and, while endeavouring to uphold the rules of discipline, to pacify if possible the people, and to arrange such a basis of reconciliation as might restore peace to the distracted Church. The milder Anselmo might perhaps have succeeded in this errand of charity, but the unbending Hildebrand was not likely to listen to aught but unconditional subjection to the canons and to Rome. The quarrel therefore waxed fiercer and deadlier; the turmoil became more inextricable as daily combats embittered both parties, and the missionaries departed, leaving Guido with scarcely a shadow of authority over his rebellious city, and the seeds of discord more widely scattered and more deeply planted than ever.

Again in 1059 a papal legation was sent with full authority to force the recalcitrant clergy to submission.

Anselmo again returned to his native city, accompanied this time by Peter Damiani. Their presence and their pretensions caused a fearful tumult, in which Damiani and Landolfo were in deadly peril. An assembly was at length held, where the legates asserted the papal pre-eminence by taking the place of honour, to the general indignation of the Milanese, who did not relish the degradation of their archbishop before the representatives of a foreign prelate. The question in debate hinged upon the authority of Rome, which was stoutly denied by the Lombards. Peter, in a long oration, showed that Rome had Christianised the rest of Western Europe, and that St. Ambrose himself had invoked the papal power as superior to his own. The pride of the Ambrosian Church gave way, and the supremacy of St. Peter was finally acknowledged. This granted, the rest followed as a matter of course, and the heretical errors of simony and marriage had to be abandoned. Peter thought himself merciful in his triumph; where all alike were guilty, punishment for the past became impossible, and he restricted himself to provisions for the future. The archbishop and his clergy signed a paper expressing their contrition in the most humiliating terms, and binding themselves and their successors, under penalty of eternal damnation, to render simony thereafter unknown. As regards the Nicolitan heresy, a significant caution was observed, for its extirpation was only promised in as far as it should be found possible; and when Arnolfo, the nephew of Guido, swore for his uncle that in future monks should be the only persons ordained without a preliminary oath that no money had been paid or received, it is observable that the maintenance of chastity was discreetly passed over. Then the archbishop and his clergy swore, in the hands of Damiani at the altar, their faithful observance of the pledge to destroy the simoniacal and Nicolitan heresies, under penalties the most tremendous; and Guido, prostrating himself on the ground, humbly deplored his negligence in the past, imposed on himself a penitence of a hundred years (redeemable at a certain sum per annum), and vowed a pilgrimage to Santiago de Compostella to atone for his sin. Not content with this, Damiani mounted the pulpit and made both priests and people take an oath to extirpate both heresies; and the clergy, before being reconciled to the Church and restored to the positions which they had forfeited by their contumacy, were forced individually, under oath, to anathematise all heresies, and especially those of simony and marriage. A penance was imposed on every one involved in simony—no allusion being made to those who were married; some, who were manifestly unfit for their sacred duties, were suspended, and the legates returned, after triumphantly accomplishing the objects of their mission.

If Damiani fancied that argumentative subtlety and paper promises, even though solemnly given in the name of God and all His saints, were to settle a question involving the fiercest passions of men, the cloistered saint knew little of human nature. The pride of the Milanese was deeply wounded by a subjection to Rome, unknown for many generations, and ill endured by men who gloried in the ancient dignity of the Ambrosian Church. When, therefore, in 1061, their townsman, Anselmo di Badagio, was elevated from the episcopate of Lucca to that of the Holy See, Milan, in common with the rest of Lombardy, eagerly embraced the cause of the anti-pope Cadalus. One of Anselmo's earliest acts as pope was to address a letter to the Milanese, affectionately exhorting them to amendment, and expressing a hope that his pontificate was to witness an extinction of the heresies which had distracted and degraded the Church. He can scarcely have entertained the confidence which he expressed, for though Landolfo and Arialdo endeavoured, with unabated zeal, to enforce the canons, the Nicolitan faction, regardless of the pledges given to Damiani, maintained the conquest with equal stubbornness. Landolfo, on a mission to Rome, was attacked at Piacenza, wounded, and forced to return. Soon after this he was prostrated by a pulmonary affection, lost his voice, and died after a lingering illness of two years. The Paterins, thus deprived of their leader, found another in the person of his brother, Erlembaldo, just then returned from a pilgrimage to the Holy Land. Gifted with every knightly accomplishment, valiant in war, sagacious in council, of a commanding presence, and endowed with eloquence to sway the passions of the multitude, he was the impersonation of a popular leader; while, in the cause to which he was now called, his deep religious convictions lent an attraction which was heightened by an unpardonable personal wrong—for, early in life, he had been betrothed to a young girl, who fell under the seductive wiles of an unprincipled priest. Yet Erlembaldo did not embark in civil strife without a hesitation which reflects honour on his character. He refused at first, but was persuaded to seek counsel of the pope. Arialdo accompanied him to Rome, and urged Alexander to adopt him as military leader in the war against sacerdotal marriage. Alexander, too, shrank from the responsibility of authorising war in such a cause, but Arialdo sought the assistance of Hildebrand, and the scruples of the pope were removed by the prospect of asserting the authority of Rome. When Erlembaldo heard the commands of the vicegerent of God, and received a sacred banner to be borne through the expected battles, he could no longer doubt as to his duty. He accepted the mission, and to it he devoted his life.

Returning to Milan with this sanction, the zeal and military experience of Erlembaldo soon made themselves felt. He enrolled secretly all the young men whom persuasion, threats, or promises could induce to follow his standard, and thus supported by an organised body, he endeavoured to enforce the decretals inhibiting simony and marriage. All recalcitrant priests presuming to officiate were torn from the altars. The riots, which seem to have ceased for a time, became, with varying fortune, more numerous and alarming than ever, and the persecution of the clergy was greatly intensified. Guido at length, after vainly endeavouring to uphold and protect the sacerdotal body, was driven from the city, and the popular reformers seemed at last to have carried their point, after a civil war which had now lasted, with short intervals, for nearly ten years.

As though to confirm the victory, Arialdo, in 1066, at a council held in Rome, procured the excommunication of his archbishop, Guido, with which he returned triumphantly to Milan. Some popular revolution among the factions, however, had brought Guido back to the city, where he maintained a precarious position. Disregarding the excommunication, he resolved to officiate in the solemn services of Pentecost (June 4th, 1066), and, braving all opposition, he appeared at the altar. Excited to fury at this unexpected contumacy, the popular party, led on by Erlembaldo and Arialdo, attacked him in the church; his followers rallied in his defence, but after a stubborn fight were forced to leave him in the hands of his enemies, by whom he was beaten nearly to death. Shocked by this outrage, many of the citizens abandoned the party of the reformers, and the nobles, taking advantage of the revulsion of feeling, again had the ascendancy. Arialdo was obliged to fly for his life, and endeavoured to conceal himself, travelling only by night. The avengers were close upon his track, however; he was betrayed by a priest, and the satellites of Guido carried him to an island in Lago Maggiore, where (27 June, 1066) they put him to death, with all the refinement of cruelty. A series of miracles prevented the attempted concealment of the martyred corpse, and ten months later Erlembaldo recovered it, fresh and untouched by corruption. Carried to Milan, it was interred with stately pomp in the monastery of San Celso, where the miracles wrought at his tomb proclaimed the sanctity of him who had died for the faith, and ere long his canonisation formally enrolled St. Arialdo in the calendar of saints.

Erlembaldo for a while remained quiet, but in secret he reconstructed his party, and, undaunted by the fate of his associate, he suddenly renewed the civil strife. Successful at first, he forced the clergy to bind themselves by fresh oaths, and expelled Guido again from the city; but the clerical party recovered its strength, and the war was carried on with varying fortune, until, in 1067, Alexander II despatched another legation with orders to harmonise, if possible, the endless strife. Cardinals Mainardo and Minuto appear to have been sincerely desirous of reconciling the angry factions. They proclaimed an amnesty, and promulgated a constitution which protected the clergy from abuse and persecution, and though they decreed suspension for married and concubinary priests, they required that none should be punished on suspicion, and laid down such regulations for trial as gave great prospect of immunity. There must have been pressing necessity for some such regulations, if we may believe the assertion of Landolfo that when Erlembaldo found his funds running low he appointed thirty judges to examine all ecclesiastics in holy orders. Those who could not procure twelve conjurators to swear with them on the Gospels as to their immaculate purity since ordination had all their property confiscated. At the same time, the rabble used to prowl around at night and throw female ornaments and articles of apparel into priests' houses; then, breaking open the doors, they would proclaim the criminality of the inmates, and plunder everything that they could lay their hands on.

Moderate men of both parties, wearied with the unceasing strife, eagerly hailed the accommodation proposed by the papal legates, and rejoiced at the prospect of peace. Erlembaldo, however, was dissatisfied, and, visiting Rome, soon aroused a fresh cause of quarrel. At the suggestion of Hildebrand he started the portentous question of investitures, and on his return he endeavoured to force both clergy and laity to take an oath that in future their archbishops should apply to the pope, and not to the emperor, for confirmation—thus securing a chief devoted to the cause of reform. Guido sought to anticipate this movement, and in 1069, old and wearied with the unending contention, he resigned his archbishopric to the subdeacon Gotefrido, who had long been his principal adviser. The latter procured his confirmation from Henry IV, but the Milanese, defrauded of their electoral privileges, refused to recognise him. Erlembaldo was not slow to take advantage of the popular feeling; a tumult was readily excited, and Gotefrido was glad to escape at night from the rebellious city. Guido added fresh confusion by asserting that he had been deceived by Gotefrido, and by endeavouring to resume his see. To this end he made a treaty with Erlembaldo, but that crafty chieftain, obtaining possession of his person, imprisoned him in the monastery of San Celso, and then proceeded to besiege Gotefrido in Castiglione. The new archbishop defended himself bravely, until, in 1071, Erlembaldo was forced to abandon the enterprise.

Meanwhile another aspirant, Azzo, installed by Erlembaldo, fared no better than his rivals. The people, unbidden guests, rushed in to his inaugural banquet, unearthed him in the corner where he had hidden himself, dragged him by the heels into the street, and, placing him in a pulpit, forced him to swear that he would make no further pretensions to the see; while the papal legate, who had presided over the solemnities, was glad to escape with his life. Azzo, however, was recognised by Rome; he was released from the obligation of his oath, and money was furnished to enable him to maintain his quarrel. On the other hand, Henry IV sent assistance to Gotefrido, which enabled him to carry on the campaign with some vigour; but he was unable to obtain a foothold in Milan. Azzo fled to Rome, and the city remained without an archbishop and under an interdict launched in 1074 by Hildebrand, who, in April 1073, had succeeded Alexander II.

The Milanese were disposed to disregard the interdict, while Erlembaldo, who now held undisputed command of the city—and, indeed, of almost all Lombardy—used every effort to enforce respect for it. At length, at Easter 1075, he resolutely prevented the solemnisation of the sacred rites, and cast out the holy chrism which the priests had persisted in preparing. This roused the populace to resistance; both parties flew to arms, and at the very commencement of the fray Erlembaldo fell mortally wounded under the shade of the papal banner, which was still the emblem of his cause, and in virtue of which he was canonised as a saintly martyr to the faith. The Milanese, sinking all past animosities, united in promptly sending an embassy to Henry IV to congratulate him on the death of the common enemy, and to request the appointment of another bishop. To this he responded by nominating Tedaldo, who was duly consecrated, notwithstanding the pretensions of his competitors, Gotefrido and Azzo. Tedaldo was the leader of the disaffected bishops who, at the Synod of Pavia in 1076, excommunicated Pope Gregory himself; and though, after the interview at Canossa in 1077, the Lombards, disgusted with Henry's voluntary humiliation before that papal power which they had learned to despise, abandoned the imperialists for a time, yet Tedaldo kept his seat until his death in 1085, notwithstanding the repeated excommunications launched against him by Gregory.

In the later years of this long and bloody controversy it is evident that the political element greatly complicated the religious ground of quarrel—that pope and emperor without made use of burgher and noble within, and the latter took sides, as respects simony and sacerdotal marriage, to further the ends of individual ambition. Still, the disputed points of discipline were the ostensible causes of the struggle, whatever might be the private aims of civic factions, or of imperial and papal rivals; and these points gave a keener purpose to the strife, and furnished an inexhaustible supply of recruits to each contending faction. Thus, about the year 1070, a conference took place at Milan between priests deputed by both sides, in which the question of marriage was argued as earnestly as though it were the source of all the intestine troubles. So when, in 1073, Gregory, shortly after his accession, addressed letters to Erlembaldo urging him to persevere in the good work, and to the Lombard bishops commanding them to assist him, the object of his labours is assumed to be the extirpation of simony and the restoration of the clergy to the purity becoming their sacred office. And when, in 1076, the schismatic bishops, under the lead of Tedaldo of Milan, met in council at Pavia to renounce all obedience to Gregory, one of the articles of accusation brought against him was that he separated husbands and wives, and preferred licentiousness to marriage, thus giving, in their grounds of complaint against him, especial prominence to his zeal for the introduction of celibacy.

Yet at last the question of sacerdotal marriage sank out of sight when the civil broils of Milan merged into the European quarrel between the empire and papacy. When, in 1093, Henry IV was driven out of Italy by the revolt of his son Conrad, and the latter was created King of Lombardy by Urban II and the Countess Matilda, the dependence of the young king upon the pope rendered impossible any further open defiance of the laws of the Church, and public marriage there, as elsewhere, was doubtless replaced by secret immorality. The triumph of the sacerdotal party was consummated at the great Council of Piacenza, held by Urban II in February 1095, to which prelates flocked from every part of Europe and the people gathered in immense numbers. If, as the chronicler informs us, four thousand ecclesiastics and thirty thousand laymen assembled on the occasion, and the sessions were held in the open air because no building could contain the thronging masses, we may reasonably attribute so unprecedented an assemblage to the wild religious ardour which was about to culminate in the first Crusade. That council condemned Nicolitism in the most absolute and peremptory manner, and there is no reason to believe that the power of so formidable a demonstration was lightly disregarded. Yet in Milan, as we shall see elsewhere throughout Europe, the custom of sacerdotal marriage had become so thoroughly established that it could not be eradicated suddenly. It continued to survive stubbornly after every attempt at repression with more or less openness as the persecution of married priests was more or less severe. A synod held in Milan in 1098 is discreetly silent as to wedlock or concubinage among ecclesiastics, though it is severe upon the concurrent vice of simony, and though its prohibition of hereditary succession in Church benefices and dignities would show that marriage among their incumbents must have been by no means infrequent. Moreover, even as late as 1152, Mainerio Boccardo, a canon of Monza, in his will specifies that certain provisions for the benefit of his brother canons shall not be enjoyed by those who are married, thus proving that the Hildebrandine reforms had not yet been successful, though Rome had long since attained its object in breaking down the independence of the Ambrosian Church. One result of the struggle had been the destruction of the temporal power of the archbishop and the conversion of the city into a republic, an example which was largely followed throughout Upper Italy.

It is not to be supposed that the story of Milan is an exceptional one. Perhaps the factions there were fiercer, and the contest more prolonged, than elsewhere; but the same causes were at work in other Italian cities, and were attended with results similar in character, if differing in intensity. In Lucca, for instance, in 1051, we find Leo IX, when confirming the possessions of the canons of the cathedral church of St. Martin, expressing the hope that God would liberate them from their married priests, who dissipated the property of the foundation, while being utterly unworthy to partake of the divine oblation. His desire that they would live in concord and harmony with their bishop was, however, not destined to be long gratified. When St. Anselmo, in 1073, accepted the episcopate at the urgent request of his friend, Gregory VII, he laboured for years to reform the dissolute lives of his clergy, until at length, finding threats and expostulations alike ineffectual, he implored the intervention of the Countess Matilda. Even the sovereign of Tuscany was unable to accomplish the submission of the recalcitrant ecclesiastics, and in 1074 St. Anselmo took advantage of the presence of Gregory VII in the city to invoke his interposition. The resolute pope, finding his personal efforts fruitless, summoned the offenders to trial before a court of bishops, presided over by the celebrated Pietro Igneo, Bishop of Albano. Being condemned and excommunicated, they resisted by force of arms, excited a rebellion in the city, drove out St. Anselmo, and joined the imperialists; and when, in 1081, Guiberto the anti-pope came to Italy, he consecrated their leader, a sub-deacon named Pietro, as bishop, in place of the exiled martyr. In Piacenza, the schismatics were guilty of excesses more deplorable, for, not content with deposing Bonizo, who had been set over them as bishop, they gave him the fullest honours of martyrdom by plucking out his eyes and then cutting him to pieces. Similar troubles occurred in Parma, Modena, Reggio, and Pistoia, and it was not until the death of their respective schismatic bishops that the Countess Matilda was able to recover her authority in those places.

CHAPTER XIV

HILDEBRAND

ALEXANDER II died 21 April, 1073, and within twenty four hours the archdeacon Hildebrand was elected as his successor—a promptitude and unanimity which showed the general recognition of his fitness for the high office. For more than twenty years he had been the power behind the throne which had directed and given purpose to the policy of Rome, and the assertion of his biographers that his disinclination for the position had alone prevented his previous elevation may readily be believed. Whether he was forced on the present occasion to assent to the choice of the conclave against his earnest resistance is, however, more problematical.

Hildebrand was the son of a poor carpenter of Soano, and had been trained in the ascetic monachism of Cluny. Gifted by nature with rare sagacity, unbending will, and indomitable spirit, imbued with the principles of the False Decretals, and firmly believing in the wildest pretensions of ecclesiastical supremacy, he had conceived a scheme of hierarchical autocracy, which he regarded not only as the imprescriptible right of the Church, but also as the perfection of human institutions. To the realisation of this ideal he devoted his life with a fiery zeal and unshaken purpose that shrank from no obstacles, and to it he was ready to sacrifice not only the men who stood in his path, but also the immutable principles of truth and justice. All considerations were as dross compared with the one object, and his own well-being and life were ventured as recklessly as the peace of the world.

Such a man could comprehend the full importance of the rule of celibacy, not alone as essential to the ascetic purity of the Church, but as necessary to the theocratic structure which he proposed to elevate on the ruins of kingdoms and empires. The priest must be a man set apart from his fellows, consecrated to the one holy purpose, reverenced by the world as a being superior to human passions and frailties, devoted, soul and body, to the interests of the Church, and distracted by no temporal cares and anxieties foreign to the welfare of the great corporation of which he was a member. We have seen the strenuous efforts which, for a quarter of a century, successive pontiffs had unceasingly made to accomplish this reform, and we have also seen how fruitlessly those efforts were expended on the passive or active resistance of the priesthood. When Hildebrand took the reins into his vigorous grasp, the change at once became manifest, and the zeal of his predecessors appears lukewarm by comparison. He had had ample leisure to note how inefficient was the ordinary machinery to accomplish the result, and he did not hesitate to call to his assistance external powers; to give to the secular princes authority over ecclesiastics at which enthusiastic Churchmen stood aghast, and to risk apparently the most precious immunities of the Church to secure the result. The end proved his wisdom, for the power delegated to the laity for a special object was readily withdrawn, after it had served its purpose, and the rebellious clerks were subdued and rendered fit instruments in the lapse of time for humiliating their temporary masters. In one respect, however, Hildebrand's policy proved a blunder. The faithful readily submitted to the restoration of clerical immunity, but the idea that ecclesiastics forfeited their privileges by sin became a favourite one with almost all heretics, as we shall see hereafter in the case of the Albigenses, Waldenses, Wickliffites, and Hussites, costing the Church many a desperate struggle.

To Gregory, as we must hereafter call him, was generally attributed, by his immediate successors, the honour of introducing, or of enforcing, the absolute chastity of the ministers of the altar. Some chroniclers mention Alexander II or Leo IX as participating in the struggle, but to his vigorous management its success was popularly conceded. He earned the tribute thoroughly, for during his whole pontificate it seems to have been ever present to his thoughts, and whatever were his preoccupations in his fearful struggle with the empire, in which he risked the present and the future of the papacy, he always had leisure to attend to the one subject in its minutest details and in the remotest corner of Christendom.

Perhaps in this there may have been an unrecognised motive urging him to action. Sprung from so humble an origin, he may have sympathised with the democratic element, which rendered the Church the only career open to peasant and plebeian. He may have felt that this was a source of hidden power, as binding the populations more closely to the Church, and as enabling it to press into service an unknown amount of fresh and vigorous talent belonging to men who would owe everything to the establishment which had raised them from nothingness, and who would have no relationships to embarrass their devotion. All this would be lost if, by legalising marriage, the hereditary transmission of benefices generally resulting should convert the Church into a separate caste of individual proprietors, having only general interests in common, and lazily luxuriating on the proceeds of former popular beneficence. To us, retrospectively philosophising, it further appears evident that if celibacy were an efficient agent in obtaining for the Church the immense temporal power and spiritual authority which it enjoyed, that very power and that authority rendered celibacy a factor not devoid of advantage to the progress of civilisation. When even the humblest priest came to be regarded as a superior being, holding the keys of heaven in his hand, and by the machinery of confession, absolution, and excommunication wielding incalculable influence over each member of his flock, it was well for both parties that the ecclesiastic should be free from the ties of family and the vulgar ambition of race. It is easy to see how the Churchmen could have selected matrimonial alliances of politic and aggrandising character; and as possession of property and hereditary transmission of benefices would have followed on the permission to marry, an ecclesiastical caste, combining temporal and spiritual power to a dangerous excess, might have repeated in Europe the distinctions between the Brahman and Sudra of India. The perpetual admission of self-made men into the hierarchy, which distinguished the Church even in times of the most aristocratic feudalism, was for ages the only practical recognition of the equality of man. If, therefore, the Church was to attain the theocratic supremacy which was the object of its ambition, sacerdotal celibacy was not only an element necessary to its success, but a safeguard against the development of an hereditary ecclesiastical aristocracy which might have proved fatal to intellectual and social progress.

What we may now readily discern to have been a means, to Gregory, however, was an end, and to the enforcement of celibacy as necessary to that object he devoted himself with unrelenting vigour. The belief that he was appointed of God, and set apart for the task of cleansing the Church of the Nicolitan heresy which had defied his predecessors, is well illustrated by the contemporary legend of some pious Pisan, who, spending the night before his election in prayer in the basilica of St. Peter, saw that holy saint himself traverse the church accompanied by Hildebrand, whom he commanded to gather some droppings of mares with which the sacred edifice was defiled, to place them in a sack, and to carry them out on his shoulders. The severe austerity of his virtue, moreover, was displayed by his admirers in the story that once, when dangerously ill, his niece came to inquire as to his health. To relieve her anxiety he played with her necklace, and jestingly asked if she wished to be married; but on his recovery he found that he could no longer weep with due contrition over his sins, and that he had lost the grace of repentance. He long and vainly searched for the cause, and finally entreated his friends to pray for him, when the Virgin appeared to one of them, and sent word to Gregory that he had fallen from grace in consequence of the infraction of his vows committed in touching the necklace of his niece.

His first movement on the subject appears to have been an epistle addressed, in November 1073, to Gebhardt, Archbishop of Salzburg, taking him severely to task for his neglect in enforcing the canons promulgated not long before in Rome, and ordering him to carry them rigidly into effect among his clergy.[1] This, no doubt, was a circular

---

[1] The fanciful purity which came to be considered requisite to the episcopal office is well illustrated by the case of Faricius, Abbot of Abingdon, who was elected to the see of Canterbury. His suffragans refused his consecration because he was a skilful leech—" tunc electus est Faricius ad archiepiscopatum, sed episcopus Lincolniensis et episcopus Salesburiensis obstiterunt, dicentes non debere archiepiscopum urinas mulierum inspicere " (De Abbat. Abbendon.—Chron. Abingdon. II. 287). The prejudice against the

letter addressed to all the prelates of Christendom, and it was but a preliminary step. Early in Lent of the next year (March 1074) he held his first synod, which adopted a canon prohibiting sacerdotal marriage, ordering that no one in future should be admitted to orders without a vow of celibacy, and renewing the legislation of Nicholas II, which commanded the people not to attend the ministrations of those whose lives were a violation of the rule. There was nothing in the terms of this more severe than what had been decreed in innumerable previous councils— indeed, it was by no means as threatening as many decretals of recent date; but Gregory was resolved that it should not remain, like them, a mere protest, and he took immediate measures to have it enforced wherever the authority of Rome extended.

The controversy as respects Italy has already been so fully described that to dilate upon it further would be superfluous. Even though Alexander II in his later years had shrunk somewhat from the contest, yet from Naples to the Tyrol the question was thoroughly understood, and its results depended more upon political revolutions than on ecclesiastical exertions. Beyond the Alps, however, the efforts of preceding popes had thus far proved wholly nugatory, and on this field Gregory now bent all his energies. The new canon was sent to all the bishops of Europe, with instructions to promulgate it throughout their respective dioceses, and to see that it was strictly obeyed; while legates were sent in every direction to support these commands with their personal supervision and exertion.

That the course which Gregory thus adopted was essentially different from that pursued by his predecessors is amply attested by the furious storm which these measures aroused. The clergy protested in the most energetic terms

---

practice of physic as incompatible with the purity of an ecclesiastic was widespread and long-lived, as chronicled in the canons of numerous councils prohibiting it (*e.g.* Concil. Claromont. ann. 1130 c. 5)—but it was not always so. In 998 Theodatus, a monk of Corvey, received the bishopric of Prague from Otho III, as a reward for curing Boleslas I, Duke of Bohemia, of paralysis, by means of a bath of wine, herbs, spices, and three living black puppies four weeks old (Paulini Dissert. Hist. p. 198); and about the year 1200, Hubert Walter, Archbishop of Canterbury, bestowed the see of St. David's on Geoffrey, Prior of Llanthony, his physician, whose skill had won his gratitude.—Girald. Cambrens. de Jur. et Stat. Menev. Eccles. Dist. VII.

that they would rather abandon their calling than their wives; they denounced Gregory as a madman and a heretic, who expected to compel men to live as angels, and who in his folly, while denying to natural affection its accustomed and proper gratification, would open the door to indiscriminate licentiousness; and they tauntingly asked where, when he should have driven them from the priesthood, he expected to find the angels who were to replace them. Even those who favoured celibacy condemned the means adopted as injudicious, contrary to the canons, and leading to scandals more injurious to the Church than the worst of heresies. Gregory paid little heed to threats or remonstrances, but sent legate after legate to accuse the bishops of their inertness, and to menace them with deposition if they should neglect to carry out the canon to the letter, and he accompanied these measures with others of even more practically efficient character.

The bishops, in fact, were placed in a most embarrassing position, which may be understood from the adventures of three prelates, who took different positions with regard to the instructions of Gregory—Otho of Constance, who leaned to the side of the clergy; St. Altmann of Passau, who was an enthusiastic papalist; and Siegfrid of Mainz, who was a trimmer afraid of both parties.

To Otho, Gregory, in 1074, sent the canons of the synod inhibiting marriage and simony, with orders to use every exertion to secure the compliance of his clergy. Otho apparently did not manifest much eagerness to undertake the unpopular task, and Gregory lost little time in calling him to account. Before the year expired, we find the pope addressing a second epistle to the bishop, angrily accusing him of disobedience in permitting the ministration of married priests, and summoning him to answer for his contumacy at a synod to be held in Rome during the approaching Lent. Nor was this all, for at the same time he wrote to the clergy and people of the diocese, informing them of the disobedience of their bishop and of his summons to trial, commanding them, in case of his persistent rebellion, to no longer obey or reverence him as bishop, and formally releasing them from all subjection to him. Otho doubtless considered it imprudent to show himself at the synod of 1075; consequently in that of 1076 he was excommunicated and deprived of his episcopal functions. During the autumn of the same year, however, the legate Altmann of Passau restored him to communion at Ulm, but without granting him the privilege of officiating. Otho disregarded this restriction, and not only persisted in exercising his functions, but openly favoured and protected the married clergy. For this Gregory absolved his flock from all obedience to him, whereupon Otho abandoned the Catholic party and formally joined the imperialists, who were then engaged in the effort to depose Gregory. From some motives of policy, the pope granted the hardened sinner three years for repentance, at the expiration of which, in 1080, he sent Altmann to Constance to superintend the election of another bishop. The new incumbent, however, proved incapable through bodily infirmity; and in 1084 Otto of Ostia was sent to Constance, and under his auspices Gebhardt was elected bishop, and duly consecrated in 1085. Evidently Gregory was not a man to abandon his purpose, and those who opposed him could not count upon perpetual immunity.

St. Altmann of Passau was renowned for his piety and the strictness of his religious observance. When the canon of 1074 reached him, he assembled his clergy, read it to them, and adjured them to pay to it the respect which was requisite. His eloquence was wasted; the clerks openly refused obedience, and defended themselves by immemorial custom, and by the fact that none of their predecessors had been called upon to endure so severe and unnatural a regulation. Finding the occasion unpropitious, the pious Altmann dissembled; he assured his clergy that he was perfectly willing to indulge them if the papal mandate would permit it, and with this he dismissed them. He allowed the matter to lie in abeyance until the high feast of St. Stephen, the patron saint of the Church, which was always attended by the magnates of the diocese. Then, without giving warning of his intentions, he suddenly mounted the pulpit, read to the assembled clergy and laity the letters of the pope, and threatened exemplary punishment for disobedience. Though thus taken at advantage and by surprise, the clerks were not disposed to submit. A terrible tumult at once arose, and the crafty saint would have been torn to pieces had it not been for the strenuous interference of the nobles, aided, as his biographer assures

us, by the assistance of God. The clergy continued their
resistance, and when, not long after, the empire and papacy
became involved in internecine strife, they sought the
protection of Henry IV, who marched upon Passau, and
drove out St. Altmann and his faction. How unbending
was this opposition, and how successfully it was maintained, are manifest from the fact that when St. Altmann
at length returned to his diocese as papal legate, about the
year 1081, even Gregory felt it necessary to use policy
rather than force, and instructed him to yield to the
pressure of the evil times, and to reserve the strict enforcement of the reform for a more fortunate period. The
political question had thus, for the moment, overshadowed
the religious one.

The archiepiscopate of Mainz was, both temporally and
spiritually, one of the most powerful of the ecclesiastical
principalities of Germany. To the Archbishop Siegfrid,
Gregory sent the canon of 1074 with instructions similar
to those contained in his epistle to Otho of Constance.
In reply, Siegfrid promised implicit obedience; but, recognising the almost insuperable difficulties of the task assigned
him, he temporised, and gave his clergy six months in
which to make up their minds, exhorting them to render
willing obedience and relieve him from the necessity of
employing coercion. At the expiration of the period, in
October 1074, he assembled a synod at Erfurt, where he
boldly insisted that they should give up their wives or
abandon their functions and their benefices. Their arguments and entreaties were in vain. Finding him immovable, they retired for consultation, when some proposed to
separate and return home at once, without further parley,
and thus elude giving sanction to the new regulations;
while bolder spirits urged that it would be better to put
the archbishop to instant death, before he could promulgate so execrable a decree, thus leaving for posterity a
shining example, which would prevent any of his successors
from attempting so abominable an enterprise.

Siegfrid's friends advised him of the turn which affairs
were likely to take. He therefore sent to his clergy a
request that they would reassemble in synod, promising
that he would take the first opportunity to apply to Rome
for a relaxation of the canon. They agreed to this, and
on meeting them the next day, Siegfrid astutely started

the question of his claims on the Thuringian tithes, which had shortly before been settled by the Saxon war. Indignant at this, the Thuringian clergy raised a tumult, flew to arms, and the synod broke up in the utmost confusion. In December, Gregory wrote to the shuffling archbishop an angry letter, reproaching him with his lukewarmness in the cause, and ordering him to present himself at the synod announced for the coming Lent. Siegfrid obediently went to Rome, but was with difficulty admitted to communion. What promises he made to obtain it were not kept, for again, in September 1075, Gregory addressed him with commands to enforce the canons. Stimulated by this, Siegfrid convoked a synod at Mainz in October, where the Bishop of Coire appeared with a papal mandate threatening him with degradation and expulsion if he failed in compelling the priests to abandon either their wives or their ministry. Thus goaded, Siegfrid did his best, but the whole body of the clergy raised such a clamour, and made demonstrations so active and so formidable, that the archbishop saw little prospect of escaping with life. The danger from his mutinous flock was more instant and pressing than that from the angry pope; his resolution gave way, and he dissolved the synod, declaring that he washed his hands of the affair, and that Gregory might deal as he saw fit with a matter which was beyond his power to control. Thus placed between the upper and the nether millstone, it is not to be wondered at if Siegfrid took refuge in the party of the imperialists, nor that his name stands at the head of the list of bishops who in 1076 passed judgment on Gregory, and pronounced that he had forfeited all claim to the papacy; neither is it surprising that Gregory lost no time in excommunicating him at the Roman synod of the same year.

These examples are sufficient to illustrate the difficulties with which Gregory had to contend, and the manner in which he endeavoured to overcome them. The incidents are by no means exceptional, and his marvellous vigour and energy in supervising the movement everywhere, encouraging the zealous co-worker and punishing the lukewarm and indifferent, are abundantly attested by his correspondence. He apparently had an eye on every corner of Europe, and lost no opportunity of enforcing his views with threats or promises, as the case might seem to demand.

It did not take long, however, to convince him that he
could count upon no efficient assistance from the hierarchy,
and that if the Church was to be purified, it must be purified from without, and not from within. To the unutterable horror of those strict Churchmen who regarded the
immunity from all temporal supervision or jurisdiction as
one of the most precious of ecclesiastical privileges, he took,
as early as 1074, the decided and unprecedented step of
authorising the laity to withdraw their obedience from all
prelates and priests who disregarded the canons of the
Holy See on the subjects of simony and incontinence.
This principle, once adopted, was followed up with his
customary unalterable resolution. In October 1074 he
wrote to a certain Count Albert, exhorting him not to
mind what the simoniacal and concubinary priests might
say, but, in spite of them, to persist in enforcing the orders
which emanated from Rome. Still more menacing was an
epistle addressed in January 1075 to Rodolf, Duke of
Swabia, and Bertolf, Duke of Carinthia, commanding
them "whatever the bishops may say or may not say
concerning this, do you in no manner receive the ministrations of those who owe promotion or ordination to simony,
or whom you know to be guilty of concubinage . . . and,
as far as you can, do you prevent, by force if necessary,
all such persons from officiating. And if any shall presume
to prate and say that it is not your business, tell them to
come to us and dispute about the obedience which we thus
enjoin upon you," and adding a bitter complaint of the
archbishops and bishops who, with rare exceptions, had
taken no steps to put an end to these execrable customs,
or to punish the guilty.

These extraordinary measures called forth indignant
denunciations on the part of ecclesiastics, for these letters
were circulars sent to all the princes on whom he could
depend, and he ensured their publicity by causing similar
orders to be published in the churches themselves. Thus
Theodoric, Bishop of Verdun, who had inclined to the
side of Gregory and had secretly left the Assembly of
Utrecht in 1076 to avoid countenancing by his presence
the excommunication then pronounced against the pope,
in a letter to Gregory bitterly reproaches his own folly
in promulgating the decretal and in not foreseeing its
effect as destructive to the peace of the Church, to the

safety of the clerical order, and as declaring a disturbance which threatened even the Christian faith. So Henry, Bishop of Speyer, indignantly denounced him as having destroyed the authority of the bishops and subjected the Church to the madness of the people; and when the bishops, at the Diet of Worms, threw off their allegiance to him, one of the reasons alleged, in Henry's letter to him, is the surrender which he had made of the Church to the laity. Yet Gregory was not to be diverted from his course, and he was at least successful in rousing the Teutonic Church from the attitude of passive resistance which threatened to render his efforts futile. The princes of Germany, who were already intriguing with Gregory for support in their perennial revolts against their sovereign, were delighted to seize the opportunity of at once obliging the pope, creating disturbance at home, and profiting by the Church property which they could manage to get into their hands by ejecting the unfortunate married priests. They accordingly proceeded to exercise, without delay and to the fullest extent, the unlimited power so suddenly granted them over a class which had hitherto successfully defied their jurisdiction; nor was it difficult to excite the people to join in the persecution of those who had always held themselves as superior beings, and who were now pronounced by the highest authority in the Church to be sinners of the worst description. The ignorant populace were naturally captivated by the idea of the vicarious mortification with which their own errors were to be redeemed by the abstinence imposed upon their pastors, and they were not unreasonably led to believe that they were themselves deeply wronged by the want of purity in their ecclesiastics. Add to this the attraction which persecution always possesses for the persecutor, and the licence of plunder so dear to a turbulent and barbarous age, and it is not difficult to comprehend the motive power of the storm which burst over the heads of the secular clergy, and which must have satisfied by its severity the stern soul of Gregory himself.

A contemporary writer, whose name has been lost, but who is supposed by Dom Martène to have been a priest of Trèves, gives us a very lively picture of the horrors which ensued, and as he shows himself friendly in principle to the reform attempted, his account may be received as trustworthy. He describes what amounted almost to a dissolution of society, slave betraying master and master slave; friend informing against friend; snares and pitfalls spread before the feet of all; faith and truth unknown. The peccant priests suffered terribly. Some, reduced to utter poverty, and unable to bear the scorn and contempt of those from whom they had been wont to receive honour and respect, wandered off as homeless exiles; others, mutilated by the indecent zeal of ardent puritans, were carried around to exhibit their shame and misery; others, tortured in lingering death, bore to the tribunal on high the testimony of blood-guiltiness against their persecutors; while others, again, in spite of danger, secretly continued the connections which exposed them to all these cruelties. In the midst of these troubles, as might be expected, the offices of religion were wholly neglected : the new-born babe received no holy baptism; the dying penitent expired without the saving viaticum; the sinner could cleanse his soul by no confession and absolution; and the devotee could no longer be strengthened by the daily sacrifice of the mass. Another writer, of nearly the same date, relates with holy horror how the laity shook off all the obedience which they owed to their pastors, and, despising the sacraments prepared by them, trod the Eucharist under foot and cast out the sacred wine, administered baptism with unlicensed hands, and substituted for the holy chrism the filthy wax collected from their own ears.

When such was the fate of the pastors, it is easy to imagine the misery inflicted on their unfortunate wives. A zealous admirer of Gregory relates with pious gratulation, as indubitable evidence of divine vengeance, how, maddened by their wrongs, some of them openly committed suicide, while others were found dead in the beds which they had sought in perfect health; and this being proof of their possession by the devil, they were denied Christian sepulture. The case of Count Manigold of Veringen affords a not uninstructive instance of the frightful passions aroused by the relentless cruelty which thus branded them as infamous, tore them from their families, and cast them adrift upon a mocking world. The count had put in force the orders of Gregory with strict severity throughout his estates in the Swabian Alps. One miserable creature, thus driven from her husband, swore that the count should undergo the same fate, and, in the blindness of her rage, she poisoned the Countess of Veringen, whose bereaved husband, overwhelmed with grief, sought no second mate.

Nor was the customary machinery of miracles wanting to stimulate the zeal of the faithful in the pious work, and to convince the doubters whose worldly wisdom or humanity might shrink from the task assigned them. Unchaste priests at mass would find sudden blasts of wind overturn the cup and scatter the sacred wine upon the ground, or the holy wafer would be miraculously snatched out of their polluted hands. The saintly virgin Herluca saw in a vision the Saviour, with his wounds profusely bleeding, and was told that if she desired to escape a repetition of the horrifying spectacle, she must no longer be present at the ministrations of Father Richard, the officiating priest of her convent—a revelation which she employed effectually upon him and his parishioners. The same holy maiden, being observed staring intently out of the window, declared, upon being questioned, that she had seen the soul of the priest of Rota carried off by demons to eternal punishment; and, on sending to his habitation, it was found that he had expired at the very moment. Puerile as these tales may seem to us, they were stern realities to those against whose weaknesses they were directed, and whose sufferings were thus enhanced by every art which bigotry could bring to bear upon the credulous passions of a barbarous populace.

It cannot be a matter of surprise if men who were thus threatened with almost every worldly evil should seek to defend themselves by means as violent as those employed by their persecutors. Their cruel intensity of fear is aptly illustrated by what occurred at Cambrai in 1077, where a man was actually burned at the stake as a heretic for declaring his adhesion to the Hildebrandine doctrine that the masses of simoniacal and concubinary priests were not to be attended by the faithful. So, in the same year, when the pseudo-emperor Rodolf of Swabia was elected by the papalists at the Diet of Forcheim as a competitor of Henry IV, he manifested his zeal to suppress the heresies of avarice and lust by refusing the ministration of a simoniacal deacon in the coronation solemnities at Mainz. The clergy of that city, who had so successfully resisted, for two years, the efforts of their archbishop, Siegfrid, to reduce them to subjection to the canons, were dismayed at the prospect of coming under the control of so pious a prince, who would indubitably degrade them or compel them to give up their wives and simoniacally acquired churches. They therefore stirred up a tumult among the citizens, who were ready to espouse their cause; and when Rodolf left his palace for vespers, he was attacked by the people. The conflict was renewed on his return, causing heavy slaughter on both sides, and though the townsmen were driven back, Rodolf was forced to leave the city.

This incident affords us a glimpse into the political aspects of the reform. In the tremendous struggle between the empire and the papacy, Gregory allied himself with all the disaffected princes of Germany, and they were careful to justify their rebellions under the specious pretext of zeal for the apostolic Church. They of course, therefore, entered heartily into his measures for the restoration of ecclesiastical discipline, and professed the sternest indignation towards those whom he placed under the ban. Thus, after Henry, in 1076, had caused his bishops to declare the degradation of Gregory, when the revolted princes held their assembly at Tribur, and in turn decreed the deposition of Henry, they used the utmost caution to exclude all who had communicated with Henry since his excommunication, together with those who had obtained preferment by simony, or who had joined in communion with married priests. The connection, indeed, became so marked that the papalists throughout Germany were stigmatised by the name of Patarini—a term which had acquired so sinister a significance in the troubles of Milan. In this state of affairs it was natural that common enmities and common dangers should unite the persecuted clergy and the hunted sovereign. Yet it is a curious illustration of the influence which the denunciations of sacerdotal marriage had exercised over the public mind, that although Henry tacitly protected the simoniacal and married ecclesiastics, and although they rallied around him and afforded him unquestionable and invaluable aid, still he never ventured openly to defend them. Writers both then and since have attributed the measure of success with which he sustained the fluctuating contest, and the consequent sufferings of the unbending pope, to the efforts of the recalcitrant clergy who resisted the yoke imposed on them by Rome. Yet Henry had formally and absolutely pledged his assistance when Gregory commenced his efforts, and had repeated the promise in 1075; and from this position he never definitely withdrew. Even when the schismatic bishops of his party, at the Synod of Brixen, in 1080, pronounced sentence of deposition on Gregory, and filled the assumed vacancy with an anti-pope, the man whom they elected did not venture to dispute the principle of Gregory's reforms, although the Lombard prelates at that very time were warmly defending their married and simoniacal clergy. Indeed, Guiberto of Ravenna, or Clement III, took occasion to express his detestation of concubinage in language nearly as strong as that of his rival, although he threatened with excommunication the presumptuous laymen who should refuse to receive the sacraments of priests who had not been regularly tried and condemned at his own papal tribunal. In thus endeavouring to place himself as a shield between the suffering priesthood and the persecuting populace, he was virtually striving to annul the reforms of Gregory, since in no other way could they be carried into effect; but he was forced to coincide with Gregory as to the principle which dictated those reforms. Notwithstanding all these precautions, however, the papalists were not disposed to allow their opponents to escape the responsibility of the alliance which brought them so much strength by dividing the Church, and no opportunity was lost of stigmatising them for the licence which they protected. When Guiberto and his cardinals were driven out of Rome in 1084 by Robert Guiscard and his Normans, the flying prelates were ridiculed, not for their cowardice, but for their shaven chins and the wives and concubines whom they publicly carried about with them.

At length Henry and his partisans appear to have felt it necessary to make some public declaration to relieve themselves from the odium of supporting and favouring a practice which was popularly regarded as a heresy and a scandal. When the papalists, under their King Hermann, at the Easter of 1085 (20 April), convened a general assembly of their faction at Quedlinburg and again forbade all commerce with women to those in orders, the imperialists lost no time in putting themselves on the same record with their rivals. Three weeks later Henry gathered around him, at Mainz, all the princes and prelates who professed allegiance to him, for the purpose of securing the succession to his eldest son, Conrad, as King of Germany, and there, in that solemn diet, marriage was formally prohibited to the priesthood. Gregory was then lying on his death-bed in the far-off castle of Salerno, and ere the news could reach him he was past the vanities of earthly triumph. Could he have known, however, that the cause for which he had risked the integrity and independence of the Church had thus received the support of its bitterest enemies, and that his unwavering purpose had thus achieved the moral victory of forcing his adversaries to range themselves under his banner, his spirit would have rejoiced, and his confidence in the ultimate success of the great theocratic system, for the maintenance of which he was thus expiring in exile, would have softened the sorrows of a life which closed in the darkness and doubt of defeat.

CHAPTER XV

CENTRAL EUROPE

HILDEBRAND had passed away, leaving to his successors the legacy of inextinguishable hate and unattained ambition. Nor was the reform for which he had laboured as yet by any means secured in practice, even though his opponents had been reduced to silence or had been forced to render a formal adhesion to the canons which he had proclaimed so boldly.

The cause of asceticism, it is true, had gained many adherents among the laity. Throughout Germany, husbands and wives separated from each other in vast numbers, and devoted themselves to the service of the Church, without taking vows or assuming ecclesiastical garments; while those who were unmarried renounced the pleasures of the world, and, placing themselves under the direction of spiritual guides, abandoned themselves entirely to religious duties. To such an extent did this prevail, that the pope was applied to for his sanction, which he eagerly granted, and the movement doubtless added strength to the party of reform. Yet but little had thus far been really gained in purifying the Church itself, notwithstanding the fearful ordeal through which its ministers had passed.

As for Germany, the indomitable energy of Henry IV, unrepressed by defeat and unchilled by misfortune, had at length achieved a virtual triumph over his banded enemies. But four bishops of the Empire—those of Wurzburg, Passau, Worms, and Constance—owned allegiance to Urban II. All the other dioceses were filled by schismatics, who rendered obedience to the anti-pope Clement. In 1089 the Catholic or papalist princes offered to lay down their arms and do homage to Henry if he would acknowledge Urban and make his peace with the true Church. The emperor, however, had a pope who suited him, and he entertained too lively a recollection of the

trials from which he was escaping to open the door to a
renewal of the papal pretensions, which he had at length
successfully defied, nor would he consent to stigmatise his
faithful prelates as schismatics. He therefore pursued his
own course, and Guiberto of Ravenna enjoyed the honours
of the popedom, checkered by alternate vicissitudes of good
and evil fortune, until removed by death in the year 1100,
his sanctity attested by the numerous miracles wrought at
his tomb, which only needed the final success of the imperialist cause to enrich the calendar with a St. Clement in place
of a St. Gregory and a St. Urban.

Under such auspices, no very zealous maintenance of
ecclesiastical discipline was to be expected. If Clement's
sensibilities were humoured by a nominal reprobation of
sacerdotal marriage, he could scarcely ask for more, or
insist that Henry should rekindle the embers of disaffection by enforcing the odious rules which had proved so
powerful a cause of trouble to their authors and his enemies.
Accordingly, it cannot surprise us to observe that Urban II,
in following out the views of his predecessors, felt it necessary to adopt measures even more violent than those which
in Gregory's hands had caused so much excitement and
confusion, but whose inefficiency was confessed by the
very effort to supplement them. In 1089, the year after
his consecration, Urban published at the Council of Amalfi
a decree by which, as usual, married ecclesiastics were
sentenced to deposition, and bishops who permitted such
irregularities were suspended; but where Gregory had
been content with ejecting husbands and wives, and with
empowering secular rulers to enforce the edict on recalcitrants, Urban, with a refinement of cruelty, reduced the
unfortunate women to slavery, and offered their servitude
as a bribe to the nobles who should aid in thus purifying
the Church. If this infamous canon did not work misery
so widespread as the comparatively milder decretals of
Gregory, it was because the power of Urban was circum-
scribed by the schism, while he was himself apparently
ashamed or afraid to promulgate it in regions where obedience was doubtful. When Pibo, Bishop of Toul, in the
same year, 1089, sent an envoy to ask his decision on
various points of discipline, including sacerdotal marriage
(the necessity of such inquiry showing the futility of
previous efforts), Urban transmitted the canons of Amalfi

in response, but omitted this provision, which well might startle the honest German mind. Perhaps, on reflection, Urban may himself have wished to disavow the atrocity, for in a subsequent council, when again attacking the ineradicable sin, he contented himself with simply forbidding all such marriages, and ordering all persons who were bound by orders or vows to be separated from their wives or concubines, and to be subjected to due penance.

Yet even in those regions of Germany which persevered in resisting Henry and in recognising Urban as pope, the persecution of twenty years was still unsuccessful, and the people had apparently relapsed into condoning the wickedness of their pastors. In an assembly held at Constance in 1094, it was deemed necessary to impose a fine on all who should be present at the services performed by priests who had transgressed the canons. When this was the case in the Catholic provinces, it is easy to imagine that in the imperialist territories the thunders of Gregory and Urban had long since been forgotten, and that marrying and giving in marriage were practised with as little scruple as ever. A fair illustration, indeed, of the amount of respect paid to the rules of discipline is afforded by a discussion on the choice of a successor to Cosmo, Bishop of Prague, who died in 1098. Duke Brecislas, in filling the vacancy with his chaplain Hermann, endeavoured to rebut the arguments of those who objected to the foreign birth of the appointee by urging that fact as a recommendation, since, as a stranger, he would not be pressed upon by a crowd of kindred nor be burdened with the care of children, thus showing that the native priesthood, as a general rule, were heads of families. For this, moreover, they could not plead ignorance, for a Bohemian penitential of the period expressly prohibits priests from having companions whose society could give rise to suspicion of any kind.

At length the duel which, for more than thirty years, Henry had so gallantly fought with the successors of St. Peter drew to a close. Ten years of supremacy he had enjoyed in Germany, and he looked forward to the peaceful decline of his unquiet life, when the treacherous calm was suddenly disturbed. Papal intrigues in 1093 had caused the parricidal revolt of his eldest born, the weak and vacillating Conrad, whose early death had then extinguished the memory of his crime. That unnatural rebellion had gained for Rome the north of Italy; and as the emperor's second son, Henry, grew to manhood, he, too, was marked as a fit instrument to pierce his father's heart, and to extend the domination of the Church by the foulest wrongs that man can perpetrate. The startling revolution which in 1105 precipitated Henry from a throne to a prison, from an absolute monarch to a captive embracing the knees of his son and pleading for his wretched life, established for ever the supremacy of the papacy over Germany. The consequent enforcement of the law of celibacy became only a question of time.

As the excuse for the rebellion was the necessity of restoring the empire to the communion of Rome, one of the first measures of the conspirators was the convocation of a council to be held at Nordhausen, 29 May, 1105, and one of the objects specified for its action was the expulsion of all married priests. The council was duly held, and duly performed its work of condemning the heresy which permitted benefices to be occupied and sacred functions exercised by those who were involved in the ties of matrimony. Pope Paschal II was not remiss in his share of the ceremony, by which he was to receive the fruits of his treacherous intrigues. The following year a great council was held at Guastalla, where, after interminable discussions as to the propriety of receiving without re-ordination those who had compromised themselves or who had been ordained by schismatics, he admitted into the fold all the repentant ecclesiastics of the party of Henry IV. The text of the canon granting this boon to the imperialist clergy bears striking testimony to the completeness of the separation which had existed between the Teutonic and the Roman Churches in stating that throughout the empire few Catholic ecclesiastics were to be found. It scarcely needed the declaration which Paschal made in 1107 at the Synod of Troyes, condemning married priests to degradation and deprivation, to show that the doctrines of Damiani and Hildebrand were thenceforth to be the law of the empire.

The question thus was definitely settled in prohibiting the priests of Germany from marrying or from retaining the wives whom they had taken previous to ordination. It was settled, indeed, in the rolls of parchment which

recorded the decrees of council and the trading bargains
of pope and kaiser, yet the perennial struggle continued,
and the parchment roll for yet awhile was powerless before
the passions of man, who did not cease to be man because
his crown was shaven and his shoulders wore cope and
stole.

Cosmo, who was Dean of Prague, who had been bred
to the Church, and had been promoted to the priesthood
in 1099, chronicles in 1118 the death of Boseteha, his wife,
in terms which show that no separation had ever occurred
between them; and five years later he alludes to his son
Henry in a manner to indicate that there was no irregularity in such relationship, nor aught that would cause him
to forfeit the respect of his contemporaries in acknowledging it.   Even more to the point is the case of a pious
priest, his friend, who, on the death of his wife (" presbytera "), made a vow that he would have no further intercourse with women.   Cosmo relates that the unaccustomed
deprivation proved harder than he had expected, and that
for some years he was tortured with burning temptation.
Finding at length that his resolution was giving way, he
resolved to imitate St. Benedict in conquering the flesh;
and having no suitable solitude for the execution of his
purpose, he took a handful of nettles to his chamber, where,
casting off his garments, he thrashed himself so unmerci-
fully that for three days he lay moribund.   Then he hung
the nettles in a conspicuous place on his wall, that he
might always have before his eyes so significant a memento
and warning.   Cosmo's admiration for this, as a rare and
almost incredible exhibition of priestly virtue and fortitude, shows how few were capable of even remaining
widowers, while the whole story proves that not only
the clergy were free to marry, but also that it was only the
voluntary vow that prevented a second marriage.   At the
close of the century Pietro, Cardinal of Santa Maria in Via
Lata, sent as legate to Bohemia by Celestin III, was much
scandalised at this state of affairs; and when a number of
postulants for holy orders were assembled in the Church
of St. Vitus at Prague, before ordaining them he pronounced a discourse on the subject of celibacy, and demanded that they should all swear to preserve continence.
Thereupon all the priests who were present rushed forward
and urged them not to assume an obligation hitherto

unknown, and when the cardinal ordered the archdeacon to repress their somewhat active demonstrations, they proceeded to pummel that unhappy official, and the tumult was with difficulty repressed by the soldiery who were summoned. The legate sentenced some of the rioters to be starved to death in prison and the rest to be exiled—a severity which broke the spirit of the Bohemian priesthood and led to the introduction of celibacy.

That this state of things was not confined to the wild Bohemian Marches, but obtained throughout Germany in general, is sufficiently attested by the fact that when Innocent II was driven out of Rome by the anti-pope Anaclet, and was wandering throughout Europe begging recognition, he held, in conjunction with the Emperor Lothair, in 1131, a council at Liège, where he procured the adoption of a canon prohibiting priestly marriage or attendance at the mass of married priests. Not only does the necessity of this fresh legislation show that previous enactments had become obsolete, but the manner in which these proceedings are referred to by the chroniclers plainly indicates that it took the Teutonic mind somewhat by surprise, and that the efforts of Gregory and Urban had not only remained without result, but had become absolutely forgotten.

If these proceedings of Innocent had any effect, it was only to make matters worse. The pious Rupert, Abbot of Duits, writing a few years later, deplores the immorality of the priesthood, who not only entered into forbidden marriages, but, knowing them to be illegal, had no scruple in multiplying the tie, considering it to be, at their pleasure, devoid of all binding force. And in Liège itself, where Innocent had held his council, Bishop Albero, whose episcopate commenced in 1135, permitted his priests to celebrate their marriages openly, so that, as we are told, the citizens rather preferred to give their daughters in marriage to them than to laymen; and the naïve remark of the chronicler, that the clergy gave up keeping concubines in secret and took wives openly, would seem to show that the cause of morality had not gained during the temporary restriction imposed by Innocent. It was not to much purpose that Albero was deprived of his see for this laxity, for the same state of things continued. No province of Germany was more orthodox than Salz-

burg, yet the archdeacon of the archiepiscopal Church
there, writing in 1175, bewails the complete demoralisation of his clergy, whom he was utterly unable to reform.
Priests who were content with their own wives and did
not take those of other men were reputed virtuous and
holy; and he complains that in his own archidiaconate he
was powerless to prevent the ordination and ministry of
the sons of priests, even while they were living in open
adultery with women whom they had taken from their
husbands. How little sympathy, indeed, all efforts to
enforce the rule called forth is instructively shown by the
wondering contempt with which a writer, strictly papalist
in his tendencies, comments upon the indiscreet reformatory zeal of Meinhard, Archbishop of Trèves. Elevated
to this lofty dignity in 1128, he at once undertook to
force his clergy to obey the rule by the most stringent
measures, and speedily became so odious that he was
obliged to leave his bishopric within the year; and the
chronicler who tells the story has only words of reprobation for the unfortunate prelate. Even as late as the
end of the twelfth century, a chronicler of the popes, writing
in Southern Germany, calls Gregory VII an enforcer of
impossibilities—" præceptor impossibilium "—because he
had endeavoured to make good the rule of celibacy; and
a Council of Ratisbon, in the thirteenth century, while
lamenting the fact that there were few priests who did not
openly keep their concubines and children in their houses,
quotes the canon of Hildebrand forbidding the laity to
attend at the ministrations of such persons, but without
venturing to hint at its enforcement.

Hungary had been Christianised at a time when the
obligation of celibacy was but lightly regarded, though it
had not as yet become obsolete. In reducing the dreaded
and barbarous Magyars to civilisation, the managers of the
movement might well smooth the path, and interpose as
few obstacles as possible to the attainment of so desirable
a consummation. It is probable, therefore, that restrictions on marriage, as applied to the priesthood, were
lightly passed over, and, not being insisted on, were disregarded by all parties. Even the decretals of Nicholas
II and the fulminations of Gregory VII appear to have
never penetrated into the kingdom of St. Stephen, for

sacerdotal celibacy seems to have been unknown among
the Hungarians until the close of the century. The first
allusion to it occurs in the Synod of Zabolcs, held in 1092,
under the auspices of St. Ladislas II, and is of a nature to
show not only that it was an innovation on established
usages, but also that the subject required tender handling
to reconcile it to the weakness of undisciplined human
nature. After the bitter denunciations and cruelly harsh
measures which the popes had been promulgating for
nearly half a century, there is an impressive contrast in
the mildness with which the Hungarian Church offered
indulgence to those legitimately united to a first wife, until
the Holy See could be consulted for a definitive decision ;
and though marriages with second wives, widows, or
divorced women were pronounced null and void, the disposition to evade a direct meeting of the question is manifested in a regulation which provided that if a priest
united himself to his female slave " uxoris in locum," the
woman should be sold ; but if he refused to part with her,
he was simply to pay her price to the bishop. Whether
or not the pope's decision was actually sought, we have
no means of knowing ; if it was, his inevitable verdict
received little respect, for the Synod of Gran, held about
the year 1099 by the Primate Seraphin of Gran, only
ventured to recommend moderation to married priests,
while its endeavour to enforce the rule prohibiting marriage
after the assumption of orders shows how utterly the
recognised discipline of the Church was neglected. The
consent of wives was also required before married priests
could be elevated to the episcopate, and after consecration
separation was strictly enjoined, affording still further
evidence of the laxity allowed to the other grades. The
iteration of the rules respecting *digami* and marriage with
widows also indicates how difficult was the effort to resusci-
tate those well-known regulations, although they were
universally admitted to be binding on all ecclesiastics.

King Coloman, whose reign extended from 1095 to 1114,
has the credit of being the first who definitely enjoined
immaculate purity on the Hungarian priesthood. His
laws, as collected by Alberic, have no dates, and therefore
we are unable to affix precise epochs to them ; but his legislation on the subject appears to have been progressive, for
we find edicts containing injunctions respecting *digami*

and irregular unions in terms which indicate that single
marriages were not interfered with; and these may reasonably be deemed earlier than other laws which formally
prohibit the elevation to the diaconate of an unmarried
man without exacting from him a vow of continence, or
of a married man without the consent of his wife. The
import of this latter condition is explained by another law,
which provided that no married man should officiate at
the altar unless his wife professed continence, and was
furnished by her husband with the means of dwelling
apart from him. As these stringent regulations form part
of the canons of a council held by Archbishop Seraphin
about the year 1109, they were probably borrowed from
that council by Coloman, and incorporated into his laws
at a period somewhat later.

I have not met with any indications of the results of
the legislation which thus combined the influence of the
temporal and ecclesiastical authorities. That it effected
little, however, is apparent from the evidence afforded by
Dalmatia, at that time a province of Hungary. Shortly
before it lost its independence, its duke, Dimitri, resolved
to assume the crown of royalty, and purchased the assent
of Gregory VII at the price of acknowledging him as feudal
superior. Gregory took advantage of Dimitri's aspirations
to further the plans of reform, of which he never lost
sight; for, in the coronation oath taken in 1076 before
Gebizo, the papal legate, the new king swore that he
would take such measures as would insure the chastity of
all ecclesiastics, from the bishop to the subdeacon. The
new dynasty did not last long, for before the end of the
century St. Ladislas united the province of Dalmatia to
the kingdom of Hungary; but neither the oath of Dimitri,
the laws of Coloman, nor the canons of the national councils
succeeded in eradicating the custom of priestly marriage.
When we find, in 1185, Urban III, in approving the acts
of the Synod of Spalatro, graciously expressing his approbation of its prohibiting the marriage of priests, and
desiring that the injunction should be extended so as to
include the diaconate, we see that marriage must have been
openly enjoyed by all ranks, that the synod had not
ventured to include in the restriction any but the highest
order, and that Urban himself did not undertake to apply
the rule to subdeacons, although they had been specially

included in Dimitri's oath. Yet still pope and synod laboured in vain, for fourteen years later, in 1199, another national council complained that priests kept both wives and benefices. It therefore commanded that those who indulged in this species of adultery should either dismiss their partners in guilt, and undergo due penance, or else should give up their churches; while no married man should be admitted to the diaconate, unless his wife would take a vow of continence before the bishop. Even yet, however, the subdiaconate is not alluded to, although the legates who presided over the council were those of Innocent III.

Of how little avail were these efforts is shown by the national council held at Vienna as late as 1267, by Cardinal Guido, legate of Clement IV. It was still found necessary to order the deprivation of priests and deacons who persisted in retaining their wives; while the special clauses respecting those who married after taking orders prove that such unions were frequent enough to require tender consideration in removing the evil. The subdiaconate, also, was declared liable to the same regulations, but the resistance of the members of that order was probably stubborn, for the canons were suspended in their favour until further instructions should be received from the pope.

Poland was equally remiss in enforcing the canons on her clergy. The leaning of the Slavonic races towards the Greek Church rendered them, in fact, peculiarly intractable, and marriage was commonly practised by the clergy at least until the close of the twelfth century. At length the efforts of Rome were extended to that distant region, and in 1197 the papal legate, Cardinal Peter of Capua, held the Synod of Lanciski, when the priests were peremptorily ordered to dismiss their wives and concubines, who, in the words of the historian, were at that time universally and openly kept. The result of this seems to have amounted to little, for in 1207 we find Innocent III sharply reproving the bishops of the province of Gnesen because married men were publicly admitted to ecclesiastical dignities, and canons took no shame in the families growing up around them. The children of priests were brought up to the sacred profession of their fathers, assisted them in their ministrations, and succeeded to their benefices. Whether or not the other disorders which Innocent designated as infecting the churches were the result of the carnal affections which thus superseded the spiritual, we may fairly doubt, in view of the abuses still prevailing in more favoured regions. The effort was continued, and was apparently at length successful, at least in the western portions of the Polish Church, for at the Council of Breslau, held in 1279, there is no mention of wives, and the constitution of Guido, legate of Clement IV, is quoted, depriving of benefices those who openly kept concubines.

The Church of Sweden was no purer than its neighbours. That the rule was recognised there at a tolerably early period is shown by the fact that when the people of Scania, about the year 1180, revolted against the exactions of Waldemar I of Denmark, they demanded to be released from the oppression of tithes, and that the clergy should be married. Singularly enough, the clerks stood by their bishop, Absalom, when he laid an interdict on the province, and the arms of Waldemar speedily subdued the revolt. Not much, however, was gained for Church discipline by this. In 1204 the Archbishop of Lunden reported to Innocent III that he had used every endeavour to enforce the canons, and had brought many of his priests to observe chastity, but that there still were many who persisted in retaining their women, whom they treated as though they were legitimate wives, with fidelity and conjugal affection. To this Innocent replied that the recalcitrants must be coerced by suspension, and, if necessary, by deprivation of benefice. How little result this achieved is evident when we find the archbishop again writing to Innocent III complaining that the Swedish priests persisted in living with their wives, and that they moreover claimed to have a papal dispensation permitting it. Innocent, in reply, cautiously abstained from pronouncing an opinion as to the validity of these pretensions until he should have an opportunity of examining the document to which they appealed. The efforts at this time were fruitless, for in 1237 Gregory IX ordered Sigund, Archbishop of Drontheim, to put an end to the public marriages of his clergy, and in 1248 we find the Cardinal of St. Sabina, as legate

of Innocent IV, holding a council at Schening, of which
the principal object was to reform these abuses, which
were so firmly established that the Swedes were considered
as schismatics of the Greek Church, in consequence of the
marriage of their priests. The council, supported by the
royal power, succeeded in forcing the Swedish ecclesiastics
to give up their wives by a liberal use of all the punishments then in vogue, together with the significant threat
of abandoning them to the tender mercies of the secular
tribunals.

In Denmark, and along the northern coasts of Germany,
there was equal delay in enforcing the canon of celibacy.
It is suggestive of some powerful intercession in favour of
the married clergy when we see Paschal II, in 1117, writing
to the King of Denmark that the rule was imperative, and
that he could admit of no exceptions to it. His insistence,
however, was of little avail. In 1266 Cardinal Guido,
legate of Clement IV, held a council at Bremen, where he
was obliged to take rigorous measures to put an end to
this Nicolitan heresy. All married priests, deacons, and
subdeacons were pronounced incapable of holding any
ecclesiastical office whatever. Children born of such unions
were declared infamous, and incapable of inheritance, and
any property received by gift or otherwise from their
fathers was confiscated. Those who permitted their
daughters, sisters, or other female relatives to contract
such marriages, or gave them up in concubinage to priests,
were excluded from the Church. That a previous struggle
had taken place on the subject is evident from the penalties
threatened against the prelates who were in the habit of
deriving a revenue from the protection of these irregularities, and from an allusion to the armed resistance, made
by the married and concubinary priests with their friends,
to all efforts to check their scandalous conduct.

In Friesland, too, the efforts of the sacerdotalists were
long set at nought. In 1219 Emo, Abbot of Wittewerum,
describing the disastrous inundations which afflicted his
country, considers them as a punishment sent to chastise
the vices of the land, and among the disorders which were
peculiarly obnoxious to the wrath of God he enumerates
the public marriage of the priests, the hereditary transmission of benefices, and the testamentary provision made

by ecclesiastics for their children out of the property which should accrue to the Church; while his references to the canon law inhibiting these practices show that these digressions were .not excusable through ignorance. The warning was unheeded, for Abbot Emo alludes incidentally, on various subsequent occasions, to the hereditary transmission of several deaneries as a matter of course. The deans in Friesland were ecclesiastics of high position, each having six or more parishes under his jurisdiction, which he governed under legatine power from the Bishop of Munster. When, in 1271, the people rose against them, exasperated by their intolerable exactions, in some temporary truce the deans gave their *children* as hostages; and when, after their expulsion, Gerard of Munster came to their assistance by excommunicating the rebels, the latter defended the movement by the argument that the deans had violated the laws of the Church by handing down their positions .from father to son, and that each generation imitated the incontinence of its predecessors. Hildebrand might have applauded this reasoning, but his days were past. The Church by this time had gained the position to which it had aspired, and no longer invoked secular assistance to enforce its laws. Even Abbot Menco, while admitting the validity of the popular argument, claimed that such questions were reserved for the decision of the Church alone, and that the people must not interfere.

After thus marking the slow progress of the Hildebrandine movement in these frontier lands of Christendom, let us see what efforts were required to establish the reform in regions less remote.

CHAPTER XVI

FRANCE

GREGORY VII had not been so engrossed in his quarrels with the Empire as to neglect the prosecution of his favourite schemes of reform elsewhere. If he displayed somewhat less of energy and zeal in dealing with the ecclesiastical foibles of other countries, it was perhaps because the political complications which gave a special zest to his efforts in Germany were wanting, and because there was no organised resistance supported by the temporal authorities. Yet the inertia of passive non-compliance long rendered his endeavours and those of his successors equally nugatory.

As early as 1056 we find Victor II, by means of his vicars at the Council of Toulouse, enjoining on the priest-hood separation from their wives, under penalty of excommunication and deprivation of function and benefice. This was followed up in 1060 by Nicholas II, who sought through his envoys to enforce the observance of his decretals on celibacy in France, and under the presidency of his legate the Council of Tours in that year adopted a canon of the most decided character. All who, since the promulgation of the decretal of 1060, had continued in the performance of their sacred functions while still preserving relations with their wives and concubines were deprived of their grades without hope of restoration; and the same irrevocable penalty was denounced against those who in the future should endeavour to combine the incompatible duties of husband and minister of Christ.

In what spirit these threats and injunctions were likely to be received may be gathered from an incident which occurred probably about this time. A French bishop, as in duty bound, excommunicated one of his deacons for marrying. The clergy of the diocese, keen to appreciate the prospect of future trouble, rallied around their persecuted brother, and rose in open rebellion against the prelate. The latter, apparently, was unable to maintain his position, and the matter was referred for adjudication to the celebrated Berenger of Tours. Although, in view of the papal jurisprudence of the period, the bishop would seem to have acted with leniency, yet Berenger blamed both parties for their precipitancy and quarrelsome humour, and decided that the excommunication of a deacon for marrying was contrary to the canons, unless rendered unavoidable by the contumacy of the offender.

Even more significant was the scene which occurred in 1074 in the Council of Paris, where all, bishops, abbots, and priests refused to obey the mandate of Hildebrand, declaring that it imposed an insupportable burden; and when the holy St. Gauthier, Abbot of Pontoise, ventured to argue that the commands of the pope must be executed, whether just or unjust, he was set upon, beaten almost to death, carried before the king, and confined until some friendly nobles procured his release.

When such was the spirit of the ecclesiastical body, there was little to be expected from any internal attempt at reform. At the stormy Synod of Poitiers, in 1078, the papal legate, Hugh, Bishop of Die, succeeded in obtaining the adoption of a canon which threatened with excommunication all who should knowingly listen to the mass of a concubinary or simoniacal priest, but this seems to have met with little response. Coercion from without was evidently requisite, and in this case, as we have seen, Gregory did not shrink from subjecting the Church to the temporal power. In Normandy, for instance, a synod held at Lisieux in 1055 had commanded the degradation of priests who resided with wives or concubines. This was, of course, ineffective, and in 1072 John, Archbishop of Rouen, held a council in his cathedral city, where he renewed that canon in terms which show how completely all orders and dignitaries were habitually liable to its penalties. The Norman clergy were not disposed to submit quietly to this abridgment of their accustomed privileges, and they expressed their dissent by raising a terrible clamour and driving their archbishop from the council with a shower of stones, from which he barely escaped alive. At length, in view of the utter failure of all ecclesiastical legislation, the laity were called in. William the Conqueror, therefore, in 1080, assisted the Archbishop of Rouen in holding a synod at Lillebonne, where the stern presence of the suzerain prevented any unseemly resistance to the adoption of most unpalatable regulations.   All who were in holy orders were forbidden, under any pretext, to keep women in their houses, and if, when accused of disobedience, they were unable to prove themselves innocent, their benefices were irretrievably forfeited.   If the accusation was made by the ecclesiastical officials, the offender was to be tried by the episcopal court, but if his parishioners or feudal superior were the complainants, he was to be brought before a mixed tribunal composed of the squires of his parish and the officials of the bishop.   This startling invasion of the dearest privileges of the Church was declared by William to proceed from no desire to interfere with the jurisdiction of his bishops, but to be a temporary expedient, rendered necessary by their negligence.   Nor is this remarkable measure the only thing that renders the Synod of Lillebonne worthy of note, for it affords us the earliest authoritative indication of a practice which subsequently became a standing disgrace to the Church.   The fifth canon declares that no priest shall be forced to give anything to the bishop or to the officers of the diocese beyond their lawful dues, and especially that no money shall be exacted on account of women kept by clerks.   A tribute known as " cullagium " became at times a recognised source of revenue, in consideration of which the weaknesses of human nature were excused, and ecclesiastics were allowed to enjoy in security the society of their concubines.   We shall see hereafter that this infamous custom continued to flourish until the sixteenth century, despite the most strenuous and repeated endeavours to remove so grievous a scandal.

It is probable that the expedient of mixed courts for the trial of married and concubinary priests was not adopted without the concurrence of Gregory, who was willing to make almost any sacrifice necessary to accomplish his purpose.   That they were organised and performed the functions delegated to them is shown by a reference in a charter of 1088 to one held at Caumont, which required a priest to abandon either his wife or his church.   So far, indeed, was Gregory from protesting against this violation of ecclesiastical immunities, that he was willing even to connive at the abuses which immediately crept into the system, and to purchase the assistance of the laity by allowing them to lay sacrilegious hands on the temporalities of the Church. Many of the nobles who thus assisted in expelling the offending clergy seized the tithes and retained them. The papal legate, Hugh, Bishop of Die—better known by his subsequent primatial dignity of Lyons—proceeded against these invaders of Church property in the usual manner, and excommunicated them as a matter of course. Gregory, however, who under ordinary circumstances would promptly have consigned the spoilers to the bottomless pit, now virtually took their side. He discreetly declined to confirm the excommunication, reproved his legate for superserviceable zeal, and ordered him to be in future more guarded and temperate in his proceedings.

Church and State—the zeal of the ecclesiastic and the avarice of the noble—vainly united to break down the stubbornness of the Norman priesthood, for marriage continued to be enjoyed as openly as ever. The only effect of the attempted reform, indeed, appeared to be that when a priest entered into matrimony he took a solemn vow never to give up his wife, a measure prompted doubtless by the fears of the bride and her kindred. The nuptials were public; male issue succeeded to benefices by a recognised primogeniture, and female children received their fathers' churches as dower, when other resources were wanting. About the beginning of the twelfth century, three enthusiastic ascetic reformers, the celebrated Robert d'Arbrissel, founder of Fontevrault, Bernard Abbot of Tiron, and Vitalis of Mortain, traversed Normandy and preached with great earnestness against these abuses, the result of which was that they nearly came to an untimely end at the hands of the indignant pastors and their more indignant spouses. On one occasion, when Bernard was preaching at Coutances, a married archdeacon assailed him, with a crowd of priests and clerks, asking how he, a monk, dead to the world, presumed to preach to the living. Bernard replied that Samson had slain his foes with the jaw-bone of a dead ass, and then proceeded with so moving a discourse on Samson, that the archdeacon was converted, and interfered to save him from the mob.

If William the Conqueror found his advantage in thus assisting the hopeless reform within his duchy of Normandy, he had no hesitation in obstructing it when his policy demanded such a course in his subject province of Brittany. During the three and a half centuries through which the Breton Church maintained its independence of the archiepiscopal see of Tours, its metropolis was Dol. Judhaël, who occupied its lofty seat, not only obtained it by simony, but sullied it by a public marriage; and when the offspring of this illicit union reached maturity he portioned them from the property of the Church. This prolonged violation of the canons attracted the attention of Gregory soon after his accession, and in 1076 he informed William that he had desposed the offender. William, however, saw fit to defend the scandal, and refused to receive Evenus, Abbot of St. Melanius, whom Gregory had appointed as successor. Judhaël, indeed, was no worse than his suffragans. For three generations the diocese of Quimper was held by father, son, and grandson; while the Bishops of Rennes, Vannes, and Nantes were openly married, and their wives enjoyed the recognised rank of countesses, as an established right. How much improvement resulted from the efforts of Gregory and his legate Hugh may be estimated from the description, in general terms, of the iniquities ascribed to the Breton clergy, both secular and regular, in the early part of the next century, by Paschal II when granting the pallium to Baldric, Archbishop of Dol. All classes are described as indulging in enormities hateful to God and man, and as having no hesitation in setting the canons at defiance. In Brittany, as in Wales and Spain, the centralising influence of Rome was at fault, and priestly marriage was persevered in long after it had been abrogated elsewhere.

In Flanders, Count Robert the Frisian and Adela, his mother, were well disposed to second the reformatory measures of Gregory, but, doubting their right to eject the offenders, they applied to him, in 1076, for instructions. His answers were unequivocal, urging them to the most prompt and summary proceedings. The spirit in which the clergy met the attack was manifested by the incident already described, when, in 1077, an unfortunate zealot was burned at the stake in Cambrai for maintaining the propriety of the papal decretals. The same disposition, though fortunately leading to less deplorable results, was exhibited in

Artois. At the instance of Adela, Robert, in 1072, had founded the priory of Watten, near St. Omer. Despite this powerful interest and patronage, the house had a severe struggle for existence, as its prior, Otfrid, lent his influence to support the reform and to enforce the decrees of Gregory. Reproaches and curses were showered upon the infant community, and it was openly threatened with fire and sword, until the unfortunate brethren felt equally insecure within their walls and abroad. At length the Countess Adela took Otfrid with her on a pilgrimage to Rome, and there the holy man procured from Gregory a confirmation of the privileges of his house. On his return, he found that this instrument only made the persecution more vehement. Accusations of all kinds were made against the priory, and its enemies succeeded in causing the brethren to be brought for trial before the local synod, where the production of the papal charter was ordered. It was at once pronounced a forgery, was taken away by force, and was retained by the bishop, Drogo of Terouane, in spite of all remonstrance.

The opposition of the clergy was not lessened by the manner in which the secular authorities exercised the power bestowed upon them. Count Robert saw the advantages derivable from the position of affairs, and seems to have been resolved to turn it thoroughly to account. Among other modes adopted was that of the " jus spolii," by which he seized the effects of dying ecclesiastics, turning their families out of doors and disinheriting the heirs. These arbitrary proceedings he defended on the ground of the incontinence of the sufferers, boldly declaring that wicked priests were no priests—as if, groaned the indignant clerks, sinful men were not men. In 1091, the Flemish priests complained of these acts to Urban II, and he vainly endeavoured to interfere on their behalf. Finding this resource fail, they appealed to their metropolitan, Renaud, Archbishop of Rheims, who by active measures succeeded in putting an end to the abuse in 1092.

Amid all this the Church proved powerless to enforce its laws, and again it called upon the feudal authority for assistance—this time in a manner by which it admitted its impotence on a question so vital. In 1099, Manasses of Rheims held a provincial synod at St. Omer, which instructed the Count of Flanders, Robert the Hierosoly-

mitan, to seize the wives of all priests who, after excommunication, declined to abandon their guilty partners;
and in this he was not to ask or wait for the assent of the
bishop of the diocese. The sturdy Crusader would doubtless have carried out this order to the letter, with all its
attendant cruelty and misery, but the clergy of the province
united in remonstrances so vehement that Manasses was
forced to abandon his position. He accordingly requested
Robert on no account to disturb the married priests and
their wives, or to permit his nobles to do so, except when
assistance was demanded by the bishops. He acknowledged the injustice he had committed in overslaughing the
constituted authorities of the Church, and deprecated the
rapine and spoliation which so ill-advised a proceeding
might cause. At the same time, he admonished his suffragans to proceed vigorously against all who married in
orders, and to call on the seigneurial power to coerce those
who should prove contumacious.

Harsh and violent as were the measures thus threatened,
there appears to have been extreme hesitation in carrying
them out. A certain clerk known as Robert of Artois
committed the unpardonable indiscretion of marrying a
widow, and openly resisted all the efforts of his bishop to
reduce him to obedience. Not only his original crime, but
his subsequent contumacious rebellion, would assuredly
justify the severest chastisement, yet both the secular and
ecclesiastical powers of the province seem to have been at
fault, for it was found necessary to ask the interference of
no less a personage than Richard, Bishop of Albano, the
papal legate in France. In 1104 the legate accordingly
addressed the Count of Flanders with the very moderate
request that the obstinate rebel and his abettors should be
held as excommunicate until they should reconcile themselves to their bishop. Robert finally appealed to Rome
itself, but in the end was obliged to succumb. Similar
was the case of two Artesian deacons who refused to abandon their wives until Lambert, the Bishop of Artois, excommunicated them, when they travelled to Rome in hopes of
reconciliation to the Church. Paschal II absolved them
on their taking a solemn oath upon the Gospels to live
chastely in future, and he sent them back to Lambert with
instructions to keep a careful watch upon them. These
cases, which chance to remain on record, show how obstin-

ately the clergy held to their wives, and how difficult it was
to convince them that the authorities of the Church were
determined to enforce the canons.   We need not therefore
be surprised to find Paschal II, after the year 1100, writing
to the clergy of Terouane expressing his astonishment that,
in spite of so many decretals of popes and canons of councils,
they still adhered to their consorts, some of them openly
and some secretly.   To remedy this, he has nothing but a
repetition of the old threat of deprivation.

The confusion which this attempted reformation caused
in France was apparently not so aggravated as we have
seen it in Germany, and yet it was sufficiently serious.
Guibert de Nogent relates that in his youth commenced the
persecution of the married priests by Rome, when a cousin
of his, a layman of flagrant and excessive licentiousness,
made himself conspicuous by his attacks on the failings of
the clergy.   The family were anxious to provide for young
Guibert, who was destined for the Church, and the cousin
used his influence with the patron of a benefice to oust
the married incumbent and bestow the preferment on
Guibert.   The priest thus forcibly ejected abandoned
neither his wife nor his functions, but relieved his mind by
excommunicating every day, in the mass, Guibert's mother
and all her family, until the good woman's fears were so
excited that she abandoned the prebend which she had
obtained with so much labour.   We can readily conceive
this incident to be a type of what was occurring in every
corner of the kingdom, when, in an age of brute force, the
reverence which was the only defence of the priesthood was
partially destroyed, and the people hardly knew whether
they were to adore their pastors as representatives of God,
or to dread them as the powerful ministers of evil.

When the religious ardour of Europe rose to the wild
excitement that culminated in the Crusades, and Pope
Urban II astutely availed himself of the movement to place
the Church in possession of a stronger influence over the
minds of men than it had ever before enjoyed, it was to no
purpose that the great Council of Clermont, in 1095, took
the opportunity to proclaim in the most solemn manner
the necessity of perfect purity in ministers of the altar, to
denounce irrevocable expulsion for contravention of the

rule, and to forbid the children of ecclesiastics from entering
the Church except as monks or canons.   It was the weighti-
est exposition of Church discipline, and was promulgated
under circumstances to give it the widest publicity and the
highest authority.   Yet within a few years we find Gaulo,
Bishop of Paris, applying to Ivo of Chartres for advice as
to what ought to be done with a canon of his Church who
had recently married, and Ivo in reply recommending as a
safe course that the marriage be held valid, but that the
offender be relieved of his stipend and functions.   His
answer, moreover, is written in a singularly undecided tone,
and an elaborate argument is presented, as though the
matter were still open to discussion, although Ivo's
laborious compilations of the canon law show that he was
thoroughly familiar with the ancient discipline which the
depravity of his generation had rendered obsolete.   Hardly
less significant is another epistle in which Ivo calls the
attention of Daimbert, Archbishop of Sens, to the conduct
of one of his dignitaries, who publicly maintained two concubines and was preparing to marry a third.   He urges
Daimbert to put an end to the scandal, and suggests that if
he is unable to accomplish it single-handed, he should
summon two or three of his suffragans to his assistance.
Either of these instances is a sufficient confession of the
utter futility of the ceaseless exertions which for half a
century the Church had been making to enforce her discipline.   Nor, perhaps, can her ill-success be wondered at
when we consider how unworthy were the hands to which
was frequently entrusted the administering of the law, and
the laxity of opinion which viewed the worst transgressions
with indulgence.   The archdeacons were the officials to
whom was specially confided the supervision over sacerdotal morals, and yet when a man occupying that responsible position, like Aldebert of Le Mans, publicly surrounded
himself with a harem, and took no shame from the resulting
crowd of offspring, so little did his conduct shock the sensibilities of the age that he was elevated to the episcopal
chair, and only the stern voice of Ivo could be heard
reproving the measureless scandal.

Equal looseness pervaded the monastic establishments.
Hildebert, Bishop of Le Mans, made numerous fruitless
attempts to restore discipline in the celebrated abbey of

Euron, the monks of which indulged in the grossest licentiousness, and successfully defied his power until he was obliged to appeal to the papal legate for assistance. Albero of Verdun, after fruitless attempts to reform the monastery of St. Paul, in his episcopal city, was obliged to turn out the monks by force and replace them with Premonstratensians, who were then in the full ardour of their new discipline. The description which Ivo of Chartres gives of the convent of St. Fara shows a promiscuous and shameless prostitution on the part of the nuns of that institution even more degrading. Instances like these could be almost indefinitely multiplied, such as that of St. Mary of Argentueil, reformed by Heloise, the great foundation of St. Denis, previous to the abbacy of Suger, and that of St. Gildas de Ruys in Brittany, as described by Abelard; who, moreover, depicts the nuns of the period, in general terms, as abandoned to the most hideous licentiousness—those who were good-looking prostituting themselves for hire, those who were not so fortunate hiring men to gratify their passions, while the older ones, who had passed the age of lust, acted as procuresses. Innocent III may therefore be absolved from the charge of exaggeration when, in ordering the reform of the nuns of St. Agatha, he alludes to their convent as a brothel which infected with its evil reputation the whole country around it. A contemporary chronicler records as a matter of special wonder that John of Salisbury, Bishop of Chartres, forced his canons to live in cloisters according to the Rule of St. Augustin; and he adds that, stimulated by this example, his uncle, John of Lisieux, and his successor, Geoffrey of Chartres, attempted the same reform, but without success. It is true that some partial reform was effected by St. Bernard, but the austerities of the new orders founded by enthusiasts like him and St. Bruno, Robert d'Arbrissel, and St. Norbert, did not cure the ineradicable vices of the older establishments.

With such examples before us, it is not difficult to believe the truth of the denunciations with which Raoul of Poitiers, whose fiery zeal gained for him the distinctive appellation of " Ardens," lashed the vices of his fellows; nor can we conclude that it was mere rhetorical amplification which led him to declare that the clergy, who should be models for their flocks, were more shameless and abandoned than those whose lives it was their duty to guide. Peter Cantor, indeed, deplores the superiority of the laity to the clergy as the greatest injury that afflicted the Church.

The natural result of such a state of morals was the prevalence of the hereditary principle against which the Church had so long and so perseveringly striven. How completely this came to be regarded as a matter of course, is shown by a contemporary charter to the ancient monastery of Bèze, by which a priest named Germain, on entering it bestowed upon it his holding, consisting of certain specified tithes. This deed of gift is careful to declare the assent of the sons of the donor, showing that the title of the monastery would not have been considered good as against the claims of Germain's descendants had they not joined in the conveyance. Even as late as 1202 we find Innocent III endeavouring to put a stop to the hereditary transmission of benefices in the bishopric of Toul, where it was practised to an extent which showed how little impression had as yet been made by the unceasing efforts of the last hundred and fifty years.

When, in the presence of so stiff-necked and evil disposed a generation, all human efforts seemed unavailing to secure respect for the canons of councils and decretals of popes, we need scarcely wonder if recourse was had to the miraculous agencies which so often proved efficacious in subduing the minds of men. Wondrous stories, accordingly, were not wanting, to show how offended Heaven sometimes gave in this world a foretaste of the wrath to come awaiting those who lived in habitual disregard of the teachings of the Church. Thus Peter the Venerable relates with much unction how a priest who had abandoned himself to carnal indulgences died amid the horrors of anticipated hell-fire. Visible to him alone, the demons chuckling around his death-bed heated the frying-pan of burning fat in which he was incontinently to be plunged, while a drop flying from the sputtering mass seared him to the bone, as a dreadful material sign that his agony was not the distempered imagining of a tortured conscience. A miracle equally significant wrung a confession of his weakness from the Dean of Minden in 1167.

If Heaven thus miraculously manifested its anger, it was equally ready to welcome back the repentant sinner. In the first energy of the reforms of St. Bernard, a priest entered the abbey of Clairvaux. The rigour of the Cistercian discipline wore out his enthusiasm; he fled from the convent, returned to his parish, and, according to the general custom (" sicut multis consuetudinis est "), took to himself a concubine, and soon saw a family increasing around him. The holy St. Bernard chanced to pass that way and accepted the priest's warm hospitality without recognising him. When the Saint was ready to depart in the morning he found that his host was absent performing his functions in the church, and, turning to one of the children, he sent him with a message to his father. Though the child had been a deaf-mute from birth, he promptly performed the errand. Roused by the miracle to a sense of his iniquity, the apostate rushed to the Saint, threw himself at his feet, confessed who he was, and entreated to be taken back to the monastery. St. Bernard, touched by his repentance, promised to call for him on his return. To this the priest objected, on the ground that he might die during the interval, but was comforted with the assurance that if he died in such a frame of mind, he would be received by God as a monk. When St. Bernard returned, the repentant sinner was dead. Inquiring as to the ceremonies of his interment, he was told that the corpse had been buried in its priestly garments; whereupon he ordered the grave to be opened, and it was found arrayed, not in its funeral robes, but in full Cistercian habit and tonsure, showing that God had fulfilled the promises made in His name.

Such was the condition of the Gallican Church when, in 1119, Calixtus II stepped from the archiepiscopal see of Vienne to the chair of St. Peter. His first great object was to end the quarrel with the empire on the subject of investitures, the vicissitudes of which rendered the papacy at the time of his accession an exile from Italy; his second was to carry out the reforms so long and so fruitlessly urged by his predecessors. To accomplish both these results he lost no time in summoning a great council to assemble at Rheims, and when it met, in November 1119, no less than fifteen archbishops, more than two hundred bishops, and numerous abbots responded to the call, representing Italy, France, Aquitaine, Spain, Germany, and England. The attempted reconciliation with the Emperor Henry V failed, but the vices and corruptions of the Church were vigorously attacked and sternly prohibited for the future. All commerce with concubines or wives was positively forbidden under pain of deprivation of benefice and function. No choice was granted the offender, for continuance in his sin after expulsion was punishable with excommunication; and the hereditary transmission of ecclesiastical dignities and property was strictly prohibited. Whether it was the lofty character of the new pope, his royal blood and French extraction, or whether the solemnity of the occasion impressed men's minds, it is not easy now to guess, but unquestionably these proceedings produced greater effect upon the Transalpine Churches than any previous efforts of the Holy See. Calixtus was long regarded as the real author of sacerdotal celibacy in France, and his memory has been embalmed in the jingling verses which express the dissatisfaction and spite of the clergy deprived of their ancestral privileges.

> O bone Calliste, nunc clerus odit te;
> Olim presbyteri poterant uxoribus uti;
> Hoc detruxisti quando tu papa fuisti,
> Ergo tuum festum nunquam celebratur honestum.

Calixtus was not a man to rest half-way, nor was he content with an empty promise of obedience. Under the pressure of his influence, the French prelates found themselves obliged to take measures for the vigorous enforcement of the canons. What those measures were, and the disposition with which they were received, may be understood from the resultant proceedings in Normandy. Geoffrey, Archbishop of Rouen, on leaving the Council of Rheims, promptly called a synod, which assembled ere the month was out. The canon prohibiting female intercourse roused abhorrence and resistance among his clergy, and they inveighed loudly against the innovation. Geoffrey singled out one who rendered himself particularly prominent in the tumult, and caused him to be seized and cast into prison; then, leaving the church, he called in his guards, whom, with acute anticipation of trouble, he had posted in readiness. The rude soldiery fell upon the unarmed priests, some of whom promptly escaped; the rest, grasping what weapons they could find, made a gallant resistance, and succeeded in beating back the assailants. A mob speedily collected, which took sides with the archbishop. Assisted

by this unexpected reinforcement, the guards again forced
their way into the church, where they beat and maltreated
the unfortunate clerks to their hearts' content; when, as
the chronicler quaintly observes, the synod broke up in
confusion, and the members fled without awaiting the
archiepiscopal benediction.

The immediate effect of the reformation thus inaugurated
may perhaps be judged with sufficient accuracy by the
incident of Abelard and Heloise, which occurred about this
period. That Abelard was a canon when that immortal love
arose, was not, in such a state of morals, any impediment to
the gratification of his passion, nor did it diminish the satisfaction of the canon Fulbert at the marriage of his niece,
for such marriages, as yet, were valid by ecclesiastical law.
In her marvellous self-abnegation, however, Heloise recognised that while the fact of his openly keeping a mistress,
and acknowledging Astrolabius as his illegitimate son,
would be no bar to his preferment, and would leave open to
him a career equal to the dreams of his ambition, yet to
admit that he had sanctified their love by marriage, and had
repaired, as far as possible, the wrong which he had committed, would ruin his prospects for ever. From a worldly
point of view it was better for him, as a Churchman, to
have the reputation of shameless immorality than that of
a loving and pious husband; and this was so evidently a
matter of course that she willingly sacrificed everything,
and practised every deceit, that he might be considered a
reckless libertine, who had refused her the only reparation
in his power. Such was the standard of morals created by
the Church, and such were the conclusions inevitably
drawn from them.

Nor were these conclusions erroneous, if we may judge
by an incident of the period. An archdeacon of Angoulême
had committed the crime of seducing the abbess of a convent in the district under his charge. When the results of
the amour could be no longer concealed, and the Count of
Angoulême ventured to remonstrate with Gérard, the
bishop of the diocese, that worthy prelate protected the
offender by dismissing the charge with a filthy jest. Yet
so far was Gérard from forfeiting the respect of his contemporaries by this laxity, that he was soon afterwards
appointed papal legate. It required the interposition of
Heaven to punish the guilty, as was seen about this time

in the diocese of Comminges, where a deacon was entangled in a guilty connection and was summoned with his paramour before the bishop, St. Bertrand. The reproof of the holy man reduced the deacon to contrition, but the woman was defiant. He escaped punishment, while she was seized by demons and expired on the spot.

Yet there are evidences that the efforts of Calixtus, and of the fathers whose assembled authority was concentrated at Rheims, did not by any means eradicate a custom which had now become traditional. Soon afterwards King Louis-le-Gros, in granting a charter to the church of St. Cornelius at Compiègne, felt it necessary to accompany the privileges bestowed with a restriction, worded as though it were a novelty, to the effect that those in holy orders connected with the foundation should have no wives—a condition which shows how little confidence existed in the mind of the sagacious prince as to the efficacy of the canons so sententiously promulgated by the rulers, and so energetically resisted by the ruled. That he was justified in this lack of confidence is evident when we see, further on in the century, an epistle of Alexander III, undated, but probably written about 1170, complaining of the canons of St. Ursmar and Antoin, who openly kept concubines in their houses, while some of them did not hesitate to marry; while as late as 1212 a Council of Paris was obliged to adopt canons forbidding clerks married in the lower orders to hold parishes while retaining their wives, and suspending from benefice and functions all those who marry while in holy orders.

One cause for this disregard of the laws so energetically promulgated is seen in the case of the Bishop of Terouane, who, about 1225, was ordered by Honorius III to enforce them against all offenders. He did so, when they had no trouble in obtaining papal letters confirming them in their benefices, and enabling them to persecute the bishop, who was obliged to appeal to Honorius for fresh authority. The Bishop of Constance had had a somewhat similar experience in 1195, when he applied to Cœlestin III for aid in ousting a deacon who while in holy orders had kept a concubine, and on her death had married a wife, retaining his benefice, in spite of all efforts to deprive him. To the good bishop's application the answer was to leave the offender in peace.

CHAPTER XVII

NORMAN ENGLAND

WE have already seen what was the condition of the Anglo-Saxon Church when William the Manzer overran the island with his horde of adventurers. Making all due allowance for the fact that our authorities are mostly of the class whose inclination would lead them to misrepresent the conquered and to exaggerate the improvement attributable to the conquest, it cannot be doubted that the standard of morality was extremely low, and that the clergy were scarcely distinguishable from the laity in purity of life or devotion to their sacred calling.

If the reformatory efforts of the popes had not penetrated into the kingdom of Edward the Confessor, it was hardly to be expected that they would excite attention amid the turmoil attendant upon the settlement of the new order of political affairs and the division of the spoils among the conquerors. Accordingly, even the vigilance of Gregory VII appears to have virtually overlooked the distant land of Britain, conscious, no doubt, that his efforts would be vain, even though the influence of Rome had been freely thrown upon the side of the Norman invader, and had been of no little assistance to him in his preparations for the desperate enterprise. In fact, though William saw fit to aid in the suppression of matrimony among the priests of his hereditary dominions, and had thereby earned the grateful praises of Gregory himself, he does not seem to have regarded the morals of his new subjects as worthy of any special attention. It is true that in his system of transferring all power from the subject to the dominant race, when Saxon bishops were to be ejected and their places filled with his own creatures, it was necessary for him to effect his purpose in a canonical way, and to procure the degradation of his victims by the Church itself, as it was impossible for him to lay unhallowed hands upon their consecrated heads, or to remove prelates from their sees on questions of mere political expediency. To accomplish this, the scandals and irregularities of their lives afforded the promptest and most effective excuse, and it was freely used. The vigour with which these changes were carried into effect is visible in the Synods of Winchester and Windsor in 1070, where numerous bishops and abbots were deprived on various pleas; and the character of the prelates removed may be assumed from the description of the Bishop of Lichfield (Chester) by Lanfranc, in a letter of the same year to Alexander II, where his public maintenance of wife and children is alleged, in addition to other crimes of which he was accused. Though a puritan, like Lanfranc, bred in the asceticism of the Abbey of Bec, might seek to enforce the canons in an individual case, as when he orders Arfastus, Bishop of Thetford, to degrade a deacon who refused to part with his wife, yet that no general effort was made to effect a reform in the ranks of the clergy is evident from an epistle addressed in 1071 to William by Alexander II, in which, while praising his zeal in suppressing the heresy of simony, and exhorting him to fresh exertion in the good work, no mention whatever is made of the kindred error of Nicolitism, which is usually inseparable in the papal diatribes of the period. Equally conclusive is the fact that when, in 1075, Lanfranc held a national council in London for the purpose of reforming the English Church, canons were passed to restrain simony, to prevent incestuous marriages, and to effect other needful changes, but nothing was said respecting sacerdotal marriage, at that time the principal object of Gregory's vigorous measures.

How thoroughly, indeed, clerical marriage and the hereditary descent of benefices were received as legitimate by common consent is manifested by a case quoted by Camden from the MS. records of the Abbey of St. Peter and St. Paul of Shrewsbury. Under the Conqueror, Roger de Montgomery in founding that house bestowed upon it the church of St. Gregory, subject to the life estate of the canons then holding it, whose prebends as they died should fall within the gift of the monks. The children of the canons, however, disputed the gift, claimed that they had a right to their fathers' holdings, and actually gave rise to a great lawsuit to defend their position.

The first steps to check the irregularities of the priesthood appear to have been taken in 1076, at the Council of Winchester, and the extreme tenderness there displayed by Lanfranc for the weakness of his flock shows how necessary was the utmost caution in treating a question evidently new, and one which deprived the English clergy of a privilege to which no taint of guilt had previously been attached. We have seen by the instance related above that when Lanfranc could act according to his own convictions, he was inclined to enforce the absolute rule of celibacy, and we may therefore conclude that on this occasion he was overruled by the convictions of his brother prelates that it was impossible to obtain obedience. All that the council would venture upon was a general declaration against the wives of men in orders, and it permitted parish priests to retain their consorts, contenting itself with forbidding future marriages, and enjoining on the bishops that they should thereafter ordain no one in the diaconate or priesthood without a pledge not to marry in future.

Such legislation could only be irritating and inconclusive. It abandoned the principle for which Rome had been contending, and thus its spirit of worldly temporising deprived it of all respect and influence. Obedience to it could therefore be evoked on no higher ground than that of an arbitrary and unjustifiable command, and accordingly it received so small a share of attention that when, some twenty-six years later, the holy Anselm, at the great Council of London in 1102, endeavoured to enforce the reform, the restrictions which he ordered were exclaimed against as unheard-of novelties, which, being impossible to human nature, could only result in indiscriminate vice, bringing disgrace upon the Church. The tenor of the canons of this council, indeed, proves that the previous injunctions had been utterly disregarded. At the same time they manifest a much stronger determination to eradicate the evil, though they are still far more lenient than the contemporary Continental legislation. No archdeacon, priest, or deacon could marry, nor, if married, could retain his wife. If a subdeacon, after professing chastity, married, he was to be subjected to the same regulation. No priest, so long as he was involved in such unholy union, could celebrate mass; if he ventured to do so, no one was to listen to him; and he was, moreover, to be deprived of all legal privileges. A profession of chastity was to be exacted at ordination to the subdiaconate and to the higher grades; and, finally, the children of priests were forbidden to inherit their father's churches.   Ineffective as was this council, it made a profound impression on the English clergy.

One symptom of weakness is observable in all this.   The council apparently did not venture to prescribe any ecclesiastical punishment for the infraction of the rules thus laid down.   If this arose from timidity, St. Anselm did not share it, for, when he proceeded to put the canons in practice, we find him threatening his contumacious ecclesiastics with deprivation for persistence in their irregularities.   A letter of instruction from him to William, Archdeacon of Canterbury, shows the earnestness with which he entered upon the reform, and also affords an instructive insight into the difficulties of the enterprise, and the misery which the forcible sundering of family ties caused among those who had never doubted the legality and propriety of their marriages.   Some ecclesiastics of rank sent their discarded wives to manors at a distance from their dwellings, and these St. Anselm directs shall not be molested if they will promise to hold no intercourse except in the presence of legitimate witnesses.   Some priests were afraid to proceed to extremities with their wives, and for these weak brethren grace is accorded until the approaching Lent, provided they do not attempt meanwhile to perform their sacred functions, and can find substitutes of undoubted chastity to minister in their places.   The kindred of the unfortunate women apparently endeavoured to avert the blow by furious menaces against those who should render obedience, and these instigators of evil are to be restrained by threats of excommunication.   Another letter to the Bishop of Hereford, who had applied for instructions on the subject, directs him to replace recalcitrant priests with monks and to stir up the laity to drive from the land the obstinate parsons and their wives.   In the enforcement of these reforms he seemed to meet with questions for which he was not prepared, for about this time we find him seeking instructions from Paschal II on several knotty points : whether a priest living with his wife can be allowed to administer the viaticum at the death-bed in the absence of one professing continence; and what is to be done with him if he refuses his ministration on the ground that he is not allowed to celebrate mass.   Paschal replies,

sensibly enough, that it is better to have the ministrations
of an unchaste priest than to die unhouselled, and that a
priest refusing his offices under such circumstances is to be
punished as a homicide of souls. This abandoned the
Hildebrandine theory and practice, and Anselm was more
consistent when he assumed that a layman could perform
baptism in preference to an unchaste priest.

Notwithstanding these zealous efforts of the primate,
and the countenance of Henry Beauclerc, in whose presence
the council had been held, Eadmer is forced sorrowfully
to admit that its canons received but scant respect. Many
of the priests adopted a kind of passive resistance, and,
locking up their churches, suspended the performance of
all sacred rites. Even in Anselm's own diocese, ecclesiastics
were found who obstinately refused either to part with
their wives or to pretermit their functions, and who, when
duly excommunicated, laughed at the sentence, and continued to pollute the Church with their unhallowed ministry.
Soon after this Anselm fell into disfavour with the king
and was exiled. His absence promised immunity, and the
clergy were not slow to avail themselves of it. In 1104
one of his friends, in writing to him, bewails the utter
demoralisation of the kingdom, of which the worst manifestation was that priests still continued to marry; and two
years later another letter informs him that those who had
apparently reformed their evil ways were all returning to
their previous life of iniquity. Finally, Henry I resolved
to turn to account this clerical backsliding, as a financial
expedient to recruit his exhausted treasury. All who were
suspected of disobedience to the canons of the Council of
London were seized and tried, and the property of those
who could be proved guilty was confiscated. By this
time Anselm had been reconciled to the king, and he
promptly interfered to check so gross a violation of ecclesiastical immunity. His remonstrances were met by
Henry with well-feigned surprise, and finally the matter
was compromised by discharging those who had not been
fined, while those who had been forced to pay were promised
three years' undisturbed possession of their positions.

That it was impossible to effect suddenly so great a
change in the habits and lives of the English clergy was,
indeed, admitted by Paschal II himself, when, in 1107, he
wrote to Anselm concerning the questions connected with

the children of priests. While reminding him of the rules of the Church, he adds that as, in England, the larger and better portion of the clergy fall within the scope of the prohibition, he grants to the primate power of dispensation, by which, in view of the sad necessity of the times, he can admit to the sacred offices those born during their parents' priesthood, who are fitted for it by their education and purity of life. A second epistle on the same subject attests the perplexity of the pope, recalling to Anselm's recollection his former injunctions, and recommending that, as there was no personal guilt involved, those of the proscribed class who were in orders should, if worthy of their positions, be allowed to retain them, without the privilege of advancement. The question, indeed, was hotly debated. There is extant a letter written about this time by Thibaut of Étampes, a dignitary of Oxford, to a certain Rosceline, who, with more zeal than discretion, had promulgated the doctrine that the sons of priests were canonically ineligible to ordination. Thibaut characterises this as not only an innovation, but a blasphemy, and seems utterly unconscious that there was any authority for such a rule.

It may be remarked that thus far the proceedings of the reformers were directed solely against the marriage of ecclesiastics. It may possibly be that this arose from general conjugal virtue, and that, satisfied with the privilege, no other disorders prevailed among the clergy; but it is more probable that the heresy of marriage was so heinous in the eyes of the sacerdotalists that it rendered all other sins venial, and that such other sins might be tacitly passed over in the endeavour to put an end to the greater enormity. Be this as it may, the stubborn wilfulness of the offenders only provoked increasing rigour on the part of the authorities. We have seen that the council of 1102 produced little result, and that when the secular power interfered to enforce its canons, the Church, jealous of its privileges, protested, so that many priests retained their wives, and marriage was still openly practised. King Henry, therefore, at length, in 1108, summoned another council to assemble in London, where he urged the bishops to prosecute the good work, and pledged his power to their support. Fortified by this and by the consent of the barons, they promulgated a series of ten canons, whose stringent nature and liberal denunciation of penalties prove that the prelates felt themselves strengthened by the royal co-operation and thus able to compel obedience. The Nicene canon was declared the unalterable law of the Church; those ecclesiastics who had disregarded the decrees of the previous council were debarred from performing their functions if longer contumacious; any priest requiring to see his wife was only to do so in the open air and in the presence of two legitimate witnesses; accusations of guilt were to be met by regular canonical purgation, a priest requiring six compurgators, a deacon four, and a subdeacon two, each of his own order. Disobedience to these canons was declared punishable with deprivation of function and benefice, expulsion from the Church, and infamy. Only eight days of grace were allowed, further persistence in wrong-doing being visited with instant excommunication, and confiscation to the bishops of the private property of the transgressors and of their women, together with the persons of the latter. A very significant clause, moreover, shows that grasping officials had discovered the speculative value of previous injunctions, and that the degrading custom of paying hush-money was already in common use, for the council required of all archdeacons and deans, under penalty of forfeiture, an oath that they would not receive money for conniving at infractions of the rule, nor permit priests who kept women to celebrate mass or to employ vicars to officiate for them.

From the account of the historian, we may assume these to be rather acts of parliament than canons of a council, and that the assembly was convened for the special purpose of devising measures for subduing the recalcitrant clergy. The temporal power was thus pledged to enforce the regulations, and as so enterprising and resolute a monarch as Henry had undertaken the reform, there can be little doubt that he prosecuted it with vigour. Anselm died in 1109, and the clergy rejoiced in the hope that their persecution would cease with the removal of their persecutor, but the king proceeded to enforce the regulations of the Council of London with more vigour than ever, and soon obtained at least an outward show of obedience. Eadmer darkly intimates that this resulted in a great increase of shocking crimes committed with those relatives whose residence was allowed, and he is at some pains to argue that Anselm and his attempted reforms were not responsible for an effect so little contemplated in their well-meant endeavours. Finally, the ardour of the king cooled off; ecclesiastical officials were found readily accessible to bribes for permitting female intercourse, and those who had grown tired of the wives from whom they had been separated found no difficulty in forming more desirable unions with new ones. Eadmer sorrowfully adds that by this time there were few indeed who continued to preserve the purity with which Anselm had laboured so strenuously to adorn his clergy.

The evil influences of this laxity in the Anglican Church were not altogether confined to Britain. At that period the Swedish bishoprics were frequently filled by Englishmen, and it is quite possible that from them was derived the laxity which, as we have seen, at a later period, caused the Swedes to be regarded as heretics adhering to the Greek schism. An incident occurring about this time shows the wisdom of the Church in her endeavours to sunder the earthly ties of her ministers. An English priest, named Edward, was promoted to the Swedish episcopate of Scaren. Unluckily, he had left a wife behind him in England, and, after a short residence in his new dignity had enabled him to collect together the treasures of his see, he absconded with them to his spouse, leaving his diocese widowed and penniless.

At length the condition of the Church in England attracted the attention of the pontiffs who had bestowed so much fruitless energy on the morals of the Continental priesthood; and Honorius II sent Cardinal John of Crema to England for the purpose of restoring its discipline. In September 1126 the legate held a council in London, where he caused the adoption of a canon menacing with degradation all those in orders who did not abstain from the society of their wives, or of other women liable to suspicion; and the expressions employed show that previous legislation had been altogether nugatory. That the cardinal's endeavours excited the opposition of at least a powerful portion of the clergy is fairly deducible from the unlucky adventure which put a sudden termination to his mission. After fiercely denouncing the concubines of priests and expatiating on the burning shame that the body of Christ should be made by one who had but just left the side of a harlot, he was that very night surprised in the company of a courtesan, though he had on the same day celebrated mass; and the suggestion that he had been entrapped by his enemies, while it did not palliate his guilt, may be assumed to indicate the power and determination of those who opposed his reforms.

The energy of the reformers and the stubborn obstinacy of the clergy are alike manifested by the Council of Westminster, held the following year, which found it necessary to repeat the prohibition and to guard it with stringent provisions, based upon those of 1108. This, however, proved as ineffectual as its predecessors, and another effort was made the next year under auspices which promised a happier result. King Henry seemed suddenly to recover the holy zeal which had lain dormant for a score of years, and in the summer of 1129 he convened a great assembly of all the bishops, archdeacons, abbots, priors, and canons of England, who found that they were summoned to meet for the purpose of putting an end to the immorality of the clergy. After long discussion, it was agreed that all who should not put away their wives by St. Andrew's Day (30 November) should be deprived of their functions, their churches, and their houses; and the assembly separated, entrusting to the zealous sovereign the execution of the decree. Perhaps Henry remembered how St. Anselm had interfered in 1106 to protect the guilty clergy from the royal extortioners; perhaps the experience of his long reign had shown him the fruitlessness of endeavouring to impose an impossible virtue on carnal-minded men. His exchequer, as usual, was in danger of collapse. The whole transaction may have been a deeply-laid scheme to extort money, or the sudden promptings of temptation may have been too powerful for his self-denial—who now can tell? We only know that he at once put into action an extended system of " cullagium," and having, by the blind simplicity of his prelates, the temporalities of nearly all the minor clergy in his power, he proceeded to traffic in exemptions shamelessly and on the largest scale. As a financial device, the plan was a good one; he realised a vast sum of money, and his afflicted priests were at least able to show their superiors a royal licence to marry or to keep their concubines in peace.

The repetition of almost identical enactments year after

year, with corresponding infinitesimal results, grows wearisome and monotonous. If, therefore, I refer to the Synod of Westminster, held in 1138, by the papal legate Alberic, Bishop of Ostia, which deprived of function and benefice all married and concubinary ecclesiastics, it is only to observe that no notice was taken of the doctrine of the invalidity of sacerdotal marriage, which at that period Innocent II was engaged in promulgating. So, if I allude to an epistle of Lucius II in 1144, reprehending the general English custom by which sons succeeded to the churches of their fathers, it is merely to chronicle the commencement of the direct efforts of the popes, fruitlessly continued during the remainder of the century, to abolish that widespread and seemingly ineradicable abuse.

What was the condition of the Church resulting from these prolonged and persistent efforts may be guessed from one or two examples. When, in 1139, Nigel, Bishop of Ely, revolted against King Stephen, he entrusted the defence of his castle of Devizes to his concubine, Maud of Ramsbury. She bravely fulfilled her charge and repulsed the assaults of the king, until he bethought him of a way to compel a surrender. Obtaining possession of Roger, son of Maud and Nigel, the unhappy youth was brought before the walls, and preparations were made to hang him in his mother's sight. At this her courage gave way, and she capitulated at once. Though the monkish chronicler stigmatises Maud as " pellex episcopi," she may probably have been his wife—in either case the publicity of the connection is a sufficient commentary on the morals and manners of the age which took no exception to the elevation of Richard Fitz-Neal, another son of the same reverend prelate, to the bishopric of London and to the post of treasurer to King Henry II.

If this be attributed to the unbridled turbulence of Stephen's reign, we may turn to the comparatively calmer times of Henry II, when Alexander III, amid his ceaseless efforts to restore the Church discipline of England, in 1171 ordered the Bishops of Exeter and Worcester and the Abbot of Feversham to examine and report as to the evil reputation of Clarembald, Abbot-elect of St. Augustine's of Canterbury. In the execution of this duty they found that that venerable patriarch had seventeen bastards in one village; purity he ridiculed as an impossibility, while even licentiousness had no attraction for his exhausted senses unless spiced with the zest of publicity. That a man whose profligacy was so openly and shamelessly defiant could be elected to the highest place in the oldest and most honoured religious community in England is a fact which lends colour to an assertion of a writer of the time of King John, that clergy and laity were indistinguishably bad, and perhaps justifies the anecdote told of Hugh, Bishop of Lincoln, who assumed that the clergy were much worse than the laity. How little these scandals shocked the public is shown by the fact that it required papal interference to cause the reformation of the nunnery of Avesbury. The abbess had borne three children, and the nuns, as the chronicler informs us, were worse than their superior, but when Alexander forced an investigation no canonical punishment was inflicted on the guilty. Such of the nuns as promised to live chastely in future were allowed to remain, and the rest were simply dismissed, while the abbess was pensioned liberally with ten marks a year to preserve her from disgrace and want. The vacancies thus created were filled with nuns from Fontevraud, who proved to be as bad as those whom they replaced. The same insensibility is manifested in a legal transaction of the period, when Witgar, the priest of Mendlesham, desired to secure the reversion of his benefice to his son Nicholas, and applied to the patron of his church, Martin, Abbot of Battle Abbey, who agreed to conform to his wishes on condition that the annual payment exacted from the church in question should be increased from ten shillings to forty. Witgar agreed, and on an appointed day, accompanied by his son, he met the abbot and his attendants at Colchester, where oaths were publicly interchanged and a formal agreement was entered into.

The efforts of Alexander and his successors were seconded by frequent national and local synods, to whose special injunctions it is scarcely worth while to refer in full. One noticeable point about them, however, is that the term " wife " disappears, and is replaced by " concubina " or " focaria "—the latter meaning a person who was a permanent occupant of the priest's hearth, but was not recognised by the authorities as a lawful wife. Deans and archdeacons were enjoined to hunt up these illegal companions, but from the frequency of the injunctions we may safely conclude that the search was not often successful, and that the officials found the duty assigned to them too difficult or too unprofitable for execution. That it was not impossible, however, when earnestly undertaken, is shown by the readiness with which King John unearthed the unfortunate creatures when it suited his policy to do so. During the long dispute over the election of Giraldus Cambrensis to the see of St. David's, the king, who was resolved that no Welshman should hold that preferment, instructed his officers, in 1202, to seize the women of all the cathedral chapter who persisted in supporting Giraldus. The measure was doubtless an efficacious one, and he repeated it when, in 1208, he persecuted the clergy in his blind impotence of wrath at the interdict set upon his kingdom by Innocent III. Discerning in these quasi-conjugal relations the tenderest spot in which to strike those who had rebelled against his authority by obeying the interdict, and at the same time as the surest and readiest means of extorting money, among his other schemes of spoliation he caused all these women to be seized, and then forced the unfortunate Churchmen to buy their partners back at exorbitant prices.

The ease, indeed, with which the eyes of the officials were blinded to that which was patent to the public was the subject of constantly recurring legislation, the reiteration and increasing violence of which bear irrefragable testimony at once to its necessity and its impotence. Not only in grave synods and pastorals was the abuse reprehended and deplored, but it offered too favourable a subject for popular animadversion to escape the shafts of satire. In the preceding century, Thomas à Becket, in a vehement attack upon simony, includes this among the many manifestations of that multiform sin—

> Symon auffert, Symon donat;
> Hunc expellit, hunc coronat;
> Hunc circumdat gravi peste,
> Illum nuptiali veste.

There were few more popular poems in the Middle Ages than the " Apocalypsis Goliæ," the more than doubtful authorship of which, at the close of the twelfth or the beginning of the thirteenth century, is claimed for Walter

Mapes in England and Gautier de Châtillon in France;
and the enduring reputation of which is attested by an
English version as late as the sixteenth century. The
author, whoever he be, inveighing against the evil courses
of the archdeacons, assumes that the extortion of the
" cullagium " was almost universal.

> Seductam nuntii fraude præambuli
> Capit focariam, ut per cubiculi
> Fortunam habeat fortunam loculi,
> Et per vehiculum omen vehiculi.
> Decano præcipit quod si presbiteri
> Per genitivos scit dativos fieri,
> Accusans faciat vocatum conteri,
> Ablatis fratribus a porta inferi.

Towards the middle of the thirteenth century, Peter de
Vinea also has his fling at the same corruption, and though
the part he took in the fierce quarrels between his master
Frederic II and the papacy renders him perhaps a prejudiced
witness, still his ample experience of the disorders of the
Church makes him an experienced one.

> Non utuntur clerici nostri vestimentis :
> Sed tenent focarias, quod clamor est gentis—
> —Dehinc reum convocant, et, turba rejecta,
> Dicunt : Ista crimina tibi sunt objecta;
> Pone libras quindecim in nostra collecta,
> Et tua flagitia non erunt detecta.
> Reus dat denarios, Fratres scriptum radunt;
> Sic infames plurimi per nummos evadunt;
> Qui totam pecuniam quam petunt non tradunt,
> Simul in infamiam et in pœnam cadunt.

The example which King John had set, however instructive, was not appreciated by the ecclesiastical authorities,
and the " focariæ " were allowed to remain virtually undisturbed, at least to such an extent as to render them almost
universal. Although by rigid Churchmen they were
regarded as mere concubines, there can be little doubt that
the tie between them and the priests was of a binding nature,
which appears to have wanted none of the rites essential to
its entire respectability. Giraldus Cambrensis, who died
at an advanced age about the year 1220, speaks of these
companions being publicly maintained by nearly all the
parish priests in England and Wales. They arranged to
have their benefices transmitted to their sons, while their
daughters were married to the sons of other priests, thus

establishing an hereditary sacerdotal caste in which marriage appears to have been a matter of course. In 1202 the Bishop of Exeter complained to Innocent III of the numerous sons of parish priests and vicars who seized their churches and claimed to hold them of right, actually appealing to Rome when they sought to interfere with them. Innocent of course ordered their removal and subjection to discipline without appeal; but the evil continued, and in 1205 we find him writing on the subject to the Bishop of Winchester, whom he required to eject the sons of priests who in many cases held their fathers' benefices. The propriety of the connection, and the hereditary ecclesiastical functions of the offspring, are quaintly alluded to in a poem of the period, wherein a logician takes a priest to task for entertaining such a partner—

> L.—Et præ tot innumeris quæ frequentas malis,
> Est tibi presbytera plus exitialis.
> P.—Malo cum presbytera pulchra fornicari,
> Servituros domino filios lucrari,
> Quam vagas satellites per antra sectari :
> Est inhonestissimum sic dehonestari.

Even the holy virgins, spouses of Christ, seem to have claimed and enjoyed the largest liberty. To this period is attributed a homily to nuns, which earnestly dissuades them from leaving their blessed state and subjecting themselves to the cares and toils inseparable from matrimony. The writer appeals to no rules of ecclesiastical law that could be enforced to prevent them from following their choice, but labours drearily to prove that they would not better their condition, either in this world or the next, by forsaking their heavenly bridegroom for an earthly one.— " And of godes brude. and his freo dohter. for ba to gederes ha is ; bicometh theow under mon and his threl to don al and drehen that him liketh."

Innocent III had not overlooked such a state of discipline, especially after the transactions between himself and John had rendered him the suzerain of England, and doubly responsible for the morals of the English Church. Thus as early as 1203 we find him expressing to the Bishop of Norwich his surprise that priests in his diocese contend that they can retain their benefices after having solemnly contracted marriage in the face of the Church. All such are peremptorily ordered to be removed without appeal, either by the bishop himself, or by his superior in cases in which he had personally conferred the preferment. His zealous efforts to effect an impossible reform are chronicled by a rhymer of the period, who enters fully into the dismay of the good pastors at the prospect of the innovation, and who argues their cause with all the sturdy common sense of the Anglo-Saxon mind.

Prisciani regula penitus cassatur,
    Sacerdos per hic et hæc olim declinabatur;
    Sed per hic solummodo nunc articulatur,
    Cum per nostrum præsulem hæc amoveatur.

Quid agant presbyteri propriis carentes?
    Alienas violant clanculo molentes,
    Nullis pro conjugiis fœminis parcentes,
    Pœnam vel infamiam nihil metuentes.

Non est Innocentius, immo nocens vere,
    Qui quod Deus docuit studet abolere;
    Jussit enim Dominus fœminas habere,
    Sed hoc noster pontifex jussit prohibere.

Gignere nos præcipit vetus testamentum;
    Ubi novum prohibet nusquam est inventum.
    A modernis latum est istud documentum,
    Ad quod nullum ratio præbet argumentum.

Nor were the English bishops remiss in seconding the efforts of the pope to break down the opposition which thus openly defied their power and ventured even to justify the heresy of sacerdotal marriage. Councils were held which passed canons more stringent than ever; bishops issued constitutions and pastorals denouncing the custom; inquests were organised to traverse the dioceses and investigate the household of every priest. The women especially were attacked. Christian sepulture was denied them; property left to them and their children by their partners in guilt was confiscated to the bishops; churching after childbirth was interdicted to them; and, if still contumacious after a due series of warnings, they were to be handed over to the secular arm for condign punishment. How much all this bustling legislation effected is best shown by the declaration of the legate, Cardinal Otto, in

1237, at the great Council of London. He deplores the fact that married men received orders and held benefices while still retaining their wives, and did not hesitate to acknowledge their children as legitimate by public deeds and witnesses. After descanting upon the evils of this neglect of discipline, he orders that all married clerks shall be deprived of preferment and benefice, that their property shall not descend to wife or children, but to their churches, and that their sons shall be incapable of holy orders unless specially dispensed for eminent merit; then, turning upon concubinary priests, he inveighs strongly against their licentiousness, and decrees that all guilty of the sin shall within thirty days dismiss their women for ever, under pain of suspension from function and benefice until full satisfaction, persistent contumacy being visited with deprivation. The archbishops and bishops are commanded to make thorough inquisition throughout all the deaneries, to bring offenders to light, and also to put an end to the iniquitous practice of ordaining the offspring of such connections as successors in their father's benefices.

This legislation produced much excitement, and the legate even had fears for his life. Some prelates, indeed, maintained that it was binding on the Church of England only during the residence of Otto, but they were overruled, and it remained, at least nominally, in force, and was frequently referred to subsequently as the recognised law in such matters. Its effect was considerable, and some of the bishops endeavoured to carry out its provisions with energy, as may be presumed from a constitution of William of Cantilupe, Bishop of Worcester, issued in 1240, ordering his officials to investigate diligently whether any of the clergy of the diocese had concubines or were married.

To this period and to the disturbance caused by these proceedings are doubtless to be attributed several satirical pieces of verse describing the excitement occurring among the unfortunate clerks thus attacked in their tenderest spot. The opening lines of one of these poems indicate the novelty and unexpectedness of the new regulations :—

> Rumor novus Angliæ partes pergiravit,
> Clericos, presbyteros omnes excitavit,
>
> . . . . . .
>
> Nasciter presbyteris hinc fera procella :
> Quisquis timet graviter pro sua puella.

The author then describes a great council, attended by more than ten thousand ecclesiastics, assembled to deliberate on the course to be pursued in so delicate a conjuncture. An old priest commences—

> Pro nostris uxoribus sumus congregati;
> Videatis provide quod sitis parati,
> Ad mandatum domini papæ vel legati,
> Respondere graviter ne sitis dampnati.

Another poem of similar character describes a chapter held by all orders and grades to consider the same question. The various speakers declare their inability to obey the new rule, except two, whose age renders them indifferent. A learned doctor exclaims—

> Omnis debit clericus habere concubinam;
> Hoc dixit qui coronam gerit auro trinam :
> Hanc igitur retinere decet disciplinam.

The general belief in the legality of the connection is shown by the remark of another—

> Surgens unus presbyter turba de totali . . .
> " Unam " dixit " teneo amore legali,
> Quam nolo demittere pro lege tali."

Another expects to escape by paying his " cullagium "—

> Duodecimus clamat magno cum clamore :
> " Non me pontifex terret minis et pavore :
> Sed ego nummos præbeam pro Dei amore,
> Ut in pace maneam cara cum uxore."

Another urges the indiscriminate immorality attending upon the attempt to enforce an impossible asceticism—

> Addidit ulterius : " Sitis memor horum,
> Si vetare præsul vult specialem torum,
> Cernet totum brevi plenum esse chorum
> Ordine sacrorum adulterorum."

And at length the discussion closes with the speech of a Dominican, who ends his remarks by predicting—

> Habebimus clerici duas concubinas :
> Monachi, canonici totidem vel trinas :
> Decani, prælati, quatuor vel quinas :
> Sic tandem leges implebimus divinas.

Notwithstanding these flights of the imagination, no organised resistance was offered to the reform. The clergy sullenly acquiesced, and submitted to a pressure which was becoming irresistible. The triumph of the sacerdotal party, however, was gradual, and no exact limit can be assigned to the recognition of the principle of celibacy. In 1250 the idea of married priests was still sufficiently prevalent to lead the populace of London to include matrimony among the accusations brought against Boniface, Archbishop of Canterbury, when his tyranny had aroused general resistance; and in 1255 Walter Kirkham, Bishop of Durham, still felt it necessary to prohibit the marriage of his clergy under pain of suspension and deprivation.

While doubtless these efforts were gradually putting an end to priestly marriage, existing unions persisted, and their results were long in disappearing. Dr. Jessopp prints a deed, to which he assigns the approximate date of 1279, granting a piece of land in Keswick to the cleric Henry of Norwich and his wife Katherine, and their legitimate children. That the transmission of benefices from father to son was recognised as illegal, while they still continued, is seen in the prohibition by Gregory IX in 1240, and by Innocent IV in 1243, of the collusive transactions through which it was sought to conceal them. Another result of the progress of the reform is found in the large demand for dispensations enabling illegitimates to enter holy orders and hold preferment, accompanied by papal injunctions to eject all such as had not so protected themselves, for these dispensations could always be had from the curia by those willing to pay the fees.

By this time, however, priestly marriage may be considered to have become nearly obsolete in England. When, in 1268, the Cardinal-legate Ottoboni held a great national council in London, and renewed the constitutions of his predecessor Otto, he made no allusion to marriage, and only denounced the practice of concubinage, which he endeavoured to eradicate by commanding all archdeacons to make a thorough inquisition annually into the morals of the clergy under their jurisdiction. These constitutions of Otto and Ottoboni long remained the law of the English Church, and we find them constantly referred to in the canons of councils and pastorals of bishops, ceaselessly labouring to effect the impossible enforcement of discipline;

even as late as 1399 the Archbishop of Canterbury ordered his suffragans to have them read and explained in the vernacular in all their episcopal synods. How hard was the task may be readily conceived when we see, in 1279, the primate Peckham, Archbishop of Canterbury, applying to Rome for assistance in prosecuting a certain bishop against whom he had long been vainly endeavouring to bring the law to bear. A concubine had confessed to having borne five children to the offender; he had himself admitted his guilt in a private interview with Peckham, for which he had afterwards claimed the seal of the confessional; yet the archbishop complains that his efforts will be unsuccessful unless he is fortified with letters from the pope himself. His strict injunctions of secrecy on his correspondent, and his evident dread lest the criminal's agents in Rome should get wind of the application, show how difficult was the enterprise, and how rarely prelates could be expected to undertake duties so arduous and so unpromising.

Perhaps the man to whom the Church owed most for his energy and activity in promoting the cause of reform was the celebrated Robert Grosseteste, Bishop of Lincoln. The leading part which he took in the political troubles of the stormy reign of Henry III has thrown his ecclesiastical character somewhat into the shade, and he is better known as the friend of Leicester than as the untiring Churchman. Notwithstanding his consistent opposition to Henry III and to the encroachments of the papacy, he was the inflexible enemy of clerical irregularities, and he enforced the decretals throughout his diocese with as firm a hand as that which he raised in defence of the rights of the nation and the privileges of the English Church. Thus, in 1251, he made a rigorous inquisition in his bishopric, forcing all his beneficed clergy to the observance of the strictest chastity, removing from their houses all suspected women, and punishing transgressors with deprivation. It is not easy to approve of his brutal expedient for testing the virtue of the inmates of his nunneries, the adoption of which could only be justified and suggested by the conviction that general licentiousness was everywhere prevalent : yet it was doubtless more efficacious than the ordeal of the Eucharist, which was frequently resorted to in special cases. Not only, however, did he thus endeavour to reform the morals of his flock, but he made the closest scrutiny into the character of applicants for ordination. In this he was largely aided by his ascetic friend and admirer, Adam de Marisco, and the correspondence between them shows not only the importance which they reasonably attached to the subject, but the sleepless vigilance required to counteract the prevalent immorality of the clergy, and the incredible laxity with which the patrons of livings bestowed the benefices in their gift.

The rule was now fairly established and generally acknowledged : concubinage, though still prevalent—nay, in fact almost universal—was not defended as a right, but was practised with what concealment was possible, and was the object of unremitting assault from councils and prelates. To enter into the details of the innumerable canons and constitutions directed against the ineradicable vice during the succeeding half-century would be unprofitable. Their endless iteration is only interesting as proving their inefficacy. A popular satirist of the reign of Edward II declares that bribery of the ecclesiastical officials insured the domestic comfort of the clergy and their female companions; while in time the canon law seems to have lost all its terrors. One of the earliest acts of the reign of Henry VII was a law empowering the ecclesiastical officials to imprison " priests, clerks, and religious men " convicted of incontinence, and guaranteeing them against prosecution by the offenders. That the aid of the secular legislator should thus have been invoked for protection under such circumstances showed the audacity resulting from long immunity, and is a confession that the ceaseless labour of four centuries had utterly failed.

In one part of England, however, the reform seems to have penetrated more slowly. We have seen above, on the testimony of Giraldus Cambrensis, that in the early part of the thirteenth century the marriage of priests and the hereditary transmission of benefices were almost universal in Wales. As in the wild fastnesses of the principality the ecclesiastical regulations seemed powerless, recourse was had to the secular law, which was employed to inflict various disabilities on offenders and their offspring, and the repetition of these shows how obstinately the custom was adhered to by the clergy until a comparatively late period. Thus, in the Gwentian and Dimetian Codes there is a provision that the son of a married priest, born after the ordination of his father, shall not share in the paternal estate ; and this provision is retained and repeated in a collection of laws which contains the date of 2 Henry IV, showing it to be posterior to the year 1400. The same collection enumerates married priests among " thirteen things corrupting the world, and which will ever remain in it ; and it can never be delivered of them." In the same spirit, the Book of Cynog, which is of uncertain date, declares, " Nor is a married priest, as he has relinquished his law, to be credited in law," and it therefore directs that the testimony of such witnesses shall not be receivable in court ; while another collection of laws, occurring in a MS. of the fifteenth century, repeats the provision—" their testimony is not to be credited in any place, and they are excluded from the law, unless they ask a pardon from the pope or a bishop, through a public penance." In fact, we may perhaps almost hazard the conclusion that, notwithstanding the efforts of both ecclesiastical and secular legislators, sacerdotal marriage scarcely became obsolete in Wales before it was once more recognised as legitimate under the Reformation.

CHAPTER XVIII

IRELAND AND SCOTLAND

In a previous section it has already been shown that the
rule of celibacy was observed by the Celtic Churches of
the British Islands during a period in which their Christianity was a model for the rest of Europe. Their religion,
however, could not preserve its purity and simplicity amid
the overwhelming barbarism of those dreary ages. From
an ancient commentary on the " Cain Patraic," or Patrick's
Law, of uncertain date, but probably belonging to the
ninth or tenth century, it would seem as though there
were at that time two classes of bishops, one bound by
monastic vows, the other permitted to marry; and, what
is somewhat singular, the law appears to favour the latter,
for the " cumad espuc," or virgin bishop, is condemned to
perpetual degradation or to the life of a hermit for offences
which the " bishop of one wife " can redeem by prompt
penance.

The Feini, prior to the advent of St. Patrick, were far
in advance of the contemporary barbarian tribes, and their
conversion to Christianity introduced a new and powerful
element of progress. It was not lasting, however, and
they lapsed into a condition but little removed from that
of savages. The marriage-tie was virtually unknown or
habitually disregarded among the laity. What was the
condition of the clergy may be inferred from the fact that
the episcopates were regarded as the private property of
certain families in which they descended by hereditary
succession. Thus, in the primatial see of Armagh, fifteen
archbishops were of one house, the last eight of whom
were married. At length Celsus, who died about the year
1130, bequeathed the dignity to his friend St. Malachy.
The kindred rose in arms at this infringement of their
rights, and two of their members successively occupied

the position, which Malachy was not able to obtain until the anger of God had miraculously destroyed the whole family.

During all this period the Irish Church had been completely independent of the central authority at Rome, but the extension of influence resulting from the labours of Hildebrand and his successors soon began to make itself felt. In the quarrels concerning the succession of Archbishop Celsus, there figures a certain Bishop Gilbert, who is described as being the first papal legate seen in Ireland. When Malachy abandoned Armagh and revived the extinct episcopate of Down, he resolved on a pilgrimage to Rome to obtain the *pallium*, a powerful instrument of papal authority, until then unknown on the island; and perhaps the opposition manifested to his wishes by his friends as well as by the authorities may be attributable to a repugnance towards the gradual encroachments of Romanising influence.

Malachy returned from Rome armed with legatine powers, and proceeded vigorously with the reforms which he had long before commenced. He held numerous councils, extirpating abuses everywhere, renovating the ancient rules of discipline and introducing new ones, bending all his energies to abrogating the national institutions and replacing them with those of Rome. The earnest asceticism of his nature, exaggerated by the training of his youth, led him to give a strongly monastic character to the Church of which he was thus the second founder. On his journey homeward from Rome, he had tarried a second time at Clairvaux to see his friend St. Bernard, and had left there four of his attendants to be exercised in the severe Cistercian discipline, that they might serve as missionaries and as models for his compatriots, who had heard, indeed, of monkhood, but had never seen it. His efforts in this respect were to a considerable extent successful, at least in a portion of the island, though his death in 1149, at the comparatively early age of fifty-four, cut short his labours before they could yield their full fruit.

The incongruous character thus imparted to the Irish Church is described by Giraldus Cambrensis some forty years later. The prelates were selected from the monasteries, and the Church was completely monastic. Chastity was the only rule of discipline thoroughly preserved, and Giraldus confesses his wonder that it could be maintained, in contradiction to all former experience, when gluttony and drunkenness were carried to excess. The monastic principle of selfishness was all-pervading, and the pastors took no care of their flocks. Among the people, marriage was still unknown, incest was of common occurrence, even the rudiments of Christian faith were left untaught, and the Church was regarded without reverence. His account of the absence of regular stipends and tithes is confirmed by the fact that an Irish bishop attending the Council of Lateran in 1179, in complaining of the condition of his native Church, stated that his only revenues were derived from three milch cows, which his flock were bound to replace as they became dry. This poverty, however apostolic in itself, can only, in an age of magnificent sacerdotalism, be regarded as an indication of a Church whose degradation could command neither the respect nor the support of its children. That the reforms of Malachy, one-sided as they were, extended only over a portion of the island, is evident from the inquiry which, a few years later, the Archbishop of Cashel addressed to Clement III as to whether the children of bishops could receive orders and hold benefices; and the exceptional character of the Irish establishment was recognised by the pope when he decided that they could, provided they were born in wedlock, and were otherwise worthy of position. This requisite of legitimacy was apparently not imposed in ignorance, for at the Council of Cashel in 1171 we find an effort made to enforce Christian marriage among the people, who are still described as indulging in unrestricted polygamy and disregarding the nearest ties of consanguinity.

When about this period the English commenced the conquest which was to lead to five centuries of cruel anarchy, they of course carried with them their civil and ecclesiastical institutions. The original conquerors—the Butlers, the Clares, and the Fitzgeralds—speedily became incorporated with the native race, and were as Irish as the O'Briens and the McCauras. Although the royal authority was limited practically to the confines of the Pale, and embraced little beyond the Ostman ports, yet it is easy to understand that the clerical licence habitual to the English spread beyond the political boundaries, and the monastic spirit of the Hibernians was grievously wounded by the unchastity which was disseminated like a contagion from the dissolute priests who followed in the wake of Strong-bow and Prince John. Not twenty years after the first invasion, a council, summoned in 1186 by John in Dublin, was troubled by a quarrel between the Saxon priests of Wexford, who mutually accused each other of publicly marrying and keeping wives. This being duly proved, they were promptly degraded, to the intense satisfaction of the Irish clergy, triumphant in their own comparative purity of morals. When, therefore, in 1205, Innocent III specially ordered his legate, Cardinal Julian, to put an end to the hereditary transmission of benefices common in Ireland, the abuse to which he referred was probably confined to the English Pale. The Church establishments, in fact, were distinct, and consequently, when an Irish synod was held in Dublin, in 1217, its canons cannot be considered as having authority beyond the narrow territory through which the king's writ would likewise run. Those canons show us that the morality of the Saxon priesthood had not improved by the example made of the priests of Wexford. The denunciations of concubinage indicate the prevalence of that vice, and the severities threatened against the unfortunate women contrast strangely with the leniency shown to their more guilty partners. That little was accomplished is indicated by an epistle of Honorius III in 1219, denouncing the laxities of the Hibernian Church, which in his eyes were equivalent to heresies. In 1250, Innocent IV ordered the Bishop of Ossory to deprive all married clerks of benefices, and to remove all priests who had succeeded to their fathers' parishes without an intermediate incumbent. This effort was equally fruitless, if we may believe the Synod of Ossory in 1320, which declares that the evil continued to flourish, open, avowed, and universal, resisting alike the authority of the Church and the efforts to repress it by severity. Whether the offenders dismissed their consorts after the thirty days' grace allowed by the synod may well be doubted. With the spread of English domination, the purity of the native Church disappeared, and so great became the general disregard of the canons that shortly before the Reformation it was not an unusual thing for Irish priests to be openly married, nor do those who were seem to have thereby forfeited the esteem of their neighbours.

In Scotland, the Christianity introduced by St. Columba had fallen into the hands of the Culdees. These were originally monks of a more than ordinary strictness of discipline, the earliest recorded allusion to whom occurs in Ireland towards the close of the eighth century—the name, Céle-dé (Keledeus, or Servus Dei), meaning simply Servant of God. In the course of time the Culdees had so relaxed their rule that they reappear in the eleventh century as an order nominally of monks, yet fulfilling the functions of the secular clergy, and enjoying free permission to marry, only abstaining from their wives when employed in the actual ministry of the altar. With marriage had come the hereditary transmission of the endowments of the Church to their children, so that the ancient abbeys and churches were well-nigh stripped of all their posses- sions, and the distinction between clergy and laity was rather a term than a fact. It may please the poet to reconstruct a world of his own, peopled by imaginary beings of angelic purity—

> Peace to their shades !   The pure Culdees
>   Were Albyn's earliest priests of God,
> Ere yet an island of her seas
>   By foot of Saxon monk was trod,
> Long ere her churchmen by bigotry
> Were barred from wedlock's holy tie.
> 'Twas then that Aodh, famed afar,
>   In Iona preached the word with power,
> And Reullura, beauty's star,
>   Was the partner of his bower—

but in sober truth the Culdees were pure so long as they kept the tradition of their founder, and it was not until they sank to the level of their savage compatriots that they transgressed the rule and became worldly and cor- rupt. In 1125 the Cardinal-legate, John of Crema, whose unlucky adventure in London has been already alluded to, visited Scotland in the execution of his reformatory mis- sion. There he found on the throne David I, a prince whose life was devoted to rescuing his subjects from their primeval barbarism. We know few details of the history of those times, but it is fair to conjecture that the exhorta- tions of the legate had a share in arousing David to a realisation of the deficiencies and the corruptions of the Scottish Church, and in guiding him to the course which he adopted in its reformation. After some fruitless efforts to restore the order of Culdees to its original condition, he resolved on the sweeping measure of removing all who should prove incorrigible. They were accordingly turned out bodily from their establishments, such property as could be traced was restored, and donations on an extended scale were made both to the old foundations and to the new ones which the royal reformer established—donations which gained for him, from an ungodly descendant, the appellation of " Ane soir sanct for the crown." These foundations were then filled with regular clergy, brought from France and England—chiefly canons of the order of St. Augustin—and the unfortunate Culdees were turned adrift unless they would promise to observe the strictness of monastic rule. That in a few places they did so is shown by references to Culdees even in the next century, but these measures were effective, and practically they and their customs disappeared together.

In a Church thus constructed from the regular clergy the heresy of marriage could find no foothold, especially as it had been so sternly punished in the expulsion of the Culdees. Still was the desired purity not yet attained. In 1181, during the long quarrel between William the Lion and the papacy on the subject of the archbishopric of St. Andrews, an interdict was pronounced on all ecclesiastics who should refuse to recognise the papal candidate John, whereupon the king persecuted those who obeyed the mandate, and the chronicler, in expatiating upon his cruelty, is careful to mention that he did not spare their children, even to babes in their mothers' arms, who were remorselessly driven into exile. The state of things indicated by this remained without improvement. In 1225, Honorius III ordered the Scottish ecclesiastics to assemble in council for the correction of the many enormities which were committed with impunity; and the council held in obedience to the papal command denounced the shameless licentiousness of the clergy as a disgrace to the Church. Inquests to detect the offenders, suspension and deprivation to punish them, were ordered with all the verbal energy of which we have already witnessed so many examples, and were attended with the same plentiful lack of success. With what disposition the clergy regarded these efforts for their improvement we may guess from the reception which they gave to the constitutions of Cardinal Ottoboni. Reference has already been made to the council held by that legate in London in 1268. The Church of Scotland had been ordered to join in this council, and had sent two bishops and two abbots as its representative delegates. These took home with them the constitutions of Ottoboni, which the clergy of Scotland utterly refused to obey.

CHAPTER XIX

WE have already seen (p. 93) that among the Visigoths of Spain the rule of celibacy had never been successfully enforced, and that during the later period of the Gothic dynasty the demoralisation of the clergy was daily increasing. The Saracenic invasion, and the subsequent struggles of the Christians, who founded petty kingdoms among the wild, mountainous regions of the north and east of the Peninsula, were not favourable to the growth of regular discipline and settled observances. The centralised sacerdotalism of Rome, which took so remarkable an extension in the ninth and tenth centuries, and which penetrated every portion of the Carlovingian empire, was powerless to intrude into the strongholds of the Jalikiah, whence the descendants of Pelayo and his companions gradually extended their frontiers from Oviedo to Toledo. Communication with the apostolic city was rare. The nominal subjection of Barcelona and Navarre to the Carlovingians, indeed, brought the eastern provinces of Spain under the domination of the Archbishops of Narbonne, and kept them, to a certain extent, under the influences which were moulding the rest of Europe; but the kingdoms of Leon and Castile grew up in complete ecclesiastical independence. Even at the close of the eleventh century a Spanish ecclesiastic describes his contemporary brethren as rude and illiterate, owning no obedience to the mother Church of Rome, and governed by the discipline of Toledo. Wild and insubordinate as was a large portion of the European clergy, the ecclesiastics of Spain were even wilder and more insubordinate. Another writer of the period, himself a canon of Compostella, and subsequently Bishop of Mondonego, speaking of his brother canons previous to the reforms of Diego Gelmirez, denounces them as reckless and violent men, ready for any crime, prompt in quarrel, and even occasionally indulging in mutual slaughter. How little, indeed, there was to distinguish the clerk from the layman is evident from a regulation promulgated by the Council of Compostella in 1113. It provides that all priests, gentlemen, and peasants shall devote themselves to wolf-hunting on every Sunday, except Easter and Pentecost, under penalty of a fine of five sols for the priest and gentleman, and one sol, or a sheep, for the peasant— visitation of the sick being the only excuse exempting the priest from the performance of this duty. Every church, moreover, was bound to furnish for the hunt, seven iron-tipped reeds. A similar condition of society is indicated at the other end of Spain, where, in 1027, the Synod of Elna, in Roussillon, had forbidden, under pain of excommunication, any one to attack a monk or a clerk who was without arms.

In such lack of social organisation it is easy to imagine that the rule of celibacy received little attention. According to Mariana, the clergy of the period were, for the most part, publicly married; and when, in 1056, the Council of Compostella specifically forbade to bishops and monks all intercourse with women, except with mothers, aunts, and sisters wearing the monastic habit, the inference is fair that even so elementary a prohibition was an innovation, and that the secular clergy, below the episcopate, were not regarded as subject to any restriction.

In the comprehensive efforts, however, made during the later half of the eleventh century by the Roman Church to bring all Christendom under its domination, the rising states of Spain were not likely to remain undisturbed in their independent isolation; nor was it to be expected that so complete a defiance of the canons would be passed unobserved by the pontiffs who were convulsing the rest of Europe in their efforts to reform the Church. Accordingly, in 1068, we find the Cardinal Hugo of Silva Candida, as legate of Alexander II, assembling a council at Gerona, and procuring the adoption of a regulation reducing to the condition of laymanship all who, in holy orders, either entered into matrimony or kept concubines; while those who should dismiss their wives were promised immunity for the past and security for the future. In 1077, Gregory VII sent a certain Bishop Amandus as his legate, with an epistle addressed to the Spaniards, in which he told them that Spain had anciently belonged to St. Peter and the Roman Church; that the carelessness of his predecessors, and the Saracenic conquest, had caused the papal rights to be forgotten, but that the time had come for them to be revindicated, and that he consequently claimed implicit obedience. Accordingly, in 1078, we find the legate presiding over another council at Gerona, which confirmed the canons of the previous one, and added several others to prevent the ordination of sons of priests and the hereditary transmission of benefices. Such slender reforms as may have resulted from these efforts were probably confined to Catalonia and Aragon; but not long afterwards influences were brought to bear upon the rest of Spain, which had a powerful effect in extending the authority of Rome over the Peninsula. Constance of Burgundy, Queen of Alfonso VI of Castile and Leon, prevailed upon her husband to ask of Gregory a legate to reform the Church, and to condemn the Gothic or Mozarabic ritual, which was jealously preserved by the people as a symbol of their independent nationality. The prayer, of course, was granted. Richard, Abbot of Marseilles, was sent, and in 1080 he held a council at Burgos, where he commanded the ordained clergy to put away their wives. The novelty and hardship of this order created great excitement. The pope, who was rightly regarded as its author, became the object of no little abuse and insult, and was held up to popular derision in innumerable lampoons.

All of these efforts were nugatory, in spite of the cloud of Cluniac monks who settled upon Spain, obtaining abbeys and bishoprics and Gallicising in many ways the national Church. The Spaniards, engaged in an interminable and often doubtful struggle with the Infidel, might well claim consideration from the Holy Father, while the independent spirit which they manifested in their resistance to the introduction of the Roman ritual was a warning that it would be prudent not to proceed too abruptly in the process of bringing them within the fold of St. Peter. Whatever be the motives, indeed, which induced such strenuous apostles of celibacy as Gregory, Urban, Paschal, and Calixtus to abstain from urging upon them the reform which was so earnestly enforced elsewhere, it is certain that little effort was made to deprive the Spanish clergy of their wives. In all the epistles of the popes up to 1130

I can find but one allusion to the subject, though communication between Spain and Italy became daily more frequent, and the papal authority was constantly exercised with greater decisiveness in the internal affairs of the Spanish Church.

When, in 1101, Diego Gelmirez succeeded in obtaining the see of Compostella, Paschal II addressed him an epistle, reproaching him with the utter contempt of discipline in his diocese, and commanding a reform. He chiefly complained of the incongruous common residence of monks and nuns, which he severely condemned and peremptorily prohibited, but he made some concession to the necessities of the time in permitting the ordination of the sons of those priests who had, " according to the ordinary custom of the country," married prior to the promulgation of what the pope significantly termed the Roman law; and he carefully abstained from ordering a separation between them and their wives, or even an enforcement of the canons for the future.

Diego, who possessed no common measure of vigour and ambition, and who needed the particular favour of the popes for the success of his plans in elevating and aggrandising his see, accordingly proceeded to reform his clergy. There is extant a minute and circumstantial contemporary history of his episcopate, written by his admiring disciples, who dwell with much instance on his labours and success in reducing to discipline the refractory canons of his cathedral seat; but in the numerous allusions to these reforms there is no mention of the enforcement of celibacy, while the fact that he would not allow them to minister at the altar without canonical vestments is made the subject of repeated gratulation and praise. The absolute silence of the authors with respect to the clergy at large shows that the reticence of Pope Paschal was not misunderstood, and that there was no effort made to bring the secular priesthood under subjection to the Roman discipline. It therefore need not surprise us that in the twenty-five canons of the Council of Compostella in 1113 there is no reference whatever to the subject, beyond an allusion to the children of ecclesiastics, whose nurses were declared entitled to clerical privileges, thus giving them a recognised and highly prized position.

That Diego's reforms, indeed, did not extend to the

abrogation of clerical marriage is evident from several incidental circumstances. Thus, in 1114, the lords of the monastery of Botoa made it over to the Church of Santiago of Compostella, reserving to themselves their life interest, with a reversion to any of their descendants who should be ecclesiastics, and who might be willing to profess celibacy, showing that the matter was optional with the secular clergy. That even the canons were bound by no absolute rules on the subject is manifested by a very curious transaction, which may be worth recounting as illustrative in several aspects of the spirit of the age. In 1127, Diego, at the head of his Galician troops, accompanied Alfonso VIII on an expedition into Portugal. On their return, the army halted at Compostella, where the archbishop received and entertained his sovereign. They were bound by the closest ties, for Diego had baptised, knighted, and crowned him, and had, moreover, constantly stood his friend throughout his stormy youth, in the endless civil wars which marked the disastrous reign of his mother, Queen Urraca. Yet, prompted by evil counsellors who were jealous of Diego, the king suddenly demanded of him an enormous sum of money, to pay off the army, under the threat of seizing and pillaging the city. After considerable resistance, Diego was forced to submit, and to pay a thousand marks of silver. He then sought a private interview, in which he solemnly and affectionately warned Alfonso of the ruin of his soul which would ensue if he did not undergo penance for thus impiously spoiling the Apostle Santiago. Alfonso listened humbly and professed entire willingness to repent but for the difficulty that he had always been taught that penitence was fruitless without restitution, and restitution he was unable and unwilling to make. Diego then suggested that he should meet the chapter and discuss the case, to which he graciously assented. When they met, Diego proposed that the king should follow the example of his father, Raymond of Galicia, in commending himself to the peculiar patronage of Santiago, and in bequeathing his body to be buried in their church, promising, moreover, that if he should do so they would pray specially for him, which, from the promise of his youth, bade fair to be no easy task. Alfonso was delighted to escape so easily: he eagerly accepted the proposition, and added that he would like to become

a canon of their Church, in order to enjoy the fullest
possible share in the masses of such holy men.   To this
the chapter assented at once; he was forthwith duly
installed as a canon of the Church which he had just
despoiled, and his conscience was set at rest, while the
Church felt that it had acquired a moral supremacy over
the spoiler.   In thus formally becoming a canon, there
could have been no assumption of celibacy, expressed or
implied.   Alfonso was but twenty-one years of age, and
in the following year he married Berengaria, daughter of
the Count of Barcelona.

In fact, in the absence of urgency on the part of Rome,
the question of sacerdotal celibacy seems to have been
virtually ignored in Spain.   How little importance was
attached to the pre-eminent sanctity of asceticism becomes
evident when we are told that in the whole of Galicia there
was no convent of nuns until Diego, in 1129, founded the
house of St. Maria of Conjo.   Equal indifference is manifest in the legislative assemblies of the Church.   The
Council of Leon and Compostella, in 1114, only prohibited
the residence of such women as were forbidden by the
canons, which, in the existing discipline of the Spanish
Church, may safely be presumed to offer no impediment
to the marriage relation; and a synod held at Palencia in
1129 is even more significant in its reticence, for it merely
provides that notorious concubines of the clergy shall be
ejected, without apparently venturing to threaten any
punishment on the reverend offenders.

Towards the close of his restless life, however, Archbishop Diego found time, amid his military, political, and
ecclesiastical schemes of aggrandisement, to undertake the
much-needed reform of a single monastery.   The Abbot
of S. Pelayo de Antealtaria was a paragon of brutish
sensuality, who wasted the revenues of his house in riotous
living and took no shame in a numerous progeny.   The
archbishop remonstrated with him long and earnestly, both
in public and private :   seven times in the general chapter
of the diocese he admonished and threatened the offender
without result.   At length, in 1130, after forbearance so
remarkable, Diego held a chapter in the abbey for his trial,
when he was proved by competent witnesses to have kept
no less than seventy concubines.   He was accordingly
deposed, but was so far from being canonically punished

that a benefice in the abbey lands was assigned for his support. A new abbot was then appointed, who swore to observe the Benedictine rule as far as he should find himself able to do so. It is a significant commentary on the state of discipline and opinion to find so weak an effort to remove and punish the grossest licentiousness characterised by the biographer of Diego with the warmest expressions of wondering admiration, as a work which doubtless gave ineffable satisfaction to the Divine Omnipotence, and which was without example in previous history.

It is very evident that the pontiffs who so energetically enforced the rule of celibacy throughout the rest of Europe were content to offer little opposition to the obstinacy of the Celtiberian priesthood. We may safely conclude, indeed, that matters were allowed to remain virtually undisturbed, and that the clergy were permitted to retain their wives. A council held in Galicia in the early part of the thirteenth century, for the purpose of reforming ecclesiastical discipline, preserves absolute silence on the subject of marriage and concubinage; in 1246, priests of Cordova were able to plead ignorance in justification of their keeping so-called concubines while performing divine service. Yet, in 1244, under pressure from the Cardinal of St. Sabina, then papal legate, public concubinarians were ordered to be suspended, deprived of their benefices, and degraded from holy orders. Notwithstanding this, some twenty years later Alfonso the Wise of Castile was obliged to formally interdict matrimony to those in holy orders. In the elaborate code drawn up by that monarch, and known as "Las Siete Partidas," there is a law punishing sacerdotal marriage with deprivation of function and benefice; while the wives, if vassals of the Church, are to be reduced to servitude, and if serfs, are to be sold and the proceeds appropriated for the benefit of the Church of the offender. The wording of the law would seem to indicate that it was an enactment intended to repress existing disorders, and not merely a well-known provision inserted in the code for the purpose of completing a compilation of statutes; while the existence in secular legislation of such invasions of the province of ecclesiastical law is a convincing proof of the continued independence of Rome asserted by the Spanish Church and State. The prelates were further authorised to command the assistance

of the secular power in enforcing these barbarous penalties
to their full measure of severity. This, if enforced, would
have put a speedy end to clerical marriage, but the Partidas
were not confirmed by the Cortes until 1348, nearly a
century later, and these provisions produced no effect at
the time. How little, indeed, the clergy were required to
abandon their customs is evident when, in 1262, Alfonso
granted to those of the diocese of Salamanca the privilege
of bequeathing all their real and personal property to their
children, grandchildren, or other descendants.

The clergy of the dominions of the crown of Aragon were
as indifferent to the canons as were those of Castile. In
Valencia a council in 1255 prohibited the residence with
priests of all women, except mothers and sisters and such
others as were beyond suspicion, but no penalty was prescribed for infractions of the rule; and the character of
the clergy with whom the council had to deal is sufficiently
shown by its complaint that the priests of the country
parishes frequented the city too much and indulged there
in disgraceful excesses, for which reason it forbids them
to visit the city more often than twice a month, and
requires them to return home the same day. Arnaldo
de Peralta, Bishop of Valencia, not long after, deplores
the utter contempt with which all previous efforts to
suppress clerical concubinage had been received, and the
prevalence of the custom by which ecclesiastics endowed
their bastards with the spoils of the Church. Yet the
only punishment he finds himself able to threaten is a
fine of thirty maravedis on public concubinarians and of
five on parish priests who connive at such offences or
neglect to report them to the bishop. Ecclesiastics, indeed, are directed to put away their children, but no
penalty is indicated for disobedience. A Council of Lerida,
about 1250, imposed a fine of fifty maravedis on public
concubinarians, alleging as a reason that money is more
prized than salvation. The Council of Gerona in 1257 was
more energetic, for it decreed the deprivation of all concubinary priests who persisted in their sin; but this apparently was not effectual, for in 1274 the threat was repeated,
with the addition that the women should be excommunicated and should receive after death the burial of
asses; and very similar was the legislation of the Council
of Peñafiel in 1302. In 1286 the Council of Urgel recites

that efforts had been made to suppress concubinage, by suspending the priest and excommunicating his companion, but this had only led to fresh scandals, for the priests had continued to officiate and had thus incurred "irregularity," while the souls of their parishioners were exposed to grave perils. To remove these evils the penalties were therefore thriftily commuted to a fine of ten gold pieces for the male offender, and of five for the female— a method which doubtless led to a profitable traffic in licences to sin. In 1314 the Council of Lerida argued ·in the same way, and restored the old fine of fifty maravedis.

However well meant these efforts were, they proved as useless as all previous ones, for in 1322 the Council of Valladolid, under the presidency of the papal legate, William, Cardinal of St. Sabina, animadverts strongly on the indecency of ecclesiastics, from the highest prelates down, officiating at the nuptials of their children, both legitimate and illegitimate. For those who publicly kept concubines it provides a graduated scale of confiscation, ending in the deprivation of the persistently contumacious who gave no prospect of amendment, the exceedingly elaborate regulations prescribed showing at once the difficulty of the subject and the importance attached to it. The acts of this council, moreover, are interesting as presenting the first authentic evidence of a custom which subsequently prevailed to some extent elsewhere, by which parishioners were wont to compel their priest to take a female consort for the purpose of protecting the virtue of their families from his assaults. The iniquity of this precaution seems to have especially scandalised the legate, and he treats the audacious laymen concerned in such transactions with much less ceremony than the concubinary clergy. The elaborate regulations promulgated by this council produced little effect. The Council of Salamanca in 1335 renews the previous repressive legislation, adding a threat of *ipso facto* excommunication for those who give Christian burial to priestly concubines, including all who are present on such occasions, who are not to be absolved until they shall have paid a fine of fifty maravedis to the cathedral church.

In Aragon, the Council of Tarragona, in 1336, out of consideration for the souls of the guilty or of their parishioners, removed the penalties of suspension and excommunication and substituted a mulct of a year's revenue of beneficed priests and a fine of ten maravedis on the unbeneficed, with a similar fine on the concubines. This leniency seems to have been misplaced, for in 1364 the Council of Urgel threatens excommunication and deprivation of benefice unless there is reasonable cause to remit the latter penalty. In Majorca the same troubles existed, and in 1364 the bishop, Antonio de Galiano, as the only method of enforcing the canons, appointed a spécial commissioner, Pedro de Carrera, to look up delinquents and punish them.

The secular power vainly interposed to check this demoralisation. In 1351 the Cortes of Castile complained that the concubines of the clergy walked shamelessly abroad, arrayed in fine garments and adorned with gold and silver, so that they could not be distinguished from married ladies, leading to frequent quarrels and fights. To remedy this King Pedro the Cruel ordered that all clerical concubines should be plainly attired and be distinguished by wearing around the head a red fillet, three fingers in breadth, under penalty for each infraction, of forfeiture of the clothes they had on and a gradually increasing fine. Of course this was ineffective, and the Cortes of 1380 asked its re-enactment, and represented that the children of such unions inherited from their father and his kinsmen, as though they were legitimate, whence it arose that the clergy could get honest widows and maidens to live with them, causing great scandal. To this King Juan I could only reply that all such legacies should be void. At length, in 1388, a national Council of Castile held at Palencia under Cardinal Pedro de Luna, papal legate, made a determined effort to eradicate the ineradicable vice. It renewed the regulations of the Council of Valladolid, which it stated were not obeyed, and added to them a clause by which all benefices were held under a sort of tenure of chastity, and subject to forfeiture. Besides this, all ecclesiastics who, within two months of death, had kept concubines were declared incapable of testating, and their property was adjudged—one-third to the fabric of their churches, one-third to the ordinary of the diocese, and one-third to the fund for the redemption of captives under the care of the Orders of Trinidad and Merced, who were empowered to seize their share. Moreover, all bishops were commanded to appoint official visitors, who were to report at annual synods, to be held thereafter, all cases of infraction of the rules. Such stringent legislation bears emphatic testimony to the magnitude and prevalence of the evils which it was designed to cure, and of the existence of such evils there is ample evidence besides what has been adduced above. In 1335 Benedict XII addressed to the Spanish prelates an earnest remonstrance on the universal corruption which characterised the whole population, lay and clerical alike, scandalising to the infidel the very name of Christians. Pedro Gomez de Albornoz, Archbishop of Seville, is equally emphatic, and even more deplorable in its details is the description given of his fellow ecclesiastics by Alvar Pelayo, Penitentiary under John XXII and Bishop of Silva in Portugal. He states that many of the clergy in holy orders throughout the Peninsula publicly associated themselves with women, frequently of noble blood, binding themselves against separation by notarial acts and solemn oaths, endowing their consorts with the goods of the Church, and celebrating with the kindred these illegal espousals as joyously as though they were legitimate nuptials. Yet even this flagrant defiance of the canons was better than the wickedness common between confessors and their penitents, or than the promiscuous and unrestrained licentiousness of those who were not fettered by the forms of marriage, whose children, as Pelayo asserts, almost rivalled in number those of the laity. Evidently the Council of Palencia had an ample field for reform, but its labours proved nugatory. In 1429 the Council of Tortosa, under the presidency of the Cardinal de Foix, papal legate, renewed the lament that the decrees of Valladolid remained unobserved, and in repeating them it added a penalty of incarceration for pertinacious offenders, indicating, moreover, one of the worst abuses to which the subject gave rise, in forbidding all officials to take bribes from those who transgressed the rules. This effort was as fruitless as all previous ones had been, and we shall see hereafter that the same state of affairs continued throughout the sixteenth century.

CHAPTER XX

GENERAL LEGISLATION

In a former section we have seen the efforts made by Calixtus II to enforce the received discipline of the Church, and we have noted the scanty measure of success which attended his labours. He himself apparently recognised that they were futile, and that some action of more decided character than had as yet been attempted was necessary to accomplish the result so long and so energetically sought, and so illusory to its ardent pursuers. On his return to Italy, and his triumph over his unfortunate rival, the anti-pope Maurice Burdino, he summoned, in 1123, the first general council of the West, to confirm the Concordat of Worms, which had just closed half a century of strife between the papacy and the empire. Nearly a thousand prelates obeyed his call, and that august assembly promulgated a canon which not only forbade matrimony to those bound by vows and holy orders, but commanded that if such marriages were contracted they should be broken, and the parties to them subjected to due penance.

This was a bold innovation. With the exception of a decretal of Urban II in 1090, to which little attention seems to have been paid, we have seen that, previous to Calixtus, while the sacrament of marriage was held incompatible with the ministry of the altar and with the enjoyment of Church property, it yet was respected and its binding force was admitted, even to the point of rendering those who assumed it unfitted for their sacred functions. At most, and as a concession to a lax and irreligious generation, the option had been allowed of abandoning either the wife or the ministry. At Rheims, Calixtus had deprived them of this choice, and had ordered their separation from their wives. He now went a step further, and by the Lateran canon he declared the sacrament of marriage to be less potent than the religious

264

vow : the engagement with the Church swallowed up and destroyed all other ties. This gave the final seal to the separation between the clergy and the laity, by declaring the priestly character to be indelible. When once admitted to orders, he became a being set apart from his fellows, consecrated to the service of God; and the impassable gulf between him and the laity bound him for ever to the exclusive interests of the Church. It is easy to perceive how important an element this irrevocable nature of sacerdotalism became in establishing and consolidating the ecclesiastical power.

The immensity of the change thus wrought in the practice, if not in the doctrine, of the Church can best be understood by comparing the formal command thus issued to the Christian world with the unqualified condemnation pronounced in earlier times against those who attempted to dissolve marriage under religious pretexts. And in all ages the Church has regarded the chastity of the monastic orders as even more imperative than that of the secular clergy.

Revolutions never go backwards. Perhaps the Lateran fathers who adopted the canon scarcely realised its logical conclusions. If they did, they at all events shrank from expressing them openly and fully, and left the faithful to draw their own deductions as to the causes and consequences of such an order. Time, however, familiarised the minds of ardent Churchmen with the idea, and it was seen that if the practice thus enjoined was correct, doctrine must be made to suit and to justify it. To this end an additional stimulus was afforded by the failure of the canon to accomplish the results anticipated from it, for the custom of sacerdotal marriage was as yet by no means eradicated. The Council of Liège, held by Innocent II in 1131, referred to in a preceding section, and those of Clermont and Rheims, over which he likewise presided, in 1130 and 1131, show how little had been accomplished, and how generally the clergy of Europe disregarded the restrictions nominally imposed upon them, and the punishments which they so easily escaped. In the canons of these councils not only is it observable that the question of marriage and celibacy is treated as though it were a matter now for the first time brought to the attention of the clergy, but also that the innovation attempted by the Council of Lateran, only seven or eight years previously, is prudently suppressed and passed over without even an allusion.

Innocent, restored to Rome and to power, was bolder than when wandering through Europe, soliciting the aid of the faithful. Surrounded by a thousand prelates at the second great Council of Lateran, in 1139, he no longer dreaded to offend the susceptibilities of the clergy, and he proceeded to justify the canon of 1123 by creating a doctrine to suit the practice there enjoined. After repeating the canons of Clermont and Rheims, he unhesitatingly pronounced that a union contracted in opposition to the rule of the Church was not a marriage. He condescends to no argument, while he admits the innovation by alleging as its object the extension of the law of continence and of the purity pleasing to God.

The abounding wickedness of a perverse generation caused this decree of the loftiest Christian tribunal to fall still-born and abortive as its forerunners had done. The Church, however, was irrevocably committed to the new doctrine and to all its consequences. When Eugenius III was driven out of Rome by Arnold of Brescia, he presided, in 1148, over a council held at Rheims, where eleven hundred bishops and abbots from Northern and Western Europe assembled to do honour to the persecuted representative of St. Peter, and to condemn the teachings of Gilbert de la Porrée. From this great assembly he procured the confirmation of the new dogma by their adoption of the Lateran canon ; while the repetition of that of Clermont and Rheims (of 1130 and 1131) shows that the evil which it was intended to repress still existed in full force. The vague assertion of Eugenius that he was but following in the footsteps of the holy fathers, and a special reference to Innocent II as his authority, render it probable that the members of the council demurred in committing themselves to the new principle, and that it was only by showing that the matter was already decided under the irrefragable authority of a general council that the consent of the Transalpine Churches was obtained.

St. Bernard himself, the impersonation of ascetic sacerdotalism, hesitated to subscribe to the new dogma, and when the monks of Chartres asked him to reconcile it with the teachings of Augustin and Gregory the Great he candidly confessed that his dialectical skill was unequal to the task. So when an abbot applied to him for advice in the case of one of his monks, who had left the convent and married, St. Bernard stigmatised the act as highly improper, but hesitated to pronounce it unlawful. He recommended that an attempt be made to convince the parties that they were perilling their salvation, and if this failed he thought that perhaps they might be separated by episcopal authority. In fact, four years after the Council of Rheims, St. Bernard reproached Eugenius with having caused the adoption of canons which no one pretended to obey. If he thought that they were enforced, he grievously erred; if he did not think so, he had sinned either by decreeing what was not to be observed or in neglecting to punish their non-observance—and no one was punished for his disobedience.

Even in Rome itself the point was still disputed. At that very time Gratian, the greatest canonist of the age, was engaged in the compilation of his " Concordia discordantium Canonum," a work undertaken to restore to the canon law the pre-eminence which it was fast losing in consequence of the recently revived study of the Justinian jurisprudence. Gratian's use of some of the Lateran canons shows that he was familiar with them, yet he distinctly declares his opposition to the new doctrine by asserting that a deacon can lawfully marry if he chooses to abandon the ministry, and that the sacrament of marriage is so potent that, even if he had vowed chastity at the time of his ordination, the violation of his vow did not affect it. The summists, however, who shortly afterwards condensed his work for practical use, discreetly forbore to allude to this, but asserted that a solemn and public vow impeded the contract of marriage and dissolved it if contracted. As the precept to vow chastity at ordination had become obsolete, they further discovered that he who accepted what implied a vow must be held to have vowed. Thus the postulant for orders, though he emitted no vow in words, yet accepted that which implied perpetual chastity, and therefore was bound by a solemn vow which was destructive of marriage. This, it is true, was reasoning in a circle, but it satisfied the schoolmen, though Gratian had known nothing of such subtleties.

While the new law was thus accepted by the schoolmen it was long in winning its way to general acceptance, nor can it be a subject of wonder if those who disregarded the acknowledged canons of the Church by marrying in orders, or by permitting such marriages in those under their charge, should neglect a rule of recent origin and of more than doubtful propriety. The Church, however, was committed to it, and, moreover, could see in its eventual recognition a more effectual means of accomplishing the long-desired object than in any expedient previously tried. By destroying all such marriages, pronouncing them null and void, inflicting an ineffaceable stigma on wife and off-spring, subjecting the woman to the certainty of being cast off without resource and without option on the part of the husband, the position of the wife of an ecclesiastic would become most unenviable; her kindred would prevent her from exposing herself to such calamities, and no priest could succeed in finding a consort above the lowest class, whose union with him would expose him to the contempt of his flock.

How slender was the immediate result of the efforts of Innocent and Eugenius, however, is manifested in the foregoing sections. If further evidence is desired it is furnished, as regards Germany, by Geroch, Provost of Reichersperg, who, writing about the middle of the century, complains that any one who would shun intercourse with Nicolitan and simoniacal heretics must quit the world, for it was full of them, and he maintains the propriety of calling them heretics because they openly defended and justified their evil courses. Indeed, so shamelessly were their transgressions displayed, that the faithful were sometimes scandalised by the sight of the priests' wives assisting their husbands in the ministry of the altar; while conventual discipline had sunk so low that nuns were in the habit of deferring their formal vows until the lassitude of old age should render the restraints thereby assumed easy to be endured, and canons led a life which was only distinguishable from that of the laity by its shamelessness. In France, Hugh, Archbishop of Rouen, complains that those who married in orders openly defended their evil practices and quoted Scripture to sustain themselves. In England, as late as 1470, Sir John Fortescue incidentally alludes to a recent case in which a priest named John Fringe, who had lived in orders for three years, procured two false witnesses to swear that he had previously been betrothed to a certain maiden, and this preliminary promise of marriage was held by the court to supersede his priestly ordination; he was ejected from the priesthood and compelled to marry the girl, with whom he lived fourteen years, until he was executed for treason by the Lancastrians during the Wars of the Roses. In Spain, as we have already seen, priestly marriage was forbidden by the secular law as late as the latter half of the thirteenth century, and priests in consequence were wont to protect their partners by entering into the most solemn compacts, the customary employment of which shows that they must have been habitually enforced by the municipal tribunals regardless of the censures of the Church.

The long pontificate of Alexander III, extending from 1159 to 1181, was absorbed for the most part by his deadly strife with Frederic Barbarossa. Yet, even before he was released from that ever-present danger, he found leisure to urge the cause of sacerdotal celibacy; and after the humiliation of his mortal enemy he devoted himself to it with a zeal which earned for him among his contemporaries the credit of establishing its observance. He who, as the legate Roland, had nearly paid, under the avenging sword of Otho of Wittelsbach, the forfeit of his life for his rude boldness at the imperial court, was little likely to abate one jot of the claims which the Church asserted on the obedience of layman and clerk; and he recognised too fully the potency of the canons of Lateran and Rheims not to insist upon their observance. The very necessity under which he found himself, however, of repeating those canons shows how utterly neglected they had been, and how successfully the clergy had thus far resisted their reception and acknowledgment. Thus when, in 1163, he held the Council of Tours, he was obliged to content himself with a canon which allowed three warnings to those who publicly kept concubines, and it was only after neglect of these warnings that they were threatened with deprivation of functions and benefice; and when, in 1172, his legates presided over the Council of Avranches, which absolved Henry II for the murder of A'Becket, the Norman clergy were emphatically reminded that those who married in holy orders must put away their wives, and this in terms which indicate that the rule had not been previously obeyed. Yet notwithstanding this formal declaration, only a few years later we find the

Archbishop of Rheims applying to him for counsel in the case of a deacon who had committed matrimony, to which Alexander of course replied that the marriage was no marriage, and that the offending ecclesiastic must be separated from the woman, and undergo due penance. The persistence of the pope, and the necessity of his urgency, are farther shown by sundry epistles to various English bishops, in which the rule is enunciated as absolute and unvarying; and he takes occasion to stigmatise such marriages with the most degrading epithet, when he graciously pardons those concerned, and permits their restitution after a long course of penitence, on their giving evidence of a reformed life.

Yet even Alexander was forced to abate somewhat of his stern determination, in consideration of the incorrigible perversity of the time, though he seems not to have remarked that he abandoned the principle by admitting exceptions, and that the reasons assigned in such individual cases might, with equal cogency, be applied to the total withdrawal of the rule. When the Calabrian bishops informed him that clerks in holy orders throughout their dioceses committed matrimony, he ordered that priests and deacons should be irrevocably separated from their wives; but, in the case of subdeacons of doubtful morals, he instructed the prelates that they should tacitly connive at the irregularity, lest, in place of one woman, many should be abused, and a greater evil be incurred, in the endeavour to avoid a less. This worldly wisdom also dictated his orders to the Bishop of Exeter, in whose diocese subdeacons were in the habit of openly marrying. He directs an examination into the lives and characters of the offenders; those whose regular habits and staid morality afford fair expectation of their chastity in celibacy are to be forcibly separated from their wives; while those whose disorderly character renders probable their general licentiousness if condemned to a single life are not to be disturbed—taking care, however, that they do not minister at the altar, or receive ecclesiastical benefices.

Alexander adopted the principle that a simple vow of chastity did not prevent marriage or render it null, but that a formal vow, or the reception of orders, created a dissolution of marriage, or a total inability to enter into it; but Celestin III carried the principle still farther, and decreed that a simple vow, while it did not dissolve an existing connection, was sufficient to prevent a future one.

Alexander did not confine himself to this portion of the question, but with ceaseless activity laboured to enforce the observance of celibacy in general, and to repress the immorality which disgraced the Church throughout Christendom—immorality which led Alain de l'Isle, the " Universal Doctor," to characterise the ecclesiastics of his time as being old men in their inefficiency and young men in their unbridled passions. Alexander's efforts were particularly directed to put an end to the practice of hereditary priesthood, and its constant consequence, hereditary benefices. If I have made little allusion to this subject during the century under consideration, it is not that the Church had relaxed her exertions to place some limit on this apparently incurable disorder, or that the passive resistance to her efforts had been less successful than we have seen it on previous occasions. The perpetual injunctions of Alexander show at once the universality of the vice and the determination of the pontiff to eradicate it. At the same time, it became a frequent, and no doubt a profitable portion of the duties of the papal chancery, to grant special dispensations when those who held such preferment, or who desired to retain their wives, underwent the dangers and expense of a journey to Rome, and were rewarded for their confidence in the benignity of the Holy Father by a rescript to their bishops, commanding their reinstatement in the benefices from which they had been ejected. The power to grant such dispensations was shrewdly reserved as the exclusive privilege of the papal court; and a high Churchman of the period assures us that there was no difficulty in obtaining them. It need not, therefore, surprise us that Alexander's successor, Lucius III, found the hereditary transmission of the priestly office claimed as an absolute right. And not only did the claims of the papal chancery thus interfere with the execution of the law by its power of granting dispensations, but its appellate jurisdiction was constantly used to avert punishment from the worst offenders. Thus Lucius III, about the year 1181, was obliged to grant to Maurice de Sully, Bishop of Paris, the right to dispossess of their benefices and functions, without appeal, certain notorious concubinarians, who, on being threatened with the applica-

tion of the law, had defied him by interposing an appeal to
Rome.   This centralisation of all power in the papal court,
and the unblushing venality of the Roman officials, meet
us in every age as the efficient obstacle to the efforts of
reforming prelates throughout Europe.

The uncertainty of this conflicting legislation, at times
enforced and at times dispensed with by the supreme
power, led to innumerable complications and endless
perplexity in private life.   Indeed, a large portion of the
canons are founded on responses given by the popes to
settle cases of peculiar difficulty arising from ignorance
or neglect of the discipline enjoined, and many of these
reveal extreme hardship inflicted on those who could be
convicted of no intentional guilt.   Perhaps the most
noteworthy instance of the troubles caused by the new
regulations was that of Bossaert d'Avesnes, which resulted
in a desperate war to determine the possession of the rich
provinces of Flanders and Hainault.   As it illustrates the
doubts which still environed these particular points, and
the conflicting decisions to which they were liable, even
from the infallibility of successive popes, it may be worth
briefly sketching here.

When Baldwin of Flanders, Emperor of Constantinople,
died in 1206, his eldest daughter Jane succeeded to his
territories of Flanders and Hainault, while his second child,
Margaret, was placed under the guardianship of Bossaert
d'Avesnes.   Bossaert was a relative of her mother, Mary
of Champagne, and though he held the comparatively
insignificant position of chantre of Tournay, he was yet a
man of great repute and influence.   With the assent and
approbation of the estates of Flanders, Margaret and
Bossaert were married, the issue of the union being three sons.
Whether the fact of his having received the subdiaconate
was publicly known or not is somewhat doubtful; but he
seems at length to have been awakened to a sense of his
uncertain position, when he went to Rome for the purpose
of obtaining a dispensation and legitimating his children.
Innocent III not only refused the application, but commanded him to restore Margaret to her relatives and to
do penance by a pilgrimage to the Holy Land.   Disregarding these injunctions, he lived openly with his wife after
his return, and was excommunicated in consequence.   At
length Margaret left him and married Guillaume de

Dampierre, while Bossaert was assassinated during a second visit to Rome, where he was seeking reconciliation to the Church.   When at last, in 1244, the Countess Jane closed her long and weary career by assuming the veil at Marquette, without leaving heirs, the children of Margaret by both marriages claimed the succession, and Margaret favoured the younger, asserting, without scruple, that her elder sons were illegitimate, while the Emperor Frederick II had no scruple in recognising the claim of the elder branch.   The difficult question was referred to St. Louis for arbitration, and in 1247 the good king assigned Flanders to Gui de Dampierre and Hainault to Jean d'Avesnes, thus recognising both marriages as legitimate.   This, of course, satisfied neither party.   Innocent IV was appealed to, and in 1248 he sent commissioners to investigate the knotty affair. They reported that the marriage of Bossaert had been contracted in the face of all Flanders, and that the d'Avesnes were legitimate, which judgment was confirmed by Innocent himself in 1252.   Thus fortified, Jean d'Avesnes resisted the proposed partition, and a bloody civil war arose. The victory of Vacheren placed the Dampierre in the hands of their half-brothers, and promised to be decisive, until Margaret called in Charles de Valois, bribing him with the offer of Hainault to complete the disinheriting of her first-born.   The war continued until Louis, returning from the East in 1255, compelled the combatants to lay down their arms, and to abide by his arbitration.

In this case we see Innocent III deciding that marriage was incompatible with the subdiaconate.   Yet it is a striking illustration of the uncertainty which still surrounded the matter to find the same pope, in 1208, commanding a subdeacon of Laon to return to the wife whom he had abandoned on taking orders, and to treat her in all respects as a wife.   Innocent is not to be suspected of any temporising concession to prevailing laxity, and yet in this case he overruled the uninterrupted tradition of the canons that married men taking orders should thenceforth treat their wives as sisters; and the doubts which experienced ecclesiastics entertained with regard to the law are visible in the fact that when the wife complained of her abandonment to the metropolitan authorities at Rheims they did not pretend to give judgment, but sent the testimony in the case at once to Innocent for his decision.

Another curious case occurring about the same time illustrates the complexity of the questions which arose and the manner in which the selfishness of ascetic zeal sometimes eluded even the very slender barriers with which the Church limited its gratification. As we have seen, it was an ancient rule that no man could assume monastic vows without the assent of his wife, with the additional condition that she must at the same time enter a nunnery. It appears that a husband desiring to become a monk, and finding his wife obstinately opposed to his designs, enlisted the services of various priests to influence her, carefully concealing from her the obligation which her assent would impose upon her to take the veil. Still she obstinately refused, until at last he threatened to castrate himself, when she yielded and went through the ceremony of placing with her own hands his head on the altar. The wife thus abandoned took to evil courses, and the husband-monk applied in person to Innocent III to learn whether he ought to remain in his order, seeing that his continence might be responsible for her unchastity. In spite of the deceit practised upon the wife, Innocent resolved his doubts in favour of the maintenance of his vows, giving as a reason that her adulteries deprived her of claim on him. At the same time, nothing was said as to compelling the woman to take the veil. In 1244, we find Innocent IV responding to the appeal of some wives, who had thus been abandoned, by granting to the Bishop of Lincoln to proceed against the husbands, who had embraced monastic life. A more conspicuous illustration of the rule occurred when the Emperor Ludwig of Bavaria, in 1328, undertook to depose John XXII as a heretic and replace him with a pope of his own. His choice fell upon Piero di Corbario, a Franciscan distinguished for piety and eloquence, who took the name of Nicholas V. He had been in the Order for forty years, and had risen to the position of Minister of the province of the Abruzzi and papal Penitentiary. Before taking the vows, however, he had been married for five years; the wife was still living, and, though she had borne the separation uncomplainingly for so long a period, she now asserted that she had never assented to his desertion, either hoping to be bought off or instigated by the papalist party. She applied to her bishop, Giovanni of Rieti, who decided that the marriage had never been annulled, and that

Piero must return to her. He had a harder fate when he was carried to his triumphant rival in Avignon and confined until his death.

In view of these perplexities, it is no wonder that even the resolute spirit of Alexander III, dismayed at the arduous nature of the struggle, or appalled at the ineradicable vices which defied even papal authority, at times shrank from the contest and was ready to abandon the principle. If we may believe Giraldus Cambrensis, who, as a contemporary intimately connected with the highest ecclesiastical authorities in England, was not likely to be mistaken, and whose long sojourn at the court of Innocent III would have afforded him ample opportunities of correcting a mis-statement, Alexander had once resolved to introduce the discipline of the Greek Church in Western Europe, permitting single marriages with virgins. To this he had obtained the assent of his whole court, except his chancellor Albert, who was afterwards pope under the name of Gregory VIII. The resistance of this dignitary was so powerful as to cause the abandonment of the project. Alexander, indeed, was not alone in this conviction. Giraldus himself was fully convinced that such a change would be most useful to the Church, though as archdeacon of St. David's he had displayed his zeal for the enforcement of the canon by measures too energetic for the degeneracy of the age, and though he occupies, in his " Gemma Ecclesiastica," twenty-one chapters with an exhortation to his clergy to abandon their evil courses. Men of high character did not hesitate to take even stronger ground against the rule. The celebrated Peter Comestor, whose orthodoxy is unquestioned, taught publicly in his lectures that the devil had never inflicted so severe a blow on the Church as in procuring the adoption of celibacy.

These were but individual opinions. The policy of the Church remained unaltered, and Alexander's successors emulated his example in endeavouring to enforce the canons. Clement III took advantage of the profound impression which the capture of Jerusalem by Saladin (Oct. 1187) produced on all Europe, when the fall of the Latin kingdom was attributed to the sins of Christendom. He preached a general reformation. Abstinence from meat on Wednesdays and Saturdays for five years, and various other kinds of mortification, were enjoined on all, to propitiate a justly offended Deity, but the clergy were the objects of special reproof. Their extreme laxity of morals, their neglect of the dress of their order, their worldly ambition and pursuits, drinking, gambling, and flocking to tournaments, and the unclerical deportment which left little difference between them and the laity, were some of the accusations brought against them. To their incontinence, however, was chiefly attributed the wrath of God, besides the measureless scandals to which their conduct exposed the Church, and they were commanded to remove all suspected females from their houses within forty days under pain of suspension from their functions and revenues. That these rebukes were not the mere angry declamation of an ascetic is shown by the declaration of Cœlestin III, a few years later, that throughout Germany the custom still prevailed of fathers substituting in their benefices their sons, born during priesthood, so that frequently parent and offspring ministered together in the same church; and the extent of the demoralisation is evident when we find the sons of priests and deacons alluded to in a constitution of Frederic Barbarossa in 1187 as a class ineligible to knighthood. The regular clergy offered no exception to the general relaxation of discipline. In 1192 Odo, Bishop of Toul, felt himself forced to deplore the wickedness of monks who left their monasteries and publicly took to themselves wives, but he could devise no better means of arresting the scandal than excommunicating them and their growing families.

Yet, with all his ardour, Clement admitted that celibacy was only a local rule of discipline, and that there was nothing really incompatible between marriage and the holy functions of the altar. The time had not yet come when the Council of Trent could erect the inviolable continence of the priesthood into an article of faith, and Clement was willing to allow that priests of the Greek Church, under his jurisdiction, could legitimately be married and could celebrate mass while their families were increasing around them.

Innocent III, who, by the fortunate conjunction of the time in which he flourished with his own matchless force of character, enjoyed perhaps the culmination of papal power and prerogative, at length brought to the struggle

an influence and a determination which could scarcely
fail to prove decisive on any question capable of a favourable
solution. By his decretals and his legates he laboured
assiduously to enforce obedience to the canons, and when
in 1215, he summoned the whole Christian world to meet
in the fourth Council of Lateran, that august assembly of
about thirteen hundred prelates, acting under his impulsion,
and reflecting his triumph over John of England and Otho
of Germany, spoke with an authority which no former
body since that of Nicæa had possessed. Its canons on
the subject before us were simple, perhaps less violent
in their tone than those of former synods, but they breathed
the air of conscious strength, and there was no man that
dared openly to gainsay them. A more rigid observance
of the rules was enjoined, and any one officiating while
suspended for contravention was punishable with perpetual
degradation and deprivation of his emoluments. Yet the
rule was admitted to be merely a local ordinance peculiar
to the Latin Church, for, in the effort made by the council
to heal the schism with Constantinople, the right of the
East to permit the marriage of its priests was acknowledged by a clause visiting with severer penalties those
who by custom were allowed to marry, and who, notwithstanding this licence, still permitted themselves illicit
indulgences. The disgraceful traffic by which in some
places prelates regularly sold permissions to sin was
denounced in the strongest terms, as a vice equal in degree
to that which it encouraged; and the common custom
of fathers obtaining preferment in their own churches for
their illegitimate offspring was reprobated as it deserved.

There is nothing novel in these canons, nor can they
in strictness be said to constitute an epoch in the history
of sacerdotal celibacy. They enunciate no new principles,
they threaten no new punishments, yet are they noteworthy as marking the settled policy of the Church at a
period when it had acquired that plenitude of power and
vigour of organisation which insured at least an outward
show of obedience to its commands. The successive
labours of so long a series of pontiffs, during more than a
century and a half, carrying with them the cumulative
authority of Rome, had gradually broken down resistance,
and the Lateran canons were the definitive expression of
its discipline on this subject. Accordingly, though we shall

see how little was accomplished in securing the purity of the priesthood, which was the ostensible object of the rule, yet hereafter there are to be found few traces of marriage in holy orders, except in the distant countries to which reference has already been made.

Yet the readiness to relax the rule when a substantial advantage was to be gained still continued, and when the effort, commenced at the Council of Lyons in 1274, to reunite the Greek Church under the supremacy of the Holy See was apparently successful, Nicholas III stoutly insisted upon the addition of " *filioque* " to the Symbol, but was discreetly silent as to separating the wives of priests from their husbands, promising in general terms that in all that merely concerned ritual observances the way should be made easy for them.

In Southern Italy, when the churches were actually brought together under the domination of Rome, priests of Greek origin were allowed to retain their wives, but married clerks of Latin parentage were not permitted to enter holy orders without separation. It not infrequently happened that the latter endeavoured to elude the prohibition by getting themselves ordained in the Greek Church, and it became necessary to denounce severe penalties not only against them, but also against the prelates who permitted it.

CHAPTER XXI

RESULTS

THE unrelaxing efforts of two centuries had at length achieved an inevitable triumph. One by one the different churches of Latin Christendom yielded to the fiat of the successor of St. Peter, and their ecclesiastics were forced to forgo the privilege of assuming the most sacred of earthly ties with the sanction of heaven and the approbation of man. Sacerdotalism vindicated its claim to exclusive obedience; the Church successfully asserted its right to command the entire life of its members, and to sunder all the bonds that might allure them to render a divided allegiance. In theory, at least, all who professed a religious life or assumed the sacred ministry were given up wholly to the awful service which they had undertaken: no selfishly personal aspirations could divert their energies from the aggrandisement of their class, nor were the temporal possessions of the establishment to be exposed to the minute but all-pervading dilapidation of the wife and family.

If these were the objects of the movement inaugurated by Damiani and Hildebrand, and followed up with such unrelenting vigour by Calixtus and Alexander and Innocent, the history of the medieval Church attests how fully they were attained. It is somewhat instructive, indeed, to observe that in the rise of the papal power to its culmination under Innocent III it was precisely the pontiffs most conspicuous for their enforcement of the rule of celibacy who were likewise most prominent in their assertion of the supremacy, temporal and spiritual, of the head of the Roman Church. Whether or not they recognised and acknowledged the connection, they laboured as though the end in view was clearly appreciated, and their triumphs on the one field were sure to be followed by corresponding successes on the other.

Yet in all this the ostensible object was always represented to be the purity of the Church and its ministers.
The other advantages were either systematically ignored
or but casually alluded to. One warning voice, indeed,
was raised, in a quarter where it would have at least commanded respectful attention had not the Church appeared
to imagine itself superior to the ordinary laws of cause
and effect. While Innocent II was labouring to enforce
his new doctrine that ordination and religious vows were
destructive of marriage, St. Bernard, the ascetic reformer
of monachism and the foremost ecclesiastic of his day,
was thundering against the revival of Manichæism. The
heresies of the Albigenses respecting marriage were to be
combated, and in performing this duty he pointed out
with startling vigour the evils to the Church and to mankind of the attempt to enforce a purity incompatible with
human nature. Deprive the Church of honourable marriage, he exclaimed, and you fill her with concubinage,
incest, and all manner of nameless vice and uncleanness.
It was still an age of faith; and while earnest men like
St. Bernard could readily anticipate the evils attendant
upon the asceticism of heretics, they could yet persuade
themselves, as the Council of Trent subsequently expressed
it, that God would not deny the gift of chastity to those
who rightly sought it in the bosom of the true Church—
though St. Bernard himself confessed that crimes which
he dared not even name commonly followed after the
fornication, adultery, and incest which specially characterised innumerable ministers of Christ. It remains for us to
see what was the success of the attempt thus deliberately
to tempt the Lord.

It is somewhat significant that when, in France, the
rule of celibacy was completely restored, strict Churchmen should have found it necessary also to revive the
hideously suggestive restriction which denied to the priest
the society of his mother or of his sister. Even in the profoundest barbarism of the tenth century, or the unbridled
licence of the eleventh; even when Damiani descanted
upon the disorders of his contemporaries with all the
cynicism of the most exalted asceticism, horrors such as
these are not alluded to. It is reserved for the advancement of the thirteenth century and the enforcement of
celibacy to show us how outraged human nature may

revenge itself and protest against the shackles imposed by zealous sacerdotalism or unreasoning bigotry. In 1208 Cardinal Guala, Innocent's legate in France, issued an order in which he not only repeated the threadbare prohibitions respecting focariæ and concubines, but commanded that even mothers and other relatives should not be allowed to reside with men in holy orders, the devil being the convenient personage on whom, as usual, was thrown the responsibility for the scandals which were known to occur frequently under such circumstances. That this decree was not allowed to pass into speedy oblivion is shown by a reference to it as still well known and in force a century later in the statutes of the Church of Tréguier. And that the necessity for it was not evanescent may be assumed from its repetition in the regulations of the see of Nismes, the date of which is uncertain, but probably attributable to the close of the fourteenth century. At the same time, we have evidence that Cardinal Guala's efforts were productive of little effect. Four years later, in 1212, we find Innocent formally authorising the prelates of France mercifully to pardon those who had been excommunicated under Guala's rules, with the suggestive proviso that the power thus conferred was not to be used for the purpose of extorting unhallowed gains. Still more significant is the fact that in the same year Innocent commissioned another legate, Cardinal Robert de Curzon, to renew the endless task of purifying the Gallican Church. Guala's efforts would seem to have already passed into oblivion, for in a council which Cardinal Robert held in Paris, he gravely promulgated a canon forbidding the priesthood from keeping their concubines so openly as to give rise to scandal, and threatening the recalcitrants with excommunication if they should persist in retaining their improper consorts for forty days after receiving notice. This was as fruitless as all previous legislation had been. No matter what decrees were issued, they were neutralised by the facility of obtaining from the Holy See letters of absolution, whenever any too zealous prelate sought to enforce them. A Formulary of the papal Penitentiary, of about the middle of the century, shows, by the number of formulæ for such cases, how frequent were the applications, and their invariable success is indicated by the fact that no formulæ are given for refusing the favour. Even more significant is the endeavour of the peccant clerics to show that the woman was not a permanent concubine; the prohibitions were construed as directed solely against durable connections, while sporadic or temporary licentiousness was evidently regarded as so much a matter of course, that it was worthy of no special reprehension. In the next century we find the rehabilitation of the sinner still more facilitated by conceding it to the bishops, for Alvar Pelayo alludes to the number of letters which, as Penitentiary under John XXII, he issued to the prelates authorising them to grant dispensations to concubinary priests to enable them to perform their functions. It was a simple matter of traffic, reduced to a system. That monachism was no less productive of sin in the depraved moral atmosphere of the age is rendered evident by other canons of the same council, which prohibit both monks and nuns from sleeping two in a bed, with the avowed object of repressing crimes against nature. It may well be asked what was the value of the continence aimed at in monastic vows when it resulted in the necessity for such regulations.

The clergy of France were not exceptional, and, unfortunately, there can be no denial of the fact that notorious and undisguised illicit unions, or still more debasing secret licentiousness, was a universal and pervading vice of the Church throughout Christendom. Its traces amid all the ecclesiastical legislation of the thirteenth, fourteenth, and fifteenth centuries are too broad and deep to be called into question, and if no evidence remained except the constant and unavailing efforts to repress it, that alone would be sufficient. National and local synods, pastoral epistles, statutes of churches, all the records of ecclesiastical discipline are full of it. Now deploring and now threatening, exhausting ingenuity in devising new regulations and more effective punishments, the prelates of those ages found themselves involved in a task as endless and as bootless as that of the Danaidæ. Occasionally, indeed, it is lost sight of momentarily, when the exactions and usurpations of the laity, or the gradual extension of secular jurisdiction, monopolised the attention of those who were bound to defend the privileges of their class; but, with these rare exceptions, it may be asserted as a general truth that scarcely a synod met, or a body of laws was drawn up to govern some local church, in which the subject did not receive a prominent position and careful consideration. It would be wearisome and unprofitable to recapitulate here the details of this fruitless iteration. Without by any means exhausting the almost limitless materials for investigation, I have collected a formidable mass of references upon the subject, but an examination of them shows so little of novelty, and so constant a recurrence to the starting-point, that no new principles can be evolved from them, and their only interest lies in their universality, and in demonstrating how resultless was the unceasing effort to remove the ineffaceable plague-spot.

Spasmodic efforts, it is true, occasionally wrought a temporary improvement, as when Alexander IV, in 1259, proclaimed to the world that licentious ecclesiastics were the cause of all the evils under which the Church was groaning, for through them the name of God was blasphemed throughout the world, the sacraments were polluted, the Catholic religion lost the reverence of the faithful, the people were deprived of the benefits of divine service, the substance of the Church was dissipated, the word of God was defiled by their impure lips, heretics were encouraged in their opposition, oppressors were emboldened to persecution, and the sacrilegious were able to expose the whole Church to mockery and contempt. To alleviate these troubles, he not only ordered the prelates of Christendom to prosecute all offences of this nature with the utmost severity, but, recognising his own court as an obstacle to reform, he surrendered his appellate jurisdiction in such cases, and forbade all appeals to Rome. His earnestness bore some fruit, and many prelates were stimulated to reform their flocks, causing large numbers of ecclesiastics to be expelled. A contemporary rhymster, Adam de la Halle (better known perhaps as Le Bossu d'Arras), thus alludes to the effects of the bull :—

> Et chascuns le pape encosa
> Quant tant de bons clers desposa.—
> —Romme a bien le tierche partie
> Des clers fais sers et amatis.

As in all similar attempts, however, the results were but transitory. Ferry, Bishop of Orleans, would scarce have been murdered, in 1299, by a knight whose daughter he had seduced, had the father felt that there was any chance of punishing the criminal by having the canons enforced against him.

In the confessed nullity of penal legislation it was natural for the Church to have recourse to her supernatural armoury, and accordingly we have ample store of legends, framed with the hope of frightening by spiritual terrors those who were indurated to canon and decretal. The dead concubine of a priest was seen chased by infernal demons, and a knight who sought to protect her had a handful of hair left in his grasp by her mad terror; and the reality of the awful scene was verified on opening her tomb and finding her tresses deficient. So a nun who had yielded to temptation and had sought to conceal her frailty by murdering her child, dying unconfessed, was seen wandering hopelessly with a burning infant clasped to her bosom, which she proclaimed was to be her torment throughout eternity. It is no wonder that the well-meant ingenuity which devised these tales met with slender reward, and that the threat of post-mortem punishment was as powerless as that of temporal penalties, for these tales were counterbalanced by other superstitions, such as that which taught that the most sinful, even among laymen, could obtain eternal salvation by the simple expedient of enveloping himself in a monastic habit on his death-bed. The Benedictines had well-authenticated cases in plenty where the most vicious of men, by adopting this plan, were rescued by St. Benedict himself from the hands of demons conducting them to eternal punishment, in spite of Satan's complaints that he was defrauded of his rights. The Franciscans contended with the Benedictines as to the efficacy of their respective patrons, and related with pride that St. Francis visited purgatory every year and carried with him to heaven the souls of his followers—a general plan of salvation which gave his vestments a decided superiority over those of the older order. As the practice became more common, it was at times recognised as equally dangerous to the welfare of the faithful and to the revenues of the Church, and was condemned as a pernicious error, but this did not deter the Carmelites from producing their miraculous scapular and the Sabbatine Bull, which, after many vicissitudes, received the final stamp of papal approbation by Clement X in 1673.

So open and avowed was the shame of the Church that the Neapolitan code, promulgated about 1231 by the enlightened Frederick II, absolutely interfered to give a quasi-legitimacy to the children of ecclesiastics, and removed, to a certain extent, their disability of inheritance. The imperial officials were ordered to assign appropriate shares in parental estates to such children, notwithstanding their illegitimacy, conditioned on the payment of an annual tax to the imperial court; and parents were not allowed to alienate their property to the prejudice of such children, any more than in cases of the offspring of lawful wedlock. The numbers and influence of the class thus protected must indeed have been great to induce such interference in their favour.

We have already seen ecclesiastical authority for the assertion that in the Spanish Peninsula the children sprung from such illicit connections rivalled in numbers the offspring of the laity. That they were numerous elsewhere may be presumed when we see Innocent IV, in 1248, forced to grant to the province of Livonia the privilege of having them eligible to holy orders, except when born of parents involved in monastic vows, for necessity alone could excuse so flagrant a departure from the canons enunciated during the preceding two centuries. A similar conclusion is deducible from the fact that, in the municipal code in force throughout Northern Germany during the thirteenth and fourteenth centuries, they were deemed of sufficient importance to be entitled to a separate place in the classification of wer-gilds, or blood-moneys; while the aim of the lawgiver to stigmatise them is manifested by his placing them below the peasant, deeming them superior only to the juggler; and that this was not a provision of transient force is clear from the commentary upon it in a body of law dating from the end of the fourteenth century. Nor is the evidence less convincing which may be drawn from the use of the old German word *pfaffenkind*, or priest's son, which became generally used as equivalent to bastard. It would not, indeed, be difficult to understand the numbers of this class of the population if ecclesiastics in general followed the example of Henry III, Bishop of Liège, whose natural children amounted to no less than sixty-five.

The direct encouragement thus given to illicit connections, by providing for the children sprung from them, neutralised one of the principal modes by which the Church endeavoured to suppress them. The innumerable canons issued during this period, forbidding and pronouncing null and void all testamentary provisions in favour of concubines and descendants, prove not only how much stress was laid upon this as an efficient means of repression, but also how little endeavour was made by the guilty parties to conceal their sin. As all testaments came within the sphere of ecclesiastical jurisdiction, it would seem that there should have been no difficulty in enforcing regulations of this kind, yet their constant repetition proves either that those who were entrusted with their execution were habitually remiss, or else that the popular feelings were in favour of the unfortunates, and interfered with the efficacy of the laws.

A single instance, out of many that might be cited, will illustrate this. In 1225 the Cardinal-legate Conrad held, at Mainz, a national council of the German empire, of which one of the canons declared that, in order to abolish the custom of ecclesiastics leaving to their concubines and children the fruits of their benefices, not only should such legacies be void, but those guilty of the attempt should lie unburied, all who endeavoured to enforce such testaments should be anathematised, and the church where it was permitted should lie under an interdict as long as the wrong was permitted. The terrible rigour of these provisions shows how deep seated was the evil aimed at; nor were they uncalled for when we see a will, executed in 1218 by no less a personage than Gotfrid, Archdeacon of Wurzburg, in which he leaves legacies to the children whom he confesses to have been born in sin, and of whom he expects his relatives to take charge. Had any earnest attempt been made to enforce the canons of the Legate, they would have been amply sufficient to eradicate the evil; yet their utter inefficiency is demonstrated by the Council of Fritzlar in 1246, and that of Cologne in 1260. The former of these was held by the Archbishop of Mainz; it has no canons directed against concubinage, which was as public as ever, but it deplores the dissipation of the temporalities of the Church by the testamentary provisions of priests in favour of their guilty partners and children, and it repeats, with additional emphasis, the regulations of 1255. The latter renews the complaint that priests not only continue their evil courses throughout life, but are not ashamed, on their death-beds, to leave their children the patrimony of Christ; and another provision is equally significant in forbidding priests to be present at the marriages of their children, or that such marriages should be solemnised with pomp and ostentation. The following year another council, held at Mainz, repeated the prohibition as to the diversion of Church property to the consorts and natural children of priests. In 1296 Boniface VIII professed to be scandalised at the horrible abuse customary in the see of Utrecht, whereby priests joined themselves to their concubines and apportioned the property of their churches among their children; while in 1342 the Synod of Olmutz was obliged to renew the prohibitions regarding the solemnisation of their children's marriages. In 1416 the Synod of Breslau deplored that the old canons were forgotten and despised, and that priests were not ashamed to bequeath to their bastards accumulations of property which would form fit portions for lofty nobles. How thoroughly, in fact, it was deemed a matter of course for the children of ecclesiastics to marry well and to have good dowries, is to be seen in Chaucer's description of the wife of " deinous Simekin," the proud miller of Trompington :—

> " A wif he hadde, comen of noble kin;
> The person of the toun hire father was.
> With hire he yaf ful many a panne of bras,
> For that Simkin shuld in his blood allie.
> She was yfostered in a nonnerie." (" The Reve's Tale.")

As time wore on, and the clergy, despite the innumerable admonitions and threats which were everywhere showered upon them, persisted in retaining their female companions, they appear, in some places, to have gradually assumed the privilege as a matter of right; and, what is even more remarkable, they seem to have had a certain measure of success in the assumption. In 1284 the papal legate, Gerard Bishop of Sabina, at the Council of Amalfi, renewed and strengthened the decretals of Alexander III respecting the concubinary priests of the Neapolitan provinces, ordering the ejection of all who should not separate from their partners within a month, suspending all prelates who should neglect to enforce the rule, and fining heavily those who, as in so many other places, made the frailties

of their subordinates a source of filthy gain. The severity
of these provisions was as unsuccessful as usual, and at
length the secular power endeavoured to come to the
assistance of the ecclesiastical authorities. The pious
Charles the Lame of Naples, whose close alliance with
Rome rendered him eager in everything that would gratify
the head of the Church, about the year 1300 imposed a
heavy fine on the concubines of priests if they persisted
in their sin for a year after excommunication. This law,
like so many similar ones, soon fell into desuetude, but in
1317, under his son, Robert the Good, the justiciary of
the Principato Citra undertook to put it into execution.
In the diocese of Marsico the clergy openly resisted these
proceedings, boldly laid their complaints before the king,
and were so energetic that Robert was obliged to issue
an ordinance directing the discontinuance of all processes
before the lay tribunals, and granting that the concubines
should be left to the care of the ecclesiastical courts alone.
These women thus, by reason of their sinful courses, came
to be invested with a quasi-ecclesiastical character, and
to enjoy the dearly prized immunities attached to that
position, at a time when the Church was vigorously striving
to uphold and extend the privileges which the civil lawyers
were systematically labouring to undermine. Nor was the
pretension thus advanced suffered to lapse. Towards the
close of the same century, Carlo Malatesta of Rimini
applied to Ancarono, a celebrated doctor of canon and civil
law ("juris canonici speculum et civilis anchora"), to
know whether he could impose penalties on the concubines
of priests, and the learned jurist replied decidedly in the
negative; while other legal authorities have not hesitated
to state that such women are fully entitled to immunity
from secular jurisdiction, as belonging to the families of
clerks—*de familia clericorum*. When a premium was thus
offered for sin, and the mistresses of priests—like the
maîtresses-en-titre of the Bourbons—acquired a certain
honourable position among their fellows from the mere
fact of their ministering to the lust of their pastors, it is
not to be wondered at if such connections multiplied and
flourished, and if the humble laity came to regard them as
an established institution.

Robert of Naples was not the only potentate who found
an organised resistance to his well-meant endeavours to

restore discipline. When, in 1410, the stout William, Bishop-elect of Paderborn, had triumphed with fire and sword over his powerful foes, the Archbishop of Cologne and the Count of Cleves, he turned his energies to the reformation of the dissolute morals of his monks. They positively refused to submit to the ejection of their women from the monasteries, and he at length found the task too impracticable even for his warlike temper. For seven long years the quarrel lasted, legal proceedings being varied by attempts at poison on the one side, and reckless devastations by the episcopal troops on the other, until the prelate, worn out by the stubbornness of his flock, was obliged to give way.

Equal success waited on the resistance of the Swiss clergy when, in 1230, the civil authorities of Zurich sacrilegiously ordered them to dismiss their women. They resolutely replied that they were flesh and blood, unequal to the task of living like angels, and unable to attend to the kitchen and other household duties. The townsmen entered into a league against them, and succeeded in driving away some of the sacerdotal consorts, when the Bishop of Constance and his chapter, allowing perhaps the pride of the churchman to get the better of ascetic zeal, interfered with a threat of excommunication on all who should presume to intervene in a matter which related specially to the Church. He absolved the leaguers from the oaths with which they were mutually bound, and thus restored security to the priestly households. About the same time, Gregory IX appointed a certain Boniface to the see of Lausanne. On his installation, the new bishop commenced with ardour to enforce the canons, but the clergy conspired against his life, and were so nearly successful that he incontinently fled, and never ventured to return.

If the irregular though permanent connections which everywhere prevailed had been the only result of the prohibition of marriage, there might perhaps have been little practical evil flowing from it, except to the Church itself and to its guilty members. When the desires of man, however, are once tempted to seek through unlawful means the relief denied to them by artificial rules, it is not easy to set bounds to the unbridled passions which, irritated by the fruitless effort at repression, are no longer restrained by a law which has been broken or a conscience which has lost its power. The records of the Middle Ages are accordingly full of the evidences that indiscriminate licence of the worst kind prevailed throughout every rank of the hierarchy.

Even supposing that this fearful immorality were not attributable to the immutable laws of nature revenging themselves for their attempted violation, it could readily be explained by the example set by the central head. Scarcely had the efforts of Nicholas and Gregory put an end to sacerdotal marriage in Rome when the morals of the Roman clergy became a disgrace to Christendom. How little the results of the reform corresponded with the hopes of the zealous puritans who had brought it about may be gathered from the martyrdom of a certain Arnolfo, who, under the pontificate of Honorius II, preached vehemently against the scandals and immorality of the ecclesiastics of the apostolic city. They succeeded in making away with him, notwithstanding the protection of Honorius and the veneration of the nobles and people who regarded him as a prophet. When such was the condition of clerical virtue, we can scarcely wonder that sufficient suffrages were given in 1130 by the sacred college to Cardinal Pier-Leone to afford him a plausible claim to the papacy, although he was notoriously stained with the foulest crimes. Apparently his children by his sister Tropea, and his being accompanied by a concubine when travelling in the capacity of papal legate, had not proved a bar to his elevation in the Church, nor to his employment in the most conspicuous and important affairs. A severer satire on the standard of ecclesiastical morality could scarcely be imagined than the inculcation by such a man, in his capacity as pope, of the canons requiring the separation of priests from their wives, on the plea of the spotless purity required for the service of the altar.

What were the influences of the papal court in the next century may be gathered from the speech which Cardinal Hugo made to the Lyonese on the occasion of the departure of Innocent IV in 1251 from their city, after a residence of eight years—" Friends, since our arrival here, we have done much for your city. When we came, we found here three or four brothels. We leave behind us but one. We must own, however, that it extends without interruption from the eastern to the western gate "—the crude cynicism of which greatly disconcerted the Lyonese ladies present. Robert Grosseteste, Bishop of Lincoln, therefore only reflected the popular conviction when, on his death-bed in 1253, inveighing against the corruption of the papal court, he applied to it 'the lines—

> Ejus avaritiæ totus non sufficit orbis,
> Ejus luxuriæ meretrix non sufficit omnis.

A hundred years later saw the popes again in France. For forty years they had bestowed on Avignon all the benefits, moral and spiritual, arising from the presence of the vicegerent of Christ, when Petrarch recorded, for the benefit of friends whom he feared to compromise by naming, the impressions produced by his long residence there in the household of a leading dignitary of the Church. Language seems too weak to express his abhorrence of that third Babylon, that Hell upon Earth, which could furnish no Noah, no Deucalion to survive the deluge that alone could cleanse its filth—and yet he intimates that fear compels him to restrain the full expression of his feelings. Chastity was a reproach and licentiousness a virtue. The aged prelates surpassed their younger brethren in wickedness as in years, apparently considering that age conferred upon them the licence to do that from which even youthful libertines shrank; while the vilest crimes were the pastimes of pontifical ease. Juvenal and Brantôme can suggest nothing more shameless or more foul. Nor was the tone of morality heightened when, fifty years later, Nicholas de Clamenges takes up the tale. His brief reference to the adulteries and vileness with which the cardinals befouled the papal court, and the obscenities in which their families imitated their example, shows that the matter was so generally understood that it needed no details.

The Great Schism perhaps could scarcely be expected to improve the morals of the papal court. Yet when the Church universal, to close that weary quarrel, agreed to receive one of the competitors as its head, surely it might have selected, as the visible representative of God upon earth, some more worthy embodiment of humanity than Balthazar Cossa, who, as John XXIII, is alone, of the three competitors, recognised in the list of popes. When the great Council of Constance in 1415 adopted the awful expedient of trying, condemning, and deposing a pope,

the catalogùe of crimes—notorious incest, adultery, defilement, homicide, and atheism—of which the fathers formally
accused him, and which he confessed without defending
himself, is fearfully suggestive of the corruption which
could not only spawn such a monster, but could elevate
him to the highest place in the hierarchy, and present him
for the veneration of Christendom. It affords a curious
insight into the notions of morality prevalent in the papal
court to observe that when he had, as chamberlain of
Boniface IX, scandalised Rome by openly keeping his
brother's wife as a concubine, the remedy adopted for the
disorder was to create him Cardinal and send him as legate
to Bologna, while the lady was conveyed to her husband
in Naples. The result of this course of procedure was that
during his sway at Bologna two hundred maids, matrons,
and widows, including a few nuns, fell victims to his brutal
lust. So obtuse, in fact, were the sensibilities of the age
that after his release from the prison to which he had been
consigned by the fathers of Constance, his successor,
Martin V, consoled him in his degradation by creating
him Dean of the Sacred College.

If the Councils of Constance and of Bâle worked some
apparent reform in the outward morality of the papacy,
their effect soon passed away. The latter half of the
fifteenth century scarcely saw a supreme pontiff without
the visible evidences of human frailty around him, the
unblushing acknowledgment of which is the fittest commentary on the tone of clerical morality. Sixtus IV was
believed to embody the utmost possible concentration of
human wickedness, until Borgia came to divide with him
the pre-eminence of evil. The success of Innocent VIII
in increasing the population of Rome was a favourite topic
with the wits of the day; but the epitaph which declared
that filth, gluttony, avarice, and sloth lay buried in his
tomb did not anticipate the immediate resurrection of the
worst of those vices in the person of his successor, Alexander VI. If the crimes of Borgia were foul, their number
and historical importance have rendered them so well
known that I may be spared more than a passing allusion
to a career which has made his name a byword. It was
reserved for Cesare Cantù to find in the criminal ambition
of his son Cæsare Borgia an argument in favour of the
celibacy which relieved the world from a succession of

papal offspring. Bishop Burchard, Alexander's master of ceremonies, naïvely remarks that he followed and improved on the example set by Innocent of giving daughters in marriage, so that all the clergy diligently set to work to get children, and, from the lowest to the highest, they publicly kept concubines with all the appearance of marriage. He adds that unless God interferes, this custom will spread to the monks, although already nearly all the convents in Rome are brothels, without any one taking exception to it.

Such men as Alexander can hardly be deemed exceptional, save inasmuch as brilliant talents and native force of character might enable them to excel their contemporaries in guilt as in ambition. They were the natural product of a system which for four centuries had bent the unremitting energies of the Church to securing temporal power and wealth, with exemption from the duties and liabilities of the citizen. Such were the fruits of the successful theocracy of Hildebrand, which, entrusting irresponsible authority to fallible humanity, came to regard ecclesiastical aggrandisement as a full atonement for all and every crime. That the infection had spread even to the ultimate fibres of the establishment can readily be believed, for the supremacy of the papal authority gave it the power of controlling the character of every parish in Christendom. We shall see hereafter, as we have already seen, how that power was habitually abused, and how the nullification of the canons was a recognised source of income to the successor of St. Peter and his needy officials. The evil was one that had long been recognised and complained of since Hincmar of Rheims so emphatically denounced it. St. Bernard declared that Rome was the acknowledged refuge of all ambitious and licentious men who desired either promotion or to retain the preferment which they had forfeited. In the fiery zeal with which he warns his protégé, Eugenius III, not to be deceived by such suitors, he shows us how useless were local efforts at reformation when they could be so readily set aside and rendered nugatory by the venal influences at work in the apostolic court. But the abuse was too profitable to be suppressed, and it continued until after the Reformation had shown the necessity for some decent reticence in the exercise of powers no longer regarded as wholly irresponsible.

My object has been to consider the subject of ascetic
celibacy as a portion simply of ecclesiastical history, and
yet I cannot well conclude this section without a hasty
glance at its influence on society at large. That influence,
as far as the secular clergy were its instruments, was
evidently one of almost unmixed evil. The parish priest,
if honestly ascetic, was thereby deprived of the wholesome common bond of human affections and sympathies,
and was rendered less efficient for good in consoling the
sorrows and aiding the struggles of his flock. If, on the
other hand, he was a hypocrite, or if he had found too late
that the burden he had assumed was too heavy for his
strength, the denial of the natural institution of marriage
was the source of immeasurable corruption to those entrusted
to his charge, who looked up to him not only as a spiritual
director, but as a superior being who could absolve them
from sin, and whose partnership in guilt was in itself an
absolution. That such was the condition of innumerable
parishes throughout Europe there is unfortunately no
reason to doubt, and all of the severer churchmen of the
period, in attacking the vices of the clergy, give us to
understand that either their example led the laity into
evil, or that their immorality rendered it impossible for
them to correct the vices of the flocks. As Cæsarius of
Heisterbach says, " Since the priesthood mostly lead evil
and incontinent lives, they soothe rather than stimulate
the consciences of the worldly." The incongruity of this
may perhaps explain to some extent the anomaly of the
practical grossness of the Middle Ages, combined with the
theoretical ascetic purity which was held out as the duty
of every Christian who desired to be acceptable to his
Creator.

The curious contrasts and confusion of the standard of
morality, arising from this striving against nature, are
well illustrated by a homily of the thirteenth century
against marriage, addressed to youthful nuns, which exhausts all the arguments that the ingenuity of the writer
could suggest. On the one hand he appeals to the pride
which could be so well gratified by the exalted state of
virginity; he pictures the superior bliss vouchsafed in
heaven to those who were stained by no earthly contamination, confidently promising them a higher rank
and more direct communing with the Father than would be

bestowed on the married and the widowed; he rapturously dwells upon the inward peace, the holy ecstasy which are the portion of those who, wedded to Christ, keep pure their mystic marriage vow; and his ascetic fervour exhausts itself in depicting the spiritual delights of a life of religious seclusion. On the other hand, mingled inextricably with these exalted visions of beatific mysticism, he presents in startling contrasts the retribution awaiting the sin of licentiousness and the evils inseparable from a life of domestic marriage. With a crude nastiness that is almost inconceivable, he minutely describes all the discomforts and suffering, physical and mental, attendant upon wifehood and maternity, entering into every detail and gloating over every revolting circumstance that his prurient imagination can suggest. The licence of Shakespeare, the plain speaking of Chaucer, Boccaccio, and the mediæval trouvères show us what our ancestors were, and what they were is easily explained when such a medley of mysticism and grossness could be poured into the pure ears of innocent young girls by their spiritual director.

Thus, with the fearful immorality of which we have seen such ample evidence, the Church still presented the same exaggerated asceticism as her guiding principle. The rhapsodies of St. John Chrysostom and St. Aldhelm were rivalled in an age when the priest was forbidden to live in the same house as his mother, because experience had shown the danger of such propinquity. How the estimate placed on purity increased as virtue diminished is fairly illustrated in a characteristic legend which was very popular with ecclesiastical teachers in the thirteenth and fourteenth centuries. It relates how a pagan, entering a heathen temple, saw Satan seated in state on a throne. One of the princes of Hell entered, worshipped his master, and proceeded to give an account of his work. For thirty days he had been engaged in provoking a war, wherein many battles had been fought with heavy slaughter. Satan sharply reproached him with accomplishing so little in the time, and ordered him to be severely punished. Another then approached the throne and reported that he had devoted twenty days to raising tempests at sea, whereby navies had been wrecked and multitudes drowned. He was likewise reproved and punished for wasting his time. A third had for ten days been engaged in troubling the wedding festivity of a city, causing strife and murder, and he was similarly treated. A fourth then entered and recounted how for forty years he had been occupied in tempting a hermit to yield to fleshly desire, and how he had that night succeeded. Then Satan arose and placed his crown on the head of the new-comer, seating him on the throne as one who had worthily achieved a signal triumph. The spectator, thus seeing the high estimate placed by the Evil One on ascetic chastity, was immediately converted, and forthwith became a monk.

While thus attaching so fanciful a holiness to virginity, the Church came practically to erect a most singular standard of morality, the influence of which could but be most deplorable on the mass of the laity. In the earlier days of celibacy the rule was regarded by the severer ecclesiastics as simply an expression of the necessity of purity in the minister of God. Theophilus of Alexandria, in the fifth century, decided that a man who as lector had been punished for unchastity and had subsequently risen to the priesthood must be expelled on account of his previous sin. We have seen, however, how, when celibacy was revived under Damiani and Hildebrand, the question of immorality virtually disappeared, and the essential point became, not that a priest should be chaste, but that he should be unmarried, and this was finally adopted as the recognised law of the Church. In 1213 the Archbishop of Lunden inquired of Innocent III whether a man who had had two concubines was ineligible to orders as a *digamus*, and the pontiff could only reply that no matter how many concubines a man might have, either at one time or in succession, he did not incur the disability of digamy. When such was the result of seven centuries of assiduous sacerdotalism in a Church which was daily growing in authority; when the people thus saw that sexual excesses were no bar to ecclesiastical preferment in that Church which made extravagant pretensions to purity; when the strict rules which forbade ordination to a layman who had married a widow were relaxed in favour of those who were stained with notorious impurity, it is no wonder that the popular perceptions of morality became blunted, and that the laity did not deny themselves the indulgences which they saw tacitly allowed to their spiritual guides.

Nor was it only in stimulating this general laxity of

principle that the influence of the Church was disastrous.
The personal evil wrought by a dissolute priesthood was
a wide-spreading contagion.   The abuse of the awful
authority given by the altar and the confessional was
a subject of sorrowful and indignant denunciation in too
many synods for a reasonable doubt to be entertained
of its frequency or of the corruption which it spread
through innumerable parishes and nunneries.   The almost
entire practical immunity with which these and similar
scandals were perpetrated led to an undisguised and
cynical profligacy which the severer Churchmen acknowledged to exercise a most deleterious influence on the morals
of the laity, who thus saw the exemplars of evil in those
who should have been their patterns of virtue.   In his bull
of 1259, Alexander IV does not hesitate to declare that the
people, instead of being reformed, are absolutely corrupted
by their pastors.   Thomas of Cantinpré, one of the early
lights of the Dominican order, indeed, is authority for the
legend which represents the devil as thanking the prelates
of the Church for conducting all Christendom to hell; and
the conviction which thus expressed itself is justified by
the reproach of Gregory X, who, in dismissing the second
Council of Lyons, in 1274, told his assembled dignitaries
that they were the ruin of the world.   Unfortunately, his
threat to reform them if they did not reform themselves
remained unexecuted, and the complaint was repeated
again and again.

That this state of things was clearly understood by the
laity is only too visibly reflected in contemporary records.
When, in 1374, the dancing mania, one of those strange
epidemics which afflicted the Middle Ages, broke out
through Germany and Flanders, the populace called to
mind the forgotten regulations of Damiani and Hildebrand, and found a ready explanation of the visitation by
assuming it to be a consequence of the vitiated baptism
of the people by a concubinary priesthood.   Chaucer,
with his wide range of observation and shrewd native
sense, took a less superstitious and more practical view of
the evil, and in the admirable sermon which forms his
" Persone's Tale " he records the convictions which every
pure-minded man must have felt with regard to the
demoralising tendencies of the sacerdotal licentiousness
of the time.

How instinctively, indeed, the popular mind assumed the immorality of the pastor is illustrated by a passage in the earliest French pastoral that has reached us, dating from the latter half of the thirteenth century—

> WARNIERS.   Segneur je sui trop courechiés.
> GUIOS. Comment?
> WARNIERS.   Mehalès est agute,
>   M'amie, et s'a esté dechute;
>   Car on dist que ch'est de no prestre.
> ROGAUS.   En non Dieu !   Warnier, bien puet estre;
>   Car ele i aloit trop souvent.
> WARNIERS.   Hé, las ! jou avoie en couvent
>   De li temprement espouser.
> GUIOS.   Tu te pués bien trop dolouser,
>   Biaus très dous amis; ne te caille,
>   Car ja ne meteras maaille,
>   Que bien sai, à l'enfant warder.

Those who were heretically disposed were keen to take advantage of a weakness so general and so universally understood. The author of the " Creed of Piers Ploughman " does not hesitate to assert with Gregory X that the clergy were the corruption of the world—

> For falshed of freres
> Hath fullich encombred
> Manye of this maner men,
> And made hem to leven
> Her charité and chastité,
> And shosen hem to lustes,
> And waxen to werly,
> And wayven the trewethe,
> And leven the love of her God.

The widely received feeling on this subject, perhaps, finds its fittest expression in a satire on the mendicant friars, written by a Franciscan novice who became disgusted with the order and turned Wickliffite. The exaggerated purity and mortification of the early followers of the blessed St. Francis had long since yielded to the temptations which attended on the magnificent success of the institution, and the mystic aspirations which earned for it the name of the Seraphic Order degenerated into sloth and crime which took advantage of the opportunities afforded by the privilege to hear confessions. The grosser accusations of the writer are perhaps unfit for quotation, but the spirit in which the friars were regarded is sufficiently indicated by the following lines :—

For when the gode man is fro hame
And the frere comes to oure dame,
He spares, nauther for synne ne shame,
That he ne dos his will.

.   .   .   .

Ich man that here shal lede his life
That has a faire doghter or a wyfe
Be war that no frer ham shryfe
Nauther loude ne still.

When such was the moral condition of the priesthood, and such were the influences which it cast upon the flocks entrusted to its guidance, it is not to be wondered at if those who deplored so disgraceful a state of things, and whose respect for the canons precluded them from recommending the natural and appropriate remedy of marriage, should regard an organised system of concubinage as a safeguard. However deplorable such an alternative might be in itself, it was surely preferable to the mischief which the unquenched and ungoverned passions of a pastor might inflict upon his parish; and the instances of this were too numerous and too glaring to admit of much hesitation in electing between the two evils. Even Gerson, the leader of mystic ascetics, who recorded his unbounded admiration for the purity of celibacy in his " Dialogus Naturæ et Sophiæ de Castitate Clericorum," saw and appreciated its practical evils, and had no scruple in recommending concubinage as a preventive, which, though scandalous in itself, might serve to prevent greater scandals. It therefore requires no great stretch of credulity to believe the assertion of Sleidan, that in some of the Swiss Cantons it was the custom to oblige a new pastor, on entering upon his functions, to select a concubine, as a necessary protection to the virtue of his female parishioners, and to the peace of the families entrusted to his spiritual direction. Indeed, we have already seen (p. 261), on the authority of the Council of Valladolid in 1322, that such a practice was not uncommon in Spain.

In thus reviewing the influences which a nominally celibate clergy exercised over those entrusted to their care, it is perhaps scarcely too much to conclude that they were largely responsible for the laxity of morals which is a characteristic of mediæval society. No one who has attentively examined the records left to us of that society can call in question the extreme prevalence of the licentiousness which everywhere infected it. Christianity had arisen as the great reformer of a world utterly corrupt. How earnestly its reform was directed to correcting sexual immorality is visible in the persistence with which the Apostles condemned and forbade a sin that the Gentiles scarcely regarded as a sin. The early Church was consequently pure, and its very asceticism is a measure of the energy of its protest against the all-pervading licence which surrounded it. Its teachings, as we have seen, remained unchanged. Fornication continued to be a mortal sin, yet the period of its unquestioned domination over the conscience of Europe was the very period in which licence among the Teutonic races was most unchecked. A Church which, though founded on the Gospel, and wielding the illimitable power of the Roman hierarchy, could yet allow the feudal principle to extend to the " jus primæ noctis " or " droit de marquette," and whose ministers in their character of temporal seigneurs could even occasionally claim the disgusting right themselves,[1] was evidently exercising its influence not for good but for evil.

[1] There is a tradition that the Abbey of Montariol lost its sovereignty over the inhabitants of the village of that name in consequence of a revolt caused by the monks exacting this feudal right in all its odious cynicism, in place of receiving a payment in commutation as was frequently done. The Abbé Marcellin, in his edition of Le Bret's Histoire de Montauban (I. 362–74) seems to me to have successfully proved its falsity. He admits, however, that in his researches on the subject he has found one case in which an ecclesiastic undertook to enforce his rights to the letter. The President Boyer, writing in the sixteenth century (Decisiones, No. 17, Decis. 297) asserts that he had seen the proceedings of a lawsuit in which " Rector seu curatus parochialis prætendebat ex consuetudine primam habere sponsæ cognitionem " (Eschbach, Introduction à l'Étude du Droit, § 174).

The existence of this feudal right has been the subject of no little debate, to the acerbity of which religious as well as scientific partisanship has contributed. Allusions to it in nearly every land of Christendom are too widely spread, however, to render it doubtful that such a right was claimed and exercised, if not universally, at least in certain times and places. The student can find abundant proof of this in Ducange, s.v. *Marcheta*, and in Lagrèze's Histoire du Devil dans les Pyrénées (Paris, 1867, pp. 384–425), who, however, denies that ecclesiastics were ever guilty of exacting it.

Documentary evidence of the custom is not wholly wanting. In Béarn, the seigneurs of Lobier claimed it of their *questaus* or serfs.— " Item. Quant auguns de tals maisons se mariden, dabant que

There is no injustice in holding the Church responsible for the lax morality of the laity. It had assumed the right to regulate the consciences of men and to make them account for every action and even for every thought. When it promptly caused the burning of those who ventured on any dissidence in doctrinal opinion or in matters of pure speculation, it could not plead lack of authority to control them in practical virtue. Its machinery was all-pervading, and its power autocratic. It had taught that the priest was to be venerated as the representative of God and that his commands were to be implicitly obeyed. It had armed him with the fearful weapon of the confessional, and by authorising him to grant absolution and to pronounce excommunication, it had delegated to him the keys of heaven and hell. By removing him from the jurisdiction of the secular courts it had proclaimed him as superior to all temporal authority. Through ages of faith the populations had humbly received these

---

conexer lors molhers, sou tenguts de las presentar per la prumère noeyt audit senhor de Lobier per en far a son plaser, ou autrement lou valhar cert tribut," and the first child born, if a male, was free " per so qui poeyre star engendrat de las obres deudit senhor de Lobier en ladite prumère noeyt et de sous suditz plasers " (Mazure et Hatoulet, Fors de Béarn, p. 172, Pau, 1847). This document is of the sixteenth century: in Catalonia it was not until about the same period that the custom was definitely abolished. When, in 1462, the peasants and nobles endeavoured to settle their differences, one of the complaints of the former was that some seigneurs claimed the first night of a peasant bride, or to pass over her when she was in bed as a symbol of his right. To this the lords replied that they did not know or believe in the existence of such a servitude, but, if it was so, they renounced and abolished it as unjust and indecent (E. de Hinujusa, Annales Internationales d'Histoire, 2° Section, p. 224, Paris, 1902). In spite of this disclaimer, the grievance continued, and it was left for Ferdinand of Aragon, in his arbitral sentence of 1486, to put an end to it.—" Item, sententiam arbitram e declaram que los dits senyors no pugan . . . la primera nit que los pages pren muller dormir ab ella o en senyal de senyoria, la nit de las bodas, apres que la muller sera colgada en lo lit, passar sobre aquell, sobre la dita muller " (Pragmaticas e altres Drets de Cathalunya, Lib. IV. Tit. xiii. § 2, n. 9. Barcelona, 1589).
The servitude was known as *Ferma despoli forçada*. Pujades, writing some three centuries ago, seeks the fanciful explanation of it and of other *mals usus* by attributing them to the Moorish tyranny over Christian vassals, and that the *pages de remensa*, or predial serfs, who remained subject to these customs, were those who refused to aid in throwing off the domination of the infidel.—Crónica universal del Principado de Cataluña, IV. 332 (Barcelona, 1832).

teachings and bowed to these assumptions, until they entered into the texture of the daily life of every man. While thus grasping supremacy and using it to the utmost possibility of worldly advantage, the Church therefore could not absolve itself from the responsibilities inseparably connected with power, and chief among these reponsibilities is to be numbered the moral training of the nations thus subjected to its will. While the corruption of the teachers thus had necessarily entailed the corruption of the taught, it is not too much to say that the tireless energy devoted to the acquisition and maintenance of power, privileges, and wealth, if properly directed, under all the advantages of the situation, would have sufficed to render mediæval society the purest that the world has ever seen.

That the contrary was notoriously the case resulted naturally from the fact that the Church, after the long struggle which finally left it supreme over Europe, contented itself with the worldly advantages derivable from the wealth and authority which surpassed its anticipations. If, then, it could secure a verbal submission to its doctrines of purity, it was willing to issue countless commands of chastity and tacitly to connive at their perpetual infraction. The taint of corruption infected equally its own ministers and the peoples committed to their charge, and the sacerdotal theory gradually came to regard with more and more indifference obedience to the Gospel in comparison with obedience to man and subservience to the temporal interests of the hierarchy. As absolution and indulgence grew to be a marketable commodity, it even became the interest of the traders in salvation to have a brisk demand for their wares. When infraction of the divine precepts could be redeemed with a few pence or with the performance of ceremonies that had lost their significance, it is not surprising if priest and people at length were led to look upon the violation of the Decalogue with the eye of the merchant and customer rather than with the spirit of the great Lawgiver.

The first impulse in the reaction of the sixteenth century was to recur to the Gospel and to interpret its commands in accordance with the immutable principles of human conscience rather than with the cunningly devised subtleties of scholastic theology. The reformers thus stood face to face with God, and, needing no intermediary to negotiate with Him, vice and sin reappeared to them in all their hideous deformity and attended with all their inevitable consequences. For the first time since primitive Christianity was absorbed in sacerdotalism, were the doctrines of morality enforced as the primal laws of man's being and of human society, and the world was made to see, by the energetic action of Puritan sects, that virtue was possible as the rule of life in large communities. We may smile at the eccentricities of Puritanism, but the rescue of modern civilisation from the long heritage of ancient vice, and the decency which characterises modern society, may fairly be attributed to the force of that fierce reaction against the splendid corruptions of the mediæval Church.

In considering, however, the influence of the regular clergy, or monastic orders, we find a more complex array of motives and results. The earlier foundations of the West, as we have seen, to a great extent neutralised the inherent selfishness of monachism by the regulations which prescribed a due proportion of labour to be mingled with prayer. The duty which man owes to the world was to some extent recognised as not incompatible with the duty which he owed to his God, and civilisation has had few more efficient instruments than the self-denying work of the earnest men who, from Columba to Adalbert, sowed the seeds of Christianity and culture among the frontier lands of Christendom. When discipline such as these men inculcated could be enforced, the benefits of monachism far outweighed its evils. All the peaceful arts, from agriculture to music, owed to the Benedictines their preservation or their advancement, and it would be difficult to estimate exactly the influence for good which resulted from institutions to which the thoughtful and studious could safely retire from a turbulent and barbarous world. These institutions, however, from their own inherent defects, carried in them the germs of corruption. The claims to supereminent sanctity, carrying with it the power of efficacious intercession with God, were inevitably used as means for the accumulation of wealth wrung from the fears or superstition of the sinner. With wealth came the abandonment of labour; and idleness and luxury were the prolific parents of licence. True-hearted men were not wanting to combat the irrepressible evil. From Chrodegang to St. Vincent de Paul, the history of monachism is full of illustrious names of those who devoted themselves to the mission of reforming abuses and restoring the ideal of the perfect monk, dead to the seductions of the world, and living only to do the work which he deems most acceptable to God. Many of these mistakenly assumed that exaggerated mortification was the only gateway to salvation, and the only cure for the frightful immorality which pervaded so many monastic establishments. Others, with a truer insight into the living principles of Christianity, sought to turn the enthusiasm of their disciples to account in works of perennial mercy and charity, at a period when no other organisations existed for the succour of the helpless and miserable.

Yet when we reflect how large a proportion of the wealth and intellect of Europe was absorbed in the religious houses, it will be seen that the system was a most cumbrous and imperfect one, which gave but a slender return for the magnitude of the means which it involved. Still, it was the only system existing, and possibly the only one which could exist in so rude a structure of society, individualised to a degree which destroyed all sense of public responsibility and precluded all idea of a state created for the well-being of its component parts. Thus, the monastery became the shelter of the wayfarer, and the dispenser of alms to the needy. It was the principal school of the poor and humble; and while the Universities of Oxford and Paris were devoting their energies to unprofitable dialectics and the subtle disputations of Aristotelian logic, in multitudes of abbey libraries quiet monks were multiplying priceless manuscripts, and preserving to after ages the treasures of the past. When fanciful asceticism did not forbid the healing of the sick, monks laboured fearlessly in hospitals and pest-houses, and distributed among the many the benefactions which they had wrung from the late repentance of the few. As time wore on, even the religious teaching of the public passed almost exclusively into their hands, and to the followers of Dominic and Francis of Assisi the people owed such insight as they could obtain into the promises of the gospel. If the enthusiasm which prompted labours so strenuous did not shrink from lighting the fires of persecution, we must remember that religious zeal, accompanied by irresponsible power, has one invariable history.

While thus, in various ways, the ascetic spirit led to institutions which promoted the progress of civilisation, in others it necessarily had a directly opposite tendency. Nothing contributes more strongly to the extension of knowledge and of culture than the striving for material comfort and individual advancement in worldly well-being. Luxury and ambition thus have their uses in stimulating the inquiring and inventive faculties of man, in rendering the forces of nature subservient to our use, and in softening the rugged asperities which are incompatible with the regular administration of law. Every instinct of human nature has its destined purpose in life, and the perfect man is to be found in the proportionate cultivation of each element of his character, not in the exaggerated development of those faculties which are deemed primarily good, nor in the entire repression of those which are evil only when their prominence destroys the balance of the whole. The ascetic selected for eradication one group of human aspirations, which was the most useful under proper discipline, and not perhaps the worst even in its ordinary excess. Only those who have studied the varied aspects of mediæval society can rightly estimate the enormous influence which the Church possessed, in those ages of faith, to mould the average habits of thought in any desired direction. It can readily be seen that if the tireless preaching of the vanity of human things and the beatitude of mortification occasionally produced such extravagances as those of the flagellants, the spirit which now and then burst forth in such eruption must have been an element of no little power in the forces which governed society at large, and must have exercised a most depressing influence in restraining the general advance of civilisation. Not only did it thus more or less weigh down the efforts of almost every man, but the ardent minds that would otherwise have been leaders in the race of progress were the ones most likely, under the pervading spirit of the age, to be the foremost in maceration and self-denial; while those who would not yield to the seduction were either silenced or wasted their wisdom on a generation which believed too much to believe in them. When idleness was holy, earnest workers had little chance.

The effect of monastic asceticism in moulding the character may be seen in the admiring picture drawn by a disciple in the fifteenth century of a shining light of the Carthusian Order in the monastery of Vallis Dei, near Seez in Normandy. He had every virtue, he was an earnest reader and transcriber of MSS., and he practised mortifications even greater than those prescribed by the severe rules of the order. He rarely slept on the couch provided for each brother, but passed his nights in prayer on the steps of the altar. In the hair shirt worn next his skin he cultivated lice and maggots so assiduously that they were often seen crawling over his face, and he scourged himself for every unhallowed wandering thought. He had preserved his virginity to old age, and his life had been passed in the Church, yet in his daily confessions he accused himself of every sin possible to man, and he rigorously performed whatever penance was assigned to him. With all this maceration, the flesh would still assert itself, and he was tormented with evil desires which the sharp cords of the discipline failed to subdue. His office of procurator of the abbey required him to make frequent visits on business to the neighbouring town, and he never left the gates of his retreat without lamenting and expressing the fear that he should not return to it the same as he left it. If we consider what might have been effected by the energies of thousands of men such as this, had those energies not been absorbed in lifelong asceticism, we may conceive in some measure the retardation of human progress wrought by the influence of monachism.

Another result which may fairly be attributed to the ascetic teachings of the Church is the slow growth of population during the mediæval period. Notwithstanding the gross and flagrant disregard of the rule, it was impossible to immure in convents men and women by the hundred thousand during successive generations without retarding greatly the rate of increase of the species. The rudeness of the arts and sciences, war, pestilence and famine were doubtless efficient causes, yet they were less efficient than enforced celibacy. This is evident when we see the rapid rate of growth established on the abrogation or even relaxation of the rule. The suppression of the monastic orders in France followed soon after the reforms by which Joseph II discouraged them throughout the Austrian empire, and the result is visible in the enormous increase of European population which followed, notwithstanding the fearful destruction of life in the Napoleonic wars. It is calculated that in 1788 Europe numbered 144,561,000 souls, which within fifty years had been augmented to 253,622,000, or about seventy-five per cent. Of late years the birth-rate has decreased in consequence of the severity of conscription in the military monarchies, but the enormous growth in the half-century following the French Revolution is the best commentary on the influences which for so many ages kept the population almost stationary.

It required the unbelief of the fifteenth century to give free rein to the rising commercial energies and the craving for material improvement that paved the way for the decadence of ascetic sacerdotalism. The corruptions of the Church, which indirectly caused and accompanied that awakening of the human mind, will be alluded to hereafter, when we come to consider the movements leading to the Protestant Reformation. At present we must turn aside for a moment to consider one or two external developments of the religious activity of the Middle Ages.

CHAPTER XXII

THE MILITARY ORDERS

THE military orders were the natural expression of the admixture of religious and warlike enthusiasm, reacting on each other, which produced and was fostered by the Crusades. When bishops considered that they rendered a service acceptable to God in leading vast hosts to slaughter the Paynim, it was an easy transition for soldiers to turn monks, and to consecrate their swords to the bloody work of avenging their Redeemer.

When the Hospitallers—Knights of St. John of Jerusalem, of Rhodes, or of Malta—first emerged from their humble position of ministering to the afflictions of their fellow-pilgrims, and commenced to assume a military organisation under Raymond du Puy, about the year 1120, their statutes required the three ordinary monastic vows of poverty, obedience, and chastity. In fact, they were at first Benedictines; but when they became numerous enough to form a separate body, they adopted the rule of St. Augustin.

When the rule for the Templars—" Regula pauperum commilitonum sanctæ civitatis "—was adopted in 1128, at the Council of Troyes, it contained no special injunction to administer a vow of celibacy, but the context shows that such a condition was understood as a matter of course. Some little difficulty was evidently experienced at first, since, from the nature of the case, novices had to be trained warriors who must frequently have been bound by family ties, and whose education had not been such as to fit them for the restraints of their new life. Married men, it is true, were admitted, but only on condition that both husband and wife should bind themselves to bequeath all their property to the order; they were to lead an honest life, but the husband was not permitted to live with the brethren, nor to wear the white mantle of the order. It is probable that the perpetual nature of the obligations assumed was not easy to be enforced upon the fierce members of the brotherhood, for, in 1183, Lucius III, in confirming the privileges of the order, specially commands that no one who enters it shall be allowed to return to the world.

The history of these two orders is too well known to require it to be traced minutely here. If, with the growth of their reputation and wealth, the austere ascetism of their early days was lost, and if luxury and vice took the place of religious enthusiasm and soldierly devotion to the Cross, they but obeyed the universal law which in human institutions is so apt to render corruption the consequence of prosperity. One conclusion may, however, be drawn from the proceedings by which the powerful Order of the Temple was extinguished at the commencement of the fourteenth century. Notwithstanding the open and scandalous licentiousness of the order, it is a little singular that the interminable articles of accusation against the members contain no allusion to unchastity, while crimes most fantastic, practices most beastly, and charges most frivolous are heaped upon them in strange confusion. As the object of those who conducted the prosecution was to excite a popular abhorrence that would justify the purposed spoliation, it is evident that the simple infraction of vows of chastity was regarded as so venial a fault and so much a matter of course that its proof could in no way serve the end of rousing indignation against the accused.

It is somewhat remarkable that the same century which saw the foundation of the Orders of the Hospital and Temple also witnessed one which, although bound by the rule of St. Augustin, and subjected to the ordinary vows of obedience, property in common, and inability to return to the world, yet allowed to its members the option of selecting either marriage or celibacy, and even of contracting second marriages. This was the Spanish Order of Santiago. What we have seen of the want of respect paid by the Spanish Church to asceticism may lessen surprise at the founding of an order based upon such regulations, yet it is difficult to understand how so great a violation of established principles could be sanctioned by Alexander III, who confirmed the order in 1175, or by Innocent III and Honorius III, who formally approved its privileges.

The example was one of evil import in the Peninsula. The Council of Valladolid in 1322 felt itself obliged to denounce under severe penalties the practice of dowering children with the possessions of the community, in which the military orders followed the precedent set them by the Church. During the universal licence of the fifteenth century, when ascetic vows became a mockery, and the profligacy of those who took them exposed all such observances to contempt, the military orders formed no exception to the general shamelessness. In 1429 the Council of Tortosa deplored the destruction and waste of the temporal possessions of the religious knights from the general concubinage in which they indulged, and to effect a cure it promulgated regulations of peculiar severity, threatening with a liberal hand the penalties of excommunication and degradation. These proved as powerless as usual, and not long after a more sensible remedy was adopted by Eugenius IV when he released the ancient and renowned Order of Calatrava from the obligation of celibacy, for reasons which would have led him to extend the privilege of marriage to the whole Church, had the purity of ecclesiastics been truly the object of the rule. He recounts with sorrow the disorderly lives of the knights, and, quoting the text which says that it is better to marry than to burn, he grants the privilege of marriage because he deems it preferable to live with a wife than with a mistress.

This apparently did not extend to the *comendadores* of the order, for we hear, in 1538, of negotiations for them and for those of the Order of Alcántara, with Paul III, for permission to marry. He conceded the dispensation, but when they found the price demanded, they refused to pay it, and the matter was left unsettled. Presumably the privileges granted by Eugenius IV were extended to the Order of Montesa, founded in Valencia in 1319, on the ruins of the Temple, for it was affiliated with the Order of Calatrava, from which its members were drawn. A writer towards the close of the sixteenth century tells us that there had then been fourteen Masters who had vowed chastity, and none of them had married until the present one, Don Cesar de Borja, who was married.

Similar arguments were employed to extend the same privilege to the Orders of Avis and of Jesus Christ, of Portugal. The former was founded in 1147 by Alfonso I,

under the Cistercian rule, and chastity was one of its
fundamental obligations; the latter was the continuation
of the Order of the Temple, which, preserved in Portugal
by the humanity of King Dionysius, assumed in the fourteenth century the name of Jesus. Both institutions
became incurably corrupted; their preceptories were dens
of avowed and scandalous prostitution, and their promiscuous amours filled the kingdom with hate and dissension. When at length, in 1496, King Emanuel applied
to Alexander VI to grant the privilege of marriage, in
hopes of reforming the orders, it is interesting to observe
how instinctively the minds of men turned to this as the
sole efficient remedy for the immorality which all united
in attributing to the hopeless attempt to enforce a purity
impossible in the existing condition of society. Alexander
assented to the request, and bestowed on the orders the
right of marriage on the same conditions as those enjoined
on the Knights of Santiago. It is true that Osorius doubts
whether the benefits of the change were not exceeded by
its evils, as he states that it lowered the character of the
orders, opened the door to unworthy members, and led to
the dissipation of their property.

There was another Portuguese order of a somewhat
different character. Twenty years after founding the
Knights of Avis, Alfonso I, in 1167, to commemorate his
miraculous victory over the Moors at Santarem, instituted
the Order of St. Michael. The knights were allowed to
marry once; if widowed, they were obliged to embrace
celibacy; and the Abbot of Alcobaça, who was the superior
of the order, was empowered to excommunicate them for
irregularity of life, to compel them to give up their mistresses. They were moreover bound to perform the same
religious exercises as lay brothers of the Cistercians. The
order is interesting as forming a curious link between the
secular, religious, and military elements of the period.

During all this, the Knights of St. John adhered to
their ancient statutes, and endeavoured from time to time
to reform the profligacy which seemed inseparable from
the institution. When the ascetic Antonio Fluviano, who
held the grand mastership from 1421 to 1437, promulgated a regulation that any one guilty of public concubinage
should receive three warnings, with severe penalties for
contumacy, it suggests a condition of morals by no means

creditable to the brethren. So, a century later, the stern Villiers de l'Isle-Adam was forced to declare that any one openly acknowledging an illegitimate child should be for ever after incapacitated for office, benefice, or dignity. What the knights were soon afterwards, the scandalous pages of Brantôme sufficiently attest, and that the succeeding century did not witness an improvement may be inferred from the dictum of an eminent casuist that the mistresses of the members of such orders were not bound to make restitution of the moneys received from their lovers.

The Marian or Teutonic Order, perhaps the most wealthy and powerful of all, was founded in 1190, and adopted the rule of the Templars as regards its religious government, with that of the Hospitallers to regulate its duties of charity and hospitality. The three vows of chastity, obedience, and poverty were essential, and no one had power to dispense from either of them. For a full century of its existence it was sorely oppressed with poverty, but at length, when transferred from the Holy Land to North-eastern Germany, it bore a prominent part in Christianising those regions, and what it won by the sword it retained possession of in its own right. With wealth came indolence and luxury, and the order became corrupt, as others had been. Its history offers nothing of special interest to us until, in 1525, the Grand Master Albert of Brandenburg went over to Lutheranism with many of his knights, founded the hereditary dukedom of Prussia, and married—of which more hereafter. Those of the order who adhered to Catholicism maintained the organisation on the rich possessions which the piety of ages had bestowed upon them throughout Germany, until this worn-out relic of the past disappeared in the convulsions of the Napoleonic wars, though the Archduke Wilhelm of Austria is—or recently was—reckoned as Grand Master, performing the occasional ceremony of admitting members in assemblages of mail-clad knights. How completely the remnant of the order, still existing in Austria, has become a mere matter of social distinction is seen in the concession made in 1886 by Leo XIII, at the request of the Emperor Franz Joseph, that in future the knights shall take only simple and not solemn vows.

CHAPTER XXIII

THE HERESIES

ALLUSION has already been made to the introduction of Manichæism into Western Europe through Bulgaria and Lombardy. Notwithstanding its stern and unrelenting suppression wherever it was discovered during the eleventh and twelfth centuries, its votaries multiplied in secret. The disorders of the clergy, their oppression of the people, and their quarrels with the nobles over their temporal possessions made them many enemies among the laity; and the simplicity of the Manichæan belief, its freedom from aspirations for temporal aggrandisement, and its denunciations of the immorality and grasping avidity of the priesthood, found for it an appreciative audience and made ready converts. Towards the close of the twelfth century the south of France was discovered to be filled with heretics, among whom the names of Cathari, Paterins, Albigenses, etc., concealed the more odious appellation of Manichæans.

It is not our province to trace out in detail the bloody vicissitudes of the Albigensian Crusades and of the Inquisition which completed their work. It is sufficient for our purpose to indicate the identity of the Catharan belief with that of the ancient sect which we have seen to exercise so powerful an influence in moulding and encouraging the asceticism of the early Church. The Dualistic principle was fully recognised. No necessity was regarded as justifying the use of meat, or even of eggs and cheese, or in fact of anything which had its origin in animal propagation. Marriage was an abomination and a mortal sin, which could not be intensified by adultery or other excesses.

Engrafted on these errors were others more practically dangerous, as they were the inevitable protest against the all-absorbing sacerdotalism which by this time had become the distinguishing characteristic of the Church. In denying the existence of purgatory and the efficacy of prayers for the dead and the invocation of saints, a mortal blow was aimed against the system to which the Church owed its firmest hold on the souls and purses of the people. In reviving the Hildebrandine doctrine that the sacraments were not to be administered by ecclesiastics in a state of sin, and in exaggerating it into an incompatibility between sin and holding Church preferment, a most dangerous and revolutionary turn was given to the widespread discontent with which the excesses of the clergy were regarded. So sure a hold, indeed, had such views upon the popular feeling, that we find them reappear with every heresy, transmitted with regular filiation through the Waldenses, the Wickliffites, and the Hussites, so that in every age, from Gregory to the Reformation, the measures with which he broke down the independence of the local clergy returned to plague their inventors.

Yet with all this, the heretics to outward appearance long continued unexceptionably orthodox. Industrious and sober, none were more devoted to all the observances of the Church, none more regular at mass and confession, more devout at the altar, or more liberal at the offertory. Hidden beneath this fair seeming, their heresy was only the more dangerous, as it attracted converts with unexampled rapidity. Priests gave up their churches to join the society, wives left their husbands, and husbands abandoned their wives; and when questioned as to their renunciation of the duties and privileges of marriage, they all professed to be bound by a vow of chastity. Yet if so ardent a combatant as St. Bernard is to be believed, their rigorous asceticism was only a cloak for libertinism. It is possible that the enthusiastic self-mortification of the sectaries led them to test their resolution by the dangerous experiments common among the early Christians, and possibly also with the same deplorable results. St. Bernard at least argues that constant companionship of the sexes without sin would require a greater miracle than raising the dead, and as these heretics could not perform the lesser prodigy, it was reasonable to presume that they failed of the greater—and his conclusion is not unlikely to be true. Be this as it may, the virtue of these puritan sects rendered chastity dangerous to the orthodox, for the celebrated Peter Cantor relates as a fact within his own knowledge, that honest matrons who resisted the attempts of priests to seduce them were accused of Manichæism and condemned as heretics.

The orthodox polemics, in controverting the exaggerated asceticism of these heretics, had a narrow and a difficult path to tread. Their own authorities had so exalted the praises of virgin purity, that it was not easy to meet the arguments of those who merely carried out the same principle somewhat further, in fearlessly following out the premises to their logical conclusion. There is extant a curious tract, being a dialogue between a Catholic and a Paterin, in which the latter of course has the worst of the disputation, yet he presses his adversary hard with the texts which were customarily cited by the orthodox advocates of clerical celibacy—" qui habent uxores sint tanquam non habentes," " qui non reliquerit uxorem et filios propter me non est me dignus," etc.; and the Catholic can only elude their force by giving to them metaphorical explanations very different from those which of old had been assumed in the canons requiring the separation of man and wife on ordination. How difficult of definition was the distinction in this matter between orthodoxy and heresy is shown in the case of Heinrich Minneke, Provost of the Cistercian nunnery of Neuwerke in Goslar, burnt as a Manichæan in 1222, when one of the articles of accusation against him was that his praises of virginity seemed a condemnation of matrimony. It was fortunate for St. Jerome that he did not live in the thirteenth century.

The stubborn resistance of the Albigenses to the enormous odds brought against them shows the unconquerable vitality of the anti-sacerdotal spirit which was then so widely diffused throughout Southern Europe. In a different shape it had already manifested itself during the first half of the twelfth century, when Pierre de Bruys infected all the South of France with the heresy called, after him and his most noted follower, the Petrobrusian or Henrician. This was an uncompromising revolt against the whole system of Roman Christianity. It not only abrogated pædo-baptism, and promulgated heretical notions respecting the Eucharist, but it abolished the visible symbols and ceremonies which formed so large a portion of the sacerdotal fabric—churches, crucifixes, chanting, fasting, gifts and offerings for the dead, and even the mass. But little is known respecting the Petrobrusians, except what can be derived from the refutation of their errors by Peter the Venerable. He says nothing specifically respecting their views upon ascetic celibacy, but we may assume that this was one of the doctrinal and practical corruptions which they assailed, from a passage in which, describing their excesses, he complains of the public eating of flesh on Passion Sunday, the cruel flagellation of priests, the imprisonment of monks, and their being forced to marry by threats and torments. Even after de Bruys was burned alive in 1126, his disciple, Henry, boldly carried on the contest, and the papal legate, Cardinal Alberic, sent for St. Bernard to assist him in suppressing the heretics. The latter, in a letter written in 1147 to the Count of Toulouse, describes the religious condition of his territories as most deplorable in consequence of the prevalence of the heresy—the churches were without congregations, the pastors without flocks, the people without pastors, the sacraments without reverence, the dying without consolation, and the new-born without baptism. Even making allowance for some exaggeration in all this, there can be no doubt that the heresy received extensive popular support and that it was professed publicly without disguise. At Alby it was dominant, so that when the Cardinal-legate went there, the people received him in derision with asses and drums, and when he preached, scarce thirty persons assembled to hear him; but two days later St. Bernard so affected them with his eloquence that they renounced their errors. He was less successful at Vertfeuil, where resided a hundred knights-banneret, who refused to listen to him, and whom he cursed, in consequence whereof they all perished miserably. Though St. Bernard was forced to return to Clairvaux without accomplishing the extirpation of the heresy, Henry was finally captured, and probably died in prison.

It was probably another branch of the same sect which was discovered at Liège in 1144, described as brought thither from the south and pervading all France and the neighbouring countries. Its followers denied the efficacy of baptism, of the Eucharist, and of the imposition of hands; they rejected not only oaths and vows, but marriage itself, and denied that the Holy Spirit could be gained except through good works. These heretics, however, had not in them the spirit of martyrdom, and speedily recanted on being discovered.

It was a period of transition, in which scholastic theology was beginning to assume shape, at the hands of the teachers in the University of Paris, and men's minds were easily led astray by any one who proclaimed a new form of belief. This explains the career of the crazy heresiarch, Éon de l'Étoile. During one of the epidemics of maceration and fanaticism which form such curious episodes in mediæval history, Éon, born of a noble Breton family, abandoned himself to the savage life of a hermit in the wilderness. Drawn by a vision to attend divine service, his excited mysticism caught the words which ended the recitation of the collect, " Per *eum* qui venturus est judicare vivos et mortuos ; " and the resemblance of " eum " to his own name inspired him with the revelation that he was the Son of God. Men's minds were ready for any extravagance, and Éon soon had disciples who adored him as a deity incarnate. Nothing can be wilder than the tales which are related of him by eye-witnesses—the aureole of glory which surrounded him, the countless wealth which was at the disposal of his followers, the rich but unsubstantial banquets which were served at his bidding by invisible hands, the superhuman velocity of his movements when eluding those who were bent on his capture. Éon declared war upon the churches, which monopolised the wealth of the people while neglecting the duties for which they had been enriched ; and he pillaged them of their treasures, which he distributed lavishly to the poor. Hugues, Archbishop of Rouen, who prided himself on his theological ability, sought to convert the heretics by an elaborate refutation of their tenets, among which he enumerated promiscuous licentiousness and disregard of clerical celibacy. Daniel, he gravely assured them, symbolises virginity, Noah continence, and Job marriage. Then, quoting Ezekiel xiv. 13–20, wherein Jehovah, threatening the land with destruction, says, " Though these three men, Noah, Daniel, and Job, were in it, they should deliver but their own souls through their righteousness," he proceeded triumphantly to the conclusion that recantation alone could save the heretics from their merited fate. More efficacious were the troops sent to quell the disturbances, who drove Éon to Aquitaine for refuge, but when he reappeared in Champagne he was captured and carried before Eugenius III at the Council of Rouen, in 1148. There he boldly proclaimed his mission and his power. Exhibiting a forked staff which he carried, he declared that when he held it with the fork upwards, God ruled heaven and hell, and he governed the earth; but that when he reversed its position, then he had at command two-thirds of the universe, and left only the remaining third to God. He was pronounced hopelessly insane, but this would not have saved him had not his captor, the Archbishop of Rheims, represented that his life had been pledged to him on his surrender. He was therefore delivered to Suger, Abbot of St. Denis, to be imprisoned, and he soon afterwards died. Even this did not shake the faith of his disciples. Many of them, in their fierce fanaticism, preferred the stake to recantation, and numbers were thus put to death before the heresy could be extinguished.

When, about the middle of the twelfth century, the sudden death of a companion so impressed Peter Waldo of Lyons that he distributed his fortune among the poor, and devoted himself to preaching the supereminent merits of poverty, nothing was further from his thoughts than the founding of a new heresy. Ardent disciples gathered around him, disseminating his views, which spread with rapidity; but their intention was to establish a society within the Church, and they applied, between 1181 and 1185, to Lucius III for the papal authorisation. Lucius, however, took exception to their going barefoot, to their neglect of the tonsure, and to their retaining the society of women. They were stubborn, and he condemned them as heretics. The enthusiasm which the Church might have turned to so much account, as it subsequently did that of the Franciscans and Dominicans, was thus diverted to unorthodox channels, and speedily arrayed itself in opposition. The character of the revolt is shown in a passage of the *Nobla Leyczon*, which declares that all the popes, cardinals, bishops, and abbots together cannot obtain pardon for a single mortal sin; thus leading directly to the conclusion that no intercessor could be of avail between God and man—

Ma yo aus o dire, car se troba en ver,
Que tuit li papa que foron de Silvestre entro en aquest,
Et tuit li cardinal et tuit li vesque e tuit li aba,
Tuit aquisti ensemp non han tan de potesta,
Que ilh poissan perdonar un sol pecca mortal.
Solament Dio perdona, que autre non ho po far.

Still, they did not even yet consider themselves as
separated from the Church, for they consented to submit
their peculiar doctrines to the chances of a disputation,
presided over by an orthodox priest. Of course, the
decision went against them, and a portion of the " Poor
Men of Lyons " submitted to the result. The remainder,
however, maintained their faith as rigidly as ever. From
Bernard de Font-Cauld, who records this disputation, and
from Alain de l'Isle, another contemporary, who wrote in
confutation of their errors, we have a minute account of
their peculiarities of belief. Their principal heresy was
a strict adherence to the Hildebrandine doctrine that
neither reverence nor obedience was due to priests in mortal
sin, whose ministrations to the living and whose prayers
for the dead were equally to be despised. In the existing
condition of sacerdotal morals, this necessarily destroyed
all reverence for the Church at large, and Bernard and
Alain had no hesitation in proving it to be most dangerously
heterodox. Their recurrence to Scripture, moreover, as
the sole foundation of Christian belief, with the claim of
private interpretation, was necessarily destructive to all
the forms of sacerdotalism, and led them to entertain many
other heretical tenets. They admitted no distinction
between clergy and laity. Every member of the sect,
male or female, was a priest, entitled to preach and to hear
confessions. Purgatory was denied, and the power of
absolution derided. Lying and swearing were mortal sins,
and homicide was not excusable under any circumstances.
Yet naturally they did not repudiate the ascetic principles
of the Church, and they regarded continence as counselled,
though not commanded, by the Christian dispensation—

La ley velha maudi lo ventre que fruc non a porta,
Ma la novella conselha gardar vergeneta.

Though marriage is praised and its purity is to be preserved—

Gardes ferm lo matrimoni, aquel noble convent,

thus showing their disapproval of the Manichæan doctrines of the Cathari. A sect which existed through centuries of persecution, concealed in scattered communities without a head, of course varied considerably in its tenets. In the earlier period the Waldenses recognised vows of chastity and treated the seduction of nuns as incest. Later they held that, in view of the Greek custom, the Latin Church erred in prescribing celibacy to the priesthood, and their ministers, or *barbes*, were married. With incredible fortitude they maintained their faith and, when came the Reformation, at the Synod of Chanforans those of the Valleys adopted most of the Protestant tenets and declared that the rule of virginity was a precept of Satan.

The Teutonic tendency to mysticism contributed its share of heresy, which bears some relation to our subject. Ortlieb of Strassburg is supposed to have been a disciple of Amaury of Bène, whose pantheistic speculations were condemned by the University of Paris in 1204. Ortlieb carried them to Germany, where they gave rise to a sect calling itself the Brethren of the Free Spirit, and variously known as Ortlibenses, Begghards, Beguines, and Picards. From their pantheism they drew the deduction that man is God, leading to the conclusion that he is impeccable, and that whatever he may do is without sin. While this doubtless led to excesses on the part of those incapable of self-restraint, it was accompanied with the austere condemnation of all sexual indulgence, save for the exclusive object of procuring offspring. It was taught that a woman in marrying should feel the deepest sorrow for the loss of her virginity, and that no one was perfect in whom promiscuous nudity could excite passion or shame. This served as a test, and was so successfully endured that an antagonistic writer can only explain their resistance to such temptation by the assistance of Satan. The sect was condemned by the Council of Cologne in 1306, and by the General Council of Vienne in 1312; it was ruthlessly persecuted by the ecclesiastical authorities and by the Inquisition, whenever that organisation managed to get a foothold in Germany, but it maintained its existence with remarkable tenacity. It was evidently a branch of the Brethren of the Free Spirit which appeared, in 1411, in Flanders, under the name of Men of Intelligence, under the lead of Giles Cautor and William of Hilderniss. They were accused of pantheism, of rejecting priestly ministrations, and of teaching that whatever they did was the work of the spirit, so that there was no sin in the grossest licentiousness. Cardinal Pierre d'Ailly, as Bishop of Cambrai, speedily suppressed them, and tradition related that the inquisitor he employed, Hendrik Selle, was saved only by a miracle from the vengeance of the heretics. As the fifteenth century advanced, the unsettled spiritual condition of Bohemia, under Hussite domination, seemed to offer a favourable field for proselytism, and it was attempted by a missionary of the sect, known as " Pichardus." He speedily gathered numerous disciples of both sexes, to whom he taught the pre-eminent virtue of nudity, and gave them the name of Adamites. They settled on an island in the river Luznic, and speedily came in collision with the neighbouring inhabitants. In an expedition from the island they slew two hundred peasants, which attracted the attention of Lizka. He made short work with them; fifty of those who escaped the sword were burnt at Klokot, and the rest were gradually hunted down, sharing the same fate, which they endured with song and laughter.

There was another heretical sect which, in the opening years of the fourteenth century, attained a terrible notoriety through the exploits and fate of its leader, Dolcino. It was an unauthorised offshoot of the stricter or Spiritual Franciscans, and was founded by Gherardo Segarelli, who was burnt in 1300. Its members styled themselves apostles; they were wanderers, subsisting on charity, and teaching an austerity which, in imitation of the follies of some of the early Christians, required the crucial test of the sexes lying together in nakedness. Persecution naturally induced antagonism, and Dolcino, who succeeded Segarelli in the perilous dignity of heresiarch, foretold the downfall of the existing Church establishment, to be followed by an age of charity and love under a saintly pope. He proclaimed himself the special envoy of God, and virtually declared war upon the existing organisation of both Church and State. Withdrawing, with some fourteen hundred followers, to fastnesses in the lower Alps, he resisted four crusades directed against him, but a fifth, in 1307, was successful, and he perished by the most dreadful death that fear and hate could devise. The wandering disciples, however, continued to give occasional occupation to the Inquisition for a hundred years, and we hear of them in regions so far apart as Lubeck and farther Spain.

There may possibly have been some connection between the Apostles and John of Pirna, who in 1341 taught the most revolutionary doctrines. According to him, the pope was antichrist and Rome was the whore of Babylon and the church of Satan. The Silesians listened eagerly to his denunciations of the clergy, and the citizens of Breslau, with their magistrates, openly embraced his heresy. When the inquisitor, John of Schweidnitz, was sent thither by the Holy Office of Cracow, the people rose in defence of their leader and put the inquisitor to death. John of Pirna appears to have maintained his position, but after his death the Church enjoyed the pious satisfaction of exhuming his body, burning it, and scattering the ashes to the winds. It was easier to do this than to destroy the leaven which was working everywhere in men's minds. No sooner were its manifestations repressed in one quarter than they displayed themselves in another.

In 1395 Jean de Varennes, a priest of the province of Rheims, was accused of various heretical teachings, the most serious of which was a revival of the old doctrine that the sacraments were vitiated in unworthy hands. He had not the zeal of martyrdom, and was easily brought to recantation, but his heresy has some interest for us as indicating the prevalent morality of the priesthood at the time. The concubinary priest was popularly known as a *prêtre marié*, and this was so universal that Jean did not hesitate to assume that all Christians were practically unbaptized.

In the ineradicable corruption of the Church, indeed, every effort to purify it could only lead to a heresy. Wickliffe, in his zeal to repress the disorders which had brought the Church into disrepute, swept away bishop, cardinal, and pope, the priesthood being the culminating point in his system of ecclesiastical polity. The temporalities which weighed down the spiritual aspirations of the Church were to be abandoned, and with them the abuses by which the worldly ambition of churchmen was sustained—indulgences, simony, image-worship, the power of excommunication, and the other devices by which the authority to bind and to loose had been converted into broad acres or current coin of the realm. The monastic orders in general were the objects of his special aversion, as having no justification in the precepts of Christ, and his repeated attacks upon them have a bitterness which shows not only his deep-rooted aversion, but his sense of their importance as a bulwark of the abuses which he assailed. He reduced holy orders to two—the priesthood and diaconate—but he maintained the indelible character of ordination as separating the recipient from his fellows, and he urged that all ministers of Christ should live in saintly poverty. All this was unreasonable enough in a perverse and stiff-necked generation, but his unpardonable error was his revival of the doctrine of Gregory VII regarding the ministrations of unfaithful priests, which he carried out resolutely to its logical consequences. According to him, a wicked priest could not perform his sacred functions, and forfeited both his spiritualities and temporalities, of which laymen were justified in depriving him. Nay more, priest and bishop were no longer priest or bishop if they lived in mortal sin, and his definition of mortal sin was such as to render it scarce possible for any one to escape.

What his opinions were on the subject of clerical celibacy was a moot point after his death. Thomas of Walden, the confessor of Henry V, in his refutation of the Wickliffite doctrines, approved by Martin V in 1427, says that the general belief was that Wickliffe was opposed to it, while some asserted that he was strongly in favour of it. Walden admits that he had found in Wickliffe's writings high praise of priestly chastity, but he had at last met, in the tract *De Officio Pastorali*, a passage condemning celibacy. Yet had Wickliffe taught this doctrine it would have been as widely known as his other errors, it would have been condemned in the repeated proceedings taken against him and his teachings, and it would not have been left for Thomas of Walden to discover it in one of the numerous writings which passed from hand to hand as the works of the heresiarch. Wickliffe was too earnest and sincere in his convictions to leave any one in doubt as to his belief on any point that he thought worth discussion.

What his views were on this subject can perhaps best be sought in the most mature of his authentic works, the Trialogus. No one can read the chapters on Sensuality and Chastity without seeing that the whole line of argument is directed towards proving the superiority of

virginity over marriage, even to the fanciful etymology of
" cœlibatus " from the state of the " beati in cœlo " ; while
in the chapter on the Riches of the Clergy they are regarded
as virgins betrothed to Christ, and the vow of chastity
which they take is likened to their similar vow of poverty,
and not to be infringed. Wickliffe's austerity, in fact,
was deeply tinged with asceticism, and in aiming to restore
the primitive simplicity of the Church, he had no thought
of relegating its ministers to the carnalities of family life,
which would render impossible the Apostolic poverty that
was his ideal. Even the laity, in his scheme, were to be
so rendered superior to the lusts of the flesh that he pronounced those who married from any other motive than
that of having offspring to be not truly married.

It is easier to start a movement than to restrain it.
Wickliffe might deny the authority of tradition, and yet
preserve his respect for the tradition of celibacy, but his
followers could not observe the distinction. They could
see, if he could not, that the structure of sacerdotalism,
to the overthrow of which he devoted himself, could not
be destroyed without abrogating the rule which separated
the priest from his fellow-men, and which severed all other
ties in binding him to the Church. In 1394, only ten years
after Wickliffe's death, the Lollards, by that time a powerful party, with strong revolutionary tendencies, presented
to Parliament a petition for the thorough reformation of
the Church, containing twelve conclusions indicating the
points on which they desired change. Of these, the third
denounced the rule of celibacy as the cause of the worst
disorders, and argued the necessity of its abrogation ; while
the eleventh attacked the vows of nuns as even more
injurious, and demanded permission for their marriage
with but scanty show of respect. This became the received
doctrine of the sect, for in a declaration made in 1400 by
Arundel, Archbishop of Canterbury, concerning the Lollard
heresies, we find enumerated the belief that those in holy
orders could take to themselves wives without sin, and
that monks and nuns were at liberty to abandon their
profession, and marry at pleasure.

The fierce persecutions of Henry V, to repress what he
rightly considered as a formidable source of civil rebellion
as well as heresy, succeeded in depriving the sect of political
power; yet its religious doctrines still continued to exist

among the people, and even sometimes obtained public expression. They unquestionably tended strongly to shake the popular reverence for Rome, and had no little influence in paving the way for the revolt of the sixteenth century.

John Huss was rather a reformer than a heresiarch. Admirer though he was of Wickliffe, even to the point of wishing to risk damnation with him, he avoided the doctrinal errors of the Englishman on the subject of the Eucharist. Yet his predestinarian views were unorthodox, and he shared in some degree Wickliffe's Gregorian ideas as to the effect of mortal sin in divesting the priesthood of all claim to sacredness or respect. According to his enemies, he asserted that no one could be the vicar of Christ or of Peter unless he were an humble imitator of the virtues of him whom he claimed to represent; and a pope who was given to avarice was only the representative of Judas Iscariot. His friend, Jerome of Prague, maintained with his latest breath that Huss was thoroughly orthodox, and was only inspired by indignation at seeing the wealth of the Church, which was the patrimony of the poor, lavished on prostitutes, feasting, hunting, rich apparel, and other unseemly extravagance. In the Bohemian clergy he had an ample target for his assaults, for they were in no respect better than their neighbours. During the latter half of the fourteenth century scarce a synod was held which did not denounce their vices; gambling, drunkenness, usury, simony, and concubinage; and when, to put an end to the latter irregularity, a strict visitation was made throughout the archiepiscopal diocese of Prague, the cunning rogues sent away or secreted their partners in guilt, and openly recalled them as soon as the storm had passed. The following year, Archbishop Sbinco peremptorily commanded that all concubines should be dismissed within six days, under pain of perpetual imprisonment, but this was evidently regarded as a mere *brutum fulmen*, for the next year a new device was resorted to, by pronouncing all concubinary priests to be heretics. All this might certainly seem to warrant any effort that might be made to accomplish what the authorities so signally failed in doing, but that any individual should assert the right of private judgment in reforming the Church in its head and its members threatened results too formidable to the whole structure of sacerdotalism, and the condemnation of Huss was inevitable. Still, like Wickliffe, he was a devout believer in ascetic purity. His denunciations of the wealth and disorders of the clergy raised so great an excitement throughout Bohemia that King Wenceslas was forced to issue a decree depriving immoral ecclesiastics of their revenues. The partisans of Huss took a lively interest in the enforcement of this law, and brought the unhappy ecclesiastics before the tribunals with a pertinacity which amounted to the persecution of an inquisition.

Unlike the Lollards, the Hussites maintained the strictness of the founder's views on the subject of celibacy. If the fiercer Taborites cruelly revenged their wrongs upon the religious orders, it was to punish the minions of Rome, and not to manifest their contempt for asceticism; and, at the same time, even the milder Calixtins treated all lapses from clerical virtue among themselves with a severity which proved their sincerity and earnestness, and which had long been a stranger to the administration of the Church. One of the complaints against the priesthood formulated in the proclamation of Procopius and the other chiefs in 1431, at the assembling of the Council of Bâle, was that the clergy were all fornicators, committing adultery with men's wives, or having wives and " presbyterissæ " of their own. In the " Compactata," or terms of reunion with the Catholic Church, agreed upon, in 1436, at the Council of Bâle, there is no allusion to priestly marriage, the four points upon which the Bohemians insisted being merely : (1st), communion in both elements; (2nd), the reformation of ecclesiastical morals; (3rd), free preaching of the Scripture; and (4th), the secularisation of Church property. Rome refused to ratify the agreement, though there was nothing save the communion in both elements to distinguish the Bohemian from the orthodox Church, and when, in 1562, the Emperor Ferdinand endeavoured to procure from the Council of Trent the use of the cup for the Utraquists or Calixtins of Bohemia, he urged in their favour that they would not admit the ministrations of any priest who did not lead a celibate life.

One fragment of the Hussites, however, held wholly aloof from reconciliation to Rome and professed to uphold in their purity the doctrines of their founder, though they

denied the real presence in the elements of the Eucharist.
These were the remains of the fiercer sect, known as the
Taborites, who were virtually destroyed at the battle of
Lipan in 1434. They called themselves the Orthodox
Brethren, but were stigmatised by their adversaries with
the opprobrious name of Picardi, from a belief that they
were related to the heretics exterminated by Ziska. In
process of time they admitted the validity of priestly
marriage, though it was discouraged among them in view
of the dangers to which they were exposed and the constant
risk of martyrdom incurred by all who ventured to be conspicuous among them, for Hussite and Catholic alike sought
their extermination. Yet they bravely maintained their
existence, until the Reformation, when they eagerly
fraternised with Luther, such minor differences as existed
in the organisation of the respective Churches being amic-
ably regulated in 1570 by the agreement of Sendomir.
Still it was not until the commencement of the seventeenth
century that priestly celibacy was wholly abolished and
that even the bishops of the Brethren were married. In
the triumphant Catholic reaction, after the disastrous battle
of the Weiss Berg in 1620, many of the pastors became more
or less sincere converts, and, in the lack of Catholic priests,
were allowed to retain their positions, but were obliged to
expel their wives and children.

While thus trampling out these successive revolts, the
Church was blind to the lesson taught by their perpetual
recurrence. The minds of men were gradually learning to
estimate at its true value the claim of the hierarchy to
veneration, and at the same time the vices of the establishment were yearly becoming more odious, and its oppression
more onerous. The explosion might be delayed by attempts
at partial reformation, but it was inevitable.

CHAPTER XXIV

THE FIFTEENTH CENTURY

NEITHER the assaults of heretics nor the constant efforts at partial reform attempted by individual prelates had thus far proved of any avail. As time wore on, the Church sank deeper into the mire of corruption, and its struggles to extricate itself grew feebler and more hopeless. We have seen that, early in the fifteenth century, Gerson advised an organised system of concubinage as preferable to the indiscriminate licentiousness which was everywhere prevalent. Even more suggestive are the declarations of Nicholas de Clamenges, Rector of the University of Paris and Secretary of the anti-pope Benedict XIII. He does not hesitate to say that the vices of the clergy were so universal that those who adhered to the rule of chastity were the objects of the most degrading and disgusting suspicions, so little faith was there in the possible purity of any ecclesiastic. He also records the extension of a custom to which I have already alluded when he states that in a majority of parishes the people insisted on their pastors keeping concubines, and that even this was a precaution insufficient for the peace and honour of their families. Elsewhere he describes the mass of the clergy as wholly abandoned to worldly ambition and vices, oppressing and despoiling those subjected to them, and spending their ill-gotten gains in the vilest excesses, while they ridiculed unsparingly such few pious souls as endeavoured to live according to the light of the gospel. Another tract which passes under his name declares that in most of the dioceses the parish priests openly kept concubines, which they were permitted to do on payment of a tax to their bishops. Nunneries were brothels, and to take the veil was simply another mode of becoming a public prostitute. Cardinal Peter d'Ailly declares that he does not dare to describe the immorality of the nunneries. In a similar indignant mood Gerson stigmatises the nunneries of his time as houses of prostitution, the monasteries as centres of trade and amusement, the cathedral churches as dens of ravishers and robbers, and the priesthood at large as habitual concubinarians. That he felt these evils to be inseparable from the condition of the Church is evident when, in an argument to prove the necessity of celibacy, he is driven to the assertion that it is better to tolerate incontinent priests than to have no priests at all. He argues that the clergy are worthy of as many sentences of damnation as they seduce souls to perdition by their corrupt example, and he asks, when he who destroys himself by his own sins is to be condemned, whether he who draws with him numerous others is not still more worthy of perdition. Theodoric a Niem represents the bishops of Scandinavia as carrying with them their concubines on their pastoral visitations, and as inflicting penalties on such of the parish priests as they found living without similar companions, while these women habitually took precedence in church of the wives of the neighbouring gentry—and he adds that the clergy of the south of Europe were no better. Theodoric Vrie, a learned and pious Churchman of Saxony, is equally unsparing in his denunciations of the Teutonic clergy— and, indeed, the testimony of the writers of the period is so unanimous that their descriptions of clerical vices cannot be regarded as the mere rhetorical declamation of disappointed reformers.

It was evident that the efforts of local synods were fruitless to eradicate evils so general and so deeply rooted, while the necessity for some reform became every day more apparent. Though Lollardry had been crushed in England under the stern hand of Henry V, yet it was reappearing in Bohemia in a form even more threatening. The Council of Pisa had not succeeded in healing the Great Schism, and there arose a general demand for an Œcumenic Council in which the Church Universal should assemble for the purpose of purifying itself, of eradicating heresy, and of settling definitely the pretensions of the three claimants to the papacy. John XXIII yielded to the pressure, and the call for the Council of Constance went forth in his name and in that of the Emperor Sigismund.

So powerful a body had never before been gathered together in Europe. It claimed to be the supreme representative of the Church, and though it acknowledged John XXIII as the lawful successor of St. Peter, it had no scruples in arraigning, trying, condemning, and deposing him—an awful expression of its supremacy, without precedent in the past and without imitation in succeeding ages.   As regards heresy, it did the best it could, according to the lights of its age, by burning John Huss and Jerome of Prague.   Its functions as a reformer, however, required for their exercise more nerve than even the condemnation of a pope.   Many members were thoroughly penetrated with the conviction that reform was of instant necessity, and such men as Gerson, Peter d'Ailly of Cambrai, and Nicholas de Clamenges were prepared to shrink from none of the means requisite for so hallowed an end.   However, in the existing corruption of the body from which representatives were drawn such men could scarcely form a controlling majority.   After the council had been in session for nearly two years, the reformers began to despair of effecting anything, and Clamenges did not hesitate to assert that nothing was to be expected from men who would regard reform as the greatest calamity that could befall themselves; while another of the members of the council declared that every one wanted such a reform as should allow him to retain his own particular form of iniquity.   These estimates, indeed, of the character of the majority of the good fathers of Constance are borne out by the contemporary accounts of the multitudes who flocked to it to ply their trades among the assembled dignitaries of the Church, showing that they were by no means all devoted to mortifying the flesh.

The feelings of those who sincerely desired reform, as they saw the prospect rapidly fading before their eyes, may be estimated by a sermon of a sturdy Gascon abbot, Bernhardus Baptisatus, preached before the council in August 1517, about three months before the conservatives succeeded in carrying their point by electing Martin V. He denounces the members of the council as Pharisees, falsely pretending to be devout in order to elude the punishment due to their crimes.   The masses and processions, which were the main business of the assemblage, he declares to be valueless in the eyes of God, for most of those who so busily took part in them were involved solely in worldly cares, laughing, cheating, sleeping, or demoralising the rest with their ungodly conversation. The Holy Spirit did not hold the acts of the council acceptable, nor dwell with its unrighteous members. Such a convocation could have but one result.

It is easy therefore to understand the influences that were brought to bear to defeat the expectations of the reformers : how the subject could be postponed until after the questions connected with the papacy and with heresy were disposed of ; and how, after the election of Martin V, those who shrank from all reform could assume that it might safely be entrusted to the hands of a pontiff so able, so energetic, and so virtuous. In all this they were successful. The council closed its weary sessions, 22 April, 1418, and during its three years and a half of labour it had only found leisure to regulate the dress of ecclesiastics, the unclerical cut of whose sleeves was especially distasteful to the representative body of Christendom.

Still, the reformers had made a stubborn fight, and had procured the appointment of a commission to consider all reformatory propositions and prepare a general scheme for the adoption of the council. This body laboured as diligently as though its deliberations were to be crowned with practical results, and various projects of reform proposed by it have been preserved. In one of these the severest measures of repression were suggested to put an end to the scandal of concubinage which was openly practised in the majority of dioceses. Under this scheme, while all the canonical punishments heretofore decreed were maintained in full vigour, deprivation was pronounced against all holders of ecclesiastical preferment, from bishops down, who should not within one month eject their guilty partners ; their positions were declared vacant *ipso jure*, and their successors were to be immediately appointed. Those who did not hold benefices were similarly to be declared ineligible to preferment. It appears that scandals had arisen in many places from the Hildebrandine and Wickliffite heresy, whereby parishioners declined the ministrations of those who were living in open and notorious sin ; and to avoid these, while the commission declined to pass an opinion on the propriety of such action, it advised that such private judgment should not be exercised. In another elaborate system of reform, which bears the marks of mature deliberation, the attempt was made to eradicate the long-standing abuse of admitting to preferment the illegitimate children of ecclesiastics, and it was declared that papal dispensations should no longer be recognised except in cases of peculiar fitness or high rank. The same code of discipline struck a significant blow at the inviolability of the monastic profession when it endeavoured to check the prevailing and deplorable licentiousness of the nunneries by decreeing that no woman should be admitted to the vows below the age of twenty, and that all vows taken at a younger age should be null and void. These projects are interesting merely as indicating the direction in which the reforming portion of the Church desired to move, and as showing that even they did not propose to remove the celibacy which was the chief cause of the evils they so sincerely deplored.

Martin V had assumed the responsibility of reforming the Church, and he did, in fact, attempt it after some fashion, though he apparently took to heart Dante's axiom—

> Lunga promessa, con l'attender corto
> Ti farà trionfar nel' alto seggio.

In 1422 Cardinal Branda of Piacenza, his legate, when sent to Germany to preach a crusade against the Hussites, was honoured with the title of Reformer General, and full powers were given to him to effect this part of his mission. The letters-patent of the pope bear ample testimony to the depravity of the Teutonic Church, while the constitution which Branda promulgated declares that in a portion of the priesthood there was scarcely left a trace of decency or morality. According to this document, concubinage, simony, neglect of sacred functions, gambling, drinking, fighting, buffoonery, and kindred pursuits, were the prevalent vices of the ministers of Christ; but the punishments which he enacted for their suppression—repetitions of those which we have seen proclaimed so many times before—were powerless to overcome the evils, which had become part and parcel of the Church itself. This condition of affairs was not the result of any abandonment of the attempt to enforce the canons. Local synods were meeting every year, and scarcely one of them failed to call attention to the subject, devising fresh penalties to effect the impossible. The result is shown in the lament of the Council of Cologne in 1423.

What was the condition of clerical morals in Italy soon after this may be learned from a single instance. When Ambrose was made General of the austere order of Camaldoli he set vigorously to work to reform the laxity which had almost ruined it. One of his abbots was noted for abounding licentiousness; not content with ordinary amours, he was wont to visit the nunneries in his district to indulge in promiscuous intercourse with the virgins dedicated to God. Yet Ambrose in taking him to task did not venture to punish him for his misdeeds, but promised him full pardon for the past and to take him into favour, if he would only abstain for the future—a task which ought to be easy, as he was now old, and should be content with having long lived evilly, and be ready to dedicate his few remaining years to the service of God. When a reformer who enjoyed the special friendship and protection of Eugenius IV was forced to be so moderate with such a criminal, it is easy to imagine what was the tone of morality in the Church at large.

While the Armagnacs and Burgundians were rivalling the English in carrying desolation into every corner of France, it could not be expected that the peaceful virtues could flourish, or sempiternal corruption be reformed. Accordingly, it need not surprise us to see Hardouin, Bishop of Angers, despondingly admit, in 1428, that licentiousness had become so habitual among his clergy that it was no longer reputed to be a sin; that concubinage was public and undisguised, and that the patrimony of Christ was wasted in supporting the guilty partners of the priesthood. That gambling, swearing, drunkenness, and all manner of unclerical conduct should accompany these disorders, is too probable to require the concurrent testimony which the worthy bishop affords us. Alain Chartier, Archdeacon of Paris and Secretary to Charles VI and Charles VII, confirms this in a more general way, when he attributes to enforced celibacy and the temporal endowments of the Church the vices and crimes which rendered the clergy so odious and contemptible to the laity that he looks forward to the speedy advent of Antichrist to wipe out the whole system in universal ruin. Apparently its corruption was too deep-seated to hope for any milder means of reformation. To this we may at least partially attribute the utter loss of respect for sacred things which rendered the churches and their pastors a special mark for pillage and persecution during the dreary civil wars of the period.

In England, which had enjoyed comparative immunity from civil strife, matters were quite as bad. At the request of Henry V, in 1414, the University of Oxford prepared a series of articles for the reformation of the Church, whose shortcomings were vehemently attacked by the Lollards. It is not easy to imagine a more humiliating confession than is contained in the 38th article, directed against priestly immorality. The carnal and undisguised profligacy of ecclesiastics is declared to be a scandal to the Church, and its impurity to be a dangerous temptation to others. It is therefore recommended that all public fornicators be suspended for a limited time from the ministry of the altar, and that some corporal chastisement be inflicted on them, in place of the trifling pecuniary mulct, which, levied in secret, had no effect in deterring them from their evil courses.

This was the outcome of the great general council, on which such hopes had been built by Christendom, but the good fathers of Constance, conscious of their shortcomings in the matter of reform, had adopted the canon *Frequens,* ordering the assembly of another general council in five years, to be followed by successors every seven years thereafter. One was accordingly convoked at Siena in 1423, to be summarily dissolved in 1424 by the presiding papal legate, when the demand for effective measures of reform in the head and members of the Church grew too unmannerly to be further evaded. The next general council was due in 1431, but Pope Martin took no steps for its assembling until at the end of 1430 it was made plain to him that Europe was determined to find, with him or without him, some means of attempting a purification felt to be necessary as a safeguard against a revolutionary uprising of the laity. Yet scarcely had the fathers fairly gathered in the Council of Bâle, when Eugenius IV, who had meanwhile succeeded to the chair of St. Peter, sent orders for its dissolution to his legate, Cardinal Giuliano Cesarini.

The legate, who had better opportunity than his master of estimating the temper of Christendom, refused obedience, and his letter explaining the reasons of his contumacy affords a curious picture of the internal condition of the

Church and of the relations existing between it and the laity. The extreme corruption of ecclesiastical morals had been the principal object in convoking the council, and had given rise to a feeling of fierce hostility towards the Church. To this was attributable the success which had attended the Hussite movement, and unless the people could have reason to anticipate amendment, there was ample cause to fear a general imitation of the Hussites. So many provincial synods were daily held without result that confidence was no longer felt in the ordinary ecclesiastical machinery; the state of the public mind grew constantly more threatening as fresh scandals were wrought by the clergy, and the hopes entertained of the council were the only restraint which prevented the breaking out of a widespread revolt. As a proof of his assertions, the legate refers to various local troubles. Magdeburg had expelled her archbishop and clergy, was preparing waggons with which to fight after the Bohemian fashion, and was said to have sent for a Hussite to command her forces. Passau had revolted against her bishop, and was even then laying close siege to his citadel. Bamberg was engaged in a violent quarrel with her bishop and chapter. These cities were regarded as the centres of formidable secret confederacies, and were believed to be negotiating with the Hussites. The good fathers evidently recognised the full magnitude of the danger. The results of the inaction of the Council of Constance were full of pregnant warnings. The reformers could no longer be brought to trust the papacy, and those who might secretly deprecate reform were fully alive to the threatening aspect of affairs. They therefore addressed themselves resolutely to the removal of the cause. All who were guilty of public concubinage were ordered to dismiss their consorts within sixty days after the promulgation of the canon, under pain of deprivation of revenue for three months. Persistent contumacy or repetition of the offence was visited with suspension from functions and stipend until satisfactory evidence should be afforded of repentance and amendment. Bishops who neglected to enforce the law were to be held as sharing the guilt which they allowed to pass unpunished; and those prelates who were above the jurisdiction of local tribunals or synods were to be remanded to Rome for trial. The council deplored the extensive prevalence of the " cullagium," by which those to whom was entrusted the administration of the Church did not hesitate to enjoy a filthy gain by selling licences to sin. A curse was pronounced on all involved in such transactions : they were to share the penalties of the guilt which they encouraged, and were, in addition, to pay a fine of double the amount of their iniquitous receipts. In the Pragmatic Sanction, moreover, agreed upon in 1438 between the Emperor Albert II and Charles VII of France, the regulation confiscating three months' revenues of concubinary priests was embodied.

Honest, well-meant legislation this; yet the fathers of the council or the princes of Christendom could hardly deceive themselves with the expectation that it would prove effectual, even if the Basilian canons had been confirmed by the Holy See and accepted by the Church at large. If legislation could accomplish the desired result, there had already been enough of it since the days of Siricius. The compilations of canon law were full of admirable regulations, by which generation after generation had endeavoured to attain the same object by every imaginable modification of inquisition and penalty. Ingenuity had been exhausted in devising laws which were only promulgated to be despised and forgotten. Something more was wanting, and that something could not be had without overturning the elaborate structure so skilfully and laboriously built up by the craft and enthusiasm of ten centuries.

How utterly impotent, in fact, were the efforts of the council is evident when, within five years after the adoption of the Basilian canons, Doctor Kokkius, in a sermon preached before the Council of Freysingen, could scarcely find words strong enough to denounce the evil courses of the clergy as a class; and when, within fifteen years, we find Nicholas V declaring that the clergy enjoyed such immunity that they scarcely regarded incontinence as a sin—which is perhaps no wonder, when he prohibited the members and officials of the Curia from keeping concubines, under pain of forfeiture of office and disability for preferment, unless they should previously have obtained letters of absolution from the Holy See—the perennial font of corruption which meets us at every turn.

Shrouded under a thin veil of formality, this in substance indicates the degrading source of revenue which was so

energetically condemned in inferior officials. The pressing
and insatiable pecuniary needs of the papal court, indeed,
rendered it impotent as a reformer, however honest the
wearer of the tiara might himself be in desiring to rescue
the Church from its infamy. Reckless expenditure and
universal venality were insuperable obstacles to any
comprehensive and effective measures of reformation.
Every one was preoccupied either in devising or in resisting
extortion. The local synods were engaged in quarrelling
over the subsidies demanded by Rome, while the chronicles
of the period are filled with complaints of the indulgences
granted year after year to raise money for various purposes.
Sometimes the objects alleged are indignantly declared to
be purely supposititious; at other times intimations are
thrown out that the collections were diverted to the private
gain of the popes and of their creatures. The opinion which
the Church in general entertained of the papal court is
manifested with sufficient distinctness in a letter from
Ernest, Archbishop of Magdeburg, to his ambassador at
Rome. The prelate states that he has deposited five
hundred florins in Fugger's bank at Augsburg, for which he
desires to procure certain bulls, one to enable him to grant
indulgences, the other to compel the chapter of Magdeburg
to allow him to dispose of the salt-works of Halle, in defiance of the vested rights of his Church—thus taking for
granted a cynicism of venality which it would be difficult
to parallel in the secular affairs of the most corrupt of
courts. Even the power to dispense from the vow of
continence was occasionally turned to account in this
manner. One of the accusations against John XXIII was
that for 600 ducats he had released Jacques de Vitry, a
Hospitaller, from his vows, had restored him to the world,
and enabled him to marry.

The aspirations of Christendom had culminated in the
Council of Bâle in the most potent form known to the
Church Universal. If the results were scarce perceptible
while the influences of the council were yet recent, and
while the antagonistic papacy was under the control of
men sincerely desirous to promote the best interests of
the Church, such as Nicholas V and Pius II, we can feel
no wonder if the darkness continued to grow thicker and
deeper under the rule of such pontiffs as Sixtus IV, Innocent
VIII, and Alexander VI. Savonarola found an inex-

haustible subject of declamation in the fearful vices of the ecclesiastics of his times, whom he describes as *ruffiani e mezzani*. In the assembly of the Trois Etats of France, held at Tours in 1484, the orator of the Estates, Jean de Rély, afterwards Bishop of Angers, in his official address to Charles VIII declared it to be notorious that the religious orders had lost all devotion, discipline, and obedience to their rule, while the canons (and he himself was a canon of Paris) had sunk far below the laity in their morals, to the great scandal of the Church. Yet what could be accomplished by an uncompromising reformer was shown when, about 1490, Niccolò Bonafede, afterwards Bishop of Chiusi, was sent to Trani as archiepiscopal vicar. He found that nearly all the priests openly kept concubines and brought up their children without shame—the primicier, in fact, had eleven in his house. Bonafede ordered that all should dismiss their companions within eight days, under penalty of forfeiture of benefice, and that the women should leave the diocese, under pain of scourging. He had already given evidence of his tenacity of purpose, and his commands were obeyed by all but one, in which case the priest was deprived of his preferment, and the unfortunate woman was duly flogged and banished.

In England, the facts developed by the examination which Innocent VIII in 1489 authorised Morton, Archbishop of Canterbury, to make into the condition of the religious houses, present a state of affairs quite as bad. Henry VII's first Parliament, in 1485, had endeavoured to accomplish some reform by passing an Act empowering the episcopal authorities to imprison all priests and monks convicted of carnal lapses, but this, like all similar legislation, whether secular or ecclesiastical, appears to have been useless. Innocent describes the monasteries, in his bull to the archbishop, as wholly fallen from their original discipline, and this is fully confirmed by the results of the visitation. The old and wealthy abbey of St. Albans, for instance, was little more than a den of prostitutes, with whom the monks lived openly and avowedly. In two priories under its jurisdiction the nuns had been turned out and their places filled with courtesans, to whom the monks of St. Albans publicly resorted, indulging in all manner of shameless and riotous living, the details of which can well be spared. These irregularities were emulated by the secular ecclesiastics. Among the records of the reign of Henry VII is a memorial from the gentlemen and farmers of Carnarvonshire, complaining that the seduction of their wives and daughters was pursued systematically by the clergy. That the prevalence of these practices was thoroughly understood is shown in a book of instructions for parish priests drawn up by a canon of Lilleshall about this period. In enumerating the causes for which a parson may shrive a man not of his own parish, he includes the case in which the penitent has committed sin with the concubine or daughter of his own parish priest.

Spain was equally infected. The Council of Aranda, in 1473, denounced bitterly the evil courses by which the clergy earned for themselves the wrath of God and the contempt of man, and it endeavoured to suppress the sempiternal vice by the means which had been so often ineffectually tried—visitations, fines, excommunication, suspension, forfeiture of benefice, and imprisonment—but all to as little purpose as before. Vainly Ferdinand and Isabella in repeated edicts sought to restrain the evil by attacking the concubines with fines, scourging, and banishment, for the male offenders were beyond their jurisdiction. The trouble continued without abatement, and the Council of Seville, in 1512, felt itself obliged to repeat as usual all the old denunciations and penalties, including those against ecclesiastics who officiated at the marriages of their children, which it prohibited for the future under a fine of 2000 maravedis—a mulct which it likewise provided for those who committed the indecency of having their children as assistants in the solemnity of the Mass. We shall see hereafter how fruitless were all these efforts to cure the incurable.

What was the condition of morals in Germany may be inferred from some proceedings of the chapter of Brunswick in 1476. The canons intimate that the commission of scandals and crimes has reached a point at which there is danger of their losing the inestimable privilege of exemption from episcopal jurisdiction. They therefore declare that for the future the canons, vicars, and officiating clergy ought not to keep their mistresses and concubines publicly in their houses, or live with them within the bounds of the church, and those who persist in doing so after three warnings shall be suspended from their prebends until they render due satisfaction. In this curious glimpse into the domestic life of the cathedral close it is evident that the worthy canons were moved by no shame for the publicity of their guilt, but only by a wholesome dread of giving to their bishop an excuse for procuring the forfeiture of their dearly prized right of self-judgment.

The Hungarian Church, by a canon dating as far back as 1382, had finally adopted a pecuniary mulct as the most efficacious mode of correcting offenders. The fine was five marks of current coin, and by granting one-half to the informer or archdeacon, and the other to the archiepiscopal chamber, it was reasonably hoped that the rule might be enforced. As might have been expected, this resulted, not in reforming the clergy, but in providing a source of revenue for the prelates, so that all parties were interested in maintaining a flourishing condition of immorality, as Jacopo della Marchia, one of the fiercest persecutors of heresy, found to his cost. In 1436 he was sent by Eugenius IV as inquisitor of Hungary and Austria to check the spread of Hussitism. His unsparing severity excited such general terror that he is said to have received the submission of fifty-five thousand converts, but when, at Fünfkirchen, he paused in his missionary labours to reform the concubinarian priests, his resolution gave way, for they repelled his interference so energetically that he was forced to fly for his life. Pope and emperor were invoked, and he was enabled to return, but we hear no more of any effort on his part to meddle with the clergy and their partners. That matters remained unaltered is shown by two synods of Gran, one in 1450 and the other in 1480, which reiterate the complaint, not only that the archdeacons and other officials kept the whole fine to themselves, but also, what was even worse, that they permitted the criminals to persevere in sin, in order to make money by allowing them to go unpunished. This state of affairs was not to be wondered at if the description of his prelates by Matthias Corvinus be correct. They were worldly princes, whose energies were devoted to wringing from their flocks fabulous revenues to be squandered in riotous living on the hordes of cooks and concubines who pandered to their appetites. The morals of the regular clergy were no better, for a diet held by Vladislas II in 1498 complained of the manner in which abbots and other monastic dignitaries enriched themselves from the revenues of their offices, and then, returning to the world, publicly took wives, to the disgrace of their order.

In Pomerania the evil had at length partially cured itself, for the female companions of the clergy seem to have been regarded as wives in all but the blessing of the Church. Benedict, Bishop of Camin, in 1492 held a synod in which he quaintly but vehemently objurgates his ecclesiastics for this wickedness; declares that no man can part such couples joined by the devil; alludes to their offspring as beasts creeping over the earth, and has his spleen peculiarly stirred by the cloths of Leyden and costly ornaments with which the fair sinners were bedecked, to the scandal of honest women. His indignation was wasted on a hardened generation, for his successor, Bishop Martin, on his accession to the see in 1499, found the custom still unchecked. The new bishop promptly summoned a synod at Sitten in 1500, where he reiterated the complaints of Benedict, adding that the priests convert the patrimony of Christ into marriage portions for their children, and procure the transmission of benefices from father to son, as though glorying in the perpetuation of their shame. What peculiarly exasperated the good prelate was that the place of honour was accorded as a matter of course to the priests and their consorts at all the merry-makings and festivities of their parishioners, which shows how fully these unions were recognised as legitimate, and apparently, for prudential reasons, encouraged by the people.

Similar customs, or worse, doubtless prevailed in Sleswick, for when Eggard was consecrated bishop in 1494, he signalised the commencement of his episcopate by forbidding his clergy to keep such female companions. The result was that before the year expired he was forced to abandon his see, and five years later he died, a miserable exile in Rome.

In fact, so loose had become the conception as to celibacy that in some places priestly marriage was quietly resumed, subject to the condition of resigning benefices. In a formulary of the fifteenth century there are formulæ for conferring parish churches, canonries, and precentorships thus vacated by the wedlock of the incumbent. Other churches had become established as hereditary, descending from father to son, and only in default of male issue did their collation revert to the bishop. The old rule rendering the bastards of priests incapable of preferment still remained on the books, but dispensations removing such disabilities for benefices without cure of souls were remanded to episcopal jurisdiction; a regular formula was provided for such cases, and, in the prevalent venality of the period, we may assume that they could be had by any applicant at a moderate price.

The monastic Orders were no better than the secular clergy. When Ximenes was made Provincial of the Franciscan Order in Spain, he set himself earnestly at work to force the brethren to live according to the rule. The "Conventuals," as the great body of the Order was called to distinguish them from the "Observantines," led disorderly lives, almost purely secular, and refused absolutely to submit to the observance of their vows. King Ferdinand being appealed to, pronounced sentence of banishment upon them, and they absolutely preferred existence in exile to the insupportable yoke of their Order. Yet they considered themselves so aggrieved that when they left Toledo they marched in procession through the Puerta Visagra with a crucifix at their head, singing the 113th Psalm, "In exitu Israel de Egypto." When Ximenes was promoted to the primatial see of Toledo, the malcontents appealed to the Vicar General of the Order in Rome, who came to Spain and warmly espoused their cause, being only forced to desist by the decided stand taken by Queen Isabella in favour of Ximenes. It was the same with the other monastic Orders. A bull of Alexander VI, issued in 1496 for the purpose of reforming the Benedictines, describes the inhabitants of many establishments of both sexes in that ancient and honoured institution as indulging in the most shameless profligacy; and marriage itself was apparently not infrequently practised. Savonarola did not hesitate to declare that nuns in their convents became worse than harlots. Even the strictest of all the orders— the Cistercian—yielded to the prevailing laxity. A general chapter, held in 1516, denounces the intolerable abuse indulged in by some abbots, who threw off all obedience to the rule, and dared to keep women under pretence of requiring their domestic services. To fully appreciate the force of this indication it is requisite to bear in mind the stringency of the regulations which forbade the foot of woman to pollute the sacred retirement of the Cistercian monasteries.

The efforts constantly made to check these abuses produced little result. A Carthusian monk, writing in 1489, deplores the fact that, while monasteries were everywhere being reformed, few if any of them maintained their morals, but returned to their old condition immediately on the death of the zealous fathers who had sought to improve them. That condition is described by a Benedictine abbot, the celebrated Trithemius, in general terms, as that of dens in which it was a crime to be without sin, their inhabitants for the most part being addicted to all manner of vices, and being monks only in name and habit.

That the clergy, as a body, had become a stench in the nostrils of the people is evident from the immense applause which greeted all attacks upon them. In 1476 a rustic prophet arose in the hamlet of Niklaushausen, in the diocese of Wurzburg, who was a fit precursor of Muncer and John of Leyden. John of Niklaushausen was a swineherd, who professed himself inspired by the Virgin Mary. From the Rhinelands to Misnia, and from Saxony to Bavaria, immense multitudes flocked to hear him, so that at times he preached to crowds of twenty and thirty thousand men. His doctrines were revolutionary, for he denounced oppression both secular and clerical; but he was particularly severe upon the vices of the ecclesiastical body. A special revelation of the Virgin had informed him that God could no longer endure them, and that the world could not, without a speedy reformation, be saved from the divine wrath consequent upon them. The unfortunate man was seized by the Bishop of Wurzburg; the fanatical zeal of his unarmed followers was easily subdued, and he expiated at the stake his revolt against the powers that were.

Such being the state of ecclesiastical morality throughout Europe, there can be little wonder if reflecting men sought occasionally to reform it in the only rational manner —not by an endless iteration of canons, obsolete as soon as published, or by ingeniously varied penalties, easily modified or compounded—but by restoring to the minister of Christ the right to indulge legitimately the affections which bigotry might pervert, but could never eradicate. Even as early as the close of the thirteenth century, the high authority of Bishop William Durand had acknowledged the inefficacy of penal legislation, and had suggested the discipline of the Greek Church as affording a remedy worthy of consideration. As the depravity of the Church increased, and as the minds of men gradually awoke from the slumber of the dark ages, and shook off the blind reverence for tradition, the suggestion presented itself with renewed force. At the Council of Constance Cardinal Zabarella did not hesitate to suggest that, if the concubinary practices of the clergy could not be suppressed, it would be better to concede to them the privilege of marriage, and shortly after the failure of the council to effect a reform had become apparent, Guillaume Saignet wrote a tract entitled "Lamentatio ob Cælibatum Sacerdotum," in which he attacked the existing system, and called forth a rejoinder from Gerson. The Carmelite, Thomas Connecte, was a wandering preacher who filled France and the Low Countries with denunciations of popular vices, both lay and clerical. His eloquence won immense applause, and his auditors were reckoned in crowds of from ten to twenty thousand souls. He was especially severe on the concubinage of all ranks of the clergy, and recommended a restoration of priestly marriage as the appropriate remedy; but when, in 1432, he ventured in Rome to lash the corruption of the Curia, he was found to be a heretic, and his career was ended at the stake. When the Council of Bâle was earnestly engaged in the endeavour to restore forgotten discipline, the Emperor Sigismund laid before it a formula of reformation which embraced the restoration of marriage to the clergy. His orator drew a fearful picture of the evils caused by the rule of celibacy—evils acknowledged by every one in the assembly—and urged that, as it had produced more injury than benefit, the wiser course would be to follow the example of the Greek Church. A majority of the Council assented to the principle, but shrank from the bold step of adopting it. Eugenius IV had just been forced to acknowledge the legitimacy of the body as an Œcumenic council; the strife with the papacy might again break forth at any moment, and it was not politic to venture on innovations too audacious. The conservatives, therefore, skilfully eluded the question by postponing it to a more favourable time, and the postponement was fatal.

One of the most celebrated members of the council, Cardinal Nicholas Tudeschi, surnamed Panormitanus, whose pre-eminence as an expounder of the canon law won for him the titles of " Canonistarum Princeps " and " Lucerna Juris," declares that the celibacy of the clergy was not essential to ordination or enjoined by divine law; and he records his unhesitating opinion that the question should be left to the option of the individual—those who had resolution to preserve their purity being the most worthy, while those who had not would be spared the guilt which disgraced them. So Æneas Sylvius, who as Pius II filled the pontifical throne from 1458 to 1464, and who knew by experience how easy it was to yield to the temptations of the flesh, is reported to have said that marriage had been denied to priests for good and sufficient reasons, but that still stronger ones now required its restoration. Indeed, when arguing before the Council of Bâle in favour of the election of Amedeus of Savoy to the papacy, he had not scrupled to declare that a married priesthood would be the salvation of many who were damned in celibacy. And we have already seen that Eugenius IV in 1441, and Alexander VI in 1496, granted permission of marriage to several military Orders, as the only mode of removing the scandalous licence prevailing among them.

This question of the power of the pope to dispense with the necessity of celibacy seems to have attracted some attention about this period. In 1505, Geoffroy Boussard, afterwards Chancellor of the University of Paris, published a tract wherein he argued that priestly continence was simply a human and not a divine ordinance, and that the pope was fully empowered to relax the rule in special cases, though he could not abolish wholly an institution of such long continuance which had received the assent of so many holy fathers and general councils. At the same time, one of his arguments in favour of its enforcement shows how little respect was left in the minds of all thinking men for the claims of the Church to veneration. He quotes Bonaventura to the effect that if bishops and arch-bishops had licence to marry they would rob the Church of all its property, and none would be left for the poor, for, he adds, " since already they seize the goods of the Church for the benefit of distant relatives, what would they not do if they had legitimate children of their own ? "

When the advantages and the necessity of celibacy thus

were doubted by the highest authorities in the Church, it is no wonder if those who were disposed to question the traditions of the past were led to reject it altogether. In 1479 John Ruchrath, of Oberwesel, graduate of Tubingen, and doctor of theology, in his capacity of preacher at Worms openly disseminated doctrines which differed in the main but little from those of Wickliffe and Huss. He denied the authority of popes, councils, and the fathers of the Church to regulate matters either of faith or discipline. The Scripture was the only standard, and no one had a right to interpret it for his brethren. The received observances of religion, prayers, fasts, indulgences, were all swept away, and universal liberty of conscience proclaimed to all. Of course, sacerdotal celibacy shared the same fate, as a superstitious observance contrived by papal ingenuity in opposition to evangelical simplicity. Thus his intrepid logic far outstripped the views of his predecessors, and Luther afterwards acknowledged the similarity between his teachings and those of John of Oberwesel. Yet he had not the spirit of martyrdom, and the Inquisition speedily forced him to a recantation, which was of little avail, for he soon after perished miserably in the dungeon into which he had been thrust.

Still more remarkable as an indication of the growing spirit of independence was an event which in July 1485 disturbed the stagnation of the centre of theological orthodoxy—the Sorbonne. A certain Jean Laillier, priest and licentiate in theology, aspiring to the doctorate, prepared his thesis or " Sorbonique," in which he broached various propositions savouring strongly of extreme Lollardry. He denied the supremacy of the pope, and indeed reduced the hierarchy to the level of simple priesthood; he rejected confession, absolution, and indulgences; he refused to acknowledge the authority of tradition and legends, and insisted that the fasts enjoined by the Church had no claim to observance. Celibacy was not likely to escape so audacious an inquirer, and accordingly among his postulates were three, declaring that a priest clandestinely married required no penitence; that the Eastern clergy committed no sin in marrying, nor would the priests of the Western Church if they were to follow that example; and that celibacy originated in 1073, in the decretals of Gregory VII, whose power to introduce the rule he more than questioned.

The Sorbonne, as might be anticipated, refused the doctorate to so rank a heretic, and Laillier had the boldness not only to preach his doctrines publicly, but even to appeal to the Parlement for the purpose of forcing his admission to the Sorbonne. The Parlement referred the matter to the Bishop of Paris and to the Inquisitor. A long controversy followed, and it required the interposition of Innocent VIII before Laillier could be punished and forced to recant. In Poland, too, there were symptoms of similar revolt against the established ordinances of the Church, as shown in a book published at Cracow in 1504, " De Matrimonia Sacerdotum."

The corruption of the Church establishment, in fact, had reached a point which the dawning enlightenment of the age could not much longer endure. The power which had been entrusted to it, when it was the only representative of culture and progress, had been devoted to selfish purposes, and had become the instrument of oppression in all the details of daily life. The immunity which had been serviceable through centuries of anarchy had become the shield of vices. The wealth so freely lavished upon it by the veneration of Christendom was wasted in excesses. All efforts at reformation from within had failed; all attempts at reformation from without had been successfully crushed and sternly punished. Intoxicated with centuries of domination, the muttered thunders of growing popular discontent were unheeded, while its corruptions were displayed before the people with more careless cynicism. There appeared to be no desire on the part of the majority of the clergy to make even a pretence of the virtue and piety on which were based their claims for reverence, while the laity were daily growing less reverent, were rising in intelligence, and were becoming more inclined to question where their fathers had been content to believe. Such a complication could have but one result.

CHAPTER XXV

THE REFORMATION IN GERMANY

THE opening of the sixteenth century witnessed an ominous breaking down of the landmarks of thought. The revival of letters, which was fast rendering learning the possession of all men in place of the special province of the legal and clerical professions; the discovery of America, which destroyed reverence for primeval tradition, and accustomed men's minds to the idea that startling novelties might yet be truths; the invention of printing, which placed within the reach of all inquirers who had a tincture of education the sacred writings for investigation and interpretation, and enabled the thinker and the innovator at once to command an audience and disseminate his views in remote regions; the European wars, commencing with the Neapolitan conquest of Charles VIII, which brought the nations into closer contact with each other, and carried the seeds of culture, civilisation, and unbelief from Italy to the farthest Thule—all these causes, with others less notable, had been silently but effectually wearing out the remnants of that pious and unquestioning veneration which for ages had lain like a spell on the human mind.

In this bustling movement of politics and commerce, arts and arms, science and letters, religion could not expect to escape the spirit of universal inquiry. Even before opinion had advanced far enough to justify examination into doctrinal points and dogmas, there was a general readiness to regard the shortcomings of sacerdotalism, in the administration of its sacred trust, with a freedom of criticism which could not long fail to destroy the respect for claims of irrefragable authority. The disposition to criticise the abuses of the ecclesiastical system, to note its shortcomings, and to apply remedial measures was general, and savoured little of the respect which the Church had for so many centuries inculcated as one of the first of Christian

duties. Its past services were forgotten in present wrongs.
Its pretensions had at one time enabled it to be the protector of the feeble and the sole defence of the helpless,
but that time had passed. Settled institutions were fast
replacing anarchy throughout Europe, and its all-pervading
authority would no longer have been in place, even if exercised for the common benefit. When it was notorious,
however, that the powers and immunities claimed by the
Church were largely employed for evil rather than for
good, their anachronism became too palpable, and their
destruction was only a question of time.

Signs of the coming storm were not wanting. In 1510
a series of complaints against the tyranny and extortion
of Rome was solemnly presented to the Emperor. The
German churches, it was asserted, were confided by the
successors of St. Peter to the care of those who were better
fitted to be keepers of mules than pastors of men, and the
pope was significantly told that he should act more tenderly
and kindly to his children of Teutonic race, lest there
might arise a persecution against the priesthood, or a
general defection from the Holy See, after the manner of
the Hussites. The Emperor was warned, in his efforts to
obtain the desired reform, not to incur the censures and
enmity of the pope, in terms which show that only the
political effects of excommunication were dreaded, and
that its spiritual thunders had lost their terrors.   He was
further cautioned against the priests in general, and the
mendicant friars in particular, in a manner denoting how
little reverence was left for them in the popular mind, and
how thoroughly the whole ecclesiastical system had become
a burden and reproach, and no longer an integral part
of every man's life and the great motive power of
Christendom.

It was evident that the age was rapidly outstripping
the Church, and that the latter, to maintain its influence
and position, must conform to the necessities of progress
and enlightenment. On previous occasions it had done so,
and had, with marvellous tact and readiness, adapted itself
to the exigencies of the situation in the long series of
vicissitudes which had ended by placing it supreme over
Europe. But centuries of almost uninterrupted prosperity
had hardened it. The corruption which attends upon

wealth had rendered wealth a necessity, and that wealth could only be had by perpetuating and increasing the abuses which caused ominous murmurs of discontent in those nations not hardy enough to set limits to the authority of the Holy See. The Church had lost its suppleness, and was immovable. A reform such as was demanded, while increasing its influence over the souls of men, would have deprived it of control over their purses; reform meant poverty. The sumpter-mule loaded with gold, wrung from the humble pittance of the Westphalian peasant, under pretext of prosecuting the war against the infidel, would no longer cross the Alps to stimulate with its treasure the mighty genius of Michael Angelo, or the fascinating tenderness of Raphael; to provide princely revenues for the bastards of a pope, or to pay mercenaries who were to win them cities and lordships; to fill the antechamber of a cardinal with parasites, and to deck his mistresses with the silks and jewels of Ind; to feed needy men of letters and scurrilous poets; to soothe the itching palms of the Rota, and to enable all Rome to live on the tribute so cunningly exacted of the barbarian. The wretched ending of the Council of Bâle rendered any internal reformation impossible which did not derive its initiative and inspiration from Rome. In Rome, it would have required the energy of Hildebrand, the stern self-reliance of Innocent, the unworldly asceticism of Celestin combined, even to essay a reform which threatened destruction so complete to all the interests accumulated by sacerdotalism around the Eternal City. Leo X was neither Hildebrand, nor Innocent, nor Celestin. With his voluptuous nature, elegant culture, and easy temper, it is no wonder that he failed to read aright the signs of the times, and that he did not even recognise the necessity which should impose upon him a task so utterly beyond his powers. The fifth Council of Lateran had no practical result. Blindly he plunged on : money must be had at any cost, until the methods employed in marketing the St. Peter's indulgence attracted the attention of Luther, and Teutonic insubordination burst forth at the sound of his voice.

It would be a mistake to credit Luther with the Reformation. His bold spirit and masculine character gave to him the front place, and drew around him the less daring minds who were glad to have a leader to whom to refer their doubts, and on whom their responsibility might partly rest; yet Luther was but the exponent of a public sentiment which had long been gaining strength, and which in any case would not have lacked expression. In that great movement of the human mind he was not the cause, but the instrument. Had his great opponent Erasmus enjoyed the physical vigour and practical boldness of Luther, he would have been handed down as the heresiarch of the sixteenth century. He too had borne his full share in preparing the minds of men for what was to come. The whole structure of sacerdotalism felt the blows of his irreverential spirit, which boldly declared that the Scriptures alone contained what was necessary to salvation. Theological subtleties and priestly observances were alike useless or worse than useless. For the living, it was idle to attend Mass; for the dead, it was folly to look to such a means for extrication from purgatory. The confessional was to be visited only as a formal prerequisite to partaking of the Eucharist; pilgrimages and the veneration of relics were ridiculed with a reckless freedom which showed how shaken was the reverence of the past. Nothing, indeed, can give us a more thorough conviction of the readiness of the public to welcome a radical change than the wealth of indignant bitterness which Erasmus, himself a canon regular and a priest, heaps upon all orders of the Church, and the immense applause which everywhere greeted his attacks. His sarcastic humour, his biting satire, his exquisite ridicule, nowhere find a more congenial subject than the vices of the monks, the priests, the prelates, the cardinals, and even of the pope himself, until even Luther, as late as 1517, feels constrained to deplore that the evils which afflicted the Church should be thus exposed to derision. It affords a curious illustration of the times to read those writings which a century earlier might have led him to share the fate of John Huss and Jerome of Prague, and to reflect that he was not only the admiration of both the learned and the vulgar of Europe, but also the petted *protégé* of king and kaiser, the correspondent of popes, and finally the champion of the system which he had so ruthlessly reviled, and which he never ceased to deplore. The extraordinary favour with which his works were received by all classes shows how fully he was justified in the indignation which he so unsparingly lavished on clerical abuses, and how eagerly the public appreciated one who could so well express that which was felt by all. Equally significant was the popularity of the "Epistolæ Obscurorum Virorum," in which the learned wits of the new school poured forth upon the clergy a broad and homely ridicule which exactly suited the taste of the age; while Cornelius Agrippa more than rivalled Erasmus in the wealth of vigorous denunciation with which he lashed the vices of all the orders of ecclesiastics, from the pope to the béguine.

Not less indicative of the dangerous state of opinion was an address delivered in the diet held at Augsburg in 1518, when the legates of Leo X appealed to Germany for a tithe to assist in carrying on the war against the Turk. The orator who replied to them did not restrain his indignation at the deplorable condition of the Church, which he attributed solely to the worldly ambition of the popes. Since they had united temporal with spiritual dominion—or, rather, since they had allowed temporal interests to divert them wholly from their spiritual duties —all had gone amiss. Christendom was despoiled from without, and filled with tumult within. Religion was openly contemned; Christ was daily bought and sold; the sheep were shorn, and the pastor took no care of them. He did not even hesitate to charge, with emphasis and at much detail, that the money extorted from Germany under pious pretexts was squandered in Italy on the private quarrels and for the aggrandisement of the papal houses and those of the members of the sacred college. All other nations were protected from papal rapacity and tyranny by formal agreements. Germany alone was surrendered defenceless, and not only were her bishops plundered, but even the smallest benefice could not be confirmed without the recipient running the gauntlet of a horde of officials whose exactions forced him to sell the very furniture of his church. As the rules of law and the dictates of justice were equally disregarded, the popular sentiment was becoming openly hostile to the Church. A state of feeling which dictated and permitted such a declaration from the supreme representative body of the empire, when brought into collision with the pretensions of the Holy See, now more exaggerated than ever, could have but one result— revolution.

With all this licence, Germany was still, by the force of circumstances, less independent of the papacy than any other Tramontane power. The fractioning of the empire since the death of Barbarossa, carefully stimulated by papal intrigues, had deprived it of unity and prevented the consolidation of a power capable of resisting the encroachments of the Curia, which sucked the life-blood of both priest and peasant, and rendered the very name of Rome hateful to all, but especially to Teutonic ecclesiastics. What was going on elsewhere in Europe may be guessed from the humiliating conditions exacted in 1517 of Silvester Darius, the papal collector, on his assuming the functions of his important office in England. He bound himself by oath not to execute any letters or mandates of the pope injurious to the king, the kingdom, or the laws; not to transmit from England to Rome, without a special royal licence, any gold, or silver, or bills of exchange; not to leave the kingdom himself without a special licence under the great seal; with other less notable restrictions, the practical effect of all being to place him and his duties wholly under the control of the king. The position of England had changed since the days of Innocent and John. Had the dissensions of Germany permitted equal progress, Luther might perhaps have only been known as an obscure but learned orthodox doctor, and the inevitable revolt of half of Christendom have been postponed for a century.

It is not my province to follow in detail the vicissitudes of the Reformation, but only to indicate briefly its relations with sacerdotal asceticism. Luther at first, like Wickliffe and Huss, paid no attention to the subject. In fact, when, on 31 October, 1517, he nailed on the church door of Wittenberg his celebrated ninety-five propositions, nothing was further from his expectations than to create a heresy, a schism, or even a general reform in the Church. He had simply in view to vindicate his ideas on the subject of justification, derived from St. Augustin, against the Thomist doctrines which had been exaggerated into the monstrous abuses of Tetzel and his fellows. In the general movement of the human mind at that period so much had been said that was inimical to the received practices of the Church, without calling forth the thunders of Rome, that men seemed to think the day of toleration had at last come. The hierarchy sat serenely upon their thrones, and in the confidence of unassailable power appeared willing to allow any freedom of speculation which did not assail their temporal privileges. Yet amid the general agitation and opposition to Rome which pervaded society, it was impossible for a bold and self-reliant spirit such as Luther's not to advance step by step in a career of which the ultimate goal was as little foreseen by himself as by others. Still his progress was wonderfully slow. Even in 1519 he still considered himself within the pale of the Church : in a letter to Leo X he protested before God that he did not seek in any way to attack the power of either the pope or the Roman Church, which he held to be supreme over all in heaven and earth, save Jesus Christ alone; and in the same year, in a sermon on matrimony, he alluded not unfavourably to the life of virginity. Events soon after forced him to further and more dangerous innovations, yet when Leo X, in June 1520, issued his celebrated bull, "Exsurge Domine," to crush the rising heresy, in the forty-one errors enumerated as taught by Luther there is no allusion to any doctrine specially inimical to ascetic celibacy. At almost the same moment, however, Luther, in his address to the Christian nobles of Germany, proposed that through the intervention of a general council the privilege of marriage should be granted to parish priests, and this was speedily followed by the suggestion that vows of chastity taken before the age of eighteen should be invalid.

The papal condemnation, followed as it was by the public burning of his writings, aroused Luther to a more active and aggressive hostility than he had previously manifested. In his book "De Captivitate Babylonica Ecclesiæ " he attacked the sacrament of ordination, denied that it separated the priest from his fellows, and ridiculed the rule concerning *digami*, which excluded from the priesthood a man who had been the husband of any but a virgin, while another who had polluted himself with six hundred concubines was eligible to the episcopate or papacy. Finally, on 10 December, 1530, he proclaimed war to the knife by burning at Wittenberg the books of the canon law, and justifying his act by a manifesto recapitulating the damnable doctrines contained in them. Among these he enumerates the prohibition of sacerdotal marriage as the origin and cause of excessive vice and scandal. As he said himself, hitherto he had only been playing at controversy with the pope, but this was the beginning of serious work. Soon after this, in a controversy with Ambrogio Catarino, he stigmatised the rule of celibacy as angelical in appearance, but devilish in reality, and invented by Satan as a fertile source of sin and perdition.

In the mighty movement which was agitating men's minds, Luther had been anticipated in this. As early as 1518, a monk of Dantzic named James Knade abandoned his order, married, and publicly preached resistance to Rome. It is evident that in this he had the support of the people, for though he was imprisoned and tried by the ecclesiastical authorities, the only punishment inflicted on him was banishment. In the multitude of other questions more interesting to the immediate disputants this point of discipline seems to have attracted but little attention until 1521, when during Luther's enforced seclusion in the Wartburg, Bartholomew Bernhardi, pastor of Kammerich, near Wittenberg, put the heresiarch's views into action in the most practical way by obtaining the consent of his parish and celebrating his nuptials with all due solemnity. Albert, Archbishop of Mainz and Magdeburg, addressed to Frederic, Elector of Saxony, a demand for the rendition of the culprit, which that prudent patron of the Reformation skilfully eluded, and Bernhardi published a short defence or apology in which he denounced the rule of celibacy as a "frivolam traditiunculam." He argued the matter, quoting the texts which since his time have been generally employed in support of sacerdotal marriage : he referred to Peter and Philip, Spiridion of Cyprus, and Hilary of Poitiers, as examples of married bishops; quoted the story of Paphnutius, and relied on the authority of the Greek Church. This apparently did not satisfy the archbishop, for Bernhardi felt obliged to address a second apology to Frederic of Saxony, to whom he appealed for protection against the displeasure of his ecclesiastical superiors. In spite of molestation, he continued in the exercise of his priestly functions until death. Less fortunate were his immediate imitators. A priest of Mansfield who took to himself a wife was thrown into prison at Halle by Albert of Mainz, and Jacob Siedeler, pastor of Glashütten, in Misnia, who was guilty of the same crime, perished miserably in the dungeon of Stolpen, to which he was committed by Duke George of Saxony.

The enthusiastic Carlostadt, relieved for the time from the restraint of Luther's cooler wisdom, threw himself with zeal into this new movement of reform, and lost no time in justifying it by a treatise in which he argued strenuously in favour of priestly marriage, and energetically denounced the monastic vows as idle and vain. Luther, however, in his retreat, seems not yet prepared to take any very decided position. In a letter of 17 January, 1522, to Wolfgang Fabricius Capito, one of the officials of the Archbishop of Mainz, and a favourer of the Reformation, he takes the latter severely to task with respect to his action in a case of the kind—probably that of the priest of Mansfield alluded to above. The man had been set at liberty, but forced to separate himself from his wife, and Capito had defended himself on the ground that the woman was a harlot. Luther asks him why he had been so earnest with a single strumpet, when he had taken no action with so many under his jurisdiction in Halberstadt, Mainz, and Magdeburg, and adds that when the priest had acknowledged the woman as his wife there should have been nothing further done. He proceeds to say, however, that he does not ask for the freedom of sacerdotal marriage, and that he is not prepared to take any general position concerning it, except that it is lawful under God. Either with or without his approbation, however, his friends lost no time in enforcing the new dogma, which they proclaimed to the world in the most authoritative manner. During the same year Luther's own Augustinian Order held a provincial synod at Wittenberg, in which they formally threw open the doors of the monasteries, and permitted all who desired it to return to the world, declaring that in Christ there was no distinction between Jew and Greek, monk and layman, and that a vow in opposition to the Gospel was no vow, but an impiety. Ceremonies, observances, and dress were pronounced futile; those who chose to abide by the established rule were free to do so, but their preferences were not to be a law to their fellows. Those who were fitted for preaching the Word were advised to depart; those who remained were obliged to perform the manual labour which had been so prominent a portion of primitive Teutonic monasticism, and mendicancy was strictly forbidden. In a few short and simple canons a radical rebellion thus declared itself in the heart of an ancient and powerful order, and principles were promulgated which were totally at variance with sacerdotalism in all its protean forms.

This broad spirit of toleration did not suit the views of the more progressive reformers. In Luther's own Augustinian convent at Wittenberg, one of his most zealous adherents, Gabriel Zwilling, preached against monachism in general, taking the ground that salvation required the renunciation of their vows by all who had been ensnared into assuming the cowl; and so great was his success that thirteen monks at once abandoned the convent. Yet even on Luther's return to Wittenberg he at first took no part in the movement. He retained his Augustinian habit, and continued his residence in the convent; but before the close of the year (1522) he put forth his work " De Votis Monasticis," in which he fully and finally adopted the views of his friends, and showed himself as an uncompromising enemy of monasticism. How difficult it was for him, however, to shake off the habitudes in which he had been trained is shown by the fact that, even at the end of 1523, he still sometimes preached in his cowl and sometimes without it.

Notwithstanding the zealous opposition of the orthodox ecclesiastical authorities, the doctrine and practice of Wittenberg were not long in finding earnest defenders and imitators. But few such marriages, it is true, are recorded in 1522, although Balthazar Sturmius, an Augustinian monk of Saxony, committed the bolder indiscretion of marrying a widow of Franconia. In that year, however, we find Franz von Sickingen, knight-errant and condottiere, who was then a power in the state, advocating the emancipation and marriage of the religious orders, in a letter to his father-in-law, Diedrich von Henthschuchsheyn. Still more important was the movement inaugurated in Switzerland by Ulrich Zwingli, who, with ten other monks of Nôtre-Dame-des-Hermites, on 2 July, 1522, addressed to Hugo von Hohenlandemberg, Bishop of Constance, a petition requesting the privilege of marriage. The petitioners boldly argued the matter, citing the usual Scriptural authorities, and adjured the bishop in the most pressing terms to grant their request. They warned him that a refusal might entail ruinous disorders on the whole sacerdotal body, and that, unless he seized the opportunity to guide the movement, it might speedily assume a most disastrous shape. They asserted, indeed, that not only in Switzerland, but elsewhere, it was generally believed that a majority of ecclesiastics had already chosen their future wives, and that a return to the old order of things was beyond the power of man to accomplish. This was followed, on 13 July, by a similar memorial addressed to the Government of the Swiss Confederacy. The signers frankly admitted their inability to preserve chastity, and asked the State to protect them in their marriages if the bishop allowed them to marry.

In this assertion, Zwingli and his companions followed perhaps rather the dictates of their hopes than of their judgment, for the revolution was by no means as universal or immediate as their threats or warnings would indicate. Its progress, nevertheless, was rapid and decided. In Zurich the secular authorities gave permission to all nuns to abandon their cloisters; in 1523, Leo Judæ, Zwingli's foremost disciple, and parish priest of St. Peters, married a former béguine, and in 1524 Zwingli himself married Anna Reinhart, widow of Hans Meyer, with whom he had been living as man and wife since 1522. In Germany, Luther, whom we have seen in the earlier part of 1522 still giving but a qualified assent to the daring innovation of his followers, in February 1523 wrote to Spalatin in favour of a married pastor who was seeking preferment at the hands of the Elector Frederic; and in April 1523 he himself officiated and preached a sermon in favour of matrimony to a multitude of distinguished friends at the wedding of Wenceslas Link, vicar of the Augustinian Order, one of his oldest and most valued supporters, who had stood unflinchingly by him when arraigned by Cardinal Caietano before the Emperor Maximilian at the Diet of Augsburg. Not less important was the countenance given to the innovation, two days later, by the Elector Frederic, who consented to act as sponsor at the baptism of the first-born of Franz Gunther, pastor of Loch, the ceremony being performed by the honest chronicler Spalatin himself.

It is curious to see in Spalatin's diary how each successive marriage is recorded as a matter of the utmost interest, the hopes of the reformers being strengthened by every accession to the ranks of those who dared to defy the rules which had been deemed irreversible for centuries. Nor was it an act without danger, for no open rupture had as yet taken place between the temporal power of any state and the central authority at Rome. Even in electoral Saxony, though Duke Frederic, by a cautious course of passive resistance, afforded protection to the heretics, yet he still considered himself a Catholic, and the ritual of his chapel was unaltered. Elsewhere the ecclesiastical power was bent on asserting its supremacy over the licentious apostates who ventured to sully their vows and prostitute the sacrament of marriage by their incestuous unions. The old charge of promiscuous intercourse was resorted to in their case, as it has been with almost every heresy in every age, for the purpose of exciting popular odium, and, wherever the discipline of the Church could be enforced, it was done unsparingly. The temper of these endeavours to repress the movement is well illustrated by the regulations promulgated under the authority of the Cardinal-legate Campeggio, when in 1524 he succeeded in uniting a number of reactionary princes at the Assembly of Ratisbon. Deploring the sacrilege committed in the marriages of priests and monks, which were becoming extremely common, he granted permission to the secular powers to seize all such apostates and deliver them to the ecclesiastical officials, significantly restraining them, however, from inflicting torture. The officials were empowered to condemn the offenders to perpetual imprisonment, or to hand them over to the secular arm—a decent euphemism for a frightful death; and any negligence on the part of the ordinaries exposed those officers to the pains and penalties of heresy.

In spite of all this, however, the votaries of marriage had the support and sympathy of the great body of the people. It shows how widely diffused and strongly implanted was the conviction of the evils of celibacy when those who four centuries earlier had so cruelly persecuted their pastors for not discarding their wives now urged them to marriage, and were ready to protect them from the consequences of the act. Thus, during the summer of 1524, Wolfgang Fabricius Capito, provost of St. Thomas and priest of the church of St. Peter at Strassburg, whom we have seen two years earlier prosecuting a married priest, took to himself

a wife, by the request of his parishioners; and, when the
chapter of canons endeavoured to interfere with him, the
threatening aspect of the populace warned them to desist.
Nor was this the only case, for Bishop William undertook
to excommunicate all the married priests of Strassburg,
when the senate of the city resolutely espoused their cause,
and even the authority of the legate Campeggio could not
reconcile the quarrel.

Even higher protection was sometimes not wanting.
When Adrian VI, in 1522, reproached the Diet of Nürnberg
with the inobservance of the decree of Worms and the
consequent growth of Lutheranism, and King Ferdinand,
in the name of the German states, replied that a council
for the reformation of the Church was the only remedy,
the question of married priests arose for discussion. The
German princes alleged that they could find in the civil
and municipal laws no provisions for the punishment of
such transgressions, and that the canons of discipline
could only be enforced by the ecclesiastical authorities
themselves, who ought not to be interfered with in the
discharge of their duty by the secular authorities. This
was scant encouragement, but even this was often denied
in practice. When, in 1523, Conrad von Tungen, Bishop
of Wurzburg, threw into prison two of his canons, the
doctors John Apel and Frederic Fischer, for the crime of
marrying nuns, the Council of Regency at Nürnberg forced
him to liberate them in a few weeks. The latter fact
is the more remarkable, since but a short time previously
(6 March, 1523) the Imperial Diet at Nürnberg, under the
auspices of the same Regency, had expressed its desire to
give every assistance to the ecclesiastical authority in
enforcing the canons. In a decree on the subject of the
religious disturbances it adopted the canon law on celibacy
as part of the civil law, pronouncing sentence of imprisonment and confiscation on all members of the clergy who
should marry, and ordering the civil power in all cases to
assist the ecclesiastical in its efforts to punish offenders.

In the Low Countries, under the Regency of Margaret
of Austria, the civil power not only assisted but stimulated
the ecclesiastical to its duty. A conspicuous case was that
of Jan de Backer (Pistorius) of Woerden, who had married,
abandoned the priesthood, and supported himself by
manual labour, until the preaching of the St. Peter's

indulgence in Woerden induced him to resume the tonsure and priestly functions in order to combat it. It illustrates the disciplinary looseness of the pre-Reformation period that he seems not to have been disturbed in his apostacy and marriage, but the Lutheran revolt had created a different temper. He was arrested and carried to The Hague, where he was tried by the inquisitors of Louvain, who earnestly endeavoured to induce him to abandon his wife and recant his errors as to papal authority, purgatory, etc., but in vain. There was nothing left to do with him but to burn him alive, which was executed accordingly, 15 September, 1525.

The emancipation of nuns excited considerable public interest, and in many instances was effected by aid from without. A certain Leonhard Kopp, who was a determined enemy of monachism, rendered himself somewhat notorious by exploits of the kind. One of the earliest instances was that by which, on Easter Eve, 1523, at considerable risk, he succeeded in carrying off from the convent of Nimptschen, in Misnia, eight young virgins of noble birth, all of whom were subsequently married, and one of whom was Catharine von Bora. The example was contagious. Before the month was out six nuns, all of noble blood, left the abbey of Sormitz, and soon after eight escaped from that of Peutwitz, at Weissenfels. Monks enfranchised themselves with still less trouble. At Nürnberg, in 1524, the Augustinians in a body threw off their cowls and proclaimed themselves citizens.

Finally, Luther gave the last and most unquestionable proof of his adhesion to the practice of sacerdotal marriage by espousing Catharine von Bora, whom we have seen escaping, two years before, from the convent of Nimptschen. Scandal, it would seem, had been busy with the intimacy between the pious doctor and the fair renegade, who had spent nearly the whole period of her liberty at Wittenberg, and Luther, with the practical decision of character which distinguished him, suddenly resolved to put the most effectual stop to rumours which his enemies doubtless were delighted to circulate. On the evening of 13 June, 1525, without consulting his friends, he invited to supper Pomeranius, Lucas Cranach, and Apellus, and had the marriage ceremony performed. It took his followers completely by surprise; many of them disapproved of it, and Justus

Jonas, in communicating the fact to Spalatin, characterises it as a startling event, and evidently feels that his correspondent will require the most incontrovertible evidence of the fact, when he declares that he himself had been present and had seen the bridegroom in the marriage bed. If the portraits after Lucas Cranach given in Mayer's Dissertation on Catharine be faithful likenesses, it was scarcely the beauty of his bride that led Luther to take this step, for her features seem rather African than European.

When Luther had once decided for himself on the propriety of sacerdotal marriage, he was not likely to stop half-way. Some of the reformers were disposed to adopt the principles of the early Church, and, while permitting married priests to officiate, denied to them the right to marry a second time or to espouse any but virgins, declaring all *digami* worthy of death and calling upon the people to drive them out. Against these Luther, in 1528, took up the cudgels vigorously, arguing the question in all its bearings, and arriving at the conclusion that only bigamists were to be shunned or deemed unworthy of holy orders. Yet at the same time his thoroughly practical mind prevented him from losing sight of some of the evils inseparable from the revolution which he had wrought in an institution so deeply affecting daily life as monasticism. As late as 1543, in a letter to Spalatin, while congratulating him on the desire expressed by some nuns to leave their convent, he cautions them not to do so unless they have a certainty or at least a speedy prospect of marriage. He complains of the number of such cases in which he had been obliged to support the fugitives, and he concludes by declaring that old women who had no chance of finding husbands had much better remain in their cloisters.

It is not difficult to explain why there was so ready and general an acquiescence in the abrogation of a rule established by the veneration of so many centuries. Not only had the doctrines of the reformers taken a deep and firm hold of the popular heart throughout Germany, destroying the reverence for tradition and antiquity, and releasing the human mind from the crushing obligation of blind obedience, but there were other motives, natural if not particularly creditable. The ecclesiastical foundations had long neglected the duties of charity, hospitality, and education, on which were grounded their claims to their broad lands and rich revenues. While, therefore, the temporal princes might be delighted with the opportunity of secularising and seizing the Church possessions, the people might reasonably hope that the increase of their rulers' wealth would alleviate their own burdens, as well as release them from the direct oppression which many of them suffered from the religious establishments. Even more potential was the disgust everywhere felt for the flagrant immorality of the priesthood. The dread experienced by every husband and father lest wife and daughter might at any moment fall victims to the lust of those who had every opportunity for the gratification of unholy passions led them to welcome the change, in the hope that it would result in restoring decency and virtue to a class which had long seemed to regard its sacred character as the shield and instrument of crime.

The moral character of the clergy, indeed, had not improved during the busy and eventful years which marked the first quarter of the sixteenth century. There is a curious little tract, printed in Cologne in 1505, with the approbation of the faculty, which is directed against concubinage in general, but particularly against that of the priests. Its laborious accumulation of authorities to prove that licentiousness is a sin is abundant evidence of the existing demoralisation, while the practices which it combats, of guilty ecclesiastics granting absolution to each other and mutually dispensing themselves from confession, show how easily the safeguards with which the Church had sought to surround her ministers were eluded. The degradation of the priesthood, indeed, can readily be measured when, in the little town of Hof, in the Vogtland, three priests could be found defiling the sacredness of Ash Wednesday by fiercely fighting over a courtesan in a house of ill-fame; or when Leo X, in a feeble effort at reform, was obliged to argue that systematic licentiousness was not rendered excusable because its prevalence amounted to a custom, or because it was openly tolerated by those whose duty was to repress it. In fact, a clause in the Concordat with Francis I in 1516, renewing and enhancing the former punishments for public concubinage, would almost justify the presumption that the principal result of the rule of celibacy was to afford to the officials a regular revenue derived from the sale of licences to sin—the old abuse, which rises before us in every age from the time of Damiani and Hildebrand, and which, since John XXII had framed the tariff of absolutions for crime known as the "Taxes of the Penitentiary," had the authority of the papacy itself to justify it. In the oldest form in which this has reached us, issued by Benedict XII in 1338, absolution and dispensation for a concubinary priest are rated at only four *gros tournois*, or less than half a florin, and the same price is named for the absolution of one who has been suspended for adultery. In a somewhat later tax-list, dispensation for the son of a priest to be admitted to orders and preferment is rated at twelve *gros*, but if he desired a bishopric, it cost thirty. It is no wonder that reforming bishops and councils found their efforts baffled when the only result was to increase the revenues of the papal chancery by stimulating the demand for its interference.

That no concealment was thought necessary, and that sensual indulgence was not deemed derogatory in any way to the character of a Christian prelate, may be reasonably deduced from the panegyric of Gerard of Nimeguen on Philip of Burgundy, grand-uncle of Charles V, a learned and accomplished man, who filled the important see of Utrecht from 1517 to 1524. Gerard alludes to the amorous propensities and promiscuous intrigues of his patron without reserve, and as his book was dedicated to the Archduchess Margaret, sister of Charles V, it is evident that he did not feel his remarks to be defamatory. The good prelate, too, no doubt represented the convictions of a large portion of his class, when he was wont to smile at those who urged the propriety of celibacy, and to declare his belief in the impossibility of chastity among men who, like the clergy, were pampered with high living and tempted by indolence. Those who professed to keep their vows inviolate he denounced as hypocrites of the worst description, and he deemed them far worse than their brethren who sought to avoid unnecessary scandal by decently keeping their concubines at home.

Even this reticence, however, was considered unnecessary by a large portion of the clergy. In 1512, the Bishop of Ratisbon issued a series of canons in which, after quoting the Basilian regulations, he adds that many of his ecclesiastics maintain their concubines so openly that it would appear as though they saw neither sin nor scandal in such conduct, and that their evil example was the efficient cause of corrupting the faithful. In Switzerland the same abuses were quite as prevalent, if we may believe a memorial presented, in 1533, by the citizens of Lausanne, complaining of the conduct of their clergy. They rebuked the incontinence of the priests, whose numerous children were accustomed to earn a living by beggary in the streets, but the canons were the subjects of their especial objurgation. The dean of the chapter had defied an excommunication launched at him for buying a house near the church in which to keep his mistress; others of the canons had taken to themselves the wives of citizens and refused to give them up; but the quaintest grievance of which they had been guilty was the injury which their competition inflicted on the public brothel of the town. What was the condition of clerical morality in Italy may be gathered from the stories of Bishop Bandello, who, as a Dominican and a prelate, may fairly be deemed to represent the tone of the thinking and educated classes of society. The cynical levity with which he narrates scandalous tales about monks and priests shows that in the public mind sacerdotal immorality was regarded almost as a matter of course.

The powerful influence of all this on the progress of the Reformation was freely admitted by the authorities of the Church. When the legate Campeggio was sent to Germany to check the spread of heresy, in his reformatory edict issued at Ratisbon in 1524 he declared that the efforts of the Lutherans had no little justification in the detestable morals and lives of the clergy, and this is confirmed by his unsparing denunciation of their licentiousness, drunkenness, quarrels, and tavern-haunting; their traffic in absolution for enormous offences; their unclerical habits and hideous blasphemy; their indulgence in incantations and dabbling in witchcraft. Very significant is his declaration that the canonical punishments shall be inflicted on concubinary priests, in spite of all custom to the contrary or all connivance on the part of the prelates.

How little, indeed, licentious ecclesiastics might reasonably dread the canonical punishments is illustrated in the report by the celebrated jurisconsult Grillandus of a case which came before him while he was auditor of the papal vicar in Rome. A Spanish priest and doctor of canon law, residing in the Christian capital, became enamoured of several young nuns at once, and endeavoured to seduce them by teaching them that, as they and he were alike spouses of Christ, carnal affection between them was their duty.   Failing in this, he sought to compel the assistance of God in his designs, and, being a man of literary culture, he composed a number of prayers of singular obscenity, and bribed various ignorant priests to recite them amid the ineffable mysteries of the Mass, hoping thus to obtain the aid of Heaven in overcoming the chastity of his intended victims.   At length he chanced to offer one of these prayers to a priest of somewhat better character, who was sufficiently shocked by it to communicate with the authorities.   Brought before Grillandus, the guilty Spaniard sought to justify himself by alleging various Scriptural texts, but upon being warned that such a defence would subject him to a prosecution for heresy, he recanted and acknowledged his errors. For this complicated mingling of lust and sacrilege his only punishment was a short banishment from Rome.   When the papal court set such an example, what was to be expected of less enlightened regions?

How keenly these evils were felt by the people, and how instinctively they were referred to the rule of celibacy as to their proper origin, is shown by an incidental allusion in the formula of complaint laid before the pope by the Imperial Diet held at Nürnberg early in 1522, before the heresy of priestly marriage had spread beyond the vicinity of Wittenberg.   The diet, in recounting the evils arising from the ecclesiastical jurisdiction which allowed clerical offenders to enjoy virtual immunity, adduced, among other grievances, the licence afforded to those who, debarred by the canons from marriage, abandoned themselves night and day to attempts upon the virtue of the wives and daughters of the laity, sometimes gaining their ends by flattery and presents, and sometimes taking advantage of the opportunities offered by the confessional.   It was not uncommon, indeed, for women to be openly carried off by their priests, while their husbands and fathers were threatened with vengeance if they should attempt to recover them.   As regards the sale to ecclesiastics of licences to indulge in habitual lust, the diet declared it to be a regular and settled matter, reduced to the form of an annual tax, which in most dioceses was exacted of all the clergy without exception, so that when those who perchance lived chastely demurred at the payment, they were told that the bishop must have the money, and that after it was handed over they might take their choice whether to keep concubines or not.   In the face of this condition of ecclesiastical morality, it required some obtuseness for Adrian VI to compare Luther to Mahomet, the one seeking to attract to his party the carnal-minded by permitting marriage, even as the other had established polygamy, and, further, to abuse him for uniting the ministers of Christ with the vilest harlots.

Among the diverse opinions of existing evils and their remedy, it is interesting to see what was the view of the subject taken by those ecclesiastics whose purity of life removed them from all temptation to indulgence, and who yet were not personally interested in upholding the gigantic but decaying structure of sacerdotalism.   Of these men Erasmus may be taken as the representative.   His opinion on all the questions of the day was too eagerly desired for him to escape the necessity of pronouncing his verdict on the innovation portended by the one or two marriages which took place near Wittenberg in 1521, and accordingly, in 1522, from his retreat in Bâle he issued a short dissertation on the subject, which, although addressed merely to Bishop Christopher of that city, was evidently intended for a European audience.   In this essay, after sketching the rise of celibacy and attributing it to the purity and fervour of the early Christians, he proceeds to depict the altered condition of the Church.   Among the innumerable multitude of priests who crowd the monasteries, the chapters, and the parishes, he declares that there are few indeed whose lives are pure, even as respects open and avowed concubinage, without penetrating into the mysteries. of secret intrigue.   As, therefore, there is no Scriptural injunction of celibacy, he concludes that, however desirable it might be to have ministers free from the cares of marriage and devoting themselves solely to the service of God, yet, since it seems impossible to conquer the rebellious flesh, it would · be better to allow those who cannot control themselves to have wives with whom they could live in virtuous peace, bringing up their children in the fear of God, and earning the respect of their flocks.   No more startling evidence, indeed, of the demoralisation of the period could be given than the cautious fear which Erasmus expresses lest such a change should be opposed by the episcopal officials, who would object to the diminution of their unhallowed gains levied on the concubines of the clergy.

When such was the condition of ecclesiastical morality, and such were the opinions of all except those directly interested in upholding the old order of things, it is no wonder if the people were disposed to look with favour on the marriage of their pastors, and if the rejection of celibacy gave a fresh impetus to the cause of Lutheranism. In the early days of all sects, it is only those of ardent faith and pure zeal who are likely to embrace a new belief, with all the attendant risks of persecution and contumely. The laxity of life allowed to the Catholic clergy would attract to its ranks and retain those whose aim was sensual indulgence. Thus necessarily the reformers who married would present for contrast regular and chaste lives and well-ordered households, purified by the dread of the ever-impending troubles to which the accident of a day might at any time expose them. The comparison thus was in every way favourable to the new ideas, and they flourished accordingly.

Nor, perhaps, were the worldly inducements to which I have before alluded less powerful in their own way in advancing the cause. Shortly before Luther's marriage, whatever influence was derivable from an aristocratic example was obtained when the Baron of Heydeck, a knight of the Teutonic Order, renounced his vows and publicly espoused a nun of Ligny. This may possibly have encouraged his superior, Albert of Brandenburg, Grand Master of the Order, to execute his remarkably successful coup d'état, in changing his religion and seizing the estates of the order, thus practically founding the state which chance and talent have exalted until it has been able to realise the dream of a united Germany. The liberty of marriage which he thus assumed was soon turned to account in his advantageous alliance with Frederic, King of Denmark, whose daughter Dorothea he espoused, the Bishop of Szamland officiating as his proxy, and the actual marriage being celebrated 14 June, 1526.

Luther may reasonably be held excusable for counselling and aiding a transaction which lent such incalculable strength to the struggling cause of the Reformation, and it is not to be wondered at if he endeavoured to follow it up with another of a similar character. The nephew of the Duke of Prussia, also named Albert of Brandenburg, occupied the highest place in the Teutonic hierarchy, as Archbishop both of Mainz and Magdeburg, in the latter of which powerful sees the Lutheran heresies had taken deep root. Luther sought to induce the archbishop to follow his uncle's example; to take possession in his own right of the Magdeburg territories, and to transmit them to the posterity with which Heaven could not fail to bless his prospective marriage—a scheme which received the warm approbation of the leading nobles of the diocese. Albert thought seriously of the project, especially as the Peasants' War then raging was directed particularly against the lands of the Church, but he finally abandoned it, and his flock had to work out their reformation without his assistance.

Perhaps some plans of territorial aggrandisement may have stimulated the zeal of the Count of Embden, who boasted that he had assisted and encouraged the marriage of no fewer than five hundred monks and nuns; yet the process of secularising the monastic foundations was in many places by no means sudden or violent. Thus, when the Abbot of Ilgenthal in Saxony died in 1526, the Elector John simply forbade the election of a successor, and placed the abbey in charge of a prefect, while the remaining monks were liberally supplied until they one after another died out; and in 1529, when Philip, Count of Waldeck, took possession of the ancient monastery of Hainscheidt, he caused all the monks to be supported during life.

Through all this period the hope had never been abandoned of such an arrangement as would prevent an irrevocable separation in the Church. Moderate and temperate men on both sides were ready to make such concessions of form as would enable Christendom to remain united, as the great vital truths on which all were agreed so far outweighed the points of divergence. Whether these hopes were well or ill founded was to be determined at the Diet of Augsburg, to which, in June 1530, both parties were summoned for the purpose of submitting their differences to the emperor. Charles came to Germany in the full flush of his recent extraordinary triumphs, the most powerful prince since the days of Charlemagne. Europe was at length at peace, even the Turk only looming in the East as a probable, not as an existing, enemy. But Charles, newly crowned at Bologna, came ostensibly as the steadfast ally of the pope, and Clement VII had not the slightest intention of renouncing the traditional and imprescriptible rights of the Holy See. The Catholic princes of Germany, too, had their grounds of private quarrel with their Protestant peers, and, holding an unquestioned majority, were not disposed to abandon their position. The Protestant princes, on the other hand, were firm in their new-found faith, and, however disposed to avert the threatened storm by the sacrifice of non-essentials, their convictions were too strong for them to retrace the steps which they had taken during so many long and weary years. It is evident that, with such materials on either side, no reunion was probable; and, even had an accommodation on points of doctrine been possible, there was one subject which scarcely seemed to admit of satisfactory compromise. In the states of the reform the downfall of monachism had placed in the hands of the temporal powers large bodies of sequestrated abbey lands. To the Catholic it was sacrilege to leave these in the hands of the spoiler; the Protestant would not willingly give up the spoil.

The contest was opened by the Protestants submitting a statement of their belief, divided into two parts, the one devoted to points of faith, the other to matters of practice. Prepared principally by Melanchthon, it presents their tenets in the mildest and least objectionable form, and becoming the recognised standard of their creed, it has attained a world-wide renown under the name of the Confession of Augsburg. The questions of celibacy and monastic vows were ably and temperately argued; their post-scriptural origin was shown, and the reasons which induced the reformers to reject them were placed in a light as little offensive as possible. At first a counter-statement was anticipated from the Catholics, and negotiations were expected to be carried on by a comparison of the two, but they took higher ground, and contented themselves with drawing up a refutation of the Confession. The emperor was firm. His aspirations for the universal monarchy, which ever eluded his grasp, did not comport with encouraging independence of thought and freedom of religious belief. In his theory, uniformity of religion was a necessary element of the political system which was to make him sovereign of

Europe, and he would listen to no compromise. He was inclined to summary measures, but the Catholic princes were hardly prepared for the consequences of an immediate rupture, and, after a threatening interval, another effort was made to effect a reconciliation. Conferences between the leading theologians on both sides took place, and the Lutherans, warned of their danger, were more disposed than ever to make concessions and to accept such terms as the stronger party were willing to offer them. At length, on 8 September, the draft of a proposed plan of accord was laid before the Diet. In this the points in dispute were referred to that future Œcumenic council which had so long been demanded as the panacea for all ecclesiastical ills, and which, after more than thirty years of continued expectation, was destined to fail so miserably in reconciling difficulties. Such monasteries as had not been destroyed were to be maintained in the exercise of the customary rites and observances of religion. Abbots and communities who had been ejected were to be allowed to return ; and all religious houses which had been emptied of their occupants were to be placed in the hands of officers appointed by the emperor, who were to administer their possessions until the future council should decide upon all the points relating to monachism ; the Protestants thus relieving themselves of the accusation that they were actuated by motives of worldly gain. Similar proposals were made with regard to communion in the two elements and clerical marriage. These were left as open questions for the council to settle, while a phrase of doubtful import subjected them in the meantime to the governments of the several states. The concessions in this project, however, though they might suit the views of the temperate doctors and princes in Germany, and though even the Roman Curia might be willing to grant them in order to save its threatened temporal power over the Teutonic states, did not suit the policy of Charles, who regarded the Church as simply one of the instruments with which he was to build up his universal empire. It was not difficult for him, therefore, to bring to naught all such schemes of conciliation. The restoration of all abbots and monks was ordered ; restitution of Church lands was commanded, or their delivery to the emperor, to be held until the assembling of the future council ; and when the Diet adjourned, Charles issued a decree enjoining on all married priests to abstain from their wives, to eject them, and to seek absolution from their ordinaries.

The threatening aspect of affairs warned the Protestant princes that no time was to be lost in making provision for mutual defence, and ere the year was out the famous League of Schmalkalden enabled them to present a united front to the powers which they had virtually defied. Into the political history of that eventful time it is not my province to enter. Suffice it to say that they were able to maintain their position, and in their own states to oppose the reactionary movement which at times seemed to be on the point of destroying all that had been accomplished.

In this their task was complicated by the extravagances of those whose enthusiasm, unbalanced by reason, carried them beyond restraint. If Luther had found it no easy task to break the chains which for so many ages had kept in check the spirit of free inquiry, he discovered that it was impossible to control that spirit once let loose; and the wild excesses of Anabaptism were at once the exaggeration and the opprobrium of Lutheranism. Originally earnest and self-denying, the primitive Anabaptists had captivated the fiery soul of Carlostadt, while Luther was in his Patmos of Wartburg. The ensuing development was in some sort a resuscitation of the Brethren of the Free Spirit, remnants of whom doubtless existed in many hidden quarters. The inner light was the guide which every man should follow, and this was to result in the Kingdom of God, wherein all should be equal and live in brotherly affection, without subjection to government of any kind. These alluring dreams spread through the populations with amazing rapidity, calling forth the severest repression by the authorities, who recognised in them the danger not only to religion, but to the whole social organisation. The sectaries manifested the sincerity of their convictions by the steadfast cheerfulness with which they endured imprisonment, torture, and the stake; but this ardent fanaticism also found expression in lawless licentiousness among those who mistook the impulses of the flesh for the dictates of the spirit. There is doubtless much exaggeration in the description of the *igneum baptisma* by which in Munster John Mathison encouraged promiscuous licence among the elect, but the history of mystic ardour furnishes too many examples of such aberrations for us to question the probability of their occurrence among such an assemblage of disordered and disorderly minds.

Luther, moreover, was quite as resolute in setting limits to his movement as Rome had been in forbidding all progress, and the Anabaptists were to him enemies as detestable as Catholics. The Protestant princes, moreover, had too much worldly wisdom to imperil their dangerous career by any alliance with fanatics whose extravagances provoked opposition so general. The cause of the Reformation, therefore, although it suffered no little from so portentous an illustration of the dangers resulting from the destruction of the ancient barriers, escaped all contamination in itself, and its leaders pursued their course undeviatingly.

Meanwhile the League of Schmalkalden accomplished its purpose. Henry VIII and Francis I were eager to seize the opportunity of encouraging dissension in the empire. The Turk became more menacing than ever. Charles, always ready to yield for a time when opposition was impolitic, gracefully abandoned the position assumed at Augsburg; and the negotiations of Schweinfurth and Nürnberg resulted in the decree of the Diet of Ratisbon in 1532, by which, until the assembling of the future council, all religious disturbances were prohibited, and the imperial chamber was commanded to undertake no prosecutions on account of heresy. Toleration was thus practically established for the moment, but the abbots and monks who had been ejected, and who had been anticipating their restoration, became naturally restive. Charles cunningly sent from Italy full powers to the chamber to decide as to what causes arose from religious disputes, and what were simply civil or criminal. Thus entrusted with the interpretation of the Ratisbon decree, the chamber assumed that claims on Church lands were not included in the forbidden class, while old edicts prohibiting the observances of Lutheranism brought all religious questions within the scope of criminal law. The promised toleration was thus practically denied, but, fortunately for the Protestants, Ferdinand was anxiously negotiating for their recognition of his dignity as King of the Romans, and by the Transaction of Cadam in 1533 he purchased the coveted homage by accepting their construction of the edict of Ratisbon.

Still the Protestants complained of persecution and the

Catholics of proselytism. The ensuing fifteen years were
filled with a series of bootless negotiations, pretended settle-
ments, quarrels, recriminations, and mutual encroachments,
which year after year occupied the successive Diets, and
kept Germany constantly trembling on the verge of a
desolating civil war. It would be useless to disturb the
dust that covers these forgotten transactions, which can
teach us nothing save that the Protestants still refused to
recognise that the schism was past human power to heal;
that Rome, recovering from her temporary hesitation, would
not abate one jot of her pretensions to save her supremacy
over half of Christendom; and that Charles, as a wily
politician, was always ready in adversity to abandon with a
good grace that which he had arrogantly seized in prosperity.
How eager, indeed, were the Protestants to effect some
compromise which should relieve them from their exceptional position is strikingly manifest in the Articles which
Melanchthon and his friends in 1535 submitted to Francis I,
after the Sorbonne had refused to enter into a disputation or
conference with them.   In this document all non-essentials
were abandoned;   doctrinal dissidences were skilfully
evaded, and stress only was laid upon such regulations as
should remove the external corruption of the Church.
Melanchthon proposed that the monastic orders should be
continued, but that the vows should not be perpetual, so
that religion might not be disgraced by the excesses of those
who had mistaken their vocation. So, as regards priestly
celibacy, he proposed that, as human nature rendered it
impossible to supply the multitude of parishes with men
able to live in continence, those who could not preserve
their purity should be allowed to marry; while, to prevent
the dilapidation of Church property, the higher positions
should be reserved to men of mature age who could lead a
single life. The Sorbonne, in reply, condescended to no
argument, but contented itself with asserting that the
Protestants desired the subversion of all religion, while, on
the other hand, Melanchthon had the satisfaction of being
proclaimed a traitor by the Germans.

In all this the only point which possesses special interest
for us is another authoritative attempt at reconciling the
irreconcilable which occurred in 1540 and 1541. It was
suggested that all parties should unite on the basis of
sacerdotal marriage, the use of the cup by the laity, and the

rejection of the authority of the Holy See. Matters reached such a point that the legate Morone reported, in July 1540, that he was ready to run away in despair; the three great ecclesiastical electors and all the episcopate except the Bishop of Trent, and the princes except the Dukes of Bavaria and Brunswick, were in favour of it, while France would undoubtedly follow the example, while he distrusted the assurances of Charles and King Ferdinand that they would not abandon the papacy. If Charles had only had Germany in view, he might well have been tempted to follow in the footsteps of Henry VIII and found an independent Church under his supremacy, but his interests in Spain and Italy bound him to the papacy, and he was sincere in his pledges to Morone. He was anxious, however, to put an end to the religious strife, and after a conference between Melanchthon and Dr. Eck at Worms, Charles himself presented to the Diet of Ratisbon in 1541 a statement of the questions in dispute, with propositions for mutual concession and compromise. In the course of this he reviewed the practice of the Church in various ages with regard to sacerdotal celibacy, admitting that the enforcement of it was not in accordance with the ancient canons, and indicating a willingness to see it abrogated. The Protestants, who were ready to make many sacrifices for peace, hailed this intimation with triumph, stoutly insisting on the repeal of the obnoxious rule, which they stigmatised as unjust and pernicious. So nearly did the parties at length approach each other that there appeared every reason to anticipate a successful result to the effort, when Paul III interfered and pronounced all the proceedings null and void, as the Church alone had power to regulate its internal affairs. The expectations excited by these negotiations naturally stimulated the desire of the people for a change in the discipline of the Church, and the next year we find Paul III obliged to exhort the Bishop of Merseberg, under threats of ejection, to resist the clamours of his subjects, who demanded the abrogation of priestly celibacy and the use of the cup for the laity. The Council of Trent, he said, had been called to consider these matters, and immediate change was especially inadmissible.

Charles had long recognised that the perpetual menace of a powerful confederation such as the Schmalkaldic League, entertaining constant relations with the external enemies of the empire, was incompatible with the peace of Germany and with an imperial power such as he was resolved to wield. The time at last came for the development of his plans. The skill of Alva and the treachery of Maurice of Saxony were crowned with success. The Battle of Muhlberg broke the power of the Protestants utterly, and laid them helpless at his feet. Yet the progress of the new ideas had already placed them beyond the control of even the triumphant Charles, though he had the Elector of Saxony and the Landgrave of Hesse in his dungeons. When, at the Diet of Augsburg in 1548, he proposed the curious arrangement known as the *Interim*, by which he hoped to keep matters quiet until the final verdict of that Œcumenic council which constantly vanished in the distance, he felt it necessary to permit all married priests to retain their wives until the question should be decided by the future council. An expression of a slight preference for celibacy, moreover, was significant both in what it said and what it left unsaid.

The Interim, of course, satisfied neither party. The Catholics regarded it as an unauthorised reformation, the Protestants as disguised popery. Charles, however, in the plenitude of his power, obliged many of the Lutheran states to accept it; while, as regards the Catholics, he was perhaps not sorry to show the pope that he too, like Henry VIII, could regulate the consciences of his subjects and prescribe their religious faith. He had broken with Paul III; the Council of Trent, against his wishes, had been removed to Bologna on a frivolous pretext; and a schism like that of England was apparently again impending. At the least, Charles might not unreasonably desire to manifest that at last he was independent of that papal power with which mutual necessities had so long enforced the closest relations, and to prove that deference to his wishes was henceforth to be the price of his all-important support. He demanded that legates should be sent to Germany armed with extraordinary powers, among which was included authority to grant dispensations to married priests. Paul III referred the request to the Sacred College, and to the council then sitting at Bologna, and it was unanimously replied that it should be granted, with the limitation that monks should not be included, and that priests thus permitted to retain their wives should not exercise their functions or enjoy the fruits of their benefices. That Paul forthwith despatched three nuncios trusted with authority to do this shows not only the disposition which then existed to relax the rigour of the canons respecting celibacy, but also the importance which the question had assumed in the religious disputes of the time, though an absolute refusal was soon afterwards returned to the request of a German prince (supposed to be the Duke of Bavaria) requesting for his subjects the use of the cup, priestly marriage, and the relaxation of the obligation of fasting.

Temporary expedients and compromises such as these are interesting merely as they mark the progress of opinion. Paltry makeshifts to elude the decision of that which had to be decided, they exercised little real influence on the history of the time. It is true that when Charles, in 1551, at the Diet of Augsburg, issued a call for the reassembling of the Council of Trent, he confirmed the Interim until that council should decide all unsettled questions, yet this confirmation was destined to be effective for a period ludicrously brief. A fresh treason of Maurice of Saxony undid all that his former plotting had accomplished; and, while Henry II was winning at the expense of the empire the delusive title of Conqueror, Charles found himself reduced to the hard necessity of restoring all that his crooked policy had for so many years been devoted to extorting. The Transaction of Passau, signed 2 August, 1552, gave full liberty of conscience to the Lutheran states, until a national council or diet should devise means of restoring the unity of the Church; and in case such means could not be agreed upon, then the rights guaranteed by the Transaction were granted in perpetuity. If Charles was disposed to withdraw the concessions thus exacted of him, the miserable siege of Metz and the increasing desire for abdication prevented him from attempting it; and, at the Diet of Augsburg, in 1555, the states and cities of the Augsburg Confession were confirmed in their right to enjoy the practice of their religion in peace.

The long struggle thus was over. The public law of Germany at last recognised the legality of the transactions based upon the Reformation, and not the least in importance among those transactions were the marriages of the ministers of Christ.

CHAPTER XXVI

THE ENGLISH CHURCH

THE abrogation of celibacy in England was a process of far more perplexity and intricacy than in any other country which adopted the Reformation. Perhaps this may be partially explained by the temperament of the race, whose spirit of independence made them quick to feel and impatient to suffer the manifold evils of the sacerdotal system, while their reverential conservatism rendered them less disposed to adopt a radical cure than their Continental neighbours.

In no country of Europe had the pretensions of the papal power been more resolutely set aside. In no country had ecclesiastical abuses been more earnestly attacked or more persistently held up for popular odium, and the applause which greeted all who boldly denounced the shortcomings of priest and prelate shows how keenly the people felt the evils to which they were exposed. William Langlande, the monk of Malvern, was no heretic, yet he was unsparing in his reprobation of the corruptions of the Church :

> " Right so out of holi chirche,
> Alle yveles springeth,
> There inparfit preesthode is,
> Prechours and techeris
>   .   .   .
> And prechours after silver,
> Executours and sodenes,
> Somonours and hir lemmannes;
> That that with gile was geten,
> Ungraciousliche is despended;
> So harlotes and hores
> Arn holpe with swiche goodes,
> And Goddes folk, for defaute thereof,
> For-faren and spillen."

And he boldly prophesied the violent downfall of the whole fabric :

" Right so, ye clerkes,
For youre coveitise, er longe,
Shal thei demen *dos ecclesiæ*,
And youre pride depose.
Deposuit potentes de sede, etc.

.   .   .   .   .

Leveth it wel ye bisshopes
The lordshipe of your londes
For evere shul ye lese,
And lyven as *levitici*," etc.

But while the people greeted these assaults with the keenest
pleasure, they were attached to the old observances, and
were in no haste to see the predictions of the poet fulfilled.
A little sharp persecution was sufficient to suppress all
outward show of Lollardry, and there was no chance in
England for the fierce revolutionary enthusiasm of the
Taborites.

As the sixteenth century opened, John Colet did good
work in disturbing the stagnation of the schools by his
contempt for the petrified theological science of the schoolmen. His endeavour to revert to the Scriptures as the
sole source of religious belief was a step in advance, while
he was unsparing in his denunciations of the corruptions
which were as rife in the English Church, as we have seen
them elsewhere. Yet Colet, though at one time taxed
with heretical leanings, kept carefully within the pale of
orthodoxy, and seems never to have entertained the idea
that the evils which he deplored were to be attacked save
by a renewal of the fruitless iteration of obsolete canons.
Perhaps, however, his friend and disciple, Sir Thomas
More, is the best example of this frame of mind in England's
worthiest men, the besetting weakness of which made the
English Reformation a struggle whose vicissitudes can
scarce be said to have even yet reached their final development.

Before Luther had raised the standard of revolt, More
keenly appreciated the derelictions of the Church, and
allowed his wit to satirise its vices with a freedom which
showed the scantiest respect for the sanctity claimed by
its hierarchy. Yet when Luther came with his heresies
to sweep away all abuses, More's gentle and tender spirit
was roused to a vulgarity of vituperation which earned
for him a distinguished place among the foul-mouthed
polemics of the time, and which is absolutely unfit for

translation. As regards ascetic observances, before the
Lutheran movement More seems to have inclined towards
condemning all practices that were not in accordance with
human nature, though he appears willing to admit that
there may be some special sanctity, though not wisdom,
in conquering nature. After the commencement of the
Reformation, however, his views underwent a reaction,
and he not only defended monastic vows, but he even
went so far as to argue that by the recent marriages of the
Saxon reformers God had manifested his signal displeasure,
for in the old law true priests could be joined only to
the chastest virgins, while God permitted these false
pastors to take to wife none but public strumpets. If he
accused Luther of sweeping away the venerable traditions
of man and of God, he showed how conscientious was this
rigid conservatism when he laid his head upon the block
in testimony for the principal creation and bulwark of
tradition—the papal supremacy.

A community thus halting between an acute perception
of existing evils and a resolute determination not to remove
them was exactly in the temper to render the great movement of the sixteenth century as disastrous to themselves
as possible. How to meet the inevitable under such conditions was a problem which might well tax the acutest
intellect, and Wolsey, whose fate it was to undertake the
task, seems to have been inspired with more than his
customary audacious ingenuity in seeking the solution.

Wolsey himself was no ascetic, as the popular inscrip-
tion over the door of his palace—" Domus meretricium
Domini Cardinalis "—sufficiently attests. A visitation of
the religious houses undertaken in 1511 by Archbishop
Warham had revealed all the old iniquities, without calling
forth any remedy beyond an admonition. In 1518, Wolsey
himself had attempted a systematic reformation in his
diocese of York, and had revived the ancient canons
punishing concubinage among his priesthood; and in 1519
we find him applying to Leo X for a bull conferring special
power to correct the enormities of the clergy. When, in
1523, he proposed a general visitation for the reformation
of the ecclesiastical body, Fox, Bishop of Winchester,
urged it as in the highest degree necessary, stating that he
himself had for three years been devoting all his energies
to restore discipline in his diocese, and that his efforts

had been so utterly fruitless that he had abandoned all hope of any change for the better. Cranmer, indeed, in his " Confutation of Unwritten Verities," did not hesitate to say that " within my memory, which is above thirty years, and also by the information of others that be twenty years elder than I, I could never perceive or learn that any one priest, under the pope's kingdom, was ever punished for advoutry by his ordinary." It may readily be believed, therefore, that Wolsey fully recognised the utter inefficiency of the worn-out weapons of discipline. Yet he was too shrewd a statesman not to foresee that reformation from within or from without must come, and, in taking the initiative, he commenced by quietly and indirectly attacking the monastic orders. As a munificent patron of letters, it was natural that he should emulate Merton and Wykeham in founding a college at Oxford; and " Cardinal's College," now Christ Church, became the lever with which to topple over the vast monastic system of England.

The development of the plan was characteristically insidious. By a bull of 3 April, 1524 (confirmed by Henry, 10 May), Clement VII authorised him to suppress the priory of St. Frediswood at Oxford, and to remove the monks, for the purpose of converting it into a " Collegium Clericorum Seculorum." This was followed by a bull, dated 21 August of the same year, empowering him as legate to make inquisition and reformation in all religious houses throughout the kingdom, to incarcerate and punish the inmates, and to deprive them of their property and privileges, all grants or charters to the contrary notwithstanding. The real purport of this extraordinary commission is shown by the speedy issue of yet another bull, dated 11 September, conceding to him the confiscation of monasteries to the amount of 3000 ducats annual rental, for the endowment of his college, and alleging as a reason for the measure that many establishments had not more than five or six inmates.

The affair was now fully in train, and proceeded with accelerating momentum. On 3 July, 1525, Henry confirmed the incorporation of the college; his letters-patent of 1 May, 1526, enumerate eighteen monasteries suppressed for its benefit, while other letters of 10 May grant seventy-one churches or rectories for its support, and yet other grants are alluded to as made in letters which have not been preserved. In 1528 these were followed by various other donations of religious houses and manors, and during the same year Wolsey founded another Cardinal's College at Ipswich, which became a fresh source of absorption.

Had Henry VIII entertained any preconceived design of suppressing the religious houses, his impatient temper would scarcely have allowed him to remain so long a witness of this spoliation without taking his share and carrying the matter out with his accustomed boldness and disregard of consequences. At length, however, he claimed his portion, and procured from Clement a bull, dated 2 November, 1528, conceding to him, for the benefit of the old foundations of the King's Colleges at Cambridge and Windsor, the suppression of monasteries to the annual value of 8000 ducats. This was followed by another, a few days later, empowering Wolsey and Campeggio, co-legates in the affair of Queen Katherine's divorce, to unite to other monasteries all those containing less than twelve inmates—thus authorising the suppression of the latter, of which the number was very large. Another bull of the same date (12 November) attacked the larger abbeys, which had thus far escaped. It ordered the two cardinals, under request from the king, to inquire into the propriety of suppressing the rich monasteries enjoying over 10,000 ducats per annum, for the purpose of converting them into bishoprics, on the plea that the seventeen sees of the kingdom were insufficient for the spiritual wants of the people. The report of the cardinals apparently seconded the views of Henry, for Clement granted to them, 29 May, 1529, the power of creating and arranging bishoprics at their discretion, and of sacrificing additional monasteries when necessary to provide adequate revenues. It is probable that the monks who had been unceremoniously deprived of their possessions did not in all cases submit without resistance, for the bull of 12 November, 1528, respecting the smaller houses, was repeated 31 August, 1529, with the suggestive addition of authority to call in the assistance of the secular arm.

Wolsey was now tottering to his fall. Process against him was commenced on 9 October, 1529, and on the 18th the Great Seal was delivered to More. His power, how-ever, had lasted long enough to break down all the safe-guards which had for so many centuries grown around the sacred precincts of ecclesiastical property; and the rich foundations which covered so large a portion of English territory lay defenceless before the cupidity of a despot who rarely allowed any consideration, human or divine, to interfere with his wishes, whose extravagance rendered him eager to find new sources of supply for an exhausted treasury, and whose temper had been aroused by the active support lent by the preaching friars to the party of Queen Katherine in the affair of the divorce. Yet it is creditable to Henry's self-command that the blow did not fall sooner, although it came at last.

It is not my province to enter into the details of Henry's miserable quarrel with Rome, which, except in its results, is from every point of view one of the most humiliating pages of English history. The year 1532 saw the proclamation of the king commanding the support of his subjects in the impending rupture, and the subscription of the clergy to a paper which, with unparalleled servility, placed the whole ecclesiastical constitution of the kingdom in his absolute power. The following year his long-protracted divorce from Katherine of Aragon was consummated; the annates were withdrawn from the pope, and Henry assumed the title of Supreme Head of the Church of England. In 1535 an obedient Parliament confirmed the acts of the sovereign, and forbade the promulgation of any canons by synods or convocations without his approval. The power of the pope was abolished by proclamation, and universities and prelates rivalled each other in obsequiously transferring to Henry the reverence due to Rome.

The greater portion of the monasteries, which had already experienced a foretaste of the wrath to come, hastened to proclaim their adhesion to the new theological autocracy, and means not the most gentle were found to persuade the remainder. The Carthusians of the Charter House of London gave especial trouble, and the contest between them and the king affords a vivid picture of the times. There is something very affecting in the account given by Strype of the humble but resolute resignation with which the prior and his monks prepared themselves for martyrdom in vindication of the papal supremacy. Their courage was soon put to the test. Between the 27th of April and the 4th of August, 1535, the prior and eleven of his monks were put to death with all the horrors of the punishment for high treason; but neither this nor the efforts of a new and more loyal prior were able to produce submission. In 1536, ten of the most unyielding were sent to other houses, where several of them were subsequently executed, and in 1537, ten more were thrown into Newgate, where nine of them died almost immediately —it is to be presumed from the rigour of their confinement and the foulness of the gaol. In 1539, the few that remained were expelled; the house was seized and used as an arsenal, until it was given to Sir Edward North, who changed it into a residence, pulling down the cloisters and converting the church into his parlour. The Observantine Franciscans were equally resolute, and, moreover, persistently adhered to the cause of Katherine of Aragon. After unsuccessful attempts to win them over, some two hundred of them were sent to prison, where they mostly perished, and in 1537 eight of them who survived were allowed to leave England.

The direct relations of the regular Orders with the papacy rendered it impossible to regard them otherwise than as a source of disaffection and danger in the new order of things. Their destruction thus seemed to be a political necessity, the desire for which was enhanced by the relief promised to Henry's exhausted treasury through the secularisation of their property. As a rule, their establishments were not unpopular, and, little as Henry recked of any opposition to his will, some excuse was necessary to win over public opinion to such harsh measures. The most effective means for this was a visitation which should expose the secret turpitude of monasticism, and accordingly, in 1535, commissions were issued to examine into the foundation, title, history, condition of discipline, and number and character of inmates of all religious orders. Thomas Cromwell had no difficulty in finding visitors who should supply the material desired. In the summer and autumn of 1535, three commissioners—John Ap Rice and Doctors Legh and Layton—were busily engaged with the religious houses of the south of England. Of these, Ap Rice, to judge by his reports, was inclined to be fairminded, while the others were unscrupulously eager to meet the wishes of their master, and their reports were filled with descriptions of foul disorders. They were consequently selected to continue the work in the north, which, under pressure of limited time, was so hurriedly performed that the investigation must have been merely nominal. Parliament was to meet on 4 February, 1536, and their work must be completed in time to lay before it. Commencing 22 December, in about six weeks they reported on a hundred and fifty-five houses in the province of York and the dioceses of Coventry, Lichfield, and Norwich, including a few scattered ones elsewhere. Only about forty per cent. of the houses in these districts were visited, and of the hundred and fifty-five there were forty-three against which nothing more serious than superstition was alleged— probably on account of well-timed liberality exhibited to the visitors. The rest were described as more or less vicious.

The result of this visitation, exaggerated by subsequent writers, has been to blacken unduly the memory of English monasticism. No one familiar with the mendacity of public papers of that age places confidence in their unsupported statements when there was an object to be gained, and nothing in the character of Henry's selected agents tends to prevent a wholesome attitude of doubt. Besides, in some cases there happens to be evidence contradicting the statements of the visitors. Thus, in October 1535, Layton reports to Cromwell : " The prior of Dover and his monks are as bad as others. Sodomy there is none, for they have no lack of women. The Abbot of Langdon is worse than all the rest, the drunkennest knave living. His canons are as bad as he, without a spark of virtue." The result of this was the immediate surrender of the houses of Langdon, Dover, and Folkestone, but the commissioners who received the surrender wrote to Cromwell 16 November : " The house of Langdon is in decay, the abbot unthrifty, and his convent ignorant. Dover is well repaired, and the prior has reduced the debt from £180 to £100, of whose nowe case divers of the honest inhabitants of Dover show themselves very sorry. Folkestone is a little house, well repaired, and the prior a good husbandman beloved of his neighbours." Still more compromising is the fact that, on 24 April, 1536, a commission was issued to some prominent men in each county to make a new survey of the monasteries. Reports of these commissioners, in June, for Leicestershire, Warwickshire, Rutland, and Hunts are extant, and they almost uniformly represent the inmates

to be of good conversation; in fact, it is especially significant that in Leicestershire, two—Garendon and Gracedieu,
which had been the subject of particular animadversion by
Legh and Layton—were reported on favourably.

In this conflict of testimony we must therefore rely on
antecedent and circumstantial evidence, and we may not
accept as proven Father Gasquet's pious and laborious
rehabilitation. All contemporary authorities agree that
the pre-Reformation Church was steeped in worldliness.
The English monasteries were not likely to have improved
since Archbishop Morton described their condition, half
a century earlier, as similarly deplorable, or Wolsey at a
later period; nor is there any ground for imagining them
as better than their Continental brethren, whose lapses
were the subject of bitter reprehension by censors of their
own faith. The Franciscan, Dr. Thomas Murner, who
was subsequently one of Luther's most vituperative
opponents, in his *Narrenbeschwerung* assumes as a matter
of course that all parish priests kept concubines, and all
priests and monks meddle with men's wives, while in the
nunneries she who has most children is reckoned the
abbess. A more sober witness is Abbot Trithemius, whose
description of the houses of his own Benedictine Order
we have seen above. Scarce anything, indeed, can be
conceived worse than the condition of the German convents as detailed in a document drawn up by order of the
Emperor Ferdinand in 1562, to stimulate the Council of
Trent to action. In Italy there is ample evidence that
the regular Orders were no better; and as for France, it
is sufficient to refer to the description, by the Council of
Paris in 1521, of the entire absence of discipline in capi-
tular and conventual life. In fact, the whole conventual
system was so corrupt that, as we shall see, the cardinals
whom Paul III in 1538 charged to draw up a plan of
reform for the Church proposed to abolish all the conventual Orders, in order to relieve the people of their evil
example, and to place the nunneries under episcopal jurisdiction. That public opinion in England took the same
view of the monastic establishments would appear from
the travels of Nicander Nucius, who visited England about
1545, and who, in relating the story of their suppression,
gives as damaging an account of their morality as Bishop
Burnet or any of those who have been classed as their

special defamers. The impartial student may therefore not unreasonably conclude that, in view of the state of monastic morals everywhere else in Christendom, the assertion that England was an exception requires stronger evidence than has been produced.

That a portion at least of the people were eager for the secularisation of the religious houses is apparent from the virulence of the assault upon them in the notorious document known as " The Beggars' Petition." It calculates that, besides the tithes, one-third of the kingdom was ecclesiastical property, and that these vast possessions were devoted to the support of a body of men who found their sole serious occupation in destroying the peace of families and corrupting the virtue of women. The economical injury to the Commonwealth, and the interference with the royal prerogative of the ecclesiastical system, were argued with much cogency, and the king was entreated to destroy it by the most summary methods. That any one should venture to publish so violent an attack upon the existing Church, at a time when punishment so prompt followed all indiscretions of this nature, renders this production peculiarly significant both as to the temper of the educated portion of the people and the presumed intentions of the king.[1]

[1] As published in the Harleian Miscellany, "The Beggars' Petition " bears the date of 1538, but internal evidence would assign it to a time anterior to the suppression of the monasteries, and Burnet attributes it to the period under consideration, saying that it was written by Simon Fish, of Gray's Inn, that it took mightily with the public, and that when it was handed to the king by Ann Boleyn, "he lik'd it well, and would not suffer anything to be done to the author " (Hist. Reform. I. 160). Froude, indeed, assigns it to the date of 1528, and states that Wolsey issued a proclamation against it, and further, that Simon Fish, the author, died in 1528 (Hist. Engl. Ch. VI.), while Strype (Eccles. Memorials I. 165) includes it in a list of books prohibited by Cuthbert, Bishop of London, in 1526. In the edition of 1546, the date of 1524 is attributed to it.

The tone of that which was thus equally agreeable to the court and to the city may be judged from the following extracts, which are by no means the plainest spoken that might be selected.

" § 13. Yea, and what do they more ? Truly, nothing but apply themselves by all the sleights they may to have to do with every man's wife, every man's daughter, and every man's maid; that cuckoldry should reign over all among your subjects; that no man should know his own child; that their bastards might inherit the possessions of every man, to put the right-begotten

Whether the reports of the visitors were true or false, they served the purpose of those who procured them. The Parliament which met 4 February, 1536, was composed almost exclusively of members selected by the court and presumably submissive to the royal will. Yet, when a bill was introduced suppressing all houses whose landed revenues did not exceed £200, it seems to have taken the House by surprise. There were hesitation and delay, and tradition relates that it required the personal urgency of the king, accompanied by threats and the reading of the reports of the visitors, to obtain its enactment. To justify it, the preamble recites that " manifest sin, vicious, carnal and abominable living is daily used and committed commonly in such little and small abbeys, priories and religious houses of monks, canons and nuns, where the congregation of such religious persons is under the number of twelve persons," and that this increases in spite of continual visitations during the past two hundred years, so that the only hope of amendment is to transfer their inmates to the " diverse and great solemn monasteries of this realm wherein (thanks be to God) religion is right well kept and observed." The distinction between the " great solemn monasteries," which were praised, and the small ones, which were reviled, was a trifle illogical, but probably no one ventured to criticise the inconsistency, and the bill was passed.

Three hundred and seventy-six houses were swept away by this Act, and the " Court of Augmentations of the King's Revenue " was established to take charge of the

---

children clean beside their inheritance, in subversion of all estates and godly order.

" § 16. Who is she that will set her hands to work to get threepence a day and may have at least twenty-pence a day to sleep an hour with a friar, a monk, or a priest? Who is he that would labour for a groat a day, and may have a least twelve-pence a day to be a bawd to a priest, a monk, or a friar?

" § 31. Wherefore, if your grace will set their sturdy loobies abroad in the world, to get them wives of their own, to get their living with their labour, in the sweat of their faces, according to the commandment of God, *Gen*. iii., to give other idle people, by their example, occasion to go to labour; tye these holy, idle thieves to the carts to be whipped naked about every market-town, till they will fall to labour, that they may, by their importunate begging, not take away the alms that the good Christian people would give unto us sore, impotent, miserable people your bedemen."

lands and goods thus summarily escheated. The rents which thus fell to the king were valued at £32,000 a year, and the movable property at £100,000, while the commissioners were popularly supposed to have been " as careful to enrich themselves as to increase the King's revenue." Stokesley, Bishop of London, remarked concerning the transaction that " these lesser houses were as thorns soon plucked up, but the great abbeys were like petrified old oaks; yet they must needs follow, and so would others do in Christendom before many years were passed." But Stokesley, however true a prophet in the general scope of his observation, was mistaken as to the extreme facility of eradicating the humble thorns. The country was not so easily reconciled to the change as the versatile, more intelligent, and less reverent inhabitants of the cities. Henry, unluckily, not only had not abrogated Purgatory by proclamation, but had specially recommended the continuance of prayers and masses for the dead, and thousands were struck with dread as to the future prospects of themselves and their dearest kindred when there should be few to offer the sacrifice of the Mass for the benefit of departed souls, to say nothing of those which had been paid for and not yet celebrated. The traveller and the mendicant, too, missed the ever open door and the coarse but abundant fare which smoothed the path of the humble wayfarer. Discontent spread widely, and was soon manifested openly. To meet this, most of the lands were sold at a very moderate price to the neighbouring gentry, under condition of exercising free hospitality to supply the wants of those who had hitherto been dependent on conventual charity.

The plan was only partially successful, and soon another element of trouble made itself apparent. Of the monks whose houses were suppressed, those who desired to continue a monastic life were transferred to the larger foundations, while the rest took " capacities," under promise of a reasonable allowance for their journey home. They received only forty shillings and a gown, and with this slender provision it was estimated that about ten thousand were turned adrift upon the world, in which their previous life had incapacitated them from earning a support. The result is visible in the Act for the punishment of " sturdy vagabonds and beggars," passed by Parliament in this same year, inflicting a graduated scale of penalties, of which hanging was the one threatened for a third offence.

This was a dangerous addition to society when discontent was smouldering and ready to burst into flame. The result was soon apparent. After harvest-time great disturbances convulsed the kingdom. A rising, reported as consisting of twenty thousand men, in Lincolnshire, was put down by the Duke of Suffolk with a heavy force and free promises of pardon. In the north matters were even more serious. The clergy there were less tractable than their southern brethren, and some Injunctions savouring strongly of Protestantism aroused their susceptibilities afresh. Unwilling to submit without a struggle, they held a convocation, in which they denied the royal supremacy and proclaimed their obedience to the pope. This was rank rebellion, especially as Paul III, on 30 August, 1535, had issued his bull of excommunication against Henry, and self-preservation therefore demanded the immediate suppression of the recalcitrants. They would hardly, indeed, have ventured on assuming a position of such dangerous opposition without the assurance of popular support, nor were their expectations or labours disappointed. The "Pilgrimage of Grace," according to report, soon numbered forty thousand men. Although Skipton and Scarborough bravely resisted a desperate siege, the success of the insurgents at York, Hull, and Pomfret Castle was encouraging, and risings in Lancashire, Durham, and Westmoreland gave to the insurrection an aspect of the most menacing character. Good fortune and skilful strategy, however, saved the Duke of Norfolk and his little army from defeat ; the winter was rapidly approaching, and at length a proclamation of general amnesty, issued by the king on 9 December, induced a dispersion of the rebels. The year 1537 saw another rising in the north, but this time it numbered only eight thousand men. Repulsed at Carlisle, and cut to pieces by Norfolk, the insurgents were quickly put down, and other disturbances of minor importance were even more readily suppressed.

Strengthened by these triumphs over the disaffected, Henry proceeded, in 1537, to make the acknowledgment of papal authority a crime liable to the penalties of a præmunire ; and, as resistance was no longer to be dreaded,

he commenced to take possession of some of the larger
houses. These did not come within the scope of the Act
of Parliament, and therefore were made the subject of
special transactions. The abbots resigned, either from
having been implicated in the late insurrections, or feeling
that their evil lives would not bear investigation, or doubtless, in many cases, from a clear perception of the doom
impending in the near future, which rendered it prudent
to make the best terms possible while yet there was time.
Thus in these cases the monks were generally pensioned
with eight marks a year, while some of the abbots secured
a revenue of 400 or 500 marks. In an agreement which
has been preserved, the monks were to receive pensions
varying from 53s. 4d. to £4 a year, according to their age.
In some cases, indeed, according to Bishop Latimer, in a
sermon preached before Edward VI, the royal exchequer
was relieved by finding preferment for most unworthy
objects : " However bad the reports of them were, some
were made bishops and others put into good dignities in
the Church, that so the king might save their pensions
that otherwise were to be paid them." An effectual means,
moreover, of inducing voluntary surrenders was by stop-
ping their source of support, and thus starving them out.
Richard, Bishop of Dover, one of the commissioners in
Wales, writes to Cromwell, 23 May, 1538 : " I thinke
before the yere be owt ther schall be very fewe howsis
abill to lyve, but schall be glade to giffe up their howseis
and provide for them selvys otherwise, for their thei schall
have no living." In anticipation of the impending doom,
many of the abbots and priors had sold everything that
was saleable, from lands and leases down to spits and
kitchen utensils, leaving their houses completely denuded.
The letters of the commissioners are full of complaints
respecting this sharp practice, and of their efforts to
trace the property. Another mode of compelling surrenders was by threatening the strict enforcement of the
rules of the Order. Thus, in the official report of the
surrender of the Austin Friars of Gloucester, we find the
alternative given them, when " the seyd freeres seyed . . .
as the worlde ys nowe they war not abull to kepe them
and leffe in ther howseys, wherfore voluntaryly they gaffe
ther howseys into the vesytores handes to the kynges use.
The vesytor seyd to them, ' thynke nott, nor hereafter

reportt nott, that ye be suppresseyd, for I have noo such auctoryte to suppresse yow, but only to reforme yow, wherfor yf ye woll be reformeyd, accordeyng to good order, ye may contynew for all me.' They seyd they war nott abull to contynew," whereupon they were ejected.

In the year 1538 the work proceeded with increased rapidity, no less than 158 surrenders of the larger houses being enrolled. Many of the abbots were attainted of treason and executed, and the abbey lands forfeited. Means not of the nicest kind were taken to increase the disrepute of the monastic orders, and they retaliated in the same way. Thus, the Abbot of Crossed-Friars, in London, was surprised in the day-time with a woman under the worst possible circumstances, giving rise to a lawsuit more curious than decent; while, on the other hand, the Abbess of Chepstow accused Dr. London, one of the visitors, of corrupting her nuns. Public opinion, however, did not move fast enough for the rapacity of those in power, and strenuous exertions were made to stimulate it. All the foul stories that could be found or invented respecting the abbeys were raked together; but these proving insufficient, the impostures concerning relics and images were investigated with great success, and many singular exposures were made which gave the king fresh warrant for his arbitrary measures, and placed the religious houses in a more defenceless position than ever.

Despite all this, in the session of 1539 all the twenty-eight parliamentary abbots had their writs, and no less than twenty sat in the House of Lords. Yet the influence of the court and the progress of public opinion were shown in an Act which confirmed the suppressions of the larger houses not embraced in the former Act, as well as all that might thereafter be suppressed, forfeited, or resigned, and on 9 May, 1540, by special enactment, the ancient Order of the Knights of St. John was broken up, pensions being granted to the grand prior and some of the principal dignitaries. These measures consummated the ruin of the monastic system in England. Henceforth it was altogether at the king's mercy, and his character was not one to temper power with moderation. In 1539 there are upon record fifty-seven surrenders of the great abbeys, and a large number in 1540, the good house of Godstow being the last of the great monasteries to fall. Of the old monastic system this left only the chantries, free chapels, collegiate churches, hospitals, etc., which were gradually absorbed during the succeeding years, until the necessities of the king prompted a sweeping measure for their destruction. Accordingly in 1545 a bill was brought in placing them all at his disposition, together with the property of all guilds and fraternities. There were some indications of opposition, but the king pleaded the expenditures of the French and Scottish wars, and solemnly promised his Parliament " that all should be done for the glory of God and common profit of the realm," whereupon it was passed. It is computed that the number of monasteries suppressed by these various measures was 645; of colleges, 90; of chantries and free chapels, 2374; and of hospitals, 110.

A vast amount of property thus passed into the hands of the court. The clear yearly rental of the suppressed houses alone was rated at £131,607 6s. 4d.—an immense sum in those days; but Burnet states that in reality it was almost tenfold the amount. Small as may have been the good effected by these enormous possessions in the hands of the monks, it was even more worthless under the management of its new masters. Henry admitted the heavy responsibility which he assumed in thus seizing the wealth which had been dedicated to pious uses, and he entertained magnificent schemes for devoting it to the public benefit, but his own extravagance and the grasping avarice of needy courtiers wrought out a result ridiculously mean. Thus he designed to set aside a rental of £18,000 for the support of eighteen " Byshopprychys to be new made." For this purpose he obtained full power from Parliament in 1539, and in 1540 he established one on the remains of the Abbey of Westminster. Those of Chester, Gloucester, and Peterborough were established in 1541, and in 1543 those of Oxford and Bristol, and one of them, that of Westminster, was suppressed in 1550, leaving only five as the result. The people were quieted by assurances that taxes would be abrogated for ever and the kingdom kept in a most efficient state of defence; but subsidies and benevolences were immediately exacted with more frequency and energy than ever. Splendid foundations were promised for institutions of learning, but little was given; a moderate sum was expended in improving the sea-ports, while broad manors and rich farms were granted to favourites at almost nominal prices; and the ill-gotten wealth abstracted from the Church disappeared without leaving traces except in the sudden and overgrown fortunes of those gentlemen who were fortunate or prompt enough to make use of the golden opportunity, and who to obtain them had no scruple in openly tendering bribes and shares in the spoil to Cromwell, the omnipotent favourite of the king. The complaints of the people, who found their new masters harder than the old, may be estimated from some specimens printed by Strype.

If it be asked what became of the "holy idle thieves" and "sturdy loobies" whom the Beggars' Petition so earnestly desired to be thrown upon the world, the answer may be found in the legislation of Edward VI. It was impossible that the sudden and violent overthrow of a system on which nearly all charitable relief was based could be effected without causing infinite misery during the period of transition, no matter how tenderly the interests of the poor might be guarded. In the organisation of the Catholic Church all benevolence finds its expression through ecclesiastical instrumentalities, and the immense possessions of the mediæval establishment had been confided to it largely in its capacity of the universal almoner. In seizing these possessions the State was morally bound to assume the corresponding obligations, but time was required for the adjustment, and the greedy rulers, during the minority of Edward VI, were much more intent upon increasing their acquisitions than in listening to the demands of humanity. By his first Parliament, in 1547, an Act was passed confirming that of 1545, concerning the hospitals, chantries, guilds, etc., under which all remnants that had escaped the rapacity of the late sovereign were placed at the mercy of the Protector Somerset and his colleagues of the Council, who speedily absorbed not only them, but everything that could be stripped from the parish churches. In the preamble of this Act, one of its objects was specified to be the "better provision for the poor and needy," thus recognising the responsibility of the State to replace the assistance which had been afforded by the Church and the guilds, but Parliament a few weeks earlier had already taken measures, not to relieve the sufferings of the poor, but to repress the vagabondage which had necessarily resulted from the destruction of the monasteries. In this Act the magnitude of the evil is indicated by the rigorously inhuman measures deemed necessary for its abatement. Every able-bodied man loitering in any place for three days without working or offering to work was held to be a vagabond; he was to be branded on the breast with a letter V, and be adjudged as a slave for two years to any one who would bring him before a justice of the peace. This substitute for clerical almsgiving was deemed sufficient for the time, and it was not until five years later, in 1552, that a practical effort was made to alleviate the miseries of poverty by a poor law, the commencement of a series which has since burdened England with ever-increasing weight.

The monastic establishments of Ireland shared the same fate. Rymer gives the text of a commission for the suppression of a nunnery of the diocese of Dublin in 1535. The insubordination of the island, however, rendered it difficult to carry out the measure everywhere, and finally, in 1541, it was accomplished by virtually granting their lands to the native chieftains. These were good Catholics, but they could not resist the temptation. They joined eagerly in grasping the spoil, and the desirable political object was effected of detaching them, for the time, from the foreign alliances with the Catholic Powers, which threatened serious evils.

It is a striking proof of Henry's strength of will and intense individuality of character, that, in thus tearing up by the roots the whole system of monachism, he did not yield one jot to the powerful section of his supporters who had pledged themselves to the logical sequence of his acts—the abrogation of sacerdotal celibacy in general. While every reason of policy and statesmanship urged him to grant the privilege of marriage to the secular clergy, whom he forced to transfer to him the allegiance formerly rendered to Rome, while his chief religious advisers at home and his Protestant allies abroad used every endeavour to wring from him this concession, he steadily and persistently refused it to the end, and we can only guess whether his firmness arose from conscientious conviction or from the pride of a controversialist.

Notwithstanding his immovable resolution on this point, his power seemed ineffectual to stay the progress of the new ideas. An assembly held by his order in May 1530, to condemn the heretical doctrines disseminated in certain books, shows how openly the advocates of clerical marriage had promulgated their views while yet Wolsey was prime minister and Henry gloried in the title of Defender of the Faith. Numerous books were denounced in which celibacy was ridiculed, its sanctity disproved, and its evil influences commented upon in the most irreverent manner. These doctrines were sometimes carried into practice, and the orthodox clergy had little ceremony in visiting them with the sharpest penalties of the canons. It was about this time that Stokesley, Bishop of London, condemned to imprisonment for life Thomas Patmore, the incumbent of Hadlam in Hertfordshire, for encouraging his curate to marry and permitting him subsequently to officiate; and the unfortunate man actually lay for three years in gaol, until released by the intercession of Cranmer.

If the reforming polemics were thus bold while Henry was yet orthodox, it may readily be imagined how keenly they watched the progress of his quarrel with the pope, and how loud became their utterances as he gradually threw off his allegiance to Rome and persecuted all who hesitated to follow in his footsteps. He soon showed, however, that he allowed none to precede him, and that all consciences were to be measured by the royal ell-wand. Thus his proceedings against the Carthusians and Franciscans in 1534 were varied by a proclamation directed against seditious books and priestly marriages. As we have seen, some unions had taken place, and all who had committed the indiscretion were deprived of their functions and reduced to the laity, though the marriages seem to have been recognised as valid. Future transgressions, moreover, were threatened with the royal indignation and further punishment—words of serious import at such a time and under such a monarch.

In spite of all this, the chief advisers of Henry did not scruple to connive at infractions of the proclamation. Both Cranmer and Cromwell favoured the Reformation: the former was himself secretly married, and even ventured to urge the king to reconsider his views on priestly celibacy; while the latter, though, as a layman, without any such personal motive, was disposed to relax the strictness of the rule of celibacy. During the visitation of the monasteries, for instance, the Abbot of Walden had little hesitation in confessing to Ap Rice, the visitor, that he was secretly married, and asked to be secured from molestation. The confidence thus manifested in the friendly disposition of the vicar-general was satisfactorily responded to. Cromwell replied, merely warning him to " use his remedy " without, if possible, causing scandal. A singular petition, addressed to him in 1536 by the secular clergy of the diocese of Bangor, illustrates forcibly both the confidence felt in his intentions and the necessity of the Abbot of Walden's " remedy " in the immorality which prevailed. There had been a visitation in which the petitioners admit that many of them had been found in fault, and as their women had been consequently taken away, they pray the vicar-general to devise some means by which their consorts may be restored. They do not venture to ask directly for marriage, but decency forbids the supposition that they could openly request Cromwell to authorise a system of concubinage. Nothing can be more humiliating than their confession of the relations existing between themselves, as ministers of Christ, and the flocks entrusted to their spiritual care. After pleading that without women they cannot keep house and exercise hospitality, they add : " We ourselves shall be driven to seek our living at alehouses and taverns, for mansions upon the benefices and vicarages we have none. *And as for gentlemen and substantial honest men, for fear of inconvenience, knowing our frailty and accustomed liberty, they will in no wise board us in their houses.*"

The tendencies thus exhibited by the king's advisers called forth the remonstrances of the Conservatives. In June 1536 the Lower House of Convocation presented a memorial inveighing strongly against the progress of heresy, and among the obnoxious opinions condemned was " that it is preached and taught that all things awght to be in comen and that Priests shuld have wiffes," and they added that books containing heretical opinions were printed " cum privilegio," were openly sold among the people, and were not condemned by those in authority. Possibly it was in consequence of this that in the following November Henry issued a circular letter to his bishops in which he commanded them—" Whereas we be advertised that divers Priests have presumed to marry themselves contrary

to the custom of our Church of England, Our Pleasure is,
Ye shall make secret enquiry within your Diocess, whether
there be any such resiant within the same or not "—and
any such offenders who had presumed to continue the
performance of their sacred functions were ordered to be
reported to him or to be arrested and sent to London.
Curiously enough, there is no reference to the subject in
the " Articles devised by the Kinges Highnes Majestie to
stablyshe Christen Quietnes and Unitie amonge us," issued
by Henry in this year.

Notwithstanding the ominous threat in the letter to
the bishops, there appears about this period to have been
great uncertainty in the public mind respecting the state
of the law and the king's intentions.   Two letters happen
to have been preserved, written within a few days of each
other, in June 1537, to Cromwell, which reveal the condition of opinion at the time.   One of these complains that
the vicar of Mendlesham, in Suffolk, has brought home a
wife and children, whom he claims to be lawfully his own,
and that it is permitted by the king.   Although " thys
acte by hym done is in thys countre a monstre, and many
do growdge at it," yet, not knowing the king's pleasure,
no proceedings can be had, and appeal is therefore made
for authority to prosecute, lest " hys ensample wnpon-
nyched shall be occasion for other carnall evyll dysposed
prestes to do in lyke manner."   The other letter is from an
unfortunate priest who had recently married, supposing it
to be lawful.   The " noyse of the peopull," however, had
just informed him that a royal order had commanded the
separation of such unions, and he had at once sent his wife
to her friends, three-score miles away.   He therefore
hastens to make his peace, protesting he had sinned through
ignorance, though he makes bold to argue that " yf the
kyngys grace could have founde yt laufull that prestys
mught have byn maryd, they wold have byn to the crowne
dubbyll and dubbyll faythefull; furste in love, secondly
for fere that the byschoppe of Rome schuld sette yn hys
powre unto ther desolacyon."

It is evident from these letters that there was still a
genuine popular antipathy to clerical marriage, and yet
that the royal supremacy was so firmly established by
Henry's ruthless persecutions that this antipathy was held
subject to the pleasure of the court, and could at any

moment have been dissipated by proclamation. In fact, the only wonder is that any convictions remained in the minds of those who had seen the objects of their profoundest veneration made the sport of avarice and derision. Stately churches torn to pieces, the stone sold to sacrilegious builders, the lead put up at auction to the highest bidder, the consecrated bells cast into cannon, the sacred vessels melted down, the holy relics snatched from the shrines and treated as old bones and offal, the venerated images burned at Smithfield—all this could have left little sentiment of respect for worn-out religious observances in those who watched and saw the sacrilege remain unpunished.

Notwithstanding the reforming influences with which he was surrounded, Henry sternly adhered to the position which he had assumed. When, in 1538, the princes of the Schmalkaldic League offered to place him at its head, and even to alter, if possible, the Augsburg Confession so as to make it a common basis of union for all the elements of opposition to Rome, Henry was well inclined to obtain the political advantages of the position tendered him, but hesitated to accept it until all doctrinal questions should be settled. The three points on which the Germans insisted were the communion in both elements, the worship in the vulgar tongue, and the marriage of the clergy. In the Convocation of that year a series of questions was submitted for decision embracing the contested points, and the clergy decided in favour of celibacy, private masses, and communion in one element. Thus sustained, Henry was firm, and the ambassadors of the League spent two months in conferences with the English bishops and doctors without result. On their departure (5 August, 1538), they addressed him a letter arguing the subjects in debate—the refusal of the cup, private masses, and sacerdotal celibacy—to which Henry replied at some length, defending his position on these topics with no little skill and dexterity, and refusing his assent finally. The reformers, however, did not yet despair, and the royal preachers even ventured occasionally to debate the propriety of clerical marriage freely before him in their sermons, but in vain. An epistle which Melanchthon addressed to him in April 1539, arguing the same questions again, had no better effect.

In the spring of 1539 Henry renewed negotiations with the German princes, and his envoys, in soliciting another visit from deputies of the League, held out some vague promises of his yielding on the point of celibacy. The Germans, in turn, to show their earnest desire for union with England, submitted a series of propositions in which they suggested that the marriage of priests might be left to the discretion of the pope, and that if it were to be prohibited only persons advanced in life should be ordained. Both parties, however, were too firmly set in their opinions for accord to be possible. Notwithstanding any seeming hesitation caused by the policy of the moment, Henry's mind was fully made up, and the consequences of endeavouring to persuade him against his prejudices soon became apparent. Even while the negotiations were in progress he had issued a series of injunctions degrading from the priesthood all married clergy, and threatening with imprisonment and his displeasure all who should thereafter marry. Argumentation confirmed his opinions, and he proceeded to enforce them on his subjects in his own savage manner, " for though on all other points he had set up the doctrines of the Augsburg Confession," yet on these he had committed himself as a controversialist, and the worst passions of polemical authorship—the true " odium theologicum "—acting through his irresponsible despotism, rendered him the cruellest of persecutors. But a few weeks after receiving the letter of Melanchthon, he answered it in cruel fashion.

In May a new Parliament met, chosen under great excitement, for the people were inflamed on the subject of religion, and animosities ran high. The principal object of the session was known to be a settlement of the national Church, and as the reformers were in a minority against the court, the temper of the Houses was not likely to be encouraging for them. On 5 May, a week after its assembling, a committee was appointed, at the king's request, to take into consideration the differences of religious opinion. On the 16th, the Duke of Norfolk, who was not a member of the committee, reported that no agreement could be arrived at, and he therefore laid before the House of Lords, for full discussion, articles embracing—(1) Transubstantiation; (2) Communion in both kinds; (3) Vows of Chastity; (4) Private Masses;

(5) Sacerdotal Marriages; and (6) Auricular Confession. Cranmer opposed them stoutly, arguing against them for three days, and especially endeavouring to controvert the third and fifth, which enjoined celibacy, but his efforts and those of his friends were vain, when pitted against the known wishes of the king, who himself took an active part in the debate, and argued in favour of the articles with much vigour. Under such circumstances, the adoption of the Six Articles was a foregone conclusion. On 30 May the Chancellor reported that the House had agreed upon them, and that it was the king's pleasure " that some penal statute should be enacted to compel all his subjects who were in any way dissenters or contradicters of these articles to obey them." The framing of such a bill was entrusted to two committees, one under the lead of Cranmer, the other under that of the Archbishop of York, and they were instructed to lay their respective plans before the king within forty-eight hours. Of course the report of the Archbishop of York was adopted. Introduced on 7 June, Cranmer again resisted it gallantly, but it passed both Houses by the 14th, and received the royal assent on the 28th. It was entitled " An Act for abolishing Diversity of Opinions in certain Articles concerning Christian Religion," and it stands as a monument of the cruel legislation of a barbarous age. The Third Article was " that Priests after the order of Priesthood might not marry by the Law of God "; the Fourth, " that Vows of Chastity ought to be observed by the Law of God," and those who obstinately preached or disputed against them were adjudged felons, to suffer death without benefit of clergy. Any opposition, either in word or writing, subjected the offender to imprisonment during the king's pleasure, and a repetition of the offence constituted a felony, to be expiated with the life of the culprit. Priestly marriages were declared void, and a priest persisting in living with his wife was to be executed as a felon. Concubinage was punishable with deprivation of benefice and property, and imprisonment, for a first offence; a second lapse was visited with a felon's death, while in all cases the wife or concubine shared the fate of her partner in guilt. Quarterly sessions were provided, to be held by the bishops and other commissioners appointed by the king, for the purpose of enforcing these laws, and the accused were

entitled to trial by jury. Vows of chastity were only binding on those who had taken them of their own free will when over twenty-one years of age. According to the Act, the wives of priests were to be put away by 24 June, but on that day, as the Act was not yet signed, an order was mercifully made extending the time to 12 July.

Cranmer argued, reasonably enough, that it was a great hardship, in the case of the ejected monks, to insist on the observance of the vow of chastity, when those of poverty and obedience were dispensed with, and when the unfortunates had been forcibly deprived of all the advantages, safeguards, and protection of monastic life. The matter, however, was not decided by reason, but by the whimsical perversity of a self-opinionated man, who unfortunately had the power to condense his polemical notions in the blood of his subjects.

To comprehend the full iniquity of this savage measure, we must remember the rapid progress which the new opinions had been making in England for twenty years; the tacit encouragement given them by the suppression of the religious houses, and by the influence of the king's confidential advisers; and the hopes naturally excited by Henry's quarrel with Rome and negotiations with the League of Schmalkalden. In spite, therefore, of the comparatively mild punishments hitherto imposed on priestly marriage, which were no doubt practically obsolete, such unions may safely be assumed as numerous. Even Cranmer himself, the primate of Henry's Church, was twice married, his second wife, then living, the niece of Osiander, being kept under a decent veil of secrecy in his palace. When, after his fruitless resistance to the Six Articles, the bill was passed, he sent his wife to her friends in Germany, until the death of his master enabled him to bring her back and acknowledge her openly; but vast numbers of unfortunate pastors could not have had the opportunity, and perhaps lacked the self-control, thus to arrange their domestic affairs. Even the gentle Melanchthon was moved from his ordinary equanimity, and ventured to address to his royal correspondent a remonstrance expressing his horror of the cruelty which could condemn to the scaffold a man whose sole guilt consisted in not abandoning the wife to whom he had promised fidelity through good and evil, before God and man—a cruelty which could find no precedent in any code that man had previously dared to frame.

As might be expected, numerous divorces of married priests followed this Draconian legislation, and these divorces were held good by the Act of 1549, which under Edward VI granted full liberty in the premises to ecclesiastics. Even Henry, however, began to feel that he had gone too far, and the influence of Cromwell was sufficient to prevent the harshest features of the law from being enforced in all their odious severity, especially as the projected marriage with Ann of Cleves and the alliance with the German Lutherans rendered active persecution in the highest degree impolitic. When the comedy of Henry's fourth marriage culminated in the tragedy of Cromwell's ruin (June 1540), the reactionary elements again gathered strength. There can be little doubt that the atrocity of the law had greatly interfered with its efficient execution and had aroused popular feeling, for now, although the Vicar-General was removed, the Catholics passed with alacrity a bill moderating the Act of the Six Articles, in so far as it related to marriage and concubinage. For capital punishment was substituted the milder penalty of confiscation to the king of all the property and revenue of the offenders.

The Six Articles, as thus modified, remained the law of England during the concluding years of Henry's reign, nor is it likely that any one ventured to urge upon him seriously a relaxation of the principles to which he had committed himself thus definitely. The fall of Cromwell and the danger to which Cranmer was exposed for several years were sufficient to insure him against troublesome remonstrants, even if his increasing irritability and capriciousness had not made those around him daily more alive to the danger of thwarting or resisting his idlest humour. How little progress, indeed, the Reformation had thus far made in England is shown in a letter written in 1546 by John Hooper, afterwards Bishop of Gloucester and Worcester, during the exile into which he was forced by the Act of the Six Articles: " Our king has destroyed the pope, but not popery; he has expelled all the monks and nuns, and pulled down their monasteries; he has caused all their possessions to be transferred into his exchequer, and yet they are bound, even the frail female sex, by the king's command, to perpetual chastity. England has at this time at least ten thousand nuns, not one of whom is allowed to marry. The impious Mass, the most shameful celibacy of the clergy, the invocation of saints, auricular confession, superstitious abstinence from meats, and purgatory, were never before held by the people in greater esteem than at the present moment."

On 28 January, 1547, Henry VIII died, and Edward VI succeeded to the perilous throne. Not yet ten years of age, his government of course received its direction from those around him, and the rivalry between the Protector Somerset and the Chancellor Wriothesley, Earl of Southampton, threw the former into the hands of the progressives, as the latter was the acknowledged head of the reactionary party. The ruin of Southampton and the triumph of Somerset, strengthened by his successful campaign in Scotland, soon began to develop their natural consequences on the religion of the country. Under the auspices of Cranmer, a Convocation was assembled, which was empowered to decide all questions in controversy. When the primate was anxious to again enjoy the solace of his wife's company and to relieve both her and himself from the stigma of concubinage, it is easy to understand that the subject of celibacy would receive early and appropriate attention; and so confident were the reformers of success that they did not hesitate to enter into matrimony without waiting for any formal sanction. Accordingly, on 17 December, 1547, a proposition was submitted to the effect that all canons, statutes, laws, decrees, usages, and customs interfering with or prohibiting marriage should be abrogated, and it was carried by a vote of 53 to 22. No time was lost. Two days afterwards a bill was introduced in the Commons permitting married men to be priests and to hold benefices. It was received with so much favour that it was read twice the same day, and on the 21st it was sent up to the Lords; but in the Upper House it raised debates so prolonged that, as the members were determined to adjourn before Christmas, it was laid aside. This might be the more readily agreed to, since on the 23rd an Act was approved which abolished numerous severe laws of the former reign, including the statute of the Six Articles, and was immediately followed by another granting the use of the cup to the laity and prohibiting private Masses.

The repeal of the Six Articles left the marriage of the clergy subject to the previous laws of Henry, imposing on it various pains and penalties, but with the votes recorded in Convocation and Parliament, it is not likely that much vigour was displayed in their enforcement. Those interested could thus afford to await the reassembling of the Houses, which did not take place until 24 November, 1548, but they claimed the reward of their patience by an early hearing in the session. On December 3 a bill was introduced, similar to that of the previous year, rendering married men eligible to the priesthood; it passed second reading on the 5th, and third reading on the 6th. Apparently encouraged by the favourable reception accorded to it, the friends of the measure resolved on demanding further privileges. The bill was therefore laid aside, and on the next day a new one was presented which granted the additional liberty of marriage to those already in orders. It conceded to the established opinions the fact that it were better that the clergy should live chaste and single, yet, " as great filthiness of living had followed on the laws that compelled chastity and prohibited marriage," therefore all laws and canons inhibiting sacerdotal matrimony should be abolished. This bill, after full discussion, was read a second and third time on the 10th and 12th, and was sent up to the Lords on the 13th. Again the Upper House was in no haste to pass it. It lay on the table until 9 February, 1549, when it was stoutly contested, and after being recommitted, it finally passed on the 19th, with the votes of nine bishops recorded against it.

Cranmer and his friends were now at full liberty to establish the innovation by committing the clergy individually to marriage, and by enlisting the popular feeling in its support. During the discussion they had not been idle. Much controversial writing had occurred on both sides, in which Poynette, afterwards Bishop of Winchester, took an active part, while Bale, Bishop of Ossory, distinguished himself on the same side by raking together all the foul stories that could be collected concerning the celibate clergy—a scandalous material not likely to be lacking in either quantity or quality. Burnet declares that no law passed during the reign of Edward excited more contradiction and censure, and the matrimonialists soon found that, even with the Act of Parliament in their favour, their course was not wholly a smooth one. Cranmer ordered a visitation in his province, and directed as one of the points for inquiry and animadversion, " Whether any do contemn married priests, and, for that they be married, will not receive the Communion or other sacraments at their hands," which distinctly reveals the difficulties encountered in eradicating the convictions of centuries from the popular mind. Sanders says, and with every appearance of probability, that the Archbishop of York united with Cranmer in ordering a visitation of the whole kingdom, during which the visitors investigated particularly the morals of the clergy, and used every argument to impel them to marriage, not only declaring celibacy to be most dangerous to salvation, but intimating that all who adhered to it would be regarded as papists and enemies of the king. The active interest which Cranmer took in the question is manifested by the fact that when Dr. Richard Smith, who had fled to Scotland in consequence of having endeavoured to stir up a tumult at Oxford against Peter Martyr, desired to make his peace and return, the inducement which he offered to the Archbishop of Canterbury to obtain for him the King's pardon was that he would write a book in favour of priestly marriage, as he had previously done against it.

The reformers speedily found that they were not to escape without opposition. The masses of the people throughout England were in a state of discontent. The vast body of abbey lands acquired by the gentry and now enclosed bore hard upon many; the raising of rents showed that secular landlords were less charitable than the ancient proprietors of the soil; the increase of sheep-husbandry threw many farm labourers out of employ; and the savage enactments, already alluded to, against the unfortunate expelled monks show how large an element of influential disaffection was actively at work in the substratum of society. Those priests who disapproved of the rapid Protestantising process adopted by the court could hardly fail to take advantage of opportunities so tempting, and they accordingly fanned the spark into a flame. The enforcement of the new liturgy, on Whitsunday, 1549, seemed the signal of revolt. Numerous risings took place, which were readily quelled, until one in Devonshire assumed alarming proportions. Ten thousand men in arms made demands for relief in religious as well as temporal matters. Lord Russel, unable to meet them in the field, endeavoured to gain time by negotiation, and offered to receive their complaints. These were fifteen in number, of which several demanded the restoration of points of the old religion, and one insisted on the revival of the Six Articles. On their refusal, another set was drawn up, in which not only were the Six Articles called for, but also a special provision enforcing the celibacy of the clergy. This was likewise rejected; but during the delay another rising occurred in Norfolk, reckoned at twenty thousand men, and yet another of less formidable dimensions in Yorkshire. Russel finally scattered the men of Devon, while the Earl of Warwick succeeded in suppressing the rebels of Norfolk, when the promise of an amnesty caused the Yorkshiremen to disperse.

The question of open resistance thus was settled. Cranmer and his friends had now leisure to consolidate their advantages and organise a system that should be permanent. In 1551, he and Ridley prepared with great care a series of forty-two articles, embodying the faith of the Church of England, which was adopted by the Convocation in 1552, and was ordered to be signed by all men in orders and all candidates for ordination. Burnet speaks of it as bringing the Anglican doctrine and worship to perfection. It remained unaltered during the rest of Edward's reign, and under Elizabeth it was only modified verbally in the recension which resulted in the famous Thirty-nine Articles—the foundation-stone of the Episcopalian edifice. Of these forty-two articles, the thirty-first declared that " Bishops, priests, and deacons are not commanded by God's law to vow the estate of a single life or to abstain from marriage."

The canon law had thus invested the marriage of the clergy with all the sanctity that the union of man and wife could possess. Yet still the deep-seated conviction of the people as to the impropriety of such proceedings remained, troubling the repose of those who had entered into matrimony, and doubtless operating as a restraint upon the numbers of the imitators of Cranmer. Among the interrogatories drawn up by John Hooper for the visitation of his diocese of Gloucester, in 1552, is one which inquires whether any midwife refuses to attend the confinement of women who are married to ministers of the Church—a suggestion which indicates how rooted was the popular aversion from such matches. If Strype's description of the clergy of the period indeed be correct, there was nothing in the character of the body to overcome the popular aversion in consideration of its purity and devotion to its sacred duties. The Act of 1549 had to a certain extent justified these prejudices by admitting the preferableness of a single life in the ministers of Christ, and it was resolved to remove every possible stigma by a solemn declaration of Parliament. A bill was therefore prepared and speedily passed (10 February, 1552), which reveals how strong was the popular opposition, and how uncertain the position of the wives and children of the clergy. It declares " that many took occasion, from the words in the Act formerly made about this matter, to say that it was only permitted, as usury and other unlawful things were, for the avoidance of greater evils, who thereupon spoke slanderously of such marriages, and accounted the children begotten in them to be bastards, to the high dishonour of the king and Parliament, and the learned clergy of the realm, who had determined that the laws against priests' marriages were most unlawful by the law of God; to which they had not only given their assent in the Convocation, but signed it with their hands. These slanders did also occasion that the Word of God was not heard with due reverence." It was therefore enacted " That such marriages made according to the rules prescribed in the Book of Service should be esteemed good and valid, and that the children begot in them should be inheritable according to law."

A still further confirmation of the question was designed in a body of ecclesiastical law which was for several years in preparation by various commissions appointed for the purpose. In this it was proposed to make the abrogation of celibacy even more distinctly a matter of faith, for in the second Title among the various heresies condemned is that which, through the suggestion of the Devil, asserts that admission to holy orders takes away the right to marry. This work, however, though completed, had not yet received the royal assent when the death of Edward VI caused it to pass out of sight until 1571, when it was printed by Foxe and brought to the attention of Parliament, but was laid aside owing to the opposition of Queen Elizabeth.

If the Protestants indulged in any day-dreams as to the permanency of their institutions, they were not long in finding that a change of rulers was destined to cause other changes disastrous to their hopes. Even the funeral of Edward, on the 8 August, 1553, afforded them a foretaste of what was in store. Although Cranmer insisted that the public ceremonies in Westminster Abbey should be conducted according to the reformed rites, Queen Mary, still resident in the Tower, had private obsequies performed with the Roman ritual, where Gardiner celebrated mortuary Mass in presence of the queen and some four hundred attendants. When the incense was carried around, after the Gospel, it chanced that the chaplain who bore it was a married man, and the zealous Dr. Weston snatched it from him, exclaiming, " Shamest thou not to do thine office, having a wife as thou hast? The queen will not be censed by such as thou ! "

Trifling as was this incident, it foreboded the wrath to come. Though Mary was not crowned until 1 October, she had issued writs for a Parliament to assemble on the 10th, and as an entire change in the religious institutions of the country was intended, we may not uncharitably believe the assertion that every means of influence and intimidation was employed to secure the return of reactionary members. These efforts were crowned with complete success. The Houses had not sat for three weeks, when a bill was sent down from the Lords repealing all the Acts of Edward's reign concerning religion, including specifically those which permitted the marriage of priests and legitimated their offspring; and after a debate of six days it passed the Commons.

The effect of this was, of course, to revive the statute of the Six Articles, and to place all married priests at the mercy of the queen; and as soon as she felt that she could safely exercise her power, she brought it to bear upon the offenders. A day or two after the dissolution of Parliament she commenced by issuing a proclamation inhibiting married priests from officiating. The Spanish marriage being agreed upon and the resultant insurrection of Sir Thomas Wyatt being suppressed, Mary recognised her own strength, and her Romanising tendencies, which had previously been somewhat restrained, became openly manifested. On 4 March, 1554, she issued a letter to her bishops, of which the object was to restore the condition of affairs under Henry VIII, except that the royal prerogatives as head of the Church were expressly disavowed. It contained eighteen articles, to be strictly enforced throughout all dioceses. Of these the seventh ordered that the bishops should by summary process remove and deprive all priests who had been married or had lived scandalously, sequestrating their revenues during the proceedings. Article VIII provided that widowers, or those who promised to live in the strictest chastity, should be treated with leniency, and receive livings at some distance from their previous abode, being properly supported meanwhile; while Article IX directed that those who suffered deprivation should not on that account be allowed to live with their wives, and that due punishment should be inflicted for all contumacy.

No time was lost in carrying out these regulations. By the 9th of the same month a commission was already in session at York, which cited the clergy to appear before it on the 12th. From an appeal which is extant, by one Simon Pope, rector of Warmington, it appears that men were deprived without citation or opportunity for defence; and that this was not infrequent is probable from the proceedings commenced against offenders of the highest class, designed and well fitted to strike terror into the hearts of the humbler parsons. On the 16th a commission was issued to the Bishops of Winchester (Stephen Gardiner), London (Bonner), Durham, St. Asaph's, Chichester, and Llandaff, to investigate the cases of the Archbishop of York and the Bishops of St. Davids, Chester, and Bristol, who, according to report, had given a most pernicious example by taking wives, in contempt of God, to the damage of their own souls, and to the scandal of all men. Any three of the commissioners were empowered to summon the accused before them, and to ascertain the truth of the report without legal delays or unnecessary circumlocution. If it were found correct, then they were authorised to remove the offenders at once and for ever from their dignities, and also to impose penance at discretion. This was scant measure of justice, considering that the marriage of these prelates had been contracted under sanction of law, and, if that law had recently been repealed, that at least the option of conforming to the new order of things could not decently be denied; yet even this mockery of a trial was apparently withheld, for the *congé d'élire* for their successors is dated 18 March, only two days after the commission was appointed. Neither party, in fact, had much ceremony in dealing with bishops. Five had been deprived under Edward VI; under Mary there were fourteen deprivations, and under Elizabeth fifteen.

During the summer the bishops went on their visitations. The articles prepared by Bonner for his diocese are extant, among which we find directions to inquire particularly of the people whether their pastors are married, and, if separated, whether any communication or intercourse takes place between them and their wives; also whether any one, lay or clerical, ventures to defend sacerdotal matrimony. Few of the weaker brethren could escape an inquisition so searching as this, and though some controversy arose, and a few tracts were printed in defence of priestly marriage, such men as Bonner were not likely to shrink from the thorough prosecution of the work which they had undertaken.

When the Convocation assembled in this year, it was therefore to be expected that only orthodox opinions would find expression. Accordingly, the Lower House presented to the bishops an humble petition praying for the restoration of the old usages, among the points of which are requests that married priests be forcibly separated from their wives, and that those who endeavour to abandon their order be subjected to special animadversion. This clause shows that many unfortunates preferred to give up their positions and lose the means of livelihood, rather than quit the wives to whom they had sworn fidelity, demanding, as we shall see, much subsequent conflicting legislation. The social complications resulting from the change of religion are also indicated in the request that married nuns may be divorced, and that the pretended wives of priests have full liberty to marry again.

Everything being thus prepared, the purification of the Church from married heretics was prosecuted with vigour.

Archbishop Parker states that there were in England some 16,000 clergymen, of whom 12,000 were deprived on this account, many of them most summarily; some on common report, without trial, others without being summoned to appear before their judges, and others again while lying in gaol for not obeying the summons. Some renounced their wives, and were yet deprived, while those who were deprived were also, as we have seen, forced to part from their wives. We can readily believe that the most ordinary forms of justice were set aside, in view of the illegal and indecorous haste of the proceedings against the married bishops described above, but Parker's estimate of the number of sufferers is greatly exaggerated. According to the latest investigator, Mr. Frere, the number of beneficed clergy deprived in London was 150, to whom perhaps about half as many unbeneficed may be added. At Canterbury, where the records seem complete, the number was 68; in Norfolk, 343. The registers elsewhere are mostly too imperfect to allow of satisfactory estimates, but the general conclusion is drawn that throughout the kingdom about one in every five or six beneficed priests was deprived, substantially all for marriage, and of these a certain proportion succeeded in being reconciled and restored. It is probable, therefore, that the list throughout England would not exceed three thousand; but this is sufficient to indicate that the privilege of wedlock had been embraced with considerable eagerness.

The proceedings in the case of John Turner, rector of St. Leonard's, London, would seem to show that the extremity of humiliation was inflicted on these unfortunates. Cited on 16 March to answer to the charge of being a married man, he confessed the accusation, and we find him on 19 March condemned to lose his benefice and be suspended from all priestly functions, to be divorced from his wife, and to undergo such further punishment as the canons required. The sentence of divorce soon followed, and on 14 May he was obliged to do penance in his late church in Eastcheap, holding a lighted candle in his hand and solemnly declaring to the assembled congregation—" Good people, I am come hither, at this present time, to declare unto you my sorrowful and penitent heart, for that, being a priest, I have presumed to marry one Amy German, widow; and, under pretence of that matrimony, contrary to the canons and custom of the Universal Church, have kept her as my wife, and lived contrary to the canons and ordinances of the Church, and to the evil example of good Christian people; whereby now, being ashamed of my former wicked living here, I ask Almighty God mercy and forgiveness, and the whole Church, and am sorry and penitent even from the bottom of my heart therefor. And in token hereof, I am here, as you see, to declare and show unto you my repentance : that before God, on the latter day, you may testify with me of the same. And I most heartily and humbly pray and desire you all, whom by this evil example doing I have greatly offended, that for your part you will forgive me, and remember me in your prayers, that God may give me grace, that hereafter I may live a continent life, according to His laws and the godly ordinances of our mother the holy Catholic Church, through and by His grace. And do here, before you all, openly promise for to do during my life." Such scenes as these were well calculated to produce the effect desired upon the people, but we can only guess at the terrorism which was requisite to force educated and respectable men to submit to such degradation.

All this was done by the royal authority wielding the ecclesiastical power usurped by Henry VIII. Strictly speaking, it was highly irregular and uncanonical, but as the papal supremacy was yet in abeyance, it could not be accomplished otherwise. At last, however, the kingdom was ripe for reconciliation with Rome. In calling the Parliament of 1554, the queen issued a circular letter to the sheriffs commanding them to admonish the people to return members " of the wise, grave, and Catholic sort." Her wishes were fulfilled, and ere the year was out Cardinal Pole was installed with full legatine powers, and Julius III had issued his bull of indulgence, reuniting England to the Church from which she had been violently severed. An obedient Parliament lost no time in repealing all statutes adverse to the claims of the Holy See, but its subserviency had limits, and one class largely interested in the reforms of Henry had sufficient influence to maintain its heretical rights. The Church lands granted or sold to laymen were not restored. Indeed, the queen, in calling the Parliament, had felt it necessary to contradict the rumour that she and Philip intended the " alteration of any particular man's possessions." Though the transactions by which they had been acquired were wholly illegal, though no duration of possession could bar the imprescriptible rights of the Church, yet the nobles and country gentlemen enriched by the spoliation were too numerous and powerful, and the reclamation of the kingdom was too important, to incur any peril by unseasonably insisting on reparation for Henry's injustice. The abbatial manors and rich priories, the chantries, hospitals, and colleges, were therefore left in the impious hands of those who had been fortunate enough to secure them, and the miserable remnants of the religious orders were left to the conscience of the queen, who made haste to get rid of such fragments of the spoil as had been retained by the Crown.

Whatever tacit understanding there may have been on this delicate subject between Queen Mary and Pope Julius was not assented to by the imperious Caraffa, who shortly afterwards ascended the chair of St. Peter. Elected 23 May, 1555, he lost no time in proclaiming the imprescriptible rights of the Church, and by his bull " injunctum nobis," issued 21 June, he pronounced null and void " de apostolicæ potestatis plenitudine " all transactions by which ecclesiastical possessions had passed into the hands of laymen, who were duly threatened with excommunication for prolonged attempts to hold their unhallowed acquisitions. The effort, of course, was fruitless, but the spirit in which the English Protestants watched the apparent opening of a breach between England and Rome is well expressed in a letter of 23 August, 1555, from Sir Richard Morrison to Henry Bullinger : " This anti-Paul, Paul of the apostasy, the servant of the devil, this antichrist newly created at Rome, thinks it but a very small plunder that is offered to him, that he is again permitted in England to tyrannise over our consciences, unless the revenues be restored to the monasteries, that is, the pigsties; the patrimony, as he calls it, of the souls that are now serving in the fifth of purgatory. Our ambassadors, who went to Rome for the purpose of bringing back the wolf upon the sheep of Christ, are now with the Emperor, and bring us these demands of the chief pontiff : God grant that he may urge them in every possible way." The hopes of the reformers, however, were disappointed, for Paul IV gave way, and on the reassembling of Parliament, 23 October, 1555, a bull was read by which the pope assented to the arrangement agreed to by Cardinal Pole, confirming the Church lands to their new possessors.

Cardinal Pole, indeed, was not remiss in giving the sanction of the papal authority to all that had been done. Convoking a synod, he issued in 1555 his Legatine Constitutions, by which all marriages of those included in the prohibited orders were declared null and void. Such apostates were ordered to be separated by ecclesiastical censures and by whatever legal processes might be required; all who dared to justify such marriages or to remain obstinately in their unholy bonds were to be prosecuted rigorously and punished according to the ancient canons, which were revived and declared to be in full force in order to prevent similar scandals for the future. As the queen had decreed by special warrant that all canons adopted by synods should have the full effect of laws binding on the clergy, these constitutions at once restored matters to their pristine condition. It was doubtless in order to mark in the most conspicuous manner his detestation of clerical marriage that Pole descended to the pettiness of ordering the body of Peter Martyr's wife to be dug up from its resting-place, near the tomb of St. Frideswide in Christ's Church, Oxford, and to be buried in a dunghill.

It was easy to pass decrees; it was doubtless gratifying to eject married priests by the thousand and to grant their livings to hungry reactionaries or to the crowd of needy churchmen whom Italy had ever ready to supply the spiritual wants and collect the tithes of the faithful. All this was readily accomplished, but the difficulty lay in overcoming the eternal instincts of human nature. The struggle to effect this commenced at once.

It was, indeed, hardly to be expected that those who had entered into matrimony with the full conviction of its sanctity would willingly abandon all intercourse with their wives, although they might yield a forced assent to the pressure of the laws, the prospect of poverty, and the certainty of infamous punishment. Accordingly, we find that the necessity at once arose of watching the " reconciled " priests, who continued to do in secret what they could no longer practise openly. Some, indeed, found the restrictions so onerous that they endeavoured to release themselves from the bonds of the Church rather than submit longer to the separation from their wives; and this apparently threatened so great a dearth in the ranks of the clergy that Cardinal Pole, as Archbishop of Canterbury, in 1556 forbade the withdrawal of any one from the mysteries and functions of the altar, under pain of the law.

Notwithstanding all this legislation, royal, parliamentary, and ecclesiastical, the question refused to settle itself, and the Convocation which assembled on 1 January, 1557, was obliged to publish an elaborate series of articles, which demonstrated that previous enactments had either not been properly observed, or that they had failed in effecting their purpose. Thus the prohibition of marriage to those in priests' orders was formally renewed. Such of the married clergy who had undergone penance and had been restored, as still persisted in holding intercourse with their separated wives, were to be deprived irrevocably of their office, and only to be admitted to lay communion—thus reversing the policy of Cardinal Pole's injunctions. As all priests who had been married were obnoxious to the people, they were to be removed from the priesthood; or at least, on account of the scarcity of ministers, to act only as curates, and to be incapable of holding benefices until a proper course of penance should have washed away their sins. Even then, in no case were they to officiate in the dioceses wherein they had been married, but were to be removed to a distance of at least sixty miles; and if detected in any intercourse with their wives, they were to incur severe punishment, a single interchange of words being sufficient to call down the penalty. To ensure the observance of these rules, all synods were directed to make special inquiry into the lives of these unfortunates, who were thus to exist under a perpetual surveillance, at the mercy of inimical spies and informers. This may, perhaps, be considered a moderate expiation for men who, in those days of fierce religious convictions, possessed that flexibility of faith which enabled them to change their belief with every dynastic accident.

If the rigid rules now introduced were successful in nothing else, they at all events succeeded in restoring the old troubles with the old canons. Denied the lawful gratification of human instincts, the clergy immediately returned to the habits which had acquired for them so much odium in times past, and the rulers of the Church at once found themselves embarked in the sempiternal struggle with immorality in all its shapes and disguises. If the scandalous chronicles of the period be worthy of credit, neither Gardiner nor Bonner, nor other active promoters of the canons, were without the visible evidences of the frailty of the flesh; and though they were above the reach of correction, the minor clergy were not so fortunate. The Convocation of 1557, which issued the stringent regulations just quoted, was also obliged to promulgate articles concerning the residence of women with priests, and the punishment of licentiousness, similar to those which we have seen reproduced so regularly for ten centuries. Cardinal Pole, too, in his visitation of the same year, directed inquiries to be made on these points in a manner which shows that they were existing and not merely anticipated evils.

Fortunately for the character of the Anglican clergy, the reign of reaction was short. On 17 November, 1558, Queen Mary closed her unhappy life, and Cardinal Pole followed her within sixteen hours. The Marian persecution had been long enough and sharp enough to give to heresy all the attractions of martyrdom, thus increasing its fervour and enlarging its circle of earnest disciples; and the sudden termination of that persecution, before it had time to accomplish its work of extirpation, left the reformers more zealous and dangerous than ever. Heresy had likewise been favoured by the discontent of the people arising from the disastrous and expensive war with France, which aided the improvident restoration of the Church lands in impoverishing the exchequer and in rendering necessary heavy subsidies from the nation, repaid only by cruelty and misfortune. Dread of Spanish influence also had a firm hold of the imagination of the masses, while the Church itself was especially unpopular, as the conviction was general that the ill-success of Mary's administration was attributable to the control exercised by ecclesiastics over the public affairs. Under such auspices the royal power passed into the hands of a princess who, though by nature leaning to the Catholic faith and disposed to tread in the footsteps of her father, was yet placed by the circumstances of her birth in implacable hostility to Rome, and who held her throne only on the tenure of waging eternal warfare with reaction. The reformers felt that the doom of Catholicism was sealed. Emerging from their hiding-places and hastening back from exile, the religious refugees proceeded at once to practise the rites of Edward VI. Elizabeth, however, after ordering some changes in the Roman observances, forbade, on 27 December, all further innovations until the meeting of Parliament, which was convoked for 23 January, 1559.

Parliament assembled on the appointed day, and sat until 8 May. It at once passed Acts resuming the ecclesiastical crown lands and restoring the royal supremacy in ecclesiastical matters, and it repealed all Mary's legislation concerning the power of the papacy. Several other bills were adopted modifying the religion of the kingdom, with a view to discovering some middle term which should unite the people in a common form of belief and worship. Anxious to avoid all extremes, it negatived the measures introduced by the ardent friends of the Reformation, and among the unsuccessful attempts was one which proposed to restore all priests who had been deprived on account of marriage. This, indeed, was laid aside by the special command of the queen herself.

The question of clerical marriage was thus left in a most perplexed and unsatisfactory condition. The Six Articles had been repealed by Edward VI, and had been virtually revived by Mary; but Mary's efforts had been to restore the independent jurisdiction of the Church, and she had therefore not continued to regard the Six Articles as in force, the canons of synods and the legatine constitutions of Pole being the law of her ecclesiastical establishment. This was now all swept away; a statute to fill the void was refused, and men were left to draw their own deductions and act at their own peril. Elizabeth refused the sanction of law to sacerdotal marriage, and would not restore the deprived priests, yet she did not enforce any prohibitory regulations, and even promoted many married men. Dr. Parker, the religious adviser of Ann Boleyn, who had left him in charge of her daughter's spiritual education, was married, and one of Elizabeth's earliest acts was to nominate him for the vacant primacy of Canterbury, which, after long resistance, he was forced to accept. The uncertainty of the situation and the anxiety of those interested are well illustrated by a letter to Dr.

Parker, dated 30 April, just before the rising of Parliament, from Dr. Sandys, afterwards Bishop of Worcester : " The bill is in hand to restore men to their livings; how it will speed I know not. . . . Nihil est statutum de conjugio sacerdotum, sed tanquam relictum in medio. Lever was married now of late. The queen's majesty will wink at it, but not stablish it by law, which is nothing else but to bastard our children." In this Dr. Sandys spoke nothing but truth, and those who were married were obliged formally to have their children legitimated, as even Dr. Parker found it necessary to do this in the case of his son Matthew.

At length Elizabeth made up her mind, and in the exercise of her royal supremacy she asked for no Act of Parliament to confirm her decree. Archbishop Parker has the credit of being the most efficient agent in overcoming her repugnance to the measure, and the ungracious manner in which she finally accorded the permission shows how strong were the prejudices which he had to encounter. In June 1559 she issued a series of " Injunctions to the Clergy and Laity " which restored the national religion to nearly the same position as that adopted by Edward VI, and it is curious to observe that when she comes to speak of sacerdotal matrimony she carefully avoids the responsibility of sanctioning it herself, but assumes that the law of Edward is still in force. All that she does, therefore, is to surround it with such limitations and restrictions as shall prevent its abuse, and although this form had perhaps the advantage of establishing the legality of all pre-existing marriages, yet the regulations promulgated were degrading in the highest degree, and the reason assigned for permitting it could only be regarded as affixing a stigma on every pastor who confessed the weakness of his flesh by seeking a wife.

From the temper of these regulations it is manifest that if Elizabeth yielded to the advice of her counsellors and to the pressure of the times, she did not give up her private convictions or prejudices, and that she desired to make the marriage of her clergy as unpopular and disagreeable as possible. It was probably for the purpose of meeting her objections that the order for a return of the clergy, issued by Archbishop Parker, 1 October, 1561, contained in the blanks issued the unusual entry classifying them as married or unmarried, and Strype informs us that in the Archdeaconry of London the returns show the ministry for the most part to have been filled with married men. Even the haughty spirit of the Tudor thus could not restrain the progress which had now fairly set in. Those around her who controlled the public affairs were all committed to the Reformation, and were resolved that every point gained should be made secure. When, therefore, in 1563, there was published a recension of the Forty-two Articles issued by Edward VI in 1552, resulting in the well-known Thirty-nine Articles of the Church of England, care was taken that the one relating to the liberty of marriage should be made more emphatic than before. Not content with the simple proposition of the original that " bishops, priests, and deacons are not commanded by God's law either to vow the estate of a single life, or to abstain from marriage," the emphatic corollary was added, " Therefore it is lawful for them as for all other Christian men to marry at their own discretion, as they shall judge the same to serve better to godliness "—such as we find it preserved to the present day. This specific declaration in a special article marks the necessity which was felt to place the matter beyond controversy, as a rule of practice. The articles on justification and works of supererogation (Arts. XI and XIX) would have sufficed, so far as principle was concerned.

This was not an empty form. Not only the right to marry at their own discretion, thus expressly declared, did much to relieve them from the degrading conditions laid down by the Queen, but the revival and strengthening of the article marked a victory gained over the reaction. When in 1559 the Queen appointed a commission to visit all the churches of England and enforce compliance with the order of things then existing, the articles prepared for its guidance enjoin no investigation into opinions respecting priestly marriage, showing that to be an open question, concerning which every man might hold his private belief. After the adoption of the Thirty-nine Articles, however, this latitude was no longer allowed. In 1567 Archbishop Parker's articles of instruction for the visitation of that year enumerate, among the heretical doctrines to be inquired after, the assertion that the Word of God commands abstinence from marriage on the part of ministers of the Church. As we shall see, it was about the same time

that the Council of Trent likewise erected the question of
clerical marriage into a point of belief.

Yet Elizabeth never overcame her repugnance to the
marriage of the clergy, nor is it, perhaps, to be wondered
at, when we consider the contempt in which she held the
Church of which she was the head, and her general aversion
from sanctioning in others the matrimony which she was
herself always toying with and never contracting. When
she made her favourites of both sexes suffer for any legalised
indiscretions of the kind, it is scarcely surprising that she
always looked with disfavour on those of the clergy who
availed themselves of the privilege which circumstances
had extorted from her, and which she would fain have
withheld. When Archbishop Parker ventured to remonstrate with her on her popish tendencies, she sharply told
him that " she repented of having made any married
bishops." This was a cutting rejoinder, but even more
pointed was the insolence from which his life-long services
could not protect his wife. The first time the Queen
visited the archiepiscopal palace, on her departure she
turned to thank Mrs. Parker : " And you—madam I
may not call you, mistress I am ashamed to call you, so I
know not what to call you—but, howsoever, I thank you."
So, in Ipswich, in August 1561, she found great fault with
the marriage of the clergy, and especially with the number
of wives and children in cathedrals and colleges—a feeling
possibly justified by occasional disorders not unlikely to
occur. In 1563 we find Sir John Bourne complaining to
the Privy Council that the Dean and Chapter of Worcester
had broken up the large organ, the pride of the cathedral,
which had cost £200; the metal pipes whereof were melted
into dishes and divided among the wives of the prebendaries,
and the case used to make bedsteads for them; the copes
and ornaments, he added, would likewise have been distributed had not some of the unmarried men prevented it,
" and as by their Habit and Apparel you might know the
Priests wives, and by their Gate in the Market and the
Streets from an hundred other Women : so in the Congregation and Cathedral Church they were easy to be
known by placing themselves above all other of the most
ancient and honest Calling of the said City." There was
no lack of persons to pour such stories into the queen's ear,
and, with her well-known tendencies, it is no wonder that

her counsellors found it difficult to restrain her to the simple order which she issued from Ipswich, declaring " that no manner of person, being either the head or member of any college or cathedral church within this realm, shall, from the time of the notification hereof in the same college, have, or be permitted to have, within the precinct of any such college, his wife, or other woman, to abide and dwell in the same, or to frequent and haunt any lodging within the same college, upon pain that whosoever shall do to the contrary shall forfeit all ecclesiastical promotions in any cathedral or collegiate church within the realm." Burghley, in sending this royal mandate to Parker, remarks, " Her Majesty continueth very evil affected to the state of matrimony in the clergy. And if [I] were not therein very stiff, her Majesty would openly and utterly condemn and forbid it. In the end, for her satisfaction, this injunction now sent to your Grace is devised. The good order thereof shall do no harm. I have devised to send it in this sort to your Grace for your province ;- and to the Archbishop of York for his ; so as it shall not be promulgated to be popular." It is doubtless to this occurrence that we may attribute the last relic of clerical celibacy enforced among Protestants, that of the fellows of the English universities.

This injunction of Queen Elizabeth caused no little excitement. Though Burghley had prudently endeavoured to prevent its becoming " popular," yet Cox, Bishop of Ely, in remonstrating against its cruelty to those whom it affected in his cathedral seat, shows that it was speedily known to all men, and that it gave exceeding comfort to the reactionaries : " What rejoicing and jeering the adversaries make ! How the godly ministers are discouraged, I will pass over." In the universities, where crowds of young men were collected, there might be some colourable excuse for the regulation, but in the splendid and spacious buildings connected with the cathedrals some milder remedy might easily have been found, and the mandate was particularly unpalatable to married bishops. Parker himself, who was individually interested in the matter, made a personal appeal to the queen, the result of which was to wound him deeply, as well as to show him how extreme were her prejudices on the subject. He pours forth his feelings in a letter to Burghley describing the interview : " I was in an horror to hear such words to come from her mild nature and Christianly learned conscience, as she spake of God's holy ordinance and institution of matrimony. I marvel that our states in that behalf cannot please her Highness, which we doubt nothing at all to please God's sacred Majesty." He deplores the effect which it must produce on the people : " We alone of our time openly brought in hatred, shamed and traduced before the malicious and ignorant people, as beasts without knowledge to Godward, in using this liberty of his word, as men of effrenate intemperency, without discretion or any godly disposition worthy to serve in our state. Insomuch that the Queen's Highness expressed to me a repentance that we were thus appointed in office, wishing it had been otherwise." The interview had evidently been stormy, and Parker had been made to feel the full force of Elizabeth's perverseness—" I have neither joy of house, land, or name, so abased by my natural sovereign good lady, for whose service and honour I would not think it cost to spend my life "—and he even goes so far as to threaten resistance : " I would be sorry that the clergy should have cause to show disobedience, with *oportet Deo obedire magis quam hominibus*. And what instillers soever there be, there be enough of this contemned flock which will not shrink to offer their blood to the defence of Christ's verity, if it be either openly impugned or secretly suggilled." Evidently, before Parker could have been driven to such scarcely covered threats, there must have been an intimation by the angry queen that she would recall the permission to marry, which, in the existing state of the law, she could readily have done.

The same spirit which rendered the marriage of a pastor dependent on the approbation of the neighbouring squires caused the retention of ancient rules, which prove the profound distrust still entertained as to the discretion and morality of the clergy, and the difficulty with which the Anglican Church threw off the traditions of Catholicism. Thus, even in 1571, Grindal, Archbishop of York, promulgates a modification of the canon of Nicæa, forbidding the residence with unmarried ministers of women under the age of sixty, except relatives closely connected by blood. Indeed, in some remote corners of the kingdom the old licence was kept up. Archbishop Parker, about the year

1565, in speaking of the diocese of Bangor, states : " I hear that diocese to be much out of order, both having no preaching there and pensionary concubinary openly continued, notwithstanding liberty of marriage granted." It evidently required time to accustom the clergy to the substitution of the new privileges for the old.

Although sacerdotal marriage was now fully sanctioned by the organic canon law of the Church, yet it was still exposed to serious impediments of a worldly character. When thus frowned upon by her who was in reality, if not in name, supreme head of the Church ; when the wife of the primate himself could be exposed to such indelible impertinence ; when the marriage of every unfortunate parson was subjected to degrading conditions, and when it was assumed that his bride must be a woman at service, the influences affecting the matrimonial alliances of the clergy must have been of the worst description. The higher classes of society would naturally model their opinions on those of the sovereign, while the lower orders had not as yet shaken off the prejudices in favour of celibacy implanted in them by the custom of centuries. Making due allowance for polemical bitterness, there is therefore no doubt much truth in the sarcastic account which Sanders gives of the wives of the Elizabethan clergy. Taking advantage of the refusal of Parliament to formally legalise such marriages—a refusal which could not but greatly affect the minds of the people—he assumes that the wives were concubines and the children illegitimate in the eyes of the law ; consequently decent women refused to undergo the obloquy attached to a union with a minister of the Church, who was therefore forced to take as his spouse any one who would consent to accept him. The wives of prelates were ostracised ; not received at court, and sharing in no way the dignities of their husbands, they were kept closely at home for the mere gratification of animal passion. The members of universities had been wholly unsuccessful in their efforts to obtain the same licence, which was only granted to the heads of colleges, under condition that their wives should reside elsewhere, and should rarely pollute with their presence the learned precincts.

The accuracy of this sarcastic description is confirmed by a statement made by Percival Wiburn for the benefit of his friends in Zurich, subsequent to the adoption of the

Thirty-nine Articles. He asserts that " the marriage of priests was counted unlawful in the times of Queen Mary, and was also forbidden by a public statute of the realm, which is also in force at this day; although by permission of Queen Elizabeth clergymen may have their wives, provided only they marry by the advice and assent of the bishop and two justices of the peace, as they call them. The lords bishops are forbidden to have their wives with them in their palaces; as are also the deans, canons, presbyters, and other ministers of the Church, within colleges, or the precincts of cathedral churches." It is not a little curious, indeed, to observe that, in spite of the formal declaration in the Thirty-nine Articles, the absence of a special Act of Parliament long caused the question to remain a doubtful one in the public mind. As late as July 1566, Lawrence Humphrey and Thomas Sampson, two zealous Protestants, in denouncing " some straws and chips of the popish religion " which still defaced the Anglican Church, state that " the marriage of the clergy is now allowed and sanctioned by the public laws of the kingdom, but their children are by some persons regarded as illegitimate "; in answer to which, Bishops Grindal and Horn rejoined that " the wives of the clergy are not separated from their husbands, and their marriage is esteemed honourable by all, the papists always excepted." The matter evidently was still regarded as a subject of controversy, not yet decided beyond appeal; and the experience of the previous quarter of a century had accustomed men to too many vicissitudes for them to feel safe with so slender a guarantee as the Articles afforded. The Catholics still constituted a very large proportion of the population, and they scarcely concealed their feelings towards the innovation. When Sir John Bourne quarrelled with Dr. Sandys, Bishop of Worcester, among the formal articles of accusation which he presented to the Privy Council was the assertion that the Bishop in a sermon had ridiculed celibacy and had decried the virtue of unmarried priests. The knight apparently believed that this would be damaging to the bishop, and the latter seems likewise to have thought so, for in his answer he emphatically denied it, retorting that his adversary was a papist who had Mass celebrated in his house and who was in the habit of applying the most opprobrious epithets to the wives of priests. So when in 1569 the Catholics of the North rose in insurrection under the Earls of Westmorland and Northumberland, one of the grievances of which they complained was the marriage of the ministers of Christ. During the whole of this transition period the question was evidently one which occupied largely the public mind, and in the diversity of opinion it was not easy to see what the ultimate decision might be. When an irrevocable step such as marriage was legal only during the pleasure of a capricious woman, whose assent was known to have been extorted from her, it is no wonder that it should be looked upon with disfavour by all prudent relatives of women inclined to venture on it.

Such a state of feeling could not but react most injuriously on the character of the great body of the clergy. It deprived them of the respect due to their sacred calling, and consequently reduced them to the level of such scant respect as was accorded to them. How long this lasted, and how materially it degraded the ministers of Christ as a body, cannot be questioned by any one who recalls the description of the rural clergy in the brilliant third chapter of Macaulay's " History of England." In 1686 an author complains that the rector is an object of contempt and ridicule for all above the rank of the neighbouring peasants ; that gentle blood would be held polluted by any connection with the Church, and that girls of good family were taught with equal earnestness not to marry clergymen, nor to sacrifice their reputation by amorous indiscretions— two misfortunes which were commonly regarded as equal.

Thus eagerly accepted and grudgingly bestowed, the privilege of marriage established itself in the Church of England by connivance rather than as a right ; and the evil influences of the prejudices thus fostered were not extinguished for generations.

CHAPTER XXVII

CALVINISM

IN the easy toleration which preceded the Reformation, Luther's precursor, Jacques Lefèvre d'Etaples, in 1512 published his Commentaries on the Pauline Epistles. The work was a significant portent of the era about to open. For the first time the traditional scholastic exegesis was cast aside for a treatment in which tradition was rejected and independent judgment was exercised as a matter of right. As in so much else, the full import of this was not recognised until the Lutheran revolt showed the necessity of strict adherence to the ancient ways and of shackling human thought with additional rigour. It was not until after Luther's condemnation by the Sorbonne, in 1521, that the Commentaries were censured and twenty-five heretical errors were discovered in them; even then the favour of Francis I protected their author from the prosecution commenced against him in 1523. Many a hardy thinker had been burnt for less. Lefèvre denied justification by either faith or works, for God alone justifies; religious Orders only awaken pride and imperil Christian love—it would be better that there were none, but, while they exist, monks should work with their hands, as did the apostles; confession and forgiveness of sins were originally mutual between brethren—the modern custom is due to the absence of faith, but Christ may accept it; celibacy in itself is better than marriage, but priests and deacons were permitted to marry until the time of Gregory VII; the Greek Church has retained the apostolic custom of marriage, while the other Churches adopted celibacy, whereby many, through incontinence, fall into the snares of the devil.

The seed thus scattered fell into fruitful soil, and as early as 1525, Clement VII, in a brief addressed to the Regent Louise of Savoy, enumerates among the "Lutheran" errors spreading through France the stigmatising of the

canons enjoining clerical celibacy as Satanic. By the time
when Jean Calvin formulated the system of theology which
bears his name, sacerdotal marriage had thus everywhere
become recognised as one of the inevitable incidents of the
revolt against Rome, and that the French Huguenots
should accept it was therefore a matter of course.

Calvin himself manifested his contempt for all the ancient
prejudices by marrying, in 1539, Idelette de Bure, the
widow of the Anabaptist Jean Stordeur, whom he had
converted. The Huguenot Confession of Faith was drawn
up by him, and was adopted by the first national synod,
held at Paris in 1559. Of course the Genevan views of
justification swept away all the accumulated observances
of sacerdotalism, and ascetic celibacy shared the fate of the
rest. The discipline of the Calvinist Church with regard
to the morality of its ministers was necessarily severe. The
peculiar purity expected of a pastor's household was shown
by the rule which enjoined any Church officer whose wife
was convicted of adultery to dismiss her absolutely, under
pain of deposition, while laymen, under such circumstances,
were exhorted to be reconciled to their guilty partners.
Any lapse from virtue on the part of a minister was visited
with peremptory deposition; nor was this a mere idle
threat, such as were too many of the innumerable decrees
of the Catholic councils quoted above, for the proceedings
of various synods show that it was carried sternly into
execution. A list of such vagrant and deposed ministers
was even kept and published to the churches, with personal
descriptions of the individuals, that they might not be able
to impose on the unwary. Indeed, the national synod of
Lyons, in 1563, went so far as to punish those ministers
who brought contempt upon the Church by unfitting
marriages; and, though this was omitted from the final
code of discipline, it shows the exceeding strictness with
which the internal economy of the ecclesiastical establishment of the Huguenots was regulated.

The relations of the Catholic Church with its apostates
were somewhat confused, and they varied with the political
exigencies of the situation. Ecclesiastics who left the
Catholic communion did not hesitate to enter into matrimony; and when the desolation of civil war rendered
a forced tolerance of the new religion necessary, their
position was a source of considerable debate, varying with

the fluctuations of the tangled politics of the time. The Edict of Pacification of Amboise, in March 1562, was held by the Huguenots to legalise the marriages of these apostates, but the explanatory declaration of August 1563 ordered their reclamation by the Church under pain of exile. When the Spanish alliance gave fresh assurances of triumph to the Catholics, this was enforced with increased severity. The Edict of Roussillon, in 1564, commands that all priests, monks, and nuns who had abandoned their profession and entered into matrimony shall sunder their unhallowed bonds and return to their duties. Recalcitrants were required to leave the kingdom within two months, under pain, in the case of men, of condemnation to the galleys for life, and in that of women, of perpetual imprisonment. As most of the Calvinist ministers necessarily belonged to the class thus assailed, the effect of this legislation in stimulating the troubles of the kingdom can readily be perceived.

The dismal strife of the succeeding ten years at length showed that, in spite of the Tridentine canons, the toleration of this iniquity was a necessity. Thus in the Edicts of Pacification issued by Henry III in 1576 and 1577 there is a provision which admits as valid the marriages theretofore contracted by all priests or religious persons of either sex. The issue of such unions was declared competent to inherit the personalty of the parents and such realty as either parent might have acquired, but was incapable of other inheritance, direct or collateral.

The Church was obliged to submit to this temporising tolerance of evil, and condescended to entreaty, since force was no longer permitted. In 1581 the Council of Rouen, while deploring the number of monks and nuns who had left their convents, apostatised, and married, directs that they shall be tempted back, treated with kindness, and pardon be sought for them from the Holy See. In the final settlement of the religious troubles, the concessions made by Henry III were renewed and somewhat amplified by the Edict of Nantes in 1598. When the reaction came, however, these provisions were held to be only retrospective in their action, and were not admitted as legalising subsequent marriages. Thus in 1628 a knight of Malta, in 1630 a nun, and in 1640 a priest of Nevers, who had embraced Calvinism, ventured on matrimony, but were separated from their spouses and the marriages were pronounced null. These decisions were based on the principle that the celibacy of ecclesiastics was prescribed by municipal as well as by canon law, and that a priest in abjuring his religion did not escape from the obligations imposed upon him by the laws of the kingdom.

In Scotland, as in France, the question of sacerdotal marriage may be considered as having virtually been settled in advance. Lollardry had not been confined to the southern portion of Great Britain. It had penetrated into Scotland, and had received the countenance of those whose position and influence were well calculated to aid in its dissemination among the people. In 1494, thirty of these heretics, known as "the Lollards of Kyle," were prosecuted before James IV by Robert Blacater, Archbishop of Glasgow. Their station may be estimated from the fact that they escaped the punishment due to their sins by the favour of the monarch, "for divers of them were his great familiars." The thirty-four articles of accusation mostly charged them with Wickliffite tendencies, and their views on the question of celibacy are manifested in the twenty-second article, which accuses them of asserting "that Priests may have wives according to the constitution of the Law and of the Primitive Christian Church."

The soil was thus ready for the plough of the Reformation; while the temper of the Scottish race gave warrant that when the mighty movement should reach them, it would be marked by that stern and uncompromising spirit which alone could satisfy conscientious and fiery bigots, who would regard all half-measures as pacts with Satan. Nor was there lacking ample cause to excite in the minds of all men the desire for a sweeping and effectual reform. Corruption had extended through every fibre of the Scottish Church as all-pervading as that which we have traced throughout the rest of Christendom.

Not long after the year 1530, and before the new heresy had obtained a foothold, William Arith, a Dominican, ventured to assail the vices of his fellow-churchmen. In a sermon preached at St. Andrews, with the approbation of the heads of the universities, he alluded to the false miracles with which the people were deceived, and the abuses practised at shrines to which credulous devotion was invited. " As of late dayes," he proceeded, " our Lady of Karsgreng hath hopped from one green hillock to another : But, honest men of St. Andrewes, if ye love your wives and daughters, hold them at home, or else send them in good honest company; for if ye knew what miracles were wrought there, ye would thank neither God nor our Lady." In another sermon, arguing that the disorders of the clergy should be subjected to the jurisdiction of the civil authorities, he introduced an anecdote respecting Prior Patrick Hepburn, afterwards Bishop of Murray. That prelate once, in merry discourse with his gentlemen, asked of them the number of their mistresses, and what proportion of the fair dames were married. The first who answered confessed to five, of whom two were bound in wedlock; the next boasted of seven, with three married women among them; and so on until the turn came to Hepburn himself, who, proud of his *bonnes fortunes*, declared that although he was the youngest man there, his mistresses numbered twelve, of whom seven were men's wives. Yet Arith was a good Catholic, who, on being driven from Scotland for his plain speaking, suffered imprisonment in England under Henry VIII for maintaining the supremacy of the pope.

How little concealment was thought requisite with regard to these scandals is exemplified in the case of Alexander Ferrers, which occurred about the same time. Taken prisoner by the English and immured for seven years in the Tower of London, he returned home to find that his wife had been consoled and his substance dissipated in his absence by a neighbouring priest, for the which cause he not unnaturally " spake more liberally of priests than they could bear." By this time heresy was spreading, and severe measures of repression were considered necessary. It was therefore not difficult to have the man's disrespectful remarks construed as savouring of Lutheranism, and he was accordingly brought up for trial at St. Andrews. The first article of accusation read to him was that he despised the Mass, whereto he answered, " I heare more Masses in eight dayes than three bishops there sitting say in a yeare." The next article accused him of contemning the sacraments. " The priests," replied he, " were the most contemnors of the sacraments, especially of matri-

mony." "And that he witnessed by many of the priests
there present, and named the man's wife with whom they
had meddled, and especially Sir John Dungwaill, who had
seven years together abused his own wife and consumed
his substance, and said: because I complain of such
injuries, I am here summoned and accused as one that is
worthy to be burnt: For God's sake, said he, will ye take
wives of your own, that I and others whom ye have abused
may be revenged on you." Old Gawain Dunbar, Bishop
of Aberdeen, not relishing this public accusation, sought to
justify himself, exclaiming, "Carle, thou shalt not know
my wife"; but the prisoner turned the tables on him,
"My lord, ye are too old, but by the grace of God I shall
drink with your daughter or I depart." "And thereat
there was smiling of the best and loud laughter of some,
for the bishop had a daughter married with Andrew Balfour
in that town." The prelates who sat in judgment found
that they were exchanging places with the accused, and,
fearful of further revelations from the reckless Alexander,
commanded him to depart; but he refused, unless each one
should contribute something to replace the goods which
his wife's paramour had consumed, and finally, to stop his
evil tongue, they paid him and bade him be gone.

All prelates, however, were not so sensitive. When
Cardinal Beatoun, Archbishop of St. Andrews, primate of
Scotland, and virtual governor of the realm, about the
year 1546 married his eldest daughter to the eldest son of
the Earl of Crawford, he caused the nuptials to be celebrated with regal magnificence, and in the marriage articles,
signed with his own hand, he did not hesitate to call her
"my daughter." It is not difficult, therefore, to credit the
story that the night before his assassination was passed
with his mistress, Marion Ogilby, who was seen leaving
his chamber not long before Norman Leslie and Kirkaldy
of Grange forced their way into his castle. His successor
in the see of St. Andrew, John Hamilton, was equally
notorious for his licentiousness; and men wondered, not
at his immorality, but at his taste in preferring to all his
other concubines one whose only attraction seemed to be
the zest given to sin by the fact that she was the wife of
one of his kindred.

This is testimony from hostile witnesses, and we might
perhaps impugn their evidence on that ground, were it not

that the Catholic Church of Scotland itself admitted the abandoned morals of its members when the rapid progress of Calvinism at length drove it in self-defence to attempt a reform which was its only chancé of salvation. In the last Parliament held by James V before his death in 1542, an Act was passed exhorting the prelates and ecclesiastics in general to take measures " for reforming of their lyvis, and for avoyding of the opin sclander that is gevin to the haill estates throucht the spirituale mens ungodly and dissolut lyves." Nothing was then done, in spite of this solemn warning, though the countenance afforded to the Reformers by the Regent Arran, strengthened by his alliance with Henry VIII, was daily causing the heresy to assume more dangerous proportions. When, therefore, the Catholic party, rallying after the murder of Cardinal Beatoun, at length triumphed with the aid of France, and sent the young Queen of Scots to marry Francis II, they seemed to recognise that they could only maintain their advantage by meeting public opinion in endeavouring to reform the Church. Accordingly, in November 1549, a council was convoked at Edinburgh, of which the first canon declares that the licentiousness of the clergy had given rise to the gravest scandals, to repress which the rules enjoined by the Council of Bâle must be strictly enforced and universally obeyed. The second canon is no less significant in ordering that prelates and other ecclesiastics shall not live with their illegitimate children, nor provide for them or promote them in the paternal churches, nor marry their daughters to barons by endowing them with the patrimony of Christ, nor cause their sons to be made barons by the same means.

This was of small avail. Ten years afterwards, the progress of heresy becoming ever more alarming, another council was held, in March 1559, to devise means to put a stop to the encroachments of the enemy. To this assembly the Catholic nobles addressed an earnest prayer for reformation. After alluding to the proceedings of the Parliament of 1542, they add, " And siclyk remembring in diverss of the lait provinciale counsales haldin within this realm, that poynt has been treittet of, and sindrie statutis synodale maid therupon, of the quhilks nevertheless thar hes folowit nan or litill fruitt as yitt, bot rathare the said estate is deteriorate . . . it is maist expedient therefore that thai presentlie condescend to seik reformation of thir lyvis . . . and naymlie that oppin and manifest sins and notor offencis be forborn and abstenit fra in tyme to cum." In this request they had been anticipated by the Reformers, who the previous year, in a supplication addressed to the Queen-regent, included among their demands " That the wicked, slanderous, and detestable life of Prelats and of the State Ecclesiasticall may be reformed, that the people by them have not occasion (as of many dayes they have had) to contemne their Ministrie and the Preaching whereof they should be Messengers."

The council, thus urged by friend and foe, recognised the extreme necessity of the case, and did its best to cure the immedicable disease. Its first canon reaffirmed the observance of the Bâle regulations, and appointed a commission empowered to enforce them; and, that nothing should interfere with its efficiency, the Archbishops of St. Andrews and Glasgow made a special renunciation of their exemption from the jurisdiction of the council. The second canon, in forbidding the residence of illegitimate children with their clerical fathers, endeavoured to procure obedience to the rule ordered by the council of 1549, by permitting it for four days in each quarter, and by a penalty for infractions of £200 in the case of an archbishop, £100 in that of a bishop, and leaving the mulct to be imposed on inferior ecclesiastics at the discretion of the officials. The third canon prohibited the promotion of children in their fathers' benefices, and supplicated the Queen-regent to obtain of the pope that no dispensations should be granted to evade the rule. The fourth canon inhibited ecclesiastics from marrying their daughters to barons and lairds, and endowing them with Church lands, or making their sons barons or lairds with more than £100 annual income, under pain of fine to the amount of the dowry or lands abstracted from the Church; and all grants of Church lands or tithes to concubines or children were pronounced null and void.

When such legislation was necessary, the disorders which it was intended to repress are acknowledged in terms admitting neither of palliation nor excuse. The extent of the evil especially alluded to in the latter canons is further exemplified by the fact that during the thirty years immediately following the establishment of the Reformation in Scotland more letters of legitimation were taken

out than were issued in the two subsequent centuries.
These were given to the sons of the clergy who were
allowed to retain their benefices, and who then made over
the property to their natural children.

Such being the state of morals among the ministers
of the old religion, it is easy to appreciate the immense
advantage enjoyed by the Reformers. They made good
use of it. Knox loses no opportunity of stigmatising the
" pestilent Papists and Masse-mongers " as " adulterers and
whoremasters," who were thus perpetually held up to the
people for execration, while the individual wrongs from
which so many suffered were noised about and made the
subject of constantly increasing popular indignation. Yet
the abrogation of celibacy occupies less space in the history
of the Scottish Reformation than in that of any other
people who threw off the allegiance to Rome.

The remote position of Scotland and its comparative
barbarism rendered it in some degree inaccessible to the
early doctrines of Luther and Zwingli. Before it began
to show a trace of the new ideas, clerical marriage had long
passed out of the region of disputation with the Reformers,
and was firmly established as one of the inseparable results
of the doctrine of justification professed by all the reformed
Churches. Not only was it thus accepted as a matter of
course by all the converts to the new faith, but that faith,
when once introduced, spread in Scotland with a rapidity
proportioned to the earnest character of the people. The
permission to read the Scriptures in the vulgar tongue,
granted by Parliament in 1543, doubtless had much to do
with this; the leaning of the Regent Arran to the same
side gave it additional impetus, and the savage fierceness
with which the Reformers were prepared to vindicate their
belief is shown by the murder of Cardinal Beatoun, which
was countenanced and justified by Knox himself. Powerful
nobles soon saw in it the means of emancipating themselves from the vacillating control of the Regent; nor was
the central authority strengthened when, in 1554, the reins
of power were wrested from the feeble Arran and confided
to the queen-dowager, Mary of Guise, who found herself
obliged to encourage each party by turns, and to balance
one against the other, to prevent either Catholic or Calvinist
from obtaining control over the state. Then, too, as in

Germany and England, the temporal possessions of the Church were a powerful temptation to its destruction. From the great Duke of Chatelleraut to the laird of some insignificant peel, all were needy and all eager for a share in the spoil. When, in 1560, an assembly of the nobles at Edinburgh listened to a disputation on the Mass, and the Catholic doctors were unable to defend it as a propitiatory sacrifice, the first exclamation of the lords revealed the secret tendencies of their thoughts : " We have been miserably deceived heretofore ; for if the Mass may not obtain remission of sins to the quick and to the dead, wherefore were all the Abbies so richly doted and endowed with our Temporall lands ? "

Of course, less selfish purposes were put forward to enlist the support of the people. On 1 January, 1559, when the storm was gathering, but before it had burst, the inmates of the religious houses found affixed to their gates a proclamation in the name of " The Blinde, Crooked, Lame, Widows, Orphans, and all other Poor, so visited by the hand of God as cannot work," ordering the monks to leave the patrimony intended to relieve the suffering, but usurped by indolent shavelings, giving them until Whit-Sunday to make their exit, after which they would be ejected by force, and ending with the significant warning : " Let him, therefore, that hath before stolen, steal no more, but rather let him work with his hands that he may be helpfull to the poore."

Such a cry could hardly fail to be popular, but when the threat was carried into execution, the blind and the crooked, the widow and orphan received so small a share of the spoil that they were worse off than before. As we have already seen in England, the destruction of the Scottish monasteries was the commencement of the necessity of making some public provision for paupers. The nobles seized the lion's share ; the rest fell to the crown, subject to the payment of the very moderate stipends assigned to the comparatively few ministers required by the new establishment, and these stipends were so irregularly paid that the unfortunate ministers were frequently in danger of starvation, and were constantly besieging the court with their dolorous complaints. Where the lands and revenues went is indicated with grim humour by Knox, in describing the resistance offered in 1560 to the adoption of his Book of Discipline by those who had professed great zeal for the Lord Jesus. Lord Erskine had been one of the first and most consistent of the " Lords of the Congregation," yet he also refused to sign the book— " And no wonder, for besides that he had a very evill woman to his wife, if the Poore, the Schooles, and the Ministerie of the Church had their owne, his Kitchin would lack two parts and more of that which he unjustly now possesseth."

Yet, when compared with the rich abbatial manors of England or the princely foundations of Germany, the spoil of the Church was mean indeed. Knox had resided much abroad, and had seen the vast wealth which the piety of ages had showered upon the Church in the most opulent lands of Europe, yet his simplicity or fanaticism finds source of wondering comment in the homespun luxury of the unfortunate monks whom he assisted in dispossessing. When the destruction of the monasteries (1559) commenced by a brawl in Perth, caused by a sermon preached by Knox, and three prominent convents were broken up, he expatiates on the extravagance revealed to sight : " And in very deed the Grey-Friers was a place so well provided that unless honest men had seen the same, we would have feared to have reported what provision they had, their sheets, blankets, beds and coverlets were such that no Earle in Scotland had better : Their naperie was fine ; they were but 8 persons in the Convent, and yet they had 8 puncheons of salt beef (consider the time of the yeere, the eleventh of May), wine, beere, and ale, beside store of victuals belonging thereto." Imagine an abbot of St. Albans or an abbess of Poissy reduced to the coverlets and salt beef which the stern Calvinist deemed an indulgence so great as to be incredible !

Still, in so impoverished a country as the Scotland of that period even these poor spoils were a motive sufficient to prove a powerful aid to the conquering party in the struggle. And yet, amid all the miserable ambitions of the Erskines and Murrays, the Huntleys and Bothwells, who occupied the prominent places in the court and camp, we should do grievous wrong to the spirit which triumphed at last over the force and fraud of the Guises, if we attributed to temporal motives alone the movement which expelled licentious prelates and drove Queen Mary to the fateful refuge of Fotheringay. The selfish aims of the nobles would have been fruitless but for the zealous earnestness of the people, led by men of iron nature, who doubted themselves as little as they doubted their God, and who, in the death-struggle with Antichrist, were as ready to suffer as they were ruthless to inflict. Nor can the disorders of the Catholic clergy be rightly imputed to the temperament of the race, for the Reformers, who carried with them so large a portion of the middle and lower classes, preached a system of rigid morality to which the world had been a stranger since the virtues of the Germanic tribes had been lost in the overthrow of the Empire; and they not merely preached it, but obtained its embodiment in a code of repressive laws which their vigilant authority strictly enforced.

I have said above that the question of celibacy appears but rarely in the course of the contest, yet, notwithstanding the causes which rendered it a less prominent subject of debate than elsewhere, it occasionally rises to view. The first instance of clerical marriage that I find recorded occurred in 1538, when Thomas Coklaw, parish priest of Tillibodie, married a widow of the same village named Margaret Jameson. This, however, was not done openly and defiantly, as in Germany, but in secret, and the married couple continued to dwell apart. That the infraction of the canons was not without danger was shown by the result, for, when it became known, Coklaw was tried by the Bishop of Dunblane and condemned to perpetual imprisonment; but his relatives broke open his dungeon, and he escaped to England. When, early in the following year, a group of Reformers, including Dean Thomas Forret, Friar John Killore, Friar John Beverege, and others, were put on trial, their presence at this wedding was one of the crimes for which they were executed upon Castle Hill at Edinburgh. In fact, the abrogation of the rule of celibacy, in Scotland as elsewhere, was necessarily one of the leading points at issue between the Reformers and the Catholics. Thus, when George Wishart, one of the early heretics who ventured openly to preach the Lord Jesus, was seized, in spite of powerful protectors, and after a prolonged captivity was brought for trial before Cardinal Beatoun in 1545, in the accusation against him Article 14 asserted, " Thou false Hereticke hast taught plainly against

the Vows of Monks, Friers, Nuns, and Priests, saying,
That whosoever was bound to such like Vows, they vowed
themselves to the state of damnation. Moreover, That it
was lawfull for Priests to marry wives and not to live sole."
Wishart tacitly confessed the truth of this impeachment by
rejoining, " But as many as have not the gift of chastity,
nor yet for the Gospel have overcome the concupiscence of
the flesh, and have vowed chastity; ye have experience,
although I should hold my tongue, to what inconveniences
they have exposed themselves." He was accordingly
condemned as an incorrigible heretic, and promptly burnt.
Yet when, in 1547, John Knox held his disputation with
Dean Wynrame and Friar Arbuckle, though the nine
articles drawn up for discussion ranged from the supremacy
of the pope and the existence of purgatory to the payment
of tithes, the subject of vows of chastity was not even
mentioned.

Still, as late as 1558 the trial of Walter Mill shows that
the question was even yet agitated in the controversies
between the polemics of the two parties. Mill had been
a priest, and had married, and the first of the articles of
accusation against him was that he asserted the lawfulness of sacerdotal marriage. To this he boldly assented,
declaring that he regarded matrimony as a blessed bond,
open for all men to enter, and that it were better for priests
to marry than to vow chastity and not preserve it, as they
were wont to do. Condemned to the stake, the unfortunate
old man commanded the sympathies of the people, even
in the archiepiscopal town of St. Andrews. No one could
be found to act as executioner, until at length one of the
servants of the archbishop consented to fill the abhorrent
office; but when a rope was sought with which to bind the
wretched sufferer to the stake, no one would furnish it,
and the tragedy was necessarily postponed. Equally
unsuccessful was the next day's search, until the archbishop,
fearing to lose his victim, gave the cords of his own pavilion,
and the sentence was carried into effect. Even after the
sacrifice, the popular feeling was manifested by raising a
pile of stones as a monument on the place of torture, and as
often as these were cast aside by the priests they were
replaced by the people, until the followers of the archbishop
carried them off by night, and used them for building.

These incidents show us that the question received its

share of attention in the controversy by which each side endeavoured to secure the support of the nation, but it makes no appearance in public negotiations and declarations. Thus, in 1558, when the growing strength of the Lords of the Congregation led the Catholics to offer concessions, which were rejected by the conscious power of the Reformers, there was no allusion to celibacy on either side. In fact, between the respective leaders the questions were almost purely personal and political, while among the conscientiously religious supporters of either party opinions were too rigidly defined for argument. Convictions were too divergent and too firm for compromise or concession to be possible, and Catholic and Calvinist grimly recognised, as by a tacit understanding, the alternative of extermination. When the English alliance at last drove the Catholics to the wall, and in July 1560 there assembled the Parliament to which by the Articles of Leith was referred the duty of effecting a settlement of the kingdom, the vanquished party made no struggle against their fate. Such Catholic prelates and lords as took their seats refrained from all debate, and allowed the victors to arrange the temporal and spiritual affairs of the kingdom at their pleasure.

In this settlement, our subject affords a curious comparison between the English and Scotch Churches. In the former, at a period even later than this, it was considered necessary to embody a renunciation of celibacy in the organic law, which has been maintained to the present day. In the latter, ecclesiastical marriage had become already so firmly established in the minds of the Reformers that it was accepted as a matter of course, which needed no special confirmation. Although laws were passed prohibiting the Mass and abolishing the supremacy of the pope, none was thought necessary to legalise the marriages of the clergy. Even in Knox's Confession of Faith, adopted by Parliament on 17 July, there is no direct allusion to the matter. The only passage which can be construed as having any bearing upon it occurs in Chapter XIV, when considering " What works are reputed good before God " : " And evill works we affirme not onely those that are expressly done against God's commandment, but those also that in matters of religion and worshipping of God have no assurance, but the invention and opinion of man, which

God from the beginning hath ever rejected, as by the prophet Isaiah and by our Master Christ Jesus we are taught in these words—*In vain do they worship me, teaching doctrines which are precepts of Men.*"

Nothing more, in fact, was needed when the triumph of the new ideas was so complete that Knox could exultingly exclaim, "For what Adulterer, what Fornicator, what known Masse-monger or pestilent Papist durst have been seen in publike within any Reformed Town within this Realme before that the Queen arrived? . . . For while the Papists were so confounded that none within the Realme durst avow the hearing or saying of Masse then the thieves of Tiddisdale durst avow their stouth or stealing in the presence of any upright judge." When persecution thus had changed sides, no minister could feel that his nuptials required special authorisation. How thoroughly, indeed, they were legitimated is shown by a curious little incident occurring in 1563. A minister named Baron made complaint to the General Assembly that his wife, an English woman named Anne Goodacre, "after great rebellions by her committed," had left him and taken refuge in England, whereupon he requested the Assembly to have her brought back to him. Spotswood, the Superintendent of Lothian, with Knox and Craig, actually wrote to Archbishop Parker officially asking him to have the woman sought for and sent to Scotland; but Parker, considering it to be an international question and beyond his sphere, prudently referred the request to Secretary Cecil.

It were foreign to our object to enter into the dark details of Mary's short and disastrous reign. The intrigues of the camarilla, the boyish weakness of Darnley, the subtlety of Rizzio, and the coarse ambition of Huntley and Bothwell, were alike harmless against the earnest reverence of the people for the new faith; and the expiring struggles of Catholicism were too feeble to give any practical importance to the vain attempts at reaction.

CHAPTER XXVIII

THE COUNCIL OF TRENT

IT has already been observed that the dissolute and un-Christian life of the priesthood was one of the efficient causes which led to the success of the Reformation. At an early period in the movement, the Catholic Church felt the necessity of purifying itself, if it was to retain the veneration of the people; and the veneration of the people was now not merely a source of revenue, but a condition of the very existence of the stupendous structure of Latin Christianity. As soon as it became clearly apparent that Lutheranism was not to be suppressed by the ordinary machinery, and that it was spreading with a rapidity which portended the worst results, an effort was made to remove the reproach which incorrigible immorality had entailed upon the Church. Allusion has been made above to the stringent measures of reform proclaimed by the legate Campeggio at Ratisbon in 1524, in which he acknowledged that the new heresy had no little excuse in the detestable morals and abandoned lives of the clergy—a truth repeatedly admitted by the ecclesiastical authorities. His well-meant endeavours had little result, and we have seen that, some years later, Erasmus still urged the abolition of the rule of celibacy as the only practicable mode of removing the scandal.

Not long afterwards the Gallican Church made a strenuous effort of the same nature to check the spread of Lutheranism. In 1521, before it had to encounter a hostile heresy, the Council of Paris had deplored the pervading corruptions with exceeding candour. The condition of conventual discipline was such as to threaten the very existence of the system, and the customary denunciations of ineradicable abuses were freely published. In 1528 the Cardinal-legate Duprat, Chancellor of France, held a council in Paris, where he condemned, seriatim, the new doctrines as heresies, and elevated the rule of celibacy to the dignity of a point of faith. He also caused the adoption of a series of canons designed to remove from the Church the disgrace caused by the laxity of clerical morals and manners. The bishops were instructed to enforce the decrees of the councils and of the fathers until concubinage and incontinence should be completely exterminated, and a rule was laid down which would have been eventually effectual if conscientiously carried out. No one was thereafter to be admitted to holy orders without written testimony as to his age and moral character from his parish priest, substantiated by the oaths of two or three approved witnesses. At the same time similar councils were held at Bourges by the Cardinal Archbishop Tournon, and at Lyons by Claude, Bishop of Macon. To what extent these excellent rules were put in force may be guessed by a description of the French clergy in 1560, as portrayed by Monluc, Bishop of Valence, in a speech before the Royal Council. The parish priests were for the most part engrossed in worldly pursuits, and had obtained their preferment by illicit means, nor did there seem much prospect of an improvement so long as the prelates were in the habit of bestowing the benefices within their gift on their lackeys, barbers, cooks, and other serving-men, rendering the ecclesiastics as a body an object of contempt to the people. We need therefore not be surprised to find in the councils of the period a repetition of all the old injunctions, showing that the maintenance of improper consorts and the disgrace of priestly families were undiminished evils. This description of the French clergy is most emphatically extended to the whole Church in the project for reformation drawn up by order of Paul III in 1583, and to these evils are attributed the innumerable scandals which afflicted the faithful, as well as the contempt in which the ecclesiastical body was held and the virtual extinction of all reverence for the services of religion. No improvement, however, was to be expected as long as a concubinary priest could obtain from the papal chancery for seven *gros tournois* letters of absolution and dispensation which specially set aside the decrees of bishops and local councils.

In 1530 Clement VII addressed himself vigorously to the task of putting an end to the scandalous practice of hereditary transmission of benefices, which he describes as almost universal. A special bull was issued, prohibiting the children of priests or monks from enjoying any preferment in their father's benefices, and, recognising that the Roman Curia was one of the chief obstacles to all reform, he provided that if he or his successors should grant dispensations permitting such infraction of the canons, they should be considered as issued unwittingly, and be held null and void. Like so many others, this bull seems to have been forgotten almost as soon as issued, and the pecuniary needs of the Roman court rendered it unable to abandon so lucrative a source of revenue. Even as soon as 1538 the cardinals to whom Paul III committed the task of drawing up the project of reformation cautiously intimate that they hear of such dispensations being granted, and to this they attribute a large share of the troubles of the Church and the enmity felt towards the Holy See. This warning passed unheeded, and, as we have seen, in 1559 a Scottish council prayed the queen-regent to use her influence with the pope to prevent dispensations being granted to enable illegitimate children to hold preferment in their fathers' benefices, while in 1562 the frequency and readiness with which such dispensations were still obtained are enumerated in a list of abuses laid before the Council of Trent by Sebastian, King of Portugal, as one of the matters requiring reformation by the supreme power of the council. To this and similar appeals the papal legates loftily replied that laws were not to be prescribed to the Holy See; and the motive for the refusal is easily comprehended when we see that in the "Taxes of the Penitentiary" the price for a dispensation admitting the bastard of a priest to holy orders was a ducat and a carlino.

In Spain, Ribadeneira, the disciple of Ignatius Loyola, tells us that the priestly concubines were accustomed to pledge their faith to their consorts as if united in wedlock, and that they wore the distinguishing costume of married women, as though glorying in their shame, which so scandalised St. Ignatius on his return, in 1535, to his native land, that he exerted his influence with the temporal authorities to procure the enactment and enforcement of sundry laws which relieved the Spanish Church of so great an opprobrium. We may reasonably, however, doubt the success of his efforts. Some ten years later, Alphonso de Castro asserts that the priesthood was one of the efficient causes of the spread of heresy, and that it would be difficult for orthodoxy to maintain itself without the direct interposition of God, in view of the scandalous lives and general worthlessness of all orders of ecclesiastics, whose excessive numbers, turpitude, and ignorance exposed them to contempt. His contemporary, the canon lawyer Bernardius Déaz de Luzo, indeed, finds in the universality of concubinage a reason for its partial condonation, for, while deploring its frequency, he warns judges not to be over-severe in its repression, since so few are found guiltless, and there is danger that those who are restrained from it may be forced into darker sins. How difficult, under such circumstances, was any reform may be gathered from a memorial presented in 1556 to Philip II, by Inquisitor-General Valdés. He relates that when he became Archbishop of Seville, in 1546, he found the clergy and the dignitaries of the cathedral so demoralised that they had no shame in their children and grandchildren : their women lived with them openly, as though married, and accompanied them to church, while many kept in their houses public gaming-tables, which were the resort of disorderly characters. To remedy these evils he instituted vigorous measures of reform, but in this he was greatly impeded and put to much expense by appeals and suits in Rome and in Granada, and in the Royal Council and before apostolic judges. In view of the facility with which absolutions and dispensations could be procured, it is easy to see how readily a persistent reformer could be embroiled with the Holy See.

About the same time, Herman von Wied, Archbishop of Cologne, undertook the reformation of his extensive diocese. He assembled a council, which issued a series of 275 canons, prescribing minutely the functions, duties, and obligations of all grades of the clergy. As regards the delicate subject of concubinage, he contented himself with quoting the Nicene canon prohibiting the residence of women not nearly connected by blood, and added that if the degeneracy of the times prevented the enforcement of a regulation so strict, at all events he forbade the companionship of females obnoxious to suspicion. The good archbishop himself could hardly have expected that so mild an allocution would have much effect upon a perverse and hardened generation, but custom had so established itself that even the loftiest prelates shrank from encountering the risk attendant upon an attempt to enforce the canons. This is seen when, in 1537, Matthew,

Archbishop of Salzburg, assembled his provincial synod, which, recognising the urgent necessity of preserving the Church and protecting the people, adopted a series of reformatory decrees. Afraid of promulgating them, it resolved to suppress them for the present, under the pretext that the approaching General Council would regulate the discipline of the Church at large; and the archbishop contented himself with a pastoral letter addressed to his suffragans, in which he urged upon them to consider the contamination to which the laity were exposed through the vices of their pastors, and timidly suggested that if the clergy could not restrain their passions, they should at all events indulge them secretly, so that scandal might be avoided and the punishment of their transgressions be left to an avenging God.

This timidity finds its explanation in the report by the papal nuncio Morone of an interview, in 1542, with the Archbishop of Mainz, on the subject of the reform of the clergy, which was acknowledged to be the pressing question of the hour. The archbishop flatly admitted his impotence; until the Council should be held no reformation was possible. Priestly concubinage, he said, could not be suppressed without great scandals—in fact, persuasion was the only course open, for the clergy of Mainz, Trèves, and Cologne had formed so strong an organisation for mutual defence that they would all rise in resistance if the least of them were prosecuted.

In the Council of Trent itself, the Bishop of St. Mark, in opening its proceedings with a speech, 6 January, 1546, drew a fearful picture of the corruption of the world, which had reached a degree that posterity might possibly equal but not exceed. This he assured the assembled fathers was attributable solely to the wickedness of the pastors, who drew their flocks with them into the abyss of sin. The Lutheran heresy had been provoked by their own guilt, and its suppression was only to be hoped for by their own reformation. At a later session, the Bavarian orator, August Baumgartner, told the assembled fathers that the progress of the Reformation was attributable to the scandalous lives of the clergy, whose excesses he could not describe without offending the chaste ears of his auditory. He even asserted that out of a hundred priests there were not more than three or four who were not either married or concubinarians—a statement repeated in a consultation on the subject of ecclesiastical reform drawn up in 1562 by order of the Emperor Ferdinand, with the addition that the clergy would rather see the whole structure of the Church destroyed than submit to even the most moderate measure of reform.

It is not to be wondered at, therefore, that the Christian world had long and earnestly demanded the convocation of an Œcumenic council which should represent all parties, should have full powers to reconcile all differences, and should give to the ancient Church the purification thus recognised as the only efficient means of healing the schism. This was a remedy to the last degree distasteful to the Holy See. The recollections of Constance and Basle were full of pregnant warnings as to the almost inevitable antagonism between the Vicegerent of Christ and an independent representative body, believing itself to act under the direct inspiration of the Holy Ghost, claiming autocratic supremacy in the Church, and convoked for the special purpose of reforming abuses the most of which were fruitful sources of revenue to the papal court. Such a body, if assembled in Germany, would be the pope's master; if in Italy, his tool; and it behoved him to act warily if he desired to meet the unanimous demand of Christendom without risking the sacrifice of his most cherished prerogatives. Had the council been called in the early days of the Reformation, it could hardly have prevented the separation of the Churches; yet, in the temper which then existed, it would probably have effected as thorough a purification of the ecclesiastical establishment as was possible in so corrupt an age. By delaying it until the reactionary movement had fairly set in, the chances of troublesome puritans gaining the ascendancy were greatly diminished, and the papal court exposed itself to little danger when, under the urgent pressure of the Emperor, it at length, in 1536, proposed to convoke the long desired assembly at Mantua.

A place so completely under papal influence was not likely to meet the views of the opposition, and it is not surprising that both the Lutherans and Henry VIII refused to connect themselves with such a council. The latter, indeed, in his epistle of 8 April, 1538, to Charles V, expressed himself more forcibly than elegantly : " Nowe, if he [the pope] calle us to one of his owne townes, we be afraid to be at suche an hostes table. We saye, Better to ryse a hungred, then to goo thense with oure bellyes fulle." The formality of its opening, 17 May, 1537, was therefore an empty ceremony; its transfer to Vicenza was little more; and, as no delegates presented themselves up to 1 May, 1538, it was prorogued until Easter 1539, with the promise of selecting a satisfactory place for the meeting. The pressure still continued until, in May 1542, Paul finally convoked it to assemble at Trent. The Reformers were no better satisfied than before. They had so long professed their readiness to submit all the questions in dispute to a free and unbiassed general council that they could not refuse absolutely to countenance it; but they were now so completely established as a separate organisation that they had little to hope and everything to fear from the appeal which they had themselves provoked, and nothing which Rome could now offer would have brought them into willing attendance upon such a body. They accordingly kept aloof, and on the assembling of the council, 22 November, 1542, its numbers were so scanty that it could accomplish nothing, and it was accordingly suspended in July 1543. When again convoked, 15 March, 1545, but twenty bishops and a few ambassadors were present; these waited with what patience they might command for accessions, which were so tardy in arriving that when at length the assembly was formally opened, on 13 December, the number had increased by only five. For fifteen months the council continued its sessions, completely under the control of the pope, and occupied for the most part with formulating as Catholic doctrine the speculations of the schoolmen, which thus far had been generally accepted without authoritative confirmation save incidentally at the Council of Florence in 1439. As these constituted the principal dogmas against which the Reformation was a protest, the labours of the fathers were directed, not to effect a reunion of the Church, but to erect an impassable barrier between Latin and Reformed Christianity.

The appeals of the German bishops and of the imperial ambassadors for some effective efforts at reform became at length too pressing, and to evade them, in March 1547, the council was transferred to Bologna, against the earnest protest of the Emperor and the Spaniards, who refused to follow. At Bologna little was done except to dispute over the sharp protests of the emperor and to adjourn the council from time to time, until, after falling into universal contempt, it was suspended in 1549. Julius III, who received the tiara on 22 February, 1550, signalised his accession by convoking it again at Trent; and there it once more assembled on 1 May, 1551.

At that time Lutheranism in Germany was under the heel of Charles V; Maurice of Saxony was ripening his schemes of revolt, and concealing them with the dexterity in which he was unrivalled; it was the policy of both that Protestant theologians should take part in the discussions— of the one, that they should there receive their sentence; of the other, that their presence might assist in cloaking his designs. The flight from Innsbruck, followed by the Transaction of Passau, changed the face of affairs. The Lutheran doctors rejoicingly shook the dust from their feet as they departed from Trent, complaining that they had been treated as criminals on trial, not as venerable members of a body assembled to decide the gravest questions relating to this life and that to come. Other symptoms of revolt among the Catholic nations were visible, and on 28 April, 1552, the council again broke up.

Ten years passed; the faithful impatiently demanded the continuation of the work which had only been commenced, and at last the pressure became so strong that Pius IV was obliged to reassemble the council. His bull bears the date November 1560, but it was not until twenty years after Trent had witnessed the first convocation that the holy men again gathered within its walls, and on 18 January, 1562, the council resumed its oft-interrupted sessions. The states of the Augsburg Confession had been politely invited to participate in the proceedings, but they declined with the scantiest of courtesy.

During these long-protracted preliminaries there were times when those who sincerely desired the restoration of the Church could not restrain their impatience. In 1536, Paul III, who earnestly admitted the necessity of some reform, called to his aid nine of his prelates most eminent for virtue and piety, as a commission to prepare a scheme for internal reformation. According to a papal historian, his object in this was to stop the mouths of the heretics who found in the Roman court an inexhaustible subject of declamation. For two years the commission laboured at its work, and finally produced the " Consilium de emendanda ecclesia," to which allusion has been made above.

The stern and unbending Cardinal Caraffa was head of the commission, assisted by such men as Contarini, Sadoleto, and Reginald Pole. They seem to have been inspired with a sincere desire to root out the chief abuses which gave such power to the assaults of the Protestants, and the result of their labours affords us a picture of ecclesiastical corruptions almost as damaging to the Church as the complaints of the Diet of Nürnberg. As regards celibacy, they were disposed to make no concession; indeed, they protest against the facility with which men in holy orders were able to purchase from the Roman Curia dispensations to marry. It is significant, however, that they had so little confidence in the possibility of purifying the conventual religious Orders that they actually recommended their abolition. To prevent individual cases of suffering, they proposed that the convents should not be immediately abolished, but that all novices should be discharged and no more be admitted, thus allowing the Orders to die out gradually, as had been done in Saxony; and meanwhile they urged that, to prevent further scandals, all nunneries should be removed from the supervision and direction of monks, and be handed over to the ordinaries. The " Consilium," in fact, was so candid a confession of most of the abuses charged upon the Church by the reformers that Luther forthwith translated it and published it with a commentary, as an effective pamphlet in aid of his cause. Caraffa himself, after he had attained the papacy, under the name of Paul IV, quietly put his own work, in 1559, into the Index Librorum Prohibitorum.

However earnest Paul may have been, the changes recommended in the " Consilium " attacked too many vested interests for even the papal power to give it effect. The project therefore was dropped, and only resulted in rendering still more clamorous the call for a reform in the head and members of the Church. As, moreover, it had shown the powerlessness of the papacy to overcome acknowledged abuses, the only hope of a radical change, such as was needful, was seen to lie in the untrammelled debates of a great assembly, which should meet as a parliament of the nations; and the prospect of this grew more and more distant. While the project of transferring the council from

Trent was being matured, it occurred to the papal court that possibly the objections to that measure and the pressure on the council for a thorough reformation might be averted by showing a disposition on the part of Rome to undertake the task of cleansing the Augean stable. It was also recognised as an important gain if the council could be confined to the harmless task of defining questions of faith, while the substantial powers involved in reforming the corruptions of the Church could be claimed and exercised by the pope. Accordingly Pius III drew up an elaborate bull designed to limit some of the more flagrant pecuniary abuses which existed, and exhorting the bishops to correct the morals of their subordinates. This was sent to the legates at Trent, but they and their confidants unanimously agreed that, in the existing temper of the council, the promulgation of such a document would be in the highest degree imprudent. It was accordingly suppressed, and only saw the light in the nineteenth century. In its failure the Church lost but little, for it touched the evils of the time with a tender and hesitating hand, and would have proved utterly inefficacious.

At length, when shortly afterwards the unmannerly urgency of the Germans, clamouring for decided measures of reform, was met by the translation of the council to Bologna in 1547, and men despaired of further results from it, Charles V resolved to take the matter into his own hands, and to effect, for his own dominions at least, that which had been vainly expected of the council for Christendom. The "Interim," which has already been alluded to, was intended to answer this purpose, as far as Lutheranism was concerned, in healing the breach of religion. The other great object of the council, the restoration of the neglected discipline of the Church, he attempted to effect by means of the secular authority of the empire acting on the regular machinery of the Teutonic ecclesiastical establishment. How utterly neglected that discipline had become is inferable from an expression in the important and carefully drawn project which had been laid by Charles before the Diet of Ratisbon in 1541, to the effect that if the canon requiring celibacy was to be enforced, it would be necessary also to revive those canons which punished incontinence, thus admitting that there existed no check whatever upon either priestly marriage or immorality.

To accomplish this desirable revival of discipline he

accordingly caused the adoption by the Diet of Augsburg of a code of reformation, well adapted, if enforced, to restore the long-forgotten purity of the Church, while at the same time it acknowledged that the degeneracy of the times rendered impossible the resuscitation of the ancient canons in their strictness. Thus, after reciting the canon of Neocæsarea (see p. 17), it adds that, as such severity was now impracticable, those in holy orders convicted of impurity should be separated from their concubines, and visited with suspension from function and benefice proportioned to the gravity of the offence. A repetition of the fault was punishable with increased severity, and incorrigible sinners who were found to be incapable of reformation were finally to be deprived of their benefices. As concubines were threatened with immediate excommunication, it is evident that a severity was designed towards them which was not ventured on with respect to their more guilty partners. Relaxation of the rules is also observable in the section which, despite the Nicene canon, permitted the residence of women over forty years of age, whose character and conduct relieved them from suspicion. The imperative injunctions of chastity laid upon the regular clergy, canons, and nuns show not only the determination to remove the prevailing scandals, but also the magnitude and extent of the evil.

Nor was this all. Local councils were ordered for the purpose of embodying these decrees in their statutes and of carrying out with energy the reformation so earnestly desired. Thus, in November 1548, about five months after the diet, a synod assembled at Augsburg, which inveighed bitterly against the unclerical dress and pomp of the clergy, their habits of drunkenness, gluttony, licentiousness, tavern-lounging, and general disregard of discipline; and adopted a canon embracing the regulations enacted by the Emperor. The Archbishop of Trèves did not wait for his synod, but issued, 30 October, a mandate especially directed against concubinary priests, in which he announced his intention of carrying out the reform commanded by Charles. He could find no reason more self-evident for the dislike and contempt felt by the people for so many of the clergy than the immorality of their lives, differing little, except in legality, from open marriage. " This vice, existing everywhere throughout our diocese, in consequence of the licence of the times and the neglect of the officials, we must eradicate. Therefore all of you, of what grade soever, shall dismiss your concubines within nine days, removing them beyond the bounds of your parishes, and be no longer seen to associate with loose and wanton women. Those who neglect this order shall be suspended from office and benefice, their concubines shall be excommunicated, and they themselves be brought before our synod to be presently held."

These were brave words, but when, some three weeks later, the synod had assembled, and the malefactors had perchance been brought before it, the good bishop apparently found that his flock was not disposed to submit quietly to the curtailment of privileges which had almost become imprescriptible. His tone accordingly was softened, for though he deprecated their immorality more strongly than ever, and asserted his intention of enforcing his mandate, he condescended to argue at much length on the propriety of chastity, and even descended to entreaty, beseeching them to preserve the purity so essential to the character of the Church, the absence of which had drawn upon the clergy an odium which could scarce be described in words. How slender was his success may be inferred from the fact that the next year he felt it necessary to hold another synod, in which he renewed and confirmed the proceedings of the former one, and endeavoured to reduce the monks and nuns of his diocese to some kind of subjection to the rules of discipline.

The Archbishop of Cologne was as energetic as his brother of Trèves, with about equal success. On 1 September he issued the Augsburg Formula of Reformation, with a call for a synod to be held on 2 October. At the same time he manifested his sense of the primary importance of correcting clerical immorality by promulgating a special mandate respecting concubinage. He asserted this to be the chief cause of the contempt popularly felt for the Church, and he ordered all ecclesiastics to send their women beyond the bounds of their parishes within nine days, under the penalties provided in the imperial decree. The synod was held at the time indicated, and, though it adopted no regular canons, it accepted the Augsburg Formula and the mandate of the archbishop, with a trifling alteration.

This proved utterly ineffectual, for in March 1549 he assembled a provincial council, in which he deplored the licence of the times, which rendered the strictness of the ancient canons unadvisable, and he announced that it had been decided to proceed gradually with the intended reforms. As to the morals of the clergy, he stated that everywhere the cure of souls was delegated to improper persons, many of them living in the foulness of concubinage, in perpetual drunkenness, and in other infamous vices, encouraged by the negligence of bishops and the thirst of archdeacons for unhallowed gains. The unions of those who, infected by the new heresies, did not hesitate to enter into matrimony, were of course pronounced illicit and impious, their offspring illegitimate, and the parents anathematised; but for those who remained in the Church, yet submitted to no restraint upon their passions, a more merciful spirit was shown, for the punishments ordered by the Diet of Augsburg were somewhat lightened in their favour. The extreme licence of the period may be understood from another canon directed against the comedians, who, not content with the ordinary theatres, were in the habit of visiting the nunneries, where their profane plays and amatory acting excited to unholy desires the virgins dedicated to God. No one acquainted with the coarseness of the drama of that rude age can doubt the propriety of the archbishop's reproof. Supplementary synods were also held, in October 1549 and February 1550, to perfect the details of a very thorough inquisitorial visitation of the whole province.

This visitation, so pompously heralded, did not take place. At a synod held in October 1550 the archbishop made sundry lame excuses for its postponement. Another synod was assembled in February 1551, at which we hear nothing more of it; but the prelates of the diocese were requested to collect such ancient and forgotten canons as they could find, which might be deemed advantageous in the future; and with this the work of reformation in the province of Cologne appears to end.

In 1549, Ernest, Archbishop of Salzburg, assembled the synod of his extensive province, but when his clergy understood that it was intended to confirm the reformatory edict of the emperor, they had the audacity to present a petition praying that the clause ordering the removal of their concubines should not be enforced. They declared that the attempt to do so would be attended with serious difficulty, and that it would lead to greater evils than it sought to remove, and they asked that the consideration of the matter should be referred to the general council, the re-assembling of which was no longer dreaded. The synod, with a proper sense of its dignity, refused to receive the shameless petition, and listened rather to those of its members who complained of the practice of the officials in receiving bribes for permitting illicit indulgences, and the representations of Duke William, of Bavaria, who asserted that the Lutheran heresy had been caused by the scandalous corruption of the Church. A canon was accordingly adopted which renewed the regulations of Basle and ordered the speedy removal of all recognised and notorious concubines.

In October and November 1548, and April 1549, the Bishops of Paderborn, Wurzburg, and Strassburg held synods which adopted the reformatory measures decreed at Augsburg. These were preparatory to the metropolitan synod of Mainz, assembled in May 1549, which commanded that no one should thereafter be admitted to orders without a preliminary examination by his bishop on the subject of doctrine and testimonials from the people as to purity of character. After thus wisely providing for the future, attention was directed to the present. It was declared intolerable that, in spite of the reiterated prohibitions of the fathers and councils, concubines should be universally kept; the Basilian canon was therefore revived, and its enforcement strictly enjoined on the ordinaries, who were forbidden in any manner to connive at these disorders for the sake of profit.

The pressure was continued, for when Cambrai, which owed temporal obedience to the emperor, while ecclesiastically it formed part of the province of Rheims, neglected to adopt the Formula of Augsburg for two years, it was not allowed to escape. In October 1550 a synod was finally assembled there under stringent orders from Charles, and the Formula was published, together with an elaborate series of canons which would have been well adapted to correct abuses that were not incorrigible.

Charles had thus exerted all the resources of his imperial supremacy, and, whether willingly or not, the powerful prelates who ruled the German Church had united in carrying out his views. The temporal and spiritual authorities had thus been concentrated upon the vices of the Church, and if its reformation had been possible, in the existing condition of its organisation, some improvement must have resulted from these combined and persistent efforts. How nugatory were the results may be guessed from a memorial presented in 1558, by the University of Louvain, to Philip II, exhorting him to grant no toleration to the heretics, but at the same time urging upon him the absolute necessity of some comprehensive system of reform to purify the Church, all the orders of which were given over utterly to the twin vices of avarice and licentiousness. The same testimony is borne by a consultation drawn up in 1562 by order of the Emperor Ferdinand. After alluding to the efforts at reform made by Paul III and Charles V, it declares that their only result has been to make the condition of clerical morality worse than before, exciting the hatred of the people for their priests to an incredible pitch, and doing more to inflame the ardour of heresy than all the teaching of Christian truth can do to restrain it.

As the failure of all efforts to improve clerical morality under the existing rules of discipline was thus found to be complete, there arose in the minds of thinking men a conviction, such as Erasmus had already declared, that, since all other measures had proved fruitless, the only mode of securing a virtuous clergy was to remove the prohibition of marriage. At the Polish Diet of 1552 petitions praying for sacerdotal matrimony were presented, and, though they failed in their object, the Diet of 1556 authorised King Sigismund Augustus to address Paul IV with a request, in the name of the nation, to grant it as well as communion in both elements.

The dissension thus existing within the Church is exhibited in a volume published in 1558 by Stanislas Hosius, Bishop of Ermeland earnestly arguing against communion in both elements, clerical marriage, and the use of the vulgar tongue in worship. As regards celibacy, he assumes that it had been maintained unbrokenly for fifteen hundred years, and was not now to be abandoned to gratify a few disorderly monks. The example of the Greek Church he meets by pointing out that the Greeks were suffered to be persecuted by the Turks; the argument that marriage would purify the Church he silences with the observation that many married men are adulterers; and he holds it to be a doubting of

God to suppose that the gift of continence would be denied to those who properly seek it. In spite of the logic of polemics such as Hosius, the opinions of the innovators continued to gain ground, until at length they won over even the highest dignitaries of the empire, and in 1560 the Emperor Ferdinand himself undertook their advocacy with the pope, after having for some years countenanced the practice within his own territories.

Almost immediately on the consecration of Pius IV, in addressing to him an argument for the reassembling of the Council of Trent or the convocation of a new council, Ferdinand seized the opportunity to ask especially for the communication of the cup to the laity and permission for the clergy to marry. The latter of these points he considered to be the only remedy for the fearful immorality of the Church, for, though all flesh was corrupt, the corruption of the priesthood surpassed that of all other men. That he had not waited for the papal assent to favour these innovations within his own dominions is shown by his statement that the Archbishop of Salzburg had recently, in a synod, earnestly called upon him to put a stop to the progress which they were making, but, he added, his long experience in such matters had shown him what was possible and what impossible, and he had accordingly set forth the difficulties of the task in a paper addressed to the archbishop, a copy of which he enclosed to the pope.

The nuncio Commendone, in transmitting this document to Rome, accompanied it with a letter from the Cardinal Bishop of Augsburg, recommending the postponement of the question until the reassembling of the Council of Trent, and, as Pius answered it in this sense, no further action was taken, though Ferdinand made haste to repeat his demand, in view of the impatience of both clergy and people, who could ill brook the delays inseparable from the discussion of the subject in so unwieldy a body. When Commendone, moreover, passed through Cleves on his way to the council, then about to be reopened, the Duke of Cleves earnestly besought him to lend his influence to the accomplishment of the measure, urging as a reason that in the whole of his dominions—and he was sovereign of three populous duchies—there could not be found five priests who did not keep concubines. In order to secure his favour for the approaching council, Commendone did not scruple to hold out expectations that the concessions would be granted.

During the progress of the Reformation, when the fate of the Catholic Church of Germany had sometimes seemed to hang in the balance, no princes had earned a larger title to the gratitude of Rome than the powerful Dukes of Bavaria, who were the leaders of the reaction. Yet now the influence of that important region was thrown in favour of the abrogation of celibacy, and Duke Albert was the first who boldly brought the matter before the council by a demand for ecclesiastical marriage, presented on 27 June, 1562. To this the evasive answer was returned that the council would take such action as would be found to redound to the glory of God and to the benefit of the Church. During the same year the Emperor Ferdinand also repeatedly urged its consideration. A plan for the reform of the Church presented by his delegates not only called attention to the necessity of purifying the morals of the regular and secular clergy, but demanded that, to some nations at least, the privilege of sacerdotal marriage should be conceded. Another elaborate paper argued the question with much temperate force, and declared that many priests had already married for the purpose of escaping the corruptions of celibacy, while studiously preserving themselves from the errors of Lutheranism. Out of a hundred parish priests scarcely once could be found who was not either openly or secretly married, and it was necessary to tolerate them to prevent the utter destruction of the Church.

A third document is extant, without date, which was laid before the cardinals of the papal court by the emperor, in which the question was argued at considerable length and with much vehemence. After asserting that, from the records of the primitive Church, celibacy was not then recognised as imperative, it proceeded to declare that, if marriage ever were permissible, the present carnal and licentious age rendered it a necessity, for not one Catholic priest out of fifty could be found who lived chastely. All were asserted to be notoriously dissolute, scandalising the people and inflicting great damage on the Church. The request was made not so much to satisfy the priests who desired marriage as to meet the wishes of the laity, for many patrons of livings refused presentation to all but married men. However preferable a single life might be for the clergy, it therefore was thought better to give it up than to leave open the door to the scandalous impurities traceable to celibacy. Another weighty reason was alleged in the great scarcity of priests, caused alone by the prohibition of marriage, in proof of which it was urged that the Catholic schools of divinity were all but empty and the episcopal function of ordination nearly disused, while the Lutheran colleges were crowded by those who subsequently obtained admission into the true Church, where they worked incredible mischief. The argument that the temporal possessions of the Church would be imperilled by sacerdotal matrimony was met by indignantly denouncing the worldly wisdom which would protect such perishable interests at the cost of innumerable souls sacrificed by the existing condition of affairs. For these and other reasons, it asked that marriage should in future be allowed to all the priesthood, whether already in orders or to be subsequently admitted; that married men of good character and education should be ordained to supply the want of pastors; that those who had contracted matrimony, in contravention of the canons, should no longer be ejected, seeing that it was most absurd to turn out men because they were married, while retaining notorious concubinarians, and that if, with equal justice, both classes should be dismissed, the people would be left almost, if not entirely, destitute of spiritual guides. The paper concluded by asserting that if the prayer be granted, the clergy could be retained in the Church and in the faith, to the great benefit of their flocks, and that the scandal of promiscuous licentiousness, which had involved the Church in so much disgrace, would be removed.

This vivid sketch of the condition of the Church, with the evils which were everywhere felt, and the remedies which suggested themselves to clear-sighted and impartial men, was as ineffectual as similar efforts had been, for to all such arguments the Council of Trent was deaf. France, too, was more than willing to see celibacy abolished. M. de Lanssac, the French ambassador, was ordered to place himself in close relations with the representatives of the emperor, and to unite with them in seeking the relaxation of all regulations which tended to prevent the reunion of the Protestants, while the Gallican bishops were commanded to show themselves reasonable and yielding in such matters : and when Lanssac reported the demands of the emperor, comprehending clerical marriage among other changes, Charles IX assented to them in terms of warm commendation. The Cardinal of Lorraine, moreover, was instructed to urge some measures efficient to reform the licentious lives of the ecclesiastics, which spread corruption and debauchery among the people, while permission for priestly marriage was recommended as one of the means essential to recall the heretics to the bosom of the true Church. As a compromise, however, the French prelates contented themselves with suggesting that none but elderly men should be eligible to the priesthood, and that the testimony of the people in favour of their moral character should be a prerequisite to ordination, in hopes that by such means the necessary purification of the clergy at least could be effected, while the sharpest measures should be adopted to punish their licentiousness.

All this was useless, and, in fact, it is difficult to imagine how any one could expect a reform of this nature from a body composed of prelates all of whom were obliged by Pius IV, in a decree of 4 September, 1560, to solemnly swear to a profession of faith containing a specific declaration that the vows of chastity inferred on entering into holy orders, or assumed in embracing monastic life, were to be strictly observed and enforced. The question thus was prejudged, and the council was more likely to listen to Bartholomew à Martyribus, the Archbishop of Bracara, who laid before it a paper containing the points which, in his opinion, required reformation, among which were the revival of the canons respecting concubinary bishops and priests, the prohibition of sons succeeding to their fathers' benefices, and the excommunication of confessors who debauched their fair penitents—though when the sturdy archbishop in a stormy debate declared that "illustrissimi cardinales egent illustrissima reformatione," he doubtless was held to be a most uncourtly and impracticable reformer.

Despite all the urgency from without, it was not until 8 February, 1563, after the council had been in session for more than a year, that the theologians at last arranged for disputation the articles on matrimony, and laid them before the council for discussion. They were divided into five classes, of which the fourth was devoted to the bearing of the subject on the clergy, consisting of two propositions—

the fifth and sixth—artfully drawn up to justify rejection, while preserving the appearance of presenting the subject for deliberation—That matrimony was preferable to celibacy, and that God bestowed grace on the married rather than on the single.—That the priests of the Western Church could lawfully contract marriage, notwithstanding the canons; that to deny this was to condemn matrimony, and that all were at liberty to marry who did not feel themselves disgraced with the gift of chastity.

The disputation on the various questions connected with matrimony commenced the next day, and was continued at intervals for six months. Meanwhile, there were negotiations on foot between Rome and Vienna, negotiations complicated by various factors. The pope and the Curia were wrathful at the reforms enacted and projected by the council, and were anxious to dissolve it at any cost, while the Emperor Ferdinand was resolved to prolong its sessions until he should obtain his desires. Then he had had his son Maximilian, King of Bohemia, elected as King of the Romans, 24 November, 1562, sorely against the will of Pius IV, who had vainly threatened to deprive the Lutheran electors of their votes and then secretly to restore them on condition of their electing Philip II of Spain. Failing in this, as the Holy See claimed the right of confirming the election, he demanded that Maximilian should take an oath practically of allegiance to Rome, which was naturally refused. Maximilian, in fact, had long been suspected of Lutheran proclivities; in 1557 we find him described as keeping a married Lutheran preacher, while the most influential members of his court were Lutherans, and he felt the necessity of friendly relations with the Lutheran princes, whose support against the Turk was indispensable. The ecclesiastical electors (Mainz, Trèves, and Cologne) had hesitated to give him their votes till they had assurances which satisfied them, but not the more incredulous Curia. Philip II seems to have had no aspirations for the imperial crown, but he was fanatically opposed to any concessions to the heretics, whether these concerned the use of the cup or priestly marriage, and through his representatives at Rome and Trent he ceaselessly brought to bear against them the utmost weight of his great influence.

Our knowledge of the moves in this complicated game is but fragmentary. We hear of a letter, in April 1562, in which Ferdinand claims priestly marriage as a thing promised to him by Pius in order to have an end put to the council, and other letters in which he threatens that if his requests are denied he will assemble a national council and proclaim an Interim worse than that of Charles V; or else that Germany would withdraw from the Roman obedience, as there was no other remedy to satisfy his people. These threats greatly troubled the pope, who begged Philip to send to Germany a personage of importance to represent that if Ferdinand separated himself from the Holy See he would become a heretic and his children would be incapacitated from inheriting his dominions. Not relying on Philip's intervention, in May he sent Cardinal Morone ostensibly as legate to the council, but with instructions to tarry there only twenty-four hours, and hasten to Vienna. In reporting this to Philip, his ambassador, Vargas, expresses the liveliest apprehensions that it would result in the concession of the cup to the laity and marriage to priests, so earnestly demanded by the Germans and French, for the pope had shown himself so yielding and so inclined to make the grant, and he could readily control the council if he did not care himself to take the responsibility of what would set the world ablaze. What terms were reached between Ferdinand and Morone it is impossible to say, but that a bargain was concluded was generally understood. In fact, in March 1564 Pius admitted in consistory that he had made promises to Ferdinand in order to hasten the dissolution of the council. Possibly it was in concert with this that, as reported in August 1563 by the nuncio Delfini from Vienna, the three ecclesiastical electors, the Archbishop of Salzburg, and the Duke of Bavaria held a conference, in which it was resolved to unite with the emperor in an appeal for bulls permitting priestly marriage and communion in both elements. In pursuance of this, early in September Ferdinand wrote to his ambassadors at Trent that he had called together in Vienna the deputies of the electors and princes of the empire, who, after mature deliberation, had determined to ask these concessions of the pope and not of the council. He enclosed a protocol of the demand, but as it was not fully settled, it was to be communicated to no one but to Philip's ambassador, the Count of Luna, whereupon Philip persuaded him to withhold it until after the council should be dissolved. A further move in the game, with the same purpose, was a promise, later in the autumn, by Pius, that when the council should be out of the way he would send a legate, with full powers to dispense in the matters of the cup, of clerical marriage, and of the retention of Church lands, while Maximilian should treat with the Protestants for their return to the Church under these concessions.

Evidently the honest Germans were ill fitted to cope with Italian diplomacy. Relying on papal promises, they held their hands off from the council, which enabled the pope to control it absolutely through his legates. Accordingly it went on its accustomed way to render the breach with Protestantism as impassable as possible. Pallavicini doubtless correctly represents its views when he remarks, concerning the princes who exerted themselves to secure sacerdotal marriage, that they seemed to consider that the council had been convoked for the purpose not of condemning but of contenting the heretics, whom they proposed to convert by gratifying in place of repressing their contumacious desires.

The result of thus skilfully shielding the council from all pressure from Germany and France was that the question of retaining sacerdotal celibacy was prevented from becoming the subject of serious debate. This, indeed, was a foregone conclusion. In the minute account, transmitted from day to day by Archbishop Calini to Cardinal Cornaro, in which all the details of internal discussion and external intrigue attainable by a quick-witted member of the council were reported, there is no allusion to the matter. No debates or diversity of opinion are mentioned, no intimation that the matter was regarded as open to a doubt, and even the appeals made by the emperor and other potentates are passed over in silence, for the very sufficient reason that the papal legates, who controlled all the business of the council, refused to allow them to be read. In their reply to the emperor's remonstrances, indeed, they declared that to have such a subject publicly broached in the council would create a fearful scandal throughout Christendom, and Pius IV approved of their answer as the best that could be given. It is no wonder, therefore, that in the correspondence of the nuncio Visconti the only allusion to the matter is a simple reference, under date of 22 March, 1563, to the demand previously made by the Duke of Bavaria.

In fact, when, on March 4, the 5th and 6th articles were reached, they were both unanimously pronounced heretical without any prolonged debate. Doctor Juan de Ludeña pronounced a " disputation " on the subject, the tone of which showed that the result was already decided, and that the only disposition of the council was to vilify those who desired the abrogation of celibacy. A discussion, however, then arose as to the power of the pope to dispense the clergy, both regular and secular, from the obligation of celibacy, and on this point there was considerable diversity of opinion, occupying numerous successive meetings in its settlement. The majority were in favour of the papal power, and its exercise in the existing condition of the Church was even recommended by those who recognised the evils of the system, but shrank from the responsibility of themselves introducing the innovation. This was promptly rebuked by the conservatives, according to Fra Paolo, with the remark that a prudent physician would not attempt to cure one disease by bringing on a greater. It was not, however, until 11 November that the canons on matrimony were finally adopted and formally published. Of these there are two relating to our subject. The first one pronounced the dread anathema on all who should dare to assert that clerks in holy orders, monks, or nuns could contract marriage, or that such a marriage was valid, since God would not deny the gift of chastity to those who rightly sought it, nor would He expose us to temptation beyond our strength. The other similarly anathematised all who dared to assert that the married state was more worthy than virginity, or that it was not better to live in celibacy than married. In the preliminary congregation, held 13 October, they had been adopted without a dissenting voice, save that the Archbishop of Sens and the Bishop of Verdun desired the words " non obstante lege ecclesiastica vel voto " to be omitted from the ninth canon. The tenth canon, though directed against the Protestants, was by no means uncalled-for among Catholics. About this period the Spanish Inquisition commenced to treat as a heresy the assertion that the married state is preferable to the celibacy prescribed for the clergy, when the number of cases which speedily appeared in the records and continued for nearly a century show how widely spread and persistent among the people was this belief.

Thus, while keeping the Germans and French quiet with delusive promises, the Church devoted its energies to the miserable task of separating itself as widely as possible from those who had left it. Its rulers seemed to imagine that their only hope of safety lay in entrenching themselves behind the exaggerations of those particular points of policy which had afforded to their adversaries the fairest chances of attack. The faithful throughout Germany might suffer from the absence of the ministers of Christ, or might endure yet more from the unrestrained passions of wolves in sheep's clothing let loose among their wives and daughters, but the Church militant in this conjuncture dreaded even more to lose the aid of that monastic army which, in theory at least, had no earthly object but the service of St. Peter; it selfishly feared that the parish priest who might legitimately see his fireside surrounded by a happy group of wife and children would lose the devotion which a man without ties should entertain for the prosperity and glory of the ecclesiastical establishment; and perhaps, more than all, it saw with terror avaricious princes eager for the secularisation of that immense property to which it owed so large a portion of the splendour which dazzled mankind, of the influence which rendered it powerful, and of the luxury which made its high places attractive to the ambitious and able men who controlled its destiny. To put an end, therefore, at once and for ever, to the mutterings of dissatisfaction among those who compared the domestic life of the Protestant pastors with the reckless self-indulgence of the ministers of the old religion, it was resolved to place the canon of celibacy in a position where none of the orthodox should dare to attack it, and to accomplish this the simple rule of discipline was elevated to the dignity of a point of belief. As the Church had already been forced, in defending the rule from the assaults of the Reformers, to attribute to it apostolic origin, we may not perhaps be surprised that it was made a point of doctrine, but we cannot easily appreciate the reasons that would justify the anathema launched against all who regarded the marriage of those in holy orders as binding. The dissolution of such marriages, as we have seen, was not suggested until the middle of the twelfth century, and the decision of the council thus condemned as heretics the whole body of the Church during three-quarters of its previous existence.

Although the doctrinal canon threw the responsibility of priestly unchastity upon God, yet, as the council had so peremptorily refused to adopt the remedy urged by the princes of the empire, it did not hesitate to employ human means to remove, if possible, the scandals which God had permitted to afflict the Church. The decree of reformation, published in December 1563, contained provisions intended to curb the vice which the Tridentine fathers, with all their reliance on Divine power, well knew to be ineradicable. These provisions, however, were little more than a repetition of what we have seen enacted in every century since Siricius. Any ecclesiastic guilty of keeping a concubine or woman liable to suspicion was admonished; disregarding this first warning, he was deprived of one-third of his revenue; if still contumacious, suspension from functions and benefice followed; and a persistence in guilt was then visited with irrevocable deprivation. No appeal from a sentence could gain exemption; these cases were removed from the jurisdiction of inferior officials and confided to the bishops, who were enjoined to be prompt and severe in their decisions; while guilty bishops were liable to suspension by their provincial synods, and, if irreclaimable, were sent to Rome for punishment. The illegitimate children of priests were pronounced incapable of preferment. Those already in orders, if employed in their fathers' parishes, were required, under pain of deprivation, to exchange their positions within three months for preferment eleswhere, and any provision made by a clerical parent for the benefit of his children was pronounced to be a fraud.

Such were the regulations which this great general council of the Catholic Church considered sufficient to relieve the establishment of the curse which had hung around it for a thousand years. There is nothing in them that had not been tried a hundred times before, with what success the foregoing pages may attest. In some respects, indeed, they were not as prompt and efficacious as the decrees which Charles V and his bishops had promulgated a few years previous, and which had proved so lamentably inefficient. There were not wanting enlightened members of the council who bitterly felt the inadequacy of what they were doing, but the undignified haste of the closing sessions and the domination of Rome rendered them unable to accomplish more. As the Bishop of Astorga said in a letter to

Granvelle, "They are not as we would have wished, to correct the abuses and scandals of the Church, which cause so many to fall into error, but we have to do what we are permitted to do, not what we would wish to do." Heretics, indeed, who asserted that there was in reality no intention of suppressing concubinage, could point in justification to the curious fact that, while previous councils had provided heavy penalties against the concubines of priests, that of Trent passed them over as though they were guiltless.

Within two months after the dissolution of the council, Ferdinand and Albert of Bavaria presented to the pope their requests, which were more moderate than might have been expected. The two papers were essentially the same. In the name of the princes of the empire, after demanding the communion in both elements for the laity, they proceeded to argue earnestly for the other concession. In place of asking, as before, the privilege for the clergy at large, they now reduced their entreaties to the simple request of allowing such Catholic priests as had entered into matrimony to retain their wives and perform their functions, which they assured the pope was absolutely essential to the preservation of the fragments of the Church still doing battle with the prevailing heresies throughout Germany. They likewise asked that in such places as could not obtain a sufficiency of pastors, the bishops should be empowered to ordain married laymen of approved piety, learning, and fitness.

These appeals were successful as far as communion in both elements was concerned, for on 16 April Pius granted that concession under certain conditions. The subject of priestly marriage, however, he still postponed, and on 17 June we find Ferdinand writing to Cardinal Morone to express his thanks for what he had obtained, and to urge the other subject on the consideration of the papal court. He had instructed his ambassador, he said, to press it earnestly, and he besought the Cardinal to aid in so pious and advantageous a work.

Nor was this the only means which Ferdinand, then verging rapidly to the grave, adopted to attain the object of his unwearied pursuit. Georg Witzel had thrown aside the monastic gown in 1531 to embrace the errors of Lutheranism, but had returned to the old religion. His

learning and piety earned for him a deserved reputation,
and elevated him to the position of imperial councillor,
where his talents were devoted to the endless task of bringing about a reconciliation between the Churches. George
Cassander, equally eminent, had never incurred the imputation of apostacy, but had laboured with tireless industry
to convert his erring brethren from heresy to the true faith.
Men like these might perhaps be heard when the voice of
princes and prelates, actuated by motives of personal
advantage, met a deaf ear; and Ferdinand applied to them
for disquisitions on the subject. Before their labours were
concluded the monarch was dead (25 July, 1564), but his
son Maximilian II inherited his father's ideas, and gladly
made use of the opinions which the learned Catholic doctors
had no hesitation in expressing.

Both took strong ground against celibacy. Cassander,
while defending the Church for originally introducing the
rule, deplored the terrible and abominable scandals which
its untimely enforcement caused throughout the Church,
and he urged that the reasons which had led to its introduction not only existed no longer, but had even become
arguments for its abrogation, since now the choice lay only
between married priests and concubinarians. He declared
it to be the source of numerous evils, chief among which
was promiscuous and unbridled licentiousness, and he added
that the already scanty ranks of the priesthood were
deprived of the accessions which were so necessary, since
men of a religious turn of mind were prevented from taking
orders by the universal wickedness which prevailed under
the excuse of celibacy, while pious parents kept their sons
from entering the Church for fear of debauching their
morals. On the other hand, those who sought a life of
ease and licence were attracted to the holy calling which
they disgraced. He was even willing to permit marriage
in orders, arguing that it was only a question of canon law,
in which faith and doctrine were not involved. As regards
the monastic orders, while fully appreciating the principles
upon which the system was founded, he warmly deplored
the corruption engendered by wealth and luxury. Though
the convents contained many pious and holy men, still for
the most part religion was forgotten in the observance of
ceremonies that had lost their significance, and nothing
could be more licentious and profane than the life led in

many of the monasteries. Witzel was equally severe in his denunciations of the clerical licentiousness attributable to the rule of celibacy, and concluded his tract by attacking the supineness, blindness, and perversity of the prelates who suffered such foulness to exist everywhere among the priesthood, in contempt of Christ and to the burdening of their consciences.

It was already evident that both the great objects for which the Council of Trent had ostensibly been assembled were failures; that it would effect as little for the purification of the Church as for the reconciliation of the heretics. Perhaps Maximilian felt that under these circumstances no one could deny the necessity of such changes as would at least afford a chance of the reformation that could no longer be expected of the Tridentine canons; perhaps he felt strengthened by the support of his ecclesiastical counsellors and controversialists; perhaps, with the zealous hopefulness of youth, he felt a confidence of which age and many disappointments had deprived his father; or perhaps he was encouraged by the concession to his subjects and to those of Albert of Bavaria of the communion in both elements, not knowing that in two short years it would be withdrawn. Certain it is that in a negotiation with the Bishop of Ventimiglia, papal nuncio at his court, he lost no time in renewing, with increased energy, the effort to obtain the recognition of married priests. After the departure of the nuncio, he addressed, in November 1564, a most pressing demand to Pius IV, in which he declared that the matter brooked no further postponement; that throughout Germany, and especially in his dominions, there was the greatest need of proper ministers and pastors; that there was no other measure which would retain them in the Catholic Church, from which, day by day, they were withdrawing, principally from this cause. He assured the Holy Father that the danger was constantly increasing, and that he feared that a further delay would render even this remedy powerless to prevent the total destruction of the old religion. If only this were granted to the clergy, even as the cup had been communicated to the laity, he hoped for an immediate improvement. The bishops could then exercise their authority over those who at present were beyond their control, as unrecognised by the Church; and so thoroughly was this lawless condition of affairs understood that a refuge was sought in his provinces by those disreputable pastors who were banished from the Lutheran states on account of their disorderly lives. His brother, the Archduke Charles, was equally urgent, in a letter which he addressed, a few days later, to the pope, repeating the same arguments, and assuring him that the only hope for the true religion in his dominions was to find some means of admitting the services of a married clergy.

Ferdinand and Maximilian were actuated in these persevering efforts not merely by the desire of gratifying the wishes of their people, or of remedying the depravity of the ecclesiastical body. It had been a favourite project with the father, warmly adopted by the son, to heal the differences between the two religions, and to restore to the Church its ancient and prosperous unity. In their opinion, and in that of many eminent men, the main obstacle to this was the question of celibacy. It was evidently hopeless to expect this sacrifice of the Lutheran pastors, while numerous members of the Catholic Church regarded the change as essential to the purification of their own establishment. The only mode of effecting so desirable a reconciliation was therefore to persuade the pope to exercise the power of dispensation which the Council of Trent had admitted to be inherent in his high office. It thus was left for Pius IV to extricate himself from the tangle of promises with which he had evaded the pressure from beyond the Alps. His position, in fact, was perplexing, for the council had thrown on him the responsibility, by admitting his power of dispensation, while at the same time, with little regard for consistency, it had cast the denial of sacerdotal marriage in the form of a dogma enforced with the dread anathema. In spite of this, no one on either side of the question seems to have doubted his power to dispense with the dogma, and this power thus became the storm-centre of a struggle in which the unfortunate Pius reaped to the full the results of his double-dealing policy.

The protagonist of conservatism was Philip II, the most powerful monarch of the time and the head of the only thoroughly Catholic kingdom beyond the Alps. He threw himself into it with such vigour, through a succession of envoys—Vargas, Luis de Zuñiga, Luis de Requesens, Cardinal Pacheco, Pedro de Avila—that Pacheco reported, 20 April, 1565, that Pius had conceived the idea that

Philip's purpose in urging him to refuse the German demands was that the emperor would then withdraw from the Church, so that Spain should remain the only Christian country and Philip thus be enabled to control the Holy See. Pius, in fact, at times scarce knew which way to turn. A few days earlier Pacheco had reported an audience, in which the pope asked him to obtain Philip's advice as to whether he should grant a request, repeatedly made by the emperor, to assemble a junta of learned prelates from all Christendom to consider the matter. It was not, he said, an affair of divine law, requiring a general council, but of positive law; and this at least would have the advantage of postponing a decision. Pacheco promised to write, but said that he knew that Philip would send no prelates to such a junta, as it would scandalise all Spain; and Philip would regard it as certain that, if the concession were granted to Germany, the Spanish clergy would not only want it, but would go there and renounce their nationality, in order to lead a dissolute life. To this Pius replied that he knew that all Christendom would demand it, but he could not resist the emperor without the vigorous support of Philip, whom he desired to use his influence with Maximilian to lighten the pressure. Pacheco concludes by adverting to the weakness and vacillation of Pius, who inclined first to one side and then to the other.

On the other hand, Maximilian was urging the concession with greater insistence than his father, and the indecision of Pius was exemplified in a consistory held 12 January, 1565, chiefly to consider the matter. He adverted to the grant of the cup, which Cardinal Hosius of Ermeland reported had proved of much advantage in Germany and Austria, both in retaining Catholics and winning heretics, while in Bohemia it had been received as a gift from heaven. The marriage question was still more important; the cardinal and other prelates admitted that priests were few, and still fewer were those who desired to take orders. He had met their arguments and abhorred innovations; although so pious an emperor deemed it necessary for his dominions, it would be of evil example, for, if conceded to Germany, no one knew but that it would be demanded by Spain, France, and Poland. He wished that it had been decided by the council, and that the burden had not been laid on him, for the Emperor would be offended if refused what he said was the only remedy, and he foresaw the action that might be taken in the approaching Diet. He therefore wanted the opinions, not only of the cardinals, but of many theologians, and would be greatly pleased if an assembly could be convened from all the nations. He therefore asked the cardinals to consider the importance of the affair, and to advise him freely and sincerely; he would hear all, and take such resolution as the Holy Ghost might inspire. To this appeal the only response seems to have been from Cardinal Simoneta, who briefly stated that he had been legate to the Council when the Emperor's petitions were presented, and it had been deemed wiser not to bring the matter up for debate, as it was certain that clerical marriage would be refused. The report of this consistory created great scandal in Spain, and Philip wrote a strong letter to Pius, representing that the concession would prove the destruction of Christianity and the ruin of his dominions. When Cardinal Pacheco read this to the pope he sighed and groaned; he could not but listen to so powerful a sovereign as the emperor. He was told that it would bring back Germany; that there were no priests there, and that the land was relapsing into paganism; that the approaching Diet would proclaim an Interim worse than that of Charles V; but God had helped him, for the Diet had been postponed until September, and they thus at least gained that much time. Three days after, Pacheco writes that the pope is old and weak and worn out with perplexity; he complains that he is left alone, and he will yield not only this, but all that is asked of him, unless he is strongly supported. He has postponed it as long as he can, and can do so no longer.

When Don Pedro de Avila was sent as a special envoy on the question, Philip, in his instructions of 10 June, 1565, told him that from the way in which the pope treated the matter it would appear that he was pledged to make the concession, whether it was one of the articles agreed upon with the emperor for the dissolution of the council or subsequently, and the expedients suggested for paving the way to it were inadmissible, especially the reference to the German prelates, for, even if they should not be moved by the desire to preserve their estates, they could not exercise free judgment in their anxiety to find a remedy for the condition of the provinces and under the pressure of the emperor, the princes, and the people. When the use of the cup was granted he had kept silent, but this was vastly more important, and if it was conceded he would make a great "demonstration"—a significant word in Spanish parlance.

De Avila's reports were reassuring. The pope declared that he had given no pledge as to marriage, as he had done with regard to the cup; the latter had been necessary to prevent a schism by dissolving the council. He would not grant it unless it would bring back all the heretics, and even then he would hesitate. The danger from the Diet had passed; he had dragged the matter along for six years, and would continue to do so, but he would not drive the emperor to despair. To gain time he had sent his nuncios Landriano and Guicciardini, with an offer to pay yearly 25,000 ducats in support of seminaries to supply the lack of priests, and shortly a second similar sum would be sent to keep Maximilian in good humour, for the emperor, it seems, rejected the project of seminaries while evidently keeping the money. Still uncertainty continued, and as late as 2 December, Cardinal Pacheco warns Philip to be friendly with the pope and accede to his request for co-operation in the Diet, for otherwise he will have to grant to Maximilian and other princes things which it will grieve Philip to hear.

The warning was superfluous, for in a week Pius passed away, on 9 December, having accomplished his purpose of evading without rejecting the demands of nearly all the Catholic nations beyond the Alps. His successor, St. Pius V, elected 7 January, 1566, was a man of different temper. Stern and inflexible, animated with the loftiest convictions of the power of his office as the representative of God, his policy towards heresy was not conciliation, but the extermination which he had practised as head of the Inquisition. Prompt action was necessary, for the Diet of Augsburg, to which all parties were looking for a solution of pending questions, was to be held in March. Triumphant Protestantism was in hopes of winning over Maximilian and sundering Germany from the Roman obedience. The Catholics, who were the weaker party, were disheartened and in lack of a leader who should rally their wavering ranks. They found him in the new pope, who within a week of consecration despatched a courier to intercept Cardinal Commendone, then on his return from Poland, with orders to hasten to Augsburg and instructions as to his duties there.

At the same time letters were written to Maximilian, and to the Catholic princes and prelates, couched in a very different tone from those of his predecessor. The Diet must confine itself exclusively to secular affairs, and not meddle with anything belonging to the jurisdiction of the Holy See; no interference with the rites and institutes of the Church must be suffered, nor any change be made in what the Council of Trent had decreed and the Holy See had confirmed. If this was disobeyed, Commendone was ordered to register a protest and depart. No special allusion was made to priestly marriage, nor was it required. Commendone fulfilled his mission with indefatigable dexterity, and was ably supported by the representatives of Philip II. The heretics were prevented from interjecting religious questions, and no Interim was proclaimed. Commendone assembled the Catholic prelates and princes, and urged them to accept the decrees of Trent. To this, after consultation, the Archbishop of Mainz replied, in the name of all, that they accepted without question everything that concerned faith and worship, but there were some points of discipline for the enforcement of which quieter times must be awaited. Thus, after a struggle continued at intervals for a quarter of a century, the rule of celibacy was left undisturbed, and the counter-Reformation had begun.

Still, in spite of conciliar anathemas, there was, after an interval, a certain amount of liberality in granting dispensations for marriage. A collection of decrees of the congregation of the Inquisition contains a number of examples of these, issued between 1600 and 1630 to sub-deacons and deacons and members of the military Orders, not only for prospective marriages, but for those already consummated, including the legitimation of the offspring. The most prominent instance is one of 18 December, 1625, to Archduke Leopold of Austria, who as subdeacon held the bishoprics of Strassburg and Passau. He promptly resigned the sees, and in 1626 married Claudia de' Medici, widow of Federigo, Duke of Urbino. The numerous cases of members of the religious Orders, of both sexes, who left their houses and contracted marriage among heretics, subsequently seeking return to the Church, illustrates the confusion of the period, while the benignity with which their supplications were admitted indicates how impotent was the Holy See to enforce the rules amid the exigencies of the struggle between orthodoxy and heresy in the lands remaining under the Roman obedience.

In Spain, as may readily be conceived, there was no such benignity. Bishop Simancas, about the middle of the sixteenth century, quotes authorities who held that a priest or religious who married publicly was subject to the Inquisition, as this manifested heretical belief, while, if the marriage was secret, it implied no intellectual error, and he was to be dealt with by his superiors; but Simancas asserts that both cases implied heresy, and the Inquisition had jurisdiction. The Inquisition took the same view, and its name inspired a terror discouraging to aspirants to clerical matrimony. Still, its records show that occasionally there were those who dared the risk, trusting to escape detection, and for them the usual penalties were deprivation of functions and benefice, and a longer or shorter term of service in the galleys.

CHAPTER XXIX

THE POST-TRIDENTINE CHURCH

THE great council, on which so long had hung the hopes of the Christian world, had at last been held. The reformation of the Church, postponed by the skilful policy of the popes, had been reached in the closing sessions, and had been hurriedly provided for. As we have seen, the regulations which concerned the morals of the clergy were sufficient for their purpose, if only they could be enforced, yet as they were but the hundredth repetition of an endeavour to conquer human nature, which had always previously failed, even those who enacted them could have felt little faith in their efficacy. August Baumgartner, the Bavarian ambassador, in his address to the council, 27 June, 1562, had alluded to the prevailing belief that any comprehensive effort to enforce the chastity required by the canons would result in driving the mass of the Catholic clergy over to Protestantism. Since continence was held by them to be impossible, it was thought that they would prefer to marry their concubines as Lutherans rather than give them up as Catholics. Possibly the fear of such untoward result may explain the slender effect which can be discerned from a scheme of reform so laboriously reached and so pompously heralded as the panacea for the woes which were destroying the Church.

Although Catherine de' Medicis and her sons refused to allow the council to be formally published in France, yet she permitted its decrees to be freely circulated, and her bishops were at liberty to adopt them as the code of discipline in their dioceses. In Germany we have seen how the Catholic princes, secular and ecclesiastical, accepted it at the Diet of Augsburg in 1566. Philip II, after some hesitation, ordered the reception of the council in all his dominions, which extended from Naples to the North Sea; and Poland, despite some opposition from an ambitious prelate, submitted to it before the year 1564 was ended.

476

As an authoritative exposition of the law of the Church of Christ, conceived and elaborated under the influence of the Holy Ghost, and commanded for implicit observance by the Vicegerent of God; as the expression of the needs and wants of the Catholic faith, wrought by the concentrated energy and wisdom of the leading doctors of Christendom, and transmitted for practical application through the wondrous machinery of the Catholic hierarchy, it should have had an immediate influence on the evils which it was intended to eradicate. Those evils had confessedly done much to create and foster the schism under which the Church was reeling; their magnitude was admitted by all, and no one ventured to defend or to palliate them. Their removal was acknowledged to be a necessity of the gravest character, and every adherent of Catholicism was bound to lend his aid to the good work. What, then, was accomplished by the council which had for so long a period laboured ostensibly with the object of restoring Latin Christianity to its primitive purity?

To few of the long line of popes does the Church owe so much as to St. Pius V. When he ascended the chair of St. Peter, Protestants were looking forward hopefully to the time when the lands of the Roman obedience should shrink to the two peninsulas of Italy and Spain. His pontificate was too brief to show results in checking the progress of revolt, but his resolute purpose to remove the evils that had led to it laid the foundations on which the counter-Reformation was built. It has not come within our scope to consider the abuses and corruption of the Curia which had created, throughout Latin Christendom, a detestation of the Holy See, to be reckoned among the primary causes of Luther's success, but they were inveterate, and to their removal he addressed himself with relentless vigour. That he should show equal solicitude in the harder task of reforming the morals of a dissolute clergy was to be expected, and this he lost no time in attempting, for he recognised how futile were the Tridentine utterances unless they should be unsparingly enforced. Pius IV had allowed two years to elapse in silence after the dissolution of the council, but Pius V lost no time, and on 1 April, 1566, issued a brief commanding the Ordinaries of all Churches to execute with vigour the conciliar decrees against concubinary priests. Then, as soon as the dangers of the Diet of Augsburg were

safely passed, in June he addressed to Maximilian, to
Albert of Bavaria, and to the German bishops letters in
which, after alluding to the scandalous lives of the clergy
as one of the leading causes of heretic success, he prescribed
the most active measures of reform, for otherwise what
remained of Catholicism in Germany would be extinguished.
The bishops were ordered to make visitations throughout
their dioceses, to investigate the morals of their clergy, to
expel their concubines, and to punish the refractory with all
the severity of the laws, depriving them of their benefices
and of the functions which they polluted; moreover, that
the reform might be thorough, these instructions were
accompanied with faculties which placed the regular Orders
under episcopal jurisdiction.   As in all this they would
need the support of the secular power, Maximilian and
Albert were exhorted to lend to the prelates all aid and
favour.

The immediate result of this was not encouraging.   When
Bernard Rasfelt, Bishop of Munster, in his synod of 1566
published the papal commands, the fury of his canons was
so excited that they forced him to resign his bishopric and
spend the rest of his days in obscurity.   He was succeeded
by Johann von Hoya, Bishop of Osnabruck and President
of the Imperial Chamber, a man distinguished by birth and
learning, who speedily wearied of the conflict and sought
peace by imitating the example of his subordinates.   Three
years later, in 1569, the Archbishop of Salzburg, in response
to a fresh exhortation from Pius to reform his Church,
replied that he and his suffragans had never ceased to
attempt it, but that all their efforts had been fruitless and
that he despaired of its accomplishment.

Two years after this, in 1571, we have a summary of the
condition of Germany in a confidential letter of 16 November to Philip II from Fray Francisco di Cordova, the confessor to the Empress.   The continued success of the
Protestant movement he attributes to clerical disorders.
Maximilian II, he says, " is regarded as a heretic, for he
shows favour to heretics and admits all their preachers to
audiences, which he denies to Catholics.   He and the
princes hold the pope, the cardinals, and the bishops
responsible for the failure of reform which would restore
religion.   Throughout all Germany the bishops neither
preach nor celebrate Mass nor perform ecclesiastical func-

tions, but seem to be laymen rather than clerics, while of the clergy at large there is scarce one without a wife or concubine. When the chapters elect bishops, they are required to swear that they will not reform the canons, and the monasteries are full of laymen and women. For all this there is no punishment, and the bishops and canons excuse themselves by saying that they merely live as the cardinals do. The one who is most scandalised by all this and who talks the most about it is the emperor. The details are not fit to write, but it is certain that if the clergy were reformed, Germany would accept Catholicism, for the people are disgusted with the clashing of opinions, and if the bishops would preach, the people would follow them, but as long as there is no reform, the heresies increase day by day, and little by little the heretics obtain the bishoprics and benefices. I know, he concludes, that true reform would win back many heretics and their chiefs, and I think the emperor would not be the last."

The German clergy were not without justification in shielding themselves behind the example of Rome, where Pius IV had allowed the most public and scandalous immorality to flourish unchecked under his immediate supervision. In 1538 the Consilium de Emendanda Ecclesiæ had animadverted upon the cynical licentiousness of the Roman clergy in terms which show that not much improvement had taken place since Petrarch's description of the papal court, and the intervening thirty years had not served to purify it. Pius V included this among his reformatory efforts. He at first proposed to banish all the public women who would not give a pledge of reformation by immediate marriage, and, when forced to abandon this as impracticably harsh, he restricted their residence to certain houses, and forbade their plying their vocation in the streets by day or night. Although this admitted the necessity of the evil and only sought to restrain its public manifestation, such reform was deemed insufferable. The clergy were ashamed to offer open opposition, but urged the Senate to strenuous resistance. The remonstrance presented by that body not only shows the prevalent immorality, but also the conviction that immorality was inseparable from celibacy. It was represented that, if the proposed rules were enforced, the prosperity of the city would be destroyed and the rents of houses be reduced to nothing, and it was urged that, amid so vast a number of men condemned to celibacy, under such restrictions it would be impossible to preserve the virtue of the wives and daughters of the citizens. The contest was stubbornly continued until at length Pius was driven to declare that if further difficulties were interposed he would leave the city. The Germans, moreover, were not mistaken when they included the cardinals among those whom they imitated, for Sixtus V in 1586 decreed that no one who had children, even if they were legitimate, should be eligible to the cardinalate, because in no other way could assurance be had of the observance of their vows.

If Pius V met with opposition in the task of purifying the Augean stable of Rome, St. Charles Borromeo, encouraged and stimulated by his example, found himself involved in a more dangerous quarrel when he attempted, in the equally demoralised city of Milan, to enforce respect for the decrees of Trent. In 1569 he undertook to reform the canons of S. Maria della Scala, whose licentious mode of life was a scandal to the faithful. So persistently did they deny their subjection to his archiepiscopal jurisdiction, that after a long discussion his only resource for vindicating his authority was excommunication. The contumacious canons were still indisposed to yield, and, assembling in their church, they maltreated his messenger. Thinking that his presence might bring them to reason, he ventured himself to expostulate with them, and found them drawn up in their cemetery, with arms in their hands, and supported by soldiers whom they had hired. On reaching the gate, he dismounted from his mule and advanced towards them with his cross, which he had snatched from his cross-bearer. Unabashed by this symbol at once of religion and authority, the mutinous canons rushed upon him with shouts of " Spagna ! " " Spagna ! " brandishing their weapons and discharging their fire-arms at the cross in his hands—fortunately without injuring him. Having thus driven him off, they continued for some time in open rebellion, until they were at length obliged to submit, when Pius V and Philip II united their power in support of St. Charles.

Still greater was the peril to which the saint was exposed in his quarrel with the Umiliati. They were a branch of the Benedictine Order, founded in 1180 by the Milanese who escaped the destruction of their city by Frederic Barbarossa.   Sharing in the general licence of the age, the excesses of the Umiliati became so infamous that they surpassed in turpitude the worst exploits of the unbridled youth of the city.   Supported by the decretals of Pius, in 1568 St. Charles undertook to reduce the Order to the observance of monastic rule.   The Umiliati resisted with so much energy and success that, after two years of contest, they were still defiant.   Regarding St. Charles as the cause of all their troubles, Girolamo Lignana, Provost of S. Cristoforo di Vercelli, who assumed their leadership in 1570, engaged a monk of the order named Girolamo Donati to murder him. The blackness of the deed was not relieved by the circumstances under which it was attempted.   While the holy archbishop was absorbed at midnight in his devotions, Donati stole into the oratory and discharged full upon him an arquebuss loaded with slugs.   Some of the missiles struck St. Charles, but rebounded to the floor, leaving him unhurt, and the miraculous nature of his escape was proved by the depth to which others penetrated the walls.   At this moment the policy of Philip the Catholic supported the disaffected and rebellious monks, and for some time yet they escaped the retribution due to their many crimes, but at length those concerned in the attempted murder were caught and executed, and the order of the Umiliati was broken up.

In fact, the Tridentine reform, so loudly heralded as a panacea for all the evils afflicting the Church, was everywhere confessedly a failure.   When, in 1583, President d'Espeisses presented to Henry III a memorial against the publication of the council in France, he drew one of his arguments from the greater corruption of the Italian Church, where, though the council was received without demur, yet none of its orders reforming the morals of the clergy received the least attention.   That the Tridentine canons in this respect were wholly inefficacious throughout Italy, and that the officials, with rare exceptions, did not venture to enforce them, can indeed be seen in the series of provincial councils held during the remainder of the century, from Lombardy to Naples.

The papacy had succeeded in crushing the reformers who had responded in so many Italian cities to the uprising in Germany; it had then convoked and managed at its will the great congress of Catholic Christendom which was to put an end at once and for ever to all the evils which had led to the schism; it had every opportunity and every motive for vindicating itself from the aspersions of its enemies, and yet we see it at once recur to the old machinery of local councils enacting canons whose frequency and wordy severity are the inverse measure of their efficiency. Had the promises of reform so liberally made been possible in their fulfilment, there had been no need of further legislation.   A convocation of the ecclesiastics of each province to receive and publish the decrees of Trent would have been all-sufficient.   When, therefore, we see the endless iteration with which the guilty clergy were threatened with the Tridentine canons, and with other new or revivified penalties —as at the councils of Milan in 1565 and 1582, and at those of Manfredonia in 1567, of Ravenna in 1568, of Urbino in 1569, of Florence in 1573, of Naples in 1576, of Cosenza in 1579, of Salerno in 1596, of S. Severino in 1597, and of Melfi in 1597—we can only conclude that the evil was irremediable, in spite of the well-meant efforts to suppress it or to throw off the responsibility of its existence.

In fact, the manner in which the Council of Trent was greeted by the clergy may be judged from its treatment in the archiepiscopate of Utrecht. Though Philip II had authoritatively ordered its reception in 1565, we find the Duke of Alva in May 1568 issuing his commands to the prelates of the five Churches of Utrecht to offer no further opposition to it.   Even so stern a ruler could not obtain immediate obedience, however, to so obnoxious a series of regulations, and they responded by pleading their ancient privileges.   This availed them little, for in June he replied that his instructions were positive, and he proceeded to enforce them by sending royal commissioners to the province empowered to carry them out.   In July, therefore, the Archbishop assembled his clergy, and in conjunction with the commissioners issued a series of regulations designed to give effective force to the canons of the council.   Visiting nunneries and haunting taverns, joining in dances and hunting and indecent songs were forbidden.   The clergy were ordered to shave their beards and to give up their concubines, whom they were not to retake or to replace. Even yet they did not yield, but while they were ashamed to claim the right to keep their female companions, they

demurred as to the sacrifice of their beards, and the archbishop was obliged to issue another peremptory command.

It was not, however, only concubinage which the
Council of Trent failed to extirpate.   Even the denial of
sacerdotal marriage, which it had elevated to the dignity
of a point of faith, was stubbornly opposed, and was not
accepted until after a protracted struggle.

In 1569 we find the synod of the extensive and important
province of Salzburg virtually dividing its clergy into two
classes—those who haunt the taverns under pretext of
getting their meals, but really for the purpose of indulging
in drunken riots with their parishioners, and those who
keep houses, with concubines under the guise of female
servants, whom they secretly marry, and who are openly
known by their husbands' names.   To meet this condition
of affairs, the synod devised an elaborate system by which
the richer clergy were directed to keep as domestics respectable middle-aged married women with their husbands, while
the poorer ecclesiastics were to club together for the same
purpose.   This expedient proved as fruitless as its predecessors, for in 1572 Gregory XIII complained to the
archbishop that in many places priests who were known to
be married were permitted by their bishops to celebrate
Mass and to handle the sacred elements.   In spite of all
this, the evil continued unabated, and in 1616 the Archbishop of Salzburg, in his instructions for a general visitation, ordered that all priests should remove their concubines
to a distance of at least six miles, and should not allow their
illegitimate children to live openly with them, except under
special licence from him.

In 1565, Anthony, Archbishop of Prague, promulgated
the Council of Trent in his provincial synod.   He was a
man of more than ordinary vigour;   he had been the
imperial orator at Trent, understood fully the views of the
council, and was not likely to underrate either their importance or their authority.   Armed with the Tridentine canons,
he set actively to work and instituted a very thorough
system of inquisitorial visitations, which ought to have
succeeded if success were possible.   Yet, after the lapse of
thirteen years, in a special mandate issued by him in 1578
he deplores the obstinate blindness of many of his clergy,
who still believed, with the heretics, that marriage was not
incompatible with priesthood, while those who did not

marry were guilty of the less dangerous error of maintaining concubines and children on the revenues of their benefices.

The same wilful ignorance apparently existed in the diocese of Wurzburg, for Bishop Julius, in 1584, found it necessary, in his episcopal statutes, to discountenance clerical matrimony and to prove its nullity by laboriously quoting innumerable canons and decretals; and he even condescended to remind his priesthood that in taking orders they had willingly and knowingly entered into an agreement of continence, by the consequences of which they must be prepared to abide.

A provincial synod of Gnesen, of which the date is uncertain, but which was probably held in 1577, deplored the insane audacity displayed by ecclesiastics in marrying, and threatened them with the Tridentine anathema. This warning appears to have been completely disregarded, for the Bishop of Breslau, a suffragan of the metropolis of Gnesen, in opening his diocesan synod in 1580, still complained that many of his clergy were guilty of this perversity, and he was at some pains to disavow any complicity with it, or any connivance at the licentiousness which was prevalent among the unmarried. In 1591 the synod of Olmutz asserted that many clerks in holy orders contracted pretended marriages, and were not ashamed of the families growing up publicly around them, while others indulged in scandalous concubinage with women, whom they styled housekeepers or cooks. In endeavouring to put an end to this state of affairs, the synod manifested its estimation of the morals of the priesthood by renewing the hideous suggestions which we have seen in the tenth and twelfth centuries, for pastors were allowed to have near them the female relatives authorised by the Nicene canons, but, in view of the assaults of the tempter, were prudently advised not to let them reside in their houses. The disregard of the Tridentine canon continued, and as late as 1628, at the synod of Osnabruck, the orator who opened the proceedings inveighed in the vilest terms against the female companions of the clergy, who not only occupied the position of wives, but were even dignified with the title.

Ancillary to the questions of clerical marriage and concubinage was that of the provisions made for the benefit of the offspring of such unions. The Council of Trent had decreed that all such provisions should be deemed fraudulent, but, in spite of this, the transmission of ecclesiastical property continued as before, and in 1571 Pius V found it necessary to supplement the conciliar decree with further positive legislation. In this he recognised his own Curia as the source of much of the evil by declaring null and void all dispensations granted for such purpose, and annulling all faculties for granting them. It was not only the need of preserving the possessions of the Church; the scandal of sacerdotal families required repression, and this he sought to accomplish, in 1572, by another decree pronouncing such children incapable of receiving even the private and patrimonial property of their fathers. How soon all this was forgotten is indicated by the synod of Augsburg, in 1610, which declared that it would enforce the Tridentine canon prohibiting the illegitimate sons of priests from holding preferment in their fathers' benefices, no matter what dispensations they might produce.

Thus the movement started by the vigour and inflexible purpose of Pius V had at last succeeded in enforcing the Tridentine decree which prohibited priestly marriage, and in suppressing the almost universal demand for it throughout Catholic Christendom. In this he richly earned the gratitude of the Ultramontanism which regards the Church as a hierarchical organisation, directed as much to temporal as to spiritual ends. This preponderating element at the Council of Trent, if we may believe Fra Paolo Sarpi, predicted that, if priests were allowed to marry, their affections would be concentrated on family and country instead of on the Church; their subjection to the Holy See would be diminished, the whole structure of the hierarchy be destroyed, and the pope himself would eventually become a simple Bishop of Rome. It is foreign to our purpose to discuss whether this would have occurred, and whether it would have been a misfortune to the Church and to the world, or whether, if marriage had been permitted, it might have resulted in a reunion of Christian believers. Its denial, at all events, rendered the division permanent, and it remains for us to see whether the counter-Reformation succeeded in removing the corruption which was admitted to have been one of the efficient causes in promoting the success of the Lutheran revolt.

Clear-sighted prelates were not wanting who proclaimed

that the same causes continued to operate and to produce the same effect. Anthony, Archbishop of Prague, in his synod of 1565, took occasion to declare that the misfortunes of the Church were attributable to the dissoluteness of the clergy, and that the extirpation of heresy could best be effected by reforming the depraved morals and filthy lives of ecclesiastics. At the Council of Salzburg, in 1569, Christopher Spandel, in the closing address, asked the assembled prelates what title was more contemptible or more odious than that of priest, in consequence of the licence in which the clergy as a body indulged. The clergy of France, assembled at Melun in July 1579, when addressing Henry III with a request for the publication of the Council of Trent, assured him that the heresy which afflicted Christendom was caused by the corruption of the Church, and that it could only be eradicated by a thorough reformation. Though the Inquisition took care that Spain should not be much troubled by heretics, yet the synod of Orihuella, in 1600, declared that the concubinage practised by ecclesiastics was the principal source of popular animosity against them. These complaints were general. In 1599, Cuyck, Bishop of Ruremonde, published a work aimed at concubinary priests, in which he assured them that they and their predecessors were the cause of the ruin and devastation of the Netherlands for the last thirty years, for their vices had led to the contempt felt for the clergy, and thus to the heresy which had caused the civil wars. Those who kept their vows he asserts to be as rare as the grapes that can be gleaned after the vintage or the olives left after gathering the crop; but the only remedy he can suggest is increased vigilance and severity on the part of the prelates. Evidently the Tridentine canons had thus far been a failure. In 1609, at the synod of Constance, the Rev. Dr. Hamerer, in an official oration to the assembled prelates, deplored the continued spread of heresy, which he boldly told them was caused by the perpetually increasing immorality that pervaded all classes of the priesthood. The Reformation had begun, had derived its strength, and was still prospering through their weakness, which rendered them odious to the people and made the Catholic religion a by-word and a shame. In 1610, the Bishop of Antwerp, in a synodal address, agreed with Bishop Cuyck in attributing the evils which had so grievously afflicted the Church of Flanders for nearly half a century to the same cause, and, while recounting the various successive efforts at internal reform made since the Council of Trent, he pronounced each one to have been a failure in consequence of the incurable obstinacy of the clergy. Damhouder, a celebrated jurisconsult of Flanders, whose unquestioned piety and orthodoxy gained for him the confidence of Charles V and Philip II, does not hesitate to speak of the clergy of his time as men who rarely lived up to their professions, and who as a general rule were scoundrels distinguished for their indulgence in all manner of evil. In a similar mood, the Bishop of Bois-le-Duc, in opening his synod of 1612, declared that the scandalous lives of the ecclesiastics were a source of corruption to the laity and a direct encouragement of heresy. So, in 1625, the synod of Osnabruck gave as its reason for endeavouring to enforce the Tridentine canons that the true religion was despised on account of the depraved morals of its ministers, whose crimes were a sufficient explanation of the stubbornness of the heretics. So little concealment of their frailty was thought necessary that they openly enriched their children from the patrimony of the Church, and decked their concubines with ornaments and vestments taken from the holy images, even as we have seen was the custom among the Anglo-Saxons of the tenth century.

The Thirty Years' War proved a more effectual bar to the spread of heresy than these fruitless efforts to cure the incurable malady of the Church. After the Peace of Westphalia there was no further need to appeal to the dread of proselytising Lutheranism as a stimulus to virtue, but still the same process of reasoning appears in exhortations to regain the forfeited respect of the community. Thus, in 1652, the Bishop of Munster expressed his horror at the obstinacy with which, in spite of fines, edicts, and canons, his clergy persisted in retaining their concubines, and he declared that the discordance between the professions and the practice of the priesthood rendered them a stench in the nostrils of the people and destroyed the authority of religion itself; and in 1662 the synod of Cologne deplored that the notorious want of respect felt for the ministers of Christ was the direct result of their own immorality. A doctrine even sprang up to the effect that it was not requisite to force a concubinarian to eject his companion if she was useful to him in his housekeeping or if it would be difficult for him

to obtain another servant; and this became sufficiently
formidable to entitle it to a place among the errors of belief
formally condemned by the Roman Inquisition in its decree
of March 1666.

In France the influence of the Tridentine canons had
been equally unsatisfactory. At a royal council held in
1560, which resolved upon the assembly of the States at
Orleans, Charles de Marillac, Bishop of Vienne, declared
that ecclesiastical discipline was almost obsolete, and that
no previous time had seen scandals so frequent or the life
of the clergy so reprehensible. From the proceedings of the
Huguenot synod of Poitiers, in 1560, it is evident that
priests not infrequently secretly married their concubines,
and, when the woman was a Calvinist, her equivocal position
became a matter of grave consideration with her Church.
The only result of the Colloquy of Poissy, in 1561, was that
Catherine de Medicis prevailed upon the bishops to present
a request to the king asking him to use his influence with
the pope to concede the marriage of priests and the use of
the cup by the laity. Means were found, as we have seen,
to prevent the former of these demands from being made,
while the latter, when presented, was peremptorily refused.
In the existing condition of affairs, the Council of Trent
could not reasonably be expected to effect much, for, as the
orthodox Claude d'Espence informs us, the French prelates,
like the Germans, were in the habit of collecting the " cullagium " from all their priests, and informing those who did
not keep concubines that they might do so if they liked, but
must pay the licence-money whether or no. In 1564, the
Cardinal of Lorraine, not long after his return from the
council, held a provincial synod at Rheims, where he
contented himself with declaring that the ancient canons
enjoining chastity should be enforced. The next year, 1565,
a synod held at Cambrai reduced the penalties to a minimum
and afforded every opportunity for purchasing immunity,
by enacting that those who consorted with loose women,
and who remained obdurate to warnings and reprehension,
should be punished at the pleasure of the officials. Thus
we find Pius V, 26 January, 1567, granting to Archbishop
Maximilian full power to correct the depraved morals of
his canons, in spite of the customary oath which he had taken
not to interfere with them. Pius further seized the oppor-

tunity to urge him and his suffragans to labour strenuously in the good cause, for the surest means of extirpating heresy was the reform of the clerical corruption that had occasioned it. We may assume this to have stimulated the council held the same year to disregard clerical immunity by invoking the aid of the secular arm to remove the concubines of its clergy—a course again suggested as late as 1631. The terms in which Claude, Bishop of Evreux, at his synod of 1576, announced his intention of taking steps to eject those who for the future should persist in their immorality show not only that such measures were even yet an innovation, but also indicate little probability of their being successful. The Council of Rheims, in 1583, while proclaiming that the Tridentine canons shall be enforced on all concubinary priests, manifests a reasonable doubt as to the amount of respect which they will receive in threatening that those who are contumacious shall be subdued by the secular arm. The Council of Tours, in the same year, deplores that the whole ecclesiastical body is regarded with aversion by the good and pious on account of the scandals perpetrated by a portion of them. To cure this evil, the residence of suspected women, even when connected by blood, is forbidden, as well as of the children acknowledged to be sprung from such unions, and various penalties are denounced against offenders. The Council of Bordeaux, in 1624, earnestly warns the clergy of the province not to allow their sisters and nieces to live in their houses, and especially not to sleep in the same room with them; and various other synods held during the period repeated the well-known regulations on the subject, which are only of interest as showing how little they were respected.

Avignon and the Constat Venaissin, the portion of modern France then belonging to the Holy See, were not neglected by the vigilance of Pius V. In 1569 we find him writing to the Cardinals of Bourbon and Armagnac, his legates in charge of the territory, and also to the individual bishops, urging them to reform the corrupt and depraved morals of clergy and laity, to which the growth of heresy was largely ascribable; the clergy especially were to be looked after and be coerced with the full severity of the canons. The usual lack of success attended this, for a council held in Avignon in 1594 declares that the numerous decrees relative to the morals and habits of the clergy are either forgotten or neglected, and then proceeds, as was customary, to forbid the residence of suspected women.

No one, in fact, who is familiar with the popular literature of France during that period can avoid the conviction that the ecclesiastical body was hopelessly infected with the corruption which, emanating from the foulest court in Christendom, spread its contagion throughout the land. If Rabelais and Bonaventure des Periers reflect the depravity which was universal under Francis I, Brantôme, Beroalde de Verville, and Noël du Fail continue the record of infamy under Catherine de Medicis and her children. The genealogy of sin is carried on by Tallemant des Réaux, Bussy-Rabutin, and the crowd of memoir-writers who flourished in the Augustan age of French literature. These show us how often the high places of the hierarchy were filled with men to whom the very name of virtue was a jest, and who could not be expected to enforce on their subjects the continence to which they themselves made no pretension. Yet it would be unjust not to keep in view also the lofty piety of such a prelate as Fénelon, or the austere virtue of Antoine Arnauld and his comrades of Port Royal. While the Jesuits and so-called moral theologians were smoothing the path of sin by the casuistry of Probabilism, there sprang up to resist them the Jansenistic Rigorism, which exercised wide influence on the side of godliness, in spite of unremitting persecution by the Holy See.

It is evident from all this that the standard of ecclesiastical morals had not been raised by the efforts of the Tridentine fathers, and yet a study of the records of church discipline shows that with the increasing decency and refinement of society during the seventeenth and eighteenth centuries the open and cynical manifestations of licence among the clergy became gradually rarer. It may well be doubted, nevertheless, whether their lives were in reality much purer. A few spasmodic efforts were made to enforce the Nicene canon, prohibiting the residence of women, but they were utterly fruitless, and were so recognised by all parties; and the energies of the arch-priests and bishops were directed to regulating the character of the hand-maidens, who were admitted to be a necessary evil. The devices employed for this purpose were varied, and repeated with a frequency which shows their insufficiency; and it would be scarce worth our while to do more than indicate some sources of reference for the curious student who may wish to follow up the reiteration which we have traced already through so many successive centuries. Among them, however, one new feature shows itself, which indicates the growing respect paid to the appearance of decency—complaints that concubines are kept under the guise of sisters and nieces.

That the monastic orders had profited more than the secular clergy by the Tridentine reformation may well be doubted. Laurent de Peyrinnis, one of the heads of the Order of Minims, in 1668, issued a code of regulations in which he showed that scandal was more dreaded than sin when he promulgated an exemption from excommunication in favour of those brethren who, when about to yield to the temptations of the flesh, or to commit theft, prudently laid aside the monastic habit. Apparently this caution was exceptional, for Chiericato deplores the constant scandal given by religious, who are not ashamed to be seen entering and leaving the houses of public prostitutes. Another celebrated jurist of the Order of Minims bears testimony to the demoralisation of his brethren when he declares that if the severe punishments provided for unchastity by the statutes were enforced they would result in the destruction of all the religious congregations.

That the awful sacrifice of the Mass should be performed by a priest fresh from concubinary pollution is a sacrilege, but even more to be dreaded would be the omission of the function which would reveal his weakness to his flock. For centuries the question has troubled the Church, and it has been forced to permit the sacrilege rather than to risk the exposure. The Council of Cambrai, indeed, devised a tolerably effective remedy, about the year 1300, when it ordered celebrants to confess daily to the episcopal penitentiaries, but this was applicable only to the cathedral town and even there was too cumbrous to be enforced. Aquinas was more considerate to human frailty when he asserted that if the sinful priest could not confess before celebrating, he could qualify himself by making a vow to confess. The Council of Trent prescribes preliminary confession for a priest conscious of mortal sin, but this is not always easy, for confession is complicated with questions of jurisdiction and reserved sins, and it adds that if this is impossible, he must confess subsequently as soon as practicable. Jansenist rigour was too severe to permit this sacrilege, but even it had to provide for frailty and it offered the suggestion that the peccant ministrant should scratch his thumb with a knife, bind up his hand and proclaim himself incapacitated. The ordinary practice, however, with those who are scrupulous, seems to be to perform an act of contrition or to make a hasty confession in the sacristy before going to the altar.

In the New World the licentiousness of the priesthood, as might be expected, began to vex the infant Church as soon as it was organised among the heathen. Little more than half a century had passed since the voyages of Columbus, when Oviedo, the first chronicler of the New World, speaks of the licentiousness of the clergy as inviting the destruction of the Spanish Colonies, even as the marriage of the Greek priests had been punished by their subjection under the Turks. The earliest synods and councils which were held contain the customary denunciations of concubinage and prohibitions for ecclesiastics to keep their children in their houses, to celebrate their baptisms and nuptials, and to be assisted by them in the ministry of the altar. Many, as we are informed by the first Council of Mexico, held in 1555, brought with them from Spain their concubines under the guise of relatives. For the most part, however, they formed connections with the natives.

In fact, the institution of slavery and the subject populations among whom its ministers were scattered gave rise to fresh problems, which the Church sought perseveringly, but vainly, to solve. Thus, in New Grenada, before the conquest was fairly achieved, Bishop Barrios, of Santafé, held his first synod, in 1556, and there, after premising that the fruits of religion among the Indians depended upon the good example of their pastors, he proceeded to prohibit any priest stationed in an Indian town from having any Indian woman residing in his house; his food was to be cooked by men, or, if this was impossible, his female servant must be a married woman, residing with her husband under another roof—a provision repeated by the synod of Lima in 1585. A curious experiment in dealing with the troubles arising from slavery is seen in the Mexican canons, which directed that if an ecclesiastic had children by his slave, the ownership of the woman was to be transferred to the Church and the children were to be set free.   It will be remembered that in 1022 the Church insisted upon the continued servitude of clerical bastards whose mothers were serfs of the Church ; and the contrast between this and the regulation which proclaimed the freedom of the children as a punishment inflicted upon the father is perhaps the sorriest exhibit that could be made of the character of those who were engaged in spreading the teachings of Christ among the heathen.

While there can be no doubt that much heroic self-devotion was shown in the efforts made to convert the new subjects of Spain, it is equally unquestionable that a majority of the ecclesiastics who sought the colonies were men of evil character.   The councils held in the several provinces deplore the bad example which they set to their newly converted flocks, and the regulations which were issued time and again against their excesses show the impossibility of keeping them under control.   In Peru, for instance, when in 1581 St. Toribio commenced the quarter of a century of labour as archbishop which worthily won for him the canonisation accorded by Benedict XIII in 1726, two councils had already been held in Lima, one in 1552 and the other in 1567, which had essayed a reformation of morals.   He, in turn, lost no time in summoning a provincial council, which assembled in 1583, the decrees of which, in their denunciation of all manner of vices, show how ineffectual the previous efforts had been.   The clergy were not disposed to submit tamely to the new restraints which Toribio sought to impose, and, while the active resistance which some of them raised was subdued, the underhand management of others was so far successful that the royal assent to the proceedings of the Council was delayed till 1591.   Notwithstanding the activity of Toribio, who, between 1583 and 1604, held three provincial councils and ten diocesan synods, who three times personally visited every portion of his vast archbishopric, and who repeatedly ordered his vicars to send secret reports of concubinary and dissolute priests, he was obliged, in the provincial council of 1601, to content himself with renewing the regulations of 1583, sorrowfully observing that they had received scant obedience, and that consequently the corruption and abuses prevalent among the clergy deprived them of usefulness among their Indian parishioners.   We can thus readily understand the grief with which the honest Fray Gerónimo de Mendieta, a contemporary, after depicting the eager docility with which the natives at first welcomed Christianity, contrasts it with the hatred which sprang up for the very name of Christian when they realised the hopeless wretchedness of their position under their new taskmasters; and the Fray does not conceal the fact that this was partly owing to the character of some of the clergy, while the better ones were disheartened and discharged their trusts mechanically, without expectation of accomplishing good. This condition of morals did not improve with time. In his official report of 1736, the Marques del Castel-Fuerte, Viceroy of Peru, remarks that the greater portion of those of Spanish blood born in the colonies embraced an ecclesiastical life, as offering an easier and more assured career than any other. Surrounded by their Indian subjects, the pastors lived in luxury and licence, which their superiors did little or nothing to check. In 1728 the civil power was ordered to make an investigation into the morals of the priesthood, and especially to designate those whose concubinage was open and notorious—an invasion of the sacred immunities of the Church which provoked a storm against the secular authorities, although only an examination was proposed, and no attempt was to be made of conviction or punishment. There is therefore no reason to question the truthfulness of the description by Don Jorje Juan and Don Antonio de Ulloa, in an official report made about 1740, when they assert that the clergy of Peru, both secular and regular, live so licentiously and with such scandal and self-indulgence that, although all men have their weaknesses and human nature is fragile in Peru, yet it seems as though it were the special function of these ecclesiastics to exceed all the rest in the perverted habits of their disorderly lives—an assertion which the writers proceed to justify by abundant details of the most convincing character.

That the monastic establishments shared in the general dissoluteness we may fairly conclude when we see the precautions which St. Toribio found necessary to preserve the purity of the spouses of Christ. Thus one regulation provides that no ecclesiastic shall visit a nun without a written permission, to be granted only by the Archbishop himself, or his Provisor; and so little confidence did he feel in the guardians whom he himself appointed, that he directs that the official visitors who inspected the nunneries should not enter them without some special and urgent reason. In fact, the report of Juan and Ulloa declares that the regulars exceed the seculars in their disorders, which are so public and notorious as to fill one with horror.

A curious rule adopted by the first Council of Mexico, in 1555, shows how much more scandal was dreaded than sin. In order, as it says, to avert danger and infamy from the clerical order and from married women, it prohibits the Fiscal, or prosecuting officer, from taking cognisance of cases of adultery committed by ecclesiastics, unless the husband be a consenting party, or the adulterer makes public boast of it, or the fact is so notorious that it cannot be passed over in silence; and even when action thus is not to be avoided, in no case is the name of the woman to be mentioned in the proceedings. The Provisors, however, are not forbidden to take notice of such crimes, but are allowed to settle them, if they can, with all due discretion. As might be expected, these regulations, by giving practical immunity, led to an increase in crime, and the third Council of Mexico, in 1585, tells us that many of the clergy indulged in it, in preference to ordinary concubinage, in the confidence that they would not be prosecuted; but the amended rule adopted by the Council to meet this trouble differs so little from its predecessors that we may reasonably doubt whether it was followed by any diminution in the evil. And this, judging from Rivera's notes to his edition of 1859, is the existing state of ecclesiastical law in Mexico, although the Tridentine canon specially orders the Episcopal Ordinaries to proceed *ex officio* in all such cases, even of laymen.

CHAPTER XXX

SOLICITATION

THE Church of the post-Tridentine period was brought into the strongest competition with the Reform, which had carried away nearly half of Europe and was seriously threatening to secure the rest. The needs of the counter-Reformation rendered obligatory efforts at internal purification, which had been superfluous during the ages of unquestioned theocracy, and there was no point in which this was more imperative than in the relations between the celibate priest and his spiritual daughters in the sacrament of penance. The power of the confessional, one of the most effective instrumentalities invented by the ingenuity of man for enslaving the human mind, was peculiarly liable to abuse in sexual matters. No one can be familiar with the hideous suggestiveness of the penitentials without recognising how frequent must be the temptations arising between confessor and penitent, while their respective relations render seduction comparatively easy, and unspeakably atrocious. To deprive such relations of danger requires the confessor to be gifted with rare purity and holiness, and when these functions were confided to men such as those who composed the sacerdotal body as we have seen it throughout the Middle Ages, the result was inevitable.

The scandals of the confessional were no new source of tribulation to the Church and the people. No sooner had the early custom of public and lay confession tended to fall into the hands of the priesthood than it was found necessary to call attention to the dangers thence arising. The first Council of Toledo, in 398, forbids any familiarity between the virgins dedicated to God and their confessors. About the year 500, Symmachus calls attention to the spiritual affinity contracted between the confessor and his penitent, rendering the latter his daughter; he alludes to Silvester as having denounced guilty relations between them, and proceeds to decree not only deposition in such cases, but life-long penitence. As sacerdotal confession gradually became customary, a decretal was forged—whether to give additional authority to the practice, or to impress upon the minds of confessors the necessity of prudence—by which the name of Celestin I was used for a regulation confiscating all the possessions of the female delinquent and confining her in a monastery for life, while the seducer was warned that such sin with his spiritual daughter amounted to a grave case of adultery, for which he must be deposed and undergo penance for twelve years, provided always that the facts had become known to the people, thus indicating that scandal rather than sin was the danger most dreaded.

It was inevitable that this trouble should continue, as we have seen it do throughout the whole history of a celibate priesthood. So constantly was " solicitation "— *solicitatio ad turpiæ*, as it came to be technically called— borne in mind that the mediæval canonists recognised that a parish priest known to be addicted to it forfeited his jurisdiction over his female penitents, who were at liberty to seek another confessor. St. Bonaventura, indeed, declares that there are few parish priests free from this or from other defects that should incapacitate them. That it was the subject of frequent and indignant reprehension on the part of those who sought to elevate and purify the Church we may well believe. Calixtus II freely assumes the perdition of the priest who thus betrays the sacred confidence reposed in him, denouncing him as a lion devouring sheep, as a bear attacking a traveller who has lost his way, as a fowler spreading lures for birds and attracting them with sweet sounds, while the woman he treats not as a partner in guilt, but as an unfortunate who finds destruction where she is seeking salvation. It is observable here that the fault is assumed to lie exclusively with the confessor, and such is likewise the case in the eloquent denunciations of Savonarola, who declares that the Italian cities are full of these wolves in sheep's clothing, who are constantly seeking to entice the innocent into sin by all the arts for which their spiritual directorship affords so much scope. For this there was virtual immunity. Like all other sins, it was made a source of profit to the curia, which offered absolution and a dispensation to hold benefices for the moderate price of thirty-six *gros tournois*. For those at a distance from Rome the local episcopal courts were equally lenient, if we may judge from the case of Alonso de Valdelamar, a priest of Almodovar, tried in 1535 by Blas Ortiz, vicar-general of the Archbishop of Toledo. The charges fully proved against him embraced the seduction of two of his female penitents and his refusal of absolution to a third unless she would surrender herself to him, besides a miscellaneous assortment of crimes—theft, blasphemy, cheating with bulls of indulgence, charging penitents for absolution, and frequenting brothels. For all this he was sentenced to a fine of two ducats and the costs and fees of his trial, and to thirty days' seclusion in the church to repent of his sins and fit himself for celebrating Mass, after which he was free to resume his flagitious career. The regular Orders seem to have been equally benignant with their delinquents. In the Mexican case of Fray Juan de Valdaña, guardian of the Franciscan convent of Suchipita, who made no secret of his affairs with his penitents, it was in evidence, on his trial by the Inquisition in 1583, that when remonstrated with, he asked, what could his prelates do to him? it was only a dozen strokes of the discipline and a year's suspension from his guardianship.

The Lutheran revolt, which found in the crime euphemistically termed Solicitation a favourite point of attack, wrought a change in the view taken of it. The reforming Bishop of Verona, Matteo Ghiberti (died in 1543), decreed severe temporal punishments for all attempts on the virtue of female penitents, culminating in deprivation and perpetual imprisonment when the attempt was successful. In his case this was doubtless prompted by sincere conviction of the iniquity of the offence, but even those who thought lightly of it recognised that the time had passed for its condonation. Bernal Díaz de Lugo, in 1543, intimated that improper relations between confessor and penitent are not much worse than ordinary concubinage, but that when they become publicly known they should be visited with deprivation and imprisonment, seeing that notoriety tends to prevent men from allowing their wives and daughters to confess and exposes the sacrament of penitence to heretical assault. In the same spirit, Archbishop Carranza of Toledo, in 1558, tells us that the enemy took full advantage of this weak spot in the line of defence. As the Council of Trent assumed that God would not deny the gift of chastity to a celibate priesthood, it could scarce refer to such a matter, even if the dread of scandal arising from any allusion to it had not imposed silence, and it adopted no provisions to lessen the evil. About that time, however, a preventive effort was commenced by the invention of the confessional. Hitherto the priest had heard confessions in the open, with the penitent at his knees or seated by his side, which gave ample opportunity for temptation and solicitation. To remedy this the confessional was gradually evolved—a box in which the confessor sits, while the penitent outside pours the tale of his sin through a grille, neither being visible to the other. The earliest allusion to such a contrivance that I have met occurs in a memorial to Charles V, by Siliceo, Archbishop of Toledo, in 1547. In 1565 a Council of Valencia ordered its use, especially for the confession of women, and between 1565 and 1575 S. Carlo Borromeo introduced it in his province of Milan, while the Roman Ritual of 1614 prescribes its employment in all churches. The command was obeyed but slackly, for the innovation had to win its way against the pronounced opposition of the priesthood, who objected to this seclusion from their penitents. In Spain we find the Inquisition, between 1710 and 1720, busy in endeavouring to enforce the use of the confessional, and as late as 1781 it issued a decree to be printed and sent to all parish priests and superiors of convents, who were to post it in their sacristies. In this it alludes to its previous repeated orders and its sorrow at the evils arising from their non-observance or from the devices used to elude them, of which it gives a curious enumeration.

A drawback to the advantages of the confessional was the opportunity which it afforded for laymen to ensconce themselves and hear confessions of women, whether from jealousy, or to gratify prurient instincts, or because it enabled them to ask indecent questions. Such cases were not uncommon, and though the offenders were not liable to prosecution for solicitation, they were held subject to the Inquisition for suspicion of heresy. If the pretended confessor, however, ventured to administer absolution, he came under the savage decrees of Paul IV, Gregory XIII, and Urban VIII, which prescribed burning alive for such sacrilege, although in Spain the Inquisition humanely modified this to service in the galleys.

Mechanical devices, however, went but a little way to cure an evil so widespread and so persistent. If the mouths of mocking heretics were to be closed, some efficacious method must be found for the discovery and punishment of offenders. Yet this was surrounded with difficulties. The crime was secret and known only to the confessor and penitent, and the latter, whether she yielded or not, was deterred from volunteering a complaint by the notoriety which accompanied it, compromising her with husband or father, to say nothing of the dangerous enmity which she would excite. Strictly speaking, such matters were not covered by the seal of the confessional, but she could scarce know this in the face of assertions freely made to the contrary. The spiritual courts, moreover, which held exclusive jurisdiction, were not, as we have seen, disposed to treat the offender harshly, and a not unnatural *esprit de corps* would lead them to reject accusations which could not be supported by witnesses and were so easily discredited. Then, beyond all else, was the ever-present dread of scandal to be aroused through the publicity of open trials, with the consequence of rendering confession odious and of affording comfort to the heretic. Thus the crime, although peculiarly heinous, was almost assured of impunity.

Yet there was in Spain a tribunal which, by its impenetrable secrecy, could avert scandal and by its special procedure could hope to procure convictions. This was the Inquisition, and, though its Apostolic jurisdiction was confined to heresy, yet heresy was an elastic term which, like charity, could be made to cover a multitude of sins. Pedro Guerrero, the reforming Archbishop of Granada, chanced to represent to Paul IV the frequency of the crime and the necessity of some more efficacious means of repression. Whether or not he directly suggested the interference of the Inquisition does not appear, but Paul resolved on tentatively trying the experiment, and on 18 February, 1559, he addressed to the Inquisitors of Granada a brief in which he assumed that confessors who could so abuse their functions must hold unorthodox views as to the sacrament of penitence, rendering them suspect of heresy and subjecting them to the Holy Office. The inquisitors were thus authorised to prosecute such offenders and punish them at discretion, even to " relaxing " them to the secular arm for burning. As the case was heretical, the exemptions of the Regular Orders were withdrawn, and they were subjected to the jurisdiction of the Inquisition.

We have no records to inform us what was the result of this in Granada, but presumably it sufficed to indicate the extent of the evil and the increased efficacy of the new method for its discovery and punishment. Accordingly, Pius IV, by a bull of 14 April, 1561, addressed to Valdes, the inquisitor-general, empowered the Inquisition, throughout the Spanish dominions, to investigate and punish all confessors who solicited women in the act of confession, even to the extent of degrading and relaxing them to the secular arm for punishment at its discretion. As before, all exemptions of the monastic Orders were withdrawn.

The Inquisition was nothing loath to exercise this new power, and, to render it effective, in the next annual publication of what was known as the Edict of Faith, solicitation was included among the offences which every one having knowledge was required to denounce to the Holy Office. As this edict was solemnly published in the churches on a feast-day, at which the whole population was summoned to attend, it was a most effective means of acquainting the people with the new legislation and of inviting information from every source. Naturally it produced a sensation, although this has been absurdly exaggerated by hostile writers. This bold abandonment of the traditional policy of the Church to cover such offences with the deepest silence evoked opposition which finds expression in a memorial presented to the Inquisition. This commences by deploring the crime which converts the sacrament into a snare for the ruin of souls; but, evil as this is, the evils of publicity are greater. The crime has always existed, for men are men and women are women, but the Church has never before attempted so novel a cure. It has always been the policy to conceal the offences of the clergy and not to risk the diminution of the reverence due to them. Scandal is the very thing to be avoided; the authority of the priesthood depends upon popular estimation, which should not be imperilled. To proclaim to the world that the confessional is thus abused is to deter people from seeking it; fathers and husbands will prevent their women from confessing, respect for the sacrament will be destroyed, and Christianity will be overthrown. Besides, it is usually the women who are the tempters, and when

their advances are repelled, they will bring false charges to
ruin the innocent. Moreover, the comfort is to be considered which it will bring to the heretics, justifying their
slanders on the morals of priests and friars. Altogether the
document, which is not without learning, is a barefaced
admission that morals and religion have nothing in common,
and that the salvation of souls is of small account in comparison with the material interests of the Church.

It is easy to conceive how pressure of this kind increased;
the Inquisition in time yielded, and, on 22 May, 1571,
it instructed the tribunals that solicitation was no longer
to be included in the edict, on account of the evils which
it caused. The inquisitors were told to devise such other
means as they could and to notify prelates to instruct
confessors that when penitents confessed to having been
solicited they must be admonished to denounce the offenders
to the Holy Office. The result of this was not satisfactory
after a few years' trial, and on 2 March, 1576, an edict to
be published in future was sent to the tribunals containing
the crime of solicitation. The reason given is its great
increase, and the inquisitors are taken to task for not
acting upon the denunciations which they received. This
remained the settled policy of the Inquisition, and all who
knew, directly or indirectly, of such cases, were required
to denounce them under pain of major excommunication.

The chief sufferers under this new dispensation were the
Regular Orders, for not only was the business of confession
largely in their hands, but the temptation to abuse it was
greater than among the secular clergy, who had fuller
opportunities for less dangerous indulgence. The Inquisition, moreover, was resolute in enforcing its jurisdiction
over them, and when two Jesuit fathers, Sebastian Briviesca
and Cristóbal Trugillo, who were guilty of the offence, were
quietly conveyed out of Spain, it prosecuted and imprisoned,
in 1587, Francisco Marcen, the Provincial of Castile, with
fathers Francisco Labata and Juan López, for infraction
of the edict commanding all cases to be reported to it.
Jesuit influence was powerful in Rome; Sixtus V promptly
evoked their cases to himself, and when the Inquisition
demurred, he threatened Inquisitor-general Quiroga with
deprivation of his office and cardinalate, which brought
submission to his mandate. Encouraged by this, the
Jesuits laboured strenuously to obtain exemption for all

the religious Orders, but the whole influence of Spain was brought to bear, and after a prolonged struggle the Congregation of the Universal Inquisition, in the presence of Clement VIII, issued a decree, 3 December, 1592, declaring that the jurisdiction of the Spanish Inquisition was exclusive and that the superiors of the regulars could not exercise it. This was confirmed, in 1605, by Paul V in a general constitution, revoking the jurisdiction of superiors in all cases pertaining to the Inquisition, and the question was permanently settled.

Although Portugal had been added to the Spanish crown in 1580, the separate organisation of its Inquisition had been preserved, and it was not until 1608 that Paul V extended to it jurisdiction over solicitation in the same terms as those granted to the Spanish tribunals. That the Roman Inquisition should exercise the same power may be assumed as a matter of course.

In all these decrees the definition of the crime, as we have seen, was so loosely phrased that there was little difficulty in evading the letter of the law, for in practice it was construed that technical solicitation was confined to women and that it must be committed during the very act of confession. As early as 1577 the Supreme Council of the Spanish Inquisition ruled that there was no penalty for soliciting penitents in the place assigned for confession if there was no confession, and, soon afterwards, that if the confessor told the penitent that he did not wish to confess her, he was not to be prosecuted for soliciting her. All this opened the door to so many evasions that the effectiveness of the bulls was seriously crippled. The churches were for the most part deserted, the attitude of penitent and confessor would disarm the suspicion of any one who chanced to observe them and amorous endearments, and even incredible indecencies might easily be indulged in so long as there was no actual sacramental confession, as is shown by frequent and flagrant details in the trials. The Roman Inquisition sought to check these abuses by subjecting them to the Holy Office, in decrees of 10 July, 1614 and 6 February, 1619, but these decrees seem not to have been accepted in Spain, for de Sausa, in 1623, repeats the assertion that there must be actual confession and that the opposite opinion is destitute of all probability. In this he is supported by an experienced inquisitor, about the same time, who says that when there is an assignation and only an external appearance of confession there is no sacrament, and therefore no sacrilege.

Another and even more dangerous evasion was evolved from the words of the bulls, implying that solicitation must be in the act of confession. Probabilism and casuistry were developing rapidly, and ingenious moralists were busy in demonstrating how all the sanctions of the moral law could be evaded. It was explained that if the confessor should make his advances before confession actually commenced, or wait until after it was concluded and absolution given, there would be no irreverence to the sacrament, and consequently no suspicion of heresy for the Inquisition to punish. By no means all authorities assented to this, but it was defended by enough to render it probable, and consequently safe in practice. Then the question as to what acts and words amounted to solicitation opened a wide field for the dialectics of the casuists. The rule that whatever a priest does is to be interpreted favourably—that if he embraces a woman it is to be held that he is blessing her—was invoked to prove that winks and nods and praises of her beauty were not to be regarded as tempting her to evil. The more rigid moralists asserted that such acts were foreign to the sacrament and could only be construed as opening the way to further advances, while others held that unless the acts amounted to mortal sin they did not come within the papal bulls—that to tell the penitent that she was pretty and cultivate her friendship so as to be invited to her house might be imprudent, but were not a mortal sin. There was another question on which opinions were divided— whether a priest acting in the confessional as a pimp for the benefit of another, or urging the penitent to serve as a procuress for him, came under the definitions of the bulls.

It was evident that papal utterances of a more definite character were requisite if the efforts to suppress the crime were to have a measure of success, and in 1622 Gregory XV attempted this in the comprehensive bull *Universi Dominici Gregis*. He not only confirmed the acts of his predecessors, but extended their provisions over all the lands of the Roman obedience, constituting not only inquisitors, but also episcopal officials as special judges over all the clergy, including the exempted religious Orders, with exclusive jurisdiction, and full power to inflict punishment, even to degradation and relaxation to the secular arm. Moreover, he sought to meet all the evasions by defining that solicitation, whether for the priest himself or for another, could occur either before or after confession, and when there was a pretext of it, provided it was in a place where confessions were heard, and he included illicit and indecent talk and acts within the definition.

The success of this well-intended measure scarce corresponded with its merits. At first Spain would have none of it. The Inquisition was exceedingly sensitive as to its exclusiveness of jurisdiction, and the terms of the bull appeared to restore to the episcopal courts a cumulative cognisance of solicitation. By some means the Ordinary of Seville obtained a copy, and showed it to the inquisitors. The Supreme Council of the Inquisition took alarm, and promptly addressed a memorial to Philip IV, 14 January, 1623, dwelling eloquently upon the heinousness and frequency of the crime, the energy and vigour of the Inquisition in repressing it, and the disastrous consequences of granting concurrent jurisdiction to the bishops. Confessors would be much emboldened in their evil courses by the comparative leniency of the episcopal courts; the secrecy which kept a knowledge of these affairs from husbands and kinsmen would be destroyed, and, if the two complainants necessary for a trial should apply, one to the bishop and the other to the Inquisition, the culprit would escape. The king was therefore asked to obtain the exemption of Spain from the operation of the bull, which was speedily arranged. Then, after some delay, in 1629 the Supreme Council sent copies of the bull to the tribunals as a guide in practice. There was some trouble with bishops who claimed jurisdiction under it, but the Inquisition boldly asserted that it had a special brief conferring exclusive jurisdiction, though this it could never exhibit, and it finally made good its claim.

Elsewhere, the bull had a still more inhospitable reception. It was not accepted or published in either France or Germany. In France the assemblies of the clergy refused to receive it, declaring that it was unsuited to the customs of the country and that it tended to violate the seal of the confessional. It was even asserted to prove the fallibility of the Holy See, and an attempt to publish it, early in the eighteenth century, was suppressed. Germany was either indifferent or opposed. In 1666, Father Gobat states that the papal decrees have not been commented upon by German moralists, either because they have not been received there and there is no expectation that they will be, or because the German women cannot be expected to trouble with their complaints such exalted personages as bishops and vicars-general, and he adds that he can name a number of vicars-general who have never received such a denunciation, save one, in a single instance. Yet this absence of complaint was not due to the superior morality of the German priesthood. In 1733, Dr. Amort tells us that a few years previously the Franciscans of Bavaria had agreed to receive the bull in so far as to prohibit any of their confessors from absolving a penitent who had been solicited by one of their own Order, unless she would permit him to denounce the offender, an example which Amort wishes were followed elsewhere, as it would be very useful in repressing many scandals which afflict the German Church. As the Roman Inquisition, in 1633, had ordered all superiors of religious houses, under pain of deprivation of office and of active and passive voice, to assemble the brethren once a year and admonish them as to the observance of the bulls, this shows how completely they had been ignored.

When Gregory included illicit and indecent acts and words in his definition of solicitation, he merely opened a field of unlimited debate. Every moralist had his own standard, from the extreme of rigorism to the most abandoned laxity. Thus already, in 1635, there was a discussion whether handing a love-letter to a penitent in the confessional came under the definition; if it was to be read on the spot, it was generally so considered; if to be read subsequently, the stricter theologians condemned it, while others argued that the woman had been absolved and reconciled to God, so that the sacrament was out of the way. It was not until 1665 that Alexander VII condemned the proposition that love-letters could be thus given without incurring the penalties of solicitation. It was a received rule among moralists that *parvitas materiæ*—or the trifling character of an offence such as theft—reduced mortal sins to venial, but it was likewise agreed that there was no *parvitas materiæ* in usury or lust. Whether there was in solicitation was a disputed point until, in 1661, the Roman Inquisition decided in the negative. Still, this settled little, for at the same time it decided that praising the beauty of a penitent or giving her a present might be solicitation or not, according to intention. Thus the question of intention threw everything in doubt, and justifies Bodonus in applying it to such utterances as " Remember me, for I love you," " If I were a layman I would marry you," " Wait for me at home, for I have to speak with you about a matter of importance," and even advising a penitent to kill her husband, none of which justifies denunciation, for they may be innocent. In 1741, Benedict XIV endeavoured, in the bull *Sacramentum Pœnitentiæ*, to define the indefinable more accurately, but he could do little more than copy Gregory XV. Subsequently to this, St. Alphonso de Liguori, the most authoritative moralist of modern times, inclines to the laxist view—not wholly, but in many of the debatable cases. He follows the laxist system in construing strictly the words of the papal decrees and limiting them to the letter, not developing their spirit. The effort to subject the crime to the Inquisition, since all other jurisdictions had failed to curb it, rendered necessary the figment of suspicion of heresy arising out of flagrant contempt for the sacrament. Thus, even in lands where there was no Inquisition, and since the Inquisition has been abolished, the sacrament came to be the one thing vital; the relation between confessor and penitent and the morals involved were lost to sight. Any vileness might be committed unless it could be proved that the sacrament was made the direct instrument of seduction. This is Liguori's guide, and the only difference between him and the extreme laxists is that he sometimes brushes aside the flimsy casuistry by which they sought to justify the unjustifiable. All this discussion is not merely academic; it is of the utmost practical importance in guiding the confessor in granting or refusing absolution to a woman who has been solicited, if she declines to denounce the offender, and the net result is to prove that solicitation is a purely technical offence, which has nothing to do with morals.

Another source of perplexity in this matter, arising from the indispensable confidences of the confessional, is the difficulty of determining the limits of indecency permissible to a confessor with his penitent, so long as he abstains from positive acts about which there can be no doubt. Suggestive questions and ribald talk might be

merely for the delectation which the moralists tell us holy
men experience in discussing these matters, or they might
be for the purpose of insidiously inflaming the passions and
corrupting a prospective victim, or again they might come
within the scope allowed to the confessor of acquainting
himself accurately with the spiritual and moral condition
of the penitent.   Where the line is to be drawn is incapable
of practical definition.   It is for the confessor to decide
how far his conscience or his brutality may lead him, and
if the penitent complains, each case has to be settled on
its own merits.   This was not always by any means easy.
In 1786 a nun of the Convent of Santa Clara of Játiva
complained of Fray Vicente González, and reported a
number of irregularly indecent and wholly irrelevant
questions which he repeatedly put to her in confession.
Under the advice of the definitor of his Order, she empowered him to denounce González to the Inquisition,
whereupon the ordinary confessor of the Council intervened
and persuaded the definitor to write a letter withdrawing
the charges.   The licence which some confessors permitted
to themselves was shown in the case of Fray Vicente Sarria,
in 1773, in which his interrogations were brutally indecent
and completely superfluous, and in that of Maestro Diego de
Agumanes, in 1742, who used to discourse at length, with
a young nun, on sexual matters in a manner most provocative of passion.   In fact, the details of some of these
trials would be incredible if they were not matters of
judicial record, with every evidence of authenticity, and it
is difficult to estimate the filthy contagion which such men
spread in the confessional.

Gregory XV, in his bull of 1622, endeavoured to overcome the greatest obstacle to the punishment of offenders—
the difficulty of inducing solicited penitents to denounce
their seducers.   It was the only mode by which the crime
could be known, while the reluctance of the women was
almost insuperable.   In Spain, as we have seen, the Inquisition sought to accomplish this by the Edict of Faith,
excommunicating those who failed to do so, and by ordering
confessors to admonish their penitents as to their duty,
when, as sometimes happened, the woman would include
her sin in making another confession.   There were
authorities who denied that she was under this obligation,
arguing that no one is obliged to denounce an accomplice

when it may involve his own infamy, and it required the severest pressure to compel performance. Gregory essayed this in a clause ordering all confessors who learn that a penitent has been solicited to admonish her to denounce the culprit; any who should neglect this or teach their penitents that soliciting confessors were not to be denounced were to be duly punished by the inquisitors or ordinaries. The Spanish Inquisition, accordingly, in 1629, granted faculties to inquisitors to punish all confessors who taught such erroneous doctrine, and Urban VIII issued an encyclical ordering that when episcopal approbations were issued to confessors, they should be instructed to require denunciation by all penitents who had been solicited. It illustrates the independence of the Gallican Church that it flatly contradicted these papal utterances. In 1707, with the support of the Faculty of Douai, the Sorbonne pronounced it to be a mortal sin for a confessor to oblige a penitent to denounce a priest who had seduced her in the confessional.

In Spain, the woman who failed to denounce incurred excommunication, and consequently was incapable of absolution until she did so, a rule enforced there as early as 1571, and at a later period elsewhere. That it proved effective to some extent is seen in the fact that a large number of the cases tried by the Spanish Inquisition derived from it their origin. Even the Edict of Faith was less productive in overcoming the deep-seated repugnance of women to expose their weakness, but, at some time or other, in making a general confession, they would chance to mention a slip of this kind, when denial of absolution would compel them to act. Yet that at best this was uncertain is shown by the long interval which frequently occurred between the crime and its denunciation—in some cases twelve, fifteen, and even eighteen years.

It was doubtless with the object of overcoming the repugnance of women to expose their shame that the Roman Inquisition, by a decree of 25 July, 1624, ordered that neither the penitent nor the confessor was to be questioned as to her consent, and that if either of them volunteered the information, it was not to be entered on the record. The casuists, indeed, agreed that the woman, if interrogated, could deny, using the mental reservation that she had not so consented as to reveal it to the examiner. Be this as it may, the wholesome rule of the Roman Inquisition was long in winning its way in Spain, where the reports of the trials show that the unfortunate witness was spared nothing. Indeed, as late as 1750, instructions to commissioners appointed to take depositions in these cases require them to ascertain and record all details with the utmost minuteness, no matter how obscene they may be. Towards the close of its career, however, the Spanish Inquisition learned mercy, and instructions issued in 1816 require the examiner to warn the witness that she is not required to state whether she consented, and if she says that she did so, it is to be omitted from the record. It is likely, however, that this received scant respect, for in 1819 the Supreme Council, in ordering the arrest of Fray Juan Montes, feels it necessary to call special attention to the rule.

There was one thing which greatly reduced the pressure on the consciences of women thus seduced to denounce the delinquents—the habitual practice of the latter in granting them absolution for the sin committed. This destroyed the sin so effectually that it no longer counted before God or man; it need not be recited in any subsequent confession, and it could be denied without sin, for it no longer existed. This was an old custom both with the concubinary priesthood and soliciting confessors, and though it was deprecated by the schoolmen, the absolution was universally conceded to be valid as, indeed, it necessarily must be under the doctrine that the sacraments are not vitiated in polluted hands. In every way the practice was scandalous and demoralising; it gave the tempter an enormous advantage in overcoming the virtue of his penitent by promising her immediate pardon for their mutual sin, and it interfered greatly with the obligation of denunciation. It is therefore remarkable that Gregory XV, in his bull of 1622, should have omitted all reference to it. Apparently the abuse was so venerable and rested on foundations so dangerous to disturb that prudence counselled silence, while great canonists like Sánchez and Diana were found to argue that not only could the confessor absolve his partner in guilt, but that it was expedient for him to do so if it would soothe her conscience and avert defamation from her, and this although the relations between them were notorious. Even in 1661, when the Roman Inquisition settled sixteen questions relating to solicitation, there was no allusion ventured to this.

Had there been a sincere desire to put an end to the practice, a way could readily have been found by limiting the jurisdiction of the confessor in such cases, as had already been done by some thirteenth-century councils in the Low Countries. In 1661 the provincial synod of Cambrai revived their canons, and decreed that no confessor in such cases should have power to absolve, except *in articulo mortis*, a rule which was soon afterwards promulgated by the congregation of archpriests of the province of Mechlin. Rome was slow to follow the example. In 1665, it is true, Alexander VII, in condemning a number of propositions, included one which affirmed that absolution under such circumstances relieved the woman from the obligation to denounce, but he went no further. That such a proposition should have been defended shows the audacity of the latitudinarian moralists, but its condemnation did not affect the evil, which was left in the hands of the episcopate. In the province of Mechlin the power to grant such absolutions was specially excepted in the certificates issued to confessors, but this accomplished little, and in 1698 the synod of Namur peremptorily inhibited the abuse. In the province of Besançon a canon of 1689 declares that although the practice had long been forbidden, yet it continued to flourish, and a cure was sought in withdrawing the power to absolve such penitents—a regulation which had to be repeated in 1707. In 1709 the Cardinal de Noailles, Archbishop of Paris, forbade it in his diocese, but Pontas informs us that such absolutions were valid everywhere, except where prohibited by episcopal authority, and Dr. Amort in 1732 makes the same statement as to Germany. This discreditable condition continued until the accession of Benedict XIV, who in his constitution Sacramentum Pœnitentiæ, in 1741, denounced the device of sacrilegious ministers of Satan rather than of God in absolving their partners in guilt, and erected into a general law what had previously been mere local regulations in some dioceses. He absolutely prohibited such absolutions for the future, except *in articulo mortis* when no other priest was to be had; he pronounced them when granted to be null and void, and punished the attempt with *ipso facto* excommunication, removable only by the Holy See. In the next year, 1742, he extended these provisions to the Greek Churches in the Roman obedience, and four years later he showed how overmastering was the dread of scandal by permitting absolution *in articulo mortis* in all cases where another confessor could not be called in without exciting suspicion, which was virtually a removal of the prohibition.

These well-intentioned measures had little practical result. To what extent the bulls were admitted in the various European states I have no means of knowing, but the synod of Namur, in 1742, felt it necessary to remind confessors that they could not absolve women whom they had seduced in the confessional, and in 1768 the Bishop of Ypres was obliged to recall the attention of his clergy to the bulls of Gregory and Benedict, and to threaten their transgressors with excommunication. In 1775 the Apostolic Vicar of Cochin China had the effrontery to ask Pius VI whether the provisions of Benedict XIV applied to the Franciscan missionaries under his charge, and, if so, whether they could not be moderated, to which somewhat shameless questions Pius replied affirmatively as to the first and negatively as to the second; while the continuance of the abuse is shown by a pastoral letter of the Apostolic Vicar of Suchuen in 1803. The Spanish Inquisition, after some little delay, accepted the bull Sacramentum Pœnitentiæ, and in 1763 it told Padre Felipe Garcia Pacheco that his asserted ignorance of it did not relieve him from its operation. It produced, however, little or no practical effect. In the great majority of subsequent cases of solicitation the culprits had absolved the women, and the only result of the bull was that in their sentences they were told to secretly advise their penitents to repeat all subsequent confessions, as being invalidated, and, as for themselves, to consult their consciences as to the irregularity of celebrating Mass while under the censures of the bull. In this, as in so much else, the wholesome measures of the Holy See were virtually nullified in practice.

The confessor in search of easy victims had a resource in requiring male penitents who confessed to carnal sins to name their partners in guilt, when the knowledge thus gained could be utilised in selecting objects for solicitation. The custom was an old one, for the information thus sought might be used for good purposes as well as for evil. In the thirteenth century, Cæsarius of Heisterbach disapproves of it, for though it may sometimes be serviceable, priestly proclivity to sin, he says, renders it dangerous. Towards the close of the sixteenth century, Bartolomé de Medina declares that, if a confessor refuses absolution unless the penitent reveals the name of his accomplice, he should be denounced to the Inquisition as a heretic, and the penitent should be refused absolution until he makes the denunciation. It is somewhat remarkable that Benedict XIV should have been the first to take action on this abuse. In 1745, in a brief addressed to Portugal, he prohibited utterly, as scandalous and pernicious, the custom of inquiring the name of the accomplice, and in 1746 he decreed excommunication *latæ sententiæ*, reserved to the Holy See, on all who should teach it as being permissible. It was assumed that these briefs were confined to Portugal, and in a few months he was obliged to issue another declaring the prohibition to be general and to be enforced everywhere. Still another utterance was required in 1749, placing the offence in Portugal under the Inquisition. I have not met with any formal grant of the kind to the Spanish Inquisition, but it assumed the power and, in spite of the papal prohibitions, until its suppression there were cases brought before it of confessors who refused absolution unless the names of the guilty partners were revealed to them. The abuse seems ineradicable. Pius IX, in the bull Apostolicæ Sedis (1849), deemed it necessary to decree reserved excommunication for all who should teach it to be lawful, and various recent councils have felt called to condemn the practice. Notwithstanding all this, in modern times it is agreed that there are circumstances under which the confessor is justified in demanding the name of the accomplice under threat of withholding absolution, and as such necessity must of course be left to the discretion of the confessor, the door is kept open to the misuse of the power.

Seduction in the confessional was not wholly confined to one side. The relations of confessor and penitent expose both to temptation, and what is known as passive solicitation occurs when the woman is the tempter. As the matter is not referred to in the papal decrees, writers on the subject are very much at odds as to its treatment and what is to

be done to either party. They discuss the liability of the
confessor when the solicitation is mutual, and when he
yields to threats of making an outcry after he has rebuffed
the temptress, and they draw distinctions between yielding
on the spot and postponing the final act. An authoritative
decision was postponed until 1661, when the Roman
Inquisition decided that the confessor was to be denounced
under the papal decrees, when the solicitation was mutual,
and also when he yielded through fear, and nothing was
said about the woman. Subsequently to this Cardinal
Cozza asserts that she is not liable to denunciation; she is
not alluded to in the papal decrees, and the case, although
equally an insult to the sacrament, is so rare in comparison
with the converse, that the popes have not deemed it
worthy of special animadversion. From this we may
assume that the space devoted to the matter by the commentators, and their assertions of its frequency, may
reasonably be attributed to their desire to minimise the
guilt of confessors and exaggerate that of their penitents.
Still, such cases did sometimes occur, and I have met with
two or three in which the woman was denounced to the
Spanish Inquisition.

Classed with solicitation was a somewhat kindred abuse
of the confessional known to the Inquisition as flagellation.
This was prescribing the discipline as penance, and either
administering it personally or causing its self-infliction in
presence of the confessor, the penitent being stripped as
far as necessary. As the lash could be ordered for any
peccant portion of the body, this gave opportunity for the
vilest indecency, and it was fully exploited by those of
brutish instincts. In fact, it was not confined to the
penitent, for confessors sometimes found gratification in
making the women discipline them, like Fray Francisco
Calvo, who in 1730 denounced himself to the Inquisition
of Madrid for having caused himself to be flagellated. At
first there was considerable doubt as to whether such cases
came under the papal decrees, but it was finally decided to
be a form of solicitation, and after this conclusion had been
reached the Inquisition had no hesitation in prosecuting
flagelantes. Culprits were not treated with deserved
severity, for the records show to what an extent the abuse
was sometimes carried; cases are not infrequent, and
continue until the suppression of the Holy Office.

It remains for us to see what was the practical application of the papal decrees directed against the abuse of the sacred relation established between the confessor and his spiritual daughters. As France and Germany had refused to receive the bull of Gregory XV, the matter remained, as before, in the hands of the bishops, who for the most part were indifferent, and, as we have seen, no effective measures were taken, beyond the occasional comminatory proceedings of synods, which serve rather to prove the existence of the evil than to promise its suppression, though occasionally, it is true, a prelate like Fénelon might instruct mission priests, to whom women should confess to have been solicited, to refuse absolution unless the penitent would authorise denunciation to be made to him. As he felt it necessary, moreover, to promise protection both to the woman and the mission priest, it indicates the risk to which all those who sought to obey the papal commands were exposed.

From such desultory and local attempts no remedy could be expected of an evil so inveterate and widespread. In Italy and in Spain, however, the crime was subjected to the respective Inquisitions, which were armed with power and organisation sufficient for its suppression, if that were practicable under the conditions of human nature and the temptations and opportunities offered by the confessional to a celibate priesthood.

As regards Italy, the data are lacking to enable us to ascertain what use the Inquisition made of its faculties. The dread of scandal rendered secrecy the one essential matter. The culprit, if found guilty, was not sentenced and punished in public as an example, but in the chambers of the Holy Office, or in his convent if a member of a religious Order. No one was to know that the crime had been committed and expiated. Under such circumstances the inquirer can ask in vain for statistics or for instances to determine whether culpable leniency or wholesome severity was shown to offenders. We only know that nominally the prescribed regulations assume the crime to require stern repression. The suspicion of heresy implied in it was classed as vehement, and the culprit was obliged to abjure *de vehementi*, which assumed that he was to be burnt without ceremony in case of relapse. If he denied the accusation and the evidence was insufficient for conviction, he could be tortured, as was the practice of the Roman Inquisition in other crimes; or if he admitted the facts and denied evil purpose, he could similarly be tortured to discover his intention. If convicted, the bull of Gregory XV prescribed a wide range of punishments, according to the degree of culpability, even to the culminating rigour of the stake. Although the latter extreme may be regarded as merely a deterrent threat, never intended to be executed, yet we are told that the punishment was five or seven years in the galleys, which was sufficient to inspire wholesome fear. In 1677, moreover, the Roman Inquisition manifested a laudable desire to discover offenders by following Spanish example in an edict requiring all persons, under pain of excommunication *latæ sententiæ*, to denounce within a month all cases coming within their knowledge.

It is not stated, however, that this edict was ever repeated, as in Spain, and in practice there was much to soften the severity of the law. Obstacles to trial were interposed by a decree of the Inquisition, 17 July, 1627, providing that arrests were not to be made on the denunciation of a single penitent, but only a report was to be made to it. Two denunciations were required for arrest and imprisonment, and three or, according to some authorities, four, for conviction, the reason alleged being the untrustworthiness of female evidence and the difficulty otherwise of getting learned and conscientious men to confess women. Similarly, the punishment was much milder than the threat. For a single solicitation, duly proved, it sufficed to deprive the offender of his faculty to confess; if he had repeatedly solicited two women, deprivation of priestly functions was added; and if there had been scandal, a regular priest was to be perpetually secluded in a convent and a secular one in a hospital. If the penitent were the wife or daughter of a magnate, or if there had been many women concerned and much public scandal, then came degradation and the galleys. Considering the extreme difficulty of inducing women to denounce their confessors, it will be seen that the chances of escape were great and the danger of severe penalties small. It is true that in 1745 the Roman Inquisition decreed that soliciting confessors incurred perpetual disability for celebrating Mass, but there was always the prospect of obtaining dispensations from an indulgent Mother Church, and all this legislation seems virtually to have become a dead letter, for, as we shall see hereafter, when Leopold I of Tuscany endeavoured, in 1774, to reform the nunneries in his dominions, they were found to be the scene of the worst disorders between the nuns and their spiritual directors, and the reformatory efforts of Leopold met their chief opposition in the Roman Curia itself.

There was also always the resource, when a soliciting priest found himself in danger of denunciation, of denouncing himself, for those who spontaneously confessed were treated with exceptional leniency. According to rule, if he did this before denunciation, and had been guilty with only one woman, a severe reprimand sufficed, while if two witnesses accused him he was to be deprived of confessing. One or two cases, however, of which we chance to have the record, would seem to show that self-denunciation conferred virtual immunity. The minim, Hilario Caone, of Besançon, was domiciled in Seville. He probably had intimation that he was about to be denounced, for he fled to Rome in 1653 and confessed to the Inquisition that in the church of San Francisco de Paula of Seville he had solicited some forty women, mostly with success. For this he was merely sentenced to abjure *de vehementi*, to visit the seven privileged altars of St. Peter's, and to recite the chapters of the Virgin weekly for three years. That this was the ordinary treatment of such cases may be inferred from that of Vincenzo Barzi, in the same year, who had a similar sentence on denouncing himself.

In Spain, access to the voluminous archives of the Inquisition gives us for the first time an opportunity of acquaintance with these secrets of the confessional which the Church has always guarded so carefully from the profane, thus rendering possible a fairly accurate understanding of its attitude towards soliciting confessors. The Inquisition had accepted in good faith the jurisdiction conferred on it, but it always had a leaning in favour of clerical delinquents, and the rules which it established for this class of cases show how much more benignantly it regarded this particular suspicion of heresy than other suspicions. It is true that no ecclesiastic could be arrested on any charge by a tribunal without referring the case to the Supreme Council and awaiting its orders, so that in this respect confessors had no advantage over their brethren, but, as in Italy, two independent denunciations of solicitation were required, where one sufficed in ordinary heresy. Where denunciation

was so difficult to secure, this was a most important
advantage to the delinquents, and saved thousands of them
from trial. A woman who chanced in a general confession
to mention her sin with a previous confessor might be
refused absolution until she denounced him. If she did
so, the Inquisitors, after the introduction of postal facilities,
sent letters of inquiry to all the other tribunals, to learn
whether they had the culprit's name on their register of
solicitors. If the replies were in the negative, the papers
were filed away, and nothing more was done, unless at some
future time another denunciation was made to some
tribunal. Meanwhile the woman was left under the
impression that her seduction by her confessor was too
trivial a matter to require investigation, and the offender
was left at liberty to continue his assaults on the virtue of
his penitents. Perhaps if, after the lapse of years, a second
accusation came, the first accuser was dead and could not
make the indispensable ratification of her testimony, so
that the culprit had another respite. The records are full
of cases in which a second denunciation did not come until
ten, fifteen, and sometimes even twenty, thirty, or forty
years after the first; and there are many in which three
denunciations are specified, showing that the first victim
must have died before the second came forward. The prolonged immunity thus enjoyed by offenders whose offences
must have been habitual shows how disastrous was the
favour thus extended to them. The reason given for this
double denunciation was the assumed unreliability of
female testimony, but in ordinary heresy all witnesses were
welcome, irrespective of sex, character, and almost of age;
while if there was enmity or infamy, the accused, from
whom the knowledge of their names was withheld, had to
grope his way to identify and disable them. But in these
cases the Inquisition saved him from all this and protected
him, before it would act on the denunciation, by a searching
inquiry into the character of the witness and any possible
enmity that might exist. Regrets were expressed that
female testimony was admitted at all; it was justifiable
only because the nature of the crime admitted of no other,
and writers like Páramo discredit it in advance with the
customary monastic abuse of women.

Another favour shown to the accused was immunity
from torture. While in ordinary accusations of heresy a

single witness sufficed to expose the defendant to the rack
or strappado, in case of his denial, the confessor was
exempt, no matter how many witnesses appeared against
him. In the earlier time there was some question as to
this, and some dialectics as to fact and intention, but the
question was settled on the common-sense basis that it
would be a greater infliction for the uncertain than for
the certain, as the penalties for conviction were not equal
to torture. When, however, doctrinal errors led to solicitation, there was no hesitation in the use of torture to detect
the aberrations of Illuminism, as in the case of the priest
Manuel Madrigal, voted to torture to discover intention,
" por solicitante, Molinista y flagelante," by the tribunal
of Madrid in 1725.

There was also the broad avenue to escape in the strictness with which the formulas of the papal utterances were
construed. Solicitation is a purely technical crime, based
on inferential misbelief as to the sacrament, and it is wholly
unconnected with morals. The Church cares nothing as to
the relations between confessor and penitent so long as the
confessional and the sacrament are not involved, and even
there the confidences deemed necessary in confession, the
obligation on the confessor to acquaint himself with all
details, afford ample opportunity for pruriency, which the
casuist can approve or condemn with equal facility. All this
is one of the incidents inseparable from auricular confession,
and the Church can only make the best of it with vague
general regulations, construed and enforced by imperfect
human nature. The decisive importance attached to
locality meets one constantly in the trials of these cases.
In that of Fernandez Pujalon, parish priest of Ciempozuelos,
before the tribunal of Toledo, in 1744, he confesses to vile
indecencies committed with his penitent Sor Cayetana de
la Providencia in the convent of Santa Clara, and chanced
to mention that once, in the parlour of the convent, she
said that she never indulged in this in the confessional, but
that it was bad for Padre Colmenas and Sor Antonia Blanca,
who had illicit relations in the confessional. The tribunal
commissioned the superintendent of convents, Canon
Miguel Barba, to examine Sor Cayetana as to this when he
should next visit Ciempozuelos, which he did in 1747, but
she naturally did not care to implicate herself; Barba
discreetly did not push his investigations, and the matter

was dropped. So, in the case of Fray Joseph Rives, tried in Valencia in 1741, the evidence of two of his penitents shows the beastliness of the practices employed to inflame the passions of the women, while arguments of his advocate are devoted to prove that the precautions which he took to evade the letter of the papal decrees proved his respect for the sacrament, and that technically he was not guilty. This was unavailing, but he escaped with deprivation of his faculty to confess and three years' exile from Valencia, Bocayente, and all royal residences. It was to meet this customary line of defence that the tribunals, in their instructions as to taking testimony, always laid special stress on ascertaining the exact spot where the incriminating acts occurred; what would be guilt in the confessional would escape animadversion elsewhere.

Another favour shown to these delinquents was that, in place of being shut up *incomunicado* in the secret prison during trial, like ordinary heretics, they were at liberty and could devise means of defence. What these sometimes were is shown in the case of a priest who had been denounced, and who threatened to kill the confessor who had sent the denunciation unless he would write that the women had withdrawn their charges. More crafty was Dr. Joseph Soriano, vicar of Vinaroz, in 1796, against whom we find pending in the tribunal of Valencia two prosecutions, one for solicitation and another for the ingenious device of suborning several women to denounce him and then to retract.

When, in spite of all facilities for evasion, conviction was obtained, the punishment meted out to the criminal was singularly disproportionate to the moral turpitude of the offence and its damage to the Church and to society. In the first place, the dread of scandal shielded him from public reprobation and the shame of exposure, thus exempting him from what in Spain was one of the heaviest penalties visited on other crimes—the infamy inflicted on the lineage of one who had been penanced by the Inquisition. There was not only the secrecy in which all the operations of the Holy Office were jealously guarded, but the culprit was not exposed to view in an auto da fe as were ordinary offenders— heretics, bigamists, blasphemers, petty sorcerers, and the like. From the earliest period, as soon as the form of procedure was reduced to rule, strict injunctions were issued that the sentence was to be read in the audience-chamber with closed doors, the only witnesses present being a specified number of members of the culprit's Order, if he were a regular, or priests of parish churches, if a secular. The same instructions prescribe as the punishment in all cases abjuration for light suspicion of heresy and perpetual deprivation of the faculty of confessing, to which might be added others suited to the gravity of the offence. Thus for frailes there might be a discipline inflicted in his convent, while the sentence was read in the presence of the assembled brethren, or, if the case were especially aggravated, a previous one in the audience-chamber also; there might, further, be seclusion in a convent, suspension or deprivation of orders, of the right of voting and being voted for, as well as the last place in choir and refectory, together with penance for heavy sin, such as the discipline and prayer. For secular priests there might be exile or seclusion, or suspension or deprivation of functions and benefice, together with fines and secret discipline and fasts and prayers. As regards fines, they were a favourite penalty for all offences, as they accrued to the tribunal inflicting them. They could not be imposed on the regulars, who held nothing, but the secular priests were sometimes rich, and were valuable culprits. Thus in the case, alluded to above, of Fernandez Pujalon, parish priest of Ciempozuelos, a feature of his sentence was a fine of half his property, but his guilt was greatly enhanced by some heretical propositions that he had uttered.

Inadequate as all this may seem in comparison with the penalties habitually imposed by the Inquisition on other classes of offenders, it was rarely inflicted to the full extent, and as time wore on there appears to be a distinct tendency to regard the crime with increasing leniency. The indulgence, indeed, with which it was viewed, in spite of the rhetorical horror expressed in the utterances of popes and inquisitors, is reflected in the adjuration of a Cunha not to drive the delinquents to despair nor to impose more penalty than is just, and he thinks that it would be much better for the Inquisition to hand offenders over for punishment to their own prelates. It is impossible, in fact, not to recognise a fellow feeling and a certain amount of sympathy, as for a matter in which any priest might involve himself, but the temper in which the Inquisition exercised the jurisdiction conferred on it can best be estimated from a few illustrative cases.

In 1594, in Mexico, the Dominican Fray Thomás Maldonado was tried on the evidence of five of his penitents. He made no defence, except alleging that his conduct with them had been jocular, and he presented witnesses as to his character, especially his prior, Fray Cristóval de Sepúlveda, all of whom testified to his being a good servant of God and a man of irreproachable life. While the trial was in progress, the prior asked for his release, as the convent wanted his services to take charge of some mills, to which the tribunal promptly assented. Finally he was sentenced to abjure for light suspicion, to be deprived of confessing women, and to exile for six years from the convent of Cuyvacan. It is evident that his offence was regarded rather in the light of an indiscretion than of a crime. More severe, in 1674, was the sentence in Toledo of Fray Miguel Martin de Eugenio, whose powers of seduction had been exercised in a number of places. He was subjected to a " circular discipline " in his convent, he was deprived of confessing men and women, and was secluded for four years in a convent, where he was to have the last place in choir and refectory and to serve in the most humble positions; during the first year he had Friday fasting on bread and water, eating on the floor of the refectory, and he was deprived of voting and being voted for. As regards the galleys, the only case that I have happened to meet in which they were imposed is that of the licentiate Lorenzo de Eldora, who was suspended from orders in 1691 by the tribunal of Toledo, and condemned to the galleys for five years, with instructions to present himself to the inquisitors, at the expiration of the term, for further orders; but he was evidently deemed an incorrigible relapsed, as he had already been punished for the same offence by the Inquisition of Granada. It must have treated him with undeserved leniency, and not have deprived him of the faculty of confession.

As a rule, however, the sentences were moderate, and grew more so as time wore on. In 1647 the Valladolid tribunal considered a reprimand sufficient for Padre Antonio Escobar, S.J., who was accused by a nun of the Monasterio de la Penitencia of Salamanca—a reformatory for loose women—although he had previously been denounced in Logroño, and the testimony obtained from there revealed almost incredible brutality on his part and on that of Padre Vilarde, S.J. In 1649 the tribunal of Toledo merely deprived the licentiate Bernardo de Amor of the faculty of confessing, with four years of exile from Madrid, Toledo, and Andujar, although his offence was that of soliciting youths in the confessional.

Progressive leniency is seen in the Toledo case, in 1763, of Felipe Garcia Pacheco, a priest with various dignities, who was condemned only to seclusion in a convent for six months, and was left in the enjoyment of his dignities and the faculty of confession, although the injunction cautiously to warn his accomplices that they must repeat the confessions made to him shows that his guilt was complete. The nineteenth century saw no increase in severity. In 1816 the case of Dr. Pedro Luceta must have been especially foul, for when his sentence was read before the twelve ecclesiastics in the audience-chamber, portions of the details of his offences were ordered to be omitted; but he was only deprived of confessing, with some spiritual exercises, one year's seclusion, and five years' exile from certain places. He was ungrateful for this leniency, and broke his seclusion, which was a more serious offence than solicitation, for he was then sent to the presideo of Ceuta (implying hard labour as in the *bagne*) for the remainder of the six years, but he was allowed to return to Algeciras on the plea of ill-health. In this same year the tribunal of Santiago, in sentencing Gerónimo González, priest of Requeijo, speaks of his *enormes delitas*, but only condemned him to spiritual exercises, a suspension of three months from celebrating Mass, of one year from confessing men and perpetually women, and eight years' exile from certain places; then, within three months, on the plea of ill-health, it allowed him to reside with his parents in Requeijo, warning him to avoid the taverns and highways, which had led to his misdeeds, and ordering the priest there to keep a watch over him. The case in 1818 of Fray Antonio de la Porteria y Vela, also in the Santiago tribunal, must have been especially atrocious, for he was perpetually deprived of both confessing and preaching, but beyond this he was subjected only to temporary exile from certain places and to two months' seclusion devoted to spiritual exercises.

As in Italy, so in Spain, a favourite device to disarm severity, especially when accusation was expected, was self-denunciation, for the *espontaneado*, as he was called, earned a claim to merciful consideration, provided always that he expressed due contrition and made full confession of his misdeeds. A very large portion of the cases tried by the Inquisition are of this character; in one list of a hundred and eight, thirty-two, or thirty per cent., are *espontaneados*. The customary impulse to this is seen in the case of Fray Nicholas de Madrid, who denounced himself to the tribunal of Madrid, 8 June, 1757. He was a trifle tardy, for a denunciation against him had been received two days before.

As a matter of course, the *espontaneado* was apt to soften the details of his guilt and extenuate his offences as far as possible. In ordinary Inquisitorial procedure this only increased the culpability, for a confession which was the result of contrition was required to be complete, and the *diminuto* who partly withheld or palliated his faults was but a hardened sinner seeking to escape punishment. Confessors, however, were not ordinary criminals. It is true that, in the earlier period, during the first flush of exercising its new jurisdiction, the Inquisition pursued its ordinary course of testing the confession by examining witnesses, and if it found that the culprit was a *diminuto*, his self denunciation did not save him from the customary penalties, but this severity was gradually relaxed. About 1640, an experienced inquisitor lays down the rule that, if a confessor accuses himself before there is any evidence against him, and if the women concerned are numerous, they are examined, and if they admit it, he is deprived of confessing; if they deny, as sometimes happens, the case is suspended with a warning to him; if there is but one woman, and the case is not grave, he is reprimanded without other penalty. If he accuses himself before there is more than one denunciation against him, the penalties are lighter than if he had not done so.

It could not have been long after this that the Inquisition manifested its indifference by simply accepting the self-denunciation without examining the women. In 1669 the licentiate Fernando de Valdés denounced himself to the tribunal of Santiago for having solicited in confession, with indecent acts, seven single and three married women, to whom, in a subsequent confession, he added a pregnant woman and several others unmarried. The records were examined, and no previous accusation was found against him. Without summoning the witnesses, the tribunal reported the case to the Supreme Council, which ordered it simply to be suspended and the culprit to be reprimanded. The fact that out of so many women solicited not one accused him indicates how few were the denunciations in comparison with the offences. The indifference of the tribunals grew with time. In 1724, Fray Manuel Pablo Herraiz denounced himself to the tribunal of Toledo for a somewhat complicated illicit connection with two penitents. Inquiries were sent to the other tribunals, with negative results. Without further action, the case was laid aside, and in 1732 the fiscal or prosecuting officer reported that there was nothing more to be done with it. These cases indicate that the only danger incurred by the *espontáneado* was that some previous denunciation might be lying in the records awaiting a second, provided the tribunal took the trouble to make inquiry.

In time even this seems to have been abandoned, and so completely did it come to be understood that the *espontaneado* was not to be prosecuted, that in 1783 the Supreme Council interrogated the tribunals, asking whether they suspended such cases or dismissed the self-accuser with abjuration and absolution. So it continued until the extinction of the Inquisition. In 1815, Padre Fray Francisco Gómez Somoerotro, sacristan mayor of the Mercenarian convent of Madrid, denounced himself to that tribunal for solicitation and doctrines suspect of Molinism, and his case was suspended. In 1819 he was denounced for solicitation to the tribunal of Valladolid, and again the case was suspended.

No class of ecclesiastics privileged to hear confessions was exempt from this contaminating sin, but the great mass of culprits belonged to the regular Orders. Llorente explains that the secular priests, having comparative wealth and freedom, were able to gratify their passions in ways less dangerous, and that it was precisely the Orders that were most rigid which produced the greatest number of culprits. To verify this last assertion would require statistics of the different Orders, now unattainable, and an accurate knowledge of the degree to which they devoted themselves to the duties of the confessional. A factor in their activity was the special faculties granted to the mendicant Orders to absolve for cases reserved to the Holy See, except those included in the Cœna Domini bull and six others specified in a decree of Clement VIII in 1601—these mendicant Orders being Dominicans, Franciscans, Augustinians, Carmelites, Minims, Jesuits, and Servites. This, of course, rendered their ministrations more attractive, and secured them a larger number of penitents, which helps to explain their undue proportion of offenders. In analysing an aggregate of 3775 cases I find that the great body of the secular clergy, including parish priests, vicars, canons, etc., contributed only 981, while the regular Orders furnished 2794.

Spain was the only land in which solicitation was systematically prosecuted, where the conditions were such as to remove some of the impediments to denunciation, and where the records are accessible. If any methods could reduce the abuse to a minimum, it was there, and from what we learn as to its prevalence in Spain, we may reasonably infer that in other countries, where no such machinery existed for its discovery and repression, it was even more prevalent.

It is thus only from the records of the Inquisition that an insight can be gained into this phase of ecclesiastical development, which has always been shrouded from public view with such anxious care. In exploring these records one seems to live in a world of brutal lust, where disregard of the moral law is accepted as a matter of course by all parties, where the aim of the confessor is to inflame the passions by act and speech, or to overcome resistance by coarse violence; where women regard it as natural that the awful authority of the priesthood is to be exercised to their undoing, and their consciences are to be soothed with pardon granted in the name of God by the hypocrite who has destroyed their honour; and where the inquisitor busies himself, not with the moral and spiritual questions involved, but with ascertaining whether certain technical rules have been violated. I have spared the reader all details, for the most debased pornographic literature can have nothing more foul to offer, and the divorce of morals from religion is complete.

Morals, in fact, have nothing to do with solicitation as

viewed by the Church. The priest can indulge his passions with his penitents in safety, so long as he commits no technical offence and so long as the danger of scandal is not incurred. The Church sees nothing specially sinful in solicitation itself, notwithstanding the vehement rhetoric of papal utterances. In the forum of conscience it is classed with simple fornication—a mortal sin indeed, for in lust there is no *parvitas materiæ*, but one not calling for any special reprobation. Heinous offences are distinguished by being " reserved "—that is, absolution for them can be obtained only from the Holy See or from the sinner's prelate. The Holy See has never reserved to itself the sin of seducing a penitent in the confessional. Bishops have power in their dioceses to reserve to themselves what sins they choose, and occasionally some puritan prelate has done so with this. In 1635, while the bull of Gregory XV was still the subject of discussion, Trimarchi tells us that it was thus reserved in the provinces of Geneva and Benevento, and in some dioceses of Naples, but nowhere else. The consequence of this is that absolution can be given by any confessor, and the culprit is told that he need only confess to simple fornication, without mentioning that it has been with his spiritual daughter. He therefore obtains pardon from God on the easiest possible terms, his conscience is clear, and he is ready to repeat the offence. This forms a strange contrast with the excommunication directed against the victim who fails to denounce her seducer, for this is reserved to the Holy See, and we are expressly told that the censures of the bulls are directed against her, and not against him. May we not attribute all this to a callousness engendered by the prevalence of concubinage among a celibate priesthood, where the woman must in almost all cases necessarily be the penitent of the priest and thus be his spiritual daughter?

CHAPTER XXXI

THE CHURCH AND THE REVOLUTION

IF the Council of Trent had thus failed utterly in its efforts
to create that which had never existed—purity of morals
under the rule of celibacy—it had at length succeeded in its
more important task of putting an end to the aspirations
of the clergy for marriage. With the anathema for heresy
confronting them, few could be found so bold as openly to
dispute the propriety of a law which had been incorporated
into the articles of faith, and the ingenious sophistries and
far-fetched logic of Bellarmine were reverently received
and accepted as incontrovertible. Urbain Grandier might
endeavour to quiet the conscience of his morganatic spouse
by writing a treatise to prove the lawfulness of priestly
wedlock, but he took care to keep the manuscript carefully
locked in his desk.[1] A man of bold and independent spirit,
fortified by unfathomable learning, like Louis Ellies Du

---

[1] When Grandier was arrested and tried for sorcery, his papers
were seized, and among them was found an essay against sacerdotal
celibacy. Under torture, he confessed that he had written it for
the purpose of satisfying the conscience of a woman with whom he
had maintained marital relations for seven years (Hist. des Diables
de Loudun, pp. 85, 191). The manuscript was burnt, with its
unlucky author, but a copy was preserved, which has been printed
(Petite Bibliothèque des Curieux, Paris, 1866). In it Grandier
shows himself singularly bold for a man of his time and station.
The law of nature, or moral law, he holds to be the direct exposition
of the Divine will. By it revealed law must necessarily be interpreted, and to its standard ecclesiastical law must be made to
conform. He evidently was made to be burned as a heretic, if he
had escaped as a sorcerer. The promise of chastity exacted at
ordination he regards as extorted, and therefore as not binding on
those unable to keep it; while he does not hesitate to assume that
the rule itself was adopted and enforced on purely temporal grounds
—" de crainte qu'en remuant une pierre on n'esbranlat la puissance
papale; car hors cette considération d'Estat, l'Eglise romaine pense
assez que le célibat n'est pas d'institution divine ni nécessaire au salut,
puisqu'elle en dispense les particuliers, ce qu'elle ne pourroit faire
si le célibat avoit esté ordonné d'en haut " (pp. 34-5).

Pin, might secretly favour marriage, and perhaps might contract matrimony. Du Pin's great antagonist, Bossuet, might incur a similar imputation, and be ready to partially yield the point if thereby he might secure the reconciliation of the hostile Churches. All this, however, could have no influence on the doctrines and practice of Catholicism at large, and the principle remained unaltered and unalterable.

Yet it was impossible that the critical spirit of inquiry which marked the eighteenth century, its boldness of unbelief, and its utter want of faith in God and man, could leave unassailed this monument of primæval asceticism, while it was so busy in undermining everything to which the reverence of its predecessors had clung. Accordingly, the latter half of the century witnessed an active controversy on the subject. In 1758, a canon of Estampes, named Desforges, who had been forced to take orders by his family, published a work in two volumes in which he attempted to prove that marriage was necessary for all ranks of ecclesiastics. The book attracted attention, and by order of the Parlement it was burnt, 30 September, 1758, by the hangman, and the unlucky author was thrown into the Bastile. These proceedings were well calculated to give publicity to the work : it was reprinted at Douai in 1772; a German translation was published in 1782 at Göttingen and Munster, and an Italian one, with some omissions, had already appeared in 1770, without an acknowledged place of publication. The Abbé Villiers undertook to answer Desforges in a weak little volume, the "Apologie du Célibat Chrétien," published in 1762, which consists principally of long extracts from the Fathers, in praise of virginity. Even Italy felt the movement, and an anonymous work, entitled "Pregiudizi del Celibato," appeared in Naples in 1765, and was reprinted in Venice in 1766. Some more competent champion was necessary to answer these repeated attacks, and the learned Abate Zaccaria brought his fertile pen and his inexhaustible erudition to the rescue in his " Storia Polemica del Celibato Sacro," which saw the light in 1774, and which not long afterwards was translated into German. In 1781 appeared a new aspirant for matrimonial liberty in the Abbé Gaudin, who issued at Geneva (Lyons) his work entitled "Les inconveniens du célibat des prêtres," a treatise of considerable learning and no little bitterness against the whole structure of sacerdotalism and Roman supremacy. This was followed, in 1782, by Andreas Forster, in his " De Cœlibatu Clericorum Dissertatio," published at Dillingen, and dedicated to Pius VI, for the purpose of replying to the attacks of the innovating Catholics.

The latter, indeed, had some hope for the approaching realisation of their demands. The reforms which characterised the minority of Ferdinand IV of Naples excited the priests of Southern Italy to petition him for the right of marriage, and Serrao, the Jansenist Bishop of Potenza, does not hesitate to say that the request would have been granted if the unfriendly relations between the courts of Rome and Naples had continued much longer. The Emperor Joseph II, amid his many fruitless schemes for philosophical reform, inclined seriously to the notion of permitting marriage to the priesthood of his dominions. In an edict of 1783 he asserted incidentally that the matter was subject to his control, and the advocates of clerical marriage confidently expected that in a very short period they would see the ancient restrictions swept away by the imperial power. A mass of controversial essays and dissertations made their appearance throughout Germany, and the well-known Protestant theologian Henke took the opportunity of bringing out, in 1783, a new edition of the learned work of Calixtus, " De Conjugio Clericorum," as the most efficient aid to the good cause. It is a striking illustration of the temper of the times to observe that this work, so bitterly opposed to the orthodox doctrines and practice, is dedicated by Henke to Archdeacon Anthony Ganoczy, canon of the cathedral church of Gross-Wardein and apostolic prothonotary. The hope of success brought out other writers, and the movement made sufficient progress to cause some hesitation in Rome as to the propriety of yielding to the pressure.

Zaccaria again entered the lists, and produced, in 1785, his " Nuova Giustificazione del Celibato Sacro," in answer to the Abbé Gaudin and to an anonymous German writer whose work had produced considerable sensation. To this he was principally moved by a report that he had himself been converted by the facts and arguments advanced by the German, an imputation which he indignantly refuted in three hundred quarto pages.

The half-formed resolutions of Joseph II led to no result, and the subject slumbered for a few years, until the outbreak of the French Revolution. At an early period in that great movement the adversaries of sacerdotal asceticism bestirred themselves in bringing to public attention the evils and cruelty of the system. Already, in 1789, a mass of pamphlets appeared urging the abrogation of celibacy. In 1790 the work of the Abbé Gaudin was reprinted, and was promptly answered by the prolific Maultrot. Even in Germany the same spirit again awoke, and a Hungarian priest named Katz published at Vienna, in 1791, a " Tractatus de conjugio et cœlibatu clericorum," in which he argued strongly for a change. In Poland these doctrines made considerable progress, for in 1801 we find a little tract issued at Warsaw vehemently arguing against those who imperil their souls by violating their vows and the laws of the Church. In England a Catholic priest distinguished for talents and learning, Dr. Geddes, published in 1800 a work in which he denied the apostolic origin of celibacy, and urged that, at most, delinquents should be punished by degradation from the priesthood, without disgrace. Indeed, he argued that the rule caused more proselytes to Protestantism than any other cause.

During this period it can hardly be supposed that the defiant immorality which characterised the eighteenth century had been favourable to the purity of a celibate priesthood. That the Church, indeed, had made but scanty improvement in the character of its ministers is visible throughout the literature of the age, and I need only allude to a few instances where efforts at reform revealed the prevailing corruption.

In France the attacks upon the vow of celibacy, to which allusion has already been made, seem to have given rise to a spasmodic attempt to regulate the Church. In 1760 an *arrêt* of the Parlement of Paris prohibited the organisation of religious congregations without express royal permission, verified by that body. The assembly of the clergy in Paris in 1766 produced no notable improvement, nor was greater success obtained when the temporal power intervened in the edicts of 1766 and 1767. Further effort apparently was requisite, and in the edict of March 1768, Louis XV undertook to diminish in some degree the causes of the more flagrant disorders among the regular clergy. Men were not to be allowed to take the vows under the age of twenty-two, nor women under nineteen ; and as the smaller religious houses were especially notorious for laxness of discipline, all were suppressed which could not number at least fifteen professed monks or nuns, except those attached to larger congregations. The ecclesiastical authorities, moreover, were emphatically commanded to make a thorough visitation, and to compel the observance of the rules of discipline of the several Orders. The enforcement of this edict created no little excitement, and several of the smaller Orders narrowly escaped destruction in their endeavours to evade its provisions. That these efforts did not succeed in accomplishing their object we may well believe, even without the testimony of an eye-witness. As for the secular clergy, when Louis XV amused himself by ordering the arrest of all ecclesiastics caught frequenting brothels, the number of victims in a short time amounted to 296, of whom no fewer than 100 were priests actively engaged in the service of the altar.

When the Grand-Duke Leopold of Tuscany undertook to reform the monasteries of his dominions and to put an end, if possible, to the abuse of the confessional, it led to a long diplomatic correspondence with the papal curia as to the jurisdiction over such cases. A public document of the year 1763 had already stated that the special crime in question had become less frequent, and attributed this improvement to the exceeding laxity of morals everywhere prevalent, for few confessors would be so foolish as to attempt seduction in the confessional when there was so little risk in doing the same thing elsewhere. Specious as this reasoning might seem, the facts on which it was based were hardly borne out by the investigations of Leopold shortly after into the morals of the monastic establishments. Nothing more scandalous is to be found in the visitations of the religious houses of England under Morton and Cromwell. The spiritual directors of the nunneries had converted them virtually into harems, and such of the sisters as were proof against seduction, armed with the powers of confession and absolution, suffered every species of persecution. It was rare for them to venture on complaint, but when they did so they received no attention from their ecclesiastical superiors, and only the protection of the grand-ducal authority at length emboldened them to reveal the truth.

The prioress of S. Caterina di Pistoia declared that, with three or four exceptions, all the monks and confessors whom she had met in her long career were alike; that they treated the nuns as wives, and taught them that God had made man for woman and woman for man; and that the visitations of the bishops amounted to naught, even though they were aware of what occurred, for the mouths of the victims were sealed by the dread of excommunication threatened by their spiritual directors. When it is considered that the convents thus converted into dens of prostitution were the favourite schools to which the girls of the higher classes were sent for training and education, it can readily be imagined what were the moral influences thence radiating throughout society at large, and we can appreciate the argument above referred to, as to the ease with which the clergy could procure sexual indulgence without recourse to the confessional. Leopold's chief assistant in this struggle was Scipione de' Ricci, Bishop of Pistoia and Prato, whose experiences in the investigation caused him to induce the Council of Pistoia, in 1786, to declare the duties of the confessional wholly incompatible with the monastic state, and, in view of the improbability of any permanent reform, to propose the abolition of the monastic Orders by restricting vows to the duration of a twelvemonth—propositions which were not approved by the congregation of Tuscan prelates held at Florence in 1787, and which were scornfully condemned by Rome. Leopold, however, sought to palliate the evil by raising to the age of twenty-four the minimum limit for taking the vows, which the Council of Trent had fixed at sixteen, but the benefit of this salutary measure was neutralised by the ease with which parents desiring to get rid of their children could place them in the institutions of the neighbouring states, such as Lucca and Modena.

Rome itself was no better than its dependent provinces, despite the high personal character of some of the pontiffs. When the too early death of Clement XIV, in 1774, cut short the hopes which had been excited by his enlightened rule, St. Alphonso Liguori addressed to the conclave assembled for the election of his successor a letter urging them to make such a choice as would afford reasonable prospect of accomplishing the much-needed reform. The saint did not hesitate to characterise the discipline of the

secular clergy as most grievously lax, and to proclaim that
a general reform of the ecclesiastical body was the only way
to remove the fearful corruption of the morals of the laity.
When we hear, about this time, of two Carmelite convents
at Rome, one male and the other female, which had to be
pulled down because underground passages had been
established between them, by means of which the monks
and nuns lived in indiscriminate licentiousness, and when
we read the scandalous stories which were current in
Roman society about prelates high in the Church, we can
readily appreciate the denunciations of St. Alphonso. A
curious glimpse at the interior of conventual life is furnished
by a manual for Inquisitors, written about this period by
an official of the Holy Office of Rome. In a chapter on
nuns he describes the scandals which often cause them to
fall within the jurisdiction of the Inquisition, and prescribes
the course to be pursued with regard to the several offences.
Among those who were forced to take the veil, despair
frequently led to the denial of God, of heaven, and of hell;
feminine enmity caused accusations of sorcery and witchcraft, which threw not only the nunneries, but whole cities,
into confusion; vain-glory of sanctity suggested pretended
revelations and visions; and these latter were also not
infrequently caused by licentiousness, for in these utterances
were sometimes taught doctrines utterly subversive of
morality, of which godless confessors took advantage to
teach their spiritual daughters that there was no sin in
sexual intercourse. As in Spain, it was the practice of the
Roman Inquisition to treat the offenders mildly, partly in
consideration of the temptations to which they were exposed,
and partly to avoid scandal. The contaminating influence
on society at large, emanating from a Church so incurably
corrupted, was vastly heightened by the overgrown numbers
of the clerical body. In 1775, for example, a census of the
terra-firma provinces of Venice showed in that narrow territory
no less than 45,773 priests, or one to every fifty inhabitants,
while in the kingdom of Naples, exclusive of Sicily, there
were, in 1769, one to every seventy-six. Such overcrowding
as this was not only in itself an efficient cause of disorder,
but intensified incalculably the power of infection.

The virtues of the clergy, therefore, could offer but a
feeble barrier to the spirit of innovation when the passions
of the French Revolution were brought to bear upon the

immunities and distinctive laws of the Church. The attack commenced on that which had been the strength, but which was now the weakness, of the ecclesiastical establishment. As early as 10 August, 1789, preliminary steps were taken in the National Assembly to appropriate the property of the Church to meet the deficit which had been the efficient cause of calling together the high council of the nation. This property was estimated as covering one-fifth of the surface of France, yielding with the tithes an annual revenue of three hundred millions of francs. So vast an amount of wealth, perverted for the most part from its legitimate purposes, offered an irresistible temptation to desperate financiers, and yet it was a prelate who made the first direct attack upon it. On 10 October, 1789, Talleyrand, then Bishop of Autun, introduced a motion to the effect that it should be devoted to the national wants, subject to the proper and necessary expenses of public worship; and on 2 November the measure was adopted by a vote of 568 to 346. This settled the principle, though the details of a transaction of such magnitude were only perfected by successive acts during the two following years. One of the earliest results was the secularisation of those ecclesiastics whose labour did not entitle them to support, a preliminary necessary to the intended appropriation of their princely revenues. This was accomplished by an act of 13 February, 1790, by which the religious Orders were suppressed, monastic vows were declared void, and a moderate annuity accorded to the unfortunates thus turned adrift upon the world.

The great body of the parochial clergy, patriotic in their aspirations, and suffering from the abuses of power, had hailed the advent of the Revolution with joy; and their assistance had been invaluable in rendering the Tiers-Etat supreme in the National Assembly. These measures, however, assailing their dearest interests and privileges, aroused them to a sense of the true tendency of the movement to which they had contributed so powerfully. A breach was inevitable between them and the partisans of progress. Every forward step embittered the quarrel. It was impossible for the one party to stay its course, or for the other to assent to acts which daily became more menacing and revolutionary. Forced, therefore, into the position of reactionaries, the clergy ere long became objects of suspicion and soon after of persecution. The progressives devised a test-oath, obligatory on all ecclesiastics, which should divide those who were loyal to the Revolution from the contumacious, and lists were kept of both classes. Harmless as the oath was in appearance, when it was tendered, in December 1790, five-sixths of the clergy throughout the kingdom refused it. Those who yielded to the pressure were termed *assermentés*, the recusants *insermentés* or *réfractaires*, and the latter, of course, at once became the determined opponents of the new *régime*, the more dangerous because they were the only influential partisans of reaction belonging to the people. To their efforts were attributed the insurrections which in La Vendée and elsewhere threatened the most fearful dangers. They were accordingly exposed to severe legislation. A decree of 29 November, 1791, deprived them of their stipends and suspended their functions; another of 27 May, 1792, authorised the local authorities to exile them on the simple denunciation of twenty citizens. Under the Terror their persons were exposed to flagrant cruelties, and a *prêtre réfractaire* was generally regarded, *ipso facto*, as an enemy to the Republic.

Under these circumstances, sacerdotal marriage came to be looked upon as a powerful lever to disarm or overthrow the hostility of the Church, and also as a test of loyalty or disloyalty. Yet the steps by which this conclusion was reached were very gradual. In the early stages of the Revolution, while it was still fondly deemed that the existing institutions of France could be purified and preserved, the National Assembly was assailed with petitions asking that the privilege of marriage should be extended to the clergy. These met with no response, even after the suppression of the monastic Orders. As late as September 1790, when the Abbé Professor Cournand, of the Collège de France, made a motion in favour of sacerdotal marriage in the assembly of the district of St. Etienne du Mont in Paris, the question, after considerable debate, was laid aside as beyond the competence of that body. It was not until 3 September, 1791, that Mirabeau introduced into the Assembly a decree providing that no profession or vocation should debar a citizen from marriage or be considered as incompatible with marriage, and forbidding the public officials and notaries from refusing to ratify any marriage contract on such pretext. Though no allusion was made in this to ecclesiastics, its object was evident, and was so admitted in the eloquent speech with which he urged its adoption—a speech which contained a very telling *résumé* of the arguments in favour of priestly marriage, but which, in its glowing anticipations of the benefits to be expected from the measure, affords a somewhat lamentable contrast to the meagreness of the realisation. The principle, when once established, was considered of sufficient importance to deserve recognition in the Constitution of September 1791, a section in the preamble of which declares that the law does not recognise religious vows or any engagements contrary to the rights of nature or to the constitution; and this was followed, as Mirabeau had proposed, by a decree of 20 September, 1791, which, in enumerating the obstacles to marriage, does not allude to monastic vows or holy orders.

Professor Cournand was probably the first man of position and character to take advantage of the privilege thus permitted, and his example was followed by many ecclesiastics who had won an honourable place in the Church, in literature, and in science. Among them may be mentioned the Abbé Gaudin of the Oratoire, the author of a work already alluded to on the evils of celibacy, who in 1792 represented La Vendée in the Legislative Assembly, and who in 1805 did not hesitate to publish a little volume entitled "Avis à mon fils âgé de sept ans"—although in the preface to his work in 1781 he had described himself as long past the age of the passions. Even bishops yielded to the temptation. Loménie, coadjutor of his uncle the Archbishop of Sens, Torné, Bishop of Bourges, Massieu of Beauvais, and Lindet of Evreux were publicly married. Many nuptials of this kind were celebrated with an air of defiance. Pastors announced their approaching weddings to their flocks in florid rhetoric, as though assured of finding sympathy for the assertion of the triumph of nature over the tyranny of man. Others presented themselves with their brides at the bar of the National Convention, as though to demonstrate that they were good citizens who had thrown off all reverence for the obsolete traditions of the past.

A nation maddened and torn by the extremes of hope, of rage, and of terror, which met the triumphal march of three hundred and fifty thousand hostile bayonets with the heads of its king and queen, which blazoned forth to

Europe its irrevocable breach with the past by instituting festivals in honour of a new Supreme Being and parading a courtesan through the streets of Paris as the goddess of reason, was not likely to employ much tenderness in coercing its internal enemies, and chief among these it finally numbered the ministers of religion. To them it soon applied the marriage test. To marry was to acknowledge the supremacy of the civil authority and to sunder allegiance to foreign domination; celibacy was at the least a tacit adherence to the enemy and a mute protest against the new *régime*. Matrimony, therefore, rose into importance as at once a test and a pledge, and every effort was made to encourage it. Among the records of the revolutionary tribunal is the trial of Mahue, curé of S. Sulpice, 13 August, 1793, accused of having written a pamphlet against priestly marriage, and he was only acquitted on the ground that his crime had been committed prior to the adoption of the law of 19 July, 1793. A decree of 19 November, 1793, relieved from exile or imprisonment all priests who could show that their banns had been published, and when, soon afterwards, at the height of the popular frenzy, the Convention sent its deputies throughout France with instructions to crush out every vestige of the dreaded reaction, those emissaries made celibacy the object of their especial attacks. Thus, in the Department of the Meuse, deputy De la Croix announced that all priests who were not married should be placed under surveillance; while in Savoy the harsh measures taken against the clergy were modified in favour of those who married by permitting them to remain under surveillance. One zealous deputy ordered a pastor to be imprisoned until he could find a wife, and another released a canon from jail on his pledging himself to marry. Many of those thus forced into matrimony were decrepit with years, and chose brides whose age secured them from all suspicions of yielding to the temptations of the flesh. Such was the venerable Martin of Marseilles, who, after seeing his bishop and two priests, his intimate friends, led to the scaffold, took, at the age of seventy-six, a wife nearly sixty years old. As an unfortunate ecclesiastic, who had thus succeeded in weathering the storm, fairly expressed it, in defending himself against the reproaches of a returned *émigré* bishop, he took a wife to serve as a lightning rod. These unwilling bridegrooms not infrequently deposited with a notary or a trusty friend a protest against the violence to which they had yielded, and a declaration that their relations with their wives should be merely those of brother and sister.

Yet in this curious persecution the officials only obeyed the voice of the excited people. The press, the stage, all the organs of public opinion, were unanimous in warring with celibacy, ridiculing it as a fanatical remnant of superstition, and denouncing it as a crime against the state. The popular societies were especially vehement in promulgating these ideas. The *Congrès fraternel* of Ausch, in September 1793, ordered the local clubs to enlighten the benighted minds of the populace on the subject, and to exclude from membership all priests who should not marry within six months. A petition to the National Assembly from the republicans of Auxerre demanded that all ecclesiastics who persisted in remaining single should be banished; while a more truculent address from Condom urged imperiously that celibacy should be declared a capital crime, and that the death penalty should be enforced with relentless severity. In times so unsparing, when suspicion was conviction and conviction death, and when such were the views of those who swayed public affairs, it is not to be wondered at if many pious Churchmen, unambitious of the crown of martyrdom, thought matrimony preferable to the guillotine or the noyade.

Indeed, the only source of surprise is that so few were found to betray their convictions. In the vast body of the Gallican Church it is estimated that only about 2000 marriages of men in orders took place after the Reign of Terror had rendered it a measure of safety. In addition to this, about 500 nuns were also married; and though this proportion is larger, it is still singularly small when we consider that these poor creatures, utterly unfitted by habit or education to take care of themselves, were suddenly ejected from their peaceful retreats and cast upon a world which was raging in convulsions so terrible.[1]

[1] I have not found it easy to form a satisfactory estimate of the number of French ecclesiastics previous to the Revolution. Le Bas (Dictionnaire Encyclopédique de l'Histoire de France, V. 218) gives a table showing an aggregate of 418,206 souls, of whom 235,147 may be considered as attached to the secular service, and 183,059 to the regular Orders and canons. Of these latter, 100,451 were men and 82,608 were women. On the other hand, M. Sauvestre (Congrégations Religieuses, pp. 5, 6) quotes from the Abbé Expilly a

This is doubtless attributable to the steadfast resistance which the better part of the clergy made to the innovation, in spite of the danger of withstanding the popular frenzy, and in disregard of the laws which denounced such opposition. Even the *assermentés*, who had pledged themselves to the Revolution by taking the oath of allegiance, were mostly unfavourable to the abrogation of celibacy, and the position thus maintained by the clergy gave tone to such of the people as retained enough of devout feeling still to frequent the churches and partake of the mysteries of religion. The existence of an active and determined opposition is revealed by an act of 16 August, 1792, guaranteeing the salaries of all married priests, thus showing that in some places at least their stipends had been withheld. Many pastors, indeed, were driven from their parishes by their congregations, in consequence of marriage, to put an end to which a decree of 17 September, 1793, ordered the communes to continue payment of salaries in all such cases of ejection.

There were not wanting courageous ecclesiastics who opposed the innovation by every means in their power. Although Gobel, Bishop of Paris, a creature of the Revolution, favoured the marriages of his clergy, a portion of his curates openly and vigorously denounced them, and Gratien, Archbishop of Rouen, addressed to him a severe reproach for his criminal weakness. The same Gratien excommunicated one of his priests for marrying, and published, 24 July, 1792, an instruction directed especially against such unions. For this he was thrown into prison, where he was long confined. Fauchet of Bayeux, for the same offence, was reported to the Convention, but was fortunate enough to elude the consequences. Philibert of Sedan issued, 20 January, 1793, a pastoral in which he more cautiously argued against the practice, and, after a long persecution, he was lucky to escape with a decree of costs against him. Pastorals to the same effect were

---

statement that in 1765 there were 79,000 monks and 80,000 nuns, while he shows that other contemporary authorities reduce the number of members of religious Orders in 1789 to 52,000 of both sexes. M. Charles Chabot (Encyclopédie Monastique, p. x, Paris, 1827) computes, after elaborate tabulation, the number of ecclesiastics, regular and secular, at 407,753 persons, enjoying a revenue of 127,610,576 francs.

also promulgated by Clément of Versailles, Héraudin of Châteauroux, Sanadon of Oléron, Suzor of Tours, and others.

The Convention was not disposed to tolerate proceedings such as these. To put a stop to them, it adopted, 19 July, 1793, a law punishing with deprivation and exile all bishops who interfered in any way with the marriage of their clergy. For a while this appears to have put a stop to open opposition, but when the Reign of Terror was past, and the Catholics saw a prospect of reorganising the distracted Church, one of the earliest efforts was directed to the restoration of celibacy. On 15 March, 1795, some *assermentés* bishops, members of the Convention, issued from Paris an encyclical letter to the faithful, in which they denounced sacerdotal marriage in the strongest terms. Those who entered into such unions were declared unworthy of confidence; the fearful constraint under which they had sought refuge in matrimony was pronounced to be no justification, and even renunciation of their wives was not admitted as entitling them to absolution for the one unpardonable sin. In a second letter, issued 15 December of the same year, this denunciation was repeated in even stronger terms.

In these manifestoes the bishops did not speak by authority. They could not threaten or command, for they were acting beyond or in opposition to the law. With the progress of reaction they became bolder. In 1797 the Church ventured to hold a national council, in which it forbade the nuptial benediction to those who were in orders or were bound by monastic vows, thus reducing their marriages to the mere civil contract, and depriving them of all the sanction of religion. The local synods which, encouraged by the fall of the Directory, were held in 1800, adopted these principles as a matter of course, and took measures to enforce them. That of Bourges even prohibited the churching of women who were wives of ecclesiastics.

This condemnation of the married clergy carried despair and desolation into the households of those who had offended, and upon whom the door of reconciliation was so sternly closed. Grégoire of Blois, a leading actor in all these scenes, records the innumerable appeals received from the unfortunates, who, torn by remorse and repudiated by the Church, begged in vain for the mercy which was incompatible with the respect due to the ancient and inviolable canons.

All this, however, was merely local action. The Gallican Church had not yet been reunited to Rome. In reconstructing a system of social order, Napoleon speedily recognised the necessity of religion in the state, and, despite the opposition of those who still believed in the Republic, the Concordat of 1801 restored France to its place in the hierarchy of Latin Christianity. There is nothing in the Concordat interfering with the right of the priest, as a citizen, to contract marriage; but as, in all affairs purely ecclesiastical, the internal regulation and discipline of the Church were necessarily left to itself, the rights of the priest, as a priest, became of course subject to the received rules of the Church, which could thus refuse the nuptial benediction, and suspend the functions of any one contravening its canons. In consequence of the power thus restored, when the question soon after arose as to the legality of sacerdotal marriages contracted during the troubles, the cardinal-legate Caprara issued rescripts to those whose unions were anterior to the Concordat, depriving them of their priestly character, reducing them to the rank of laymen, and empowering the proper officials to absolve them and remarry them to the wives whom they had so irregularly wedded. This created a strong feeling of indignation among the prelates who had carried the tabernacle through the wilderness, and who, while opposing such marriages most strenuously, regarded this intervention of papal authority as a direct assault upon the liberties of the Gallican Church. Their time was past, however, and their denunciations of this duplication of the sacrament were of no avail. Yet the legality of such marriages as civil contracts, and the unimpaired right of priests to contract them, were asserted and proved by Portalis, in his masterly speech of 15 April, 1802, before the Corps Législatif, advocating the adoption of the Concordat as a law, although he admitted that the Church could withhold its sanction and could exercise its discipline while the feeling of the people rendered sacerdotal celibacy desirable.

One phase of the situation thus created was aptly illustrated in the curious affair of Prince Talleyrand's marriage, which attracted at the time the attention of Europe.

Forced into the Church by family exigencies, and elevated to the bishopric of Autun, he had earned the permanent hatred of the hierarchy by throwing himself into the revolutionary movement, where he bore a leading part in the secularisation of ecclesiastical property and utilised his episcopal functions in consecrating the Constitutional bishops. This could not be condoned, even in view of the active assistance which, as Minister of Foreign Affairs, under the Consulate, he rendered in the negotiations for the Concordat. In these he had vainly sought to introduce a clause releasing from their obligations all ecclesiastics who had contracted marriage or had otherwise renounced their clerical status—a clause which would have covered his own case—but Pius VII was obdurate, and, while promising to give to his legate Caprara faculties to absolve simple priests, he refused to comprehend bishops and members of the religious Orders.

The Concordat adopted in this shape left Talleyrand in an awkward position. A fascinating woman with a dubious past, known as Madame Grand, had for some years been his acknowledged mistress, doing the honours of his house. In the easy morality of the Directory this had caused no scandal, but Napoleon, in re-establishing order, insisted on external decency, and, moreover, when relations were resumed with foreign powers, ambassadorial ladies murmured at being obliged to associate with a concubine. He therefore offered Talleyrand the peremptory alternatives of marrying Madame Grand or of dismissing her, and Talleyrand chose the former. Two pressing applications were made to the Holy See and urged with all the force that Napoleon could bring to bear, but in each case the only outcome was a brief enabling Talleyrand to be unfrocked, to be reduced to lay communion, deprived of sacerdotal functions, and authorised to lead a secular life, without a word as to marriage. Thus checked, Talleyrand made the best of the situation. He caused the second brief to be laid before the Council of State, which duly accepted it and ordered its registration, and it was officially gazetted in a concise form stating that it restored citizen Talleyrand to secular life. All the world assumed this as conferring on him the full privileges of the laity, and it was in vain that the Holy See caused the insertion in foreign journals of a statement that it reduced him to lay communion without relieving him of his vows. His civil marriage with Madame Grand was celebrated on 10 September, 1802, and the lady had the satisfaction of styling herself Talleyrand-Périgord, or subsequently Princess of Benevento. A sacramental marriage, it is said, followed, performed quietly by the curé of Epinay, but the parish register of that place has disappeared and the assertion cannot be confirmed, though there is little reason to disbelieve it, for no one at the time, save the Curia, doubted the legal validity of the union.

The question of celibacy was not settled by the Concordat. Notwithstanding the certainty of ecclesiastical penalties following such infraction of the Tridentine articles of faith, the practice which had been introduced could not be immediately eradicated. Priests were constantly contracting marriage, and the question gave considerable trouble to the Government, which hesitated for some time as to the policy to be pursued. Portalis, in 1802, as we have seen, declared the full legality of such marriages, and the unimpaired right of ecclesiastics to contract them; and the provisions of the Code respecting marriage, adopted in 1803, make no allusions [to vows or religious engagements as causing incapacity. Yet in 1805, when Daviaux, Archbishop of Bordeaux, opposed the application of a priest named Boisset to the civil authorities for a marriage contract, Portalis, then Minister of Religious Affairs, on being appealed to, replied that the Government would not allow its officers to register such contracts. The local administrations sometimes assented to such applications and sometimes referred them to the central authority, until at length, in 1807, a definite conclusion was promulgated. This was to the effect that, although the civil law was silent as regards such marriages, yet they were condemned by public opinion. The Government considered them fraught with danger to the peace of families, as the powerful influence of the pastor could be perverted to evil purposes, and, if seduction could be followed by marriage, that influence would be liable to great abuse. The emperor therefore declared that he could not tolerate marriage on the part of those who had exercised priestly functions since the date of the Concordat. As for those who had abandoned the ministry previous to that period and had not since resumed it, he left them to their own consciences. Thus in practice, although marriage was regarded as purely a civil institution, a limitation was introduced which was not authorised by the Code, which rested solely upon the authority of the emperor, and which, far from indicating respect to the Church, was a flagrant insult.   As Napoleon withdrew himself more and more from the principles of the new order of things, we find him disposed to take even stronger ground in opposition to the civil privileges accorded to the priesthood by the Concordat.   The question of sacerdotal marriage continued to present itself under perplexing shapes, and at length the emperor, on the eve of his downfall, perhaps with a view to propitiate the sacerdotal power, proposed to apply to married priests the penalty imposed by the law on bigamy.   It was too late, however : the Empire was rapidly vanishing, and these suggestions were soon forgotten in the hurrying march of events.

CHAPTER XXXII

THE CHURCH OF TO-DAY

THE question of sacerdotal marriage was left in France, on the collapse of the Empire, in a curiously unsettled condition, giving rise to very remarkable contradictions in the judicial decisions which since then have from time to time been rendered by the tribunals as cases were brought before them.

Under the Restoration, a priest named Martin, an old *réfractaire* of 1792, committed the imprudence of marrying in 1815. Not long after he died without issue. His relatives contested the succession with the widow, and in 1817 the inferior court decided in her favour. The next year the court of appeals reversed the judgment on the ground that sacerdotal marriage had only been sanctioned indirectly by the legislation of the Revolution, and that the Charter of 1814 (Art. 6) had restored Catholicism as the religion of the state. In 1821, however, the final decision of the Court of Cassation settled the question in favour of the widow, thus legalising such unions, for the incontrovertible reason that the Code did not recognise vows or holy orders as causes incapacitating for marriage.

Even yet, however, the matter was not held to be finally disposed of. In 1828, Louis Thérèse Saturnin Dumonteil, a priest of Paris, who desired to contract marriage, failed to obtain from the courts the customary assistance required by the law to set aside the refusal of his parents, who declined their assent to his projected union. The case was argued in all its bearings on civil and ecclesiastical law, and he found the tribunals resolutely opposed to him. When the Revolution of July unsettled the public mind with visions of the revival of the principles of '89, Dumonteil endeavoured to carry out his project. The lower court decided in his favour, 26 March, 1831, but the higher courts reversed the decision, and pronounced definitely that priests could not contract civil marriage, and this in spite of the Charter of 1830, which simply affirmed Catholicism to be the religion of the majority of Frenchmen, while that of 1814 had declared it to be the religion of the state.

This curiously vexed question seemed incapable of positive solution. The case of Dumonteil apparently discouraged aspirants for clerical marriage during the next thirty years, for I have met with no allusions to any attempt in that direction until 1861. In that year M. de Brou-Laurière, a priest already debarred from his sacred functions, engaged himself in marriage with Mlle. Elizabeth Fressanges, of Deuville near Périgueux. On calling upon the mayor of the village to perform the ceremony and register the contract, that functionary refused to act. He was supported by the public authorities, and the expectant bridegroom was obliged to appeal to the tribunals to obtain his rights. The question was warmly contested and thoroughly argued, and it was not until a year had elapsed that the court of Périgueux rendered a decision ordering the mayor to perform his functions and to marry the patient couple. The case was then carried to the superior court at Bordeaux, which reversed the previous decision.

Again, in 1864, in the case of the Abbé Chataigneu, the court of Angoulême decided that a priest was, under the law of France, not competent to contract civil marriage. On the other hand, in 1870 the court of Algiers, in the case of a M. Q——, delivered an elaborate decision to the effect that in France there is no law forbidding the civil marriage of priests. Yet in 1878 the Court of Cassation confirmed a decision of the court of Rennes, pronouncing null and void the marriage of a priest, at the instance of his nephew and niece, to whom he had bequeathed his property by a will anterior to the marriage. When M. Loyson (Père Hyacinthe) married Mrs. Merriman, in 1872, the ceremony was performed in London, at the office of the registrar of marriages, and M. Loyson gave as the reason of his seeking a foreign land the refusal of the French officials to confirm the civil ceremony. So the Abbé Chavard, vicar of Marseilles, in 1874 went to Geneva for the same purpose, where he continued his priestly functions; and this leads me to regard as exceedingly improbable a public statement in the daily journals that priestly marriages occur in France at the rate of twenty or thirty a year. In fact, so lately as September 1883 there was before the courts a case which shows how uncertain is the question still in France. A certain Abbé Junqua was expelled from the Church and was condemned to three months' imprisonment for continuing to wear the priestly robes. He subsequently married and engaged in trade, when he failed, and his wife sought to secure her dowry from the bankrupt assets, but was resisted on the ground that her marriage was illegal under the Concordat, although the Church had itself deprived the husband of his ecclesiastical character. Yet at last, when in 1888 the Court of Cassation, the supreme tribunal in France, definitely decided in favour of priestly marriage, the decision was acquiesced in with scarce a remonstrance and hardly attracted attention. It is evident that the world moves.

In Switzerland I have met with two or three cases of such marriages, but they have no special significance. In one of them, occurring in Lucerne some fifty years ago, the priest left the Church in order to marry, and lived with his wife until her death, in 1880, when he permitted her to be buried as a Catholic, and had the mortification of seeing her name entered on the register, publicly exposed in the parish church, as an unmarried woman.

In Wiesbaden, in 1821, a priest named Koch, with the permission of the authorities, abandoned the priesthood and applied to the curé of the place to marry him, when, meeting with a refusal, he had the ceremony performed by a Protestant pastor, and was promptly excommunicated by the vicar of Ratisbon. Not deterred by this, in 1828 a hundred and eighty priests of Baden petitioned the secular power for permission to marry, and the Chamber of Deputies showed a disposition to grant the request. This effort was imitated in 1831 by the Catholic clergy of Silesia, but the movement was repressed by the Prussian Government; and in 1833, at Trèves, a clerical association was formed to carry out the same object. These efforts led Gregory XVI, in the encyclical Mirari vos (15 August 1832), to urge the bishops to constant vigilance and earnest effort in defence of a law of the greatest importance, against a foul conspiracy which was daily extending. Some similar movements in Austria in the next decade

led Pius IX, almost immediately after his accession to
the papal chair, in his encyclical letter Qui pluribus
(9 November, 1846), to repeat the words of his predecessor.
In 1851, moreover, he took especial pains to stigmatise a
work, published in Lima by Francisco de Paula in 1848,
entitled " Defensa de la Autoridad de los Goberinos,"
which impiously sought to decentralise the Church, and
which took strong grounds against enforced celibacy.

How immovable, indeed, is the position of the hierarchy on this matter is shown by the case of Panzini.
Panzini is, or was, a Capuchin monk, who in 1854 conceived the idea that the greater part of the evils under
which the establishment labours are the result of celibacy
and its attendant immorality. He addressed to the pope
an anonymous memorial urging him to submit the question
to the bishops then assembled in Rome, and followed this
with two similar subsequent applications. Finally, in the
troubles of 1859, anticipating the assembling of a European
congress, he resolved to print an essay on the subject,
addressed to all the bishops of the Church, thinking that
the congress would afford him an opportunity of reaching
them. The printer to whom he confided his manuscript
promptly placed the dangerous matter in the hands of
Cardinal Antonelli, when Panzini was at once thrown into
prison and delivered to the Inquisition. After a trial
which lasted six months, he was condemned to twelve
years' incarceration and perpetual suspension from the
sacerdotal functions which were his only source of livelihood. After two years of his sentence had expired, he
was released at the instance of the Italian Government,
and in 1865 he published his essay, rewritten from memory,
under the title of " Pubblica Confessione di un Prigioniero
dell' Inquisizione Romana ed origine dei mali della Chiesa
Cattolica."

Now, Panzini's persecution arose solely from his affirm-
ing that enforced celibacy is impolitic and unnatural. He
professed unbounded reverence for the Church in all
matters of faith, and claimed that the point at issue was
merely one of discipline on which the Church might make
a mistake. Even here, however, he was careful to declare
his measureless admiration for voluntary asceticism. Virginity he believed to be immensely superior to matrimony,
and he anathematised as cheerfully as the Council of Trent

could wish all who should proclaim the contrary. Even monasticism he defended as a state of perfection recommended by Christ. His sole objective point was the rigidity of the law which renders the single state indispensable to all ecclesiastics, and he essayed to prove that this is in direct antagonism to all the general principles of Catholic theology; that the purity which is its pretext is impossible to enforce, and that the effort itself is most disastrous to the Church and to the faithful. The authorities were not disposed to consider that these opinions were an allowable dissidence on matters of policy, and they hastened to brand them as heretical. In the sentence passed upon Panzini the Inquisition took occasion to stigmatise as heresy the assertion that enforced celibacy is contrary to nature, that it is a stumbling-block and the cause of perpetual transgression. That this theory was enforced in practice so long as the Church could control the secular power is shown in the case of an Italian priest who, preferring to sanctify love by marriage rather than to indulge in illicit intrigue, married and fled with his bride to Africa, seeking among the infidel the liberty denied him in Christendom. Three children blessed his union, but the unresting vigilance of the Church discovered his retreat, when, with the aid of the French consulate, he was seized, carried back to Naples, and thrown into prison to repent indefinitely of his errors.

There evidently could be no reasonable ground for expecting a change of policy in this respect on the part of the Roman Curia, and this was recognised in 1866 by some Catholic priests of Hungary, who, desiring liberty of marriage, and seeing the futility of anticipating it at the hands of their superiors, united in petitioning the National Diet for the requisite permission. Yet in spite of the extravagance of supposing that a body which, since the Council of Trent, has become so thoroughly centralised as the Church, would listen to the wishes of its lower classes, there were not wanting those who imagined that the Council of the Vatican in 1870 would adopt the discipline of the Eastern Church and permit marriage to the inferior orders. Any such expectations were destined to be disappointed as soon as the preliminary machinery of the council became known. A *congregazione centrale* was appointed by Pius IX in advance, consisting exclusively of cardinals connected with the Inquisition, and to this body was delegated the sole determination of the matters to be submitted to the council for discussion. Under this *congregazione*, and presided over by its members, were five *consulte*, to act as sub-committees on the subjects respectively confided to their deliberations. The *consulta* on faith and dogma was under the presidency of Cardinal Bilio, notorious as the compiler of the Syllabus of December 1864, and that on canons and discipline was committed to Cardinal Catarini, whose whole career had been passed in the Inquisition, and who had acquired a sinister fame by his rigorous punishment of all attempts at reform. If, as the Church asserts, the proceedings of general councils are under the immediate guidance of the Holy Ghost, it will be seen what reverent care was observed to keep Him in due subjection, and to spare the Church the scandal of being brought by thoughtless innovators into opposition with Him.

As the destined outcome of the council was simply the dogma of papal infallibility, the hopes of the anti-celibatarians were transferred to the schism precipitated by it, and known as that of the Old Catholics. In 1875 a Dean Suczinsky married the Baroness Gazewaska, and joined the schismatics, when the Prussian Government decided to protect him in the enjoyment of his temporalities, and his new brethren agreed to receive him, and thus committed themselves on the question of celibacy—a decision confirmed in 1878 by the synod of Bonn, which decreed, by a vote of seventy-five against twenty-two, that the prohibition of the canons is not an obstacle to the marriage of ecclesiastics, or to the cure of souls by married priests. It required no common conscientiousness and strength of purpose for men like von Döllinger, von Schulte, Reusch, and their companions, upheld by their intimate knowledge of the past, to sever themselves from the Church in which they had been nurtured, when so many of those on whose co-operation they had relied allowed themselves to be coerced into subscribing to a doctrine the untenability of which they had exposed. What, however, is to be the eventual outcome of their self-sacrifice time alone can determine. The struggle in France over the separation of Church and State shows that Ultramontanism is unyielding, and that the Vatican is resolved to rule or ruin. It is irreconcilable, and those who will not submit blindly to its demands have no choice but heresy or schism. This can scarce fail to broaden the movement of *Los von Rom*, which in Austria has already cost the Church so many thousand souls; and while most of these have gone over to the Evangelicals, the Old Catholics in the German portions of the Austrian Empire claim 23,000 members, and are growing at the rate of a thousand a year. In Bavaria and the Rhine lands they are said to be numerous, and in Switzerland the canton of Geneva alone numbers them at 4300. Holland has its share; and in the United States they have long been organised, having had about four thousand communicants as early as 1892. A cognate movement is on foot in France, where the uncompromising stand of the Vatican on the Law of Separation is directly provocative of schism. Akin to this is the separatist Polish National Church of America, which at the present moment is considering the question of abrogating priestly celibacy. It is useless to forecast the future, but he is blind to the portents of the times who does not recognise that there are elements at work which, if met with the eternal *non possumus*, may seriously threaten unity.

Another serious blow in the matter of marriage has been dealt by the adoption in successive Catholic states of what is known as civil marriage, by which matrimony is withdrawn from the exclusive control of the Church, and the sacrament and benediction are declared to be accidents not necessary to the legal status of husband and wife or to the legitimacy and heritable capacity of children. We have already seen that this was one of the legislative results of the French Revolution, and the example thus early set by France has been followed of late by Italy and Austria after its adoption in 1853 by Sardinia, as one of the earliest reformatory measures of Cavour. Yet the Church positively refuses to regard such marriages as entitled to respect. This is a trouble of old date, for when, in 1744, Benedict XIV was informed that in Belgium parties who were obliged by the law to present themselves before the civil magistrate and declare their intention to be man and wife frequently neglected to invoke the ministration of the priest, he pronounced such marriages to be invalid, and this was repeated by Pius VI in 1791 and Pius VII in 1808. It is therefore not surprising that when the project was under discussion in Italy, the *Unità Cattolica*, one of the papal organs, in its issue of 16 July, 1864, did not hesitate to assert that the establishment of civil matrimony was establishing the liberty of licentiousness, and that, after having scattered houses of ill-fame throughout Italy, it would convert the whole peninsula into one brothel. In a similar spirit, the papal penitentiary, 15 January, 1866, issued instructions reciting a decision of Pius IX in secret consistory, 27 September, 1852, that civil marriage without the sacrament was nothing but a foul and destructive cohabitation, whence it was deduced that the civil authorities have no power over marriage or divorce, and Pius IX followed this by an allocution of 30 October, 1866, denouncing it as leading to an organised system of scandalous concubinage. When, in May 1868, Austria followed the example of Italy, Pius within a month delivered an allocution in which he not only condemned the " abominable law," but declared it to be null and void; and Cardinal Rauscher, Archbishop of Vienna, issued a manifesto in which he not only denied that the civil contract constituted marriage, and directed that children sprung from such unions should be entered on the parish registers as neither legitimate nor illegitimate, but gave positive instructions that absolution should be denied, even *in articulo mortis*, to all parties who had cohabited in such unions—thus stigmatising them as worse than concubinage. In a similar spirit, when, in 1869, civil marriage was proclaimed under the short-lived republic of Spain, the clergy, under inspiration from the Vatican, denounced it as concubinage, and threatened to suspend the celebration of the Mass. The law, in fact, excited much popular feeling, for it made the civil ceremony essential, and declared that without it the solemnisation in church did not confer the legal status of man and wife, so that with the restoration of the monarchy it was promptly repealed, and an effort to restore it was rejected by an emphatic vote of the Cortes in February 1883. With the more liberal tendencies that have since prevailed, the matter has been again taken up, and its recognition has been the subject of fierce dissension. Leo XIII was vigorous in his opposition to the innovation. In his first encyclical, issued 21 April, 1878, he declared that " citizens, profaning the dignity of Christian marriage, have adopted legal concubinage in place of religious matrimony "; and he returned to the attack in a special encyclical on the subject, published 10 February, 1880. In this he assumes that, as " by the will of Christ the Church alone can and ought to legislate and decide concerning sacraments, so it is out of the question to attempt to transfer any, even the smallest part, of her power to the government of the state," and therefore " judicial sentences on conjugal contracts, as to whether they have been entered upon rightly or wrongly," are a direct infringement of the rights of the Church, whether those judgments be adverse or not to the canons.

The earlier passages of this encyclical are so warm and eloquent a defence of the holiness of matrimony, as the natural condition of man decreed by God, that it would probably trouble its author to explain why so exalted and divine a state should be prohibited to the ministers of the God who devised it and fitted his creatures specially for it. It is easy, however, to account for the bitter and persistent opposition of the Church to the civil marriage laws without attributing it to the control which the monopoly of the sacrament gives it over the faithful, and the lucrative nature of the business thus brought to the Curia. More important than these is the fact that under the laws the State has the power to permit clerical marriage. For more than half a century such laws had existed in France, but as the French tribunals leaned towards upholding ecclesiastical celibacy, they were acquiesced in comparatively in silence. When Italy, however, followed the example, it was seen that the temper of the Italian Government would lead to construing them in a sense favourable to priestly liberty, and hence the opposition, which has been justified and intensified by the result. Immediately on the passage of the Civil Marriage Act, Dr. Prota, of Naples, an energetic reformer within the Church, in a letter of 30 October, 1865, advised all his clerical friends to marry and to persist in the exercise of their functions, " and the more who do so at once and simultaneously the safer for all, for the bishops will venture the less to persecute you in the face of public opinion." Accordingly, cases of priestly marriage commenced to occur, and when they were contested their validity was confirmed by the tribunals. The superior courts of Genoa, Trani, and Palermo successively decided in this sense; and finally, in 1869, occurred the case of Andrea Treglia, of the diocese of Salerno, which settled the question in ·Naples. The municipal officers of Vietri refused to marry him; the court of Salerno decided against him, but when the matter was carried up to the court of appeals of Naples judgment was rendered in his favour, and he was married forthwith—thus legitimating the unions of some fifty priests who had preceded him, without the question having been settled by the tribunal of last resort. In the organ of the reforming Catholics of Naples, the *Emancipatore Cattolica*, it was not without interest to see the successive marriages chronicled with the same satisfaction as that evinced by Spalatin in the stormy days of Luther. In Austria the Church succeeded better in maintaining its hold upon those who had once entered its service. The Civil Marriage Law encouraged a number of priests to marry, but in 1891 the journals announced a decision by the High Court of Appeals, in the case of one who abandoned the Catholic faith in 1870 and who married in 1879, to the effect that a man who had vowed a life of celibacy could not be released from his vow.

Yet the whole question is one of but slender practical importance. In no country is the Catholic Church subservient to the State. It controls its own sacraments, and no government is likely to venture upon interference with it in its own sphere. While therefore it may be deprived of the power to persecute and punish those of its members who enter upon civil marriage, it yet possesses the ability to deprive them of their functions, which in most cases is equivalent to depriving them of bread; and it has an unquestioned right to expel them from its communion. The priest who marries, therefore, is virtually separated from his Church and deprived of his means of livelihood— motives which, combined with the moral forces at work to keep men within the accustomed bounds, are quite sufficient to prevent defection from growing common, or to render marriage with a priest attractive to women above the lowest class. Even in the United States, where there is no legal impediment to priestly marriage, and the tone of society is such as rather to welcome those who escape from the pale of Rome, such cases are rare, although of late years they seem to be increasing. While, therefore, the civil marriage laws of Europe unquestionably loosen the ties which in this respect bind the priest to his Church, there are still sufficient material and moral forces at work to prevent desertions from this cause from assuming any serious proportions.

The monastic Orders have not escaped the innovating spirit of modern times, and Catholic lands have followed, to a large extent, the example set in the sixteenth century by Henry VIII and the German Protestant princes. The excessive multiplication of the " religious " and the enormous accumulation of property in mortmain were recognised as an evil calling for repression as soon as the old-time veneration for the Church declined in the irreverential spirit of the eighteenth century. The expulsion of the Jesuits from Portugal, France, and Spain, between 1759 and 1767, and the suppression of the Order by Clement XIV in the bull Dominus ac Redemptor, 24 July, 1773, gave the impulse. The Emperor Joseph II, in a series of measures from 1772 to 1784, greatly reduced the religious Orders in his own dominions and suppressed the contemplative ones, which contributed nothing visible to the benefit of society. His brother, Leopold of Tuscany, desired to abolish all the Orders and replace them with one which should serve as a retreat for pious souls, but he felt himself not strong enough, and ventured only on partial measures. The French Revolution followed, with its decisive action of secularising all Church property by the decree of the National Assembly of 2 November, 1789, and the suppression of the Orders, 13 February, 1790. Germany yielded to the temptation, and by the Reichsrecess of 25 February, 1803, secularised the bishoprics and monastic foundations; everywhere but in Austria the religious houses were gradually suppressed, and their buildings were converted into barracks, prisons, insane asylums, and the like. In Spain, the Napoleonic invasion laid waste many convents, and the Cortes of Cadiz in 1813 decreed that none should be restored which had less than twelve inmates, and that there should not be more than one of each Order in any one place. The Revolution of 1820 went further, suppressing the monastic Orders and consolidating the houses of the mendicants, all of which was revoked by the reaction of 1823. In the troubles

following the death of Ferdinand VII in 1833, the Regency
was forced to rely on the Liberals : a policy was adopted
of suppressing the religious Orders and secularising Church
property, which during the ensuing fifteen years, amid
various fluctuations, gradually destroyed them. The
process was by no means always peaceable. In 1835 the
revolutionary juntas rose against them, burning many of
the houses, ejecting the inmates and slaying some of them.
The decrees of 8 March, 1836, and 29 July, 1837, extinguished the convents with few exceptions; even the nuns
were turned out and left to perish in misery, although the
funds of their convents consisted largely of the dowers
which they had brought. The Concordat of 1851, however,
re-established the Orders devoted to works of charity and
education; but the royal decrees issued in execution of
these provisions placed them under Government supervision and subject to strict limitations, in spite of which
they have flourished and multiplied largely, leading to
political vicissitudes of which the end is not as yet apparent.
In Portugal the process was more summary. The Emperor
Pedro I of Brazil, as regent for his daughter, Maria da
Gloria, by decree of 15 August, 1833, suppressed the convents and the military Orders; the promised pensions of
the ejected inmates were not paid, and they suffered the
extremity of want. When Italy ceased to be a geographical
expression and was consolidated under Victor Emanuel,
the law of 28 June, 1866, with its supplements of 15 August,
1867, and 19 June, 1873, completed the destruction of the
religious houses, confiscated their property, and pensioned
the inmates with from 144 to 600 lire per annum, according
to their position. Two exceptions were made : Monte
Cassino, the venerable mother of Western monachism, was
spared, and provision was made for its maintenance as a
national monument; while Savonarola's convent of San
Marco was preserved, rather perhaps on account of its
frescoes than of its associations. The process of eject-
ment was summary. Panzini speaks with indignation of
the files of soldiery sent to drive from their houses the
terrified nuns, who were thrown upon a world with which
they were by their training utterly unfit to cope; and early
in 1867 the journals reported that nearly all the inmates
of the monasteries were dispersed, some of them returning to their families, some of them accepting refuge

offered to them by the charitable, but most of them
clubbing together and hiring houses in which to live as
of old.

In France, under the Concordat of 1801, the re-estab-
lishment of monachism was strictly prohibited, but some
organisations succeeded in forming themselves. Charitable
associations of females were encouraged and flourished,
while male brotherhoods which proved politically dangerous
were crushed without ceremony. Even under the Restoration popular antagonism was still so strong that the efforts
made by Charles X, from 1825 to 1827, to introduce the
Jesuits and other male Orders aroused strong opposition,
and the elections of 1827 settled the question definitely in
the negative. The constitutional Government of Louis
Philippe, from 1830 to 1848, showed itself persistently
hostile; but the Second Republic was more liberal, and the
Second Empire ostentatiously sought the alliance of the
Church. After the fall of Louis Napoleon, the reactionary
Government of Marshal MacMahon continued this alliance,
and the result was seen in the enormous growth of the
regular Orders in wealth, members, and influence. This,
after republicanism had been firmly established by the will
of the people, became a serious menace to the tranquillity
of the State, for by its vital principle monachism owes its
allegiance first to the Holy See and secondarily to the
land from which its members are drawn. A long struggle
ensued, commencing with the Ferry laws on education in
1879—a struggle in which the expatriation of the monastic
Orders became merely an incident, and culminating in the
separation of Church and State. The struggle thus has
assumed the wider aspect of the internecine conflict between
mediæval theocracy on the one side and civil and religious
liberty on the other. The issue is still undecided, and it
is not for us to predict the result.

Nor has this anti-monastic movement been confined to
the Old World, for the example of Europe has been
followed in many of the former Spanish colonies. Para-
guay led the way, in 1824, by suppressing all monasteries
as useless, and Brazil, in 1829, prohibited the entrance of
men devotees, thus condemning the existing institutions to
gradual extinction. Mexico, by a series of laws from 1856
to 1863, suppressed the religious Orders and confiscated
their property. New Granada was even more prompt, by

legislation commencing in 1852 and culminating in 1863. Venezuela did the same in 1874. Ecuador in 1899 secularised all ecclesiastical property, and Nicaragua is understood to be preparing for similar action.

So general a movement in both hemispheres, by nations professing Catholicism, cannot be explained simply by greed for the overgrown possessions of the Church, although that has unquestionably borne its share in tempting governments to replenish their exhausted treasuries. It is an evidence that mediæval monasticism has outlived the influences which fostered its growth to such enormous proportions, and that, whatever may have been its services of old, they no longer correspond to the wants of the present sufficiently to justify its absorption of so large a portion of the resources and productive energies of society. It further indicates the convictions of statesmen that such corporations, dissociated from their environment by the vow of celibacy, having interests distinct from those of their fellow citizens, indissolubly bound together and owing allegiance, not to their own rulers but to a foreign chief, are politically as well as economically undesirable.

It only remains for us to consider what is the present effect of celibacy on the moral condition of the Church, and whether it has succeeded, after fifteen centuries of fruitless effort, in at last obtaining a priesthood whose chastity is more than nominal. At the commencement of the struggle, the great apostle of asceticism, St. Jerome, calmed the fears of those who dreaded a diminution of population from the spread of vows of continence, by assuring them that few would be found to persevere to the end in a task so difficult as the maintenance of virginity. Has, then, human nature changed during the interval, and has the Church been justified in its assertion at the Council of Trent that God would not withhold the gift of chastity from those who rightly seek it, or permit us to be tempted beyond our strength? It is certainly not so easy to answer this question now as we have seen it in former ages, when men were more plain-spoken and less decent, when offences against morality were committed more openly, and when they were denounced both by the Church and its enemies with a distinctness of utterance unfit for modern ears. Yet it is not impossible to find some evidence bearing on the question which may enable the impartial inquirer to arrive at a conclusion.

The Church is unquestionably violating the precept "Thou shalt not tempt the Lord thy God" when, in its reliance that the gift of chastity will accompany ordination, it confers the sub-diaconate at the age of twenty-two and the priesthood at twenty-five—or even earlier by special dispensation—and then turns loose young men, at the age when the passions are the strongest, trained in the seminary and unused to female companionship, to occupy a position in which they are brought into the closest and most dangerous relations with women who regard them as beings gifted with supernatural powers and holding in their hands the keys of heaven and hell. Whatever may have been the ardour with which the vows were taken, the youth thus exposed to temptations hitherto unknown finds his virtue rudely assailed when in the confessional female lips repeat to him the story of lustful longings, and he recognises in himself instincts and passions which are only the stronger by reason of their whilom repression. That a youthful spiritual director, before whom are thrown down all the barriers with which the prudent reserve of society surrounds the social intercourse of the sexes, should too often find that he has over-estimated his self-control, is more than probable.

This, of course, is merely *à priori* reasoning, and of itself proves nothing, except the extreme imprudence of a system which applies fire to straw and assumes that combustion will not follow. Doubtless there are cases in which the assumption is justified by the result—whole countries, indeed, where scandals are few. In Ireland, for instance, we rarely hear of immoral priests, though such cases would be relentlessly exposed by the interests adverse to Catholicism, and the proverbial chastity of the Irish women may be both a cause and a consequence of this. In the United States, also, troubles of the kind only come occasionally to public view; but here again the Church is surrounded by antagonistic Churches. At the same time it must be borne in mind that the extreme care with which the Church avoids scandal renders it impossible for one not within the pale to ascertain what may really be the relations between ecclesiastics and the female servants whom, as we shall see, they are permitted to keep in their houses.

In lands where Catholicism is dominant I fear that there can be little doubt as to this, although Ernest Renan, a witness of unquestionable impartiality, whose clerical training gave him every opportunity of observation, declares emphatically that he has known no priests but good priests, and that he has never seen even the shadow of a scandal. In spite of the Nicæan canon, on which the rule of celibacy has virtually rested, the Church, after a struggle of more than a thousand years, was forced to admit the " subintroducta mulier " as an inmate of the priest's domicile. The order of Nature on this point refused so obstinately to be set aside that the Council of Trent finally recognised women as a necessary evil, and only sought to regulate the necessity by forbidding those in holy orders from keeping in their houses or maintaining any relations with concubines or women liable to suspicion. It is true that the severe virtue of St. Charles Borromeo refused to grant to a septuagenary priest a licence for more than a year for the residence of a sister equally aged, and forced him to apply annually for its renewal; it is also true that the Council of Rome, in 1725, allowed the residence of women only within the first and second degrees of kindred; but in modern times the Tridentine canon has been interpreted as allowing the residence of female servants or housekeepers, in view of the hardship of doing without domestics and the expense of employing men. In order to meet the Tridentine caution to avoid suspicion, efforts have sometimes been made to define a minimum " canonical " age for these women, varying from thirty to fifty years, but usually placed at forty—a palliative which, as might be expected, accomplishes little, even when, as is not always the case, the rule is observed more scrupulously than by the device of dividing the canonical age and keeping two girls of twenty. The careful provisions as to the age and character of these " Marthas," and the prohibitions of manifestations of undue familiarity with them— especially in public—are scrupulously enumerated in the latest assembly of Catholic prelates, the Plenary Council of Latin America, held in Rome in 1899. These precautions are not uncalled for if there is truth in the statement that statistics submitted to the council showed that in Latin America, of 18,000 priests 3,000 were living in regular wedlock, 4,000 in concubinage with their so-called housekeepers, and some 1,500 in relations more or less open with women of doubtful reputation.

Few priests, it may be assumed, have the self-denial to live without this female companionship, which is permitted by the Church as a matter of course. Indeed, the census paper officially filled in at the Vatican and returned in January 1882 stated the population of the palace to be 500, of whom one-third were women. While, of course, it does not follow that the relations between these women and the grave dignitaries of the papal court may not have been perfectly virtuous, still, considering the age at which ordination is permitted, it would be expecting too much of human nature to believe that in at least a large number of cases among parish priests the companionship is not as fertile of sin as we have seen it to be in every previous age since the ecclesiastic has been deprived of the natural institution of marriage. The " niece " or other female inmate of the parsonage throughout Catholic Europe still excites the smile of the heretic traveller, and is looked upon as a matter of course by the parishioner, while the prelates, content if open scandal be avoided, affect to regard the arrangement as harmless, knowing that it serves as a preventive of more flagrant and more public trouble, though the fact that this companionship is made the subject of discussion and regulation at virtually every council or synod or episcopal convention held by the Church shows that privately it is recognised as a necessary evil at best. Yet the old sophistry is not forgotten, which proves that such sin is less than the infraction of ecclesiastical laws. In a tract in favour of celibacy, published at Warsaw in 1801, with the extravagant laudation of the authorities, argument is gravely made that as priestly marriage is incestuous, such adultery is vastly worse than simple licentiousness, the latter being only a lapse of the flesh, while marriage would be schism and arrogant disobedience, involving sin of a far deeper dye.

It would, of course, be vain to expect at the present day, from the rulers of the Church, the outspoken candour of the Middle Ages, when evils were denounced openly and in the coarsest terms. In those days councils could speak, because none but those connected with the Church were likely to be cognisant of their proceedings, while in the sixteenth and seventeenth centuries the immorality of ecclesiastics was so notorious that no harm could arise from admitting it in the efforts made for its correction. In modern times, however, when an external veil of decency is to be maintained before the eyes of antagonistic critics, when scandal is of all things to be avoided, and when the proceedings of ecclesiastical bodies are carefully revised at Rome before they are allowed to become public, with the consciousness that they may be spread by the Press before a world of hostile mockers, ready to jeer at the woes of the Church, only the most guarded allusions can be made to such subjects, and these only when the case is urgent. When, therefore, we see that almost every council held in modern times has deemed it necessary to insist on the supreme importance of preserving chastity—lying, swearing, stealing, and other sins not being even alluded to ; when the caution against undue familiarity with women, even devotees, is constantly urged; and when the relations between the priest and his servant are frequently indicated by directions that he must not admit her to companionship at the table, or on walks and journeys, and especially in visiting fairs and merrymakings, it would be difficult not to recognise under this guarded phraseology an admission of the actual relationship existing between the good pastors and their female inmates, and a friendly warning, *si non caste saltem caute*.

It is not often that we can obtain an inside view of these matters, especially from a source that is at once well informed and not hostile, but such a view is afforded by an indignant remonstrance addressed, in 1832, to Monseigneur Sterckx, Archbishop of Mechlin, by the Abbé Helsen, who for twenty-five years had been a popular preacher in Brussels. The abbé calls upon his prelate to enforce the Tridentine canon by banishing the women who are universally inmates of the houses of priests, and thus put a stop to the sin and the scandal which destroy the influence of the Church and spread immorality among the faithful. Even the bishops and dignitaries of the Church are not spared, and the archbishop himself is summoned to dismiss the " Petronilla " who had accompanied him from the curacy of Bouchout to the cathedral of Antwerp, and from Antwerp to the metropolitan See of Mechlin. Throughout this plain-spoken epistle the author assumes as a matter of course not only that the relations between the clergy and their servants are guilty, but that they are so recognised by every one—so notorious, indeed, as to need no proof; and as a natural consequence he regards the priesthood as a source of infection destructive to public morals. The cure is to be found in putting a stop to these irregular unions : " If women were for ever banished from the houses of ecclesiastics vowed to celibacy, I think we should not see so great a number of prostitutes who ply their trade at night in our great cities, nor so many illegitimate children who curse their destiny as they multiply more and more around us. We ridicule the seraglio of the Grand Turk and the polygamy of the Moslem, but they too, on their side, ridicule the infinite number of strumpets with whom Christian Europe is deluged, and the custom of keeping as many concubines as can be afforded. Whence comes to us this shameful trade, so hurtful to society, which is found under our religion more than under any other? We dare not doubt that it is the result of our own misconduct; we dare not accuse only the heretics and the philosophers of modern times. No, no ! the most poisonous spring is in us, among us, with us, and it will not dry up without us. Let us blush to our eyeballs; let us hide ourselves from public sight ! Oh for the times and the virtues of the primitive Church ! Why come ye not again? " That this sort of scarcely veiled concubinage is, in fact, a fruitful source of prostitution can scarcely be doubted if, as Helsen asserts, the ordinary custom is, when one of these priest's servants becomes pregnant and cannot be saved by a prudent absence, to dismiss her and take another, perhaps younger and more attractive; and that this may occur repeatedly without the ecclesiastic being subjected to any special annoyance or supervision—unless, indeed, he is so ill-advised as to take pity on the unfortunate girl and refuse to send her away. In that case he becomes a public concubinarian, liable to the canonical penalties, with which he is sometimes disciplined. As Helsen indignantly exclaims, " Would the Mahometans tolerate such infamy in their fakirs and dervishes? The Japanese, the Chinese, the Hindus in their bonzes? The pagans in their Vestals? Our ancestors in their Druids? Even the Jews and Protestants have blushed for it, since they advise their Rabbis and ministers to marry rather than thus to contaminate themselves." Helsen does not fail to allude to the public familiarity of these servants with their employers

—the familiarity condemned in almost the same words by many of the councils cited above—and it would seem the extreme of Pyrrhonism to doubt that almost universal concubinage is tolerated, even where on the surface there are no public scandals to attract the attention of the malicious.

There would therefore seem no reason to call in question the remarks of the Rev. William Chauncy Langdon, whose long residence in Italy as the agent of the American Episcopal Church gave him ample opportunity of observation. " I learned to regard a priest who had lived all his mature life openly and faithfully with a woman to whom of course he had not been married, by whom he had children now grown up, and for all of whom he was faithfully providing—with a relative respect as one who had greatly risen above the morality of his Church and of the society around him, and whose life really might be considered, on the dark moral background behind him, a source of relative light."

All this in fact may be inferred from sundry propositions presented to the Vatican Council in 1870. The Neapolitan bishops asked for legislation to check the frequency with which priests entered into civil marriage. They argued that the existing rule under which such offenders cannot be deprived until they have lain for a year under excommunication is inefficient, and that it would be much better to suspend them at once from office and benefice while awaiting the expiration of the year. The French bishops proposed that priests should be required to exclude women from their houses, or, if their services were indispensable, at least they should be of undoubted good repute and not less than forty years of age, except the near kindred permitted by the ancient canons. The German bishops also desired this question to be settled, and further suggested that, to avert the serious evils arising from the scandalous lives of priests, such offences as notorious fornication, manifest concubinage, drunkenness, and incorrigible prodigality be added to the legitimate causes for deprivation of benefice. From all this it would appear that the old scandals still flourish, and that something more efficacious is needed than the reformatory legislation of Trent. The managers of the council were of the same mind, and prepared a constitution *De vita et honestate clericorum*, in which Chapter III provided that a cleric living in concubinage or keeping a suspected woman in his house or elsewhere should be subjected to the Tridentine penalties, enforceable without the formalities of justice and solely on the strength of the facts; but bishops were warned that, to prevent the too facile aspersion of priests and the reproach to themselves of inconsiderate action, the evidence both of the offence and of the three warnings provided by the Council of Trent should be carefully preserved, to be used in case of appeal.

Slender as was this provision for the cure of immedicable evils, it was not adopted. The work for which the council was assembled was accomplished, 16 July, 1870, when it accepted the *Constitutio dogmatica de Ecclesia Christi*, defining the infallibility of the pope and his supreme jurisdiction over the whole Church. Its further existence was superfluous, and before another session was held the Italian occupation of Rome, September 20, afforded an ostensible reason for its dissolution, which was effected October 20 by its suspension.

The fact is that, if the priesthood is to be purified, some more summary process must be devised than the existing cumbrous formalities of ecclesiastical procedure. Few reforming bishops can be expected to undergo the expenses and delay incident to prosecutions, if we may judge from the recent case of Luigi Bidone, parish priest of Oliva Gessi. In 1901 he was accused before the Bishop of Tortona of keeping as a servant, with suspicion of evil relations, Angela Chiappano, a girl of twenty-two, in contravention of the synodal constitutions. The bishop ordered her dismissal, but Bidone retained her, in spite of the three successive commands, whereupon the bishop suspended him and deputed another priest to replace him. Other charges were brought against him of dissipating the parochial temporalities, and of having received 5071 lire for Masses never celebrated. The case was tried by the episcopal court, but it was not until 11 February, 1904, that he was formally deposed, nor till 17 June, 1905, that this judgment was confirmed by the Congregation of the Council of Trent. The laws exist, as of old, and can be enforced, but more than common tenacity is requisite for their enforcement, in face of the labour involved and the dread of scandal.

It is not to be supposed that the Church suffers less than formerly from the solicitation of female penitents by confessors. Indeed, the numerous utterances on the subject during the last half-century would perhaps justify the assumption that the evil is increasing rather than that the Church is more alive to the duty of its repression, for in the forum of conscience it is not regarded as a more heinous sin than of old. It is still not a reserved case, its commission does not incur excommunication, and absolution for it can be obtained from any confessor whom the culprit may select. Even the disability to celebrate Mass, prescribed in 1745, was virtually nullified by a decision of the Congregation of the Inquisition, 18 March, 1863, that it is not *latæ sententiæ*, but *ferendæ*—that is, that it does not operate of itself, but as the result of a conviction and sentence pronounced. As formerly, scandal is the one thing dreaded. All other considerations are of minor importance, and the subject is treated on the basis of the principle laid down by the Glossator : " Nothing is to be done that creates scandal . . . to avoid scandal the rigour of ecclesiastical law often yields." To this end, the proceedings in all cases are conducted with the most impressive secrecy from the beginning to the end. When a priest obtains a delegation to receive a denunciation from an accusing penitent, which we shall see is a necessary preliminary, he is sworn in presence of his bishop to perform the duty faithfully and to observe inviolate secrecy, and this oath is taken on the gospels and not by merely touching the breast, as is customary with priests. All names are scrupulously suppressed, and what testimony is shown to the accused is to be so carefully disguised as not to give him an inkling as to the witness. All papers are to be kept by the bishop in a special cabinet to which even his vicar-general is debarred access, the accuser is kept in ignorance of the result, and when the case is ended it is to be buried in oblivion. Under these circumstances it is impossible even to guess what may be the frequency of either the crime or its detection, but that it is kept in mind as an ever-present possibility is suggested by the recommendation that priests engaged in " missions " or revivals should always provide themselves with the necessary faculties to receive denunciations, and by the frequent recurrence, in the councils of the nineteenth century, of injunctions that the confessions of women shall always be heard at times and in places open to public observation.

There is the same difficulty as of old in defining the exact
limits to which the confessor may go without subjecting
himself to the definitions of the bulls of Gregory XV and
Benedict XIV.   The licence allowed in the confessional is
necessarily great, and the discretion of the confessor is a
variable quantity.   Even without evil intention on his part,
the pure-minded penitent may be scandalised, and indecency,
though perhaps not so common as in former times, would
still seem to exist.   We are told that some confessors are so
habitually scurrilous that they forget themselves without
seeking to corrupt their penitents, but the law is not simply
for the punishment of guilt, but for the prevention of scandal.
Yet imprudence is so exceedingly common and inevitable
that, if it were subject to denunciation, who would venture
to hear the confessions of women ?   The discussion still
goes on, as it did in the seventeenth century; there are
still opposing opinions of greater or less laxity, into the
details of which it is scarce worth while again to enter.
We may content ourselves with the general impressions
derived from the debate that the kind of talk which seems
to be common between the confessor and his penitent must
frequently lead to temptation difficult for average human
nature to resist ; that, amid the mass of conflicting opinions,
the priest who avoids the grosser and more direct forms of
seduction has the opportunity of attaining his object
without running much risk, and that it is not the flagitious
character of the act but the disrespect to the sacrament
which is still the subject of repression.
    The offence thus is still technical and not moral, for the
priest who learns the frailty of a penitent and visits her the
next day is not subject to denunciation.   The laxity of this
strict construction is seen in the decision of a case, 6 June,
1898, in which the laundress of a priest was accustomed to
confess to him.   On one occasion she confessed to adultery,
when he told her to wait for him in the ante-room of the
monastery.   There, after some talk about his clothes, he
made indecent advances, and subsequently when she
attended Mass he would beckon to her from his confessional
and make appointments to visit her at her house, finally
taking her and supporting her as his mistress.   The decision
by the Congregation of the Inquisition was that he was not
guilty of solicitation under the bulls, for, although some
authorities hold that a priest is guilty who makes use of

knowledge gained in the confessional, this cannot be accepted in practice, for the somewhat significant reason that it would hinder the full confession of such sins because of its imposing on the penitent the obligation of denouncing the confessor who takes advantage of the knowledge. Liguori lays down the rule that, where there is doubt, the confessor is not to be denounced; there must at least be moral certainty : appearances may deceive, while on the other hand solicitation may be so shrewdly disguised as to render it difficult of recognition or proof.

When these preliminary difficulties are solved by the confessor to whom the woman reveals the fact of her having been solicited—for it is assumed that denunciations are made only under pressure of a refusal of absolution for not denouncing—the rules of procedure are not such as to facilitate conviction and punishment. In 1867 the Congregation of the Inquisition addressed all archbishops, bishops, and ordinaries, complaining that the papal constitutions on the subject were neglected, and that abuses had crept in, both as to penitents denouncing guilty confessors and as to the punishment of the latter. It therefore urged the prelates everywhere to greater vigilance and vigour, and gave a summary of the current practice of the Inquisition, which affords us an insight into the methods deemed sufficient for the repression of this persistent and perennial abuse. The success of the Holy See since the seventeenth century in making good its claims on the obedience of the faithful is warrant sufficient for assuming that this utterance has been accepted as authoritative, and that it has nowhere been treated with the contempt shown by France and Germany for the decrees of Gregory XV.

As formerly, the woman solicited is compelled to accuse the culprit, and Pius IX in the great bull Apostolicæ Sedis, 12 October, 1869, which superseded the old bulls In Cœna Domini, included among those subject to excommunication latæ sententiæ women who neglected to do so within a month after the commission of the offence. It is, however, apparently impossible to induce them to do this, and it is only when they chance to confess their sin to some other confessor and are refused absolution that they are compelled to do it, although the rule is absolute that they are not to be interrogated as to consent. Strictly speaking, the denunciation should be made before a notary, but it is excessively difficult to secure this, and a special faculty must be obtained from the bishop to enable the confessor to take it.   When obtained, he forwards it to the bishop, keeping no copy, burning all memoranda, and returning the faculty, so that all trace of the matter shall be destroyed. The denunciation is then sent to the Roman Inquisition, and its orders are awaited.

Strict as are the injunctions to denounce, there are various ways in which they can be eluded.   Dispensations relieving the penitent from the duty can be obtained from the bishop, the Inquisition, or the Papal Penitentiary.   Danger to life, reputation, or property, whether of herself or her near kindred, relieves her of the obligation ; even close kinship, gratitude for favours received, and friendship serve as an excuse.   Confessors who do not admonish their penitents of this duty are liable to punishment, but they are advised to abstain from initiating inquiries about the matter ; they are warned not to be over-zealous in starting denunciations without close investigation, and are told not to admonish the penitent if, on the one hand, they feel convinced that she will not obey, and thus incur mortal sin, or, on the other, if her character is such as to cause apprehension that she may talk about it and thus create scandal.   Anything, in fact, which may lead to a knowledge of the affair is sufficient to prevent its prosecution.   In 1880 the Inquisition issued further instructions, saying that it often happened that denunciations contained allusions to other solicited penitents, who had not been examined, as they should have been and must be in future ; also that prosecutions frequently failed because the denunciations were not in proper form, wherefore it sent a formula to be followed in all cases.   In 1897 additional instructions were issued, relative to the investigations as to the character of the accuser and accused, which were necessary as a guide in weighing the credibility of the denunciation.

It is evident that there is no little difficulty in obtaining denunciations and in formulating them properly, but when this is accomplished the culprit is still reasonably safe, for no action is taken, except to have him watched, until three separate ones have been transmitted against him— a thing which can happen but rarely.   When such an accumulation occurs, they are duly investigated, and if he is found guilty the only punishment indicated is deprivation of the faculty of hearing confessions, leaving to the bishop the commutation of the other penalties into spiritual exercises. In practice, however, we are told that when the offender is a parish priest he is simply forbidden to hear confessions outside of his parish, and is required to resign it within a given time. Inadequate as these provisions must seem for an offence so grievous, they can be greatly reduced by self-denunciation. One who accuses himself before any evidence has been received against him escapes with spiritual penances and the advice to avoid confessing those whom he has solicited, and it is the same if a single accusation has been sent in; if there are several accusations against him and he presents himself and confesses before the trial is ended, he obtains a mitigation of the customary sentence. It would appear from all this that the active legislation on the subject of recent years is rather an indication of the prevalence of the trouble than of a sincere desire to eradicate it by measures of suitable vigour and severity.

Even the long-standing abuse of the absolution of the accomplice is still existent. Various councils in the nineteenth century felt impelled to call attention to the prohibitions uttered by Benedict XIV, and the Inquisition of recent years has found it necessary to issue repeated decrees on the subject. An obscure decision, 16 May, 1877, led to the assumption that the censures of the bull Sacramentum Pœnitentiæ could be eluded by the confessor leading his accomplice to omit allusion to their mutual sin in the confession to him in which he absolved her—either persuading her that it was no sin, or that, as it was already known to him, there was no necessity of mentioning it. To meet this the Inquisition, 19 February, 1896, decided that the excommunication could not be thus evaded, as it would virtually neutralise the bull. A decree of 9 November, 1898, specified certain cases in which the delinquent was excused from personal application to the Papal Penitentiary for absolution, but when, in 1899, a bishop in a foreign land asked whether this applied to one of his priests who had confessed to absolving an accomplice, but who declared that his duties and his poverty precluded him from appearing before the Penitentiary, the answer was in the negative. Evidently in the struggle with human nature the Church is not wholly successful.

Perhaps its success might be greater if it exerted its

powers unreservedly, but such is its dread of scandal that rather than incur the risk of publicity it prefers to shield the criminal. If the punishment cannot be secret, there must be no punishment and no admission of priestly weakness.

How powerfully and how unscrupulously its influence is exerted to this end may be judged from a few examples. In 1817, at Availles, in France, the sacristan complained to the mayor that his daughter was received every night by the curé, to the scandal of the people. The mayor thus invited entered the priest's house suddenly one night, and found the girl in *déshabille*, hidden in a corner. He drew up an official statement of the facts and forwarded it to the authorities, and the response to this was his summary dismissal from office on the ground of having violated the domicile of the curé and increased the scandal. A case which attracted much attention at the time was that of Antoine Mingrat, who as priest of Saint-Aupe, near Grenoble, created scandal by his amours, when, in place of being punished, he was transferred to Saint-Quentin. Here he was attracted by a young married woman named Marie Gérin. An unsuccessful attempt upon her virtue rendered it necessary to despatch her. He choked her to death in the parsonage, and dragged the body three-quarters of a league to the Isère, where he cut off the legs and threw the fragments into the river. Suspicion pointing to him, he was about to be arrested, when he escaped across the frontier and found refuge in Savoy. Protected by a mysterious influence, he was never surrendered, although he was condemned to death *in absentia* by the court of Grenoble, 9 December, 1822, and the only result was the persecution of the family of his victim, who had dared to complain. Similarly, in 1877, the Abbé Debra, condemned at Liège in default, for no fewer than thirty-two offences, was, after proper seclusion in a convent, given a parish in Luxembourg by the Bishop of Namur. In the case of the Abbé Mallet, which occurred in 1861, the Church was unable to save the culprit from punishment, but did what it could to conceal his crimes from the faithful. As a canon of Cambrai, he seduced three young Jewish girls and procured their confinement in convents under pretext of labouring for their conversion. One of his victims lost her reason in consequence of her sufferings, and the court of Douai con-

demned him to six years at hard labour—a sentence which
was announced by an orthodox journal thus : " M. le
chanoine Mallet de Cambrai, accusé de détournement de
mineurs pour cause de prosélytisme religieux, a été con-
damné à six ans de reclusion "—where the skilful use of
the masculine " mineurs " and the characterisation of his
offence as religious proselytism elevate the worst of criminals
into a martyr for the faith.   It is quite within the bounds of
probability that, as such a martyr, he may since the
expiration of his sentence have been enjoying, in some cure
of souls, the opportunity of repeating his missionary
experiments.

It is evident from these various causes that the criminal
records can give only the barest suggestion as to the extent
of crimes thus committed in secret by a class shielded by
influences so powerful.   The records of the *ministère de la
justice*, moreover, are not in France open to the public, and
the only mode of obtaining even an approximate idea of
the number of prosecutions in these cases is to gather them
from the journals in which they chance to appear as items
of news.   An attempt to effect this has been made by
Dr. Wahu, and, though from the nature of the case necessarily imperfect, it affords some interesting and suggestive
statistics.   His list extends from the beginning of 1861 to
April 1879, and is thus tabulated :—

1861	3 cases.
1862	2 ,,
1863	1 ,,
1864	1 ,,
1866	2 ,,
1867	3 ,,
1868	3 ,,
1869	3 ,,
1872	10 ,,
1873	6 ,,
1875	5 ,,
1876	1 ,,
1877	16 ,,
1878	35 ,,
1879 (January to April)	19 ,,

In all 110 cases, of which nearly one-half were brethren
connected with educational institutions.

The earlier years of this list must be necessarily imperfect,
and, indeed, M. Charles Sauvestre has given details of nine

cases occurring in schools in 1861, all of which have escaped
Dr. Wahu; but, after making allowance for the impossibility
of hunting up all the fugitive records of the past, the
increase during recent years is not to be regarded as indicating an increase of immorality. It rather proves how
powerful were the forces protecting the Church and repressing publicity under the Second Empire. The absence of
cases in 1870–1 is probably attributable to the preoccupations of the Franco-Prussian War and its consequent
troubles. While the presidency of M. Thiers, in 1872,
yielded ten cases, the reactionary government of Marshal
MacMahon showed but twelve cases in four years. After
the fall of MacMahon the number rapidly increases, the first
four months of 1879 affording no fewer than nineteen cases.
Whether since then this rate of progression has been maintained I have no means of knowing, but it is to be hoped
that the breaking up of the unauthorised orders and the
increased vigilance of the authorities, aided by an aroused
public sentiment, have led to a decrease in the dismal record.
One deplorable feature of many of these cases is the large
number of victims frequently represented in a single
prosecution, and that the perpetrator had often been
afforded the opportunity of continuing his crimes in successive situations. Thus, in the affair of the Abbé Debra,
at Liège, in 1877, there were thirty-two offences charged
against him; and, of those occurring in the single year
1878, Frère Marien was condemned for no fewer than 299,
Frère Mélisse, at Saint-Brice, for fifty, Frère Climène at
Candé, Mazé, and Martigné-Ferchaud, for twenty-five, and
Frère Adulphe at Guipry, Saint-Meloir-des-Ondes, and
Pleurtuit, for sixty-seven. It would be a libel on human
nature to assert that this catalogue of sin does not represent
more than an average of wickedness, and the responsibility
for the existence of so shocking a condition of morality must,
at least in part, be attributed to the rule of celibacy.

Irrespective of questions of morality, the rule of celibacy
in modern society is harmful to the State in proportion as
it contributes to the aggrandisement of those who enforce
it. A sacerdotal caste, divested of the natural ties of family
and of the world, with interests in many respects antagonistic
to the communities in which its members reside, with aims
which, from the nature of the case, must be for the temporal

advancement of its class, is apt to prove a dangerous element in the body politic, and the true interests of religion as well as of humanity are almost as likely to receive injury as benefit at its hands, especially when it is armed with the measureless power of confession and absolution, and is held in strict subjection to a hierarchy. Such a caste would seem to be the inevitable consequence of compulsory celibacy in an ecclesiastical organisation such as that of the Catholic Church, and the hierarchy based upon it can scarce fail to become the enemy of human advancement, so long as the priest continues to share the imperfections of our common nature. How little the aims of that hierarchy have changed with the lapse of ages may be seen in the pretensions which it still advances, as of old, to subject the temporal sovereignty of princes and peoples to the absolute domination of the spiritual power. The temper of Innocent III and Boniface VIII is still the leading influence in its policy, and the opportunity alone is wanting for it to revive in the twentieth century the all-pervading tyranny which it exercised in the thirteenth. Even the separation of Church and State is condemned as a heresy, and as the State is denied the privilege of defining the limits of its own authority, and as the right of the Church to use force is asserted, it would be difficult to set bounds to the empire which is its rightful heritage, and of which it is deprived by the irreligious tendencies of the age.

Yet, in spite of its reactionary efforts, and of its antagonism to the progress which has made the centuries since the Reformation the most important in the annals of civilisation, the Church has still a part to play, more or less beneficent as its rulers may be more or less sagacious. Conservatism has its uses, and mankind at large has not outgrown the necessity of the bridle as well as of the spur. There were ages in which the Church was the leader in knowledge and enlightenment; that it has become obscurantist is due to the use which it made of its leadership to so organise its temporal and spiritual domination that further development of human intelligence could only be accomplished through revolt, and it thus became the enemy in place of the friend of advancement. The policy then adopted rendered a reactionary position inevitable, because in support of its theocratic aspirations it framed a system of dogma assumed to be of divine revelation, and therefore unalterable as the will of God. Entrenched behind this, it has, with varying success, defended its position for more than three centuries. From the storms of the Revolution it emerged with centralised Ultramontanism triumphant over the particularism known as Gallicanism and Jansenism —a triumph which culminated in the Council of the Vatican. This was too complete, and since then signs have not been lacking of a growing restlessness which may be provoked to schism or may be soothed by wise concessions. The spirit of the age is not propitious for relentless discipline which will tolerate nothing but blind obedience, and the Church may find that only by yielding can it preserve its unity. The lesson of the sixteenth century should not be forgotten, when unwisdom cost it nearly half of its membership.

INDEX

577

Nicæa on, 33; how affected by introduction of celibacy, 56; as described by Salvianus, 59; equally bad in Oriental and Western Church, 60; by St. Jerome, 75; St. Augustin, 78; indicated by St. Theodore Studita, 83; St. Isidor of Seville, 89; Smaragdus, 89

Morals of bishops in Merovingian France, 91–2; of clergy in Italy in sixth century, 94; of clergy in France in eighth century, 100; of clergy in France in ninth century, 108; of clergy in England in tenth century, 132; in monasteries in eleventh century, 142; of married clergy in Milan in eleventh century, 163; clerical, in Germany in twelfth century, 203; clerical, in France in eleventh century, 218; clerical, corrupt laity, 219, 235; clerical, in England in twelfth century, 232; clerical, in England in thirteenth century, 237; clerical, in Ireland in fourteenth century, 249; clerical, in Scotland in thirteenth century, 251; clerical, in Spain in fourteenth century, 263; clerical, in Church of twelfth century, 271, 276; clerical, in Church of thirteenth century, 280; clerical, in Rome, 290; in papal court, 290–1; in mediæval Church, 296; in Bohemian Church, 325; clerical, in fifteenth century, 328, 332, 333, 338, 341; clerical, in sixteenth century, 363, 365; clerical, in English Church of sixteenth century, 380–1; in English monasteries, 385–6; clerical, in Brunswick in 1476, 339; clerical, in Bangor, 424; clerical, in Scotland, 430, 433–4, 438; clerical, in Germany, described by Cassander and Wicelius, 468–9; clerical, in Rome, in sixteenth century, 479; clerical, in post-Tridentine Church, 481; clerical, in Bohemia, 486; clerical, in Spanish colonies, 492, 493; clerical, in the Low Countries, 487; clerical, in France, 488; in the confessional, 497–8; in America, 561; clerical, in the modern Church, 559–63; have nothing to do with solicitation, according to Church views, 527

More, Sir Thomas, satirises vices of Church, 379; accusation against Luther by, 380

Morone, Cardinal, legate of Holy See, report by, 375; reports, in 1542, 446; sent to Vienna, 462; terms made with Ferdinand by, 462; requests urged by Ferdinand to, 467

Morrison, Sir Richard, on assumption of Church lands, 414

Mortal sin, Wickliffe's definition of, 323

Morton, Archbishop, visitation by, 338; calls condition of monasteries deplorable, 386

Mosaic dispensation, materialism of, 4

Mothers, residence of, forbidden in priests' houses, 109, 281

Mucius the Holy, story of blind obedience of, 78

Muhlberg, battle of, breaks power of Protestants, 376

Mulier subintroducta, 33

Muncer, John of Niklaushausen precursor of, 343

Munster, synod of, in 1566, 478; impossibility of reform in, 487; Rasfelt, Bishop of, publishes papal commands, 478

Murner, Dr. Thomas, on immoralities of priests and nuns, 386

Mutilation, practice of, 20–1; advocated by Sextus Philosophus, 21

Mylitta, 4

Mystic rewards for virginity, 294–5

NALANDA, the Sangharama (Buddhist monastery) of, 72

Namur, synod of, in 1698, 511; in 1742, 512

Nanno, Count of Verona, protects married priests, 120

Nantes, Edict of, 429

Naples, children of ecclesiastics in, 285; position of priests' concubines in, 288; clerical marriage proposed in eighteenth century in, 530; number of clergy in, 534; priestly marriage in, 554; Council of, in 1576, 482

Napoleon re-establishes religion, 542; allows Church to regulate question of marriage, 542; takes up case of Talleyrand and Madame Grand, 543; decides against priestly marriage, 544

Napoleon, Louis, fall of, 558

National Assembly and Church property, 535

Nature, crimes against, 108, 282

Nazirites, ascetic vow of, 5

Neapolitan Code, the, 285

Neocæsarea, Council of, 17

Neo-Platonism, elevated mysticism of, 20

Nestorians as missionaries, 69; controversies of, 81

Nestorius, Patriarch of Constantinople, heresy of, 68

Netherlands, troubles in, caused by clerical corruption, 486

Neustria, reforms in, 103

New Granada, suppression of monasteries in, 558–9

Nicæa, first General Council held at, 33; canon of, does not refer to celibacy, 34; no interference for some time after Council, with married priests, 37; canon of, renewed by Greek Church, 68; enforced by Gregory I., 95; enforcement of, attempted in 744, 103; enforcement in England in twelfth century, 230

Nicaragua, question of secularising Church property in, 559

Nicetas Pectoratus, defence of Greek Church by, 155

Nicholas de Clemanges (see Clemanges)

Nicholas I., orders deposition of immoral priests, 110; rules for trial of priests, 111; skilfully tacit permission of priestly marriage, 112

Nicholas II., election of, 156; canon of, on mass of non-celibate priests, 158; controlled by Hildebrand, 159; intervenes in Milanese troubles, 171; canons on celibacy renewed by, 185; enforces celibacy in France, 210